All the
PROMISES
of the Bible

Books in This Series

All the
PROMISES
of the Bible

Herbert Lockyer

ABOUT THE AUTHOR

Dr. Herbert Lockyer was born in London in 1886 and held pastorates in Scotland and England for twenty-five years before coming to the United States in 1935.

In 1937 he received the honorary Doctor of Divinity degree from Northwestern Evangelical Seminary.

In 1955 he returned to England where he lived for many years. He then returned to the United States where he continued to devote time to the writing ministry until his death in November of 1984.

ZONDERVAN®

All the Promises of the Bible
Copyright © 1962 by Zondervan

Requests for information should be addressed to:

Zondervan, *3900 Sparks Drive SE, Grand Rapids, Michigan 49546*

ISBN 0-310-28131-8

Printed in the United States of America

*Dedicated
to my
publishers,*
PAT AND BERNIE,
*as I have affectionately
known them for more than a quarter
of a Century.
How they love the Promises
and live to circulate them
in various forms!*

"Take the promises of God. Let a man feed for a month on the promises of God, and he will not talk about how poor he is. You hear people say, 'Oh, my leanness! how lean I am!' It is not their leanness, it is their *laziness*. If you would only read from Genesis to Revelation and see all the promises made by God to Abraham, to Isaac, to Jacob, to the Jews and to the Gentiles, and to all His people everywhere — if you would spend a month feeding on the precious promises of God — you wouldn't be going about complaining how poor you are. You would lift up your head and proclaim the riches of His Grace, because you couldn't help doing it!"

— DWIGHT L. MOODY

Contents

Introduction

Once an author decides to write a certain book and has settled upon its main outline, his first effort is to gather a library of authorities who have already dealt with the general aspects of his subject. Such aids to study are invaluable to a writer and act as a stimuli to thought. A perusal of the *Bibliographies* quoted at the end of the other books in this series — *All the Men of the Bible; All the Prayers of the Bible; All the Kings and Queens of the Bible; All the Miracles of the Bible* — will reveal the various religious and secular lakes in which the author fished.

When this present volume was decided upon, I immediately set about gathering the works of others in the field of divine promises, but I was disappointed over the paucity of printed help. Only one satisfactory volume came to light. The advice of the Secretary of the Evangelical Library in London was sought. He replied, "Although clearly one of the most important of all Bible subjects, it has been sadly neglected. For this reason, there is not a big range to refer to." Secretary George Williams was good enough, however, to inform me that "the classic on the subject is unquestionably that great and gracious divine, Dr. Samuel Clark." Happily, out of its countless thousands of volumes, rare and modern, The Evangelical Library had a copy of the most helpful book to loan me and what a treasure it is! The collection of verses in this volume have been recently published separately under the title of *Precious Bible Promises*, by Grosset and Dunlap, New York.

Scripture Promises, as Dr. Clark's study is named, was published more than 130 years ago. No wonder it is rare! What makes this old book so valuable is not only Dr. Clark's own "Introduction" and his classification of hundreds of promises, but a unique "Introductory Essay" by Dr. Ralph Wardlaw of Glasgow, written in 1831. As it is almost impossible to secure another copy of this precious small book, I have freely adopted and adapted many of the profitable remarks of Dr. Wardlaw on the promises as a whole, feeling that Twentieth Century Christians should benefit, as I have, from the observations of this learned divine, who lived more than a century and a half ago.

Grateful recognition is also given for help received in the compilation and exposition of many of the tabulated promises from devotional books made up of some of the most precious promises and the most important precepts of the Bible. Recommended are: *Daily Manna*, by J. Gilchrist Lawson; *Guide to the Oracles*, by Dr. Alfred Neven; *Climbing the Heights*, by Al Bryant; *The Hour of Silence — The Secret Place*, by Dr. Alexander Smellie; *Morning and Evening*, also

Daily Checkbook, by C. H. Spurgeon; *Topical Text Book*; *The Continual Burnt Offering*, by Dr. H. A. Ironside; *The Faithful Promises*, by Dr. J. R. Macduff; *The Green Pastures*, by Dr. J. R. Miller; *The Promises of Jesus*, by William J. May; *Rainbow in the Cloud*, by Lolo E. Kilfoil; *Pathway of Promise*, by J. A. M.; *Give Us This Day*, by Herbert Lockyer; *This Is the Day*, by Nell Warren Outlaw. Profitable assistance was likewise received from the "Chain References" in the *Scofield Reference Bible*. In the realm of expositional material, much use was made of *Ellicott's Bible Commentary*, Spurgeon's *Treasury of David*, and Matthew Henry's indispensable work.

The question may arise as to whether this book in your hands justifies its title of dealing with *all* the promises found in the Bible. It has been computed that there are 30,000 Bible promises. No indication is given as to how this colossal number is reached. Altogether, there are 31,173 verses making up the Bible; 23,214 verses comprising the Old Testament, and 7,959 – the New Testament. Doubtless this total of verses gave rise to the 30,000 – every verse being a promise. The magazine *Time*, of Dec. 4, 1956, carried an item to the effect that Schoolteacher Everet R. Storms, of Kitchener, Canada, reckoned the 30,000 figure to be off the mark. During his 27th reading of the Bible, this devout student tried to tally up the promises, a task which took him a year and a half. Storms came up with 7,487 promises by God to man, 2 by God the Father to God the Son, 991 by one man to another (such as the servants who promised to interpret King Nebuchadnezzar's dream), 290 by man to God. 21 promises were made by angels, one by man to an angel, and two were made by an evil spirit to the Lord. Satan made nine, as when he promised the world to Christ if He would fall down and worship him. Storms then gives us the grand total of 8,810 promises.

Scattered throughout the Bible are hundreds of definite explicit promises forming the category Peter names as "the exceeding great and precious promises" (II Peter 1:4). But when we remember that all the *prophecies* and *covenants* are promises, and that almost every verse of the 2,461 forming the Psalms is a potential promise, as are the 915 verses making up Proverbs, then it is realized what a task confronts an author when he endeavors to set forth *all* the promises of the Bible. This present writer hopes that he has succeeded in marshalling a comprehensive and representative number of the promises which are like an arranged museum of "gems and precious stones and pearls" of inestimable value in God's cabinet of spiritual jewels, and which constantly remind the Christian of his true, abiding riches. All of these gracious promises deserve to be "bound upon our fingers and written upon the table of our hearts."

All the
PROMISES
of the Bible

I

THE SUBSTANCE OF THE PROMISES

What actually constitutes a *promise?* Samuel Johnson's answer is, "A promise is the declaration of some benefit to be conferred." Webster's *Dictionary* gives us this:

1. One's pledge to another to do or not to do something specified, narrowly, a declaration which gives to the person to whom it is made a right to expect or to claim the performance or forbearance of a specified act.
2. Ground for hope, expectation or the assurance, often specified of eventual success.
3. That which is promised—

To engage to do, give, make, obtain: to make to another a promise of; also, to give one's promise to assure as "He will go, I *promise* you." To show or suggest beforehand; betoken; as, the clouds *promise* you.

A *promisee* is the person to whom a promise is made; and a *promissory note* is a written promise to pay on demand or at a fixed future time a certain sum of money to, or to the order of, a specified person or to bearer. A *breach of promise* represents the violation of one's plighted word, as is used especially of a promise to marry. For an exact nature of Bible promises, one must study the original words used to describe them. Although the word "promise" is used more than 100 times in the Bible, there are other terms implying the same thought.

The Old Testament is a record of God's promises to patriarchs, kings, prophets, Israel, lowly saints, and to the world at large. The Hebrew noun, *dahtar,* is generally rendered "word," but "promise" is found in I Kings 8:56 and Nehemiah 5:12,13.

"According to all that He *promised:* there hath not failed one *word* of all His good *promise*"

"That they should do according to the *promise.*"

A difficulty in assessing the number of Bible promises is further seen in the fact that another Hebrew word for "promise"

is *omer,* meaning "saying." This is the term used in —"Doth his promise fail for evermore?" Psalms 77:8, and employed again as "word" in passages like—

"The Lord gave the *word*" (promise). Psalm 68:11

"Thy bow was made quite naked, according to the oaths of the tribes, even thy word" (promise). Habakkuk 3:7.

The change in Psalms 105:42 R.V.—"He remembered his holy word"—reminds us that God's "Holy Word" is always a "Holy Promise." The Hebrew verb *dabhar* is usually translated "speak," but "promise" is found in many places—

"According as he hath promised."

Exodus 12:25

"All the good that I have promised them." Jeremiah 32:42.

In several places the Revised Version gives "speak" or "say," instead of "promise," e.g., "According as the Lord thy God promised him" (Deuteronomy 10:9). In his *Expository Dictionary of New Testament Words,* W. E. Vine gives us the following interpretation of the words used for "promise." Of the two nouns Vine says that there is—

EPANGELIA, which is primarily a law term, denoting a summons (*epi*—upon; *angelo,* to proclaim, announce), also meant an undertaking to do or give something, a promise. It is used only of the promises of God except in Acts 23:21, "Looking for a promise from thee." Frequently this term stands for the thing promised, and so signifies a gift graciously bestowed, not a pledge secured by negotiation; thus, in Galatians 3:14, "The promise of the Spirit" denotes "the promised Spirit" (see Luke 24:49; Acts 2:23; Ephesians 1:13). "The promise of the eternal inheritance" is "The promised inheritance." On the other hand, in Acts 1:4 "The promise of the Father" is "The promise made by the Father."

The plural "promises" is used because the one promise to Abraham was variously repeated (Galatians 3:16), "Now to Abraham and his seed were the promises made." (See Genesis 12:1-3; 13:14-17; 15:18; 17:1-14; 22:15-18). The plural is also used because it contained the germ of all subsequent promises (Romans 9:4; Hebrews 6:12; 7:6; 8:6; 11:17).

In Galatians 3, Paul shows that the promise was conditional upon faith and not upon the fulfilment of the Law. The Law was later than and inferior to, the promise, and did not annul it (Galatians 3:21) with 4:23,28). Again, "the covenants of the promise" (Ephesians 2:12) does not indicate different covenants, but a covenant often renewed, all centering in Christ as the promised Messiah-Redeemer, and comprising the blessings to be bestowed through Him.

The plural is likewise used, in Hebrews, of every promise made by God, and of special promises mentioned:

"Blessed him that had the promises." (7:6)

"Who through faith . . . obtained promises." (11:33)

For other applications of the word, see Ephesians 6:2; I Timothy 4:8; II Timothy 1:1; Hebrews 4:1; II Peter 3:4,9). Some MSS have this word meaning "message," instead of *angelia*, as in I John 1:5.

Vine goes on to state that the occurrences of the word in relation to Christ and what centers in Him, may be arranged thus:

1. The contents of the promise –
   "The promise made of God unto our fathers." Acts 26:2,3
   "He staggered not at the promise of God." Romans 4:20
   "This is the promise that he hath promised us." I John 2:25

2. The heirs of the promise –
   "The children of the promise are counted for the seed." Romans 9:8
   "To confirm the promises made unto the fathers." Romans 15:8
   "Heirs according to the promise." Galatians 3:29
   "The heirs with him of the same promise." Hebrews 11:9

3. The conditions of the promise –
   "The promise . . . through the righteousness of faith." Romans 4:13,14
   "Receive the promise of the Spirit through faith." Galatians 3:14-22
   "After ye have done the will of God, ye might receive the promise." Hebrews 10:36

EPANGELMA denotes a promise made by God –
   "Whereby are given unto us exceeding great and precious promises." II Peter 1:4

"According to His promise." II Peter 3:13

As to the three verbs that are used of the English word "promise," we have, first of all –

EPANGELLO, meaning, to announce, proclaim. In the New Testament this word has two meanings – *to profess* and *to promise*, each used in the middle voice: to promise –

1. Of Promises of God.
   "He promised that he would give it to him for a possession." Acts 7:5; also Romans 4:21
   The passive voice is found in the phrase –
   "To whom the promise was made." Galatians 3:19; also in Titus 1:2; Hebrews 6:13; 10:23; 11:11; 12:26; James 1:12; 2:5; I John 2:25

2. Of Promises Made by Men.
   "They promised to give him money." Mark 14:11
   "While they promise them liberty." II Peter 2:19

This verb is used of "profess," as in I Timothy 2:18; 6:21.

PROEPANGELLO is in the middle voice, and denotes "to promise before," and occurs twice in Paul's writings
   "Which he had promised before." Romans 1:2
   "Make up beforehand your bounty." II Corinthians 9:5

The term PROEPANGELLOMAI also means "to promise before," and is translated by the one word "afore-mentioned." II Corinthians 9:5 R.V.

HOMOLOGEO Here we have a word meaning "to agree, confess," and signifies to promise – "Whereupon he promised with an oath" (Matthew 14:7). This is the same word used for "confesses" (John 1:20 etc.). The word EXOMOLOGEO means "to agree openly, to acknowledge outwardly, or fully" and is translated "consented" in the R.V. of Luke 22:6 where the A.V. has "promised."

A further consideration of the substance or nature of a promise leads us to say that a mere mental decision to bestow a benefit is not a promise. If the resolution of the mind is to be constituted a promise, then it must be intimated to the person for whom the benefit was planned. This expression of an inward resolution can be covered to be beneficial in many ways – by a verbal declaration, or by writing, or by other ways of expressing the intention of one's mind. All God's promises are in written form in

His Word, which is the only authentic revelation of the divine mind and purpose the world has (Romans 1:2).

Once the thought-over promise is declared, then with its intimation, the promise becomes promissory or binding. The written form of the promise becomes what is known as "a promissory note," that is, a written promise to fulfill the declared benefit. Every divine promise is a "promissory note." Sometimes there is superadded to a promise the appeal to the God of Truth, as when an oath is taken in a Law-Court, "So help me God." This is supposed to indicate the sincerity of the promiser to perform his promise, which becomes a ".promissory oath." If one fails to fulfill such a solemn pledge then the violation becomes the guilt of perjury. Because of all God is in Himself, no oath is necessary, yet we read that He confirmed His promise with "an oath" (Hebrews 6:17).

It is to be regretted that we live in an age when a man's word is no longer his bond. This is a common belief that one is not bound to keep his word, that one is not habituated to regard fully a good and beneficient promise as a sacred transaction. Take as an example of "Men apt to promise are apt to forget," those who are profuse in promises before an election. Politicians tend to word their promises vaguely, so that if they are not kept, it will be no easy matter for disillusioned electors to pin-point them. This is why political promises are usually accepted with the proverbial grain of salt. Judge Darling wrote in his *Scintillac Juris:* "To convince a poor voter by common argument of promised reforms is merely to corrupt him with hope." How different are the promises of God, none of which ever corrupt a believer with unrealized hope! Earl Long, former Governor of Louisiana, who died recently was referred to as one who "promised the world to anyone who would give him a vote." A proverb has it, "To promise and give nothing is a comfort to a fool." Yet another runs: "Promises are like pie-crusts, lightly made and easily broken." A further proverb reads, "He that promises too much means nothing." Samuel Johnson says, "Promising large promises is the soul of an advertisement."

Truth, however, is the sole basis of mutual confidence, and mutual confidence, the sole bond of social life. If we make a legitimate promise and give our word that it will be realized, then, if we break our word, we become guilty of lying. We sin against the principle of moral obligation. A proverb has it, "The promise of a good man becomes a legal obligation." Do you recall Alexander Pope's tribute to Addison? –

> Statesman yet friend to truth; of soul sincere
> In action faithful, and in honour clear.
> *Who broke no promise*, served no private end,
> Who gained no title, and who lost no friend.
> Enobled to himself, by all approved,
> And praised, unenvied by the muse he loved.

Who does not covet a similar reputation as Addison's who never broke a promise. Certainly this is God's reputation, for not one of His multitudinous promises can possibly fail. Says Browning, "If we've promised them anything then let us keep our promise."

The God we love and serve is the God of Truth, and requires truth as one of the virtues of His intelligent offspring.

> "God is not a man, that he should lie; neither the son of man, that he should repent: hath he said, and shall he not do it? or hath he spoken, and shall he not make it good?" Numbers 23:19
> "The strength of Israel will not lie nor repent: for he is not a man, that he should repent." I Samuel 15:29
> "It is impossible for God to lie."
> Hebrews 6:18

This reflection of the divine character is a just and glorious tribute to God's reliability, also a sad yet just reflection on human character because the inference of the above passages is that man is capable of promising and guilty of breaking his promise and becoming a liar.

Before we leave this aspect of our study dealing with the nature of a promise, it is necessary to comment upon the difference between *a statement of fact* and *a promise.* Too often, we fail to observe the distinction between "Facts" and "Promises." A fact is a truth distinguished from a mere statement of belief. The realm of *fact* is distinct from that of *fancy*. Bible facts are to be accepted as being actual and therefore must be believed. Promises, on the other hand, are to be received and claimed. The proverb has it: "Facts are stubborn things."

When Jesus came to leave His disciples He assured them of His abiding presence –
> "Lo, I am with you alway, even unto the end of the age."
> Matthew 28:20

That was a statement of fact, although we name it as a promise, and rightly so. This was David Livingstone's favorite verse and as he was wont to say about it, "That's the word of a perfect Gentleman, and that's the end of it." Such a fact is the other side of the command to go and teach all nations. Whether we realize the Sacred Presence, or no, as we labour in the Lord's Name, the fact remains that He is with us. If some earth-born cloud arises to hide Him from our eyes, He is still near because He has stated that He will never leave nor forsake His own. Here then, is a blessed fact to be accepted by faith and constantly rested in. Then, as we shall presently prove, many promises are conditional, but the facts are not.

We readily concede that there are distinct and precious phrases like "God is love," and "God is great." We call these promises and they light up the pages of the Bible as the stars light up the nightly sky. These gracious epithets form an exceeding great army. "If I would declare and speak of them, they are more than can be numbered" (Psalm 139:17, 18). The point to remember, however, is that the majority of these statements are *facts*. No one and nothing can alter the fact that "God is love." Of course, such a blessed fact carries with it the promise that He will be loving in His treatment of saint and sinner alike.

II
THE SIMPLICITY OF THE PROMISES

The fact that all God's promises are stated in clear, simple terminology adds to their value. They are not expressed in general or ambiguous terms, but with the greatest clarity and perspicuity. It is not His will to leave His people in uncertainty concerning His kind and gracious intentions towards them. The divine promises are never wordy, nor are they couched in complex, mystifying language for "God is light, and in Him is no darkness at all" (I John 1:5). All He has to say is set forth in clear, intelligible words, so that even the wayfarer cannot err therein. If the full meaning of a promise appears doubtful in one place it is abundantly cleared up in other promises.

Neither are any of the promises expressed in any cold or reserved manner. Because he wanted no dullness or slowness to believe all that he has promised, God condescended to make use of the strongest, simplest words and phrases language could furnish. Thus we have a great variety of choice expressions to convince us of the assurances of His favor. The promises are so contrived as to meet one's objection and to remove all our doubts and fears. What else can we do but marvel at God's affection, tenderness and condescension in seeking to convince us – sinful dust and ashes – of His beneficent purpose in loving terms, so transparent. Ovid, the Latin poet wrote –

"Make a point of promising: for what harm can it do to promise? Anyone can be rich in promises."

God is rich in His promises, but He never multiplied them unnecessarily; nor was He guilty in clothing His promises with unnecessary adornment. But God differs from man, as night from day. What He has promised in terms so concise and unmistakable, He performs. His deeds match His declarations. Sidney R. Lysaght, in his *Confession of Unfaith*, written in 1900, had this gloomy aspect:

"Dreams that bring us little comfort, heavenly promises that lapse, into some remote. It – may – be, into some forlorn Perhaps."

The child of faith can give the assuring confession that "heavenly promises" are no idle dreams, no "Perhaps." He rests upon divine promise that cannot fail.

Ethical writers point out that there are certain principles or morals of moral casuistry determining whether a promise is binding or no. Paley, for instance, laid down the rule that when "the terms of a promise admit of more sense than one, it is to be performed in the sense in which the promiser apprehended the promisee to have understood and received it: it being the business of the former to be explicit, and to see to it that the latter has a correct understanding of the terms of his engagement, and of his *bona fide* intention." Such a maxim, however, is not applicable to the promises of God, for when He gave certain promises to certain individuals, He caused those to whom they were given clearly to understand the nature and extent of what He had committed Himself to do for them, as for example, His promise to Abraham and Sarah regarding a son of promise. Having made such a clear promise, God was obligated by His character to fulfill it, which He did.

What must be borne in mind is the fact that the gracious Promiser is only bound to fulfil any given promise *in His own sense*, and not in any sense which others may attach to the promise. Promises misunderstood and misapprehended result in disappointment, but the fault is entirely human for God can never be brought under obligation by our mistakes. Many of the Jews formed gross misconceptions of the clearly defined import of Old Testament prophecies regarding their coming Messiah and His reign. But when He appeared they saw no beauty in Him that they should desire Him. The divine promises had raised their hopes but their confidence was badly shaken when Jesus came as a Babe born in a stable. God's promise of a King, however, was not at fault, only the false interpretation of it by the Jewish rulers.

Another maxim in respect to human promises is that they are not binding where the performance of them is impossible. As Dr. Ralph Wardlaw says, "The promise may have been made at the time in the full persuasion of their practicability; otherwise, the making of them would be dishonorable and fraudulent; but if afterwards, and contrary to anticipation, the fulfilment is found to be beyond the promiser's power,

the obligation of necessity ceases." For instance, suppose one promises a friend a sum of money, payable at death, out of gratitude for favors, and has acquainted the friend of such a gracious intention, but yet through force of unseen circumstances finds himself impoverished with no money to leave – what then? Well, although the promisee may have a written affirmation of the promise made in all good faith, he knows that the emergence of unfavorable circumstances makes the promise void and of none effect.

Happily, such an eventuality does not apply to the promises of God for with Him "all things are possible." Certainly, He cannot promise to do anything involving the contradiction of His will or incompatible with the perfection of His moral nature. But all He has so explicitly promised, He has power to realize. To Him a promise is sure of performance. A proverb has it that there are, "No greater promisers than those who have nothing to give." God, however, is a great Promiser and has everything to give. To Him "promising is the eve of giving." As the God of the universe, all its laws are under His control and command, and nothing can stand in the way of the fulfilment of any promise He has made. Omnipotence is His, and He can never on any ground of incapacity, break down on any promise. "Hath He said, and will He not do it? hath He spoken, and will He not make it good?" (Numbers 23:19). What simplicity there is in Him and in all His promises! (II Corinthians 11:3). May ours be that simplicity of faith enabling us to take Him at His word! (II Corinthians 1:12).

III

THE STIPULATION OF THE PROMISES

Among the many striking evidences of the Bible being God's inspired, infallible Word are –

1. The remarkable sublimity, excellency and reasonableness of the great *doctrines* it teaches.
2. The strength and efficiency of those sanctions, with which it enforces its manifold *precepts*.
3. The wisdom, holiness and perfection of the *rules* of life it lays down for the sons of men.

4. The awesomeness of its *threatenings*, which act as a powerful restraint against any irregular behavior.
5. The *promises* likewise testify to Scripture as a divine original: and they are calculated to intensify our faith and confidence in God; and also to provide an incentive and encouragement to a life of piety and universal holiness. This is why Peter reasons that "the exceeding great and precious promises"

enable us to become "partakers of the divine nature."

The numerous promises throughout the Bible are not too difficult to find. In our chapter dealing with *The Scope of the Promises*, we have endeavored to classify these rich promises for the help of pilgrims. There are, however, several facts to bear in mind as we handle these promises. Certain stipulations, stated and inferred, must be observed. First of all, we take note of this characteristic feature that a promise may have more than one application. Several blessings or duties are sometimes compressed into one verse. For instance, take this "Proverb" which is also a "promise," from Solomon's collection—

"By humility and fear of the Lord are riches, and honour and life." Proverbs 22:4

Here is a verse offering the preacher a wide range of exposition. The possession and manifestation of humility and godliness and reverence can lead to both material and spiritual gains.

Then there are direct promises and particular blessings, some of which were made to all men in general, according to the rules and limitations indicated. Here are two illustrations of this truth—

"For the Lord God is a sun and a shield:
The Lord will give grace and glory;
No good thing will he withhold from them that walk uprightly."
                                         Psalm 84:11

In the plainest terms God tells us what He is in Himself, and what He is willing to bestow upon those who fulfill the stipulation laid down.

"O fear the Lord, ye His saints: for there is no want to them that fear Him.
The young lions do lack, and suffer hunger; but they that seek the Lord shall not want any good thing." Psalm 34:9, 10

How the saints of every succeeding age, irrespective of nationality or position, have staked their claim in such a rich mine of promised sustenance!

Further, there are those promises addressed to definite persons but in which all Christians may take comfort. The assurance given by Joshua of divine companionship can be experienced by us all.

"As I was with Moses, so will I be with thee; I will not fail thee, nor

forsake thee." Joshua 1:5; Deuteronomy 31:6, "He hath said, I will never leave thee, nor forsake thee." Hebrews 13:5. Here, as you can see, a particular promise given first to Moses, then to Joshua becomes a general promise for the saints of God to realize.

"He's promised never to leave us,
Never, to leave us, alone."

In the next place there are those promises given to Jews, for Jews to claim, yet the truth they contain can be appropriated by God's people today. Was it not to Israel, as God's vineyard of red wine, that He said—

"In the Lord do keep it; I will water it every moment: lest any hurt it, I will keep it night and day."
                                         Isaiah 27:3

Then it was of Jerusalem during the Kingdom-Age that God said—

"I will be unto her a wall of fire round about, and will be the glory in the midst of her." Zechariah 2:5

Coming to the New Testament we find the same divine provision and protection translated into Pauline phraseology thus—

"The God of peace shall bruise Satan under your feet shortly." Romans 16:20
"My God shall supply all your need according to His riches in glory by Christ Jesus." Philippians 4:19

Thus, for the godly Jew, and the Christian, the truth is the same, God is ever round about His own, as the mountains are round about Jerusalem.

What it is so essential to remember, however, is the rule, so often lost sight of, namely, while *all* the Bible was written *for* us, not all of it was written *to* us. Promises made to particular persons, and in cases and for reasons that equally concern other saints, are yet applicable to the comfort of all, and may be pleaded with faith and prayer. Paul thus writes—

"Whatsoever things were written aforetime were written for our learning, that we through patience and comfort of the Scriptures might have hope."
                                         Romans 15:4

A fitting illustration of this is the "great commandment" Moses gave to Israel, a commandment with the promise of possession of the good land—

"Thou shalt love the Lord thy God with all thine heart, and with all thy soul, and with all thy might."
                                         Deuteronomy 6:5, 18

Jesus took this Jewish command with promise and applied it to those of His own day and to all who would follow Him (Matthew 22:37; Mark 12:29, 30; Luke 10:27.)

Further, there are promises given to particular persons in the Bible which can be used by others for their encouragement so far as the case and circumstances agree, though not absolutely and in their whole content. Take, for example, the promise made specially to King Solomon as he entered upon his glorious reign—

> God said to Solomon, Behold this was in thine heart, and thou hast not asked riches, wealth, or honour, nor the life of thine enemies, neither yet hast asked long life; but hast asked wisdom and knowledge for thyself, that thou mayest judge my people, over whom I have made thee king. Wisdom and knowledge is granted unto thee; and I will give thee riches, and wealth, and honour, such as none of the kings before thee, neither shall there any after thee have the like.
>
> II Chronicles 1:11, 12

Within certain limits, any sovereign or ruler can re-echo Solomon's prayer for wisdom and receive it to govern their people, for it is—

> "By wisdom princes rule, and nobles, even all the judges of the earth . . . Riches and honour are with wisdom; yea, durable riches and righteousness."
> Proverbs 8:16, 18

Solomon's request for wisdom inspires believers to seek the same gift although it may not be for the same purpose Solomon used his gift—

> "If any of you lack wisdom, let him ask of God, that giveth to *all* men liberally, and upbraideth not; and it shall be given him."
>
> James 1:5, 6

Christ's promise that when the Holy Spirit came He would teach the apostles all things about Himself, and bring to their remembrance His many utterances, is a promise it is your privilege and mine to claim. Are not the Spirit's illumination, instruction and guidance for all those born anew by His power?

> "But the Comforter, which is the Holy Spirit, whom the Father will send in my name, he shall teach *you* all things, and bring all things to your remembrance whatsoever I have said unto you." John 14:16, 26

This indwelling Guest, the Redeemer sent "with us to dwell," is our unfailing Teacher and Monitor, and the same good Spirit guards us from all dangerous and fatal mistakes.

> But ye have an unction from the Holy One, and ye know all things . . . . But the anointing which ye have received of him abideth in you, and ye need not that any man teach you; but as the same anointing teacheth you of all things, and is truth, and is no lie, and even as it hath taught you, ye shall abide in Him.
>
> I John 2:20, 27

Are we among the number who daily appropriate such an unfailing Source of infallible wisdom? There is no excuse for ignorance in spiritual truth and tasks when we have the unerring Spirit so near to undertake.

It should further be stipulated that care must be taken to understand each divine promise in its true sense and rightly apply the same to our own heart and life. It is always necessary to ascertain the original setting of a promise and not view it in any unconnected and insulated fashion. All divine promises form a harmonious scheme, namely that we might "glorify God and enjoy Him forever" as the *Shorter Catechism* expresses it. All His promises have a beneficent end. While the promises are before us in rich profusion they should be examined in their respective settings, as they appear in the Bible. Often this method is not valid with promises from the *Psalms* and the *Proverbs*, since both of these sections of Scripture are like necklaces made up of separate pearls of truth. Reference is made to the promises as diamonds from a mine, each of which has its own purity and peculiar splendor, independently of all that surrounds them in the mine. It is otherwise with many diamonds of truth, the value of which often depends upon its meaning; and its meaning very often upon its connection.

For an illustration of this we turn to a definite promise given to Paul for a particular purpose in a time of trial. There was given to him "a thorn in the flesh, the messenger of Satan to buffet him, lest he should be exalted above measure." Thrice Paul besought the Lord to relieve him of this thorn, but was met with the Divine announcement, "My grace is sufficient for thee: for my strength is made perfect in weakness" (II Cor. 12:7-9). What saint among us has not found consolation in those precious words, "My grace is sufficient for thee"? When overwhelmed by the trials and tribulations of this world we read this promise and say to our despondent heart, "Up! trudge another mile." But while we have every right to appropriate and apply such an assuring promise, we must first of all interpret it in the light of its context. Certain verses, then, express the experiences of particular persons, yet what is recorded of them is for our instruction and comfort so that if we find ourselves in similar circumstances, like the saints of old we, too, can find grace and mercy. The following promise is applicable to *all* saints as well as to the Psalmist to whom it was given.

"Thou, which hast shewed me great and sore troubles, shalt quicken me again, and shalt bring me up again from the depths of the earth." Psalm 71:20. (Compare Psalm 118:6 with Hebrews 13:6.)

While it may be evident that a chosen promise has a distinct and obvious sense by itself, yet often it will be found that there are other aspects of truth to be gleaned by examining the background of the promise as given in the Sacred Record. The Bible must not be used as a mere arsenal of texts. The drift of truth is often lost by taking a verse out of its setting. There have been those who thought that the mere quotation of some text, often torn from its context and given a twist, was the last word in argument about several controversial matters such as abstinence from alcohol and Sabbath Day observance. No isolated verse is of worth except in the meaning which the Holy Spirit intended it to convey when He inspired some holy man of old to record it. A misunderstood text can result in false comfort, groundless fears, and unauthorized conduct, as for example, the snakehandling founded on Mark 16:18. Are we not instructed to "compare spiritual things with spiritual"? The whole of Scripture must interpret any part we consider and the part must be looked at in the light of the whole. It is only thus that we can arrive at "an enlarged and consistent view of the full extent and lovely harmony of divine truth: and the more our minds can embrace of this, the richer will be their satisfaction and the more stable their peace. These promises, indeed, have each their own light

and beauty; but it is only as sparks struck from the sun; and we must not be satisfied with sparks, but seek to walk in the sun's full light and warmth. The promises have each their attractive loveliness –

'Like atoms of the rainbow flutt'ring round' –

"but it is to the full arched bow itself that we look, as the blessed symbol of God's covenant of peace."

Another recognizable condition is that any chosen promise must be contemplated *practically*. A study of the New Testament proves that none of its writers bring forward either the truths or the promises of the Gospel merely for *comfort*. "There is a way of comforting," says Dr. Ralph Wardlaw, "that is anything but practical. It is rather a soothing or lulling of the spirit into an indolent and sentimental repose, than the animating of it with the joy of the Lord, which is the strength for active service." Take Paul, for example, who, when he presents a promise of comfort, at the same time excites to duty. With him, truth had to be turned to practical account. When the Apostle reminds us of the paternal relation of God to His own it is to animate them to "resist unto blood, striving against sin." To Paul, the promises were not an end in themselves but were the means to an end. "Having, therefore, these promises, dearly beloved, let us cleanse ourselves from all pollution of the flesh and spirit, perfecting holiness in the fear of God" (II Corinthians 6:16-7:1).

John, likewise, turns truth to a practical account when, after putting the saints in remembrance of what manner of the love the Father hath bestowed upon us in making us His children, checks any undue elation or elevation over our glorious hopes by instantly reminding us that such is our hope in Christ that we should purify ourselves even as Christ Himself is pure (I John 3:1-3).

Peter inspires us as he speaks of "the exceeding great and precious promises" but he does not leave us to muse over the promises as such. Why were they given? What is their ultimate purpose? Peter tells us –

"That by these promises ye might be partakers of the divine nature, having escaped the corruption of the world through lust." II Peter 1:4

At all times, our eyes must be fixed, not on a promise merely, but on Him, the only Foundation of our hopes, and in and through whom alone all the promises are made good to us: also upon the Holy Spirit the Comforter, through whose grace we discover the excellency and blessedness of the promises. The Three Persons of the ever-blessed Trinity stand ready to supplement their promises with deeds.

Doubtless you have read of the old lady who had an extremely lazy and unworthy method of using the Bible for help and guidance. When passing through a time of need her way of securing divine aid was to hold a closed Bible in her hand and pray, "O, Lord, give me the right verse to comfort me." Then she would let her Bible fall open, and the first verse her eyes lighted upon was supposed to be the one divinely given. Well, up against it one day, the dear soul prayed and acted in this fashion, and the first verse to catch her glance was, "And Judas went out and hanged himself." Quickly she closed her Bible, and said, "Lord, that is not at all fitting. Give me another verse." Eyes and Bible were again closed, and the Book opened at the place, "Go thou and do likewise." Petulant over the failure to receive the promise she felt she needed and should receive, she prayed the third time, and let her Bible open at random. This time she read, "What thou doest, do quickly." It is needless to say that this is *not* the way to use God's Word or to seek assurance therein.

While the promises form "God's Promise Box" and constitute the believer's spiritual treasure and, as we shall see, it is profitable to have them collected and classified for our enlightenment and edification, the promises, in themselves, must never be allowed to supersede or substitute our study of the Bible as a whole. Although the promises are a mine of unsearchable riches, they are only specimens of still greater spiritual wealth. Precious in themselves, they are only meant to stimulate investigation. "The believer whom these grains of precious ore shall lure to further search to the mine itself will find his pleasing toil amply repaid from the endless store which remains behind of hidden treasure."

In these days of stress and strain, there is a tendency to forego the daily period of consecutive Bible reading and study and to depend upon a collection of texts in a "promise box," or upon a selection of verses found in a "Daily Light" compilation, or upon brief paragraphs based on Scripture verses, such as those already mentioned in our *Introduction*. While these aids are commendable, however, they must never be allowed to substitute our study of the Bible as a progressive and complete revelation of the purpose of God. Fragments of truth are not sufficiently nourishing. We must feast upon the whole loaf.

Another evident stipulation is that no promise is binding if the performance of it would be *unlawful*. It is surely wrong to make a promise which, in itself, is wrong. Such a promise merits no fulfilment. If the promiser was ignorant of the unlawfulness of a promise made, the realization of it cannot possibly change wrong to right. Jephthah's terrible vow (Judges 11:30) which was a promise, was one he should not have made, seeing that the fulfilment of it in the sacrifice of his daughter meant disobedience to the divine law, "Thou shalt not kill." No divine promise comes within this category for all God's promises are in perfect harmony with the principles of moral rectitude. He cannot offer mankind anything contrary to His own righteous being. Further, because of His Omniscience and able, therefore, to read the end from the beginning, God is able to foresee all circumstances arising between the making of His promises and the time of their fulfilment. Man may not know what shall be on the morrow but God does, and no changes in our circumstances can alter His ultimate plan.

Attention is drawn to another stipulation, namely, no human promise is obligatory when it is *contrary to previous engagements*. It is possible for a person to let slip what they had formerly promised to do, and thereby bring themselves under the necessity of a counter-promise, at variance with the former. Thus one promise must be broken. But nowhere in Scripture is God found guilty of a counter-promise. As the All-Perfect One, He cannot suffer from any lapse of memory. Neither can He forget. His promises were made centuries before their fulfilment and cannot be crossed. Having infinity, all His promises go back to eternity and form one harmonious scheme of promissory kindness, gradually unfolding from the beginning till the future of time, and in regard to their final accomplishment reach forward to the close of the Church's and the world's history and embrace eternity.

A further condition governing promises is that no promise is binding if it has been extorted from the promiser by violence or fear. Any such promise is made to be broken.

Judas promised to sell his Lord for thirty pieces of silver. How different his end would have been had he courageously, repentantly, broken such a fatal promise. To regard any divine promise in this way would be the most fearful impiety. God is infinitely above all such influence. What He asks for is faith, not fear. Love inspired all of His gracious promises. He, Himself, is independent of any of His creatures. Possessed of Almightiness, He has nothing to fear even though all of the 3,000 millions of the world's population conspired to destroy Him. A word from Him could annihilate them all, just as a word gave them existence.

IV

THE SURETY OF THE PROMISES

The worth and excellency of the promises are enhanced by the evidences that every one of them can be realized. Behind every promise we have the Word and oath of Him who cannot lie, that so by these promises, we might have consolation. Christ is made our Surety, not only of all God's promises, which He ratified by His own blood (Hebrews 7:22), but of all the promises concerning His blood-washed children. As "the Truth" (John 14:6), He will ever act in harmony with His own nature.

Then the Holy Spirit witnesses to the truth of the promises by His miraculous operations when first poured out at Pentecost, and by His sanctifying influences upon the hearts of true believers since that historic Day. He it is who encourages us to accept the promises as a living hope and who furnishes us with well-provided evidences of the reliability of any God-given promise. He is also the One who can turn promises into performances. He takes all the several promises made to every exercise of grace and every performance of duty, and makes them real in experience, and a means of encouragement to be "stedfast, unmovable, always abounding in the work of the Lord" (I Corinthians 15:58).

All God's promises concerning His own, are dated, in heaven and with our finite knowledge we cannot read the time when many of them are to be fulfilled. If a friend of vast wealth and of the highest integrity gave you a promissory note saying, "Twelve months after the date of this note I promise to pay you $10,000," as the promisee, you might regret the lapse of the intervening months, yet you would certainly expect the promised sum on the date mentioned. Suppose, however, that the note read differently, say in this strain: "At my own pleasure, and in my own time, I promise to pay you, or your heirs, $10,000." Then you would expect such a sum to be forthcoming at some time or the other, provided the friend did not fail financially, change his mind, or forget, or die.

The fact that God has dated His promises according to His sovereign will and His infinite knowledge of what is best, does not in the least diminish their value, nor render their final accomplishment less certain. When some of these promises are to be realized may be unknown to us, but God never fails, never changes His mind, never forgets, and can never die. How vividly this fact is illustrated in the experiences of many of God's saints.

Abraham had the promise of a son, but long, wearisome years dragged by before Isaac was born.

David was God's anointed king, but he was a poor fugitive dwelling in caves and hunted like a partridge on the mountains, before the throne of Israel became his.

Paul was divinely assured that not one of those who sailed with him on the stormy Mediterranean should be lost; but the vessel was wrecked, and some swam ashore, "and the rest, some on boards, and some on broken pieces of ship. And so it came to pass, that they all escaped to land."

How and when God's promise may be fulfilled is beyond our ken. Often we are brought to the end of our own resources, and go all to pieces, like Paul's ship, yet at the right moment and in the right way, the Divine Promiser appears to fulfil His promise – the performance of which is as certain as His own existence. God is never *before* His time and *never* after it. He is "a very *present* help in trouble" (Psalm 46:1). Let us dwell, then, upon the manifold evidences of the surety of His promises.

Divine promises must be realized because

they are the promises of *Deity*. They are the promises of God:

> "God, which He had promised afore by his prophets in the holy scriptures, concerning his Son Jesus Christ our Lord . . . ." (Romans 1:2, 3)

Because of all He is, in Himself as *God*, He was, and is, bound to fulfil every word of His. Those prophets were not reliable messengers, if what they declared as *promises* were only empty words; and the Scriptures would not be *holy* in recording same. The witness of the New Testament, however, is eloquent with the fulfilment of the covenant God had made with His chosen –

> "I have sworn unto my servant David."
> Psalm 89:3

"The truth of God to confirm the promises made unto the fathers." Romans 15:8 As "*all* Scripture is given by inspiration of God" (II Timothy 3:16), its divine promises must be God-breathed, and therefore impossible of non-fulfilment. With such a *God* as my Father I should bid "Farewell" to any doubt and trust Him wholly. The divine promises, fountains of my perpetual refreshment, are in His heart. What more should I need?

Further, His promises are backed by His *faithfulness* which runs like a golden thread through His Word. All writers of Holy Writ combine to magnify God for His unfailing faithfulness to all generations.

> "Know therefore that the Lord thy God, He is God, the faithful God, which keepeth covenant and mercy with them that love Him and keep His commandment to a thousand generations."
> Deuteronomy 7:9

"He is faithful that promised."
> Hebrews 10:23

"Sarah received strength to conceive seed, and was delivered of a child when she was past age, because she judged Him faithful who had promised." Hebrews 11:11

"God is faithful, by whom ye were called unto the fellowship of His Son Jesus Christ our Lord."
> I Corinthians 1:9

"God is faithful, who will not suffer you to be tempted above that which ye are able." I Corinthians 10:13

"Faithful is he that calleth you, who will also do it." I Thessalonians 5:24 God's faithfulness, then, is our special ground of encouragement as we appropriate His promises.

"Great is Thy faithfulness."
> Lamentations 3:23

David would have us feed upon this divine faithfulness which is "the girdle of His reins" (Isaiah 11:5). The R.V. of "Verily thou shalt be fed." (Psalm 37:3) is "Feed upon His faithfulness."

Each line hath a treasure, each promise a pearl,
  That all if they may secure;
And we know that when time and the world pass away,
  God's Word shall forever endure.

Another guarantee of fulfilment is in the very names of God. What an evangel each one of His *Jehovah* titles contains! Among the names given to the Divine Being in the Old Testament, that of Jehovah (in the A.V. "Lord") is by far the most frequently employed, occurring no fewer than 6823 times; other designations are used less often – *Elohim* (God) 2570 times, *Adonai* (Lord) 134 times, and *Shaddai* (Almighty) 39 times. Each name or designation is a promise.

There is general recognition of the fact that *Jehovah* was the specific name of the God of the Israelites as distinguished from the deities or tribal gods of the surrounding Gentile nations. Such a name was first revealed to Moses when shepherding his flocks at Horeb.

> "The Lord (Jehovah), the God of the fathers of Israel." Exodus 3:15

"Thou alone, whose name is Jehovah."
> Psalm 83:18 R.V.

Peter, in his Pentecostal sermon, called Jesus "Lord," the word used in the Septuagint as the translation of *Jehovah*, Paul spoke of Him as "The Lord Jesus Christ."

> "Thou shalt call His name Jesus."
> Matthew 1:21

Christ, then, was Jehovah Himself become incarnate, God manifest in the flesh. Jehovah was the Covenant name, and in Christ, God was mindful of His gracious covenant.

Abraham commemorated God's deliverance and grace manifested on Mount Moriah by calling the place *Jehovah-Jireh* -- "the Lord will provide."

> "Abraham called the name of the place Jehovah-Jireh; as it is said to this day. In the mount of the Lord it shall be seen (R.V. *provided*)." Genesis 22:14

"My God shall supply all your need according to His riches in glory by (R.V. *in*) Christ Jesus." Philippians 4:19

What a dread transaction that was up to the last act, when Abraham's hand was stayed and Isaac was spared. How dramatic was God's deliverance and provision! Truly there is no Actor like God! When He steps upon the stage, all human actors are put into the shade.

"There is none like unto the God of Jeshurun, who rideth upon the heaven for thy help, and in his excellency in the skies." Deuteronomy 33:26

Paul's words are simply the New Testament version of *Jehovah-Jireh*, and the supplies which God provides for His own today are just the four things which He provided for Abraham.

1. Propitiation for guilt – a lamb for a burnt offering
2. Strength for duty – the necessary faith was supplied
3. Deliverance from danger – the ram substituted for Isaac
4. Blessing for obedience – sacrifice is always rewarded

No matter what need may arise, *Jehovah-Jireh* is a name promising relief. In ways and by means unknown and unthought of, God can interpose and effect deliverance.

Another divine title, so full of promise for those who are physically and spiritually sick, is *Jehovah-Rophi*, "The miracle healer."

"I am the Lord that healeth thee."
Exodus 15:26
"Be merciful unto me and heal my soul." Psalm 41:4
"Who healeth all thy diseases."
Psalm 103:3
"Is there no physician there?"
Jeremiah 8:22
"Thou hast no healing medicines."
Jeremiah 30:13
"I would have healed Israel."
Hosea 7:1
"Many followed Jesus, and He healed them all." Matthew 12:15
"To heal the brokenhearted." Luke 4:18
"The healing of the Nations."
Revelation 22:2

The foregoing passages, and many others, intimate that humanity collectively and individually stands in need of a Physician who is able to heal diseases of various sorts – physical, mental and moral, and that, in the Lord there is One well able to heal the sin-sick of their wounds. When, in response to the cry of Moses, God healed the bitter waters at Marah, He revealed Himself as the One always ready to act as the Physician of His people. And the character of Himself here displayed was pre-eminently that in which Jesus presented Himself to Israel when He appeared as God's Representative. What miracle-healings were His as He moved among the sick and needy!

The tragedy is that so frequently the physically and spiritually diseased will not seek the healing balm in Gilead. Divine prescriptions for relief are not followed. Israel did not follow the prescription and enjoy the promise –

"If thou wilt diligently hearken to the voice of the Lord thy God, and wilt do that which is right in his sight, and wilt give ear to his commandments and keep all his statutes, I will put none of these diseases upon thee which I have brought upon the Egyptians."
Exodus 15:26

The medicine prescribed by Jesus for all with physical ills and spiritual woes implies that men and nations must believe in His Person, rest upon His works, listen to His teaching and follow His example.

"Come unto Me, all ye that labour and are heavy laden, and I will give you rest . . . ye shall find rest unto your souls." Matthew 11:28-30

Promise is also laid up in the further divine designation of *Jehovah-Nissi*, "The Lord is my banner."

"Moses built an altar and called the name of it Jehovah-nissi." Exodus 17:15
"I am thy shield." Genesis 15:1
"Give me the shield of thy salvation."
II Samuel 23:2; Psalm 3:3
"His banner over me was love."
Song of Solomon 8:4
"A banner to them that fear thee."
Psalm 60:4
"We will set up our banners."
Psalm 20:5
"A standard for the people."
Isaiah 49:22
"Signs and wonders may be done by the name of thy holy Child Jesus."
Acts 4:30
"The captain (R.V. "Author") of their salvation." Hebrews 2:10

Banners, bearing a figure or device of some sort, and frequently inscribed, have from time immemorial been borne in front of armies – sometimes as rallying-points for the soldiers, as with the Israelites, every tribe of whom had its own particular standard. Constantine's banner bore the sign of the Cross. Across the altar Moses reared, he wrote, "The Lord is my banner," in commemoration of the recent victory over Amalek, one of the fiercest of Israel's enemies.

The banner speaks of God as a *Campaigner*, and a victorious One at that. "The Lord shall fight for you, and ye shall hold your peace." In every subsequent age hostile forces have waged war against God and Jesus Christ, and against the Church. But Jehovah is a Man of War, and eternally participates in the warfare against darkness, error and sin. The promise for our hearts is that with God's help, victory is sure. All against Him and His own are certain to be overthrown. "We are more than conquerors through him who loved us." Victory is ever of the Lord.

The promise and performance of our personal sanctification are resident in another "Jehovah" title, namely, *Jehovah-Mekaddishkem*, "The Lord our sanctification."
"The Lord that doth sanctify you."
Exodus 31:13
"Who is like thee glorious in holiness."
Exodus 15:11
"Sanctify yourselves."
II Chronicles 19:34; 30:17
"He is our holy God." Joshua 24:19
"I am the Lord that sanctify them."
Ezekiel 37:28
"Ye are holy unto the Lord." Ezra 8:28
"Sanctify them through Thy truth."
John 17:17
"Sanctified . . . by the Spirit of our God." I Corinthians 1:2; 6:11
"The very God of peace sanctify you wholly." I Thessalonians 5:23
The primary root of "sanctification" is that of *separation,* or "setting apart." It is a *separation* including a *dedication,* the general sense being the separation and dedication of an object or a person to and for God, to belong wholly to Him and to be used for His Glory.
"But know that the Lord hath set apart him that is godly for himself: the Lord will hear when I call unto him."
Psalm 4:3
The double aspect of the separation is that of separation *from* all that is antagonistic to God's holy will, and then separation *unto* Him for the witness and work as those who are His. Such a sanctification is Positional, Practical and Progressive, and in its entirety is all of God, seeing it is His provision, will and call. (See Hebrews 9:13, 14; 10:10; I Thessalonians 4:3, 7; 5:23, 24). What a

thrice-holy God has commanded, He has likewise promised, and waits to fulfill in our fully-yielded lives.

One of the most revered of divine titles to Jew and Christian alike is *Jehovah-Shalom,* "The Lord send peace" (Judges 6:24). That He is the God of Peace is seen in the fact that this attribute dominates the Bible. Definite and implied promises on the many aspects of this theme abound. To gather together all the references to "Peace" provides one with an antidote for the fear, unrest and turmoil of times like these. Run your eye over all these "peace" texts, and your song will be—

Peace, peace, sweet peace,
　Wonderful gift from above;
Oh, wonderful, wonderful peace,
　Sweet peace, the gift of God's love.

"God shall give . . . an answer of peace." Genesis 41:16
"The Lord . . . give thee peace."
Numbers 6:26
"Bless his people with peace."
Psalm 29:11
"Great peace have they that love thy law." Psalm 119:165
"Peace shall they add unto thee."
Proverbs 3:2
"All his paths are peace." Proverbs 3:17
"Length of days, and long life, and peace, shall they add unto thee."
Proverbs 3:2
"The Prince of Peace." Isaiah 9:6
"Thou wilt keep him in perfect peace."
Isaiah 26:3
"Then had thy peace been as a river."
Isaiah 48:18
"Neither shall the covenant of my peace be removed." Isaiah 54:10
"Blessed are the peacemakers."
Matthew 5:9
"Peace I leave with you, My peace I give unto you." John 14:27
"That in me ye might have peace."
John 16:33
"He is our peace." Ephesians 2:14
"The Lord himself give you peace."
II Thessalonians 3:16
"Let the peace of God rule in your hearts." Colossians 3:15
"Peace that passeth all understanding."
Philippians 4:17
"Gideon built an altar to the Lord, and called it Jehovah-Shalom."
Judges 6:24
Having received the sign that the Person who talked with him was *Jehovah,* Gideon

built an altar in commemoration of the inter-view and called it "Jehovah is Peace," mean-ing, that peace for the individual and for the nation can only be found in returning to Je-hovah, and that for both, Jehovah alone is the Author and Giver of peace. There is the further thought that Jehovah Himself *is* Peace. Peace, then, is not something but *Someone.* "He hath made peace by the blood of the cross" (Colossians 1:20), and such a peace He now gives us, and preaches to all who are afar off (Ephesians 2:17). A blood-soaked earth awaits His coming as "the Prince of Peace," to bless it with universal peace.

> "It is enough! Earth's struggles soon shall cease.
> And Jesus call us to Heaven's perfect peace."

That God is well able to perform all He has promised can be gathered from the wealth of meaning wrapped up in another *Jehovah* title, namely *Jehovah-Isabaoth,* "The Lord of hosts" (I Samuel 1:3).

> "This is God's host . . . Manhanaim."
> Genesis 32:2
> "A great host like the host of God."
> I Chronicles 12:22
> "Over the host of the Lord."
> I Chronicles 9:19
> "Very jealous for the Lord God of hosts."
> I Kings 19:10
> "The Lord of hosts is with us."
> Psalm 46:7, 11
> "Go forth with our hosts." Psalm 108:11
> "The Lord of hosts is His name."
> Amos 5:27
> "The Lord of Sabaoth." Romans 9:29
> "The Lord of hosts He is the King of Glory." Psalm 24:7, 10

Is not the plural used in this divine designa-tion so full of encouragement for our hearts? Does it not indicate God's sovereignty in ev-ery realm, and therefore His ability to fulfil every promise of His on our behalf? He is not only "Lord" but the "Lord of *Hosts,*" all hosts! He is Lord of the angelic hosts above. Having created all angelic beings, they carry out His will and purpose on our behalf, as Hezekiah learned when one angel slew those 185,000 Assyrians. God is also the Lord of all the feathered hosts of the sky. His power brought the birds into being and they willingly act as His messengers when needed, as Elijah discovered when the ravens fed him. God is likewise the Lord of all the stellar hosts, sun, moon and stars, they are His handi-work and having created them, He can con-trol them, as Joshua realized when God made the sun to stand still as he fought to vic-tory over the Amalekites. Then, God is Lord of all the animal hosts, as Daniel experienced when He closed the lions' mouths and then opened them. God is Lord over all human hosts, and would have us cease from fearing man, whose breath is in his nostrils. As to all hellish hosts, is not God supreme in this realm too? Who is the devil? He is only a dog on a leash and cannot go any further than divine permission, as the God of Job teaches.

With such a great God to back up any word of His why should we fear anyone or anything? May grace be ours to encourage ourselves in all God is in Himself!

Most precious of all the *Jehovah* titles is *Jehovah-Rohi,* "The Lord is my shepherd" (Psalm 23:1).

> "Give ear, O Shepherd of Israel."
> Psalm 80:1
> "We are the . . . sheep of His hand."
> Psalms 95:7; 100:3
> "Guided them like a flock in the wil-derness." Psalm 77:20
> "He leadeth me beside the still waters."
> Psalm 23:2
> "Maketh thy flock to rest at noon."
> Song of Solomon 1:7
> "He shall feed his flock like a shep-herd." Isaiah 40:11
> "All we like sheep have gone astray."
> Isaiah 53:6
> "All shall have one shepherd."
> Ezekiel 34:23
> "There is no shepherd." Ezekiel 34:8
> "Awake, O sword, against my shep-herd." Zechariah 13:7
> "I am the good shepherd." John 10:14
> "That great shepherd of the sheep."
> Hebrews 13:20
> "When the chief shepherd shall appear."
> I Peter 2:25; 5:4

Oriental shepherds had certain marks by which they knew their own sheep. With us, farmers have their own way of initialing or "ear-marking" their sheep so that they can identify them anywhere. Christ knows His people by certain distinguishing marks. He knows their faces, their names, their characters. His true sheep know Him, love and follow Him. They possess His dispo-sition of meekness and lowliness. As His sheep, do we believe that it is His province to lead, feed, protect and heal us? Be-cause He laid down His life for the sheep, they are precious to Him. As blood-washed ones they are carried in His bosom and fed in the most suitable pastures. Why should we charge our souls with care with such a Shepherd to protect and provide?

Another satisfying glimpse of our "Great Jehovah" is given us by Isaiah – *Jehovah-Goal-eka*, "The Lord my redeemer" (Isaiah 44:24). Is not the Bible – the crimson Book – saturated with the truth of God's redeeming grace and power? If "the life of the flesh is in the blood" (Leviticus 17:11), it is also true that "the life of the Bible is in the blood." Take the Blood out of the Bible, and how useless it becomes in imparting hope to a world of sinners lost and ruined by the fall.

"Redeem Israel to God." Psalm 25:22
"Thou hast . . . redeemed thy people" Psalm 74:2; 106:10
"He hath redeemed us from our enemies." Psalm 136:24
"Thou hast redeemed me." Psalm 31:5
"With him is plenteous redemption." Psalm 103:7
"Return unto me for I have redeemed thee." Isaiah 44:22
"Is my hand shortened . . . that it cannot redeem." Isaiah 50:2
"The holy people, the redeemed." Isaiah 62:12
"Redeemer, Thy name is from everlasting." Isaiah 63:16
"The redeemed shall walk there." Isaiah 35:9
"Saith the Lord the redeemer." Isaiah 44:6
"Shalt know that I . . . am . . . thy redeemer." Isaiah 60:16
"Ye shall be redeemed." Isaiah 52:3
"The year of my redeemed is come." Isaiah 63:4
"Their redeemer is strong." Jeremiah 50:34
"Thou hast redeemed my life." Lamentations 3:58
"He hath . . . redeemed his people." Luke 1:68
"He which should have redeemed Israel." Luke 24:21
"The redemption that is in Christ Jesus." Romans 3:24
"In whom we have redemption." Ephesians 1:7
"Christ hath redeemed us." Galatians 3:13
"Redemption through his blood." Colossians 1:14
"Redeemed us unto God by thy blood." Revelation 5:9
"Redeemed from all evil." Genesis 48:16
"Thy people . . . whom thou hast redeemed." Deuteronomy 9:26
"For I know that my redeemer liveth." Job 19:25

There are three Greek verbs translated *redeem* in the New Testament. One means *to go into the market-place to buy a captive;* another implies *to bring out of the market-place that which has been bought;* the third signifies *to set free* or *let go.* All three verbs are required to tell the whole story of sin, bondage and redemption. The first promise of redemption is to be found in the opening pages of the Bible. As soon as Adam and Eve sinned, God promised a perfect redemption in the words –
"The Seed of the Woman shall bruise the serpent's head." Genesis 3:15
At Calvary, Christ, as the Seed, destroyed Satan's power and authority and bought us back from sin's slavery, captivity and death. "Ye were bought with a price" (I Corinthians 6:20) – and what a price! He gave His life a ransom (Matthew 20:28; I Timothy 2:8). As *Elohim* is His creative name, so *Jehovah* is His redemptive and covenant-keeping name.

There is still another *Jehovah* combination, so full of promise for all who are "guilty, vile and full of sin." It is *Jehovah-Tsidkenu*, "The Lord our righteousness" (Jeremiah 23:6; 33:16).
"In righteousness and uprightness." I Kings 3:6
"By justifying the righteous." II Chronicles 6:23
"Rehearse the righteous acts of the Lord." Judges 5:11
"My righteousness is in it." Job 6:29
"Ascribe righteousness to the maker." Job 36:3
"Open to me the gates of righteousness." Psalm 118:19
"My tongue . . . shalt talk of thy righteousness." Psalm 51:14
"I will behold thy face in righteousness." Psalm 17:15
"I will make mention of thy righteousness." Psalm 71:16
"The words of my mouth are in righteousness." Proverbs 8:8
"Righteousness exalteth a nation." Proverbs 14:34
"Ye that follow after righteousness." Isaiah 51:1
"A king shall reign in righteousness." Isaiah 32:1
"Sanctified in righteousness." Isaiah 5:16
"Righteousness shall be the girdle." Isaiah 11:5

"I will bring near my righteousness."
Isaiah 46:13
"Brought forth our righteousness."
Jeremiah 51:10
"Righteousness belongeth unto thee."
Daniel 9:7
"I came not to call the righteous but sinners." Mark 2:17
"In holiness and righteousness."
Luke 1:75
"Righteousness unto God."
Romans 6:13
"Grace reign through righteousness."
Romans 5:21
"Made unto us wisdom and righteousness." I Corinthians 1:30
"The peaceable fruits of righteousness."
Hebrews 12:11
"The righteousness which is by faith."
Hebrews 11:7
"A crown of righteousness."
II Timothy 4:8
"Fine linen is the righteousness of the saints." Revelation 19:8

In his *Precious Promises*, Cunningham Geikie says: "If we look out on some fair garden in the height of June, the glory of the varied flowers, and the mingled sweetness of their odours may well delight us; but if we would enjoy the fulness of the beauties before us, and the fragrant delicacy of their perfume, we must go to each bed and border and bend lovingly over it. So with the promises; to look at them as a whole as they bloom all over the garden of God's Word, may well ravish our senses; but to know their full richness we need to look at them in detail, more closely."

This good advice is most necessary as we come to bend lovingly over the flower of divine righteousness before us in the above references in so many hues. Self-righteousness, God condemns (Isaiah 64:6; Philippians 3:9). By his own works the sinner can never be justified (Romans 3:19-21; 4:4,5). He is under God's wrath because he is ungodly, unrighteous, and holds the truth in unrighteousness (I Corinthians 1:18-32). The glorious promise of the Gospel, however, is that righteousness before God for sinful men has been provided by God and can be found by repentant and believing sinners only in Christ. Righteousness, satisfying God, is a universal need of man—a righteousness which puts a sinful soul right before God. Such a righteousness is an impossible attainment by man, whose sinful endeavors

can never gain favor with God. A sinner is absolutely helpless when it comes to working out a justifying righteousness for himself. But the promises we have considered on such a theme assure us that such a required righteousness has been divinely provided. This righteousness can never be *attained*—only *obtained* by faith (Romans 3:22; 5:18; 10:11; Philippians 3:9). It is God's free gift to the sinner and becomes his, not through any self-merit but only through Christ's merit. Our own much-vaunted self-righteousnesses are as filthy rags in the sight of a thrice-holy God, who is our Righteousness.

There is yet another Jehovah title guaranteeing the fulfilment of all He has promised on our behalf. It is *Jehovah-Shammah*, meaning, "The Lord is there" (Ezekiel 48:35). For the city, church, or Christian, the presence of God is assured.

"Behold I am with thee and will keep thee." Genesis 28:15
"The Lord was with thee."
Genesis 26:28
"Because the Lord was with him."
Genesis 39:2; 21:23
"My presence shall go with thee."
Exodus 33:14
"He it is that doth go before thee."
Deuteronomy 10:17
"Glory and honour are in his presence." I Chronicles 16:27
"Cast them out from his presence."
II Kings 24:20
"Surely I will be with thee."
Judges 6:16
"The Lord be with you." Ruth 2:4
"With thee whithersoever thou goest."
Joshua 1:9
"For thou art with me." Psalm 23:4
"Immanuel, God with us."
Matthew 1:23
"I am with you alway."
Matthew 28:20
"I will never leave you nor forsake you." Hebrews 13:5
"Thou . . . remainest for ever."
Lamentations 5:19

Christ is not only in His Church *metaphorically*, or *symbolically*, or *materially*, but *really* and *spiritually*, in the Person of His Spirit, who dwells in the hearts of His people and who makes Himself known in assemblies gathered in His Name. Does He not speak of His true Church as His habitation? (Ephesians 2:20,21). "God is in the midst of her" (Psalm 46:5). He is ever in the midst of His own. Thus, when we gather in His Name we have not to pray for His presence, but seek by the Spirit's aid to realize His presence.

"What if Thy form we cannot see,
We feel, and know that Thou art here."

Alas! too often we meet for worship, ministry and prayers and fail to realize His nearness. With Jacob we have to confess, "Surely the Lord is in this place, and I knew it not" (Genesis 28:16). In congregational worship we often sing —

Jesus, stand among us,
In Thy risen power,
Let this time of worship
Be a hallow'd hour.

Such times of worship, however, would be more hallowed, if only we had the consciousness that He *is* standing among us in all His risen power. What mighty occasions our gatherings would be if only each worshipper realized how near the Lord is! Of old, the over-powering presence of Jehovah was so evident, that the priests could not minister (I Kings 8:11; II Chronicles 5:14):

God *is* here! we feel His Presence
In this consecrated place:
But we need the soul refreshing
Of His free, unbounded grace.

Another expressive compound name of "Jehovah" is *Jehovah El Shaddai,* the exact meaning of which is uncertain. Scofield says that its etymological definition is both interesting and touching and suggests that *El* means "strength" or "The Strong One," while *Shaddai* is derived from the Hebrew word "Shad" meaning, "The Breast" and is so used of this female organ (Genesis 49:25, etc.). Other authorities affirm that *Shaddai* is derived from a root meaning "To overthrow," and could thus imply "The Destroyer," a play on the sound being found in "destruction from the Almighty" (Isaiah 13:6). It may also have the root meaning of "The Rain-Giver" or can be interpreted as "My Mountain" or "My Lord." Traditionally, *El Shaddai* is rendered "God Almighty," and thus stands for His Almightiness. *Sh,* implies "He *who* is;" and *Dai,* "all sufficient." "*All-sufficient*," better expresses both the Hebrew meaning and the characteristic use of the name in the Bible.

"I am the Almighty God."

Genesis 17:1

"God Almighty bless thee."

Genesis 28:3

"The name of God Almighty."

Exodus 6:3

"The vision of the Almighty."

Numbers 24:4

"He that is mighty." Luke 1:49

"The Lord God Almighty."

Revelation 1:8; 4:8; 11:17; 15:3; 21:22

Scofield's interpretation offers a profitable application: "*Shaddai* primarily means 'The Breasted One' and suggests God as *The Nourisher, The Strength-Giver, The Satisfier,* who pours Himself into believing lives. As fretful unsatisfied babe is not only strengthened and nourished from the mother's breast, but also quieted, rested, satisfied, so *El Shaddai* is that name of God which sets Him forth as *The Strength-Giver* and *Satisfier* of His people."

Our last Jehovah title, so full of promise, is *Jehovah-Ra-ah,* meaning "The Lord – the shepherd." As we think of Him thus, "The Shepherd Psalm" is immediately suggested. In Psalm 22, *Jehovah-Shalom* is seen making peace by the blood of His Cross. In Psalm 23, *Jehovah-Ra-ah* is shepherding those redeemed by His blood who are in the world. Promises of divine Shepherd-hood are many and varied.

"The shepherd, the stone of Israel."

Genesis 49:24

"The Lord is my shepherd." Psalm 23:1

"Give ear, O shepherd of Israel."

Psalm 80:1

"He shall feed his flock like a shepherd."

Isaiah 40:11

"I will raise up a shepherd in the land." Zechariah 16:1

"Awake, O sword, against my shepherd." Zechariah 13:7

"I am the good shepherd." John 16:14

"There shall be one fold, and one shepherd." John 10:16

"The Lord Jesus, that great shepherd of the sheep." Hebrews 13:20

"The shepherd and bishop of your souls." I Peter 2:25

"When the chief shepherd shall appear."

I Peter 5:4

The three aspects of the Divine Shepherd so rich in promise are those depicting Him as *good, great* and *chief.* The first to receive announcement of our Lord's birth were the lowly shepherds, which was most fitting, seeing that the One born in the manger came as the *Good Shepherd.* In this designation (John 10:11-29), there is emphasized the design and extent of His atoning death in its saving effect in respect to His own believing people–His sheep, in whose place He died. He saw them in peril from which they could be rescued only by the voluntary surrender of His own life.

Christ is truly called the *Good Shepherd* because by His vicarious sacrifice, He furnished the strongest proof of His love for us and of His willingness to give Himself to save us from destruction. The satanic wolf was upon us, and there was no possible way of escape, except by the Shepherd's throwing His body before the wolf's devouring jaws. How wonderful to know that the swift pursuit of the enemy has been stayed forever and that His flock shall be safely gathered into the fold.

As the *Great Shepherd*, His resurrection and exaltation are prominent (Hebrews 13:20, 21). From the Holy Spirit, Christ, as "The Good Shepherd" receives the additional title of the *Great Shepherd*, because of the efficacy of His death and His victory over it. "The God of peace" who raised His Son from the grave, assures us that the blood of the Good, Great Shepherd is the blood of the everlasting covenant, confirming and sealing both now and through all eternity the promise of the Father to save the sheep for whom the Shepherd died. Alive forevermore, the Shepherd is able to provide for and protect His sheep.

As the *Chief Shepherd*, Christ is the radiant Object of the believer's hope (I Peter 5:1-4). All who are called of God to minister the Word are under-shepherds and will be rewarded for their faithful services by the *Chief* Shepherd when He returns to gather His flock around Him. How sad it is that thousands of the flock do not allow a single beam of our Lord's return to brighten their pilgrim way in the wilderness of the world!

There are many more divine names and titles we could dwell upon, each of which imply the certainty of the fulfilment of divine promises. Our Lord Himself is described in almost 300 ways, either directly by name or indirectly by metaphor, or figure of speech, and all combined prove His power and willingness to fulfil His promised word on our behalf.

That all God's promises are sure is proven by a trinity of virtues the Bible presents of His being or nature. In Him dwell Truth, Love and Power in all their perfection. The promises are not only "exceeding great and precious" because of their varied character but because of the certainty of their fulfilment – a certainty resting upon the solid foundation of these three great aspects of the divine character.

There Is Truth

Amongst the moral excellencies which the Bible, by its universal tenor and in numberless specific instances, affirms belong to God, is Truth which covers veracity in all His statements, sincerity in all His invitations, faithfulness in all His promises and threatenings. His revealed character through the Bible is that He cannot act contrary to His nature. Neither can Christ as "The Truth," nor the Holy Spirit as "The Spirit of Truth." Because of this attribute of trustworthiness all the Holy Three are bound to fulfil their respective promises on man's behalf. A promise can be of little account if we have no confidence in the promiser, and every suspicion of his trustworthiness becomes a proportional deduction from its value. Had the Divine Promiser, the Most High God, the only true God, and the God of Truth, been found in only one instance to depart from any word of His, and to fail in the realization of it, that solitary instance would throw a gloom of uncertainty over all hopes which *all* His promises inspire.

But how encouraged we are by the absolute assurance that He has not, and cannot, fail in any instance.

"There failed not ought of *any* good thing which the Lord had spoken unto the house of Israel: *all* came to pass." Joshua 21:45

"Not *one* thing hath failed of *all* the good things which the Lord your God spake concerning you." Joshua 23:14

"According to *all* that he promised there hath not failed *one* word of *all* his good promise, which he promised by the hand of Moses his servant." I Kings 8:56

"Faithful is he that calleth you, who also will *do* it." I Thessalonians 5:24

It is, therefore, with unshaken and unshakeable security that we rest in the Lord, and in any word of His. "Faithful is he that promised" and it is this union of fidelity in the Promiser with the preciousness of blessing in His promises that completes the soul's happiness in the exercise of faith and hope.

"God is not a man, that he should lie . . . Hath he said, and shall he not do it? or hath he spoken, and shall he not make it good?

Numbers 23:19

"The strength of Israel will not lie nor repent." I Samuel 15:29

"The word of the Lord is tried."

Psalm 18:30

"I trust in thy word."

Psalm 119:42

"Thy word is true from the beginning." Psalm 119:160

"My heart standeth in awe at thy words." Psalm 119:161

"God . . . which keepeth truth for ever." Psalm 146:6

"Thy counsels of old are faithfulness and truth." Isaiah 25:1

"He cannot deny himself."

II Timothy 2:12

"God that cannot lie promised before the world began." Titus 1:2

"It is impossible for God to lie."

Hebrew 6:18

"The Lord is not slack concerning his promise." II Peter 3:9

"With whom is no variableness, neither shadow of turning." James 1:17

"For thy word's sake" is the ultimate appeal of those who can say with David as he sat before the Lord, "O Lord God, thou art that God, and thy words be true, and thou hast promised this goodness unto Thy servant" (II Samuel 7:28). All fear regarding the fulfilment of any divine promise is banished as we remember that truth enters essentially into the divine character, and that each Person in the Trinity cannot be anything else but truthful both in His words and works. Their promises are as the free and spontaneous dictates of divine goodness. None of the Divine Persons in the Godhead were obliged to make the promises they did and no power in the universe could hinder any of these Persons from breaking any of their promises, or call them to account for any breach of promise. Further, there is no higher authority to compel them to fulfil such promises which are binding upon them by those immutable principles of moral nature.

There Is Love

John, the apostle of love, gives us a brief but comprehensive statement of the divine character in the twice-repeated three-word phrase, "God is love" (I John 4:6, 18). Benevolence, then, belongs essentially and pre-eminently to God's moral nature and

is inseparably associated in its exercise with all His other perfections. All creation is stored with the most irresistible proofs that He who made the universe is good, supremely good, and not only good but righteous, kind and loving: and that this love will not suffer Him to go back upon, or to forget, what He promised.

"Thou shalt not be forgotten of me."

Isaiah 44:21

"Can a woman forget her sucking child, that she should not have compassion on the son of her womb? yea, they may forget, yet will I not forget thee."

Isaiah 49:15

"He remembered his holy promise."

Psalm 105:42

"The mercy promised to our fathers, and to remember his holy covenant."

Luke 1:72

There is only one thing our loving God ever forgets and that is the sins of the believer –

"Their sins and iniquities will I remember no more." Hebrews 10:17

There is one thing He never forgets, and that is the soul redeemed by the precious blood of His beloved son –

"Behold, I have graven thee upon the palms of my hands; thy walls are continually before Me." Isaiah 49:16

Behind all God's promises there is the love-beat of a father's heart, seeking the highest and best for those he loves. It may be hard at times when tears and trials are ours to rest in His love, and to accept His promises of protection, yet nevertheless because He is all-wise, as well as all-loving, He knows what is best for those He has promised to bless. God is His own interpreter and able, therefore, to make everything plain.

There Is Power

God's omnipotence ensures His ability to perform all that He has promised. Joel Chandler Harris in his *Nights With Uncle Remus* makes his character say –

"A promise is a promise, do you make it in de dark or de moon."

All God's promises, secret and open, are guaranteed performances, seeing all power is His in heaven and on earth.

"Abraham staggered not at the promise of God through unbelief; but was strong in faith, giving glory to God; and being fully persuaded that, what he had promised he was able also to perform."

Romans 4:19-21

A man with limited resources is capable of promise without performance. "A promise neglected is an untruth told." We have had friends who promised to help us in one direction or another but who, while they possibly meant well, through lack of ability or forgetfulness left us with an unrealized promise. With God, however, it is completely different, for His word is His bond. Behind what He offers to do there is not only His reliability but His omnipotence to execute His promise. Thus Abraham was fully persuaded that God was able to reverse the laws of nature on his behalf, in order to make him the father of many nations. Note Paul's three P's in the above verse—*Persuaded, Promised, Perform*.

May we be found sharing the weeping prophet's faith when he declared—

"Ah, Lord God, behold Thou hast made the heaven and the earth by thy great power and stretched-out arm, and there is nothing too hard for thee."

Jeremiah 32:17

Then there is the Master's tribute to God's Almightiness—

"With God all things are possible."

Mark 10:27

"Thou art the God that doest wonders." Psalm 77:14

The proverb has it, "A promise attended to is a debt settled." How we bless God because He has no unsettled debt! He is the Covenant-keeping God.

The numerous ways in which the divine promises are described afford further confidence in their fruition. Peter, for instance, speaks of them as "exceeding great and precious promises" (II Peter 1:4). These promises are indeed great in themselves seeing they were made by Him, "Who is great, and greatly to be praised" (Psalm 48:1). They are also exceeding great in number. How many there is is almost impossible to calculate. Then they are precious, for none can estimate their value. "The very excellence of their nature and the richness of their amount, make us only the more solicitous about the validity of the Word which constitutes their sole authority." They are also great and precious because of the nature and variety of the blessings they contain, the manner in which they are so clearly expressed, the certainty with which we can depend upon their fulfilment, and the happy, holy influences they have upon our minds. All the promises of God (II Corinthians 1:20) encourage believers to strive to perfect holiness in the Lord (II Corinthians 7:1).

The promises are called "good" because through them God seeks the highest good of those who love Him (II Samuel 7:28; I Kings 8:5, 6; James 1:12). "Holy" is another designation they bear (Psalm 105:42). Coming from a holy God, the promises when appropriated by faith result in holiness of life (II Peter 1:5). "Better promises" is another way of describing them. Promises under grace are infinitely better than those given under the Law. Promises of life can come from wrong sources. Ezekiel calls such promises, made by false prophets, lies (13:22). Promises to Israel related more or less to an earthly inheritance. Promises given to the redeemed are of a spiritual and eternal nature and therefore, infinitely better.

Another tribute to the surety of divine promises is their immutability and inviolability. "Immutable" means unchangeable, invariable, incapable of a change.

"The counsel of the Lord standeth for ever." Psalm 33:11

"I have sworn unto David my Servant." Psalm 39:3

"Thou art the same, and Thy years have no end." Psalm 105:27; Hebrew 1:12

"The word of our God standeth for ever." Isaiah 40:8

"I have purposed it, I will also do it." Isaiah 46:11

"I am the Lord, I change not."

Malachi 3:6

"The Scripture cannot be broken."

John 10:35

"Promise . . . confirms it with an oath." Hebrews 6:17

"The same yesterday, today, and for ever." Hebrews 13:8

"With whom there existeth no change, or declension of a shadow."

James 1:17

Because of human frailty, man is subject to change, and is often fickle in the promises he makes. Because of his unreliability, promises are as easily broken as made. How different is our great God who is ever the same!

There is another group of passages bearing on the surety of the promises we cannot afford to neglect—and what precious gems they are! There may be times when we are

tempted to think that God is slow and
tardy, and we become discouraged. But
is it not foolish to apply our human mea-
surements to Him with whom a thousand
years are as one day? All of the prophecies
and all of His dealings in history are promises. Sooner or later He overthrows the
evil and diadems the right.

"Not one thing hath failed thereof."
Joshua 23:14
"According to all that he promised."
I Kings 8:56
"Doth his promise fail for ever?"
Psalm 77:8
"My covenant will I not break."
Psalm 89:34
"He remembered his holy promise."
Psalm 105:42
"I will perform that good thing which
I have promised." Jeremiah 33:14
"When the time of the promise drew
nigh . . . the people grew and multi-
plied in Egypt." Acts 7:17
"When the fulness of the time was
come." Galatians 4:4
"The Lord is not slack concerning his
promise." II Peter 3:9

Are not such promises the breasts of consolation for our poor, tried and distressed
hearts? These promises of free grace, confirmed by the blood of Jesus, ought to be
our strength and support, and should be
our plea at the throne of grace, our confidence in hours of trial, and our rejoicing
in prospect of death. Are we making these
promises, which are so plain that a child
can understand yet so great that no angel
can fulfil them, our daily comfort? As they
are more lasting than earth and more stable
than the pillars of the heavens let us be
found searching them out and storing them
up in our minds.

Last, but by no means least, the certainty
of promise-fulfilment is emphasized by Paul's
emphatic formula of ratification which we
herewith cite in full –

"But as God is true, our word toward
you was not yea and nay. For the Son
of God, Jesus Christ, who was preached
among you by us, even by me and
Silvanus and Timothy, was not yea
and nay, but in him was yea. For
all the promises of God in him are
yea, and in him amen, unto the glory
of God by us" (II Corinthians 1:18-20.
See I Corinthians 10:8, 9, 13; II Thessalonians 3:3).

Paul sets forth the truthfulness of God in
the nature of an oath – "As God is faithful
in all his words so is my preaching, writing, and personal intercourse, true and faithful also." With the Apostles there had been
no "Yes" and "No" in the same breath;
no saying one thing yet meaning another.
It was never "yea and nay but in Christ
was yea." How could those who preached
Christ, the absolutely true Christ who enforced every precept with the emphatic
"Amen, Amen," be shamefully untruthful
and use words that paltered a double sense?
The term, "Amen, Amen," occurs 31 times
in Matthew, 14 times in Mark, 7 times
in Luke, and in its reduplicated form,
"Verily, Verily," 25 times in John. "In
Him was yea" or "in Him has been and
still is so," is His great characterizing word.
"In him is the yea, and also by his is the
amen of God for glory by our means."
Here Paul affirms that all, not some of, the
promises of God have been fulfilled and
ratified in Christ, the living, incarnate
"Amen" to those promises.

Divine promises are sure and infallible;
not yea and then nay, one thing today and
an opposite thing tomorrow; but always
"yea," and this "yea of heaven is yea indeed"; it cannot direct astray or disappoint.
This is why we can use any promise of
His as a key to unlock the closed door of
Doubting Castle. No *Giant Despair* can
hold us as we claim the promises of an
infallible, immutable God

"Because I – the Great Amen (Revelation 3:14) –live, ye shall live also."
John 14:19
"He is the Mediator of a better covenant, which was established upon better promises." Hebrews 8:6; Galatians
3:20, 21; II Timothy 1:1

While Christ lives the promises cannot fail,
and a draft presented in His name on the
bank of heaven has never yet been dishonored. Under the Law there was only
failure, but there can be none under Him.
It is said of Alexander the Great that when
one of his favorites was honored with a
magnificent gift that he exclaimed –

"This is too much for me to receive."
Alexander's reply was in generous vein –
"It is not too much for me to give."
Our God is a great and generous Giver,
but let us not stagger at any promise of
His for He says what He means and means
all He says. May we be found matching
the great promises with a great faith!

Martin Luther, overwhelmed by a promise he had been considering, wrote,

"I forgot God when I said, How can this be?"

V

THE SOURCE OF THE PROMISES

Apart from the Bible – the infallible, indestructible, inexhaustible and indispensable Book – we have no direct revelation of and from God. All we know of creation, redemption and providence comes solely from the Scriptures. Within them, the past, present and future are dealt with in unmistaken terms. They are also the only reliable source of promises for the guidance and gladness of pilgrims as they journey from *The City of Destruction* to *The Celestial City*. Viewing these promises as a whole it would seem as if they fall into three categories, namely, Heavenly, Human and Hellish.

God's Promises to Man

At this point we are only tracing beneficial promises to their divine source. Our next chapter dealing with the scope of these promises, will deal particularly with hundreds of them. Under the present section we indicate their divine source, namely, God, Christ, the Holy Spirit, angels. Spontaneity is an essential part of the meaning of the word "promise" when used of God, especially of "the promise" which comprises all the blessings of the Messianic Kingdom. God's every word of grace is a *promise*. Even His commandments are assurances of grace, conditional only upon man's willingness to obey.

The Promise Made to Adam

"I will put enmity between thee and the woman and between thy seed and her seed; it shall bruise thy head, and thou shalt bruise His heel."

Genesis 3:15

Actually, it was Satan, the one responsible for the entrance of sin into the world, who received the first promise and prophecy of redemption. The original innocence of Adam and Eve was quickly lost and they became the world's first sinners. As quickly as they sinned, however, came God's initial promise of deepest interest to each one of us as partakers of a fallen and sinful nature. As the result of the disobedience of our first parents, man's moral relation to God assumed a new aspect. Having incurred the threatened penalty, Adam and Eve forfeited the promise of life on the condition of obedience and brought upon themselves the curse. God was revealed in a new character, or there came a new manifestation of the character which had belonged to Him from eternity. It was His manifestation as a *Promiser*.

A promise was conveyed to Adam and Eve in the terms of a curse upon their malignant seducer. This first promise of deliverance from Satan's power and thraldom was fulfilled when, millenniums later, Jesus Christ came as the Promised Redeemer.

"Thou shalt conceive in thy womb, and bring forth a son, and shalt call his name JESUS." Luke 1:31; Galatians 4:4, 5

Thereafter, this first voluntary, unsolicited and gracious promise of a Saviour became the commencing point of divine revelation. Such a promise became the theme of early prophecy as Jude reminds us (verses 14, 15). With this promise of a Saviour, God made man the recipient of many promissory notes which through grace are being constantly fulfilled.

"Blessed be the God and Father of our Lord Jesus Christ, who hath blessed us with all spiritual blessings in heavenly places in Christ." Ephesians 1:3.

The Promise Made to Noah

Under the *dispensation of conscience*, as in the *dispensation of innocence*, man utterly failed, and the judgment of the flood marks the end of the second dispensation and the beginning of the third, namely, *the dispensation of human government* (Genesis 8:20-23).

"The Lord smelled a sweet savour; and the Lord said in his heart, I will not again curse the ground any more for man's sake, for the imagination of man's heart is evil from his youth; neither will I again smite any more every thing living, as I have done. While the earth remaineth, seedtime and harvest, and cold and heat, and summer and winter, and day and night shall not cease."

Under the covenant given to Noah (Genesis 8:20-9:27), man's relation to the earth under the Adamic Covenant, confirmation of the order of nature, establishment of human government, preservation of the earth against another universal judgment by water, are among its chief elements. The rainbow set in the cloud was given as the promise that the covenant made with Noah would stand. For our own hearts the message is that faith sees the bow of covenant promise whenever sense sees the cloud of affliction. Until the waters go over the earth again, the saints will have no reason to doubt the covenanting-keeping God.

The Promise Made to Abraham

What intimate knowledge of some of heaven's secrets this "Friend of God" had! Some of the greatest of Bible promises were given to this man of great faith. With Abraham commenced the *fourth dispensation of promise*, a *dispensation* extending from Genesis 12 through to Exodus 19:8. This *dispensation* must be distinguished from the *covenant* God made with His servant – the former is a mode of testing; the latter is everlasting because conditional. As Abraham turned aside from his country and kith and kin to become a pilgrim, he received the glorious promise from God –

"I will make of thee a great nation, and I will bless thee, and make thy name great; and thou shalt be a blessing: And I will bless them that bless thee, and curse him that curseth thee: and in thee shall all families of the earth be blessed." Genesis 12:1-3; 22:15-18

"All the land which thou seest to thee will I give it, and to thy seed for ever. And I will make thy seed as the dust of the earth." Genesis 13:15, 16

"Unto thy seed have I given this land, from the river of Egypt unto the great river Euphrates." Genesis 15:18

"Abraham shall surely become a great and mighty nation, and all the nations of the earth shall be blessed in him" Genesis 18:10, 18

"Now to Abraham and his seed were the promises made. He saith not, And to seeds, as of many; but as of one, And to thy seed, which is Christ." Galatians 3:16

The promise to make of Abraham a great nation is fulfilled *naturally* in the Hebrew people, "the dust of the *earth*": *spiritually*, "*heaven* . . . so shall thy seed be" – all men of faith whether Hebrew or Gentile: *nationally*, the Arab world through Ishmael (Genesis 17:18-20). Abraham himself was blessed temporally and spiritually, and his name became one of universal honor. The promise relating to the blessing and the cursing of those dealing with the Hebrew people has been wonderfully fulfilled in history even down to Hitler's brutal massacre. "It has invariably fared ill with the people who have persecuted the Jew – well with those who have protected him."

For our own hearts, comfort and confidence can be gathered from both the Abrahamic dispensation and covenant, "Thou shalt be a blessing" (Genesis 12:2). Although we were by nature cursed of God, and a curse to others, He graciously saved us and poured out His blessing upon us, and now seeks to make us channels of blessing to others. "I am thy shield" (Genesis 15:1). All who are Christ's are blessed with believing Abraham, and many of the promises made to him, God will fulfil to us. As our Shield, He is ever near to protect us and to preserve our going out and coming in. "All the land which thou seest, to thee will I give it." (Genesis 13:14, 15). This was a special promise for a memorable occasion. Abraham had behaved very generously to Lot, in giving him the choice of the land. If we deny ourselves for peace's sake, the Lord will be our upmaking portion. All Abraham saw, he could claim, even although he had to wait for the actual possession. What boundless blessings belong to us by covenant gift! All things are ours. Are we possessing our possessions?

The Promise Made to Hagar

Does not our sympathy go out to Hagar, Sarah's Egyptian maid, who had to bear the brunt of her mistress's jealousy? How disastrous in family life is polygamy! Abraham and Sarah should have waited for God to redeem His promise and give them a son. Instead they tried to hurry things on and frustrated, thereby, the divine purpose. But to Hagar the promise was given –

"I will multiply thy seed exceedingly, that it shall not be numbered for multitudes."

Genesis 16:10

"I will make of thee a great nation."
Genesis 21:18

From Ishmael, Hagar's son, we have the Arabs, so hostile to the Jews, Isaac's descendants. "Little did Sarai think," says a writer of the last decade, "when she persuaded Abram to take Hagar, that she was originating a rivalry which has run in the keenest animosity through all ages, and which oceans of blood have not quenched." How inexpedient it is to resort to any expedient that is intended to take the place of faith in God.

As for rejected Hagar herself, it may be that she would never have known God, as she came to know Him, had she never felt the anguish of the iron that entered into her soul. In her pain there came the promise that her son would be the progenitor of a great multitude, and such a promise "was virtual assurance that though, through the wrongdoing of her master and mistress, she had been led into a false position, the favour of God should rest upon her." Although Ishmael was not to be the child of promise in connection with God's purposes for Israel, yet he was the child of a promise God had made to Hagar. God's promises are as soothing as His threatenings are alarming!

Under divine direction Hagar called her son "Ishmael," meaning "God shall hear." But what did He hear? He heard the moaning of a woman's broken heart. Hagar's disconsolate sigh came up before God as a prayer, which He answered. Do we hear the prayers of such fashioning, the sighs and cries of the world's needy? If our self-satisfied hearts are deaf to such prayers we know but little of the God of Hagar.

The Promise Made to Isaac

With the birth of Isaac we come to the cross-roads in patriarchal history. While Isaac and Ishmael were of the same stock, it was Isaac who came as the child of promise and the progenitor of Christ. Abraham had received the promise –

"In Isaac shall thy seed be called."
Romans 9:7

God, who always keeps His promise, "visited Sarah," as He had said, and through divine interposition, what was naturally impossible, was achieved. Often the promises we make are broken because of our inability to fulfil them. With God,

however, it is different. He is always "able to perform" (Romans 4:21).

The promise Abraham received concerning Isaac was really an off-shoot of that first promise given in Eden concerning the Redeemed (Genesis 3:15). "The tree of promise has many branches, but the trunk of the tree is Christ." Apart from Him the promises are "Nay." Every divine promise is a check drawn upon God, but before we can cash one of these checks we must have it endorsed with the name of Jesus. We cannot cash any promise in our own name.

In a time of desolating famine, Isaac received precious promises from the Lord, which were to be fulfilled on condition that he continued to sojourn in the Land of Promise.

"The Lord appeared unto him, and said, Go not down into Egypt; dwell in the land which I shall tell thee of: Sojourn in this land, and I will be with thee, and will bless thee; for unto thee, and unto thy seed, I will give all these countries, and I will perform the oath which I sware unto Abraham thy father." Genesis 26:1-5

In this confirmation of the Abrahamic covenant given to Isaac we have a threefold promise –

1. A Promise of the Divine Presence – "I will be with thee."

The nearness of the Lord to His people at all times ought to be their greatest consolation.

2. A Promise of Blessing – "I will bless thee."

In Isaac's case the blessing carried with it the gift of a son who was to be the ancestor of the Messiah. How blessed we are because of our association with the Saviour!

3. A Promise of Territory – "I will give thee all these countries."

Because the earth is the Lord's, He retains the right to give it to whom He will. With Him, blessing is always connected with giving. Whom God blesses, He enriches with gifts material and spiritual (Proverbs 10:22). This promise of territory was given to Abraham, and now it is renewed to Isaac. "We need to have the promises that have cheered the saints of God in other ages brought home to our own hearts. The promises of God are like Jacob's well, which, though it was given originally to Joseph, was a source of refreshment to weary travellers for long generations afterwards."

The Promise Made to Jacob

Rebekah certainly knew that her favored son, Jacob, was the divinely-appointed heir to the promise made to Abraham, Genesis 25:23, and was determined to overrule the purpose of Isaac concerning his favored son, Esau. Rebekah overheard the proposal of her husband to bless Esau, and conceived the idea that Isaac should be diverted from his purpose by a spread of savory meats. Alas! she made bad use of her parental authority. "My son obey my voice" (Genesis 27:8)--which Jacob did, much to his own undoing. The bitter fruit of his obedience to his mother who was "his counsellor to do wickedly" (II Chronicles 22:3), we see in the subsequent career of this misguided son.

We all know how the story unfolds. After Rebekah's deceptive scheme was uncovered, Jacob was forced to flee to Padan-Aran. His mother who instigated the act of fraud, was now to lose her son for more than twenty years. How true it is that sin is ever followed by suffering. During his journey from Beersheba to Haran, tired and weary, Jacob laid his head upon a stone and slept, and dreamed about a ladder reaching from earth to heaven, upon which angels were ascending and descending. Then came the promise--

"The Lord stood above the ladder, and said, I am the Lord God of Abraham thy father, and the God of Isaac: the land whereon thou liest, to thee will I give it, and to thy seed: And thy seed shall be as the dust of the earth, and thou shalt spread abroad to the west, and to the east, and to the north, and to the south: and in thee and in thy seed shall all the families of the earth be blessed. Behold, I am with thee, and will keep thee in all places whither thou goest, and will bring thee again into this land: for I will not leave thee, until I have done that which I have spoken to thee of." Genesis 28:12-16

How full Jacob's dream was of Jacob's God, whose voice was full of majesty and tenderness. That dream was more than an ordinary dream. In it, Jacob learned of God's grace and heard His voice relating gracious promises for the future. The *pillow* on which his head had rested, Jacob made a *pillar*

as a memorial, not of his dream, but of the divine glory he had witnessed. A solitary stone became a fitting memorial of God's goodness and promise to the solitary wanderer (See Isaiah 35:1).

Some twenty years later Jacob heard the same divine voice assuring him of divine protection--

"The Lord said unto Jacob, Return unto the land of thy fathers, and to thy kindred; and I will be with thee."
Genesis 31:3

On the way home after such a long absence, Jacob is again accosted by the angels, and has contact with the God of his fathers, from whom came the assurance of the old-time promise:

"I will surely do thee good, and make thy seed as the sand of the sea, which cannot be numbered for multitude."
Genesis 32:12

As the result of this divine encounter both the name and nature were changed. No longer must he be *Jacob,* a supplanter, but *Israel,* a prince of God. Back at Bethel, with communion and promise restored, God assured Jacob of His great purpose--

"I am God Almighty: be fruitful and multiply: a nation and a company of nations shall be of thee, and kings shall come out of thy loins; And the land which I gave to Abraham and Isaac, to thee I will give it, and to thy seed after thee will I give the land."
Genesis 35:9-15

Back in Beersheba Jacob, now called "Israel" (Genesis 46:1), offered sacrifices unto the God of his father Isaac and again became the recipient of a divine visitation, during which the divine promise was reiterated--

"I am God, the God of thy father: fear not to go down into Egypt: for I will there make of thee a great nation. I will go down with thee into Egypt; and I will surely bring them up again."
Genesis 46:1-4

Such a promise, partially fulfilled, awaits a perfect realization. Israel will yet be His glory and the channel of blessing to all nations. As for the Promised Land, it has ever been Israel's since it was first promised. It is hers by divine gift and right and will be hers in its entirety when her Messiah returns to reign. God's promises, given to Abraham and confirmed to Isaac and Jacob, concerning His ancient people, will be fulfilled to the letter. Not one word can fail.

The Promise Made to David

This man after God's own heart was eminently blessed of God. Among Old Testament saints, David is outstanding in his knowledge and experience of God's grace and power. What sublime revelations of the divine character were granted unto him! The Psalms of this "sweet psalmist of Israel" are full of the majesty and might, protection and preservation of the Almighty. Rich promises were given to this illustrious king, who could say, "I love the Lord." To David was given *the seventh* or *Davidic covenant* (I Chronicles 17:4-15).

> "The Lord telleth thee that He will make thee an house. And when thy days are fulfilled, and thou shalt sleep with the fathers, I will set up thy seed after thee, which shall proceed out of thy bowels, and I will establish his kingdom." II Samuel 7:4-17; I Chronicles 17:7-15
> "I have made a covenant with my chosen. I have sworn unto David my servant. Thy seed will I establish for ever, and build up thy throne to all generations. Selah." Psalm 89:3, 4, 35-37.

Of such promises God said—

> "My covenant will I not break, nor alter the thing that is going out of My lips." Psalm 89:34

This great Psalm is rich in its tribute to God's faithfulness, and as the faithful God, He cannot act contrary to His character. If He failed in His promises, broke His covenants, and altered His words, He would not be worthy of our trust and confidence.

> "Thou hast performed thy words; for thou art righteous." Nehemiah 9:8

The Promise Made to Solomon

It is not within the province of this present study to discourse upon the reign, riches and ruin of Solomon who reigned in the Golden Age of Israel's history. The reader is referred to the author's volume on *All the Men of the Bible* for a fuller treatment of the son born to David and Bathsheba. In his youth, Solomon chose wisdom as the treasure most to be desired, and as has been written of him, "No fairer promise of true greatness, or more beautiful picture of juvenile piety, is known in history."

Solomon inherited from his father David the throne of the most powerful kingdom then existent. Solomon's dominions were vast, his personal character exalted, his wisdom proverbial, and Jerusalem, in his reign, renowned for its wealth and splendor. Yet this king, so eminently blessed of God, sinned against light when he married idolatrous women who brought about his ruin. "The besotted apostasy of Solomon's old age is one of the most pitiful spectacles in the Bible." Yet this man received great promises and was chosen to write three of the books forming the Bible.

> "The Lord appeared to Solomon in a dream by night: and God said, Ask what I shall give . . .
> "God said unto him, Because thou hast asked this thing (an understanding heart to judge thy people, verse 9), and hast not asked for thyself long life; neither hast asked riches for thyself, nor hast asked the life of thine enemies, but hast asked for thyself understanding to discern judgment; Behold, I have done according to thy words." I Kings 3:5-14; II Chronicles 1:7-12

When Solomon had finished the building of the Temple, and presented it to the Lord, there came the second divine appearance when the Lord assured Solomon that his dedicatory prayer had been heard and that He had hallowed the House built for the worship of His Name. Then came God's further promise to Solomon—

> "If thou wilt walk before me, as David thy father walked, in integrity of heart, and in uprightness, to do according to all that I have commanded thee, and wilt keep My statutes and judgments: Then I will establish the throne of thy kingdom upon Israel for ever, as I promised to David thy father, saying, There shall not fail thee a man upon the throne of Israel." I Kings 9:4-9; II Chronicles 7:12-22

When, in all humility, Solomon confessed his utter inability to follow his father's example in walking before God in uprightness of heart, or to govern a people that could not be numbered nor counted for multitude, seeing that he was "but a little child": not knowing how "to go out or come in," he had God's ear and favor. With largeness of heart God said: "Ask what I shall give thee," and Solomon could have taken God at His word and presented large petitions. But he scorned riches, fame, conquest, longevity. His was a single desire. All he desired was wisdom to rule and judge so great a people as Israel, and his one request was abundantly complied with.

What Solomon did not ask God for, God gave him. Overweight became his, in riches and honor, outstripping the wealth and majesty of any other king. Solomon's was the single eye for the accomplishment of a God-given task, and all the time he maintained such a single purpose, God blessed him. The lesson for our hearts is that if we put first things first, all else will be cared for by Him who waits to reward those who seek first and foremost His revealed interests (Matthew 6:33).

The Promise Made to the Israelites

In describing his solicitude for Israel, Paul, as a regenerated Hebrew, cites among the seven privileges of God's ancient people that of the promises they received –

"Who are Israelites; to whom pertaineth . . . the promises." Romans 9:4

In his sermon in the synagogue at Antioch, the Apostle, in his defense of the doctrine of justification by faith, also spoke of the glad tidings –

"How that the promise which was made unto the fathers, God hath fulfilled the same unto us their children."

Acts 13:32, 33

Before Agrippa, Paul declared that he was suffering because he had believed the old-time promises which God was now fulfilling through his teaching and work.

"I stand and am judged for the hope of the promise made of God unto our fathers: Unto which promise our twelve tribes, instantly serving God day and night, hope to come." Acts 26:6, 7

The constituent element of one of the promises given to Old Testament saints was that Gentiles, as well as Jews, would be visited by God in saving grace and mercy, as Peter emphasized in his sermon at Pentecost –

"For the promise is unto you, and to your children, and to *all* that are afar off, even as many as the Lord our God shall call." Acts 2:39

Regarding God's promises made to Israel, they were confirmed by an oath (Hebrews 6:17; psalm 89:3, 4); were associated with His covenant (Hebrews 8:6), are not annulled by the Law (Galatians 2:21; 3:17). Although the Law once reigned, now grace reigns (Romans 5:21).

Man's Promises to God

A proverb has it, "He who trusts to the promises of others is often deceived." No one has ever been deceived in the fulfilment of divine promises, none of which has ever failed. God, however, has often been deceived by man's promises, vows and covenants. The Old Testament is one long record of the way in which the creature has disappointed the Creator. That God expects man to be as true to his word, as God Himself is, can be gathered from the following Mosaic instructions –

"When a man shall make a singular vow, the person shall be for the Lord by thy estimation." Leviticus 27:2

"if a man vow a vow unto the Lord, or swear an oath to bind his woul with a bond: he shall not break his word, he shall do according to all that proceedeth out of his mouth." Numbers 30:2

"When thou shalt vow a vow unto the Lord thy God, thou shalt not be slack to pay it: for the Lord thy God will surely require it of thee . . . That which is gone out of thy lips thou shalt keep and perform; . . . according as thou hast vowed unto the Lord thy God, which thou hast promised with thy mouth." Deuteronomy 23:21, 23

"I will pay thee my vows, which my lips have uttered, and my mouth hath spoken." Psalm 66:13, 14

"When thou vowest a vow unto God, defer not to pay it; for he hath no pleasure in fools: pay that which thou hast vowed. Better it is that thou shouldest not vow, than that thou shouldest vow and not pay." Ecclesiastes 5:4, 5

From Moses we learn that promising is synonymous with vowing (Deuteronomy 23:21, 23). In this instructive passage Moses shows the voluntary nature of the obligation that is incurred by him who promises God something, or who vows unto Him. Here are two instances of those who fulfilled their promise or vow, Godward.

"Jacob vowed a vow; saying, If God will be with me, and will keep me in this way that I go, and will give me bread to eat, and raiment to put on, So that I come again to my father's house in peace; then shall the Lord be my God: And this stone, which I have set for a pillar, shall be God's house: and of all that thou shalt give me I will surely give the tenth unto thee." Genesis 28:21, 22

It may seem as if Jacob, the supplanter and deceiver, who was being forced to flee from home, was seeking to strike up a bargain with God. In this promise, while there was a desire for God's presence and protection, there was also a strong regard for temporal mercies like bread and raiment. There was a mixture of spirituality and worldliness in the motive that led Jacob to make his choice. The patriarch's promise had too much of the bargain-making spirit in it – too much of the "if" and "then." How suggestive is the contrast in the "if not" of the three Hebrew youths who went to the fiery furnace for their Lord (Daniel 3:18). Anyhow, Jacob's promise or vow is the first of which we have record, and it is interesting to know that he paid his vow and redeemed his promise (Genesis 35:7, 15).

The other instance is that of Jephthah the judge, of whom it is said that –

> "He vowed a vow unto the Lord, and said, If thou shalt without fail deliver the children of Ammon into mine hands, Then it shall be, that whatsoever cometh forth of the doors of my house to meet me, when I return in peace from the children of Ammon, shall surely be the Lord's, and I will offer it up for a burnt-offering." Judges 11:30

Returning from his God-given victory over the Ammonites, he saw the first to cross the threshold of his home, his own much-loved daughter. Without hesitation, Jephthah fulfilled his promise, saying, "I have opened my mouth unto the Lord, and I cannot go back." In a most noble fashion, his daughter replied to her father, "If thou hast opened thy mouth unto the Lord, do to me according to that which hath proceeded out of thy mouth" (Judges 11:36).

Volumes have been written on the morality or otherwise of such a solemn vow, and as to whether the daughter was actually offered up as a living sacrifice in fulfilment of the vow. What must not be forgotten is the fact that Jephthah was not impetuous and hasty in the making of his promise. It was not made in the heat of the battle with the Ammonites without weighing his words, but before he set out. While he made a hard vow, he left it to providence to choose what should first cross his threshold to be offered up as a sacrifice to God. "In his eagerness to smite the foe and thank God for it, Jephthah could not think of any particular object to name, great enough to dedicate. He shrank from measuring

what was dearest to God, and left this for Him to decide." Perhaps he hoped that God would not require the hardest of sacrifices, namely, the surrender of his only child.

What a solemn matter it is to make God a promise! Due thought should be given to all its implications before framing it into a prayer and presenting it to God. Too often we make vows without prayerful consideration. Under the influence of a powerful sermon, our hearts are stirred, and when a call to surrender or dedication is made we promise God to be wholly His, and join in singing –

> Take my life, and let it be
> Consecrated, Lord, to Thee.
> Take myself, and I will be
> Ever, only, all for Thee.

To our shame, however, we have to sadly confess that our pathway is strewn with broken vows and unrealized promises. Yet any vow the Spirit prompts, He can enable us to realize. Power is His to fulfil our holy promises, just as He fulfils His promises on our behalf.

To God manifest in flesh Peter promised, "Though all men shall be offended because of thee, yet will I never be offended." Matthew 26:33

Here is another promise made by man that came to nothing. Unconscious of his utter inability to carry out his proud boast, Peter's promise had no better foundation than human resolve which proved to be futile. When the testing came, Peter denied his Master and used an oath to confirm his denial. Spurgeon remarks that a man's promise is often like "an earthen pot broken with a stroke," or as "a blossom, which, with God's care, may come to fruit, but which, left to itself, will fall to the ground with the first wind that moves the bough."

On any divine promise we can hang time and eternity, and rely upon God to fulfil to the limit any promise we claim. On our own resolve, however, we dare not depend for our best resolves we only break. Whatever we are prompted to do for God, or to give Him, can only be realized as we depend upon Him for all necessary grace to perform what we promise. "I can do all things," but only "through Christ who strengtheneth me."

Man's Promises to His Fellow Men

Cato, the Latin philosopher, is credited with the saying, "What you are able to do to serve anyone, do not promise twice over; and do not be wordy if you wished to be esteemed as a man of discernment." It is to be feared that men of such discernment are rare these days, when wordy promises, even of those in high places, mean so little. Let us turn to a few Bible men and see how they fared in this direction.

Joshua kept his promise to the Gibeonites, even though they deceived him into making a league with them:

"We have sworn unto them by the Lord God of Israel: now therefore we may not touch them. . . . Let them live." Joshua 9:19-21

Nehemiah was another gentleman whose word was his bond, as he sought restitution for the people:

"We will restore them, and will require nothing of them; so will we do as thou sayest. Then I called the priests, and took an oath of them, that they should do according to this promise." Nehemiah 5:12

A dastardly promise Haman, the Jews' enemy, made, recoiled upon his own head and resulted in his deserved death:

"Mordecai told him of all that had happened unto him, and of the sum of the money that Haman had promised to pay to the king's treasuries for the Jews, to destroy them."
Esther 3:9; 4:7

Another promise with tragic results, given when the promiser's passions were roused, was Herod's to Salome:

"Whereupon he promised with an oath to give her whatsoever she would ask." The noble head of John the Baptist was asked for, and the weak king had to comply with such a cruel request:

"The king was sorry: nevertheless for the oath's sake, and them which sat with him at meat, he commanded it to be given her." Matthew 14:7,9

The vow of forty men who bound themselves under an oath not to eat or drink until they had killed Paul proved to be futile.

"Now they are ready, looking for a promise from thee." Acts 23:21

But such a promise was not forthcoming and Paul escaped. Here, the term for "promise" means *word*. In our relations with others may we be known for our integrity and reliability. May we seek after the Christian chivalry found in the ancient Psalm in which we have a "figure of stainless honour drawn by the ancient Jewish poet." As Ellicott comments, "In heart and tongue, in deed and word, the character of Psalm 15 is without reproach." The two aspects pertinent to the necessity of the fulfilment of honest promises are in these lines –

"Who speaketh truth in his heart" (Psalm 15:2), a phrase meaning, one who both thinks and speaks the truth, and implies the reputation Shakespeare wrote of in *Hamlet* –

"This above all: to thine ownself be true,
And it must follow as the night the day,
Thou canst not then be false to any man."

The other arrestive phrase describing a perfect gentleman is –

"He that sweareth (or promiseth) to his own hurt, and changeth not."
Psalm 15:4

The *English Prayer Book* gives us the version, "Who sweareth to his neighbour, disappointeth him not, even though it were to his own hindrance."

Christ's Promises to His Own

As we shall later see, Jesus Christ came as the long Promised One, and while here in the flesh He could lay hold of those Old Testament prophecies, which were promises, and relate them to Himself (Luke 24:25-27; 44-48). As He tabernacled among men, the testimony of those who heard Him was, "Never man spake like this man" (John 7:46). All He uttered was so full of promise. His sayings, parables and discourses, are potential promises. There are, however, a few explicit promises we can enumerate under this section. Others will be dealt with in the next chapter.

"Thy father which seeth in secret himself shall reward thee openly."
Matthew 6:4

"Seek ye first the kingdom of God, and his righteousness, and all these things shall be added unto thee."
Matthew 6:33

"Ask, and it shall be given you; seek, and ye shall find; Knock, and it shall be opened unto you." Matthew 7:7

"How much more shall your father which is in heaven, give good things to those who ask him?"
Matthew 7:11

"Come unto me, and I will give you rest." Matthew 11:28

"Whosoever shall do the will of my father which is in heaven, the same is my brother, and sister, and mother." Matthew 12:50

"Upon this rock I will build my church: and the gates of hell shall not prevail against it." Matthew 16:18

"Whosoever will lose his life for my sake shall find it." Matthew 16:25

"If ye have faith as a grain of mustard seed, ye shall say to this mountain, Remove hence to yonder place; and it shall remove; and nothing shall be impossible unto you." Matthew 17:20

"Ye which have followed me . . . shall sit upon thrones, judging the twelve tribes of Israel." Matthew 19:28

"Lo, I am with you alway, even unto the end of the world." Matthew 28:20

"Fear not, little flock: for it is your Father's good pleasure to give you the kingdom." Luke 12:32

"Peace be unto you: as my Father hath sent me, even so send I you . . . Receive ye the Holy Ghost."

John 20:21, 22

There is a sense in which John 14, 15 and 16 can be treated as one long, glorious promise for the saints of God. How permeated these great chapters are with all Christ is willing to be, and to do, for His own. The appropriation of all He has promised in this last discourse of His, would quickly end all doubt and spiritual impoverishment. He waits to fulfil His word on our behalf, and if only our love were more simple, we would "take Him at His word."

All the promises of Christ are, as John Bunyan said of one of them, "Words for a man to hang his soul upon." His promises, like His Cross, tower o'er all the wrecks of time. The saints of succeeding ages have testified to the fact that He is faithful to all His promises. Some scholars affirm that the familiar exhortation of Jesus, "Have faith in God" should be rendered, "Hold fast the faithfulness of God." Jesus came as God manifest in flesh and we can certainly hold fast to His faithfulness as a Promiser.

We trust, not only His faithfulness, but His power enabling Him to fulfill any promise on our behalf. His promises were made not only as the Carpenter of Nazareth, but as the Eternal Son of God, begotten before all worlds and who came as "God" (John 1:1, 2).

When William of Orange was coming to England, he gave written pledges to certain of his friends that they should have particular honors and certain high offices in the kingdom. But there was one of his friends, who became Lord Chamberlain of the realm, who refused any pledge. "No, sir," he said respectfully, "Your Majesty's word is enough." Can we not write over every royal promise—"Thy word, Lord, is enough"? Is not the story of past fulfilments of His promises sufficient assurance for today? All He has been as the Faithful Promiser, He is, and will ever be.

Satan's Subtle Promises

Here is our Lord's assertion as to Satan's absolute lack of integrity, truthfulness and reliability:

"He . . . abode not in the truth, because there is no truth in him. When he speaketh a lie, he speaketh of his own: for he is a liar, and the father of it." John 8:44

With such a divine estimation of Satan's character before us, what else can we do but discount the fulfilment of any promise he has made? Among the very few of his recorded promises there are those connected with Adam and Eve, and our Lord, which we might consider briefly.

Satan's Promise to Our First Parents

"The serpent said unto the woman, Ye shall not surely die: for God doth know that in the day ye eat thereof, then your eyes shall be opened, and ye shall be as gods, knowing good and evil."

Genesis 3:4, 5

We have here a three-fold promise Satan whispered in the ear of Eve, namely, (1) that she would not die, although God had declared she would; (2) that enlightenment would be hers; (3) that partaking of the forbidden fruit would result in divinity of choice. The background of man's first temptation must be kept in mind. Eden was the sphere of probation for our first parents, who were placed in circumstances in which they had freedom of choice. God did not create Adam and Eve as mere machines or robots. Endowing them with life, He gave them free-will, and the tragedy of Eden is that such a precious gift was used against the Giver.

> "Our wills are ours we know not why
> Our wills are ours, to make them
> Thine."

But because the will was not kept in harmony with the Divine Will, sin entered the world to mar God's handiwork. Sin, however, although a possibility to Adam and Eve, was not a necessity. Everything in their sphere of probation was favorable to holiness, with God giving them a clear and distinct warning respecting the terrible consequence of sin.

> "In the day thou eatest thereof thou shalt surely die." Genesis 2:17

Satan, we are told, beguiled Eve through his subtlety, but both she and her husband were deceived (II Corinthians 11:3; I Timothy 2:14), by Satan's promises. The divine restriction was limited to one tree — to all the other trees there was free access. Thus the permission was larger than the restriction. How beneficent God is! Seven days make up a week, yet He only asks for one day to be set apart specially for Himself. In the Garden, "He put a fence round one tree, but threw open large orchards in which were smiling flowers, delicious fruit and silver streams."

Our first parents fell amidst the purity and glory of Eden proving that holy surroundings are no sure barrier against the wiles of Satan. The one prohibited tree is spoken of as "the tree of the knowledge of good and evil." Man had knowledge of good so long as he kept away from the tree: the knowledge of evil came through the violation of what God had said about the tree. The record of Satan shows that he does not always appear in the same character. With his innate and accumulated wisdom he knows how to seduce the souls of men.

To Eve he came as a subtle serpent — that "old serpent," (Revelation 12:9), and in this capacity as he promised, he lied (John 8:44).

When it suits his purpose to be demonstrative, he appears as "a roaring lion" (I Peter 5:8; Mark 1:26) "seeking whom he may devour."

Seeking to make havoc of the flock of God, he is seen as a ravening wolf (Acts 20:29).

At other times he is seen in the role of apostle, so cleverly disguised that even the elect are unable to detect his presence (John 13:27, 28).

Although "the prince of darkness" he can transform himself into "an angel of light." II Corinthians 11:14

But the meanest of his portrayals is that of the slimy snake and as such he instilled his poisonous promises into the mind of Eve. Satan knows how to use words to deceive men. He can employ "lying words" (Daniel 2:9), cankerous words (II Timothy 2:17), "vain words" (Ephesians 5:6), "enticing words of man's wisdom" (I Corinthians 2:4), "great swelling words" (II Peter 2:18). But in all, Satan's words fashioned into promises, although having the inspiration of evil (Luke 8:28), are counterfeits of the divinely inspired Promises.

Satan commenced by insinuating a falsehood, "Yea, hath God said, Ye shall not eat of every tree of the garden?" This was *not* what God said, and therefore Satan, in order to represent God, coined a lie. He then went on to make a false promise to Eve: "Ye shall not surely die." After suggesting that God had not spoken at all, Satan proceeded to affirm that if God had spoken then He said something He did not mean and thus denied the truth God had uttered and so became "the liar" Jesus called him.

Since that fair yet foul promise, countless multitudes have been deceived by Satan. As he covered his promises with what appeared to be beneficial and attractive gains, as he tempted Eve, so today he hides the dagger of death in a lovely bouquet of flowers, as the assassin did who murdered President Carnot, of France. As the god of this world, Satan knows all about its pleasures and pursuits, and can use them in seemingly innocent, attractive ways to entrap saint and sinner alike. Eat the forbidden fruit, he says, and still promises, "Ye shall not surely die." As the tempter kept his promise in the ear of Eve until she violated God's command and fell, so he, as a sinner from the beginning (I John 3:8), deceives the whole world (II Corinthians 4:4; 11:3). Our only hope of deliverance from all the wiles of Satan is the invincible armor God has provided (Ephesians 6:11).

Is it not wonderful to realize that on the heel of Satan's subtle, evil promise there came God's first promise of grace to fallen man — a promise containing the whole Gospel, and the essence of the covenant grace, which in great measure was fulfilled at Calvary when Jesus bruised the serpent's head? "To us, the promise stands as a prophecy that we shall be afflicted by the powers of evil in our lower nature," says Spurgeon, "and thus be bruised in our heel: but we shall triumph in Christ, who sets His foot on the old serpent's head."

From Satan's encounter with the first Adam, in the garden, we go over to his conflict with the Last Adam in the wilderness, where the double promise of preservation and kingship was presented by Satan to the Saviour. The first temptation assailed Jesus through His bodily sufferings and was overcome by faith. In that second temptation Satan sought to appeal to the spiritual exaltation of Jesus. Jesus' faith had triumphed, now there is the endeavor to make that faith overdo itself in presumption. The Jews had a tradition that when the Messiah came, He would stand upon the roof of the sanctuary, and proclaim to Israel –

"Ye sufferers, the time of your redemption draweth nigh; and, if ye believe, rejoice in my light which is risen upon you."

Satan, cognizant of such a tradition and also of the prophecy that the Lord would suddenly come to His Temple (Malachi 3:1), urged Jesus to make a dramatic descent and appearance, assuring Him that such a short cut would not result in any physical injury. He could float unhurt on angels' wings, seeing that He had a Scripture promise guaranteeing His safety –

"He shall give his angels charge over thee, to keep thee in all thy ways. They shall bear thee up in their hands, lest thou dash thy foot against a stone."
Psalm 91:11, 12

In quoting this gracious promise, Satan omitted the important phrase "to keep thee in all thy ways." He is cunning enough to twist the Word of God, even as he did with Eve. God promises us preservation and safety only to keep us in His ways, *if* we are in them. "I, *being in the way*, the Lord led me" (Genesis 24:27).

The next promise Satan made was he would give Jesus all the kingdoms of this world, and the glory of them, if only He would fall down and worship him. Jesus was promised the throne of universal empire – and on easy terms. Our Lord Himself allowed the claim of Satan to world-kingdom. He called him, "The prince of this world" (John 12:31; 14:30.) But this unworthy prince had nothing on Him, who

is coming as "the prince of the kings of the earth." (Revelation 1:5). The apostle Paul speaks of Satan as "the god of this world" (II Corinthians 4:4), and as "the world-ruler of darkness" (Ephesians 6:12). All the tempter asked was homage rather than the adoration and worship due to God only. But Christ met Satan with great calm, for He remembered what the sinister promiser had forgotten about the ancient Psalm, "Thou shalt tread upon the lion and adder." Thus the roaring lion, who keeps no promise, was trodden upon. Satan still offers his "kingdoms" – wealth, honors, fame, position – all are accessible to us if only we will compromise. It was in this veiled fashion that he prompted Jesus not to go to the cross, but take an easier way to His kingdom. Peter, however, heard himself rebuked in almost the same formula, "Get thee behind Me, Satan" (Matthew 4:10; 16:23). He, who was tempted in all points like as we are, is our Shield against the darts of the wicked one.

The Angels and Their Promises

It is to be regretted that angelic ministry is a Bible theme so sadly neglected by many of God's people. Bishop Hall's observation on this point needs to be emphasized, "We come short of our duty to the blessed spirits if we entertain not in our hearts a high and venerable conceit of their (the angels') wonderful majesty, glory and greatness, and an awful acknowledgment and reverential awe of their presence; a holy joy, and confident assurance of their care and protection; and, lastly, a fear to do aught that might cause them to turn their faces in dislike from us."

In the volume, *All About Angels in the Bible*, I endeavored to show that the Bible introduces us to a universe peopled with spirits intermediate between God and man.

"Millions of spiritual creatures walk the earth
Unseen, both when we wake and when we sleep."

It is evident to the most casual reader of the Bible that it abounds in angelic appearances and angelic ministrations. Angels are closely associated with some of Scripture's most remarkable histories and events and have an important mission to fulfil in the consummation of the Gentile Age.

None of the angelic hierarchy, with the exception of the most distinguished Angel, spoken of as *'The* Angel of the Lord' or

"The Angel of the Covenant," whom we believe to be the Lord Jesus Christ, are found making promises on their own initiative. As God's elect messengers, or intermediaries, they are simply the conveyors of the divine promises to the sons of men. Created by God, the angels exist to carry out God's will in the world, and to assist His children in their pilgrim walk and witness. The following is a brief classification of the association of the angels with the promises.

Promises of the Law

"The chariots of God are twenty thousand, even thousands of angels: the Lord is among them as in Sinai, in the holy place." Psalm 68:17

"The angel which spake to him in the mount Sinai." Acts 7:38

"Who received the law by the disposition of angels." Acts 7:53

"To whom the promise was made, and it was ordained by angels in the hand of a mediator." Galatians 3:19

"If the word spoken by angels was stedfast." Hebrews 2:2

The above passages prove that legions of angels attended the divine manifestation at Sinai when the Law was given to Moses (Deuteronomy 32). Without doubt they were present as ministering spirits of *The Angel Jehovah*, Source of all the precepts and promises of the Law. This Law *spoken* by the angels implies that they delivered it in articulate and audible sounds.

Promise of a Son

"The angel of the Lord found Hagar by a fountain of water in the wilderness . . . The angel of the Lord said unto her, Return . . . The angel of the Lord said unto her, I will multiply thy seed exceedingly, that it shall not be numbered for multitude . . . Thou shalt bear a son, and shalt call his name Ishmael." Genesis 16:7, 9, 11

The angels reflect the graciousness, sympathy and beneficence of their Creator. Hagar's broken heart must have been consoled by the tender, solicitous approach of the angelic visitor, who revealed an intimate knowledge of Hagar's name and perilous plight. How true it is that the angels are "ministering spirits" (Hebrews 1:14).

Promise of Deliverance

"There came two angels to Sodom at even."

"The men (the two angels who had assumed human form) put forth their hand, and pulled Lot into the house to them, and shut the door."

"The angels hastened Lot . . . Haste thee, escape thither." Genesis 19:1, 10, 15, 22

When Lot pitched his tent *toward* Sodom he assumed a perilous position. Before long he was *in* Sodom and caught up in the maelstrom of its iniquity. Yet amid such putrid surroundings we have another illustration of the effectiveness of angelic ministry in the preservation of the righteous. While the angels were messengers of mercy on behalf of Lot and his two daughters, fulfilling for them the promise of deliverance from destruction, they were likewise ministers of vengeance, seeing they were sent by God, not only to witness the sin of Sodom but to punish it.

Promise As to Isaac

"The angel of the Lord called unto him out of heaven . . . I know that thou fearest God."

"The angel of the Lord called Abraham out of heaven the second time . . . I will bless thee." Genesis 22:11, 15, 17

It will be recalled that three angels in human form appeared to Abraham at Mamre and brought him the joyful tidings from the Lord about the birth of Isaac, the son of promise (Genesis 18:2). Now "the angel of the Lord" spares Isaac from sacrifice and assures Abraham of Isaac's wonderful posterity.

Promise of Guidance

"He shall send his angel before thee, and thou shalt take a wife unto my son from thence.

"The Lord, before whom I walk, will send his angel with thee, and prosper thy way." Genesis 24:7, 40

"The angel of his presence." Isaiah 63:9

What different homes our nation would have if only those desiring to set them up had the guidance and direction of heaven, as Eleazar had when he sought out the right kind of a partner for Isaac. This is the right kind of marriage made in heaven. How tragic it is when two unite in a divine institution, as marriage is, without divine guidance and benediction!

Promise of Possession

"Behold the angels of God ascending and descending . . . The land whereon thou liest, to thee will I give it, and to thy seed, and thy seed shall be as the dust of the earth."

Genesis 28:12-14

Jacob experienced intimate encounters with angels, both on his flight from home and his return to it. Angelic guardians made earth "the gate of heaven" (28:17) for lonely Jacob. See Genesis 31:11-13; 32:1. It was the *Angel Jehovah* who changed the patriarch's name from Jacob to *Israel* (Hosea 12:3-5) and who also changed the heart of Esau so that the two brothers could meet in peace.

Promise of Proclamation

"The angel of the Lord said unto Balaam, Go with the men: but only the word that I shall speak unto thee, that thou shalt speak."

Numbers 22:35; 23:26

Although a seemingly religious man, Balaam was yet a lover of the wages of unrighteousness (II Peter 2:15), and found himself reproved by an angel and rebuked by an ass. The angel of mercy who would have restrained Balaam from sinning, was rather a friend than an adversary. He obeyed the angelic voice and said to Balak, "All that the Lord speaketh that must I do."

Promise of Faithfulness

"An angel of the Lord . . . . I will never break my covenant with you . . . When the angel of the Lord spake these words unto all the children of Israel, that the people lifted up their voices, and wept." Judges 2:1-4

God had graciously undertaken for His people in preserving them and bringing them unto the Promised Land. He had kept His promise, but the people had broken theirs, and the angel proclaimed their judgment.

"An angel of the Lord . . . appeared unto Gideon, and said unto him, The Lord is with thee, thou mighty man of valour . . . The angel of God said unto him . . . I have seen an angel of the Lord face to face."

The angelic ministrations are associated with Gideon's call to deliver Israel from their fourth apostasy and servitude. Of the meal Gideon prepared for his heavenly visitor and instructor, Bishop Hall says: "Gideon intended a dinner, the angel turned it into a sacrifice."

Promise of a Nazarite Son

"The angel of the Lord appeared unto the woman and said unto her, Behold now, thou art barren, and bearest not: but thou shalt conceive and bare a son . . . The angel of God came again unto the woman as she sat in the field . . . The angel of the Lord said unto Manoah, Of all that I said unto the woman let her beware . . . The angel of the Lord did no more appear to Manoah and his wife. Then Manoah knew that he was an angel of the Lord and said . . . we have seen God." Judges 13:3-22

Although Manoah and his wife were a most godly couple, they were childless and doubtless had prayed much over such a condition. Prayer was heard, and in a most needy period of Israelite history, a son was given to these two like-minded hearts. He became the mighty Samson – troubler of Israel's foes, the Philistines. The celestial dignity of the angel, who appeared to Manoah and his wife, distinguishes Him from an ordinary angel. Here, again, we have the great Angel – Jehovah – one of the theophanic appearances of Jesus.

Promise of Sustenance

"An angel touched Elijah, and said unto him, Arise and eat . . . The angel of the Lord came again the second time, and touched him, and said, Arise and eat: because the journey is too great for thee . . . The angel of the Lord said to Elijah the Tishbite, Arise, go out to meet the messengers of the King of Samaria." I Kings 19:4,5; II Kings 1:3-15

To have an angel as a cook and host was no mean honor. Throughout his career as a prophet, Elijah, the rugged son of the wilderness, was accustomed to divine and angelic provision and protection. At his translation, he was taken up to heaven in a chariot with its horses of fire. Gill, the commentator says that, "Angels are meant by *chariots*, and they are called *chariots* because they have appeared in such form, and because, like chariots of war, they are the strength and protection of the Lord's people, and because of their swiftness in doing His work" II Kings 2:17;

6:16; Psalm 68:17, 18).

Promise of Preservation

"Blessed be God . . . who hath sent his angel, and delivered his servants that trusted in him." Daniel 3:28

"My God hath sent his angel, and hath shut the lions' mouths that they have not hurt me." Daniel 6:22

How varied are the activities of the angels. One prepared a meal for Elijah, here another preserved the three Hebrew youths from being burned to death, and doubtless it was the same angel who restrained the natural hunger of the ferocious lions so that Daniel could have a restful night. Gabriel, one of the highest in the angelic hierarchy, was the one who revealed to Daniel God's plan for the nations (Daniel 8:16-19; 9:21).

Promise of Interpretation

"The angel that talked with me said unto me, I will shew thee what these shall be . . . The angel of the Lord answered and said, O Lord of hosts, how long wilt Thou not have mercy on Jerusalem, and on the cities of Judah? . . . The angel communed with me . . . The angel of the Lord protested unto Joshua." Zechariah 1:9, 11, 12; 3:6, etc.

In *Zechariah*, a book rich in symbols, angelic appearances and activities are conspicuous. On this occasion, however, they are related to God's prophetic plan regarding Jerusalem, the restoration of true religion and the coming of the Messiah. As God's representatives, the angels are able to impart unerring instruction and knowledge.

"The angel that talked with me answered and said unto me, Knowest thou not what these things be?" 4:5

Promise of a Forerunner

"There appeared unto Zacharias an angel of the Lord . . . who said, Fear not, Zacharias: for thy prayer is heard: and thy wife Elisabeth shall bear thee a son, and thou shalt call his name John . . . The angel answering said unto him, I am Gabriel that stands in the presence of God, and am sent to speak unto thee, and to shew thee glad tidings." Luke 1:11, 13, 19

The mission of angels is carried over into the New Testament, in which they appear just as active as in the Old Testament. To Gabriel was the honor given of announcing to Zach-

arias and Elisabeth, the end of barrenness, and the birth of a son, who would become the forerunner of the predicted Messiah, who was to say of John the Baptist, "There is none greater" (Luke 7:28).

Promise of a Saviour

"In the sixth month the angel Gabriel was sent from God . . . to a virgin . . . and said, Hail, thou that art highly favoured, for the Lord is with thee: blessed art thou among women . . . thou shalt . . . bring forth a son, and shalt call his name JESUS . . . The angel answered and said to Mary, The Holy Ghost shall come upon thee, and the power of the Highest shall overshadow thee: therefore also that holy thing which shall be born of thee shall be called the Son of God." Luke 1:26-38 See Matthew 1:20

Gabriel's prediction was fully realized and Jesus came into the world as its only Babe who never had a human father. "With God nothing shall be impossible." Thus Jesus, conceived of the Holy Spirit and born of the Virgin, appeared as the Saviour of the world, as the angel of the Lord announced, and a myriad of angels rejoiced over (Luke 2:9, 10, 13).

Promise of Fulfilled Prophecy

"The angel of the Lord appeared to Joseph in a dream, saying, Arise, and take the young child and his mother, and flee into Egypt . . . that it might be fulfilled which was spoken of the Lord by the prophet, saying, Out of Egypt have I called my son." Matthew 2:13, 14; Hosea 11:1

Abiding in the presence of God, the angels are instructed in many of His secrets and, in turn, are commissioned to transmit what they receive from Him for the enlightenment of men.

Promise of Resurrection

"The angel of the Lord descended from heaven, and came and rolled back the stone from the door, and sat upon it . . . The angel answered . . . Fear not ye, for I know that ye seek Jesus, which was crucified. He is not here: for He is risen as he said." Matthew 28:2, 5; Luke 24:23

The mighty, heavy boulder was no problem to an angel. From that which the friends of Jesus feared, the angel made a seat. Then, with what joy this heavenly witness to Christ's resurrection must have proclaimed such a fact. Note his phrase "as He said." The disciples did not believe Him when He said that He would rise again. But the angel knew He would triumph over the grave, even as He had declared.

Promises of Deliverance from Prison

"The angel of the Lord by night opened the prison doors, and brought them forth, and said, Go, stand and speak in the temple to the people all the words of the life." Acts 5:19, 20

"The angel of the Lord came upon him, and a light shined in the prison: and he smote Peter in his side, and raised him up, saying, Arise up quickly . . . Gird thyself, and bind on thy sandals . . . It was true which was done by the angel . . . The Lord hath sent his angel, and hath delivered me out of the hand of Herod." Acts 12:7-15

Those who were responsible for Peter and John being thrown into prison were the Sadducees who did not believe in the resurrection and of the existence of angels. The interposition of the latter on behalf of the apostles must have caused the unbelieving Sadducees to reflect. Mantled with divine power, angels find locked prison doors no barrier. Neither were the strong prison guards whom the angels were able to paralyze in some miraculous way.

Promise of Courage

"There stood by me this night, the angel of God, whose I am, and whom I serve, Saying, Fear not, Paul: thou must be brought before Caesar: and lo, God hath given thee all them that sail with thee."

Acts 27:23, 24

The crises of life either break or make a man. During the terrible storm that beset the ship taking Paul and other prisoners to Rome, all around the apostle became panic-stricken. Paul's moral ascendancy, however, dominated the situation. He infused courage and cheer into crew and captives alike, and commanded the crisis because of the divine assurance he had received through the medium of an angel.

The question may be asked, Have we any reason to believe that the manifold angelic ministry continues until this day? The testimony of the Bible is that it does. The angels "are ministering spirits, sent forth to minister for them who shall be heirs of salvation" (Hebrews 1:14). As all the blood-washed are these *heirs*, then they can lay claim to promised angelic ministrations. As in the Lord Jesus we have One always near, although unseen, so in angels we have guardian attendants, though not perceived (Matthew 18:10).

If wicked spirits have power over the thoughts for evil, why should we question the great influence good angels have over us in a heavenly direction? Saintly Samuel Rutherford said, "I doubt not but good angels suggest good counsels, tender holy motives, offer pious thoughts; yea, refresh the often-parched spirits of gracious men with inward joy." Heirs of salvation! Heirs of God and joint-heirs with Christ! No wonder that angels watch over us to keep us in all our ways.

The Holy Spirit and His Promises

Among the numerous titles of the Holy Spirit describing His personality and performances, there is the suggestive one Paul gave us in his Ephesian letter:

"Ye were sealed with that Holy Spirit of promise." Ephesians 1:14

Why is He thus named? First of all, He came as the Promised One. He came as the Promise of the Father and of the Son.

"I will pray the Father, and He shall give you another Comforter . . . even the Spirit of Truth." John 14:16, 26

"Wait for the Promise of the Father, which, saith He, ye heard of from Me." Acts 1:4

"The gift of the Holy Spirit. For the Promise is unto you, and to your children, and to all that are afar off, even as many as the Lord our God shall call." Acts 2:39

On the Day of Pentecost, the divine promise was realized, and the Holy Spirit came in the plenitude of His power and brought into being the mystic fabric–the Church of the Living God. It was then that Joel's prophecy was partially fulfilled (2:28-31). The final fulfilment will be experienced in the day of Israel's exultation and blessing. (Isaiah 2:2-4; Micah 4:1-7)

He is also called "The Holy Spirit of promise" because by Him the promises of redemption and sanctification are coined into the reality of experience. All the Father and the Son made objective and possible, the Spirit makes subjective and actual in the lives of the redeemed. He is the Promise or Pledge of better and more perfect work in His present inworking in us. He is but "the earnest" of the divine purpose to claim in complete possession that which God has purchased. Actually, the Spirit is God's "Promissory Note" of a full and final settlement.

Further, He is "The Holy Spirit of promise," seeing He inspired holy men of old to record the thousands of promises the Bible holds. He it was who put words into their mouths and taught them what to say. (Exodus 4:15, 16; II Timothy 3:16)

"The Spirit of Christ which was in the prophets did signify when they testified beforehand." I Peter 1:11

"Holy men of God spake as they were moved by the Holy Spirit." II Peter 1:21

Perhaps *The Psalms* contain more gracious promises than any other book of the Bible. How permeated they are with all God is willing to be and do for His children! As the bulk of these *Psalms*, with their rich promises, came from the heart and pen of David, the sweet Psalmist of Israel, it is interesting to note that he claimed the inspiration of the Spirit for all his work. Of Psalm 18, David could write:

"The Spirit of the Lord spake by me, and his word was in my tongue." II Samuel 23:2 and chapter 22 with Psalm 18

While we could profitably explore *all* the utterances of the Spirit through those He chose and inspired, and dwell upon the promises, facts, revelation and threatenings they contain, there are seven explicit promises of the Spirit we feel constrained to draw attention to, namely the seven to be found in the Master's letters to the seven churches. (Revelation 2-3) Here is the order of these "Overcomer" promises. An exposition of these letters, as such, is not within the province of our present study. That each follow a marked pattern ending with a promise is clearly evident.

1. The Promise to Ephesus

"The Spirit saith unto the church: To him that overcometh will I give to eat of the tree of life, which is in the paradise of God." Revelation 2:2

The Lord in heaven, and the Spirit on earth make the true Church their special subject of care. Each letter proves their present oversight of the Church, and ends with promises and rewards to those within the Church who overcome the world, flesh and the devil. Each promise could be stud-

ied in the light of the letter containing it. The first promise to the overcomer contains an evident allusion to the Garden of Eden, with the tree of life in its midst (Genesis 2). Walter Scott says, "Adam had not to overcome in the Garden, he had simply to obey and keep his innocence, and the test of an innocent creature's obedience was the prohibition against eating of the symbolical tree of knowledge of good and evil."

For the Christian overcomer the scene presented is far more glorious than Eden. In the coming Paradise, expression of heaven's blessedness, there is the tree of life of which one may freely eat, and no tree of good and evil, the symbol of creative responsibility. For victors in the fight there is eternal life without alloy and without fear of failure. There, conquerors are to enjoy an everlasting feast. Overcoming false prophets and their evil teaching: Overcoming our own faintness of heart and tendency to decline from our first love, we have the promise of an unending walk with God in Paradise.

2. The Promise to Smyrna

"The Spirit saith unto the churches: he that overcometh shall not be hurt of the second death."

Revelation 2:11

This second letter came from Him "which was dead, and is alive again," and was addressed to those who were about to die for their faith (Revelation 2:8, 10). Overcomers in Smyrna required endurance suited to the death struggle. What conflict raged between light and darkness! Allegiance to Christ then meant loss of character, possessions and life itself, and the faithful required strong faith and clear spiritual trust of Him who would not forsake His valiant saints. Many of them were called upon to die terrible deaths, even as their Master had died, but the promise enabling them to die triumphantly was deliverance from "the second death" which issues in "the lake of fire" (Revelation 20:14; 21:8). For such overcomers there was the promise of the crown or completeness of life for evermore. To escape the hurt of the second, eternal death is a prize worth fighting for throughout a lifetime with Satan and sin dogging our heels.

3. The Promise to Pergamos

"The Spirit saith unto the churches: To him that overcomes, to him will I give of the hidden manna: and I will give to him a white stone, and on the stone a new name written, which no one knows but he that receives it."

Revelation 2:17

Here, again, that promise is personalized, "To *him* that overcomes." Even a company of overcomers is formed by the exercise of faith and spiritual energy of each one. Often we have to fight the good fight of faith alone. What peculiar sweetness characterizes this promise! The twice repeated "I give," enhances the value of the promised rewards. First of all, the overcomer is to feast on "the hidden manna." Israel's manna, spoken of as "angel's food," and "the bread of God" (Psalm 78:25; John 6:33) was certainly not "hidden," since it lay on the face of the ground round the camp where it could be seen and gathered. There was, however, manna hid in a "golden pot" and for some 500 years. This "hidden manna" told its tale of Christ in humiliation, but to God alone (Exodus 16:33; Hebrews 9:4). Such a pot was hid from the gaze of the people. The reward of the future is the feasting upon the moral beauties and perfections of Him who is presently hid from our eyes. He who enables His saints to fight and overcome, will, in all His fulness, be their reward.

The second part of the promise speaks of a white stone with its new name unknown to any, save the possessor of the stone. What are we to understand by this particular stone bearing its secret name? Walter Scott, in his *Exposition of Revelation,* gives us this most instructive explanation:

> A "white stone" was largely employed in the social life and judicial customs of the ancients. Days of festivity were noted by a *white* stone; days of calamity by a *black* stone. A host's appreciation of a special guest was indicated by a white stone with a name or message written on it. A *white* stone meant acquittal! A *black* stone condemnation in the courts of justice.

The Spirit promises the overcomer a white stone bearing the new name known only to the happy recipient. Can this suggest the mighty Victor's personal delight in each one of the conquering band, following Him in the train of His triumph? As to the *new* name, alone known to the overcomer, can this mean that Christ will be known in a special and peculiar way to each of those to be rewarded? Is there to be a secret communication of love and intelligence be-

tween Christ and the overcomer, in joy which none can share, a reserved token of appreciative love? Scott says:

> In the glory of the hidden manna is the expression of *our appreciation* of Christ in His humiliation; while the white stone equally sets forth *His* appreciation of us as overcomers. His and our individual path here are points respectively set forth in the glory by the symbols of the "manna" and the "stone."

4. The Promise to Thyatira

"He that overcometh . . . I will give him the morning star. He that hath an ear, let him hear what the Spirit saith unto the Churches." Revelation 1:26-29

It will be noted that in the first three letters, the voice of the Spirit precedes the promise to the overcomer, while in the last four letters, the promise precedes the voice. In the first group of letters, the Church as a whole is called to repent. "In the second group the hopeless condition of the Church is but too apparent, and hence a remnant company is marked off from the mass, whose one and only hope is centered on the personal return of the Lord from heaven. Now from the fact of the call to hear being placed *after* the words of cheer to the overcomers in the last four churches, we gather none save overcomers or conquerors hear the voice of the Spirit."

What a rich promise is here offered: "I will give to him the morning star." Overcomers are to have a personal interest in Christ Himself. "In His character as the 'Sun of Righteousness' to Israel He heals His people and brings in blessing, but in His character as the 'Bright and Morning Star' He appears before the sun rises to His own alone." Until the day break, and the shadows flee away, what a joy it is to see in Jesus "The Morning Star," which is never far from "The Sun." Are we holding fast that truth, grace; hope and love which the Lord has given us? If so, then ours is the assurance of the dawn of coming glory. "He that makes thee overcome evil, and persevere in righteousness, has therein given thee the morning star."

5. The Promise to Sardis

"He that overcometh, the same shall be clothed in white raiment; and I will not blot out his name out of the book of life, but I will confess his name before my Father, and before his angels. He that hath an ear, let him hear what the Spirit saith unto the Churches." Revelation 3:5, 6

As warriors of the cross, may grace be ours to fight on, never halting until victory is complete, and that eternal reward crowning a life of warfare is ours. The white raiment speaks of perfect purity, more perfect than the undefiled garments of a few in Sardis. Yes, and the white raiment speaks of reward becoming a conqueror, and priestly array. No speck or stain shall rest on the garment of white.

"The book of life" mentioned here is not the same to be found in Revelation 13:8, in which the names of true believers are recorded. In the promise before us "the book of life" is the record of Christian *profession*—not the record of *reality* as in 13:8. In the former true and false are found: in the latter the true only. Many who have not persevered and overcome will find their names erased in the register of Christian profession when life's records are to be scanned by the all-searching eye of the Lord of the churches. If we never shrink from confessing His name, He will not be ashamed to single us out in the august presence of the Father and His angels and confess our name before the grand assembly.

6. The Promise to Philadelphia

"Him that overcometh will I make a pillar in the temple of my God, and he shall go no more out: and I will write upon him the name of my God, which is new Jerusalem, which cometh down out of heaven from my God: and I will write upon him my new name. He that hath an ear, let him hear what the Spirit saith unto the churches."
Revelation 3:12, 13

Here and now, an open door, no man can shut, faces the overcomer (3:8). It is the open door of communion with the Father, and the open door into all the mysteries of the Word. None of its promises or precepts are closed to the faithful. What a bountiful promise is this sixth one, offered to those in Philadelphia, who although weak, yet pursued! In spite of so much to test

their faith they held fast with a tight and tightening grip Christ's Word, name, patience and return. The Holy Spirit promised that earth's weakness would be exchanged for heaven's stability: "Him will I make a *pillar*." Then there is a fixed and eternal abode. "He shall go no more at all out." As to bearing God's name, what a privilege it will be for each one of the conquering band to bear such a privileged name, indicating a special relationship with Him amid heavenly blessedness.

7. The Promise to Laodicea

"He that overcomes, to him will I give to sit with me in my throne: as I also have overcome, and have sat down with my Father in his throne. He that hath an ear, let him hear what the Spirit saith unto the churches." Revelation 3:21, 22

A "throne" is the sign and symbol of royal authority and dominion, and the Laodicean conqueror was promised association with Christ in His Kingdom and glory. Overcomers are to share Christ's throne, even as He shares His Father's throne. On the difference between the two thrones mentioned in this portion, Ellicott observes: "My throne, saith Christ: this is the condition of glorified saints who sit with Christ in His throne. But My Father's, that is, God's throne, is the power of divine majesty. Herein none may sit but God, and the God-Man Jesus Christ. The promise of sharing the throne is the climax of an ascending series of glorious promises, which carry the thought from the Garden of Eden (2:7) through the wilderness (2:17), the temple (3:12), to the throne. The promise bears marked resemblance to the language of Paul (Ephesians 2-6).

"The crowning promise is made to the most unpleasing of the churches. But it is well that thus the despondency which often succeeds the sudden collapse of self-satisfied imaginations should be met by so bright a prospect. The highest place is within the reach of the lowest: the faintest spark of grace may be fanned into the mightiest flame of divine love."

VI

THE SECURITY OF THE PROMISES

Spurgeon tells us that He believed all the promises of God but that many of them

he had personally tried and proved." I have seen that they are true, for they have been fulfilled in me." The question before us in this chapter is, "How can we secure many of the Bible promises and make them our very own?" Are the experiences of men of old of any use to us in this modern age? The Psalmist could say, "I sought the Lord, and He heard me," and again, "This poor man cried, and the Lord heard him." Can the same confidence of answered prayer be ours? If so, how?

We must not overlook the principle that, while many of the promises can be claimed by those who love God and are called according to His purpose, the fulfilment of such is dependent upon becoming more alive to the conditions attached to many of these promises which must be met. Promises contingent upon a condition will be realized as the respective condition is fulfilled. In the acquisition or appropriation of any promise, we must first of all bear in mind the difference between an *absolute promise,* that is, an unconditional promise: and a *conditional promise,* meaning a promise that cannot be secured unless the specified condition is met. *Absolute promises* are those unconnected with the requirement of anything on the part of the promisee, in order to their fulfilment. Such a promise is a naked agreement and in law means, a contract without *quid pro quo,* that is, something given or taken as equivalent to another. An illustration of an *absolute promise* is seen in God's promise to provide a guilty race with the ground and means of reconciliation. "I will never leave thee" is another of the *absolute* promises of heaven.

Conditional promises, of which there are many, are those dependent for their fulfilment upon the carrying out of certain requirements, expressly stated. For instance, take this one:

"Truly God is good to Israel."

Psalm 73:1

It would be altogether wrong to say, "Well, God was good to Israel, unworthy though she proved to be, therefore, I know He will be good to me." Such a promise of goodness is dependent upon fulfilment of the important attached condition:

"Even to such as are of a clean heart."

If we are confident that ours is the "clean heart," then there is nothing in the way to a realization of God's goodness. Take another illustration of conditional blessing offered to Israel:

"Neither will I make the feet of Israel move any more out of the land which

I gave their fathers. . . ."

To stop there and claim divine protection would have been sheer folly because the promise was dependent upon the condition of obedience.

"Only *if* they will observe to do according to all that I have commanded them, and according to all the law that my servant Moses commanded them."

II Kings 21:8

The people, however, as the narrative shows, failed to comply with the specific condition and they had to forfeit occupancy of the land (II Kings 21:12-15).

The root meaning of the Greek term for "promise" is "to announce oneself," hence to signify to "offer one's services" and "to engage oneself voluntarily to render a service," and is associated in Rabbinical usage with "assurance." In the gospels "promise" carries the thought of this assurance—

"Behold, I send the promise of my Father upon you." Luke 24:29

The "promise" here refers to the gift of the Holy Spirit (Acts 1:4; 2:23, 29; Galatians 3:14; Ephesians 1:13). The same word is used in the unfulfilled promise of Christ's return (II Peter 3:4). In Christian experience a "promise" is translated into "assurance" when any declared condition is recognized and realized.

God has made great promises to men, the sum total of the promises being: His rest, eternal life and eternal goodness. The only true rest of the soul and of all souls is *His* rest:

"Come unto me, all ye that labour and are heavy laden, and I will give you rest . . . Ye shall find rest unto your souls." Matthew 11:28, 29

In order to enter into and to enjoy this rest it is imperative to *come, take,* and *find.* The forfeiting of such a promise is a terrible calamity. To "come short of" the true rest, what greater loss than this could befall the human spirit?

The Epistle to the Hebrews is rich in its passages which make mention not only of the promises of old being fulfilled in Christ, but likewise fulfilled for us as we carry out the provisions laid down. "Lest . . . any of you should seem to come short of the promise" (4:1). Some of the blessings of God are bestowed irrespective of our choice or effort, such as life, intellect and the material elements. But others depend upon our effort, and the rest of soul is one for which we must strive–*agonize*–

as the word means. A glance at other references confirms the necessity of diligence and endeavor, if certain promises are to become real in experience.

"Be not slothful, but followers of them who through faith and patience inherit the promises." Hebrews 6:12

While God made promises to Abraham, it was only after patient endurance that he obtained or realized the promises (see Genesis 15:6). Although the promises are divine in origin, they are unavailing unless we receive them by faith. As we shall presently see, it is only as we believe the promises that we can inherit them. Then we certainly need *patience* ere some promises are fulfilled. George Mueller believed God would answer prayer for an unsaved friend, but had to wait forty years for God to grant his desire. We must not lose heart if God seems slow to fulfil a promise we daily claim. In patience, we must possess our souls, for God is never late.

The word "slothful" in the text means *sluggish* and is the same word used in the previous chapter, "Ye are dull of hearing" (v. 11). There it is applied to lack of interest in the apprehension of truth. Here, the word is related to Christian hope and life. If truth is not welcomed and inherited, there will be no spiritual vigor in Christian walk and witness. Dr. E. Schuyler English comments: "Diligence toward heavenly things will rout sluggardliness in earthly exercises, and in such a way we all need to be followers or, better, imitators of others who, through faith and patience, have inherited the promises of God." Abraham was long tried but he was richly rewarded. Patient waiters are never disappointed because God's promises cannot fail of their accomplishment.

"After he had patiently endured, he obtained the promise." Hebrews 6:15

As we are discovering, Abraham is before us for special mention as the most illustrious example of those who "inherit the promises." (See John 8:58.) The assurance given to Abraham was confirmed by an oath, and in the promise lay included the appearance of Christ. While the promises made to Abraham were essentially one, the various parts were progressively fulfilled (see Genesis 12:3; 15; 22:17). Abraham, however, having patiently waited, obtained the promise, or the promised gift. Ellicott remarks: "Though some portions of the promise received a partial accomplishment

in Abraham's life, it is not this that the writer has in view (Hebrews 6:12, 11:13). The promise made to Abraham was substantially and really that which embraced all Messianic hope (Hebrews 6:15): of this promise not Abraham's son only, but all 'they which are of faith' (Galatians 3:7, 29), Abraham's spiritual seed, are the heirs."

Abraham, it is said, obtained the promise after much patient endurance. God tried him by delaying to fulfil His promise; Satan tried him by testing; men tried him by jealousy, distrust, and opposition; Hagar tried him by condemning her mistress; Sarah, his wife, tried him by her peevishness; but Abraham patiently waited. As a man of great faith, "he did not question God's veracity, nor limit His power, nor doubt his faithfulness, nor grieve His love; but bowed to divine sovereignty, submitted to divine wisdom, and was silent under delays, waiting the Lord's time." Do we imitate his example? How Abraham's endurance condemns a hasty spirit, reproves a murmuring spirit, commends a patient spirit, and encourages quiet submission to God's will and way.

"Blessed him that had the promises." Hebrews 7:6

Melchisedec, the great and mysterious character, blessed Abraham, who was already the recipient of the promises of God (Genesis 12:2, 3, 7). "What greater blessing could any man have than such promises?" asks Dr. English. "Yet Melchisedec's superiority demonstrated itself in that Abraham gave tithes to him, and received his blessing without rebuke. And beyond all contradiction 'the less is blessed of the better' — a truth so obvious as to require no comment whatever." We have no right, of course, to seek the blessing of a promise unless we are willing to fulfil its conditions. How true it is that all who believe and claim the promises are richly blessed of the Lord! How gracious He is to make us the recipients of His promises so loaded with benefits!

"They which are called might receive the promise of eternal inheritance." Hebrews 9:15

Christ's death, as a ransom for sin, was also a sacrifice inaugurating the new covenant, containing the promise of the eternal inheritance. Some promises are not valid until death takes place, as in the case of a friend promising and willing another a legacy on death. Christ was promised as the Sin-Offering, and as the result of His death there is remission of sin and eternal life for all who believe.

"The heirs with him of the same promise."Hebrews 11:9

By faith, Abraham sojourned in "a land of the promise." He came into and dwelt in a land which the promise made his own (Genesis 12:7). As Vaughan expresses it, "Abraham made his home once for all, well aware that it was to be his home–expecting no change in this respect all his life long –in tents, moveable, shifting abodes–here today, there tomorrow–with, as did also in their turn, Isaac and Jacob, the heirs with him of the same promise." All three were co-heirs of the same promise given by God to each of the patriarchs (Genesis 12:7; 13:15; 17:18; 26:3; 35:12). While the land was Abraham's by promise, for a century he was only a stranger and pilgrim in it. When he died, all he owned of the land was a field in Machpelah. Yet he died in faith, not receiving the promises, but having seen them afar off (Hebrews 11:13). Believing God, Abraham knew that both the earthly possession and the heavenly estate would be realized. Abraham looked for the glorious city whose "Architect and Maker is God" (Revelation 21)

"These all, having obtained a good report through faith, received not the promise." Hebrews 11:39

Here the promise, anticipated by many but which none of them received, was the coming of the Messiah as the Saviour of the world. Prophets and kings (Luke 10:24; I Peter 1:10; Jude 14, 15) did not live to see God's Anointed One. Yet accepting the hope of redemption and of resurrection, they died in faith and were accepted by God in virtue of Calvary. They looked forward to the Cross, just as we look back to it. The three passages which must be kept together are:

"Having patiently endured, Abraham obtained the promise." Hebrews 6:15

"Ye have need of endurance, that having done the will of God ye may receive the promise." Hebrews 10:36

"Having obtained a good report through faith, received not the promise." Hebrews 11:39

To Old Testament saints the promised blessing of redemption was future–they obtained it, but not within the limits of this present life. They had it "on credit." To all, saved by grace, "the promised blessing is present, revealed to us in its true nature, obtained for us once for all; for we know that eternal redemption has been won through Christ's entering for us once for all into the heavenly sanctuary (Hebrews 9:12), and to us the perfection has come, in that through Him we draw near to God" (Hebrews 7:11, 19). Ere long, the Church Triumphant above and the Church Militant on earth will sing in unison–

> Joy to the world! The Lord is come;
> Let earth receive her King;
> Let every heart prepare him room
> And Heaven and nature sing.

There is one other passage we can consider along with the foregoing. Paul speaks of the promise being made of none effect (Romans 4:14). In his exposition of *Justification*, the apostle's contention is that adherence to the Law nullifies God's work of grace. The promise to bless all, through the righteousness of faith, is made of none effect by the work of the Law. What we must remember, however, even though we are under grace, is that many promises are conditional, and that failure on our part to comply with the condition abrogates these promises. The tragedy is that so many wonderful promises of God are rendered of none effect in experience because of sin, unbelief and disobedience.

This leads us to another thought in connection with the security or appropriation of the promises, namely, their immediate function and ultimate goal. The *immediate* purpose of acquired promises is the meeting of our varied needs. The ultimate design of the promises is the separation of our lives from anything unworthy of the Divine Promiser.

"Having these promises . . . let us cleanse ourselves." II Corinthians 7:1 Any given promise should make us more pure. No specific promise, even though related to material needs should not be claimed apart from the sanctifying influence, the granting of the promise, is able to exercise in our life. The promise of "the blessed hope" of our Lord's return results in holiness of life (I John 3:1-3).

Promises, to be effective both materially and spiritually, must be possessed by faith –proven by obedience–presented in prayer.

Possessed by Faith

We live a life of faith upon promises. Today the riches of any nation consists in the credit that is given to notes, bonds, assignments, etc. Likewise, the riches of the Christian life are in the notes under God's hand. A nation can default in its bonds. With God, however, it is impossible for any promise of His to fail. The Bible presents a formidable array of passages proving that faith, which is the medium of a right relationship Godward, is also the condition on which depends the security and enjoyment of promised blessings.

"The promise by faith of Jesus Christ might be given to them that believe." Galatians 3:22

"The promise . . . through the righteousness of faith." Romans 4:13

"Therefore it is of faith . . . to the end the promise might be sure to all the seed." Romans 4:16

"Through faith and patience inherit the promises." Hebrews 6:12

"Who through faith . . . obtained the promises." Hebrews 11:33

"Let him ask in faith, nothing wavering." James 1:5

We have already considered Abraham –

"Who staggered not at the promise of God through unbelief." Romans 4:20

It was staggering enough for a man about a hundred years old to be told that his wife, not much younger, would give birth to a son. Yet such was Abraham's faith, who against hope believed in hope, that the physically impossible did not trouble him. God had promised a son of promise and that was the end of the matter as far as Abraham was concerned. He was not weak in faith. The same applies to Sarah (Hebrews 11:11):

"Through faith also Sarah herself received strength to conceive seed, and was delivered of a child when she was past age, because she judged him faithful who had promised."

Possibly some of the promises of God stagger us. They appear to be too good to be true. But God never mocks the human heart. He says what He means and means all He says. Our difficulty is the failure to meet the great promises with a great faith. But as we believe God, we prove Him to be faithful to His Word.

Faith confidently expects the fulfilment of the Divine word –

"Be it unto me according to thy word." Luke 1:38

"Blessed is she that believed: for there shall be a performance of those things which were told her of the Lord." Luke 1:45

"Wait for the promise of the Father." Acts 1:4

"Nevertheless we, according to his promise, look for new heavens and a new earth, wherein dwelleth righteousness." II Peter 3:13

A promise is God's bond and is intended to set our minds at rest. Trusting God's word, then, we need fear no foe, or dread any trouble. We are not only saved but *safe*.

"I will trust in thy word." Psalm 119:42

Trusting God's naked promise may be difficult yet it is obtainable. It is unsafe and improper to trust our feelings or fancies, or to be guided by appearances. Our guide is God's Word, and this should be the object of our trust.

If we seek to claim a promise for wrong ends, to consume upon our own lusts, and not for God's honor, then we ask amiss and cannot receive the promise.

"Ye ask and receive not, because ye ask amiss." James 4:3

All promises, whether temporal or spiritual, are realized by faith, love and obedience. The promises of grace and glory far outweigh those associated with material things. For all who enquire after God, there is the promise of a new heart (Ezekiel 36:26, 27). There is a promise of wisdom for all who will search for it (Proverbs 2:4, 5). There is the promise of the Spirit for those who ask for Him (Luke 11:13). There is the promise of rest for all who labor and are heavy laden (Matthew 11:28). There is the promise of the increase of grace for those who persevere unto the end (John 15:16).

We have two notable instances of the lack of expectation. There is Zacharias, who refused to believe that his desire for a son, and God's promise of one, was about to be granted (Luke 1:13, 18). Then there were those "gathered together praying" for Peter's release, yet could not credit the fact that "he stood before the gate, and continued knocking" (Acts 12:5, 12-16).

Spurgeon in his most helpful arrangement of the precious promises for daily use, known as *Faith's Checkbook*, says that –

A promise of God may very instructively be compared to a check payable to order. It is given to the believer with the view of bestowing upon him some good thing. It is not meant that he should read it over comfortably, and then have done with it. No, he is to treat the promise as a reality, as a man treats a check. He is to take the promise, and endorse it with his own name, by personally receiving it as true. He is by faith to *accept* it as his own. He sets to his seal that God is true, and true as to this particular word of promise. He goes further and believes that he has the blessing in having the sure promise of it, and therefore he puts his name to it to testify to the receipt of the blessing.

This done, he must believingly *present* the promise to the Lord, as a man presents a check at the counter of the bank. He must plead it by prayer, expecting to have it fulfilled. If he has come to heaven's bank at the right date, he will receive the promised amount at once. If the date should happen to be further on, he must patiently wait till its arrival; but meanwhile he may count the promise as money, for the bank is sure to pay when the due time arrives.

Some fail to place the endorsement of faith upon the check, and so they get nothing; others are slack in presenting it, and these also receive nothing. This is not the fault of the promise, but of those who do not act with it in a common-sense, business-like manner.

Further on in the *Preface* of his devotional volume containing 365 brief, experimental comments on the promises which Spurgeon has chosen, the renowned preacher tells us that so many of these promises are true because they were fulfilled in his own experience during a time of "wading in the surf of controversy," and also when "sharp bodily pain succeeded mental depression, accompanied both by bereavement, and affliction in the person of one dear as life. Never were the promises of Jehovah so precious to me as at this hour." Thus it was to help other sufferers that Spurgeon prepared this comforting book.

The sight of the promises themselves is good for the eyes of faith; the more we study the words of grace, the more grace we shall derive from the words. To the cheering Scriptures I have added testimonies of my own, the fruit of trial and experience. I believe the promises of God, but many of them I have persoanlly tried and proved.

But while the promises of God are to be appropriated by faith, this does not discharge us from the diligent use of all proper and lawful means. God has promised us food and raiment, but the slothful and careless should not expect to benefit from such a promise.

"The soul of the sluggard desireth, and hath nothing: but the soul of the diligent shall be made fat." Proverbs 13:4

A further observation is that faith is manifested in works. "Faith without works is dead" (James 2:20). Many promises are associated, conditionally, with particular duties.

"Godliness is profitable unto all things, having promise of the life that *now* is, and that which is to come."

II Timothy 4:8

If we do not seek after godliness, then we are not in the right condition of soul to claim the promise. Many promises are linked to diligence and to various kindred virtues.

"The hand of the diligent maketh rich."

Proverbs 10:4

God cannot condone indolence and sloth. Although God miraculously supplied the manna, the people had to gather it daily.

"If any man will not work, neither shall he eat." II Thessalonians 3:10

Then some promises are associated with the legitimate and liberal use of what has been already bestowed, as indicated in the promise—

"Honour the Lord with thy substance . . . so shall thy barns be filled with plenty." Proverbs 3:9

"Bring ye all the tithes into the storehouse . . . I will pour you out a blessing, that there shall not be room enough to receive it." Malachi 3:10

Is it not presumptuous to expect God to fulfil a promise if conditions connected with it are violated or neglected? We must not only believe a promise, but work out by grace, all it expects of us.

Proved by Obedience

Faith and obedience are the two legs a Christian walks with. The Bible's insistence upon *obedience* is marked. It was because the first man disobeyed God that sin entered the world. But through the obedience of the Man Christ Jesus, there is life for evermore (Romans 5:19). When God commanded the children of Israel to go in and possess the land it was as good as theirs, for already God had "lifted up" His hand to give it them. But the promise was made of none effect through their disobedience (Romans 10:21).

"Ezra had prepared his heart to seek the law of the Lord, and to *do* it."

Ezra 7:10

"If ye be willing and obedient, ye shall eat of the good of the land."

Isaiah 1:19

"All that the Lord hath said will we do, and be obedient." Exodus 24:7

"A blessing, if ye obey . . . a curse if ye will not obey." Deuteronomy 11:27, 28

"To obey is better than sacrifice."

I Samuel 15:22

"Obey my voice, and I will be your God." Jeremiah 7:23

"After ye have done the will of God, ye might receive the promise."

Hebrews 10:36

In His teaching and example on "Humility" our Lord associated joy with knowledge of His Word – both being contingent upon obedience.

"If ye know these things, happy are ye if ye *do* them." John 13:17

As we approach a promise demanding obedience to the expressed wish and will of God, is ours the joy springing from a willingness to obey? Obedience is not only a virtue of high importance, it is also the supreme test of faith. We cannot read the annals of the Old Testament without realizing how vital obedience was. Take Abraham, for example, in whose experience obedience formed a relationship not to be broken. The patriarch was made a blessing to the world because of his obedience to God's voice, promises, statutes and laws:

"In thy seed shall all the nations of the earth be blessed, because thou hast obeyed my voice." Genesis 22:18

"In thy seed shall all the nations of the earth be blessed: because that Abraham obeyed my voice and kept my charge." Genesis 26:4-5

Obedience and disobedience are offered as points of contrast between the saved and the unsaved. A true Christian is a "child of obedience" (I Peter 1:14 R.V.). A sinner is "a child of disobedience" (Ephesians 2:2). Those who are the Lord's are not only elected unto obedience (I Peter 1:2), their obedience is a condition of promised answer to prayer –

"Whatsoever we ask, we receive of him, because we keep his commandments, and *do* those things that are pleasing in his sight." I John 3:22

Obedience likewise results in the promised knowledge of the Lord –

"Hereby we do know that we know him, *if we keep* his commandments."

I John 2:3

Obedience is also a test of mutual indwelling and of abiding love –

"He that keepeth his commandments dwelleth in him, and he in him."

I John 3:24

"If ye keep my commandments, ye shall abide in my love." John 15:10

The prophet reminds us that obedience to all the promises of God issues in a peace as full and as abundant as the sea –

"O that thou hadst hearkened to my commandments! then had thy peace been as a river, and righteousness as the waves of the sea." Isaiah 48:18

Claiming a promise, then, we must honestly face any condition attached to it, and by the grace of Him, who was obedient unto the death of the cross, fulfil the expressed stipulation. If we fail to obey, we fail to obtain.

Presented in Prayer

How comforting it is to take God's exceeding great and precious promises and turn them into prayer! Does it not please God when we plead His promises?

"Put me in remembrance: let us plead together: declare thou, that thou mayest be justified." Isaiah 43:26

Think of the way some of the saints of old turned promises into prayers –

"Jacob said, O God of my father Abraham, and God of my father, Isaac, the Lord which saidst unto me, Return unto thy country, and to thy kindred, and I will deal with thee . . . Thou saidst, I will surely do thee good." Genesis 32:9-12

Then in David's great prayer he pleads a divine promise –

"Let it even be established, that thy name may be magnified for ever . . . Now Lord, thou art God, and had promised this goodness unto thy servant."

I Chronicles 1:23, 26, 27

Promises which strengthen our faith and prompt our obedience also enforce our pleas. We can go with the promises to God, firmly depending upon His faithfulness to answer our demands accordingly. A promise is a note under His own hand, and He will acknowledge His own handwriting. Thus as we rest in, and upon, Him, we are assured that He will not be unmindful of His promise.

Promise, prayer and performance cover our advancement in the spiritual life. The promise and performance are the Lord's but prayer must come from us. Promises are ineffectual and their performance is inoperative, if prayer on our part is lacking.

"I will yet for this be enquired of by the house of Israel, to do it for them."

Ezekiel 36:37

W. C. Proctor says that, "The promises of God should be the basis of all our prayers, for they are alike our warrant for asking and our security for receiving. It is not safe for us to ask anything that lies beyond their all-embracing scope, for we have no authority to do so; but we may confidently ask for whatever is included in them, for He never fails to fulfil them."

"Thou hast promised this goodness unto thy servant; therefore now let it please thee to bless the house of thy servant . . . Do as thou hast said." II Samuel 7:28, 29

The keynote of that wonderful Psalm, which magnifies the Word of God, is found in David's prayer –

"Remember the word unto thy servant, upon which thou hast caused me to hope." 119:49

The petition, "according to thy word," occurs twelve times (25, 28, 41, 58, 76, 107, 116, 149, 154, 169, 170), while the declaration, "I hope in thy word," is repeated six times (42, 43, 74, 81, 114, 147).

A concluding thought is that God's unfailing promises are given to stimulate prayer, not to supersede it; for, while everything good for us is promised in answer to believing prayer, nothing is promised apart from it. The "fire" of our prayers must be fed with the "fuel" of divine promises. Persuaded of the promises, we plead them and then possess them.

"When Daniel understood by the books the number of the years . . . for the accomplishing of the desolations of Jerusalem, even seventy years, he set his face unto the Lord God to seek by prayer and supplications their fulfilment." Daniel 9:2, 3 R.V.

Suppose we take a repeated promise like –

"I will never leave thee, nor forsake thee." Hebrews 13:5

It is essential, not only to believe and claim it, but to constantly pray that ours will be the unfailing realization of His promised presence. We must be careful to have a life in which there is nothing displeasing to His holy will.

VII
THE SCOPE OF THE PROMISES

We come now to a suggested classification of the multitudinous, all-embracing promises of God: and as the reader can see, because of the importance of this aspect of our study, this chapter forms the bulk of the book. How embarrassed with spiritual riches we are, as we seek to group in order, all that God has promised to be and to do! Looking at the promises as a whole, as they bloom all over the Garden of God's Word, we find our senses ravished; but to know their full richness, we need to look at them in detail, more closely.

The divine promises comprehend a rich and endless variety. They embrace time and eternity, and therefore cover all temporal and spiritual needs and thus cover all that may be necessary. As we are to discover, there is a promise for every need. These promises are scattered throughout the Bible like diamonds in a mine of gold. Many of them are of a more special and appropriate nature. Others are associated with the history of particular individuals. Yet even these, related to persons in peculiar circumstances are for the saints of God in general. For instance, the promise God gave to Moses, and then to Joshua (Deuteronomy 31:7, 8; Joshua 1:8), is generalized and given as the ground of trust and as a source of comfort to all the people of God (Hebrews 13:5).

In fact, the different promises resemble "a well-furnished provision store containing food for all, for every description of ailment, for every variety of need; and at the same time they are a well-filled and well-assorted medicine chart with means of relief and healing for all kinds of spiritual complaints." A remarkable feature of the divine promises is that they contain gifts and graces of all kinds of the most excellent nature and suited to every circumstance of our mortal life. As man is a tripartite being, made up of spirit, soul and body, the necessities of his complex, present life must be provided for, as well as the security of life beyond the grave. This is why Paul reminds us of the wide, complete coverage of the promises –

"Godliness is profitable . . . for this life . . . and that which is to come."

I Timothy 4:8

One satisfying aspect, then, of God's promises is that abundant care has been taken of life both here and hereafter. Full provision has been made for the Christian's peace, joy and comfort in this world and in that which is to come. The promises cover both worlds and include all things that pertain to life and godliness. They also inspire the assurance that the several necessaries and conveniences of life will be granted as divine wisdom deems best to bestow. God, because of His knowledge of all the various trials and tribulations His own are exposed to, encourages them with various promises related to needs as they arise. These promises tell the redeemed in unmistakable terms that they shall either be preserved from life's afflictions, or if they have to endure them, God will support them through them all, using all for His glory and the good of His own; and that in His own way and time He will deliver them.

> "Many are the afflictions of the righteous but the Lord delivereth him out of them all." Psalm 34:19

The promises, then, are exceeding great and precious because of their number, contents and variety, or diversity. It is most difficult to calculate the vast array of consolations provided for our confidence and comfort. The promises relating to our temporary adversities pale into insignificance alongside those spiritual and eternal blessings, so fully expressed in the Gospel of divine grace. As we approach the absorbing study of the *scope* of God's promises, it must again be emphasized that the classified promises should be studied in their original connection, if one desires to experience the utmost spiritual good any of them can yield. The setting around a promise makes it more vivid, just "as a diamond is enhanced in its beauty by an exquisite platinum setting. This also heightens the interest in the jewel as well as in the search for the way whereby one may claim it for one's own."

The Bible, as we have already indicated, must never be treated as a kind of lottery, which alas! it is when opened at random, and a verse is taken that happens to catch our eye as being God's message for our heart in a time of special need. This can become a most delusive and mischievous practice. Any single promise is only a delectable sweetmeat and should not interfere with a fuller meal. A promise should be an appetizer, exciting the desire for something more substantial.

THE PROMISES AND THE JEWISH WORLD

While it is perfectly true that all Scripture has been written for us, that is, for all classes of people and sections of the human race--"written for our learning, that we through patience and comfort of the Scriptures must have hope" (Romans 15:4), yet *all* Scripture was not written about *all* people in general. Different portions refer to different sections of the human populace. As Dr. W. Graham Scroggie puts it, "The Divine Spirit has divided men into three classes--The Jews, the Gentiles and the Church of God, and to gather up all that Scripture has to say concerning each of them, is to get a magnificent view of God's dispensational doings."

It is the Apostle Paul who reminds us that there are three streams flowing into the broad river of humanity, and who urges us to be charitable to all --

> "Give none offence, neither to the Jews, nor to the Gentiles, nor to the Church of God." I Corinthians 10:32

And the contents of the Bible, as we are to see, cover these three sections which must be consistently distinguished if we are to be delivered from those heresies that are the direct outcome of denial or ignorance of the divine dispensational purpose:

There are the Jews, a nation chosen by God for His own design, an elect people separated from all the other peoples of the earth.

There are the Gentiles, the rest of the mankind, apart from the Jews. Finally, in the elect Kingdom, all earthly kingdoms are to be incorporated and assimilated.

There is the Church of God, composed of both regenerated Jews and Gentiles, an elect people gathered out from all nations.

To apply indiscriminately to all peoples, the promises, prophecies and responsibilities of each group is to lose sight of the divine order and beauty of the divine plan, and to hopelessly confuse the divine interpretation of the Bible. There are the Jews or Israelites (John 4:22; Romans 3:1, 2; 9:4, 5); The Gentiles, or "Dogs" (Mark 7:27, 28; Ephesians 2:11, 12; 4:17, 18); the Church of God (Ephesians 1:22, 23; 5:29, 33).

The promises to Israel are not collective and impersonal, and largely without condition, that they seem to belong naturally to the Church. Israel is *not* the Church.

There may be a sense in which promises for the Jew can be applied to the Christian, but the difference must be preserved between *application* and *interpretation*. In the study of any portion of the Bible it is first of all *interpretation*, not *application*. After arriving at the interpretation of a passage we can make any application we like, within the realm of reason. Certainly, the Church can enjoy the *Life-Interest* of many Jewish promises, so long as it is remembered that the *capital* belongs to the Jews and will be collected by them at the appropriate time.

The folly of *Amillennialism* from Augustine's time on, has been the wholesale robbery of Jewish promises. The contention of the *Amillennialist*, who is one believing that we are now in the Millennium, is that there is no future for the Jews. God has finished with them as a separate people. Therefore, all their blessings have been transferred to the Church. Thus Jewish promises are misappropriated. As for the *curses*, Amillennialists leave these to the poor Jews. We do not rightly divide the Word of Truth, if we make specific promises apply to all men in general. When God says that a particular blessing is for a Jew, then it is for him, and for no one else. The same applies to Gentile promises, and the Church's promises.

Promises covering Israel's past, present and future are scattered with prodigal hand throughout the Bible, with the majority of the promises yet to be realized. The possession of Canaan, the growth of the nation, universal blessing through the race, are examples of promises of which the patriarchs did not receive the outward fulness.

> "These all died in faith, not having received the promises, but having seen them afar off, and were persuaded of them, and embraced them, and confessed that they were strangers and pilgrims on the earth." Hebrews 11:13

Westcott remarks, "On the one hand, Abraham 'obtained the promise' because the birth of Isaac was the beginning of its fulfilment (Hebrews 6:15): on the other hand he is one of the fathers who 'received not the promise' but with a true faith looked for a fulfilment of the promise which was not granted to them (Hebrews 11:39)."

Although we are tempted to linger over the various aspects of the romantic history of the Jews, our present purpose in keeping with the design of this book, is to trace the promises related to God's ancient people, a few of which have already been noticed in *God's promises to man*. Perhaps we can pause to point out the significance of the different names of those to whom abundant promises were given. They are known as—

Hebrews

This original name of the chosen people was first applied to Abraham, the father of the Jewish race, and is the Gentile designation of both Abraham and his descendants—

"Abraham the Hebrew." Genesis 14:13 The first Jew then was a Gentile. The term *Hebrew*, means "belonging to Eber." Eber was the great-grandson of Shem (Genesis 10:21-24), and it was from this stock that Abraham and our Lord descended (Luke 3:35). Applied to Abraham, *Hebrew* signifies "the emigrant" or "one who has crossed over," alluding to his crossing over the Euphrates to Egypt. It was a term full of divine promise seeing that the essence of its meaning is "separation," and was used thereafter to distinguish the Jewish race from surrounding nations. In the New Testament the word is used to signify those who retained the Hebrew tongue and lived in Palestine (Acts 6:1 R.V.). Fausset remarks that the term *Hebrew* expresses the language and nationality of original Jews in contrast to Hellenists, that is, Greek-speaking Jews.

The Seed of Abraham

This further title of promise is closely identified with the previous one, and is applied to Jews and Christians alike—

> "If ye be Christ's, then are ye Abraham's seed, and heirs according to the promise." Galatians 3:29

All, springing from Abraham—father of all who believe—are spoken of as his *seed*. Failure to distinguish between his three seeds, and the promises made to each, has resulted in confusion of interpretation.

There is the National Seed, represented in Ishmael and his posterity.

There is the Covenant Seed, seen in Isaac and his posterity.

There is the Spiritual Seed covering all the children of faith.

Jacob

The original name of the progenitor of the Twelve Tribes, is also used as a gen-

eral designation of all his descendants, being employed in the characteristic sense of natural posterity –
> "O house of Jacob, come ye, and let us walk in the light of the Lord."
> Isaiah 2:5

Israel

Numerous promises are related to this most common of Jewish titles, originally bestowed upon Jacob himself, and then transferred to his descendants during, and after, his lifetime –
> "Thy name shall be called no more Jacob, but Israel: for as a prince hast thou power with God and with men, and hast prevailed." Genesis 32:28
> "Israel strengthened himself, and sat upon his bed." Genesis 48:4

Used *characteristically*, "Jacob" indicates the national posterity of Abraham, Isaac and Jacob. "Israel" is the term implying the spiritual part of the nation.
> "The Lord sent a word into Jacob, and it hath lighted upon Israel." Isaiah 9:8

The divine message was only comprehended by the spiritually-minded of the nation. Generally speaking the term, "Israelite," means a member of the theocracy and an heir of the promises, and expressive of the high theocratic privileges of descent from Jacob conveys a two-fold significance:

1. A Particularly Honorable Designation
> "Who are Israelites to whom pertaineth . . . the promises." Romans 9:4
> "I also am an Israelite." Romans 11:1
> "Are they Israelites? so am I."
> II Corinthians 11:22

2. A Sign of High Moral Qualities
> "Behold an Israelite indeed, in whom is no guile." John 1:47

It is interesting to observe that God describes Himself as the *Holy One of Israel* 32 times, and as *The God of Israel*, 29 times.

Jews

Originally, this title described those who were descended from Judah, the son of Jacob. These were the inhabitants of Judea. Then it was applied to the Kingdom, or Tribe, of Judah in the South, thereby distinguishing it from the Israelites of the North.
> "All the Jews that were in Moab," etc.
> Jeremiah 40:11

After the period of the Captivity, the title *Jews* was extended and applied to all the national descendants of Abraham, and used

in contrast to *Greeks,* or *Gentiles.* In course of time, the name *Jew* became synonymous with Israelites. Saul of Tarsus, although a Benjamite, claimed to be a Jew –
> "I am a man which am a Jew of Tarsus." Acts 21:39
> "I am verily a man which am a Jew."
> Acts 22:3

Paul also used the term to denote an adherent of the Jewish faith, as distinguished from the Christian faith –
> "Unto the Jews I became as a Jew, that I might gain the Jews." I Corinthians 9:20

Without doubt, the preservation of the Jews through the centuries is "The Miracle of History," and is a subject one would like to linger over. But our effort is to show that such a "history," called His-story, that is, God's story of choice, love, patience, grace and blessing, is likewise loaded with His promises. The leading points in Israel's history are full of promises as the following passages prove:

1. As the seed of Abraham – Romans 4
2. As the family under Jacob – Genesis 49
3. As the nation under Moses –
   Exodus 12-14
4. As the kingdom under Saul –
   I Samuel 10
5. As captives –
   Under Shalmaneser – 10 tribes –
   II Kings 17.
   Under Nebuchadnezzar - 2 tribes –
   II Kings 25
6. As a restored remnant under Cyrus –
   Ezra 2
7. As a nation dispersed under Titus –
   Luke 21:24
8. As a nation regathered – Isaiah 11:12
9. As a nation full of blessing – Ezekiel

In spite of the many backslidings of Israel, divine promises concerning her have never been abrogated. She was brought into being for the manifold purpose of –

1. Witnessing to the unity of God in the midst of universal idolatry –
> "Here, O Israel: The Lord our God is one Lord." Deuteronomy 6:4-5
> "Ye are my witnesses . . . that I, even I, am the Lord." Isaiah 43:10-12

2. Illustrating the blessedness of serving the true God.
> "Happy art thou, O Israel: who is like unto Thee, O people saved by the Lord." Deuteronomy 33:26-29
> "What one nation in the earth is like Thy people Israel?" I Chronicles 17:20-21
> "Happy is that people, that is in such

a case: yea, happy is that people, whose God is the Lord." Psalm 144:15

3. Producing and preserving the Scriptures –
"Behold, I have taught you statutes and judgments." Deuteronomy 4:5-8
"Unto them were committed the oracles of God." Romans 3:1, 2

4. Preparing the way for the Messiah –
"Out of thee shall he come forth unto me, that is to be a ruler in Israel."
Micah 5:2; Matthew 2:5-12

The promises under this section will be fully dealt with later on. Suffice it to say at this point that the supreme mission of Israel was to produce the Messiah, and so to form the Scriptures that when He came He would be instantly recognized so that men could say, "Here is the promise – here is the performance – here is the Scriptures – here is the Saviour."

"Concerning His Son Jesus Christ our Lord, which was made of the seed of David, according to the flesh."
Romans 1:3

5. Providing a sinful and sinning world with salvation –
"In thee shall all families of the earth be blessed." Genesis 12:2, 3
"All the nations of the earth shall be blessed in him." Genesis 18:18
"In thy seed shall all the nations of the earth be blessed." Genesis 18:18
"The Scripture . . . preached before the gospel unto Abraham, saying, In thee shall all nations be blessed."
Galatians 3:8

When our Lord declared that "Salvation is of the Jews" (John 4:22), He did not only infer that they produced Him as the Saviour of the world, but that they themselves were to act as the salt of the earth, preserving it from moral putrefaction. As the Jews were dispersed throughout the world they became the media of divine communication to the Gentiles and they played a great part in the distribution of the good news. What needless controversy would have been saved if only God's plan of Israel's election had been regarded as *inclusive* and not *exclusive* – that He chose *one* nation through whom He might bless *all* nations.

"This is Jerusalem: I have set it in the midst of the nations and countries that are round about her."
Ezekiel 5:5; 36:20, 23

"If the fall of them be the riches of the world, and the diminishing of them

the riches of the Gentiles; how much more their fulness? Romans 11:12

Dispersed, denationalized, dispossessed, and discredited, the Jews have been divinely preserved, and all God's promises concerning their present and future destiny will be abundantly fulfilled. The preservation of the three Hebrew youths as they were made to pass through the fiery furnace (Daniel 3:19-25), affords a prophecy and a promise of God's preservation of His own chosen people.

"He made it again another vessel, as seemed good to the potter to make it."
Jeremiah 18:4

Let us now examine the numerous and explicit promises concerning the restoration and future blessing of the Jews. Scripture is emphatic in its testimony that Jews, as such, are to be restored to their own land, privileges, and favor with God. While some of the promises received a partial fulfilment when the Jews were restored to Jerusalem after the Babylonian Captivity, and also in their recent national renaissance, complete restoration is yet future.

"I will bring them against this land: and I will build them, and not pull them down! and I will plant them, and not pluck them up." Jeremiah 24:6; 30:10, 11
"I will plant them upon their land, and they shall no more be pulled up out of the land which I have given them, saith the Lord thy God." Amos 9:13-15

In the promise of final restitution Israel will be "set in the midst of the nations" (Ezekiel 5:8; Acts 3:19-21; 15-17), in Jerusalem "the center of the earth" (Ezekiel 38:12). Dr. C. J. Rolls says: "Palestine became the *nerve center* of the earth in the day of Abraham. Later on, the country became the *truth center* because of Moses and the Prophets. Ultimately it became the *salvation center* by the manifestation of Christ. His rejection led to its becoming the *storm center* as it has continued to be through many centuries. The Scriptures predict that it is to be the *peace center* under the Messianic Kingdom: and it will be the *glory center* in a new universe yet to be experienced."

Meantime the Hebrew Christian is "a candlestick of witness within Jewry," and when Christ returns to earth, "the Hebrew Christian remnant will be the means by which He will accomplish the spiritual regeneration of the Jewish people that will be saved out of the final catastrophe which is to befall the Holy Land in what is referred to in the Old Testament as 'the hour of Jacob's trouble.'" Briefly stated, the promises regarding Israel's restoration can be summarized thus:

1. They are to be regathered in unbelief.

Presently, the Jews are returning to their own land but alas! returning in their spiritual blindness (Romans 11:25, 26). Before their national converison, it would seem as if severe judgment is to overtake them (Ezekiel 20:34-38; 36:24-27).

2. They are to be refined in holiness.

Destined for great purposes, the Jews are to be subjected to tremendous tests. God is to cast them into the melting pot (Ezekiel 22:19-22) and cause them to go through the refiner's fire (Zechariah 13:9; Malachi 3:1-3. See also Jeremiah 30:4-7; Daniel 12:1; Matthew 24:21-31).

3. They are to be restored to favor.

As the result of the refining processes, the Jews will become wholly the Lord's, and promised blessings will then be fully realized. God's age-long controversy with His people will be at an end (Ezekiel 36:24-27; Isaiah 66:8; Zechariah 12:10; 14:4; I Corinthians 15:8).

4. They will be reunited in love.

Schism is to give way to blissful unity, as the promise of the "Two Sticks" vividly portrays (Ezekiel 37:15-32).

"Ephraim shall not envy Judah, and Judah shall not vex Ephraim." Isaiah 11:13; Jeremiah 3:18

5. They are to be readjusted in privilege.

All the promises as to Israel's future glories, depicted in such glowing terms, are to be consummated during the Millenial Age. All their theocratic privileges are to be restored. Mark these aspects in your Bible—

"Israel will be free from war, international strife, and friction (Isaiah 2:1-4; Micah 4:1-4).

Her cities are to be rebuilt and her land divinely replenished (Amos 9:14, 15; Jeremiah 31:27, 28).

All her past sorrow and anguish are to give way to joy and satisfaction (Jeremiah 30:10-14; Isaiah 61:4-9).

A new covenant will be entered into and enjoyed. All broken covenants will be forgotten (Jeremiah 31:31-34).

Israel will be distinguished by righteousness and glory and have a new name (Isaiah 62:1-4). The Lord's presence and blessing will be hers (Zechariah 8:23). Rest and quietness will be experienced and favor among all peoples will be hers (Zechariah 3:20).

Thus the promise is that the Jews, strange and solitary as they may be, with a drama of long and mournful history, will yet become the media of salvation to a troubled world. Prophecy depicts them as the evangelists of the coming Kingdom. They are to be safely inhabited in Jerusalem (Zechariah 14:11)—a land sacred to the heart of every true Jew. Gentile heels will no longer tread its sacred dust for the time of Gentile domination is to cease (Luke 21:24). God has promised to deliver them "out of all places where they have been scattered in the cloudy and dark day" (Ezekiel 34:12). In spite of all the bloody purges they have experienced, the Jews live on, in the same silent, mysterious and indestructible way. Presently scattered and peeled among the nations, country nor climate can change them, and before them there is the glorious prospect of their Jerusalem (Ezekiel 37; Hosea 1:10, 11; 3:4, 5). It is because of the divine promises and purposes yet to be fulfilled that the Jew must remain "The Indestructible Jew."

God has never lost His interest in the Jew, who is ever the index-finger of prophecy. Our present obligation is to labor for the salvation of the Jew, for when it comes to the Gospel, the Jew has the primacy—"To the Jew *first*"(Romans 1:16). Jewish missions should head the list in our missionary interest and giving. Alas! however, Jewish evangelization is sadly neglected by the Church.

THE PROMISES AND THE GENTILE WORLD

Paul is our authority for affirming that the Gentiles, as well as the Jews, are the recipients of divine promises—

"That the Gentiles should be fellow heirs, and of the same body, and partakers of His promise in Christ by the gospel." Ephesians 3:6

In respect to the great Gentile world, the coverage of promises for such is both wide and varied. It may help us to understand the specific Gentile promises, if we can settle *who* and *what* the Gentiles are. The terms, *Gentiles, heathen* and *nations* are equivalent, as used in the Old Testament; and correspond to *Greeks* and *peoples* in the New Testament. *Uncircumcised* (Isaiah 52:1 – *Uncircumcision* (Romans 2:26) – *Strangers* (Isaiah 14:1; 60:10) are further terms used of the same people. Taken together, these designations describe all non-Israelite people from the Israelites.

Cruden observes that "the Hebrews, or Jews, called the Gentiles by the general name of *Goiim*, which signified those nations that had not received the *Faith*, or the Law of God. All who are not Jews and circumcised are *Goiim*." While it was God Himself who separated the Jews from the Gentiles, there was no thought of one group being superior to the other. The Gentiles were simply non-Jewish, and were not despised for that reason. With the passage of time, however, the Jewish attitude toward Gentiles gradually changed until they became regarded with scorn and hatred. They were treated as "dogs," unclean, and enemies of God's people, to whom the knowledge of God was denied. Such a Jewish attitude is understandable when we realize something of what the Jews suffered at the hands of their Gentile captors.

The first occurrence of the word *Gentile* is in connection with the Flood, when the only people left alive were Gentiles (Genesis 10:5), but who, as such, received gracious promises from God (Genesis 8:21, 22; 9). The inhabitants of the earth, now some 2,500,000,000, the majority of whom are Gentiles, are descended from the three sons of Noah, Japheth, Shem and Ham.

JAPHETH, who had seven sons, and seven grandsons by two of his sons, Gomer and Javan (10:2-4) through his posterity, possessed Europe.

Gomer, the eldest son of Japheth, became the father or progenitor of the ancient Cimmerians, who settled on the northern shores of the Red Sea. The modern and familiar name of "Crimea," or the "Cimbri," of ancient times, are derived from the Cimmerians, the immediate descendants of Gomer. The Gauls and Celts of ancient times, and of more modern date, the Germans, French and British, are descended from the same stock.

Magog was the progenitor of the ancient Scythians or Mongolian tribes, who settled on the Caucasus and the Caspian Sea, and whose descendants predominate in modern Russia (Ezekiel 38:2; 39:6; Revelation 20:8).

Madai, Japheth's third son, has been identified with the Medes who were allied to the Persians in after years (Isaiah 13:17).

Javin is reckoned to be the ancient name for Greece, Javin being the progenitor of those who peopled Greece and Syria (Daniel 8:21).

Tubal has been identified as the modern Russian city of Tobolsk, the capital of Asiatic Russia. Tubal's descendants then, peopled the region of the Red Sea, from whence they spread north and south. A branch of the race peopled Spain.

Meshech, connected with Gog and Magog (Ezekiel 38; 39), is the modern Moscow, the metropolis of the Russian Empire.

Tiras was, in all probability, the progenitor of the Thracians.

So much for the sons of Japheth, as they spread abroad. As for his seven grandsons, as they colonized still further, we have –

Ashkenaz, the descendants of whom settled in the Northern and Southern sides of the Black Sea.

Riphath became the father of the tribes who located on the Rhipean, or Carpathian Mountains, far north of Tiras or Thrace.

Togarmah. The Armenians assert that they are descended from "Targom" or Togarmah of Scripture.

Elishah. A portion of the Greek race inhabiting the cities of the Aegean Sea bore this name (Ezekiel 27:7).

Tarshish is identified as Tuscany, in Italy. There was, however, an Eastern and a Western City of this name.

Kittim, or *Chittim*. This is the ancient name for the noted island of Cyprus. In Scripture, the name denotes the islands and sea coast of the Mediterranean under the yoke of Rome (Daniel 11:30).

Dodanim is believed by some scholars to signify an ancient Greek race.

SHEM, Noah's second son, became the founder of the Western Nations of Asia, called "Semitic Nations." Here again, the names of the sons and grandsons are significant.

Elam is the ancient name for Persia.

Asshur was the progenitor of the Assyrians.

Arphaxad. His descendants peopled the north of Assyria.

Lud. His descendants settled in Asia Minor.

Aram is the Biblical designation of Suria (Numbers 23:7).

Several of the names under SHEM, as Salah, Peleg, must be read simply as heads of races.

Eber or *Heber*, As we have already noticed it was from this stem of the Gentile family that the Hebrews sprang. Most of the other names refer to tribes inhabiting various parts of Arabia.

HAM, the youngest son of Noah, means "black," "burnt," "warm" and is thus peculiarly significant of the sun-baked regions allotted to this branch of the family. The four sons of Ham, his grandson, and great-grandsons have been identified as follows:

Cush. This name has been wrongly translated "Ethiopia" (Isaiah 18:1). The Cushites settled on the Nile and on the Euphrates.

Migraim. This plural name denotes Upper and Lower Egypt.

Phut is the progenitor of the Africans, known as the Libyans, and from whom the Moors are descended.

Canaan became a general designation of the nations inhabiting the country from the Mediterranean on the West, to Jordan on the East, prior to Israel's occupation.

Seba, Havilah, Sabtah, Rammah, Sabtechah, Sheba and *Dedan* all refer to those who settled at, or near, the Persian Gulf.

Babel, Erech, Accad and *Calneh* became the names of four cities originally constituting the strength of the Babylonian Kingdom.

Nineveh, Rehoboth, Calah and *Resen* became names of four cities originally constituting the strength of the Assyrian Kingdom.

Ludim, Anamin, Lehabim, Naphtuhim, Pathrusim, Casluhim, with their Hebrew dual ending, represent various African tribes or nations.

Philistim. From this branch settling on the Western border of Canaan, there came the "Philistines."

Caphtorim. The original inhabitants of the isle of Crete, also known as Candia, once a mighty kingdom of a hundred cities, as Homer sang, are supposed to have descendants from Caphtorium.

Thus, as Walter Scott, to whose outline we are indebted at this point, observes, "This tenth chapter of Genesis is a very remarkable one. Before God leaves, as it were, the nations to themselves and begins to deal with Israel, His chosen people from Abraham downward, He takes a loving farewell of all the nations of the earth, as much as to say, 'I am going to leave you for a while, but I love you: I have created you: I have ordered your future.' Then their different genealogies are traced. From then on, attention is focused on the Semitic line."

Having briefly traced the rise and development of the multitudinous Gentile peoples, we are now better able to deal with the Promises associated with every phase of their whole history. Let us look, first of all, at various expressive "Gentile" phrases, to which Promises of Blessing or of Judgment are attached.

The Isles of the Gentiles

"These were the isles of the Gentiles divided in their lands." Genesis 10:5
The word for "isles" signifies "coasts," and implies that the descendants of Japheth settled along the coast-lands. Thus the "isles" represent the Mediterranean, Caspian and Black Seas. The promise is that these isles are to be visited and blessed of the Lord –

"Surely the isles shall wait for me."
Isaiah 60:9; Zephaniah 2:11
Are there not still millions in these "isles" waiting for Him?

The Forces of the Gentiles

"The forces of the Gentiles shall come unto Thee." Isaiah 60:5
"Therefore thy gates shall be open continually; and they shall not be shut day nor night; that men may bring unto thee the forces of the Gentiles, and that their kings may be bought." Isaiah 60:11
By "forces" we are to understand riches, possessions. The R.V. translates the phrase, "The wealth of the nations." Taken in its context, it describes the promise of affluence coming to the Jews from surrounding nations during the Millennium. The LXX Version gives us "the power of the nations." If only we could see the power of the nations harnessed to God's chariot in our day, what a different world it would be.

The Milk of the Gentiles

"Thou shalt suck the milk of the Gentiles, and shalt suck the breasts of kings."
Isaiah 60:16
A similar phrase is "the riches of the Gentiles" (61:6), and represents abundance and strength. Later on we read of "the glory of the Gentiles like a flowing stream" (66:12). When Paul refers to "the riches of the Gentiles" (Romans 11:12), he has in mind the conversion of the Gentiles, made possible by Jewish rejection of Christ. The opening of the door of salvation to the Gentiles added to the world's spiritual wealth

in that a greater number was included in God's purpose and promise of Grace. The saints in the Gentile churches were their most precious possession.

The Destroyer of the Gentiles

"The destroyer of the Gentiles is on his way." Jeremiah 4:7

The "lion" referred to in the passage as the "destroyer" is the symbol of the Assyrian monarchy. This Chaldean invader was to destroy Zion, even as he had many Gentile peoples. The devil, however, is likened unto a "lion" (I Peter 5:8), and what a "destroyer" of nations he is. Think of the millions killed and massacred during the last World War! But yet another "Lion" (Revelation 5:5) is to come and when He does it will be as the "Destroyer" of godless nations (Revelation 19:15). In Him, we have the prospect and promise of peaceful universal sovereignty.

The Horns of the Gentiles

"These are come to fray them, to cast out the horns of the Gentiles, which lifted up their horn over the land of Judah to scatter it." Zechariah 1:21

"Horn," in Scripture, is used as a symbol of a Gentile king. The vision then, that Zechariah records is of the four Gentile empires – Babylon, Medo-Persian, Greece and Rome – represented by the four horns, scattering the people of God. We have also phrases like "the princes of the Gentiles" and "the kings of the Gentiles" (Matthew 20:25; Luke 22:25), all of whom will have to bow to Christ when He returns as "the prince of the kings of the earth." Revelation 1:5.

The Way of the Gentiles

"Go not into the way of the Gentiles." Matthew 10:5

This prohibition did not mean that the Gentiles were to be denied participation in the promise of the Gospel. While on the earth, our Lord recognized the priority of Israel – "to the Jew first, and also to the Gentile." But as Ellicott remarks: "It was necessary for His disciples to learn how to share His pity for the lost sheep of the house of Israel before they could enter into His yearnings after the sheep that were 'not of this fold.'" The salvation of Gentiles is enshrined in many an Old Testament promise (Isaiah 40:5).

The Times of the Gentiles

"Until the times of the Gentiles be fulfilled." Luke 21:24

We have the promise that the Gentile Age, with all its warring activities, is to cease. Gentile monarchy commenced with Judah's servitude under Nebuchadnezzar, to whom was divinely delegated a world-empire.

"I have given all these lands into the hands of Nebuchadnezzar the king of Babylon." Jeremiah 27:7-8

The promise is that Gentile world-rule will be destroyed when Christ returns in glory and fashions the kingdoms of this world into His own world-kingdom (Revelation 11:15). Then, His kingdom is to stretch from shore to shore.

The Fulness of the Gentiles

"Until the fulness of the Gentiles be come in." Romans 11:25

This phrase is to be distinguished from the previous one. Here we have the promise of salvation for the Gentiles. Since Pentecost, Christ has been gathering in His "other sheep" (John 10:16). Now, the world at large is the object of God's redeeming love (John 3:16).

The Will of the Gentiles

"The will of the Gentiles when we walked in lasciviousness." I Peter 4:3

The "will" here represents the "life" of the Gentiles or "the manner of the Gentiles" (Galatians 2:14), or "the vanities of the Gentiles" (Jeremiah 14:22). Such phrases represent the ungodly lives and ways of Gentile unbelievers. Choice must be made between "the will of God" and "the will of the Gentiles" (I Peter 4:1, 3). Peter outlines many promises of blessing for those who choose the sweet will of God.

Promises of deliverance from the guilt and government of sin in the lives of all Gentiles, willing to repent and turn to the Saviour of the world, are resident in a few interesting designations. For instance, God is described as –

The God of the Gentiles

"Is he the God of the Jews only? is he not also of the Gentiles? Yea, of Gentiles also." Romans 3:29

As "the God of all flesh" (see Jeremiah 14:22), He cannot be guilty of partiality. What a blessed promise this is for all Gentile sinners thronging the World! This God of love waits to be their God. As "the

King of the nations," God's overruling power is described. (Jeremiah 10:7; Psalm 113:4)

A Light to Lighten the Gentiles

"A light to lighten the Gentiles, and the glory of thy people Israel." Luke 2:32 In Simeon's prophecy and promise of Christ, as the world's Redeemer, the Gentiles are given the first place. He came as "the Light of the World." The tragedy is that multitudes of both Gentiles and Jews are still blinded by the god of this world. The promise of a full redemption is theirs but they will not claim the promise. The prophet speaks of "the veil that is spread over the nations" (Isaiah 25:7). How this darkening veil persists! May grace be ours to increase our efforts to bring the lost to Him who is "the desire of all nations" (Haggai 2:7).

Scofield in connecting the Old Testament promise with its New Testament repetition (Isaiah 42:6 with Luke 2:32) says that Christ is promised to the Gentiles in a three-fold way:

1. As the *Light*, bringing salvation to the Gentiles (Luke 2:32; Acts 13:47, 48).
2. As the *Root* of Jesse, reigning over the Gentiles in His Kingdom (Isaiah 11:10; Romans 15:12). He saves Gentiles – a distinctive feature of this present age (Romans 11:17-24; Ephesians 2:11-12). He reigns over the Gentiles in the coming Kingdom-Age (Psalms 2 and 8; Zechariah 12:8).
3. As the *Head* of the Body. Believing Gentiles together with believing Jews, constitute "the Church which is His Body" (Ephesians 1:23; 3:6).

The Apostle to the Gentiles

Paul, a Jew, was specially ordained of God to proclaim all the promises of the Gospel to the great Gentile world. It is for this reason he is described as:

"The apostle to the Gentiles."
Romans 11:13
"The minister of Jesus Christ to the Gentiles." Romans 15:16
"A teacher of the Gentiles." I Timothy 2:7
"A preacher, and an apostle, and a teacher of the Gentiles." II Timothy 1:11
Paul was ever conscious that this was the distinctive work for which God saved him (Acts 22:21; Galatians 2:7-9; Ephesians 3:1). How grateful those of us who are Gentiles should be that Paul was obedient to the heavenly vision, resulting in Europe receiving the Gospel.

Reviewing Gentile history, which is incidental in Scripture, we find promises of a varying nature associated with each epoch. The time of *Gentile Antiquation*, stretching from Adam to Abraham, and embracing Gentile development, degradation and dispersion, provides us with many a glimpse of the divine heart. As the human race progressed, so did the sin of those comprising it. Yet mercy was mixed with judgment; and God gave a sinning humanity many a rainbow of promise during the 2,000 years of history marked by failure.

To Satan, whose subtlety was responsible for sin's entrance into the newly created world, there was given the promise of Christ who would nullify his power:

"I will put enmity between thee and the woman, and between thy seed and her seed; it shall bruise thy head, and thou shalt bruise his heel." Genesis 3:15
To Adam and Eve, the first on earth to be deceived by Satan, there came the mournful promise of sorrow and death:

"Unto the woman God said, I will greatly multiply thy sorrow and thy conception . . . Unto Adam God said . . . cursed is the ground for thy sake; in sorrow shall thou eat of it all the days of thy life." Genesis 3:16-19
To Cain, the world's first murderer, there was given the promise of divine protection in his ostracism:

"The Lord said unto him, Therefore whosoever slayeth Cain, vengeance shall be taken on him sevenfold. And the Lord set a mark upon Cain, lest any finding him should slay him." Genesis 4:15
To Noah, through whom God re-peopled the earth again after the terrible destruction of the Flood, many promises were given. There was the promise of an established covenant:

"But with thee will I establish My covenant." Genesis 6:18; 9:13-17
There was the promise of freedom from further curse:

"I will not again curse the ground any more for man's sake." Genesis 8:21
There was the promise of enlargement through Japheth:

"God shall enlarge Japheth."
Genesis 9:27
The development of government, science and art through the centuries is the indisputable fulfilment of such a Japhetic promise.

There was the promise of Shem's peculiar relation to Jehovah:

"Blessed be the Lord God of

Shem." Genesis 9:26

From this point on, attention is focussed upon the line of Shem from whom sprang Abraham, the Hebrew race, and Jesus Christ.

There was the promise of Ham's inferior and servile posterity –

"Cursed by Canaan: a servant of servants shall he be unto his brethren."
Genesis 9:22, 25-27

In these days, when we are witnessing the upsurge of Nationalism among the Hamilic races, it would seem as if they are determined to reverse the divine edict.

The Time of *Gentile Exclusion*, from Abraham to Nebuchadnezzar, is another period characterized by divine promises, beneficial and otherwise. To enumerate them all would require more space than we can allocate. With the great and glorious promise God gave to Abram that he would be the father of a new nation (Genesis 12:1-3), the human race became separated into two sections. With Abraham commenced the Jewish race; the rest of mankind became the Gentile race, and promises for both are scattered through the portion of Scripture from Genesis 12 to the book of Daniel.

Such an exclusion of the nations through the choice of Israel did not mean that God was going to turn the Gentiles adrift. His sole purpose of separating them was that through the Jews, whom He raised up to magnify His name, He might ultimately include all in His great purpose of grace. *Exclusion* meant *inclusion*.

"In thee shall *all* the families of the earth be blessed." Genesis 12:3; 17:9
"I will give thee all these countries."
Genesis 26:3-5
"In thy seed shall all the families of the earth be blessed." Genesis 28:14.
(Follow chain of Israel-Covenant references in the Scofield Bible.)

The time of *Gentile domination* is a period reaching from Nebuchadnezzar right over until the return of Christ to the earth as its rightful Lord and King. It was about 606 B.C. that God permitted world power to pass into the hands of Nebuchadnezzar (Jeremiah 27:5-7; 39:7). Is it not somewhat striking that almost the same language is used of the commencement of Gentile monarchy, as of its consummation?

"Thou, O king, art a king of kings; the God of heaven hath given thee a kingdom, power, and strength, and glory." Daniel 2:37
"The kingdoms of this world are be-

come the kingdoms of our Lord, and of his Christ . . . King of kings and Lord of lords." Revelation 11:15; 19:16

How crowded with promises the period in between these two world-dominions is! There are promises made to Babylon's monarch, promises regarding Jewish dispersion and re-establishment in their own land, promises concerning succeeding empires, promises related to the coming of God's King and of His universal sway when He reigns from shore to shore (Isaiah 63:1-6). At present, we are living in "the times of the Gentiles," meaning that the nations of the world, with the exception of the newly-formed nation of Israeli, are Gentile in nature and government. This Gentile Age, however, will end with the return of Christ to the earth, as He Himself taught (Matthew 24:14).

Christ is the *Stone* (Daniel 2:45; Isaiah 28:16), cut out of the mountain without hands, signifying His divine origin, who will appear in power and glory to end the Gentile reign in judgment (See Isaiah 63:1-6; Daniel 11:35; Zechariah 12:1-9, etc.).

"The stone that smote the image became a great mountain, and filled the whole earth." Daniel 2:35

Christ's return to earth is an event, personal and corporeal, and not a mere process. When He appears He will consummate and destroy the present Gentile, political world-system (Daniel 2:34-35 with Revelation 19:11), and after this judgment (Matthew 25:31-46) produce world-wide Gentile conversion, and participation in the blessings of His Kingdom (Isaiah 2:2-4; 11:10; 60:3; Zechariah 8:3, 20, 23; 14:16-21). Then the promise of Gabriel will be realized to the full –

"He shall be great, and shall be called the Son of the Highest: and the Lord God shall give unto Him the throne of His Father David:
And He shall reign over the house of Jacob for ever; and of His kingdom there shall be no end." Luke 1:32, 33

Paul declared that Christ came to confirm the promises made unto the fathers (Romans 15:8). He came, labored and died in confirmation of many of those promises, all of which He confirmed, but all of which have not been fulfilled. Those relating to the future of His Church, of Israel, and of the Gentile world await fulfilment.

Dean Alford says, "Among the mysteries of the new heaven and new earth, this is set before us: that, besides the glorified Church there shall still be dwelling on renewed earth, nations organized under kings, and saved by means of the heavenly city."

"The nations shall walk by its light, and the kings of the earth bring their glory to it." Revelation 21:24

At last, the sovereign rule of Christ is acknowledged. The seat of His government is in the midst of the city, and millennial kings and nations, then basking in the bright light of the ever-glorious city, gladly render their homage to Him who will then reign without a rival.

Meantime the promise of *Gentile salvation* is being realized. In this present dispensation of grace there are no distinctions or exclusions whatever. God does not segregate mankind into Jews and Gentiles, Catholics and Protestants. All are sinners in His sight and can only be saved upon the acceptance of His terms. His design in this age is to gather out a people for His name –a people, or Church, composed only of regenerated Jews and Gentiles. Thus, all the promises of salvation are related to those who repent and believe, whether heathen or civilized, Jew or Gentile, Catholic or Protestant. There is no difference as to nationality or religion for –

"All have sinned and come short of the glory of God." Romans 3:23

"God so loved the world that *whosoever* believeth in him should not perish but have everlasting life." John 3:16

"There is no respect of persons with God." Romans 2:11

"This is a faithful saying, and worthy of all acceptation, that Christ Jesus came into the world to save sinners."

I Timothy 1:15

As Gentiles outnumber the Jews by millions, naturally there are more Gentiles than Jews being brought into the true Church. It is wrong, however, to refer to the Church as "the Gentile Bride of Christ," seeing this mystic body is composed of both Jew and Gentile, as Paul teaches:

"He hath broken down the middle wall of partition between us." Ephesians 2:21

"There is neither Jew nor Greek . . . all one in Christ Jesus." Galatians 3:28

Our solemn obligation, as grace continues to "reign," is to obey the Saviour's commission to preach the Gospel to *every* creature. We are to go out into His world in which there are countless millions still in spiritual darkness and beseech them to be reconciled to Him, who would have all men to be saved.

There are other aspects of Gentile history to which promises of good or evil are associated, and which we cannot afford to neglect in our study of the international realm. For a fuller treatment of the empires and nations in the Bible, with their rise and fall, and the history of their kings and rulers and of their respective influence upon the empires they represented, the reader is referred to the author's volume–*All the Kings and Queens of the Bible*.

From ancient times when mankind was divided up into nations, there have been kings, rulers and presidents. Melchisedec is the first one in the Bible to be mentioned as a *King* (Genesis 14:18). The tragedy is that from the beginning of national life there has been a constant record of devastating wars involving both Jews and Gentiles, the latter being more conspicuously warlike than the former. Ambition and covetousness have resulted in horrible wars and captivities with their inevitable harvest of desolation, anguish and sorrow for multitudes of innocent people. The Apostle James leaves us in no doubt as to the root-cause of the clash among rulers:

"From whence come wars and fightings among you? Come they not hence, even of your lusts that war in your members? Ye lust, and have not: ye kill, and desire to have, and cannot obtain: ye fight and war, yet ye have not, because ye ask not." James 4:1, 2

Gathering together what the Bible says about kings and rulers, and the divine promises and precepts concerning them, these facts stand out for all modern and future monarchs to observe:

1. *God overrules in their choice.* From the human point of view hereditary and elections appear to decide who is to reign or rule, but God is always in the shadows overruling in the affairs of nations and men.

"Thou shalt in any wise set him king over thee, whom the Lord thy God shall choose." Deuteronomy 17:15

"Howbeit the Lord God of Israel chose me before all the house of thy father to be king over Israel for ever."

I Chronicles 28:5

"There is no power but of God: the powers that be are ordained of God." Romans 13:1

"Now therefore behold the king whom

ye have chosen . . . Behold, the Lord hath set a king over you."

I Samuel 12:13

"He removeth kings, and setteth up kings." Daniel 2:21

"The Most High ruleth in the kingdom of men, and setteth up over it the basest of men." Daniel 4:17

Reference to the contest where the above verses are found indicates promise of success if the Omnipotent God is recognized, and threat of defeat, if He is despised. Nebuchadnezzar, one of the mightiest of kings, had to be reminded that God is omnipotent when it comes to the rise and fall of sovereigns.

"Rulest not Thou over all the kingdoms of the nations." II Chronicles 20:6

"His kingdom ruleth over all."

Psalm 103:19

When we read that God sets up the basest of men to reign and attaches a promise of divine favor to the beneficent reign, we are to understand that He permits them to be chosen. Without doubt Adolph Hitler was one of the basest of men, a child of hell, yet God permitted him to reach his position of supreme power from which he cast the world into its most devastating war. This is a mystery which heaven alone will reveal. Faith rests in confidence on the promise that God possesses infinite wisdom and therefore knows what He is about. Rulers may appear to rule, but God overrules.

"By me kings reign, and princes decree justice." Proverbs 8:15

When the time comes for any cruel, godless ruler to be deposed, God will crush him, even as He did Hitler. All rulers are dependent upon His sovereignty.

"Thou wilt prolong the king's life: and his years as many generations."

Psalms 61:6

"I will surely rend the kingdom from thee, and will give it to thy servant."

I Kings 11:11

Often kings exercised their power arbitrarily and had to be reminded that any promise of a prosperous reign depended upon their endeavor to emulate divine justice and righteousness in rule.

"Saul said unto the footmen that stood about him, Turn and slay the priests of the Lord." I Samuel 22:17, 18

"The king said, Do as he hath said, and fall upon him, and bury him."

I Kings 2:23, 25, 31

Before there was any expressed desire on Israel's part for a king, such as surrounding nations possessed, God gave Moses a profile of the kind of king He was willing to bless—

"His heart be not lifted up among his brethren, and that he turn not aside from the commandment to the right hand, or to the left. . . ."

Then comes the divine promise of blessing—

"To the end that he may prolong his days in his kingdom, he, and his children, in the midst of Israel."

Deuteronomy 17:14-20

Rulers were also counseled to remember that the success of their rule depended, not upon their own prowess or strength, but solely upon the Lord. Promises were attached to the full recognition of Him as the Source of all prosperity, and to the determination of rulers to serve Him and also those they governed. Addressing the Australian Parliament at Melbourne in February, 1951, Queen Elizabeth II said, "It is my resolve under God that I shall not only rule but serve. That is not only the tradition of my family. It describes, I believe, the modern character of the British Crown." What a different history of the nations would have been written if only all crowned heads from early monarchial times had, under God, served Him and those they governed!

"There is no king saved by the multitude of an host: a mighty man (or monarch) is not delivered by his great strength . . . He is our help and our shield." Psalm 33:16, 20

David, warrior and writer, knew what he was talking about, for although he became a great king he was yet severely punished for numbering his soldiers indicating, thereby, that deliverance from his enemies was wholly dependent upon a host of brave fighters. But God has never promised to be on the side of big battalions. National security is not the outcome of strong fighting forces, or the possession of the most deadly weapons. No king is immune from defeat and disaster because of what he has, whether much or little. National prosperity and peace are ordained by God.

"Woe to them that go down to Egypt for help; and stay upon horses, and trust in chariots, because they are many; and in horsemen, because they are very strong: but they look not unto the Holy One of Israel, neither seek the Lord!"

Isaiah 31:1

"Some trust in chariots, and some in horses: but we will remember the name of the Lord our God." Psalm 20:7

King Hezekiah received the promise of deliverance from the overwhelming forces of Assyria because he recognized his utter inability to do anything apart from God. In the end God did it all. Hezekiah had not to raise a finger in his defense. The Assyrian host of 185,000 were slain by one angel.

"Hezekiah prayed before the Lord and said, O Lord God of Israel, which dwellest between the cherubim, thou art God, even thou alone, of all the kingdoms of the earth: thou hast made heaven and earth. . . . The Lord said, I will defend this city, to save it, for mine own sake, and for my servant David's sake. And it came to pass that night, that the angel of the Lord went out, and smote in the camp of the Assyrians an hundred four score and five thousand: and when Hezekiah arose early in the morning, behold, they were all dead corpses"
II Kings 19:14-19, 34, 35

A firm, unshakeable faith in God, and the recognition of Him in every phase of national life, then, is the strongest and most impregnable defense any nation can have.

Further, God has promised that kings can prolong their reign if covetousness is hated. Augustine once wrote, "Abolish justice and what are kingdoms but robberies?" Sacrificing all justice and honor, kings, lustful for more power and possessions, built up kingdoms on robbery.

"The prince that wanteth understanding is also a great oppressor: but he that hateth covetousness shall prolong his days." Proverbs 28:16

God, who is able to reprove kings (I Chronicles 16:21), is the avowed enemy of covetousness in any shape or form. John Milton, the blind poet said, "God gave us kings in His wrath." If He did, it was because of covetousness. Israel's first king was given thus in anger –

"I gave thee a king in mine anger, and took him away in my wrath."
Hosea 13:11

Israel coveted all the glitter and glory, pomp and pride of Gentile kings and demanded of Samuel –

"Make us a king to judge us like all the nations." I Samuel 8:5; 10:19

Thus the people rejected Theocracy for monarchy, with dire results as their future history proves. The avarice and pride of rulers have deeply stained the earth with the ruby blood of millions.

Divine rules for rulers to obey with promises of divine favor if God is honored in national life are scattered throughout the Bible. Monarchs and rulers must fear God and rule in the fear of God.

"He that ruleth over men must be just, ruling in the fear of God."
II Samuel 23:3

These words were among the last spoken by King David, whose reign was an honored one. While guilty of a dark sin marring his royal influence, in the main, David was just and sought to rule in the fear of God. The bent of his life was Godward. This illustrious king left a promise for all those willing to rule as unto God:

"He shall be as the light of the morning, when the sun riseth, even a morning without clouds; as the tender grey upspringing out of the earth by clear shining after rain."

How different civilization would have been if only all kings had kept David's precept and promise in mind! Rulers are exhorted to promote the interest of divine institutions:

"The Lord God of heaven . . . hath charged me to build him an house at Jerusalem." Ezra 1:2-4; 6:1-12. See Isaiah 49:23

Rulers should maintain the cause of the poor and the oppressed –

"The words of King Lemuel . . . Open thy mouth for the dumb in the cause of all such as are appointed to destruction. Open thy mouth, judge righteously, and plead the cause of the poor and needy." Proverbs 31:1, 8, 9

Judgment must never be perverted –

"Pervert not the judgment of any of the afflicted." Proverbs 31:5

All matters relating to subjects must be fully investigated –

"The honour of kings is to search out a matter." Proverbs 25:2

There are warnings against all kinds of evil –

"Give not . . . thy ways to that which destroyeth kings. It is not for kings to drink wine; nor for princes strong drink." Proverbs 31:3, 4

"It is an abomination to kings to commit wickedness: for the throne is established by righteousness."
Proverbs 16:12

"Excellent speech becometh not a fool: much less do lying lips a prince."
Proverbs 17:7

"If a ruler hearken to lies, all his servants are wicked." Proverbs 29:12

"A king that sitteth in the throne of judgment scattereth away all evil with his eyes." Proverbs 20:8

"Righteous lips are the delight of kings." Proverbs 16:13

The foregoing injunctions prove that the influence of a ruler's reign depends upon his morals. Often when a ruler's ways are corrupt and his judgments warped, national life becomes the mirror of his own life. The witness of history, Bible and secular, shows that when kings are godly and wise, and pledge allegiance to the King of kings, then their reign is most beneficial to their subjects. Not only so, but promised blessedness is for those who reign in truth and righteousness. If only all sovereigns and potentates could have grace poured into their lips (Psalm 46), favor the wise (Proverbs 14:35), honor the diligent (Proverbs 22:20), keep the divine Law (I Kings 2:3), study the Scriptures (Deuteronomy 17:19), serve Christ (Psalm 2:10-12), how enriched their lives would be.

The tragedy is that through the centuries so many of the kings of the earth have set themselves and the rulers have taken counsel together against the Lord (Psalm 2:2). Divine restraints have been discarded. The language employed by the Psalmist describes a deliberate and planned hostility to God on the part of the earthly rulers. They are unified in their determination to abolish all restraints. Then the rage and rejection depicted carry a prophetic significance. Ere Christ returns to earth as the King of kings, earth-rulers will be cemented into a godless confederacy. Their every action will be against God. But the promise is that His King, His beloved Son, will take unto Himself His power and reign.

"The Lord hath broken the staff of the wicked, and the sceptre of the rulers."
Isaiah 14:5

Shakespeare expressed the sentiment that "Time's glory is to calm contending kings." Time, however, is not calming contentious kings. What bitter contention characterizes the meeting of the rulers of nations today! How utterly godless some of these rulers are! But He who sits in the heavens laughs, and He can afford to laugh for His day is coming, and when it does, all will bow before Him and recognize His supremacy as the World-Emperor. If only those who have the destinies of nations in their hands would presently acknowledge God's sovereignty and make the patriotic prayer of Daniel, prime minister of Babylon, their own cry:

"O Lord, to us belongeth confusion of face, to our kings, to our princes, and to our fathers, because we have sinned against thee." Daniel 9:3-19

Our attitude toward the kings and rulers of earth, whether they are godly or ungodly, is clearly defined in Scripture. We are not to speak evil of them (Job 34:18; II Peter 2:10) pay necessary tribute to them (Matthew 22:21; Romans 13:6, 7), not despise but honor them (Romans 13:7; I Peter 2:17; Jude 8), fear and reverence them (Proverbs 24:21; I Samuel 24:8; I Kings 1:23, 31), respect their divine ordination (Romans 13:2), and obey them (Romans 13:1, 3; I Peter 2:13). When Peter wrote:

"Submit yourselves . . . to the king, as supreme,"

he was addressing slaves of Caesar, to whom Jesus said everything had to be rendered which were his. Whether we believe in the divine right of kings or not, the fact remains that it is the will of God that the citizens of a country must be subject to decrees its ruler makes. If the rule is tyrannical, then the saints are to await patiently the day of divine deliverance and vengeance.

In lands governed by atheistic, communistic rulers, it may be hard for the saints in such countries to obey the apostolic exhortation to pray for them (I Timothy 2:1, 2). Can prayer avail against those who abuse their authority? When they endeavor to destroy all that is of the Christian faith how can those under communism lead a quiet and peaceable life in all godliness and honesty? Believers in Russia and China may feel it useless to concentrate prayer effort upon their godless rulers, interceding for their recognition of divine wisdom in all their deliberations, but pray they must. Is not the God they pray to, the Lord God Omnipotent with power to set up or depose earthly rulers? Prayerfully they can await the coming of His peaceful Kingdom.

We now come to examine a few promises related to *war*, which will not be abolished until the Prince of Peace takes over the government of the earth. Ever since humanity was divided up into nations, and there appeared kings, princes and rulers, there have been feuds and conflicts between them, resulting in terrible bloodshed. Monarchs and wars have been – and still are –

synonymous. What holocausts of destruction the world has experienced! Millions have looked up to heaven through their blinding tears and cried, "O God, why do men make wars?" Our Lord declared that until the Gentile Age has run its course "wars and rumours of wars" can be expected (Matthew 24:6). But the bright promise is that when "the Son of God goes forth to war," the bloody wars of earth will end.

"He maketh wars to cease unto the end of the earth." Psalm 46:9

"The nations . . . shall beat their swords into ploughshares, and their spears into pruning hooks: nation shall not lift up sword against nation, neither shall they learn war any more." Isaiah 2:4

Summit conferences for rulers to meet and plan for peace in our time are to be commended. The U.N.O. in New York was conceived to banish war from the earth, yet since its inception we have had nothing but a succession of wars and the rape of nations like Hungary and Tibet by larger, power-hungry nations. Certainly we should pray for statesmen as they explore the avenues of peace but with our Bibles open before us we know that any respite from war will only be temporary. The prerogative of world-peace belongs to Him who is coming to break the bow asunder. The recurring personal pronoun in the promise of the Psalmist must not be lost sight of—"He . . . He . . . He." The abolition of war, and the complete destruction of the munitions of war, await the return of Jesus Christ to earth. Meantime, our attitude should be that of supreme confidence in the realization of the promise of ultimate divine sovereignty—

"Be still, and know that I am God. I will be exalted among the nations, I will be exalted on the earth."

Psalm 46:10

"Scatter thou the people that delight in war." Psalm 68:30

"For the kingdom is the Lord's: and he is governor among the nations." Psalm 22:28

F. W. Boreham, in *The Ivory Spires*, says: "It is clear that those who would abolish war must provide the youth of the nations with avenues of adventurous service that will stir their pulses no less wildly than the call of the bugle and the beat of drum." But such a noble ideal is impossible of realization seeing that the great nations of the earth are presently occupied in the production of the most horrible and hellish weapons of war ever conceived, leaving little money or desire for "avenues of adventurous service."

The dread of an atomic war has gripped the hearts of multitudes. Ominous threats keep the world jittery, for if there is another world-conflict, it will mean near annihilation for many nations. If God should permit another war in our time, are there Promises we can cling to if wardrums should beat again? Yes, there are many we can hide in our heart. A wonderful feature of *war-promises* given thousands of years ago, is that they have brought consolation and strength to the saints caught up in the horrors of war in succeeding ages. Such promises, nay all kinds of promises, are inexhaustible. With passing generations they seem to hold a deeper meaning and greater truth. During the last World War, many Old Testament promises seemed to be as fresh as ever, and imparted tireless power of endurance and strength of courage amid the sacrifice and carnage of war.

"The Lord your God is he that goeth with you, to fight for you against your enemies, to save you."

Deuteronomy 20:4

"The Lord thy God walketh in the midst of thy camp, to deliver thee, and to give up thine enemies before thee."

Deuteronomy 23:14

"The Lord shall cause thine enemies that rise up against thee to be smitten before thy face." Deuteronomy 28:7

"Lord, it is nothing with thee to help, whether with many, or with them that have no power: help us O Lord our God: for we rest on thee, and in thy name we go against this multitude. O Lord, thou art our God; let not man prevail against thee."

II Chronicles 15:11

"He shall deliver thee . . . in war from the power of the sword." Job 5:20

"Though an host should encamp against me, my heart shall not fear: though war should rise against me, in this will I be confident . . . He shall hide me in his pavilion." Psalm 27:3, 6

"Through God we shall do valiantly: for he it is that shall tread down our enemies." Psalm 60:11

"That we should be saved from our enemies . . . That he would grant unto us, that we being delivered out of the hand of our enemies might serve him without fear." Luke 1:71, 74

"We may boldly say, The Lord is my helper, and I will not fear what men shall do unto me." Hebrews 13:6

While the above, and similar promises, do not guarantee immunity from the sorrows of war, they nevertheless imply that if we should be swept along by the current of war, we have a source of consolation and hope, of which the godless are ignorant (Proverbs 3:24-26).

"He shall redeem thee . . . in war from the power of the sword." Job 5:20

Through the ages the instruments of war have become more deadly, until misdirected ingenuity and science have succeeded in creating the most fearful implements of destruction ever known. Present day nuclear missiles are too frightful to contemplate. But Job's promise declares that God is able to preserve both man and family produce in time of war. True, Christians perish as well as non-Christians when battles rage, but for Christians who perish by the way, there is the consolation that warring forces are not able to kill the soul (Matthew 10:28). Bombs only deliver believers from the sordidness of earth. For them, sudden death is sudden glory. Some of the early martyrs could kiss the flames encircling them, seeing they only hastened their entrance into heaven.

"Fear not: for they that be with us are more than they that be with them." II Kings 6:16

The young man who was disturbed by the overwhelming host with horses and chariots surrounding Samaria, had to be reminded by Elisha that there were mightier, invisible hosts acting as the city's bodyguard. Do we believe that greater is He that is for us than any arrayed against us? (Read II Chronicles 32:7; Psalm 55:18; Romans 8:31).

"No weapon (even nuclear ones) that is formed against thee shall prosper." Isaiah 54:17

While this is a promise directly related to restored Israel, like many other of her promises, we can claim the *life-rent* of it. God is still able to break the bow and cut the spear in sunder. Modern weapons of war are indeed fearful and diabolical, but He knows how to bring them to naught. Often He rallies the forces of nature to combat the cruelty of men. It was thus that God used the snow against Napoleon and the miracle-mists at Dunkirk.

"Shall your brethren go to war, and shall ye sit here?" Numbers 32:6

Whenever war breaks loose upon a nation, the vexing question of Christian participation inevitably arises. Pacifists and conscientious objectors become conspicuous as they affirm their unwillingness to take up arms against man. War is anti-Christian, it is said, and dismetrically opposed to the witness and teachings of Christ. In our democracy such individual conscience is respected. Still, the problem is, What should be the attitude of a Christian when war arises? Is he, like the children of Gad and the children of Reuben, to sit in comfort, while others go out to bleed and die? A Christian, although a citizen of heaven, is likewise a citizen of earth, and must decide whether or no he has corresponding responsibilities, and should be in subjection to the powers that be. Peter gives us clear instructions on this matter:

> Having your conversation honest among the Gentiles; that, whereas they speak against you as evil-doers, they may by your good works, which they shall behold, glorify God in the day of visitation. Submit yourselves to every ordinance of man for the Lord's sake: whether it be to the king, as supreme; Or unto governors, as unto them that are sent by him for the punishment of evil-doers, and for the praise of them that do well. For so is the will of God, that with well-doing ye may put to silence the ignorance of foolish men: As free, and not using your liberty for a cloak of maliciousness, but as the servants of God. Honour all men. Love the brotherhood. Fear God. Honour the king. Servants, be subject to your masters with all fear; not only to the good and gentle, but also to the froward. For this is thankworthy, if a man for conscience toward God endure grief, suffering wrongfully. For what glory is it, if, when ye be buffeted for your faults, ye shall take it patiently? but if, when ye do well, and suffer for it, ye take it patiently, this is acceptable with God. For even hereunto were ye called; because Christ also suffered for us, leaving us an example, that ye should follow his steps; Who did no sin, neither was guile found in his mouth; Who, when he was reviled, reviled not again; when he suffered, he threatened not; but committed himself to him that judgeth righteously; Who his own self bare our sins in his own body on the tree, that we, being dead to sins, should live unto righteousness: by whose stripes ye were healed. For ye were as sheep going astray; but are now returned unto the Shepherd and Bishop of your souls. I Peter 2:12-25

You cannot enforce Christian ethics in a non-Christian world. They that take the sword must perish by the sword. Some of the godliest men were soldiers, and fought and died for their country's honor. To these, like General Gordon, the Promises of divine succor were most precious.

One of the grim casualties of any war is the capture and plight of prisoners. From ancient times captors have been guilty of inhuman treatment toward their captives. The Philistines delighted in the degradation they made Samson to suffer when they put out his eyes, bound him with fetters of brass, and made him grind in the wretched prison house (Judges 16:21). A similar fate overtook King Zedekiah at the hands of the king of Babylon (Jeremiah 52:11). Jeremiah the Prophet begged to be kept from a death-infested prison (Jeremiah 37:15, 20). In Bible times, then, prisoners were subjected to extreme suffering. Promises, either of deliverance from prison or of grace to bear such a trial, if deliverance was not forthcoming, however, were graciously given:

"Let the sighing of the prisoner come before thee: According to the greatness of thy power preserve thou those that are appointed to death." Psalm 79:11
"To hear the sighing of the prisoners; to loose those that are appointed to death." Psalm 102:20
"His feet they hurt with fetters: He was laid in chains of iron (margin – His soul entered into the iron,) Until the time that his word came to pass. The word of Jehovah tried him, The king sent and loosed him." Psalm 105:19, 20
"The captive exile hasteneth that he may be loosed, and that he should not die in the pit." Isaiah 51:14

A pit, as a prison, was prevalent in the East. Usually prisoners were let down through a hole into a narrow pit, where they were confined at the pleasure of their tyrannical masters. The writer remembers how he shuddered on viewing the "Bottle Dungeon" at St. Andrews, Scotland, in which saintly Samuel Rutherford was forced to suffer. Isaiah made it clear that no captive wants to die in such a prison.

What vile prisons countless multitudes were forced to suffer in during the last World War! German and Japanese prison camps, and Russian slave camps were most cruel and inhuman, and against all international agreement. To the credit of America, Great Britain and France, they were more humane in their treatment of their war prisoners. Recently I listened to the Rt. Rev. John Leonard Wilson relate his harrowing experiences at the hands of the Japanese. In 1942, while Bishop of Singapore, he was suspected of being a spy, imprisoned and tortured by the secret police. The film, *Singapore Story*, describing the bishop's brutal treatment, made one weep over man's inhumanity to man. Now, the Bishop of Birmingham, Dr. Wilson radiates the forgiving spirit of his Master and testifies to the absence of hatred in his heart even when he was being so cruelly beaten.

In such painful and pitiable conditions what was the bishop's hope, and of thousands like him who loved the Lord? Why, the divine promises of Him who is never deaf to the sighing of the prisoner sustained them. Describing the privations and threatened hunger of the prison, Isaiah gives us one of those blessed "Buts" of the Bible –

"But I am the Lord thy God." Isaiah 51:14, 15
"He bringeth out those which are bound with chains." Psalm 68:6
"He brought them out of darkness and the shadow of death, and brake their bands in sunder." Psalm 107:14
"Thus saith the Lord, Even the captives of the mighty shall be taken away, and the prey of the terrible shall be delivered." Isaiah 49:24, 25

A captive people like Israel never treated God's promises as if they were curiosities of a museum. When captives of the mighty rulers, the words of the prophets were the source of comfort and hope in exile. God was made to take the prey from the mighty, and through His servant He promised to contend with those who ill-treated His own. When war breaks loose upon the world, men and women and children in conquered countries become prisoners, and many languish and die. What a terrible blot on civilization was the brutal massacre of more than five million helpless Jews by Adolph Hitler! Cruel aggressors, however, merit the judgment of heaven. The humiliating end of Hitler and Mussolini fittingly illustrated the divine condemnation –

"I will feed them that oppress thee with their own flesh, and they be drunken with their own blood, as with sweet wine." Isaiah 49:26

The Romans had a singular method of fettering their prisoners. The one end of a long chain was fixed about the right arm of the prisoner, and the other end was fastened to the left arm of a soldier. Thus a prisoner was always attended and guarded, which occasioned one of the most pathetic and affecting strokes of true oratory ever displayed either in the Grecian or Roman senate:

> "I would to God, that not only thou, but also all that hear me this day, were both almost, and altogether such as I am, except these bonds." Acts 26:29

Can we not imagine how Paul would accompany his words with the parade and dangling of his chains? Yet his bonds were a blessing, for they gave the apostle great opportunities of winning his guards for the Lord. "Because that for the hope of Israel I am bound with this chain." We can really picture him proclaiming such a hope to his changing guard. Grace was his to fashion a pulpit out of his prison. That both Paul and Peter endured imprisonments yet received promised succor and deliverance is fully dealt with in the author's volume on *All the Miracles of the Bible.*

> "The king . . . changed his prison garments." II Kings 25:29

The King of Babylon acted most graciously when it came to the release of Jehoiachin, his royal prisoner. Read the context (27-30) and note the handsome treatment Jehoiachin received, and which continued all the days of his life. How pleased he must have been when, by the edict of Evil-Merodach, he discarded his prison garb and once again donned his royal attire and went forth to enjoy the promise of freedom! His coarse clothes, symbol of captivity, were exchanged for gold and purple, symbols of royalty. Does this not supply us with a picture of grace? The moment our head is lifted up out of the prison-house of sin by our heavenly King, we cast off the rags of sin and bondage and put on His priceless robe of righteousness. Paul refers to this change of raiment as a "putting off" and a "putting on." The tragedy is that we ofttimes cling to our old clothes. We continue to look like prisoners, instead of living as princes.

> "I was in prison and ye came to Me."
> Matthew 25:36

Civil prisons testify to the reality of sin. Society demands them as a means of punishment for crime. All within our national prisons are there because they deserve to suffer. Modern prisons, especially in democratic countries, are far removed from the cold barbarity once associated with them. Liberty is given to messengers of Christ to visit our prisons and to influence the prisoners to live a better life. What trophies of grace have come from a prison cell! In His Olivet discourse, our Lord affirms that in caring for the needy, whether in or out of prison, we are actually ministering unto Him. "Ye did it unto me." The first man to receive the Crucified Saviour was a criminal who was dying for his evil deeds. Let us constantly pray for prison chaplains and Christian workers as they deal with those whose sin has produced bondage. As Bibles are to be found in prison cells, at least in countries where the Bible is revered, let us also pray that God will bless and use His silent messenger for the transformation of sin-burdened lives (See I Peter 3:19).

> "The Lord . . . despiseth not his prisoners." Psalm 69:33

The Bible uses a prison in various ways. It represents the grave of Christ, with the promise of resurrection (Isaiah 53:8). Those who are in bondage by reason of their own lusts are among the prisoners the Lord came to bring out of the prison-house of sin (Isaiah 42:7). God's power over Satan is proved by the latter's presence in prison for a thousand years (Revelation 20:1,7). Paul speaks of himself, not as the prisoner of Nero, but as the prisoner of the Lord (Ephesians 3:1; 4:1). Those of Smyrna, who were cast into prison because of their allegiance to Christ, were likewise His prisoners (Revelation 2:10). But unto such the promise was given that the Lord will not despise or leave them to rot unforgotten. He hears their sighs and has His own way of delivering them, as Peter proved when the prison doors opened of their own accord.

> "Turn ye to the strong hold, ye prisoners of hope." Zechariah 9:12

Here the narrative is directly related to the re-gathering of Israel, and her re-establishment as a nation. The figure of speech is therefore most expressive. Scattered as they were among the nations, the Jews were upheld amid much suffering by God's promised deliverance. They believed that He would bring them to "the strong hold" of their own land, and render them double blessing. For their tears, God would give them triumph. Glory was to compensate their grief. As prisoners in many lands, the Jews still hope on. National resurgence has resulted in freedom.

The saints of God are likewise "prisoners of hope." Their redeemed spirits are within the prison of the body, yearning for freedom. Fettered by the world and the flesh, they cannot serve the Lord as they should or would like. At Christ's coming, however, they leap out of their bodily prison, leaving their chains behind (Philippians 3:20, 21).

For those who labor for peace in a war-weary world there are a few encouraging promises for them to rest in –

"To the counsellors of peace is joy."

Proverbs 12:20

"Blessed are the peacemakers: for they shall be called the sons of God."

Matthew 5:9

"He that will love life, and see good days, let him refrain his tongue from evil, and his lips that they seek no guile: Let him eschew evil, and do good: let him seek peace, and pursue it." I Peter 3:10, 11

If the Prince of Peace Himself is not recognized and revered by war-like nations, how can there be the universal peace millions sigh for? How apt are the prophet's words in more ways than one –

"Peace, peace to him that is afar off, and to him that is near saith the Lord; and I will heal him.

But the wicked are like the troubled sea, when it cannot rest, whose waters cast up mire and dirt.

There is no peace, saith my God, to the wicked." Isaiah 57:19-23

THE PROMISES AND THE NATURAL WORLD

In his appeal to the men of Athens, Paul, using as his text the altar inscription, *To An Unknown God*, declared that such a God was –

"The God that made the world and all things therein, He, being Lord of heaven and earth, dwelleth not in temples made with hands . . . He giveth to all life, and breath, and all things." Acts 17:24-26

The heart-inspiring truth emphasized throughout the Bible is that God, as the Lord of nature and of providence, promises an abundance of good things as the seasons, which He has determined, come and go (Acts 17:26). The universe offers itself to view as earth, sky and sea.

1. *He Is the Creator and Controller of the Sea.*

"The sea is His, and He made it, and His hands formed the dry land."

Psalm 95:4-5; Revelation 21:1

"In six days Jehovah made heaven and earth, the sea and all that in them is."

Exodus 20:11

"The Lord caused the sea to go back."

Exodus 14:21; Proverbs 8:29

"He shall have dominion from sea to sea." Psalm 72:8; 66:6; Matthew 8:26

2. *He is the Creator and Controller of the Sky.*

"God . . . Who rideth upon the heavens for thy help, and in his excellency on the skies." Deuteronomy 33:26

"Canst thou with him spread out the sky?" Job 37:18

"The heavens declare the glory of God: and the firmament showeth his handiwork." Psalm 19:1

"By his Spirit he garnished the heavens." Job 26:13

3. *He Is the Creator and Controller of*

the Earth.

"The earth is the Lord's, and the fulness thereof: The world, and they that dwell therein. He hath founded it upon the seas, and established it upon the floods." Psalm 24:1, 2

"Every beast of the forest is mine, and the cattle upon a thousand hills. I know all the birds of the mountains; and the wild beasts of the field are mine. If I were hungry, I would not tell thee; For the world is mine, and the fulness thereof." Psalm 50:10-12

"The silver is mine and the gold is mine, saith the Lord of hosts."

Haggai 2:8

"Behold, all souls are mine."

Ezekiel 18:4

"Shall not the judge of all the earth do right?" Genesis 18:25

All the foregoing evidences of divine ownership and sovereignty prove that as a servant is dependent on his master, so is all of nature upon her Lord. Nature is not her own governess. She does not follow her own will, but her Lord's will. She does not express her own thoughts, but His thought and purpose. For instance, the sun rises every day at the right moment – who is the thinker? The sun? No; but the God who created it. The bee builds her comb according to the severest principles of geometry – who is the mathematician? The bee? No; but the God who created it. Thus nature has no thought, no will of her own; she is entirely under the control of her Lord. What a magnificent display of God's dominion in His own world Job gives us! Read this absorbing and incomparable description (Job 37-41).

Neither is nature her own support. Brought

into being by God, she lives on His bounty, as a child on the table of its father. "Nature can originate nothing; she must receive all. Left to her own resources, she would reduce herself to penury in one day. Were she called upon to feed the creatures on her surface for one single hour, she would turn bankrupt the next. In her relation to God, she incessantly receives." It is for this reason that God has given us so many gracious nature-promises. Throughout the Bible there are assurances that He will continue to supply through nature, His handmaid, all that is required for mankind, and for the beasts of the field and the fowls of the air. His promises likewise cover the seasons of the year, and all the forces of nature.

Divine greatness is seen, not only in the provision of nature herself, but in all her unfailing bounty. The blessing of Jacob for his son Joseph, carries the promise of nature's gifts for all the offspring of God—

"Blessed of Jehovah be his land,
For the precious things of Heaven, for the dew,
For the deep that coucheth beneath,
For the precious things of the fruit of the sun,
For the precious things of the growth of the moons, (or months)
For the precious things of the everlasting hills,
For the precious things of the earth and the fulness thereof, and the good will of him that dwelt in the bush."

Deuteronomy 33:13-16

For nature, emerging from beneath her watery covering, there was the divine promise that never again would a flood destroy the earth. The bow set in the cloud was to be the enduring remembrance-token. Encircling the heavens with its belt of golden hues, it was to testify of God's promise, and appears as a lasting memorial of His covenant throughout all generations. Since Noah's day different parts of the earth have experienced devastating floods, but ever and anon the beautiful rainbow appears to remind sinful man that God "shall no more destroy all flesh." The rainbow is also a remembrance to Himself of His gracious promise, "I will look upon it that I may remember the everlasting covenant." Such a bow of promise was also to be the pledge of the perpetuity of nature's blessings.

"While the earth remaineth, seedtime and harvest, and cold and heat, and sum-mer and winter, and day and night shall not cease." Genesis 8:22

"The fountain of Jacob shall be upon a land of corn and wine; also his heavens shall drop down dew."

Deuteronomy 33:28

"If the clouds be full of rain, they empty themselves upon the earth."

Ecclesiastes 11:3

"If God so clothe the grass of the field."

Matthew 6:30

Is it not wonderful how, with amazing regularity, God meets the needs of the millions on earth in succeeding generations? True, there is poverty amid plenty. Multitudes in some parts of the world live on the verge of starvation, while others have enough and to spare. But this is no break-down of nature. It comes about through man's unequal distribution of nature's bounties.

The storms and winds may rise and rage but—

"He maketh the storm a calm, so that the waves thereof are still."

Psalm 107:23-30

He who controls the skies and atmospheric conditions can empty the clouds of rain, or permit drought—

"I will give you rain in due season."

Deuteronomy 11:14

"He shut up the heavens, so that there be no rain; and the land shall not yield its fruit." Deuteronomy 11:17

"The Lord sent thunder and rain that day." I Samuel 12:18

"The appearance of the bow that is in the cloud in the day of rain."

Ezekiel 1:28

There may be times when it seems as if the part of the country we live in has too much rain, and the sigh escapes us for a drier, sunnier clime. But as James Whitcomb Riley puts it—

It is no use to grumble and complain;
It's just as cheap and easy to rejoice;
When God sorts out the weather and sends rain —
Why, rain's my choice.

Then as Autumn comes round, and we have our harvest festival, does the same not bring with it the verification of the promise given to Noah? Do not our hearts gratefully sing to the Lord of the harvest —

All good things around us,
Are sent from heaven above.

The tragedy is that although the good seed is fed and watered by God's Almighty hand, and He sends the beneficial snow in winter, He gets little thanks from man. The ever-recurring summers, autumns, winters and springs, with all each season produces, are taken as a matter of course. The majority, blessed by nature, do not magnify the Lord, for all things bright and beautiful and good. God's promise of unceasing supply is not recognized.

In the Bible there are various *promised harvests* – harvests both of joy and judgment. The natural world is made to illustrate the judicial realm.

"They joy before thee according to the joy in harvest." Isaiah 9:3

In the narrative, Isaiah uses this illustration from nature as a promise of a divine Child as Israel's only hope. Knowing something of the harvest Christ is to gather as the result of His victory over the forces of hell, we, too, joy before the Lord according to the joy of harvest. As the farmer rejoices over his gathered crop, at the Judgment Seat, as laborers in the Master's vineyard, we likewise can know the joy of harvest (I Thessalonians 2:19, 20). Will you have sheaves to rejoice over at that harvest time?

"He that gathereth in summer is a wise son; but he that sleepeth in harvest is a son that causeth shame."

Proverbs 10:5

Among the Proverbs of Solomon, all of which are potential promises, there are striking illustrations of the contrast between the wisdom of righteousness and the folly of wickedness. To gather a harvest as the summer fades is an evidence of wisdom. We speak of making hay while the sun shines. When the harvest is ripe, there is little time for sleep or indulgence in pleasures associated with slacker days. To sleep in harvest, then, brings loss and shame to the reaper. We are still in the summertime of grace. Ere long, the bitter winter of the Great Tribulation will overtake a guilty world. While the Saviour tarries, it is harvest-time for soul-winning. God forbid that shame should be ours when we see the Lord of the harvest! The fields are white unto harvest, but are we at ease in Zion? Are we sleeping instead of gleaning? Because of the need and peril of the loss, we dare not sleep as do others.

"The harvest is past, the ingathering of summer fruits is ended."

Jeremiah 8:20 R.V.

Jeremiah, the Prophet of Tears, had a unique way of employing forceful metaphors in his endeavor to bring a backsliding nation back to God. In spite of his weeping eyes,

however, his was a fruitless task. Ceaselessly he preached that if the people would but repent, God would save them from the aggression of the Babylonians. But hopelessly and fanatically attached to their idols, the people were doomed. The harvest of grace and the summer of acceptance were ended, and those to whom he addressed his tear-drenched messages were not saved from their idolatry and consequent destruction. The promises of reconciliation to God were spurned. In this Gospel Age, an incentive to a more aggressive evangelism is the fact that the harvest is not past, and the summer of salvation is not ended. The door of mercy is still ajar. May grace be ours then to "rescue the perishing, care for the dying, weep o'er the erring one, tell them of Jesus the mighty to save."

"Put ye in the sickle for the harvest is ripe." Joel 3:13

The Bible likens a people ripened by sin for destruction to a harvest ready for the sickle of God's vengeance.

"He will cut off the springs with pruning hooks, and the spreading branches will be take away and cut down." Isaiah 18:4-7

What a bloody harvest awaits a guilty, godless earth! The vision of Armageddon is terrible to contemplate (Ezekiel 39). What destruction will overtake the multitudes when "the harvest is ripe" (Revelation 14:15)? The promised sickle of judgment will be in the pierced hand of the Son of Man. Rejecting Him, men thrust a reed into His hands, and then drive those cruel nails through them. But when those scarred hands lay hold of the sickle, woe betide the rejectors thronging the earth! None will escape the dread vengeance of those days. Blessed be God, all who are His will escape such a horrible harvest. Having been reaped in grace, they will not experience the sickle of slaughter.

"I also will keep thee from the hour of trial, that hour which is to come upon the whole world, to try them that dwell upon the earth." Revelation 3:10

"Pray ye therefore the Lord of the harvest." Matthew 9:38

A great ingathering of souls is called a *harvest*. Since the inception of the Church, the harvest has been plenteous. Unnumbered multitudes in heaven and on earth have been garnered. As the corn of wheat, Jesus fell into the ground and died. But much fruit is now the Lord's. What we presently fail to realize is that the fields of opportunity are white unto harvest. The ingathering is slow for the laborers are few. The burden of our Lord should be for Him to thrust forth laborers into the field. Are we interceding as we should for more godly ministers, more flaming evangelists, more sacrificial missionaries, more consecrated Christian workers? Whether we sow or reap, let us keep the Judgment Seat before us, where sowers and reapers are to rejoice together (John 4:35-38).

"The harvest is the end of the age."
Matthew 13:39

The day of final reckoning is likened unto a harvest, when both nature and the wicked will be ripe for divine judgment (II Peter 3:5-7). In the Parable of the Tares, our Lord makes it clear that angel-reapers are to gather in the wicked for burning. The wheat – all who are the Lord's – will have been gathered in. At the end of this Gentile Age, when the Lord returns to earth to consummate the Age and usher in His millennial reign, all offensive to His mind and will is to be judicially dealt with. A similar judgment-harvest awaits the wicked dead at the setting up of the Great White Throne (Revelation 20:11-15). Satan, the enemy-sower of tares, is to eternally suffer with his dupes as they wail and gnash their teeth.

"They that sow in tears shall reap in joy.
He that goeth forth and weepeth, bearing seed for sowing,
Shall doubtless come again with joy, bringing his sheaves with him."
Psalm 126:5-6

What a contrast is here presented – *tears* and *joy!* The tears are to be the media of the joy. If we sow in weeping, we have the promise of a joyful harvest. Says C. H. Spurgeon, "When thine eyes are dim with silver tears, think of the golden corn. Bear cheerfully the present toil and disappointment, for the harvest day will fully recompense thee . . . . Seed steeped in the tears of earnest anxiety will come up all the sooner . . . . Our heavenly seed could not fitly be sown laughing. Deep sorrow and concern for the souls of others are a far more fit accompaniment of godly teaching than anything like levity." The hymn reminds us that –

"God's choicest wreaths,
Are wet with tears."

There is another aspect that must be dealt with ere we leave this section taken up with the natural world and its specific promises. While, as we have seen, God has promised seed time and harvest with food sufficient for mankind, He has likewise promised famine and destitution for those who disobey His laws, as well as the laws of nature. Wherever there is life, food, in some form or another, is absolutely necessary for the nourishment and continuance of that life. Without food, both man and beast die. Thus Bible facts as to famine are worthy of note. Famine is divinely sent:

"He called for a famine upon the land;
He brake the whole staff of bread."
Psalm 105:16

Famine comes as one of four sore judgments of God:

"How much more when I send my four sore judgments upon Jerusalem, the sword, and the famine, and the evil beasts, and the pestilence to cut off from it man and beast." Ezekiel 15:13, 20

Bible famines were the result of different causes: The withholding of God's blessing (Hosea 2:8, 9; Haggai 1:6); want of seasonable and necessary rain (I Kings 17:1; Jeremiah 14:1-4; Amos 4:7); rotting of seed in the ground (Joel 1:17); swarms of destructive insects (Deuteronomy 28:28, 42; Joel 1:4); blasting and mildew (Amos 4:9; Haggai 2:17); devastation by enemies (Deuteronomy 28:33-51). Such famines were often long (Genesis 41:27; II Kings 8:12), severe (Genesis 12:10; I Kings 18:2; Jeremiah 52:6), followed by pestilence (Jeremiah 42:17; Ezekiel 7:15; Matthew 24:7), and illustrative of the dearth of the means of grace (Amos 8:11, 12).

Among Bible promises are those indicating that God is able to provide for His people during a period of famine.

"I have commanded the ravens to feed thee there . . . . I have commanded a widow there to sustain thee."
I Kings 17:4, 9

"The Lord is my Shepherd, I shall not want." Psalm 23:1

The Bible presents distinguishing features of famines:

"There was a famine in the land: and Abraham went down into Egypt to sojourn there; for the famine was sore in the land." Genesis 12:10

In this first recorded famine, we have an insight into the grievousness of such a blight. Widespread scarcity of food, disease, misery and death are famine features. At all times, famines are indeed dreadful and are to be feared. No end is so terrible as that of being slowly starved to death. "When all the land of Egypt was famished, the people cried to Pharaoh for bread." Genesis 41:55

Since Abraham's day, the world has witnessed many a sore famine. What tragic stories history holds of multitudes in different lands perishing from starvation! We have the record of a Bible famine when parents were forced to eat their own children (II Kings 6:24-31). The question arises in some hearts, "How can God be a God of love and compassion, and allow such a terrible situation to prevail?"

"In famine he will redeem thee from death . . . . At destruction and famine thou shalt laugh." Job 5:20,22.

"To keep them alive in famine."

Psalm 33:19

"In the days of famine thou shalt be satisfied." Psalm 37:19

If only Elimelech had had these promises before him he would have remained in Bethlehem and not have gone down to Moab for bread (Ruth 1:1, 2). Need can never throttle God. He is able to provide a table even in a wilderness (Psalm 23:5). As we have seen, Elijah came to experience that God is able to use ravens as food-carriers, when it comes to feeding a hungry prophet in a time of famine. No matter what scarcity prevails, God is able to preserve His own. Crops may fail, or be destroyed by blight, or war; God's larder is never empty.

"I will punish them . . . by the famine."

Jeremiah 44:13

Some famines came, as we have indicated, as the manifestation of divine wrath. For his sin in numbering the people, David was given a choice of punishment – famine, flight, or pestilence. The latter fell upon 70,000 men (II Samuel 24:10-25). Famine, as a medium of judgment, proves the Omnipotence of God as the Creator as well as that of the Righteous Judge. Scattering food so bountifully, for the physical good of man and beast, God can also withhold the fruits and forces of nature, upon which all are so dependent. With a regal hand God bestows, and with a righteous hand He blasts. Would that the hordes of earth who, although fed with amazing regularity by God's Almighty hand, yet sin with impunity, might learn His power to transform plenty into poverty. Famine can displace His favor.

"I shall send upon them the evil arrows of famine, that are for destruction."

Ezekiel 5:16

While Ezekiel makes it clear that *famine* is one of the divine judgments for sin, what impresses us in this verse is the promised "evil arrows." What are these arrows disastrous in their mission? Gnawing of the bowels, unappeased hunger, wasting of body, loss of sleep, torture of mind, a living death, extreme inertia, and anguish over others similarly smitten. What evil arrows! Surely it is better to be slain than starve – to die suddenly than gradually as the famine-stricken do. The redeemed are promised deliverance from these evil arrows. So long as we have plenty, let us share what we have with the needy.

"I will send a famine in the land, not a famine of bread, nor a thirst for water, but of hearing the words of God."

Amos 8:11

Amos, along with other prophets, declares that there is a worse famine than scarcity of food. Surely these are days when there is a famine of hearing the words of God. Hardly ten per cent of the British people darken a church door. There are plenty of Bibles about (never so many as now) and churches in abundance, but what a famine of the Word! We have a glut of pleasing, inoffensive sermonettes, book reviews, political and topical talks, religious homilies, but a famine of sane, Scriptural exposition. What a nation of spiritually starved souls ours is! An abundance of bread, water and money, but an empty spiritual cupboard. Hungry souls wait to be fed with the Bread of Life, but pulpits, in general, lack pastors who are able to feed a hungry flock.

"There shall be famines . . . in many places." Matthew 24:7

If "famines" are to be one of the signs heralding the return of Christ to earth, then surely coming events are casting their shadows before them. What horrible famines stalk different parts of the earth! We think of millions who hardly have enough to keep body and soul together in heathen countries. Then how terrible is the plight of the refugees of war. But famines past and present are not to be compared to the sorrows about to overtake a godless earth. What a trinity of grief awaits a world from which the true Church will be missing – famines, pestilence, earthquakes! Earth's travail, however, will cease when Jesus comes to usher in His reign of peace and prosperity. Throughout the Millennium, the earth will bask in plenty. No more pinched faces, starved bodies, living skeletons, when Christ is here as King of kings.

"Who shall separate us from the love of Christ, shall . . . famine?" Romans 8:35

Away from his father, the prodigal son found himself without food or friends. "There arose a mighty famine in that land" (Luke 15:14). But hunger helped to drive the wayward boy home, where the fatted calf awaited him. Many a saint has had to endure the pangs of starvation through no fault of his own. For Christ's sake they were killed all the day long. Being His did not bring immunity from the terrible end the gaunt figure of famine produces. They had the promise of their bread and water being sure, yet in divine providence suffered want. Yet triumph was theirs. Dying of empty stomachs, parched lips, and emaciated frames, they were victorious. Famine could come and reap its cruel harvest but these valiant warriors had hidden manna to feed upon. The Bread of Life was their stay, and no one and nothing could separate them from Him. Whatever lack may afflict us, He remains as our sufficiency.

THE PROMISES AND THE CHRISTIAN WORLD

We have now reached the bulk of Bible promises, related as they are to the Lord and His own. It has been computed that there are more than 800 of these promises in the New Testament alone. If this be true, then we have waters of promised blessing to swim in. As we come to enumerate and expound the vast array of promises with the Christian outlook, we are amazed at their inexhaustibleness. Theirs is a thought none can reach, or tongue declare. This is particularly true of the promises associated with the depth of the widsom and riches of the unsearchable grace of our Lord Jesus Christ. If only we could fully explore and interpret these promises and thereby help others to see the wealth they contain. "Their great glory is that no one can read into them more truth and power and grace than is really there."

It is said that when Nansen was exploring the Arctic Seas he came to places where his longest sounding lines were not long enough to reach the ocean bed. All he could do was to mark on his charts the depths he had sounded and then add, "Deeper than that." When we feel we have exhausted thought and language in exploring the wealth of the riches of Christ's promises, we have to add, "Greater than that; truer than that; more sure and abiding than that." Such is the nature of any divine promise that each time we claim it we discover treasure hitherto unknown.

Historians say that Christopher Columbus discovered the American Continent. After weeks on the ocean all he ever saw was a few small islands lying off the coast of America. He never heard the thunder of Niagara, never saw the towering heights of the Rocky Mountains or the grandeur of the Grand Canyon, or the vast prairies of the Middle West. True, Columbus came home with tales of a land of fabulous wealth, but how little he knew of the real, exhaustless wealth of the new world. Is it not so in relation to the divine promises? All we can see is the coast-line of the land, but the land waiting to be possessed and the riches waiting to be discovered are hid from us. "We see horizons, but we know that a horizon is not a boundary, and when we reach the horizon there will be other horizons and beyond those still greater and wider horizons." These promises shine more and more unto the perfect day.

Further, age and experience enable one to fathom more deeply the hidden riches within so many of the promises. Believers, young in years, can lay hold of the blessed promise: "Where I am, there ye may be also" (John 14:3) – and be thrilled with the thought of heavenly bliss. But to aged saints in the sunset years of life, who are not far away from the pearly gates, such an assuring promise is more meaningful. They have come to cling, not so much to the Master's words themselves, but to their inner significance and reality. Eagerly and confidently they await the call to the mansions above, when their Lord's promise of heaven will be fully realized.

To sectionalize all the promises under this last aspect of our general study is by no means an easy task. Different amplifications have been attempted as, for example, the lists to be found in Samuel Clarke's *Precious Bible Promises*. It may be that the following outline we have planned, which is by no means exhaustive, may prove to be helpful, both for devotional and study purposes:

Promises Relative to Christ
Promises Relative to the Christian
  Scriptures
Promises Relative to the Christian
  Church
Promises Relative to Christian
  Doctrines

Promises Relative to Christ

Because there are hundreds of definite prophecies or promises of Christ in the Bible, as well as hundreds more of implied references and types and symbols, displaying His glory and grace, it would require a book in itself to rightly arrange all of these Messianic references, sparkling with diamond rays upon the sacred page. Perhaps a twofold general division will prove serviceable. First of all, we have –

The Promised Person. Under this section we can consider many of the specific predictions of Christ, along with their definite fulfilment.

The Person' Promised. In this category we can place a few of the many names, types and metaphors, all of which are necessary to extol His matchless worth and beauty. Everywhere there are hidden Messianic intimations which are not clearly visible on the surface of the verse.

The Promised Person

After God's first promise of Christ as "the seed of the woman" (Genesis 3:15), He is never lost sight of in the Old Testament as the Promised One. In all of its 39 books, there is the air of expectancy. *Someone* is coming! Hundreds of years before Christ came God graciously unveiled Him. It has been asserted that exclusive of numberless typical predictions of Him, that "the prophecies and references to Christ in Old Testament Scriptures, which are expressly cited in the New Testament, either as predictions fulfilled in Him, or as provisions applied to Him, number not less than 333." Therefore, it is with utmost confidence that we can affirm that He dominates the Old Testament, and is before us as the One who is the Substance of its messages and the Goal of its hope. All its avenues lead to Him. He is the Golden Thread binding the diverse books together, giving them an amazing *unity . . .*

We have our Lord's own authority for the fact that He is the Key to Old Testament promises, profiles and pictures.

"In the volume of the book it is written of Me." Hebrews 10:7

Commenting on this statement Martin Luther asked, *"What book*, and *what person?"* The Reformer answered his own question – "There is only one Book – the Bible; and only one Person – Christ." The pre-eminent purpose then, of the pre-eminent Book, is to magnify and extol the pre-eminent Person of our blessed Lord.

"Beginning at Moses and all the prophets, he expounded unto them *in all the Scriptures* the things concerning *Himself . . .* All things must be fulfilled, which were written *in the Law of Moses*, and *in the Prophets*, and *in the Psalms* concerning *me."* Luke 24:27, 44

Christ and the Bible then are inseparably wedded. The Written Word and the Living Word are one. Christ is the secret of the structural, historical, prophetical, doctrinal and spiritual aspects of the Bible. Christ gives value to the Bible, not the Bible to Christ. Dr. A. J. Gordon of Boston, well known in his day for his Christ-honoring ministry, used to tell of a jig-saw puzzle he once gave his children when he went away on a short preaching mission. Returning, Dr. Gordon went to see how the young folks had progressed with the puzzle and was surprised they had finished it so soon.

"How did you manage to put it together so quickly?" asked the father.

"Because we found a man on the back," was the joyful reply.

In our quest for Truth, whether we deal with facts or figures, Prophecies or Promises, let us realize that the secret of interpretation is to find the Man Christ Jesus on the back, because all Scripture exists to reveal Him. It brings sustenance to our souls when we discover how Christ and the Scriptures are similarly presented. For instance, think of these features –

Both are called the *Word of God.*
"His name is called the Word of God."
Revelation 19:13; John 1:1
"The Word of God, which liveth and abideth for ever." I Peter 1:23

Both are spoken of as *Truth.*
"I am the Truth." John 14:6 "Full of . . . truth." John 1:14
"All thy commandments are truth." Psalm 119:151

Both are described as *Light.*
"In Him was life, and the life was the light of men." John 1:4; 8:12
"The law is light." Proverbs 6:23; Psalm 119:105

Both are defined as *Life.*
"I am the Life."
John 14:6; John 5:11, 20
"Holding forth the word of life. . . ."
Philippians 2:16

Both are praised as being *precious.*

"Unto you which believe he is precious." I Peter 2:7

"Exceeding great and precious promises." II Peter 1:4

Both are extolled as being *wonderful*.

"His name shall be called Wonderful." Isaiah 9:6

"Thy testimonies are wonderful."
Psalm 119:129

Both are written of as being *tried*.

"I lay in Zion . . . a tried stone."
Isaiah 28:16

"The word of the Lord is tried."
Psalm 18:30

Both are presented as being *everlasting*.

"The Lord shall endure for ever."
Psalm 9:7

"The Word of the Lord endureth for ever." I Peter 1:25.

Both are said to contribute to our *salvation*.

"Born of God." I John 5:18. "Born again . . . by the word of God."
I Peter 1:23

"Wherefore he is able to save."
Hebrews 7:25

"The engrafted word which is able to save your souls." James 1:21

Both are channels of *cleansing*.

"The blood of Jesus Christ his Son cleanseth us from all sin."
I John 1:7

"Now are ye clean through the word."
John 15:3

Both are able to *sanctify*.

"By which will we are sanctified."
Hebrews 10:10

"Sanctify them through thy truth."
John 17:17

Both can result in *healing*.

"He healed them." Matthew 4:24

"He sent his word and healed them."
Psalm 107:20

It was this complete identification between Christ and the Bible that constrained Joseph Hart to write:

> The Scriptures and the Word
>   Bear one tremendous name,
> The Living and the Written Word
>   In all things are the same.

Dr. W. Graham Scroggie gives us this profitable analysis:

The Old Testament – the Christ of Prophecy

The Gospels – the Christ of History

The Acts and the Epistles – the Christ of Experience

The Revelation – the Christ of Glory

Old Testament prophecies of Christ prove that "the Incarnate Word was in the Prophetic Word which is a perpetual witness to His divine origin and character." Prophecies are actually promises. Any divine prophecy is a promise that God will perform all that the prophecy presents. Generally speaking, these Messianic promises set forth these aspects of the Promised Person –

His Royal and Human Pedigree

His Deity and Uniqueness

His Redemptive and Governmental Program

We herewith cite these outstanding Old Testament Messianic promises along with their New Testament performances.

As the eternal Son of God –

Promise – "Thou art My Son: this day I have begotten Thee." Psalm 2:7

Performance – "He shall be called the Son of the Highest. . . . He shall be called the Son of God." Luke 1:32, 35

"Thou art my Son." Acts 13:30-39

As the Seed of the woman –

Promise – "I will put enmity between thee and the woman, and between thy seed and her seed: it shall bruise thy head, and thou shalt bruise his heel." Genesis 3:15

Performance – "When the fulness of the time was come, God sent forth his Son, made of a woman." Galatians 4:4

"Mary was found with child of the Holy Spirit." Matthew 1:18

As the Seed of Abraham –

Promise – "I will establish my covenant between me and thee and thy seed after thee." Genesis 17:7

"In thy seed shall all the nations of the earth be blessed." Genesis 22:18

Performance – "Now to Abraham and his seed were the promises made."
Galatians 3:16

"Jesus Christ . . . the son of Abraham." Matthew 1:1

As the Seed of Isaac –

Promise – "In Isaac shall thy seed be called." Genesis 21:12, 13

Performance – "Of whom it was said, That in Isaac shall thy seed be called."
Hebrews 11:16-19

As the Seed of David –

Promise – "The Lord hath sworn in truth unto David; he will not turn from it: Of the fruit of thy body will I set upon thy throne." Psalm 132:11

Performance – "Jesus Christ, the Son of David." Matthew 1:1

"I will raise unto David a righteous Branch." Jeremiah 23:5

"David . . . Of this man's seed hath God according to his promise raised unto Israel a Saviour, Jesus."

Acts 13:23

"Jesus Christ . . . of the seed of David." Romans 1:3

As to His Birth at a set time –

Promise – "The sceptre shall not depart from Judah, nor a lawgiver from between his feet, until Shiloh come."

Genesis 49:10

"After threescore and two weeks shall Messiah be cut off, but not for Himself." Daniel 9:24-26

Performance – "It came to pass in those days." Luke 2:1

"When the fulness of the time was come God sent forth his Son, made of a woman." Galatians 4:4

As to His Birth of a virgin –

Promise – "Behold a virgin shall conceive, and bear a Son, and shall call His name Immanuel." Isaiah 7:14

Performance – "When as His mother Mary was espoused to Joseph, before they came together, she was found with child of the Holy Spirit." Matthew 1:18

As to His being named Immanuel.

Promise – "Call His name Immanuel."

Isaiah 7:14

Performance – "They shall call his name Immanuel, which being interpreted is, God with us."

Matthew 1:22, 23

As to His coming in the Lord's Name –

Promise – "Blessed be he that cometh in the name of the Lord."

Psalm 118:26

Performance – "Blessed is he that cometh in the name of the Lord; Hosanna in the highest."

Matthew 21:9

As to His Birth in Bethlehem –

Promise – "But thou Beth-lehem Ephratah, though thou be little among the thousands of Judah, yet out of thee shall He come forth unto Me that is to be ruler in Israel." Micah 5:2

Performance – "Now when Jesus was born in Bethlehem of Judea in the days of Herod the King."

Matthew 2:1; Luke 2:4-6

As to those adoring Him –

Promise – "The kings of Tarshish and out of the isles shall bring thee presents . . . offer gifts." Psalm 72:10

Performance – "The wise men . . . presented unto Him gifts."

Matthew 2:1-11

As to the massacre of infant innocents –

Promise – "A voice was heard in Ramah, lamentation, and bitter weeping . . . for her children." Jeremiah 31:15

Performance – "Then Herod . . . slew all the children . . . Rachel weeping for her children." Matthew 2:16-18

As to His being called out of Egypt –

Promise – "I loved him, and called my Son out of Egypt." Hosea 11:1

Performance – "Out of Egypt have I called my Son." Matthew 2:15

As to His forerunner –

Promise – "Prepare ye the way of the Lord, make straight in the desert a highway for our God." Isaiah 40:3

"My messenger, he shall prepare the way before me." Malachi 3:1

Performance – "John the Baptist . . . The voice of one crying in the wilderness, Prepare ye the way of the Lord."

Matthew 3:1,3; Luke 1:17

As to His Anointing with the Spirit –

Promise – "Anointed with the oil of gladness above thy fellows."

Psalm 45:7

"The Spirit of the Lord shall rest upon him." Isaiah 11:2

"The Spirit of the lord God is upon me." Isaiah 61:1

Performance – "God giveth not the Spirit by measure unto him."

John 3;34

"God anointed Jesus of Nazareth with the Holy Spirit and with power."

Acts 10:38

As to His likeness to Moses as a Prophet –

Promise – "The Lord thy God will raise up unto thee a prophet . . . like unto me." Deuteronomy 18:15

Performance – "A prophet . . . like unto me; Him shall ye hear."

Acts 3:20-23

As to His Melchizedek succession –

Promise – "Thou art a priest for ever after the order of Melchizedek."

Psalm 110:4

Performance – "So also Christ . . . Thou art a priest for ever after the order of Melchizedek."

Hebrews 5:5, 6

As to His entrance into public ministry –

Promise – "To preach good tidings unto the meek . . . to bind up the broken-hearted . . . to proclaim the acceptable

year of the Lord." Isaiah 61:1-2
Performance—"Jesus came to Nazareth
. . . opened the book. He found the
place where it was written . . . I
must preach the kingdom of God to
other cities also." Luke 4:16-21, 43
As to His Galilean ministry—
Promise—"In Galilee of the nations.
The people that walked in darkness
have seen a great light." Isaiah 9:1, 2
Performance—"Jesus departed into
Galilee . . . Galilee of the Gentiles,
The people which sat in darkness saw
a great light." Matthew 4:12-17, 23
As to His entrance into Jerusalem—
Promise—"Shout, O daughter of Jerusalem, Behold thy king cometh unto
thee." Zechariah 9:9
Performance—"When they drew nigh
unto Jerusalem . . . Behold thy King
cometh unto you, meek, and sitting
upon an ass." Matthew 21:1-11
As to His appearance in the Temple—
Promise—"I will fill this house with
glory." Haggai 2:7, 9
Performance—"Jesus went into the
temple of God."
                   Matthew 21:12; Luke 2:27-32
As to His accepted poverty—
Promise—"As a root out of dry
ground: he hath no form nor comeli-
ness: and when we shall see him,
there is no beauty that we should desire him." Isaiah 53:2
Performance—"Jesus said . . . The Son
of Man hath nowhere to lay his head."
                                      Luke 9:58
As to His manifest meekness—
Promise—"He shall not cry, nor lift
up, nor cause his voice to be heard
in the street." Isaiah 42:2
Performance—"Jesus . . . charged them
that they should not make him known
. . . He shall not strive."
                                  Matthew 12:15-21
As to His tender compassion—
Promise—"He shall gently lead those
that are with young. . . . A bruised
reed shall he not break."
                            Isaiah 40:11; 42:3
Performance—"Jesus . . . a bruised
reed shall he not break."
                                  Matthew 12:20
"Touched with the feeling of our in-
firmities." Hebrews 4:15
As to His guileless nature—
Promise—"Because he had done no
violence, neither was any deceit in

his mouth." Isaiah 53:9
Performance—"Who did no sin, neither
was guile found in his mouth."
                                   I Peter 2:22
As to His unflagging zeal—
Promise—"The zeal of thine house hath
eaten me up." Psalm 69:9
Performance—"His disciples remembered that it was written, The zeal
of thine house hath eaten me up."
                                   John 2:17
As to His parabolic teaching—
Promise—"I will open my mouth in
a parable, I will utter dark sayings
of old." Psalm 78:2
Performance—"I will open my mouth
in parables: I will utter things which
have been kept secret." Matthew 13:35
As to His miraculous ministry—
Promise—"God will come . . . Then
the eyes of the blind shall be opened,
and the ears of the deaf shall be un-
stopped." Isaiah 35:4-6
Performance—"Jesus answered . .
The blind receive their sight."
                     Matthew 11:4-6; John 11:47
As to His undeserved reproach—
Promise—"A reproach of men, and
despised of the people. All that see
me shall laugh me to scorn. Because
for thy sake I have borne reproach
. . . The reproaches of them that
reproached thee fall upon me."
                            Psalm 69:7, 9, 26
Performance—"Even Christ pleased
not himself; but as it is written, The
reproaches of them that reproached
thee fell on me." Romans 15:3
As to His rejection by His brethren—
Promise—"I am become a stranger unto
my brethren, and an alien unto my
mother's children."
                     Psalm 69:8; Isaiah 63:3, 5
Performance—"He came unto his own,
and his own received him not . . .
His brethren therefore said unto him,
Depart hence." John 1:11; 7:3
"Neither did his brethren believe in
him." John 7:5
As a Stone of stumbling to the Jews—
Promise—"He shall be . . . a stone
of stumbling and for a rock of of-
fence to both the house of Israel."
                                   Isaiah 8:14
Performance—"They stumbled at that
stumbling stone." Romans 9:32, 33
"A stone of stumbling, and a rock
of offence." I Peter 2:8

As to His encounter with Jewish hatred –
Promise – "They that hate me without a cause are more than the hairs of my head." Psalm 69:4
"To him whom man despiseth, to him whom the nation abhorreth."
Isaiah 49:7
Performance – "He that hateth me . . . They have both seen and hated both me and my Father." John 15:23-25
As to His rejection by Jewish rulers –
Promise – "The stone which the builders refused is become the head stone of the corner." Psalm 118:22
Performance – "Jesus saith unto them . . . The stone which the builders rejected, the same is become the head of the corner."
Matthew 21:42
As to His rejection by Jews and Gentiles –
Promise – "The kings of the earth set themselves, and the rulers take counsel together, against the Lord, and his anointed." Psalm 2:1, 2
Performance – "Pilate and Herod were made friends together for before they were at enmity between themselves."
Luke 23:12
"The Gentiles, and the people of Israel, were gathered together."
Acts 4;25-29
As to His betrayal by a friend –
Promise – "Yea, mine own familiar friend in whom I trusted, which did eat of my bread, hath lifted up his heel against me." Psalm 41:9
"It was not an enemy that reproached me . . . it was those . . . mine acquaintance." Psalm 55:12-14
Performance – "He that eateth bread with me hath lifted up his heel against me . . . One of you shall betray me."
John 13:18, 21
As to the disciples forsaking Him –
Promise – "Smite the shepherd, and the sheep shall be scattered abroad."
Zechariah 13:7
Performance – "I will smite the shepherd, and the sheep of the flock shall be scattered abroad." Matthew 26:31
As to His sale for thirty pieces of silver –
Promise – "They weighed for my price thirty pieces of silver." Zechariah 11:12
Performance – "They covenanted with him for thirty pieces of silver."
Matthew 26:15
As to Judas' successor –
Promise – "Let his days be few; and

let another take his office."
Psalm 109:8
Performance – "His bishopric let another take." Acts 1:20
As to the price of the potter's field –
Promise – "I took the thirty pieces of silver, and cast them to the potter in the house of the Lord."
Zechariah 11:13
Performance – "They took counsel, and bought with them the potter's field to bury strangers in." Matthew 27:7
As to His extreme suffering –
Promise – "I am poured out like water, and all my bones are out of joint: my heart is like wax: it is melted in the midst of my bowels." Psalm 22:1-21
Performance – "Being in an agony he prayed more earnestly: and his sweat was as it were great drops of blood falling down to the ground."
Luke 22:44
As to His substitutionary sufferings –
Promise – "Surely he hath borne our griefs . . . our sorrows . . . our transgressions . . . our iniquities . . . our peace." Isaiah 53:4, 5
Performance – "Even as the Son of man came not to be ministered unto but to minister, and to give his life a ransom for many." Matthew 20:28
As to His demeanor in suffering –
Promise – "He was oppressed, and he was afflicted, yet he opened not his mouth." Isaiah 53:7
Performance – "But Jesus held his peace." Matthew 26:63.
"He answered nothing . . . He answered him to never a word."
Matthew 27:12, 14
As to His being smitten on the cheek –
Promise – "They shall smite the judge of Israel with a rod upon the cheek."
Micah 5:1
Performance – "They took the reed, and smote him on the head."
Matthew 27:30
As to His marred visage –
Promise – "His visage was so marred more than any man, and his form more than the sons of men." Isaiah 52:14
Performance – "Then came Jesus forth, wearing the crown of thorns and the purple robe." John 19:5
As to His scourging –
Promise – "I gave my back to the smiters, and my cheeks to them that plucked off the hair: I hid not my face from

shame and spitting." Isaiah 50:6

Performance – "Some began to spit on him, and to cover his face, and to buffet him." Mark 14:65

"Then Pilate therefore took Jesus, and scourged Him." John 19:1

As to His being nailed to a cross –

Promise – "They pierced my hands and my feet." Psalm 22:16. "He was afflicted." Isaiah 59:7

Performance – "Where they crucified him, and two others with him."
John 19:18
"Except I shall see in his hands the prints of the nails." John 20:25

As to His being forsaken of God –

Promise – "My God, my God, why hast thou forsaken me? Why art thou so far from helping me and from the words of my roaring?" Psalm 22:1

Performance – "About the ninth hour Jesus cried with a loud voice saying . . . My God, My God, why hast thou forsaken me?" Matthew 27:46

As to the mocking of His crucifiers –

Promise – "They shoot out the lip, they shake the head, saying, He trusted in the Lord that he would deliver him: let him deliver him, seeing he delighted in him." Psalm 22:7, 8

Performance – "They that passed by wagged their heads saying . . . He trusted in God: let him deliver him now, if he will save him."
Matthew 27:39-44

As to the opiates offered Him –

Promise – "They gave me also gall for meat: and in my thirst they gave me vinegar." Psalm 69:21

Performance – "They gave him vinegar to drink mingled with gall . . . One . . . took a sponge, and filled it with vinegar . . . and gave him to drink."
Matthew 27:27, 48

As to His parted garments –

Promise – "They parted my garments among them, and cast lots upon my vesture." Psalm 22:18

Performance – "That it might be fulfilled which was spoken by the prophet, They parted my garments among them, and upon my vesture did they cast lots." Matthew 27:35; John 19:24

As to His intercession for His crucifiers –

Promise – "He made intercession for the transgressors." Isaiah 53:12

Performance – "Then said Jesus, Father, forgive them; for they know not what they do." Luke 23:34

As to His ultimate death –

Promise – "He hath poured out his soul unto death." Isaiah 53:12

Performance – "Jesus when he had cried out again with a loud voice, yielded up the ghost." Matthew 27:50

As to His bones not being broken –

Promise – "Neither shall ye break a bone thereof." Exodus 12:46

"He keepeth all his bones; not one of them is broken." Psalm 34:20

Performance – "They break not his legs . . . A bone of him shall not be broken." John 19:32-36

As to His being pierced –

Promise – "They shall look upon me whom they have pierced."
Zechariah 12:10

Performance – "One of the soldiers pierced his side . . . They shall look on him whom they pierced."
John 19:34, 36

As to His burial –

Promise – "He made his grave with the wicked, and with the rich in his death."
Isaiah 53:9

Performance – "When Joseph had taken the body . . . he laid it in his own new tomb." Matthew 27:57-60

As to His deliverance from corruption –

Promise – "Thou wilt not . . . suffer thine Holy One to see corruption."
Psalm 16:10

Performance – "Neither wilt thou suffer thine Holy One to see corruption . . . Neither did his flesh see corruption." Acts 2:27, 31

As to His glorious Resurrection –

Promise – "For thou wilt not leave my soul in hell (or grave)." Psalm 16:10

"The dead shall live . . . my dead body shall they arise." Isaiah 26:19

Performance – "He is not here but risen . . . The Lord is risen indeed." Luke 24:6, 31; I Corinthians 15

As to His Ascension –

Promise – "Thou hast ascended on high, thou hast led captivity captive."
Psalm 68:18

Performance – "He was parted from them, and carried up into heaven."
Luke 24:51

"He was taken up." Acts 1:9

As to His presence at God's right hand –
Promise – "The Lord said unto my Lord, Sit thou on my right hand."
Psalm 110:1
Performance – "The Lord said unto my Lord, Sit thou on my right hand."
Matthew 22:44
"Sat down on the right hand of the majesty on high." Hebrews 1:3

As to the exercise of His priestly office –
Promise – "He shall be a priest upon his throne." Zechariah 6:13
Performance – "Christ . . . who also maketh intercession for us."
Romans 8:34; Hebrews 7:25

As to His being the Chief Corner Stone –
Promise – "A precious corner stone, a sure foundation."
Isaiah 28:16; Psalm 118:22
Performance – "Behold I lay in Zion, a chief corner stone elect, precious."
I Peter 2:2, 7; Matthew 21:42

As to His being King in Zion –
Promise – "Yet have I set my king upon my holy hill of Zion." Psalm 2:6
Performance – "The Lord God shall give unto him the throne of his father David." Luke 1:32; John 18:33-37

As to His salvation of Gentiles –
Promise – "A root of Jesse . . . to it shall the Gentiles seek." Isaiah 11:10
"He shall bring forth judgment to the Gentiles." Isaiah 42:1
Performance – "That on the Gentiles was poured out the gift of the Holy Spirit." Acts 10:45; John 10:16

As to His righteous Government –
Promise – "The sceptre of thy kingdom is a right sceptre. Thou lovest righteousness." Psalm 45:6, 7
Performance – "My judgment is just."
John 5:30
"In righteousness he doth judge."
Revelation 19:11

As to His universal dominion –
Promise – "He shall have dominion also from sea to sea, and from the river unto the ends of the earth." Psalm 72:8
"There was given unto him dominion, glory, and a kingdom, that all people, nations, and languages should serve him." Daniel 7:14
Performance – "At the name of Jesus every knee should bow . . . that every tongue should confess that Jesus is Lord." Philippians 2:10, 11

As to the perpetuity of His Kingdom –
Promise – "The throne of David . . . to establish it with judgment and with justice from henceforth even for ever."
Isaiah 9:7
"His dominion is an everlasting dominion." Daniel 7:14
Performance – "He shall reign over the house of Jacob for ever: and of his kingdom there shall be no end." Luke 1:33

One cannot meditate upon the foregoing selected Messianic citations without realizing how the Lord Jesus Christ permeates the Bible. How wonderfully He is woven into the texture of such a divine revelation! He is everything from A to Z in the Bible. These first and last letters of the Greek alphabet are used by Jesus Himself – "I am the First and the Last" (Revelation 22:13). Whether we think of creation, revelation, redemption, or experience, Christ is "the beginning and the end" and all in between. How expressive are the lines of T. W. H. Myers, particularly of the Bible –

"Christ is the end, for Christ was the beginning, Christ was the beginning for the end is Christ."

The Person Promised

Having considered evidence of the indissoluble union between Christ and Scripture, let us now think of the Promised One Himself. Throughout Scripture there are hundreds of profiles of our blessed Lord, both direct and implied, and it takes them all to declare all that He is in Himself, and all that He is willing to accomplish, in and through His own true followers. C. H. Spurgeon used to say that no matter what gate of Scripture he opened, he always scampered over the fields to Christ. May such a holy scamper be ours! To look for Christ in all we read is to add delight to our Bible study. Cameos of our Lord are before us in truth and type, in promise and parable, in fact and figure, and as we now look at a few of His conspicuous profiles may our love for Him be intensified and our zeal to serve Him be quickened by the Holy Spirit, who ever glorifies Christ. Latent in every profile of our adorable Lord is a promise of all we can appropriate by faith.

He Is God's Display Cabinet

"Him God raised up the third day, and shewed him openly; Not to all the people, but unto witnesses chosen before of God."
Acts 10:40; I Corinthians 15:1-8

Raised again from the dead according to the Old Testament promise, God boldly revealed His Son to worshiping hearts. How glad they were when they saw their Lord! Something lived in every hue of Him, Christless eyes could not see.

"But he could not be hid." Mark 7:24
"But if our gospel be hid, it is hid to them that are lost: In whom the god of this world hath blinded the minds of them which believe not, lest the light of the glorious gospel of Christ, who is the image of God, should shine unto them." II Corinthians 4:3, 4

Jeremy Taylor wrote of the believer as "a mysterious cabinet of the Trinity." How true it is of Jesus, heaven loves to display, that He is a "mysterious cabinet." As a show-case of gems in a jeweler's establishment indicates the precious goods that can be purchased within so, reverently, Jesus is heaven's show case. God is not ashamed nor afraid to expose His victorious Son to view. "He shewed him openly." Proudly He displayed Him as the Conqueror of Satan, sin and sickness. The Father loved to draw attention to His Son who could not be holden of death, who was raised from the dead by the power of God. Such a conquest cannot be hid.

Are we showing Him openly? Or are we ashamed to confess we are His – hiding such a Light under a bushel? If He has undisturbed sway over our lives then, all unconsciously, they will exhibit His wealth and worth. His beauty will be seen in all of our ways. Read John 14:8-12; Colossians 1:15, 16; Hebrews 1:3.

He Is Our Abiding Companion

"My presence shall go with thee, and I shall give thee rest. And he said unto him, If thy presence go not with me, carry us not up hence." Exodus 33:14, 15
"Lo, I am with you alway, even unto the end . . ." Matthew 28:20
"Jesus himself drew near, and went with them." Luke 24:15
"I will never leave thee nor forsake thee."
                                    Hebrews 13:5

The promises of the Lord are all precious, and He will not be slack fulfilling any one of them. There is something, however, better than His promises, namely, His realized Presence. Amid all the separations life may hold for us, there is One of whose companionship we can be certain until traveling days are done. "Thou remainest." As the Lord promised Moses that He would favor His servant with His presence, so we can experience how the same Presence is our glory,

yielding us support under losses, crosses, and bereavements. The Lord was with Moses and he persevered, with Joshua, and he conquered, with David, and he reached the throne, with Paul, and he was more than a conqueror. No one and nothing can act as a substitute for the Lord's abiding presence. Did not Jesus say that the Father and He would make their abode with us? We have the gracious promise that He will never leave us, never leave us alone. Anyone but the Lord would have left us long ago, but He is so long-suffering. We can rely on Him to go through the whole journey of life with us and to be our Support in every trial, our Comfort in every sorrow, our Deliverer in every danger. He will never forsake His redeemed people for His great name's sake. Having loved His own, He will love and accompany them unto the end. Read Exodus 33:12-23; Matthew 28:16-20; Hebrews 13:5-8.

He Is Heaven's Breach Repairer

"The repairer of the breach, the restorer of paths to dwell in." Isaiah 58:12
"To bind up the broken-hearted."
                                    Isaiah 61:1
"He healeth the broken in heart, and bindeth up their wounds." Psalm 147:3
"The Lord bindeth up the breach of his people." Isaiah 30:26

Actually, Isaiah gives us two profiles of Him whose skilful hands can bind up that which is broken. He is a *Repairer* and *Restorer*. Who else could have repaired the terrible breach sin caused between God and man? But at Calvary the breach was repaired and the broken-hearted Saviour provided a world bruised and broken by sin with a perfect salvation. Now there is access into the holiest of all by His blood.

Have you a breach that needs to be repaired? Is there some torn relationship in home, business or church that requires mending? Then why not seek the aid of the heavenly Repairer whose loving, tender hands can bring broken ends together and make fellowship whole again? Read Ephesians 2:11-18; Colossians 1:20-23; Genesis 33:8-15.

He Is Our Eternal Refuge

Outstanding among the numerous metaphors describing the provision and preservation the Lord makes possible for His own are those portraying Him as our Refuge, Tower, Pavilion, Fortress, Hiding Place and Covert. As these glimpses of Him are manifold we cite a few of the more prominent references, leaving the reader to pursue this

cameo of Him with the aid of a concordance.
"The Eternal God is our refuge."

Deuteronomy 33:27
"My high tower and refuge."

II Samuel 22:3
"I will be a refuge for the oppressed."

Psalm 9:9
"Because the Lord is our refuge."

Psalms 14:6; 46:1; 48:3
"In thy wings will I make my refuge."

Psalms 57:1; 59:16; 62:7
"O Lord, my refuge in affliction."

Jeremiah 16:19
"The name of the Lord is a strong
tower." Proverbs 18:10
"God is my high tower."

II Samuel 22:3; Psalms 18:2; 144:2
"The Lord is my fortress."

Psalms 18:2; 31:3; 91:2; 144:2
"He shall hide me in His pavilion."

Psalm 27:5
"He shall keep them secretly in a pa-
vilion." Psalm 31:20
"Trust in the covert of his wings."

Psalm 61:4
"A man shall be a covert from the
tempest." Isaiah 32:2

Common to all these promises is the thought
that in the Lord we have an impregnable
Fortress or Hiding Place, and that in Him we
are safe and unassailable. Six cities of refuge
were provided by Joshua for Israel (Joshua
20), and any Jew slaying another unwittingly
could flee to one of these cities and know what
it was to be safe from the avenger all the
time the high priest lived. Because our Refuge is the Great High Priest, we have the assurance that ours is an eternal security (John
10:28). In Him we are both saved and safe.

How comforting it is to know that when pursued by sin, doubt, perplexity and sorrow,
that we have in Him who became the Man of
Sorrows a safe hiding place! "Other refuge
have I none." Having such an Omnipotent
Person as our Fortress or Tower, what ade-
quate protection is ours against all foes
and fears assailing us. Read Deuteronomy
33:24-29; Joshua 20; Psalms 46; 48.

He Is Our Imperishable Rock

Similar to the similes of our Lord we
have just considered is that of the conspicuous one – The Rock. Such a figure of
speech is used to express durability, shade,
rest, and refreshment.

"Trust ye in the Lord for ever: for
in the Lord Jehovah is everlasting
strength." Isaiah 26:4
The Hebrew of the last two words reads

"the Rock of Ages–" the phrase which inspired Toplady to write his famous hymn.
"Thou blest Rock of Ages, I'm hiding in
Thee." A writer describes many of the
ancient buildings of Oxford University as being "leprous with age," meaning that many
of them are seriously crumbling away. But
the Lord, as our Rock, is unchanged by
age. He cannot crumble or decay, but is
ever new and whole.

"He is our Rock, his work is perfect
. . . just and right is he."

Deuteronomy 32:4
"The Lord liveth; and blessed be my
rock; and exalted be the God of my
salvation." II Samuel 22:47
Because He is perfect, just and righteous,
we can trust the salvation He has provided
to offer sufficient protection. In Him and
upon His merit and atoning grace we rest,
and know that shelter from wrath is ours.

"The Lord is my rock and my fortress." Psalm 18:2
Altogether there are seven profiles of our
Lord in this great promise. Perhaps it was
this verse which inspired Martin Luther to
write that renowned battle hymn of his, "A
Mighty Fortress Is Our God." No evil can
reach the soul sheltering in this Rock-
Fortress.

"Be thou my strong rock." Psalm 31:2
Since He is a strong Rock, in Him we have
a strong and safe defense from ourselves,
the world and the devil. The storms may
rage, but He who has endured throughout
the ages will shield us. So we pray,

"Lead me to the Rock that is higher
than I" (Psalm 61:2).
How blessed it is to realize that He is higher
than all our needs, the cares and crises
of this world, and the threats of men.

"The shadow of a great rock in a weary
land." Isaiah 32:2
To desert travelers a massive rock affords
much needed protection from the burning
sun, in the shadow it casts. At such, the
traveler can shelter and rest. One such
traveler writes, "Journeying one night in
the wilderness of Central Africa in a section plagued by ravenous beasts, we found
no place of safety till we came to the
shadow of a great rock where we sat down
with our backs to the rock and building
at our feet a fire, found rest and refreshing
for the next day's still weary journey."

As travelers in this desert below, when
our strength fails and we feel that we cannot go on further, how refreshing it is to

lean back in His shadow and upon Him. To the Israelites, the smitten rock represented refreshment to slake their thirst in their wilderness pilgrimage. Out of the rock there flowed the life-giving water.

"They drank of the rock that followed them; and that rock was Christ."

I Corinthians 10:4

There are those expositors who suggest that the water supernaturally supplied as Moses smote the rock (Numbers 20), flowed on and followed the people all through their forty years of wandering. This we do know, that Christ, as our spiritual Rock, follows us over life's journey so that at any moment we can stoop and drink and live. Read Deuteronomy 32:12-20; Psalm 18; I Corinthians 10:1-6.

He Is the Expert Carpenter

"The carpenter encourageth the goldsmith." Isaiah 41:7

"The carpenter stretched out his rule." Isaiah 44:13

"Is not this the carpenter?" Mark 6:3; Matthew 13:55

What a suggestive profile of Him, who came to mend a world broken by sin! If legend be true, Joseph died when Jesus was but a lad, and the burden of the carpenter's shop in Nazareth fell upon His young shoulders. If this be so then at that bench we have "the toil of divinity, revealing the divinity of toil." For something like fifteen years Jesus earned His own bread, and it may be, the bread of others, by the strength of His arms and the sweat of His brow. Can we not imagine how the farmers would bring their implements for repair, and how perfectly He would mend the broken goods of the housewives and the broken toys of children? Thus, He was not removed from the toils and trials of life, for He touched it at every point.

How fitting it was to give Him wood and nails when He died! As the Carpenter, He was used to them, as He made and mended things. More than ever, this old broken world of ours needs the encouraging, skillful workmanship of the Carpenter of Galilee. If only men would allow His pierced hands to repair all that sin and war have broken, what a different world ours would be! Can it be that yours is a broken life, or a broken home? If so, then why not call in heaven's Carpenter to repair the damage? He is willing and able to mend the broken things of life, and His service is free. This High Priest

can repair any breach. Read II Kings 3:5; 22:5, 6; II Chronicles 24:9-12; Ezra 9:5-9; Isaiah 61:1-3; Ephesians 2:10.

He Is the Affluent One

The same Lord over all is rich unto all that call upon him. Romans 10:12

"Rich, yet for our sakes he became poor." II Corinthians 8:9

"Rich in mercy . . . The exceeding riches of His grace . . . The unsearchable riches of Christ." Ephesians 2:4, 7; 3:8

"Now unto him that is able to do exceeding abundantly above all that we ask or think." Ephesians 3:20

"The fulness of him that filleth all in all." Ephesians 1:23

These, and many other similar promises, emphasize the great truth of our Lord's affluence. We read of this one and the other being the richest person in the world. But the wealth of any man fades into insignificance alongside Christ's vast possessions. Who is rich in every sphere? What inexhaustible treasures are His, and how He loves to share them with His own. Giving never impoverishes Him, just as withholding could not enrich Him. Paul, who was poor yet possessed all things, was forever drawing on his Master's bank. The apostle proves what a large heart Jesus has, and that there are no barriers or restrictions when it comes to the scattering of His wealth. Jew and Gentile can share in His bounty. Further, giving with Him is not conditioned by the merit of the recipient. All is so freely given because of His grace. There is one condition that must be observed, however, if we desire to possess His bounty – we must call upon Him. Is spiritual impoverishment ours? If so, believe His promise and claim all you need from His inexhaustible riches of grace.

He Is the Unselfish Christ

"Even Christ pleased not himself." Romans 15:3

"I do those things that please my Father." John 8:29

"He saved others: himself he cannot save." Matthew 27:42

"Let him deny himself, and take up his cross, and follow me . . . Whosoever shall lose his life . . . shall find it." Matthew 28:24, 25.

Our gracious Lord not only preached self-abnegation, He practiced it. He never pleased Himself. Self-interests were never first with Him. In His life and death, self was crucified. Had He wished He could have saved Himself from the cross. He could have come down from it and with a word destroyed

His enemies. But had He saved Himself from those final agonies there would have been no salvation for a sinning race. Thus, because He stayed on the cross and died, we can live. With this virtue in mind, Paul gives it a very personal and practical application. If we bear His name, then we must reflect His character. Like the Master we, too, must ever strive to please God, and please our weak neighbours for their good to edification.

Alas! too many of us please ourselves. God is not first, but self. Selfish like, we live for the gratification of our own desires, forgetting the nobler path of self-denial. If we live for self we live in vain. If we live for God we live again. "*I* live, yet not *I*, but Christ liveth in me" (Galatians 2:20).

He Is the Invincible Lion

"Judah couched as a lion."
Genesis 49:4; Numbers 24:9
"Blessed be he that . . . dwelleth as a lion." Deuteronomy 33:20, 22
"He was unto me . . . as a lion in secret places." Lamentations 3:10
"I will be unto Ephraim as a lion." Hosea 5:14
"The lion of the tribe of Judah . . . hath prevailed." Revelation 5:3

Grouped around the Tabernacle, each of the twelve tribes had their own particular ensign or flag. That which distinguished Judah was the *Lion* – an ensign Britain also uses. Jesus came of the tribe of Judah, and came as its true Lion. As the king of beasts, the lion is known for its strength, fearlessness, and invincibility. Satan is also likened unto a lion – a roaring lion, seeking whom he may devour (I Peter 1:8). But he was no match for Judah's Lion. At Calvary, all the hatred of hell and of men was heaped upon Christ, as heaven's strong Lion, but He prevailed.

The promise is that we, too, can tread upon the lion (Psalm 91:13). Why should we dread any foe? Satanic forces may combine to tear us to pieces, but standing over us is God's majestic lion, who waits to deal with any who would dare to touch His redeemed ones, who also, through grace can be as bold as a lion (Proverbs 28:1).

He Is the Word We Can Handle

"Howbeit there is a kinsman nearer than I." Ruth 3:12
"Handle me, and see." Luke 24:39
"Nor handling the word of God deceitfully." II Corinthians 4:2
"Our hands have handled the Word of Life." I John 1:1

John's contact with the Lord he dearly loved was blessed and intimate. He had leaned upon the bosom of Jesus and is always spoken of as the disciple Jesus loved. After His Resurrection, our Lord invited His somewhat frightened followers to handle Him, or touch and hold Him, and prove clearly that He was no spirit or apparition, but the very same Jesus whose human form was so familiar to them. "Handle Me, and see."

John, more than the others, knew what it was to have such close contact with Jesus. He it is who gives us several glimpses of the intimate fellowship he enjoyed. He had heard Him, seen Him with his own eyes, and shared some of His innermost secrets. No wonder John goes on to say that having seen Him, he lived to show Him to others. While our actual hands have not touched Him, yet ours can be the touch of faith. As the Spirit makes Him real through the Word we can lay hold of Him, and make Him our very own. Sometimes we receive a package marked *Handle With Care.* The contents are either fragile or valuable and must not be thrown about carelessly. As we handle Jesus, it must be with pure hands.

He Is Tranquillity Supreme

"A son . . . a man of rest."
II Chronicles 22:9, 10
"In the world . . . tribulation . . . In me . . . peace." John 16:33
"I will give you rest." Matthew 11:28
"This is my rest for ever." Psalm 132:14

All that Christ is in Himself holds for us the promise of participation in His attributes so that it becomes true in more senses than one –

"As he is, so are we, in this world."
I John 4:17

While the first reference above depicts the nature of Solomon's reign, surely a greater than Solomon is here. A Son was born of Mary, who came as a Man of Rest, ever tranquil in Himself and therefore able to give rest to others. As the result of Calvary, He has rest from all His enemies; and the trend of prophecy proves that He will yet give peace and quietness to Israel in the days of His Kingdom, and also peace to the world.

It is impossible to meditate upon the earthly life of Jesus without being impressed with His serenity of soul. He was never ruffled, harassed or put out. Nothing ever disturbed Him. He was never worried, flurried or agitated. His was a "hidden calm repose."

He could sleep in a storm. Can we say that this rest of faith is ours?

He Is the Mighty Prophet

"This is Jesus the prophet of Nazareth in Galilee." Matthew 21:11

"Of a truth this is the prophet."
John 7:40

"The Lord God will raise up unto thee a prophet from the midst of thee, of thy brethren, like unto thee."
Deuteronomy 18:15, 20-22

"Jesus . . . a prophet mighty in deed and word." Luke 24:19

Coming as the promised Prophet, Jesus was without honor in His own country. The nation of which He was part would not recognize Him as the Sent-One of God. Yet the marks of a true Prophet were His. Works, words and ways testified to His authority as the Representative of God. Prophets of old brought God down to men and raised men up to God. Before God and all the people, Christ revealed Himself to be a mighty Prophet.

In ancient times, prophets functioned in a two-fold direction. They were *foretellers* and *forthtellers*. As the first, they were "seers," declaring a message for an age beyond their own. By the Spirit's inspiration they testified coming events beforehand (I Peter 1:11). As the second, they were "preachers" proclaiming stirring messages for their own times. And how their utterances blistered the consciences of men and nations! Jesus, as a prophet, was both a *Foreteller* and a Forthteller. He more than any other prophet, lifted the veil and revealed things to come. But for those around Him in the days of His flesh, He had wonderful words of life. Without fear or favor He told forth the whole counsel of God.

He Is Our Burden-Bearer

"Cast thy burden on the Lord, and he shall sustain thee." Psalm 55:22

"Thou layest the burden of all this people upon me." Numbers 11:21

"I removed his shoulder from the burden." Psalm 81:6

"His burden shall be taken off his shoulder." Isaiah 10:27; 14:25

"My burden is light." Matthew 11:30

"Bear ye one another's burdens, and so fulfil the law of Christ." Galatians 6:2

Promised as a Burden-Bearer, when He came, Jesus went about lifting the loads of others. It was His law or custom to shoulder the heavy loads of others. He carried our sorrows. He bore the sin of the world. Our iniquities were laid on Him. That heavy burden of the cross He was made to carry, was our load, but He died as our Substitute. What do we know, experimentally, about casting our burdens upon our burden-bearing Lord? There is no load too heavy for Him to shoulder, now that He has borne the heaviest load of all, namely, the sin of the world.

He Is Omnipotence in Action

"That he might make his mighty power to be known." Psalm 106:8

"Praise him in the firmament of his power." Psalm 150:1

"The Son of Man hath power."
Matthew 9:6

"All power is given unto me."
Matthew 28:18

"Upholding all things by the word of his power." Hebrews 1:3

Promises of the manifestation of divine power are too numerous to mention. Among the captivating profiles of Jesus, is that of the human personification of divine power. He moved among the sons of men as the Son of God having all power to enforce His Word. Christ's omnipotence extends to every realm. He upholds, not some things, but *all* things, by His authoritative word. Where the word of a king is, there is power; and our Sovereign Lord holds the reins of creation, redemption, prophecy, history and our personal life in His all-powerful hands.

Sometimes we hear despondent hearts moan, "Why, the world is going to pieces!" Broken, it may be, by wickedness and war, but it is still among the *all things* upheld by His power. He overrules, as well as rules, and is therefore able to make even the wrath of man to praise Him. Coming to the narrower world of our own individual life, do we believe that He is able to uphold all things by the Word of His power? As of old, He can still speak, and it is done. Trouble comes when we take the control out of His hands and transfer it to our own hands. The Almighty One, alone, is the sole Source of our strength.

He Is the Worthy Lamb

"God will provide himself a lamb."
Genesis 22:8

"Your lamb shall be without blemish."
Exodus 12:5; I Peter 1:19

"He was brought as a lamb to the slaughter." Isaiah 53:7

"Behold the lamb of God." John 1:29

"Worthy is the lamb that was slain."
Revelation 5:12

The last book of the Bible is "The Book of the Lamb." In it, Christ is spoken of more than twenty times, in different connections, as the *Lamb*. Promised as the divine Lamb, in the fulness of time, Christ was provided as the Lamb and John reminds us of how the vast angelic host, along with the living creatures and elders exalt His worthiness as God's Lamb. How worthy He was as the Lamb, freshly slain, to receive –*power*. All power is now His in heaven and on earth. *Riches*–whether spiritual or material. The wealth in every mine belongs to Him. *Wisdom*–eternal wisdom. He became Wisdom personified. *Strength*–ultimately the strength of the strongest fails, but His remains undiminished. *Honor*–every knee, says Paul, will yet acknowledge Him as Lord. *Glory*–with His ascension there came the restoration of the glory He had prayed for (John 17:1-4). *Blessing*–the fulness of every promise is now His, and if we have been washed in the blood of this Lamb then all He is, and has, can become ours.

He Is the Redeemer-Interpreter

"He opened to us the Scriptures . . . . Then opened he their understanding, that they might understand the Scriptures."

Luke 24:32, 45

"He that openeth and no man shutteth."

Revelation 3:7

"Thou art worthy to take the book, and to open the seals thereof."

Revelation 5:9

The scene before us in *The Revelation* is that of the worshipful host, singing the new song in which the Lamb is extolled for His worthiness to take the book and open its seals. Such ability and authority to open this book of judgment, or any other book of the Bible, are based upon His redemptive work. "For thou wast slain." It was as the Crucified, Risen One that He was able to expound in all the Scriptures the things concerning Himself. His life, death and resurrection enabled Him to prove that all the Old Testament promises concerning Him had been fulfilled.

If we would know how to take the Book and open its seals then a death is necessary. Sin and self must be slain, if authority is to be ours to lead others into the truth. Are we worthy to take the Book and handle its sacred truths? Is ours the practice corresponding to all its promises and precepts? Disobedience closes the door of Revelation. Implicit obedience is ever the key to open its seals.

He Was a Wizard of Words

"I have esteemed the words of his mouth more than my necessary food."

Job 23:12

"The words of the pure are pleasant words." Proverbs 15:26

"The words of a man's mouth are as deep waters." Proverbs 18:4

"The words I speak unto you . . . they are life." John 6:63

"The words of our Lord Jesus Christ."

I Timothy 6:3

As the Prince of Preachers, Jesus knew how to seek out acceptable words. His words were as goads and as nails fastened in a sure place (Ecclesiastes 12:10-11). Paul reminds us that His words were sound and wholesome–wonderful words of life. His lips were like lilies, dropping sweet-smelling myrrh; and like a thread of scarlet uttering comely speech (Song of Solomon 4:3; 5:13, 16). What would we not give to listen to the gracious words proceeding out of His mouth! And every word of His is a royal promise to believe and prove.

Vain and idle words never left those lips of His, into which grace had been poured. Every word was a benediction. Jesus was never verbose. He was never guilty of using unnecessary words or exaggerated speech. Each word, as it left His lips, was rightly coined and timed and was shot as an arrow to a given target. Life would be saved much of its friction if only we would set a watch upon our lips, and utter words acceptable in His sight (Psalm 19:14).

He Was the Homeless One

"There was no room for them in the inn." Luke 2:7

"The Son of Man hath not where to lay his head." Matthew 8:20

"We have no certain dwelling place."

I Corinthians 4:11

"Let us go forth therefore unto him without the camp . . . Here we have no continuing city." Hebrews 13:13, 14

Tragic, is it not, that He who created all the materials homes are built of, was yet denied a home of His own? He, Himself, declared that He was less fortunate than the foxes with their sheltering holes and the birds with their warm nests. The people could retire to their comfortable homes at eventide, but there was no one with decency enough to offer Jesus a bed. Out He went to the Mount of Olives, where with the darkness of the night as a blanket to cover Him He spent the lonely hours in fellowship with His Father, in whose bosom He had dwelt. What privation, ostracism and humiliation He willingly endured for our sakes.

How privileged we are to offer Him our hearts as His home and our homes as His dwelling place! How blest we are when He takes up His abode with us!

He Is the Provider of Songs

"The Lord is my . . . song." Exodus 15:1; Psalm 118:14; Isaiah 12:2

"He hath put a new song in my mouth."
Psalms 40:3; 96:1; Revelation 5:3

"I will praise the Lord with a song."
Psalm 69:30

"Ye shall have a song, as in the night."
Isaiah 30:29

"God who giveth songs in the night."
Job 35:10

"At midnight Paul and Silas . . . sang praises unto God." Acts 16:25

"Psalms and hymns and spiritual songs, singing with grace in your hearts unto the Lord." Colossians 3:16

"When they had sung an hymn."
Matthew 26:30

Is it not encouraging to have these promises of a singing heart and of the Lord as our constant Song? Many of us do not have musical voices yet we have learned how to make melody in the heart to the Lord (Ephesians 5:19).

We know that Jesus was one of that singing company that went out to the Mount of Olives. He had just broken bread with His disciples, and having explained the mystic significance of the bread and the wine, He turned aside from the chamber and went out with His own into the dark night. Where were their footsteps taking them? Their faces were set toward the Garden of Golgotha. But the marvel was that they faced the sorrowful future with a song. Surely, it is not irreverent to suggest that Jesus Himself led the chorus that night. Possibly some of those *Degree Psalms* (120-134) He knew so well, formed the hymn they sang. This we know, He came that we might have songs in the night, and therewith prove that pain need not silence praise.

He Is the One the Saints Remember

"Remember the Lord, which is great and terrible." Nehemiah 4:14

"Remember that thou magnify his work, which men behold." Job 36:24

"We will remember the name of the Lord." Psalm 20:7

"Those that remember thee in thy ways."
Isaiah 64:5

"Remember that Jesus Christ was raised." II Timothy 2:8

"Remember the words spoken of Jesus."
Jude 17

"If I do not remember thee, let my tongue cleave to the roof of my mouth."
Psalm 137:6

"He shall bring all things to your remembrance." John 14:26

"This do in remembrance of me."
I Corinthians 11:25

The Lord assures us that He ever remembers us. He never forgets the humblest of His own. But how gracious it is of Him to ask us to remember all He accomplished on our behalf, and to attach so many rich promises to such a remembrance. Truly, every day ought to be a *Remembrance Day* in a believer's life. Knowing how faulty the human memory is, and how soon we are apt to forget, Christ has left us blessed tokens of remembrance.

Dr. J. R. Miller tells the story of a mother who had lost her longed-for baby, and who would constantly go to a drawer, and taking out the baby's shoes and clothes, fondly remember the little one taken from her by death. Jesus left us the bread and wine, bidding us to remember His dying love as we partake of the elements. If, "Remembrance is a paradise from which we need not be driven," then our unfailing remembrance of Jesus Christ, and of all He accomplished on our behalf, can bring us a daily paradise. He always has us in mind. "Yet will I not forget thee." May we never be guilty of forgetting Him who died in our room and stead!

He Is the Ever-Present, All-Sufficient Friend

"The Lord spake unto Moses face to face, as a man speaketh to his friend."
Exodus 33:11

"A friend loveth at all times."
Proverbs 17:17, 18

"There is a friend that sticketh closer than a brother." Proverbs 18:24

"Faithful are the wounds of a friend."
Proverbs 27:6, 9, 17

"This is my beloved, and this is my friend." Song of Solomon 5:16

"The Lord be with you all."
II Thessalonians 3:16

How privileged we are to be called the Lord's "friends," and to have Him as our never-absent, all-bountiful Friend. Promises of His nearness to relieve and bless abound in Scripture. He is always at hand, cheering us: yes, and reproving us as any true

Friend should. As the "Lord," our Friend, He is the Master of every situation and able to undertake accordingly. How comforting it is to know that He is with us all. All? Then this includes *you*, no matter how simple, ordinary and inconspicuous you may be. All He is and has can be appropriated by each and all. How tragic it is when we neglect to take advantage of the abundant provision of such a constant Friend, or when we become His enemy through courting the friendship of the world! (James 4:4).

He Is Our Unerring Guide

"He will be our guide, even unto death."
Psalm 48:14

"Thou art the guide of my youth."
Jeremiah 3:4

"I will guide thee with mine eye."
Psalm 32:8

"Thou shalt guide me with thy counsel." Psalm 73:24

"By the springs of water shall he guide them." Isaiah 49:10; Psalm 23:2, 3

"The Lord shall guide thee continually."
Isaiah 58:11

"To guide our feet into the way of peace." Luke 1:79

"He will guide you into all truth."
John 16:13

"The Lord . . . guided them on every side." II Chronicles 32:22

"He guided them by the skilfulness of his hands." Psalm 78:52, 72

"My sheep hear my voice . . . and they follow me." John 10:27

Promises associated with divine guidance are as prolific as they are precious. How the Lord loves to reveal Himself as a safe and sufficient Guide – all of which He is! What more pleasing profile of Him could we have as we step out upon the untrodden pathway of the future! We have no conception of what the morrow may hold for us, but He has. If we do not know the way we certainly know the Guide, and with our hand in His, all will be well. Has He not promised to guide us continually, even unto death? May grace be ours to live near this infallible Guide who never takes a wrong turning, and who is our best Guardian at all times.

He Is the Ever-Welcome Visitor

"God will surely visit you."
Genesis 50:24; Exodus 13:19

"What is man . . . that thou shouldest visit him?" Job 7:17, 18

"O visit me with thy salvation."
Psalm 106:4

"God did at the first visit the Gentiles."
Acts 15:14

"Thou hast visited me in the night."
Psalm 17:3

"The day-spring hath visited us."
Luke 1:68, 71; 7:16; Psalm 65:9

"Behold I stand at the door."
Revelation 3:20

Some visitors are always wlecome; others are not. When certain people visit us we wish they would prolong their stay; with others, the sooner they leave the better. Have you ever thought of the Lord as a *Visitor*, whose visits are sometimes gladly welcomed and at other times unwanted? When He visited the sin of His people upon them they resented such a visitation. Yet how warmly received He was when He came down to visit and deliver them (Exodus 13:19). Are you grateful that as the Dayspring from on high, He visited the world with His salvation? We Gentiles would have been of all men most miserable had He not visited us (Acts 15:14).

A dreadful day of visitation awaits this godless earth, and His visit in judgment will not be an appreciated one. Do we welcome the daily visits of the Lord? Have we the joy of opening the door to Him every morning? Praise Him, He is not content to visit us! He comes to abide (Luke 24:29). Visiting our hearts in salvation, He closes the door behind Him, and remains.

He Is Our Guiding Star

"There shall come a star out of Jacob."
Numbers 24:17

"We have seen his star in the east."
Matthew 2:2, 9, 10

"Till the day-star arise in our hearts."
II Peter 1:19

"I will give him the morning star."
Revelation 2:28

"I am the bright and morning star."
Revelation 22:16

There is no more beautiful promise and profile of our Lord than this. Balaam's prophecy of Christ as a Star concerns His return to set up His kingdom. At His birth, the brilliant star, called *His Star*, guided the wise men to His feet. In the promise of Moses, Christ is the Star Himself, to guide His people Israel. With undimmed light and radiance, He will provide direction to all who follow Him.

As the Morning Star, He is the promise of a better day both for Israel and the world at large. The old philosopher has told us to "hitch our wagon to a star." We never lose our way when the wagon of our life is hitched to Him, who is the ever-shining Star.

He Is Our Commanding Captain

"In their rebellion appointed a captain."
Nehemiah 9:14

"As captain of the host of the Lord am I now come." Joshua 5:14

"David became a captain over them."
I Samuel 22:2

"God himself is with us for our captain." II Chronicles 13:12

"The captain of their salvation."
Hebrews 2:10

The word Paul uses for "captain" means princely, leader or originator, that is, one who initiates and carries through. It is the same word used of "author" (Hebrews 12:2). It was Jesus, the Captain, who initiated and carried through our salvation. The Man Joshua saw, and who declared Himself to be the Captain of the Lord's host, was doubtless Christ Himself in theophanic form. Immediately Joshua recognized the superior command of the One intercepting him and wisely accepted His divine leadership. The hosts of Israel stood before the gateway of the Promised Land. No swords were drawn on their part, yet Jericho and all the giants of the land were forced to submit as Israel went forth under the leadership of the divine Captain.

As the Captain of our Salvation, Christ valiantly met the satanic foe and triumphed gloriously over him. Now, as our Prince-Leader, He waits to lead us out of bondage into liberty. As our Captain, His orders must be obeyed, and His plans gladly executed.

He Is a Provident Husband

"For thy maker is thy husband."
Isaiah 54:4, 5

"I am an husband unto them, saith the Lord." Jeremiah 31:32

"I have espoused you to one husband . . . Christ." II Corinthians 11:2

"As a bride adorned for her husband."
Revelation 21:2

What a tender promise this is of our Lord as a Husband. Isaiah speaks of Him both as *Maker* and *Husband*. He is our Maker. We speak of those who are self-made, but actually there are no self-made men for He is the Maker of us all. Would that men knew how to bow before their marvelous Maker! As the Husband, He is related both to Israel and His Church, both of whom

are referred to as His *wife*. How unfaithful both have proved themselves to be, but as the Husband, He will win faithless ones back to His side and will forgive their evil wanderings (Isaiah 54:5-10).

But is there not another phase of His husbandhood? Has He not promised to be as a Husband to the widow, and as a Father to the fatherless? Has death robbed you of a loving, provident husband? Is your heart and home terribly vacant? Take courage; the Lord is near who offers to fill that dear one's place, and be more to you than ever a husband could be.

He is a Pitying Father

"A father of the fatherless . . . is God."
Psalm 68:5

"Like as a father pitieth his children, so the Lord pitieth them that fear him."
Psalm 103:13

"Whom the Lord loveth he correcteth: even as a father the son in whom he delighteth." Proverbs 3:12

"His name shall be called everlasting Father." Isaiah 9:6

"I am a father to Israel." Jeremiah 31:9

"Our Father which art in heaven."
Matthew 6:9

"Your Father knoweth what things ye have need of." Matthew 6:8

"Abba, Father, all things are possible unto thee." Mark 14:36

"We have received the Spirit of adoption whereby we cry Abba, Father."
Galatians 4:6

The Bible abounds in promises of the tenderheartedness of God. How kind, gentle, understanding He is. Yes, and His gentleness is able to make us great. Jesus exhibited this divine tenderness, especially as He died, when grace was His to pray for His enemies. What a precious portrait of the Lord this is – *Father*. His tenderness and patience as such carried Him to great lengths to extricate His wayward children out of trouble. All strength, wisdom and provision are His as the Father of the fatherless. While in the sense of creation, He is the Father of all, we cannot look up into His face and speak to Him as our heavenly Father unless Christ is our Saviour. The Fatherhood of God is based upon the Saviourhood of His beloved Son. Once regenerated, we have the right to cry, "Abba, Father." It was His compassion as a Father that led Him to surrender His son for the redemption of a prodigal world. Are you resting in a heavenly Father's pity and provision?

He is a Rejoicing Bridegroom

"As a bridegroom coming out of his chamber." Psalm 19:5

"As a bridegroom decketh himself with ornaments." Isaiah 61:10

"As a bridegroom rejoiceth over the bride, so shall thy God rejoice over thee."
Isaiah 62:5

"Can the children of the bridechamber mourn so long as the bridegroom is with them?" Matthew 9:15

"Behold, the bridegroom cometh."
Matthew 25:1-10

"He that hath the bride is the bridegroom." John 3:29

Here is another gracious promise, and likewise a sacred glimpse into the tender heart of our Lord. How does a bridegroom rejoice over his bride? In the first place, union is the consummation of love. The church is the Bride (Revelation 22:17), and by the Spirit, believers are joined to Christ, in a union death cannot break. As the bridegroom claims his bride at the altar, so Christ has possessed us forever. As the bridegroom promises to endow the bride with all his worldly goods, so Christ makes His own the sharers of all He possesses.

For His Church, the joyful marriage of the Lamb is not far away. How He will rejoice over His Bride when He returns for her future bliss! And what joy will be the Bride's when she eyes not his garment, but her dear Bridegroom's face. With His own around Him, and eternally united to Him, He will see of the travail of His soul and be satisfied.

He Is a Blessed Sanctuary

"Israel was his sanctuary." Psalm 114:2

"He shall be for a sanctuary."
Isaiah 8:14

"A glorious high throne from the beginning is the place of our sanctuary."
Jeremiah 17:12

"Yet will I be to them a little sanctuary." Ezekiel 12:16

"The waters issued out of the sanctuary." Ezekiel 47:12

"An habitation of God through the Spirit." Ephesians 2:22

How good of God it is to promise Himself as a Sanctuary! In the Old Testament He provided a temple for His people; in the New Testament He has a redeemed people as His temple. But the wonder of wonders is that He also is our Temple. How consoling it is to know that amid all the turmoil of the street, busy cares of the home,

hurry and confusion of our modern life, we have a little sanctuary "closer than breathing, nearer than hands or feet." No sanctuary ever surpassed the Temple Solomon built. For its marvel and magnificance it was incomparable, yet where is it today? But, blessed be our Sanctuary, He abides.

While it is fitting to gather in a house of worship, whether it be a simple or cathedral-like structure, the sphere makes little difference. Many dear shut-in ones cannot journey to a sanctuary of stone, yet hidden from earth's eyes they can take advantage of Him who offers Himself as a Sanctuary. Blessed, is it not, to have a *Person* as well as a place we can draw nigh to?

He Is the Undiscouraged Christ

"Wherefore discourage ye the heart of the children of Israel?" Numbers 32:7, 9

"Fear not, neither be discouraged."
Deuteronomy 1:21, 28

"He shall not fail nor be discouraged."
Isaiah 42:4

"Your children . . . lest they be discouraged.
Colossians 3:21

"David encouraged himself in the Lord his God." I Samuel 30:6

"He . . . encouraged them to the service of the house of the Lord." II Chronicles 35:2

What a most unusual promise of Christ Isaiah gives us! "He shall not . . . be discouraged." Because of this virtue He is the Lord of all encouragement. The Bible warns us against discouragement. The spies, save Joshua and Caleb, "Discouraged the heart of the children of Israel." But the One Isaiah portrays will never be discouraged until His final task is accomplished. Then what satisfaction will be His. Slowly, yet surely, He is reaching His goal to set judgment on the earth.

Think of Him while among men. Surely He had enough to discourage His heart. What with the failure of His own and hostile foes around Him, it would have been human if He had faltered by the way. But no, courageously He set His face toward Jerusalem. No one and nothing could keep Him back. Presently it would seem as if the world is altogether out of His control, but He is not discouraged, for He knows His day is coming. What an incentive He provides for our discouraged hearts! How apt is the exhortation of Marcus Aurelius –

"Be not uneasy, discouraged, or out of humour because practice falls short of precept in some particulars.

If you happen to be beaten, return to the charge!"

He Is the Incomparable Storyteller

"Never man spake like this man." John 7:46

"I turned to see the voice that spake." Revelation 1:12

"Without a parable spake he not unto them." Matthew 13:34

"Why speakest thou unto them in parables?" Matthew 13:10-16

"He began to speak unto them by parables." Mark 12:1

The parables of the Master were actually His promises of accomplishment. But what a matchless storyteller Jesus was! For naturalness, simplicity, conciseness and effect, His parables, metaphors and illustrations are without equal. If a parable is an earthly story with a heavenly meaning, then Jesus knew how to draw from a wide range of subjects, parables so full of spiritual import.

The story of the husbandman smote the consciences of those Pharisees who listened to it with deep conviction. They knew Christ had spoken the parable against them, and had it not been for His popularity among the common people who heard Him gladly, they would have taken Him prisoner. Christ's answer as to the question of tribute caused the people to marvel and to wonder. Those who are called to preach and teach the Word of Life, can learn much from Jesus as to the art of illustration. He never used stories merely for the sake of telling them. They were always windows to let the light in.

How tempted we are to pursue this absorbing aspect of our study and dwell upon *all* the figures of speech, direct and implied, the Bible employs to show forth His greatness, grace and goodness! Alas! however, such a fascinating meditation would require far more space than the size of this volume allows. We sincerely trust that the glimpses given of Him, who is the divine Promiser, will whet the reader's appetite for a fuller coverage of His titles and names. Feeling that it might prove helpful for Bible lovers to have a condensed list of the testimony to the Person and perfections of our adorable Redeemer, we set forth the following table, taken from Nevin's *Guide to the Oracles*, which although far from exhaustive will prove sufficient to prove that He is able to fulfil His manifold promises on behalf of His people.

Adam ....I Corinthians 15:45
Advocate .... I John 2:1
Amen .... Revelation 3:14
Angel ....Isaiah 63:9; Malachi 3:1
Ancient of Days .... Daniel 7:22
Anointed .... Psalms 2:2; 45:7

Apostle ....Hebrews 3:1
Apple Tree ....Song of Solomon 2:3
Author and Finisher of Faith Hebrews 12:2
Babe .... Luke 2:16
Beginning of the Creation
  of God .... Revelation 3:14
Begotten of the Father .... John 1:4
Beloved .... Song of Solomon 1:13;
                                        Ephesians 1:6
Bishop .... I Peter 2:25
Blessed .... I Timothy 6:15
Branch .... Zechariah 3:8
Brazen Serpent .... John 3:14
Bread of life .... John 6:48-51
Bridegroom .... Matthew 9:15
Bright Morning Star .... Revelation 22:16
Brightness of the
  Father's glory .... Hebrews 1:3
Bundle of Myrrh .... Song of Solomon
Camphire .... Song of Solomon 1:14
Captain .... Joshua 5:14;
                                        Hebrews 2:10
Child .... Isaiah 9:6
Chosen .... Matthew 12:18;
                                        Luke 23:35
Christ .... Matthew 1:16; 2:4
Consolation of Israel .... Luke 2:25
Corner-stone ...... Ephesians 2:20; I Peter 2:7
Covenant .... Isaiah 13:6
Counsellor .... Isaiah 9:6
Covert .... Isaiah 32:2
Creation .... Isaiah 43:15
Creditor .... Luke 7:41
Cyrus .... Isaiah 45:1
David ....Jeremiah 30:9;
                          Exodus 37:24, 25; Hosea 3:5
Day's-man .... Job 9:33
Day-star .... II Peter 1:10
Deliverer .... Romans 11:26
Desire of all nations .... Haggai 2:7
Dew .... Hosea 14:5
Diadem .... Isaiah 62:3
Door of sheepfold .... John 10:7
Eagle .... Deuteronomy 32:11
Elect .... Isaiah 13:1
Emmanuel .... Matthew 1:23
Ensign .... Isaiah 6:10
Eternal Life .... I John 5:20
Everlasting Father .... Isaiah 9:6
Express image, etc. .... Hebrews 1:3
Faithful witness .... Revelation 1:5;
                                        3:14; 19:11
Fatted calf .... Luke 15:23
Father of eternity .... Isaiah 9:6
Feeder ....Isaiah 60:11
Fir-tree .... Hosea 14:8
First-begotten .... Revelation 1:5
First fruits .... I Corinthians 15:23

First and last .... Revelation 2:8
Flesh .... John 1:14
Foundation .... Isaiah 28:16
Fountain .... Zechariah 13:1
Forerunner .... Hebrews 6:20
Friend of sinner .... Matthew 11:19
Gift of God .... II Corinthians 9:15
Glory of God .... Isaiah 60:5
Glorious Lord .... Isaiah 33:21
God ....John 1:1; Romans 9:5;
                I Timothy 3:10; I John 5:20
Gold .... Song of Solomon 5:11
Golden altar .... Revelation 8:3
Governor .... Matthew 2:6
Gracious .... I Peter 2:3
Guide .... Psalm 68:14
Habitation .... Psalm 91:9
Harmless .... Hebrews 7:26
Head of the church .... Colossians 1:18
Heir of all things .... Hebrews 1:2
Help .... Psalms 33:20; 40:17
Heritage .... Isaiah 58:14
Highest .... Psalm 18:13; Luke 1:32
High Priest .... Hebrews 3:1; 7:1
Most High .... Luke 8:28
Holy one of God .... Mark 1:24
Holy one of Israel .... Isaiah 41:14
Holy child .... Acts 4:30
Honeycomb .... Song of Solomon 4:11
Hope ....Acts 28:20; I Timothy 1:1
Horn of Salvation .... Psalm 18:2
Husband .... Isaiah 54:5; Jeremiah 31:32
I Am ....Exodus 3:14; John 8:58
Image of God .... Hebrews 1:3
Immanuel .... Isaiah 7:14
Immortal .... I Timothy 1:17
Inheritance .... Ezekiel 44:28
Invisible .... I Timothy 1:17
Israel .... Isaiah 44:21; 49:3
Jacob .... Isaiah 41:8; 44:1, 5
Jah .... Psalm 68:4
Jehovah .... Isaiah 26:4; 40:3
Jerusalem .... Song of Solomon 4:4
Jesus ...... Matthew 1:21; I Thessalonians 1:10
Judah .... Revelation 5:5
Judge ....Micah 5:1; Acts 10:42
King .... Matthew 21:5; 25:34
Ladder .... Genesis 28:12
Lamb .... John 1:19; Revelation 5:6
Lawgiver .... Isaiah 23:22; James 4:12
Leader .... Isaiah 55:4
Light .... John 1:9; 8:12; 12:46
Life .... John 14:6
Lion of the tribe of Judah ...... Revelation 5:5
Living God .... I Timothy 3:15
Long Suffering .... Exodus 34:6
Lord ....Romans 1:3; Revelation 17:14
Lovely .... Song of Solomon 5:16

Man ....Acts 17:31; I Timothy 2:5
Master .... Matthew 8:19; 23:6
Mediator .... I Timothy 2:5
Melchisedec .... Hebrews 7:1
Merciful .... Hebrews 2:17
Messenger .... Malachi 2:7; 3:1
Messiah .... Daniel 9:25; John 1:41
Michael .... Daniel 12:1; Revelation 12:7
Mighty God .... Isaiah 9:6; 63:1
Minister .... Hebrews 8:2
Morning Star ...... Revelation 2:28; 22:16
Moses .... Acts 3:22
Nazarite .... Matthew 1:23
Offspring of David .... Revelation 22:16
Only-begotten .... John 1:14
Ointment .... Song of Solomon 1:3
Passover .... I Corinthians 5:7
Plant of renown .... Ezekiel 34:29
Potentate .... I Timothy 6:15
Prince .... Acts 3:15; 5:31
Prophet .... Luke 4:19; Acts 3:22
Propitiation .... I John 2:2; 4:10
Power of God .... I Corinthians 1:24
Purifier .... Malachi 3:3
Physician .... Matthew 9:12
Polished shaft .... Isaiah 40:2
Priest .... Hebrews 4:14; 7:26
Ransom .... I Timothy 2:6
Reaper .... Revelation 14:15
Redeemer .... Isaiah 59:20; 60:16
Resurrection .... John 11:25
Refiner .... Malachi 3:3
Refuge .... Isaiah 25:4
Righteousness .... Jeremiah 33:6
Rock .... Deuteronomy 32:15;
                I Corinthians 10:4
Rod and branch .... Isaiah 11:1
Root of David .... Revelation 22:16
Roe and hart .... Song of Solomon 2:9
Rose of Sharon ....Song of Solomon 2:1
Ruler in Israel .... Micah 5:2
Sacrifice .... Ephesians 5:2
Salvation .... Luke 2:30
Samaritan .... Luke 10:33
Sanctification .... I Corinthians 1:30
Sanctuary .... Isaiah 8:14
Seed of Abraham .... Galatians 3:29
Seed of David .... II Timothy 2:8
Seed of the woman .... Genesis 3:15
Second man .... I Corinthians 15:47
Servant .... Isaiah 42:1, 19; 44:21
Shepherd .... John 10:11; Hebrews 13:20
Shield .... Genesis 15:1; Psalm 18:35
Shiloh .... Genesis 49:10
Solomon .... Song of Solomon 3:7; 8:11, 12

Promises Relative to the Christian Scriptures

An outstanding, characteristic feature of

the Bible is that it is not only a Book laden with divine promises for Christian pilgrims, but that it also contains a multitude of descriptions and emblems of itself, each of such being a latent promise. These manifold references the Bible uses of itself proclaim what God is prepared to do in us, for us, and through us. While the prime mission of the Bible is to testify of Christ, it has no hesitation whatever in testifying of itself. The greatest minds have witnessed to the influence and integrity of "The Impregnable Rock of Holy Scripture," to quote Wm. E. Gladstone's description. What interests us in this chapter is the remarkable way the Bible extols its own virtues. It is its own best advocate.

One of the most prominent portions in which the Bible magnifies its nature and power is the marvelous acrostic Psalm— Psalm 119. Made up of 176 verses, every verse, with the exception of verses 121, 122, 132, praises the varied ministry of God's most blessed Word. How this long and noble Psalm is devoted to the praise of that Word, and what a rich aid to meditation it is! Ruskin wrote of this Psalm:

"It is strange that of all the pieces of the Bible which my mother taught me, that which cost me most to learn, and which was to my child's mind chiefly repulsive, has now become of all most precious to me in its overflowing and glorious passion of love for the law of God."

What impresses us about the Psalm is first of all its unique construction. It is an alphabetical acrostic and certainly the most remarkable of the acrostic Psalms. Doubtless it was thus composed in order to aid the saints of old in the memorizing of the Psalm. To make it easy to remember, its contents are broken up into twenty-two short divisions or sections, all the verses in each section beginning with the same letter of the Hebrew alphabet.

Another feature of the Psalm is an apparent monotony and sameness in the ever-recurring phrases which under slightly different expressions state the same fact. It is a pleasant and profitable exercise to take up these phrases and keywords of the Psalm, occurring throughout its texture, and dwell on them in all the varying lights flashed thereon by the context in each case. Here, for instance, are some of the outstanding terms preachers could use as sermon material. The play upon words is conspicuous:

Quicken – verses 25, 37, 40, 88, 149, 156, 159. These references indicate the different ways in which God is able to manifest His vitalizing power through His word. It is "The Word of Life."

Word. Unfortunately, one English term is used for two distinct Hebrew words. "Word" occurs 42 times in this Psalm – in 23 cases standing for *daba*, meaning "Word," and in 19 cases for *imrah*, meaning "saying." An example of this can be seen in verse 103 which should read "How sweet are Thy *sayings* unto my taste." As we have already pointed out both terms are related to the word *promise*. As "The Word," there is the thought of the will of the Lord as an actual utterance expressing the divine mind.

Saying. In this repeated term there is the idea of the will of God as an actual utterance of the divine mind.

Law. Here is a word setting forth the will of God as a complete code of duty for all to observe.

Way. This much used term, linked as it is to Him who came as *The Way* (John 14:6), represents the will of God as a line of conduct – a path which our feet as pilgrims may discern and tread.

Judgments. Present and final divine judgments will be according to our response to God's revealed will in His Word. This word, therefore, denotes His will as a just judicial decision.

Statutes. This further favorite term of the Psalmist carries the idea of the divine will as a decree with legal force behind it. A government statute is backed by the power of enforcement.

Commandments. Used often, this Mosaic word is scattered not only through this Psalm, but throughout the Bible as a whole and is a word implying God's will for His creatures in the form of a Father's instructions.

Precepts. In this expressive term, God's will is treated as a charge entrusted to us to keep. As we shall see, precepts and promises are closely related.

Testimonies. The Bible sounds forth its own testimony in no uncertain notes. Such a designation suggests that God's will is set forth in human language, and is fulfilled in human experience as it testifies to the truth and justice of God.

Faithfulness. How all the psalmists magnified God for His unchanging faithfulness! "Great is thy faithfulness." It is a most profitable exercise to run over all the references to God's "faithfulness" in the book of Psalms. We have the promise that God's will is reliable and eternal.

What a beneficial aspect of Bible meditation is the gathering together of the symbols it employs to describe its message and ministry, its sublimity, simplicity and sufficiency! Here are the outstanding and attractive symbols it uses of itself and which taken together constitute a claim to the divine authorship of the Bible. How full of spiritual and practical teaching are these figures of speech!

The Bible Is a Critic

"The Word of God . . . is a discerner of the thoughts and intents of the heart."

Hebrews 4:12

While the word, "discern," frequently occurs in the Bible this is the only reference in which the peculiar Greek word *Kritikos,* from which is derived our English word *critic,* is used. The adjective used signifies that which relates to judging, fit for, or skilled in, judging; hence *critical.* The Bible is critical of our thoughts and intents, meaning, its authority to discriminate and pass judgment on our thoughts and feelings. Because of the nature of the Bible the idea of it as our critic carries the promise of criticism which is just and deserved.

Presumptuous men call themselves *critics* of the Bible and sit in judgment upon it. They forget that the Bible is the infallible critic of their actions. We recognize that Biblical Criticism is of two kinds. There are those devout Hebrew and Greek scholars who bow before the authority of Scripture and who, with much patience and prayer, search the ancient manuscripts in order to give us, as nearly as possible, the actual words used by the inspired writers of old. How we praise God for the painstaking labors of such scholars! Ours is a debt of gratitude which can never be adequately repaid for many translations before us.

The other kind of critics are those who represent what is known as *Destructive Criticism.* Their activities are unlawful and fraught with the most soul-ruining and God-dishonoring consequences. These so-called *Higher Critics* endeavor to give us a revised and improved Bible. Rejecting divine inspiration, these unworthy critics doubt the accuracy of the Bible, strike out passages as being uninspired and leave us with nothing better than a piece of patched-up forgery. Such false handlers of Scripture never reveal any of its treasures nor inspire us to grasp more firmly any of its truths. How blessed we are when we refuse to sit in judgment upon the Bible, but accepting it as a holy critic, submit to its mysterious, soul-searching power!

The Bible Is As Tender Grass

"My doctrine shall drop as the rain, my speech shall distil as the dew, as the small rain upon the tender herb, and as the showers upon the grass."

Deuteronomy 32:2

"His word was in my tongue . . . as the tender grass springing out of the earth by clear shining after rain."

II Samuel 23:2, 4

Here we have a striking symbol drawn from nature of the refreshing and reviving influences of the Scriptures. What a promise of spiritual quickening there is in the truths of the Bible being able to revive and quicken our parched hearts and the dry, barren condition of the church, just as the continuous rain brings new life to fields and lawns! How we need these showers of blessing!

Such a promise of accomplishment can be found in these verses—

"Cast thy bread upon the waters: for thou shalt find it after many days."

Ecclesiastes 11:1

"As the rain cometh down . . . watereth the earth . . . so shall my word be that goeth forth out of my mouth."

Isaiah 55:10, 11

God has declared that His life-giving Word will not return unto Him void. What authority there is in the declaration, "It shall accomplish that which I please and shall prosper in the thing whereto I sent it." Here, then, is the promise to cheer our drooping spirits when we feel that our preaching of His Word is in vain—*It shall accomplish!* Then, as Sidney Collett has reminded us in his comment on the rains and snow of which Isaiah speaks: "Here are wonderful symbols for the Bible, rising like vapour from the mighty ocean of God's eternal love; wafted by the breath of His spirit over this world of ours; regarded by men as a dark cloud which seems only to mar their enjoyment; yet falling on barren hearts at all seasons with enriching showers from the bounteous hand of Him who 'sendeth rain on the just and the unjust' (Matthew 5:43). How beautiful also to remember that the *sun* and *rain* together make the *rainbow* of God's covenant promise."

The Bible Is As Seed

"The seed is the Word of God." Luke 8:11
"Incorruptible, by the Word of God."
I Peter 1:23
"That he may give seed to the sower."
Isaiah 55:10
"He that ministereth seed to the sower."
II Corinthians 9:10

The symbol of the Bible as *seed* carries with it the promise of fruitfulness and reproduction. Seed sown in good soil multiplies itself. At times we are discouraged, for the seed seems to fall on uncongenial soil. Sometimes we are guilty of the folly of scattering the seed indiscriminately. Yet our responsibility as sowers is clearly stated. We must never withhold the precious seed.

"Blessed are ye that sow beside all waters." Isaiah 32:20
"In the morning sow thy seed, and the evening withhold not thine hand: for thou knowest not whether shall prosper, either this or that, or whether they both shall be alike good." Ecclesiastes 11:6

What we must not forget is the fact that God holds us responsible for the sowing – *not for the harvest.* The latter is God's responsibility.

"I have planted, Apollos watered; but God gave the increase."
I Corinthians 3:6

The ground, however, must be duly prepared by the warmth of our love and the tears of our compassion. Then we can claim the promise of a harvest.

"He that goeth forth and weepeth, bearing precious seed, shall doubtless come again rejoicing, bringing his sheaves with him." Psalm 126:6

The Bible Is As a Sword

"The sword of the Spirit, which is the Word of God." Ephesians 6:17
"The Word of God . . . sharper than any two-edged sword." Hebrews 4:12
"The sword of the Lord, and of Gideon." Judges 7:18
"The sword . . . There is none like that: give it me." I Samuel 21:9
"My sword shall be bathed in heaven."
Isaiah 34:5

In this militant metaphor we have the promise of conquest, victory, and dominion. The Bible as our sword is the weapon we use as soldiers against spiritual foes. It was thus that Jesus used the Scriptures in His contest with Satan in the wilderness temptation. In three different ways he assailed Jesus, but all He did was to give the enemy three thrusts of the sword. The three, "It

is written," were sufficient to defeat Satan (Matthew 4:4, 7, 10). The Word as a sharp sword in the hand of good soldiers of Jesus Christ can accomplish mighty victories (II Timothy 2:15). This is the sword which pierces the conscience and leads to an awakening. It is a sharp *two-edged* sword, meaning, it can cut both ways. If the Bible does not save, then it slays. If it fails to convert, then it condemns (Acts 2:37, 41; 7:51, 54, 57). Finally, this sword bathed in heaven, signifying its divine origin, will smite with an eternal stroke all those who persist in their rejection of the Word's authority.

The Bible Is As a Hammer

"Is not my word . . . like a hammer that breaketh in pieces?" Jeremiah 23:39
"They fasten it with nails and with hammers that it moves not."
Jeremiah 10:4
"He that smootheth with the hammer."
Isaiah 41:7
"The smith . . . fashioneth it with hammers." Isaiah 44:12
"Break down . . . with axes and hammers." Psalm 74:6

The above references reveal the dual yet opposite function of a hammer – it makes and breaks. What a useful implement the hammer is in the hands of a carpenter! With it, he can unite separate fashioned pieces of wood into a chair, table or some other article. Does not the Bible as God's Hammer exercise unifying influences? Where you have a group of persons loving the Bible and intent on studying it, and above all, applying it to the daily life, there you have, not merely several individuals, but a united body, who are *one* in Christ Jesus.

The other function of the Bible, which Jeremiah illustrates, is that of breaking hard substances into pieces. Hearts are indeed hard – gospel and truth hardened – and endeavors to break them are sometimes slow and discouraging, yet in the end regular blows tell. Our solemn task is to keep on wielding the Divine Hammer, praying that God will use it to break rock-like hearts. It was thus that the Word acted in the conversion of the jailor (Acts 16:25-34). What a brutal, hard-hearted man he was! He had to be insensitive to human feelings to retain his position. He could lash the backs of prisoners until the blood oozed forth yet never turn a hair. But the Hammer struck hard on that adamant heart and out came the broken-hearted cry –

"Sirs, what must I do to be saved?"

The promise, then, in this emblem, is that in God's own way and time the mighty weapon of His Word will be effective.

The Bible Is a Fire

"Is not my word like as a fire?"
                                    Jeremiah 23:29
"His word was in mine heart as a burning fire shut up in my bones."
                                    Jeremiah 20:9
"Did not our hearts burn within us . . . while he opened to us the Scripture?" Luke 24:32
"While I was musing the fire burned; then spake I with my tongue."
                                    Psalm 39:3

Fire, being a symbol of divine holiness, divine hatred of sin, divine empowerment, holds much promise of blessing for our cold hearts. Fire destroys, and the Bible, when believed and obeyed, destroys everything alien in your life and mine. Fire purges, refines, cleanses, and the Bible is the medium of purification.

"Now are ye clean through the word I have spoken unto you." John 15:3

Fire energizes. What is the power producing the steam so necessary for the loaded train, traveling over miles of track – it is the fire around the boiler. On the day of Pentecost, the Holy Spirit came upon the disciples as fire, empowering them to turn the world upside down. Words from their tongues of fire burned their way into the cold hearts of multitudes.

The Bible Is As a Lamp

"The word is as a lamp unto my feet, and a light unto my path." Psalm 119:105
"The entrance of thy words giveth light."
                                    Psalm 119:130
"The commandment is a lamp; and the law is light." Proverbs 6:23
"The more sure word of prophecy . . . a light that shineth in a dark place."
                                    II Peter 1:19

Promises of illumination and guidance are associated with this expressive symbol of Scripture. It will be noted that the Psalmist uses the double figure of *lamp* and *light*. While we look upon these as one, yet there is a distinction. What is the use of a lamp, costly and ornamental though it may be, if there is no light within to radiate forth? The internal life is necessary to the external lamp. The Bible as a whole is the external Lamp, but without the Spirit, the Divine Light, illuminating Scripture and shining through it, it remains dark.

The darkness of the natural heart is likened to the chaos that existed on the earth before light, life and order were established but God "Who commanded the light to shine out of darkness, hath shined in our hearts" (II Corinthians 4:6; Isaiah 8:20; Acts 17:11). Such gross darkness, however, can be dispelled by the unfailing light of God's Word. "Like the star in the East, it can lighten those who seem to be furthest away, and will lead any honest seeker to Christ; like the seven-branched candlestick in the Tabernacle, it shines with a perfect light." Sooner or later all earthly lights upon which men are prone to rely, fail, while God's Lamp shines on more and more unto the perfect day.

"The word of the Lord endureth for ever." I Peter 1:25

Guidance and direction were also in the minds of the sages of old when they wrote of Scripture as a light unto our paths.

"The cloud . . . gave light by night to thee." Exodus 14:19, 20

Just as that fiery pillar marked out the way for the Israelites, so the Bible lights up the whole pathway of God's children in their wilderness journey, and in that Light of life they must walk "till travelling days are done."

The Bible Is As a Mirror

"Beholding as in a glass the glory of the Lord." II Corinthians 3:18
"A hearer of the Word . . . is like unto a man beholding his natural face in a glass." James 1:22-25

A mirror reveals and reflects. Standing before a mirror we see ourselves as we are. A mirror never lies unless it is warped like those crazy mirrors used in shows to give people a humorous distortion of their figure. The promise of a perfect revelation both of God and ourselves is ours when we accept the Bible as the divine mirror. People shrink from the Word of God, because it tells them the truth about their sin and reveals to them not what they think they are, but what God declares them to be – "guilty before Him" (Romans 3:19). A missionary tells the story of visiting a heathen village where an aged woman was recognized as its head. In order to win his way, the missionary carried with him a bag of inexpensive gifts. As he stood before the heathen chieftainess, he wondered what kind of a present he could give her and thereby gain her interest. Turning over his gifts he came across a small mirror – something the woman had never seen. Instructing her to hold it up and look at it, the missionary soon discovered his mistake. The woman was horrified as she looked at her face and flung the mirror to the ground. Poor mirror, it could not help it. It only told the truth.

Are there not those who would destroy the Bible because of the revelation it provides of their own sinful life? Coleridge said that he loved the Bible because it "found him." Yet there is no need to fear the revelation of God's mirror for what the light reveals, the blood can cleanse. Let us be among the number often recalling the wonderful tribute of Sir Walter Scott to God's imperishable Book:

> Within that awful volume lies
> The mystery of mysteries.
> Happiest they of human race
> To whom their God has given grace
> To read, to fear, to hope, to pray,
> To lift the latch, and force the way;
> And better had they ne'er been born
> Who read to doubt, or read to scorn.

The Bible Is As a Laver

"The washing of water (*laver*) by the word." Ephesians 5:26

"Now are ye clean through the word which I have spoken unto you."
                              John 15:3

"Sanctify them through thy truth."
                              John 17:17

"Wherewithal shall a young man cleanse his way? By taking heed thereto according to thy word." Psalm 119:9

"Thy word have I hid in my heart, that I might not sin against thee."
                              Psalm 119:17

How full of promised cleansing is the Laver of the Word! The very Book, which as the mirror reveals my sin, is likewise the laver showing me how every stain can be cleansed. In the outer court of the Tabernacle there stood the Brazen Altar and The Laver. After serving at the first, the Priest, having dealt with the sacrifice, had to wash his hands (work) and his feet (walk) and thereby remove all defilement as he sought to enter the Holy Place to worship God.

"Be ye clean, that bear the vessels of the Lord." Isaiah 52:11

The Bible is the medium of cleansing in that it leads us to the only fount of cleansing, namely, the precious blood of Christ (I John 1:7, 9). Too often we maintain the whole round of Christian activities, but nothing happens. Progress and power are not ours, simply because we are not fit for God to use. It is only as we keep walking

in the light as He is in the light, that His blood constantly cleanses our hearts from all that is alien to His will. The Word must first of all work *in* us, before it can be effective *through* us.

The Bible Is As Gold and Silver

"The law of thy mouth is better unto me than thousands of gold and silver."
                              Psalm 119:17

"The statutes of the Lord are . . . more to be desired are they than gold, yea, than much fine gold." Psalm 19:10

"The words of the Lord are pure words: as silver is tried in a furnace of earth, purified seven times."
                    Psalms 12:6; 119:140; Proverbs 30:5

As gold is the most costly metal we have, the reference to the Bible as *Gold* indicates the promise of preciousness. Peter speaks of its "Exceeding great and precious promises" (II Peter 1:4). The believers at Smyrna, who loved and kept God's Word were poor, materially, but rich, spiritually. "I know thy . . . poverty: but thou art rich" (Revelation 2:9). What real and lasting wealth God has provided for us in the Scriptures! Within it are riches to which the treasures of earth are as trash. The tragedy is that with so much gold at our disposal we yet live as spiritual paupers. Heirs of such abundant wealth as the Word contains, we live as children cast off without a penny to our name. O for grace to possess our vast possessions in God and in His Word!

The Bible Is As a Word

Words are the garments of thoughts. While it is true that a thought can exist in the mind without words, such a thought can only be communicated to other minds through the media of words, whether spoken or written. The Bible, therefore, as God's *Word*, is the outer expression of His inner thought. Scripture is the revelation of the divine mind. Because of the widespread use of the emblem of "The Word," it is beyond the limit of our space to cite all the references where it is employed. Over and over again it is found in the Psalms, particularly in Psalm 119. With the aid of a concordance trace the passages where "My Word"; "The Word of God"; "His Word"; "Thy Word"; "This Word" are found and you will light upon an abundance of promises revealing the grace and goodness of God.

"The word of God is quick and powerful." Hebrews 4:12

"In his word do I hope." Psalms 130:5; 148:8

"To him that trembleth at my word."

Isaiah 66:2

"This word that came from the Lord."

Jeremiah 26:1

"Thy word have I hid in my heart."

Psalm 119:11

Already we have noted the mystic union between Christ, the Living Word; and the Bible, the Written Word. It is with profound reverence that we bow before Him seeing—

"His name is called *the Word of God.*"

Revelation 19:13

The Bible, then, and Christ, through the Bible, both reveal and express the mind and purpose of God. Having and knowing the mind of God, Christ was able to declare in language men could not fail to understand the deep things of God. Think of all that is promised for our hearts in the following combination—

Both Are the Expressions of the Mind of God

The Living Word—

"The brightness of His glory and the express image of His person."

Hebrews 1:3

The Written Word—

"I have written . . . the great things of My Law." Hosea 8:12

Both Have an Eternal Existence

The Living Word—

"Jesus Christ the same yesterday, today, and for ever." Hebrews 13:8

The Written Word—

"The word of God, which liveth and abideth for ever." I Peter 1:23

Both Came As God's Messengers to Bless a Needy World

The Living Word—

"God having raised up His Son Jesus, sent him to bless you." Acts 3:26

The Written Word—

"Blessed are they that hear the word of God and keep it." Luke 11:28

Both Partake of the Human and the Divine

The Living Word—

"God was manifest in the flesh."

I Timothy 3:16

The Written Word—

"Holy men . . . spake as they were moved by the Holy Spirit." II Peter 1:21

Both Are Infallible

The Living Word—

"In Him is no sin." I John 3:5

The Written Word—

"Every word of God is pure."

Proverbs 30:3

Both Are Sources of Life

The Living Word—

"I am . . . the Life." John 14:6

The Written Word—

"The word of God is living and powerful." Hebrews 4:12

Both Are Light

The Living Word—

"I am the light of the World."

John 8:12

The Written Word—

"The commandment . . . is light."

Proverbs 6:23

Both Are Truth

The Living Word—

"I am the truth." John 14:6

The Written Word—

"Thy word is truth." John 17:17

Both Are Food for the Soul

The Living Word—

"I am the bread of life . . . of God."

John 6:35

The Written Word—

"Man doth not live by bread only, but by every word that proceedeth out of the mouth of the Lord doth man live."

Deuteronomy 8:3

Both Must Be Received Before Salvation Is Possible

The Living Word—

"As many as received Him, to them gave He power to become the sons of God."

John 1:12

The Written Word—

"Receive with meekness the engrafted word, which is able to save your souls."

James 1:21

Both Are Associated with Irreparable Loss

The Living Word—

"If ye believe not that I am he, ye shall die in your sins." John 8:29

The Written Word—

"If they hear not Moses and the prophets, neither will they be persuaded, though one rose from the dead." Luke 16:31

Both Are Despised and Rejected by the Natural Man

The Living Word—

"He is despised and rejected of men."

Isaiah 53:3

The Written Word—

"Full well ye reject the commandment of God." Mark 7:9

Both Are Able to Judge Men

The Living Word—

"He will judge the world in righteousness, by that man whom he hath ordained." Acts 17:31

The Written Word—

"The dead were judged out of those things which were written in the books." Revelation 20:12

We come now to those emblems related to food, indicating as they do, the promise of sustenance. Job and Jeremiah could confess—

"I have esteemed the words of his mouth more than my necessary food." Job 23:12

"Thy words were found, and I did eat them." Jeremiah 15:16

If only the spiritually-starved multitudes could discover the nourishment the Bible affords! When an awakened soul cries, "I perish with hunger," then in the Word he finds food convenient for his soul. Food is of very varied kinds. There are four items necessary for our physical and spiritual maintenance which we can group under the title—

The Bible Is As Food

"I have fed you with milk." I Corinthians 3:2

"Such as have need of milk . . . he is a babe." Hebrews 5:12, 13

"As new born babes, desire the sincere milk of the word, that ye may grow thereby." I Peter 2:2

The Bible is so designed that many of its truths can be understood by the youngest. Within its sacred pages there is much to interest little children. The apostolic use of the emblem of milk is related to those who are young in faith and not necessarily to those who are young in years. *Milk* stands for the simplicities of the Gospel, which the youngest believer by the Spirit can grasp. Paul chided the Corinthians for the carnal condition preventing them from going on from the A.B.C. of the Gospel to its deeper, doctrinal truths. While milk is the only necessary food for a baby, it would be tragic if it tried to grow up on nothing else but milk. The day comes when the child is weaned and is given more solid fare so that it can develop a sturdy human frame.

Too many professing Christians are dwarfed. Separation from the world and dedication to God have not been thorough and so there is little taste for the deeper things of the Word. All teaching about the great and glorious doctrines of God are over their heads and consequently their souls are not nourished and built up. They never get away from rudimentary spiritual teaching. It is sometimes remarked that milk is good for infants and invalids. Feasting on "the strong meat" of the Word, may our minds never be corrupted from—

"The simplicity that is in Christ." II Corinthians 11:3

"Ye are strong and the Word of God abideth in you." I John 2:14

"I fed you with milk, and not meat." I Corinthians 3:2

"Strong meat belongeth to them that are of full age." Hebrews 5:12, 13

When Paul uses the emblem of "meat" he has in mind the idea of the more profound teaching of the Word to those who delight to follow on to know the Lord in a richer and fuller measure. Are we among those who are content to paddle along the shores, or are we in the company of those who love to launch out into the deep? The Bible is no mere milk-and-water Book. True, there are parts of it which are so simple that a little child may understand them (I Timothy 3:15), yet they contain truths so profound that the mightiest intellect cannot fully grasp. Dwell deep! (Jeremiah 49:8).

"Man doth not live by bread only, but by every word that proceedeth out of the mouth of the Lord doth man live." Deuteronomy 8:3

"Wherefore do ye spend money for that which is not bread?" Isaiah 55:1, 2

"Bread to the eater: so shall my word be." Isaiah 55:10

Jesus sanctified Scripture by appealing to them as He did when implying that the Word was "bread" (Matthew 4:4). Also Mark 12:10; John 7:42. He also spoke of Himself as the *Bread of Life* (John 6:33, 35). Such a description offers us the promise of daily sustenance. Ordinary bread is our staple food. We can do without fancy pastries, so long as we have plenty of wholesome bread. What nourishing bread is Scripture! It is to be hoped that we know what it is to cut off a large, daily slice of God's Loaf proving thereby its strengthening, satisfying qualities.

"Bread of Heaven,
Feed me till I want no more."

"How sweet are thy words unto my

taste, yea, sweeter than honey to my mouth." Psalm 119:103

"Sweeter also than honey and the honey-comb." Psalm 19:10

"Knowledge is pleasant unto thy soul." Proverbs 2:10; 24:13

"It was in my mouth as honey for sweetness." Ezekiel 3:3

This aspect of the Bible suggests the promise of pleasure and delight. How sweet and delightsome is a piece of bread covered with honey!

"What is sweeter than honey?" Judges 14:18

God satisfied His people of old with honey out of the rock (Psalm 81:16). David could write of the delight he found in God's Law (Psalm 1:2). The study of His Word then, is pleasurable as well as profitable. Do you find Bible meditation delightsome or a drudgery?

This emblem of "honey," however, breaks down at one point, for one can eat too much natural honey.

"It is not good to eat much honey." Proverbs 25:27

"Hast thou found honey? eat so much as is sufficient for thee, lest thou be filled therewith, and vomit it." Proverbs 25:16

But the redeemed soul can never have too much of God's *Honey* – the Word! He furnishes a rich table, not only with necessary food, but also sweets – luxuries of such a king that they cannot make us spiritually sick.

> God's Word is like the treasure hid,
> Or finest wheat in stock;
> 'Tis manna from the skies above,
> And honey from the rock.

There are still many promises *in* the Word itself which we can lay up in our hearts. These are listed herewith for the comfort they impart.

There Is the Promise of Profit

"That he may learn to fear the Lord his God, to keep all the words of this law and these statutes, to do them." Deuteronomy 17:19

"All Scripture . . . is profitable for doctrine, for reproof, for correction, for instruction in righteousness: That the man of God may be perfect, throughly furnished unto all good works." II Timothy 3:16, 17

There Is the Promise of Blessing

"Doers of the Word... shall be blessed." James 1:22-25

"Blessed are they that hear the Word of God and keep it." Luke 11:28

"Blessed is he that readeth, and they that hear the words of this prophecy." Revelation 1:3

There Is the Promise of Full Revelation

"The mystery . . . now is made manifest, and by the scriptures of the prophets." Romans 16:26

"Ye may understand my knowledge in the mystery of Christ . . . now revealed." Ephesians 2:4, 5

There Is the Promise of Joy

"Let the Word of Christ dwell in you richly in all wisdom . . . singing with grace." Colossians 3:16

"The statutes of the Lord are right, rejoicing the heart." Psalm 19:8

"I rejoice at thy Word, as one that findeth great spoil." Psalm 119:162

"If ye know these things, happy are ye if ye do them." John 13:17

There Is the Promise of Prosperity

"His delight is in the law of the Lord . . . whatsoever he doeth shall prosper." Psalm 1:2, 3

"Thy word hath quickened me." Psalm 119:50, 93, 159

"These words . . . shall be in thine heart . . . and houses full of all good things." Deuteronomy 6:6-11; 4:14

"Lay up these words in your heart . . . that your days may be multiplied." Deuteronomy 11:18-21

There Is the Promise of Witness

"Search the Scriptures . . . these are they which testify of me." John 5:39

"To him give all the prophets witness." Acts 10:43

"Shewing by the scriptures that Jesus was Christ." Acts 18:28

"I declare unto you the Gospel . . . according to the scriptures." I Corinthians 15:1-3

There Is the Promise of Sufficiency

"They have Moses and the prophets; let them hear them." Luke 16:29-31

"Thy word is true from the beginning." Psalm 119:160

"Ye shall not add unto the word which I command you, neither shall ye diminish ought from it." Deuteronomy 4:4; 12:32; Revelation 22:18

There Is the Promise of Salvation

"The word of faith . . . and shalt believe . . . thou shalt be saved." Romans 10:8-10

"By the words of thy lips I have kept me from the paths of the destroyer." Psalms 17:4; 119:41

"The law of the Lord is perfect, converting the soul." Psalm 19:8

"The holy scriptures . . . able to make the wise unto salvation."

II Timothy 3:15

There Is the Promise of Wisdom

"The testimony of the Lord is sure, making wise the simple." Psalm 19:7

"They have rejected the word of the Lord: and what wisdom is in them?" Jeremiah 8:9

"Not in the words which man's wisdom teacheth, but which the Holy Ghost teacheth." I Corinthians 2:13

There Is the Promise of Reward

"In keeping of them there is great reward." Psalm 19:11

"They are written for our admonition." I Corinthians 10:11

"Blessed are they . . . which keep those things which are written."

Revelation 1:3

There Is the Promise of Hope

"Remember the word . . . upon which thou hast caused me to hope."

Psalm 119:49

"I have hoped in thy word."

Psalm 119:74, 81, 147

"Through the scriptures . . . have hope." Romans 13:4

There Is the promise of Life

"These are written . . . that believing ye might have life through his name." John 20:31

"The righteousness of thy testimonies is everlasting; give me understanding and I shall live." Psalm 119:144

There Is the Promise of Edification

"The word of his grace, which is able to build you up." Acts 20:32; Ephesians 4:15, 16

"The word of God, which effectually worketh also in you that believe." I Thessalonians 2:13

There Is the Promise of Realized Discipleship

"If ye continue in my word, then are ye my disciples indeed." John 8:31, 32

"If . . . he will keep my words . . . we will make our abode with him." John 14:23

"If my words abide in you . . . so shall ye be my disciples." John 15:7, 8

To appropriate to the full all the promises associated with Scripture, certain definite, positive attitudes toward it must be constantly observed. For instance –

Our steps must be ordered by it. Psalm 119:133

We must not be mere hearers of it. James 1:22

It must be fully believed. John 2:22

Obedience to its demands must be given. Psalm 119:158; Luke 8:21; 11:28

The Spirit alone can unfold its truths. John 18:13; I Corinthians 2:10-11; Luke 24:45

It must be grasped as a whole. I Peter 1:20 (Scofield margin)

It must be accepted as the divine Word. I Thessalonians 2:13; Psalm 119:42

We must daily search it. John 5:39; 7:52 with Acts 17:11

Its awesomeness must be recognized. Psalm 119:161

Remembrance of it is enjoined. Isaiah 66:2; Psalm 119:16

It must not be handled deceitfully. II Corinthians 4:2; 2:17

Its truths must not be twisted. II Peter 3:16; Jeremiah 36:29-32; I Peter 2:8

How privileged we are to have such a treasure as the Bible, which like its Giver, "shall stand forever" (Isaiah 40:8). May grace be ours to rest in this infallible revelation.

Promises Relative to the Christian Church

Promised by Christ, whose death and resurrection brought her into being, the Church has abundant promises at her disposal. *The Epistles*, both Pauline and General, reveal "the exceeding great and precious promises," to which the Church of Jesus Christ can lay claim. While the Church which He said He would build is not before us in Old Testament Scriptures, nevertheless there are many promises therein she can possess, seeing such Scriptures were written for her admonition. As we have previously indicated, many of those promises relative to Israel and to Zion are so collective and impersonal, and largely without condition as, for instance, the promises of *The Psalms*, that they belong as naturally to the New Testament Church as to Israel (Psalm 84:1-2).

Distinguishing, as we do, between Israel and "The Church," it may be fitting at this point to examine the terms used of both. *Ekklesia*, is a Greek word meaning, "a calling out from" and was used among the Greeks of a body of citizens gathered to discuss the affairs of the State.

"It shall be determined in a lawful

assembly." Acts 19:39

The Septuagint Version uses the same word to designate the gathering of Israel, summoned for any definite purpose, or a gathering regarded as representative of the whole nation. It is used both of Israel and of a riotous mob.

"The church in the wilderness."

Acts 7:38

"The assembly was confused . . . Dismissed the assembly." Acts 10:32, 41

This same word is translated "congregation" in Hebrews 2:12 (R.V.) instead of the usual rendering "church."

In New Testament usage, the word has a double application when applied to Christians. First, to the whole of the company of redeemed men and women:

"I will build my Church."

Matthew 16:18

"The church which is his body."

Ephesians 1:22; 5:23

Second, when in the singular number the word refers to a company consisting of professed believers:

"If he neglect to hear thee, tell it unto the church." Matthew 18:17

"Unto the church of God which is at Corinth." I Corinthians 1:2, etc.

Derived, then, from a Greek word meaning *The Lord's,* the general New Testament term is strictly accurate in describing the Church, which is the Lord's body, formed of regenerated Jews and Gentiles.

The Divine Promise to Build the Church

"Upon this rock I will build my church."

Matthew 16:18

The Roman Church falsely interprets this passage by implying that our Lord meant that Peter was the "rock" and that he was the first Pope, the foundation of the Church. Well, Peter may be claimed as the foundation of the Roman Church, but he is certainly not the foundation of Christ's Church.

"For other foundation can no man lay than is laid, which is Jesus Christ."

I Corinthians 3:11

While "Peter" and "Rock" are one word in the dialect familiarly spoken by Christ and there appears to be a play upon the word, He did not refer to Peter in this magnificent description of His Church. In the figurative use of the word "Rock" in the Old Testament, it is always used symbolically of God, except when used of false gods to contrast to the Rock of Israel, who is the living God (Deuteronomy 32). Paul has no hesitation in identifying Christ as

"The Rock" –

"The spiritual rock that followed them: and that rock was Christ."

I Corinthians 10:4

What Christ actually meant, then, was that He would build His Church, not upon Peter, but upon Peter's heaven-given revelation of Christ's deity as "the Son of the living God." The Church is built upon Himself. "With His own blood He bought her," and having bought her, after His Ascension, He proceeded to build her. Dr. Campbell Morgan reminds us that "the Word the Lord employed was one that signified more than the mere act of building . . . It has within itself the suggestiveness of the formation of a dynasty, or an economy, which is interpreted by the words, 'My *ecclesia.'"*

Before we come to a consideration of Church promises, one further word by way of introduction is necessary, namely, the word "Church" is never used of a mere building. The nearest approach to such an application is in I Corinthians 14:19, 28, 35. Fausset remarks, *"Ecclesia,* in the New Testament, it must be noted, is never used of the building, or house of assembly, for church buildings were long after the apostolic age. It means an organized body, whose unity does not depend on its being met together in one place; not an assemblage of atoms, but members in their several places united to One Head, Christ, and forming one organic whole."

We find it hard to rid our minds of the idea that a church in apostolic times consisted of bricks and mortar and that the Apostles themselves when referring to a church did not have in mind an edifice with pulpit, chancel, pews and stained-glass windows, but a congregation or society of men and women, built together like living stones, who were content to meet in some upper-room or a private dwelling like that of Mary's, mother of John Mark, where Rhoda acted as doorkeeper. Paul preached wherever he could get a hearing. If not in synagogues, then by the riverside at Philippi, on Mars Hill at Athens, on the citadel steps in Jerusalem, in a hired house under the shadow of Caesar's throne. It was not until long years after that money began to be spent on architecture. The apostles never wasted their energies on material shrines. If only the present-day energy we devote to removing huge church mortgages and debts could be devoted to soul-winning, what a mighty spiritual force the church would be!

It is, therefore, because of the spiritual conception of the church that all her promises are related, not to buildings, but to believers, as can be proved by a study of the various ways by which the true, invisible Church is described –

The Body of Christ. Ephesians 1:22-23; Colossians 1:24

The Bride of Christ. Ephesians 5:31-33; II Corinthians 11:2-3; Revelation 19:7; 21:9; 22:17

The House of Christ. Hebrews 3:6

The House of God. I Timothy 3:15; Hebrews 13:21

The Habitation of God. Ephesians 2:19-22; I Peter 2:4-5

The Temple of God. I Corinthians 3:16-17

The Temple of the Living God. II Corinthians 6:16

God's Building. I Corinthians 3:9

God's Husbandry. I Corinthians 3:9

God's Heritage. I Peter 5:3

The Church of God. Acts 20:28

The Church of the Living God. I Timothy 3:15

The Church of the First Born. Hebrews 12:23

The Israel of God. Galatians 6:16

The Flock of God. I Peter 5:2

The City of the Living God. Hebrews 12:22

Mount Zion. Hebrews 12:22

The New Jerusalem. Revelation 21:2

Heavenly Jerusalem. Galatians 4:26; Hebrews 12:22

A Spiritual House. I Peter 2:5

The Pillow and Ground of Truth. I Timothy 3:15

The Family in Heaven and Earth. Ephesians 3:15

A Mystery. Ephesians 3:9; 5:32; Colossians 1:25-26

The Light of the World. Matthew 5:14

The Golden Candlestick. Revelation 1:20

The Salt of the Earth. Matthew 5:13

One Bread. I Corinthians 10:17

An Elect Race . . . Royal Priesthood . . . Holy Nation. I Peter 2:9

As God's Church, she had her *eternal* origin in Him. Through His sovereign act in grace, He predetermined an elect body, redeemed by the blood of His Son (Ephesians 1:4-14 etc.). Because the Church originated in Him and is the building He is rearing (I Corinthians 3:9), she is dependent upon Him for provision which is expressed in her being His arable field. He it is who cultivates her and augments her fertility.

She is His dearest treasure, the apple of His eye and His choicest gift to the world.

Foundationally, the Church commenced with Christ, her Foundation (Matthew 16:18), as the hymn expresses it –

"The Church's one Foundation,
Is Jesus Christ her Lord."

A church before Christ's *death* would have been an *unredeemed* church, a church before His *resurrection* would have been a church *without the indwelling Spirit*, a church before His *ascension* would have been a *headless Body*.

Historically, the Church commenced at Pentecost which is spoken of as "The Church's Birthday" (Acts 2). Through the coming of the Spirit, she rapidly grew, as *The Acts* clearly shows. By the end of the First Century, countless thousands had been added unto her and unto her Lord.

Here is a listing of some of the promises all those who are redeemed and regenerated and who consequently form the mystic fabric known as "The Church of the Living God," can claim.

She Was Promised by God in a Past Eternity

"God . . . gave him to be the head over all things to the church."

Ephesians 1:22

She Exists to Display the Wisdom of God

"Might be known by the church the manifold wisdom of God." Ephesians 3:10

She Manifests the Glory of God

"Unto him be glory in the church by Christ Jesus throughout all ages, world without end. Amen." Ephesians 3:21

She Was Promised by the Lord Jesus Christ

"I will build my church." Matthew 16:18

"The stone which the builders rejected, the same is become the head of the corner."

Matthew 21:41 with Psalm 118:23

The *cement* that binds believers together in the fellowship of the Church is the greatest of all Christian graces – LOVE.

"The body edifying itself (building itself up) in love." Ephesians 4:16; John 15:12

She Was Promised Christ As Her Head

"The head over all things to the church . . . The head, even Christ . . . Christ is the head of the body."

Ephesians 1:22; 4:15; 5:23

Christ is never called King of the Church. Spiritually, of course, He is her Sovereign Lord. *King* is one of the divine titles and the Church in her worship joins Israel in exalting "the king, eternal, immortal, invisible" (Psalm 10:16; I Timothy 1:17). But Christ's kingship is future and will be realized when the Church reigns with him.

She Has Promises Attendant Upon the Observation of Ordinances

"Go ye into all the world and teach all nations, baptizing them in the name of the Father, and of the Son, and of the Holy Ghost." Matthew 28:19, 20

"This do in remembrance of me." Luke 22:19, 20. (See also Mark 16:16; Acts 2:38; 22:16; Romans 6:3; I Corinthians 10:16; 11:13; 12:13 etc.).

She Can Appropriate Promised Gifts

"The gift of Christ...he gave gifts unto men." Ephesians 4:4-11; Psalm 68:18

She Has Promised Completeness in Her Head

"Ye are complete in him, which is the head." Colossians 2:10

She Has Christ As Her Promised Corner Stone

"Jesus Christ himself being the chief corner stone." Ephesians 2:20; I Peter 2:6

She Has Her Lord's Promised Love

"Christ also loved the church, and gave himself for it." Ephesians 5:25

"I am my beloved's, and his desire is toward me." Song of Solomon 7:10

His undying love for His Church is revealed in His death for her (Acts 20:28; Ephesians 5:25; Hebrews 9:12); in His desire to sanctify her (I Corinthians 6:11; Ephesians 5:26, 27); in making her the object of His grace (II Corinthians 8:1; Isaiah 27:3); in His request for her subjection to Himself (Romans 7:4; Ephesians 5:24).

She Has His Promised Care

"Nourisheth and cherisheth, even as the Lord the church." Ephesians 5:29

"The flock . . . he careth for you." I Peter 5:2, 7

She Has His Promised Protection and Preservation

"My church and the gates of hell shall not prevail against it." Matthew 16:18

"For the Lord is our defence." Psalm 89:17; Isaiah 4:5

"No weapon that is formed against thee shall prosper." Isaiah 54:17

His Church is invincible and His petition for her (John 17) assures her that all Christ wishes for her will certainly be granted. The same applies to prophetical prayers (Genesis 49; Deuteronomy 3:3). Springing from the heart of the Eternal One, she also is eternal. Men have tried – and are still trying – to destroy her, but invincible, like a mighty army, the true Church fights her foes.

She Has His Promised Presence

"There am I in the midst of them." Matthew 18:20

"He may abide with you forever." John 14:16, 21; Revelation 3:20

"I will never leave thee." Hebrews 13:5

"Our fellowship is with . . . Jesus Christ." I John 1:3

"In the midst of the seven candlesticks one like unto the Son of Man." Revelation 1:13

Alas! all too often we gather together in a building set aside for the worship of and service for the Master all unconscious of His promised presence in the midst of His own.

"Surely the Lord is in this place; and I knew it not." Genesis 28:16, 17

What need we have to pray each time we gather in His name –

> Jesus, stand among us,
> In Thy risen power,
> Let this time of worship
> Be a hallow'd hour.

She Is Promised Additions to Her Numbers

"Ye shall receive power . . . ye shall be witnesses unto me." Acts 1:8

"There were added unto them about three thousand souls." Acts 2:44

"The Lord added to the church daily such as should be saved." Acts 2:47; 4:6, etc.

While it is the Lord who chooses His people, calls them by His grace, quickens them by His Spirit, adds them to His Church, yet it is to His Church that He has committed the task of evangelism. Such evangelism is the constant proclamation of the Gospel in public and private with a view of winning men and women, young people and children to Jesus Christ, thereby helping to complete the Church, which is His Body.

She Is Promised a Spirit Unity

"That they all may be one even as we are one." John 17:21, 22

"So we, being many, are one body in Christ." Romans 12:4-8

"For we being many are one bread, and one body." I Corinthians 10:17

"For the body is one . . . being many, as one body." I Corinthians 12:12-31

"Ye are all one in Christ Jesus." Galatians 3:28

"The unity of the Spirit . . . . There is one body." Ephesians 4:3, 4

Outer unity among those naming the name of Christ is conspicuous by its absence, and the manifold denominations and sects confuses the mind of the man in the street outside the pale of the Church. Although we lustily sing on a Sunday –

"We are not divided
All one body we,"
the sad fact is that we do not worship and work as one body. Such perfect unity among the saints will not be realized until Jesus comes when all saved by grace irrespective of their denominational label, will be "caught up *together* to meet the Lord in the air."

She Is Promised Union and Communion with Christ

"I will that they also . . . be with me where I am." John 17:24
"Made nigh by the blood of Christ." Ephesians 2:13, 18
"The household of God. . . . An habitation of God." Ephesians 2:20, 22
"Ye are come unto mount Sion. . . . And to Jesus." Hebrews 12:22, 24
"Truly our followship is . . . with his Son Jesus Christ." I John 1:3
"I sat down under his shadow with great delight." Song of Solomon 2:3
To the spiritual mind *The Song of Solomon* is eloquent of the union and communion existing between Christ, as the Bridegroom, and His Church, as the Bride.

She Is Promised Punishment for Those Who Defile Her

"If any man defile the temple of God, him shall God destroy."
I Corinthians 3:17

She Is Promised a Glorious Consummation

"That where I am, there ye may be also." John 14:3
"That he might present it to himself a glorious church." Ephesians 5:27
"The king's daughter is all glorious within." Psalm 45:13
"Come ye hither." Revelation 4:1; I Thessalonians 4:13-18
"To her was granted that she should be arrayed in fine linen." Revelation 19:8
"Prepared as a bride adorned for her husband." Revelation 21:3, 9
How the true Church longs to gaze on her dear Bridegroom's face and to be with Him for ever! Is not His glorious advent "the pole star of the Church"?

She Has Manifold Promises Upon Faithful Ministers

"The Lord is his inheritance, according as the Lord thy God promised him."
Deuteronomy 10:9
"Bless, Lord, his substance, and accept the work of his hands."
Deuteronomy 33:11
"Blessed are ye that sow beside all waters." Isaiah 32:20

"I said, I have laboured in vain . . . yet surely my judgment is with the Lord, and my work with my God."
Isaiah 49:4
"I will satiate the soul of the priests with fatness." Jeremiah 31:14
"I will feed them in a good pasture."
Ezekiel 34:14
"It is not ye that speak but the Spirit of your Father which speaketh in you."
Matthew 10:20; 28:20
"Who then is that faithful and wise steward?" Luke 12:42; Ephesians 3:7-8
"I will give you a mouth and wisdom."
Luke 21:15
"He that reapeth receiveth wages, and gathereth fruit unto life eternal."
John 4:36
"Evangelists . . . pastors and teachers; for the perfecting of the saints, and the work of the ministry." Ephesians 4:11, 12
"Take heed unto thyself, and unto the doctrine." I Timothy 4:16
"Every man's work shall be made manifest." I Corinthians 3:13
The above are only a few of the many Bible references in the light of which all who are called to feed the flock of God should walk. As His representatives in a world of need, He has promised to equip them in every way.
"Even so hath the Lord ordained that they which preach the gospel should live of the gospel." I Corinthians 9:14
Here are some promises especially directed at those who minister:
"Blessed are ye that sow beside all waters." Isaiah 32:20
All who are called to minister the Word have need to constantly pray that the good Lord will deliver them from mere professionalism. While Sunday is their day for sowing the seed, Isaiah would have them know that pastors, and in fact, all who profess to be saved, are only thrice blessed as every opportunity is grasped of witnessing to God's saving grace and power. The true sower will not save his seed for set occasions. With a full, prepared basket, he will have a handful of seed ready to scatter over the soil of any soul he touches. Day in and day out, in visitation, conversation and communication, the diligent minister will drop a seed here and there, trusting the Lord of the harvest to guard the sown seed and make it fruitful.
"I have laboured in vain . . . yet surely . . . my work with my God." Isaiah

49:4; I Thessalonians 3:5

Isaiah, the Evangelical Prophet, had a true pastor's heart. Perhaps there is no other book so vitally connected with pastoral vision and virtue as Isaiah's prophecy. He knew all about the successes and sorrows of a preacher's task. Often his appeal evoked no response. Faithful in his declarations, at times they seemed to fall upon deaf ears. Knowing of his rejected witness, we can understand his complaint,

"I have laboured in vain, I have spent
my strength for nought, and in vain."

Are these lines being read by a discouraged pastor? Pure in your life, and positive in your message, you yet find yourself unwanted, unappreciated. Well, take courage! Let Isaiah's confidence be yours, "Yet surely my judgment is with the Lord, and my work with my God." If your life and labor are well pleasing to the Lord, you have His promise that your witness will not be in vain.

"I will give you pastors according to
mine heart and shall feed you with
knowledge and understanding."

Jeremiah 3:15

Promised pastors were to function as shepherds, feeding the sheep. *Pastor* and *pasture* have a vital connection. An old, illiterate woman once spoke of her pastor as, "My pasture." Well, she was not far wrong! The knowledge and understanding a true pastor provides form the pasture needy souls feed upon. A flock is always well-fed when it has a pastor "according to God's heart." Alas! too many pastors correspond to the description Jeremiah speaks of who "destroy and scatter the sheep" (10:21; 23:1, 2). A modernistic minister is not a shepherd. Giving stones for bread, how can he feed the hungry? Denying the foundational truths of Holy Writ, how can he claim to be a pastor according to God's heart? God-given men believe a God-given message and are always ready to feed hungry souls with the bread of heaven, and consequently reap the promised blessing of reward.

"Behold, I have made thy face strong
against their faces." Ezekiel 3:8

Here is a chapter every pastor should read on his knees. As a watchman, he must warn souls as from God (Ezekiel 3:17-21). To witness, however, before those who are impudent and hard-hearted is no light task, but courage is promised (3:7). What a heartening word this is for preachers who have a rebellious crowd to deal with. "Neither be dismayed at their looks" (Ezekiel 3:9).

Determination must be matched. As fearless as are the people in their rejection of a God-given message, the preacher must be just as fearless in the declaration of the truth the hard-hearted hate. To win through, pastors certainly need grace, grit and gumption. Kindly yet firmly he must continue warning the rebellious of their peril.

"They that turn many to righteousness
shall shine as the stars for ever and
ever." Daniel 12:3

While the entire passage before us is a precious promise for all soul-winners, it has a special application to pastors, seeing they have one of the greatest opportunities of turning souls to God. Wise in the winning of men, Paul knew that he would shine as the brightness of the firmament. This is why he rejoiced over the thought of meeting his Thessalonian converts at the Judgment Seat of Christ.

"What is our hope, or joy or crown
of rejoicing? Are not even ye in the
presence of our Lord Jesus Christ at
his coming?" I Thessalonians 2:19, 20

My pastor-friend, you may not have the gifts and brilliance of others. Your abilities may not be conspicuous. Fame and favor do not come to you as to others. But be patient and faithful for the promise is that if you serve God to the limit of your capacity, eternal brilliance will be yours. A good many movie and ministerial stars are having all the "shine" they will ever have. Your unnoticed work has the promise of unfading glory.

"Make full proof of thy ministry."

II Timothy 4:5

Next to Christ, Paul is conspicuous as the most ideal Preacher in the New Testament. Paul was no mere professional. He found himself in the ministry because he could not help it. And as a preacher, he ever practiced what he preached. At the end of a long, faithful and honored career, Paul, the veteran preacher, gives young Timothy some practical advice as he faces his life's task. Urging him to make full proof of his ministry, Paul points to his own example and bids Timothy keep the promise of reward before his eyes.

All who are called to minister the Word can easily discover by reading this whole chapter how to make full proof of their ministry. Preaching the whole counsel of God at all times, laboring with eternal values in view, ever alert for the souls of

men, these are among the secrets of a fruitful ministry.

"Feed the flock of God . . . the chief
    Shepherd shall appear." I Peter 5:2, 4
If pastoral counsels are to be obeyed (Hebrews 13:17), and pastors themselves held
in reputation and honor (Philippians 2:29)
and find themselves highly esteemed (I Thessalonians 5:12, 13), then there must be the
remembrance of the resemblance they bear
in this work and offices to Jesus Christ
(Hebrews 13:20; II Peter 2:25). The promise of the crown of unfading glory can only
be claimed by those shepherds who were
ensamples of the flock.

The solemn warning is that if proud, con-
ceited, domineering, fond of filthy lucre,
then the undershepherd cannot expect to
receive the promised reward from the Chief
Shepherd when He appears. The crown of
glory is only for those who laid in dust
life's glory dead. If lordly in their office
(I Peter 5:3), what do they expect from the
Lord? Crowned with self-glory on the earth,
they forfeit the right to receive the crown
of glory from the hand of the Master.

How richly blessed the Church is with a
multitude of pastors all over the world who,
although "unknown, unsung and unhon-
oured," toil on day after day so devotedly
and unselfishly! Living on the promises of
God, these sacrificial Shepherds are not affected by circumstances. Their eyes are on
the final goal.

She Has the Promise of Revival

In her present confused, divided and impoverished condition, the organized Church
is certainly in need of a mighty quickening
from above. How impotent she seems to
be in the face of national evils and of international crises! Yet there was a day when
she had power to turn the world upside
down. Let us, then, look at one or two
revival promises the Church can appropriate.

"O Lord, revive thy work in the midst
    of the years." Habakkuk 3:2
It is to be hoped that we are not among
the number who discredit any hope of revival in these dark days and who argue
that the terrible condition of things in a
world under the cloud of another world
war precludes revival. How can men concentrate upon the vital necessities of the
soul, when they have to struggle hard to
provide the necessities of life! Then pagan
forces predominate in the world and civilization is again at the cross-roads, so how
can there by any hope of better days?

Strange, is it not, that secular writers
are telling us that if the world is to be
saved from disaster, then we must have
a spiritual revival and that speedily. Church
history reveals that in the midst of the darkest years, God breaks out in blessing. Was
it not the mighty revival under John Wesley
that saved England from a bloody revolution? Well might we cry, "O Lord, do
it again!"

"Wilt thou not revive us again?"
                                        Psalm 85:6
In this Psalm we are encouraged to pray
for revival, seeing we have a God who is
willing to forgive our lapses. The Psalmist
makes it clear, however, that once we are
quickened, there must be no more relapses.
"Let them not turn again to folly." Revival, of course, is related to the Lord's
people. Anything dead cannot be revived.
Life, no matter how low, must be present
if revival is to be experienced. Sinners cannot
be revived because they are dead in sins.
The word and experience for them is "regeneration" or the impartation of divine
life. For those who are regenerated, but
who have allowed the sinister influences of
the world to rob them of spiritual power
and progress, the reviving grace of the Lord
constitutes the paramount need. How the
Church needs to have a spark fanned into
a glowing flame!

"Thou wilt revive me." Psalm 138:7;
    Hosea 6:1-3
When we speak about the necessity of
the revival of the Church, we must not
forget that what God promises to revive is
not churches as buildings, but those who
gather in them. Without a company of
born-again men and women within any
church, it is only a mere building. Therefore, as the visible Church is made up of
individuals, there cannot be a collective
revival apart from a personal revival. Each
and all within the Church must come under
the sway of God's quickening power. What
a mighty, spiritual upheaval there would
be if only *every* Christian would pray—

"O Lord, send a revival,
    And let it begin in me."
"To revive the spirit of the humble, and
    to revive the heart of the contrite ones."
                                        Isaiah 57:15
The promise, preparation and plan of revival are before us in the context. Going
back a verse we find that the stumbling
block had to be taken out of the way of
God's people. How true it is that prom-

ised revival only becomes actual as we are willing to remove all known hindrances to the manifestation of His power! Everything alien to His will must be dragged out and humbly confessed. A deep contrition because of our sins and failures must be forthcoming, if we desire God to make us channels of blessing. The difficulty is that we are not broken enough for a God, who is truly broken over the sins of the men, to use to heal a broken world.

"Will they revive the stones out of the heaps of rubbish which are burnt." Nehemiah 4:2

Sanballat, in his opposition to Nehemiah's determination to rebuild the city wall, heaped ridicule upon the "feeble Jews," as he called them. Could they, out of the debris, repair the damaged wall and gates? Tobiah further ridiculed their efforts by saying that if they did rebuild the wall, it would be such a poor job that the light tread of a fox would cause the stones to fall. But the work proceeded and was satisfactorily completed, for the people had a mind to work.

There is no doubt about God's ability to revive His living stones out of the rubbish heap of carnality. The promise is that He is well able to restore the years the locusts have eaten. A lot of "rubbish" clings to the Church. Worldly compromise has damaged the wall of testimony. The narrow gate of regeneration has been broken down. May God give us a reviving . . . to repair the desolations thereof! (Ezra 9:8, 9).

"Quicken thou me according to thy word." Psalm 119:25

Here the Psalmist is pleading the promise of revival. While the word "quicken" is used of life being given to the dead, it also implies God's power to raise up and cheer all who languish. And what is revival but God's quickening of His own! He finds them cleaving to the dust and touches them. As branches of the Vine, they trail on the ground where the sun, rain and air cannot benefit them. But when His Spirit is abroad in revival blessing, the trailing, dust-covered branches are raised to a trellis where, fully exposed to atmospheric conditions, they can become fruitful. Then it must not be forgotten that all revival comes through the medium of the Word. A revival that is not according to God's revealed will, is not a heaven-sent one. The Lord deliver us from a Bible-less, and therefore spurious, revival!

"Bring ye . . . I will pour you out a blessing." Malachi 3:10

In this further promise of revival there are two key-words to underline: *Bring — Bless.* What a vital connection between bringing and blessing Malachi emphasizes! Mark these steps in your Bible—

Robbery, Retribution, Restitution, Revival (Malachi 3:9, 10)

The Church certainly needs the opened windows of heaven. Her parched condition cries out for refreshing rain. Even her orthodoxy is dead and dry. But the condition of the promise is irrevocable—

"Bring you all the tithes into the storehouse . . . I will pour you out a blessing." Without the bringing there can be no blessing. But bringing, He blesses. His Church, then, can have a revival whenever she likes. As soon as she is prepared to pay the price, the promise of divine refreshment will be realized.

She Is Promised Divine Favor for Sabbath-Keeping

Specific promises are offered to those who keep the day, God has reserved for Himself, as unto Him.

"I was in the Spirit on the Lord's Day." Revelation 1:10

Recognizing that the *Sabbath* is a Jewish term, signifying a day set apart for religious exercises; and that under the Christian dispensation, which unites regenerated Jews and Gentiles, the Sabbath is altered from the seventh day of the week, to the first day of the week, we yet use the term in a general way. *Sabbath* means rest or cessation from labor. John speaks of "The Lord's Day" and it is His in a special sense, for it is the Day commemorating His victory over death. While all days are His, this is the one of the seven He claims for Himself. It is the day set apart for the worship of His Name and the proclamation of His Word. Such a holy day, however, only yields the utmost spiritual profit as we find outselves "in the Spirit" (Revelation 1:10).

"The Lord . . . rested the seventh day, wherefore the Lord blessed the sabbath day and hallowed it." Exodus 20:1

Originally the Sabbath was a day of worship in memory of God's work in creation. Then it was looked upon as a day of repose for man and beast, that they might not have their bodily strength exhausted by uninterrupted labor. The Sabbath was made for man, being ordained for his welfare.

Alas! modern life has turned our Sunday, a day of rest, into one of restlessness. The ceaseless whirl of cars on national highways, tens of thousands at baseball games and engaged in all kinds of sports, cinemas all ablaze, and countless ways of robbing the day of its significance and value, prove the decadent life of the Nation.

If the Creator rested on the seventh day, surely the creature has need of a day's cessation from the labor, legitimate and exacting, monopolizing the other six days of the week. Do we keep the Lord's Day free of all unnecessary work? Do we preserve it as His day? If so, then we have His promised benediction (Jeremiah 17:24, 25).

"Upon the first day . . . Paul preached."
Acts 20:7

This passage proves the use of the first day, and not the seventh, by apostolic churches. Further, we read that it was the custom of the early believers to meet together to break bread and to hear the Word expounded. Has not the Church departed from the apostolic employment of the Lord's Day? Simplicity of worship and ministry has been lost amid a good deal of ritualism and professionalism. Yet one feature still characterizes the Lord's Day, wherever it is observed by Christians, independent of their nationality, namely, the preaching of the Word. Have you ever stopped to think of the unnumbered hosts of pastors, teachers, evangelists, missionaries and workers who proclaim the Truth as each Sunday comes round? What a blessed day! And what a blessed Gospel to preach throughout its hours!

"Blessed is the man . . . that keepeth the Sabbath from polluting it."
Isaiah 56:2

In this further promise of blessing, ethical instructions laid down by God for Israel hold an application for our dispensation. Nothing can contribute to our personal happiness – which the word *blessed* means – like a Sunday kept free from worldly pollution. Spiritual, physical and mental reward is ours as we remember His Day to keep it holy. May all our Sundays be as oases in this desert world! May grace be ours to guard them against all illegitimate encroachment! A tender conscience will enable us to determine what are works of necessity.

"The first day of the week . . . came Jesus." John 20:19; Matthew 17:1

No matter where the Lord's Day finds us worshiping, there is always the realization of His presence if He is being worshiped in spirit and in truth. Not only so, worship is not valid if He is not the Center of it. Sunday only yields its richest treasures when all our hymns, prayers, readings, thoughts and messages are fragrant with His Name. How blessed it is to turn from the week and its work, worry and weeping to Him, whose presence is so gladdening. "After six days, JESUS." (Matthew 17:1). Like the disciples of old, we, too, are glad as we see the Lord and listen to His voice. May He enable us to make all our Sundays Christ-conscious, Christ-honoring days!

"Upon the first day of the week . . . lay by . . . as God hath prospered."
I Corinthians 16:2

The universal adherence to the apostolic way of giving would save the Church from financial embarrassment and from doubtful money-raising schemes. Combining this method of support laid down by Paul, along with the doctrine of Christian giving, he emphasizes later on (II Corinthians 8:1-6), we learn that each Lord's Day must witness a double surrender. First of all, our gifts to the Lord for the maintenance of His cause must be proportioned to our income. Then along with our silver, there must go ourselves. Tithes without lives are of little value to Him to whom all the silver and the gold belong. Paul commended the Corinthian believers because they first gave their own selves unto the Lord. A dedicated purse accomplishes great things for Him when with it there is a dedicated person.

Promises Relative to Christian Doctrine

Doctrine is woven into the texture of the Bible. Take away its glorious doctrines of divine love, justice, and grace, and there is little left for the soul to feast upon. While theologians have tried to systematize these doctrines, it is most profitable to go from reference to reference when dealing with any doctrine, as C. I. Scofield illustrates in his *Reference Bible*.

All we can attempt in this study of the promises of the Bible is to indicate the manifold provision God has promised in many of the great doctrines His Word proclaims. What blessed promises of present and eternal enrichment are ours, for example, in the shared attributes and virtues of the three Persons forming the TRINITY. While the actual term "Trinity" is not used in the

Bible, the fact of it dominates the Bible. "Spirit . . . God . . . Christ." Romans 8:9. (Compare Exodus 20:2 with John 20:28 and Acts 5:3,4; Matthew 3:16, 17; I Corinthians 12:3-6; Ephesians 1:3; 4:4,6; I Peter 1:2, etc.)

The promises are assured—

Because the Trinity is eternal
"The everlasting God." Romans 16:26
"Christ . . . the King Eternal."
I Timothy 1:16, 17
"The eternal Spirit." Hebrews 9:14

Because the Trinity is Holy
"The Holy one . . . the Prince of Life."
Acts 3:14, 15
"Holy, holy, holy, Lord God almighty."
Revelation 4:8
"An unction from the holy One."
I John 2:20, 27

Because the Trinity is true
"He that sent me is true." John 7:28
"The Spirit is truth." I John 5:6
"He that is true." Revelation 3:7

Because the Trinity is omnipresent
"Do not I fill heaven and earth? said the Lord." Jeremiah 23:24
"Whither shall I go from thy Spirit?"
Psalm 139:7
"Lo, I am with you alway."
Matthew 28:20

Because the Trinity is omnipotent
"I am the almighty God." Genesis 17:1; Jeremiah 32:17
"The power of the Spirit." Acts 15:19; Micah 3:8
"His Son . . . the word of his power."
Hebrews 1:3; Revelation 1:8

Because the Trinity is omniscient
"Known unto God are all his works from the beginning of the world." Acts 15:18
"He knew all . . . he knew what was in man." John 2:24, 25
"The Spirit searcheth all things, yea, the deep things of God."
I Corinthians 2:10

Because the Trinity is creative
"In the beginning God created the heavens and the earth." Genesis 1:1
"Who is the image of the invisible God . . . by him were all things created."
Colossians 1:15, 16
"By his Spirit he garnished the heavens." Job 26:13; 33:4; Genesis 1:3

Because the Trinity sanctifies
"Sanctified by God." Jude 1
"Sanctification of the Spirit."
I Peter 1:2
"The captain of our salvation . . .

he that sanctifieth." Hebrews 2:11

Because of the Trinity's spiritual operations
"The God of peace . . . making you perfect in every good work."
Hebrews 13:21
"It pleased the Father that in him should all fulness dwell." Colossians 1:19, 20
"All these worketh that one and the self-same Spirit." I Corinthians 12:11

Because the Trinity is the source of eternal life
"I give unto them eternal life."
John 10:28
"The gift of God is eternal life."
Romans 6:23
"Of the Spirit reap life everlasting."
Galatians 6:8

Because the Trinity is instructive
"The Lord God which teacheth thee to profit." Isaiah 48:17; 54:13
"I was taught it . . . by the revelation of Jesus Christ." Galatians 1:12
"The Holy Ghost . . . he shall teach you all things." John 14:26

Because of the Trinity's resurrection power
"God hath both raised up the Lord, and will also raise up us by his own power." I Corinthians 6:14
"In three days I will raise it up . . . he spake of the temple of his body."
John 2:19, 21
"The Spirit of him that raised up Jesus from the dead." Romans 8:11

Because of the Trinity's inspiration
"God, who at sundry times and in many manners spake in time past."
II Timothy 3:16; Hebrews 1:1
"Christ speaking in me."
II Corinthians 13:3
"It is not ye that speak, but the Holy Ghost." Mark 13:11; I Peter 1:11; II Peter 1:21

Because of the Trinity's work of salvation
"God hath from the beginning chosen you to salvation." II Thessalonians 2:14
"He saved us . . . Jesus Christ our Saviour." Titus 3:5, 6
"Ye have purified your souls . . . through the Spirit." I Peter 1:22, 23

Because of the Trinity's benediction
"The grace of the Lord Jesus Christ, and the love of God, and the Communion of the Holy Ghost."
II Corinthians 13:14

Because of the fellowship the Trinity offers
"Our fellowship is with the Father, and with his Son Jesus Christ."
I John 1:3

"If any fellowship of the Spirit."

Philippians 2:1

The separation of the Persons forming the Trinity and a dissertation on all the transcendant attributes of the Father, and the Son, and the Holy Spirit respectively, is a task of such magnitude as to make it impossible for inclusion in this present volume. We shall confine ourselves to many of those God possesses, realizing at the same time that these same virtues are equally attributed to Jesus Christ, and the Holy Spirit, as the foregoing list under "The Trinity" clearly proves. Because of all God is in Himself, His promises on behalf of saint and sinner alike are certain of performance. Praise Him, He is greater than His promises!

"In the beginning, God." Genesis 1:1 How full of promise is this majestic declaration opening the Scriptures! God stamped His Name and sovereignty upon the very forehead of His Book. God first! This is surely the keynote of the initial book of the Bible. God first in everything – in Creation, in redemption, in Providence, in personal experience. We may not know the hidden cares, trials, and responsibilities, but He does! God first in every phase of our life begets the assurance that any need that may arise will receive His close attention.

"Thou, God, seest me." Genesis 16:13 The realization of His omniscience produces comfort for the saint, but conviction in the sinner. The latter tries to hide from His all-seeing eye, while the Christian rejoices that such a compassionate eye is upon him. His eye is upon the sparrows – and the saints!

"God is faithful." I Corinthians 1:9 We have already seen how divine faithfulness runs like a golden thread through the Bible. As we come to consider some of the promises related to gospel doctrines, we know what to expect for He is faithful that promised.

"We ought to obey God rather than men." Acts 5:29

We cannot ask for the redemption of any promise God has made unless we are living in obedience to His revealed will. Multitudes, robbed of personal freedom, are forcibly obedient to their godless leaders. Our obedience Godward, however, is one of love. The question is sometimes asked: "Can we obey God and man at the same time?" The general answer is: "Only when the commands of men harmonize with those

of God." Yet in sad, tragic China there are still scores of saints who outwardly have to obey their atheistic rulers, but who inwardly obey God and who rest in His promise of preservation.

Then what promise there is in the doctrine of *the Fatherhood of God*. We hold that He is the Father of all only in respect to Creation. His relationship as Father towards us is based upon the redemptive work of His beloved Son. We hear a good deal about the Fatherhood of God, and the brotherhood of Man, but all too little about the Saviourhood of Christ, which is the necessary link between the two.

"Behold, what manner of love the Father hath bestowed upon us, that we should be called the sons of God." I John 3:1 "Because ye are sons, God hath sent forth the Spirit of his son into your hearts, crying, Abba, Father."

Galatians 4:6

"Ye have not received the spirit of bondage again to fear; but ye have the Spirit of adoption whereby, we cry, Abba, Father." Romans 8:15 "I will be a Father unto you, and ye shall be my sons and daughters, saith the Lord Almighty." II Corinthians 6:18 "To as many as received him, to them gave he power to become the sons of God." John 1:12 "If a son, then an heir of God through Christ." Galatians 4:7; Romans 8:17 How fittingly S. J. Coleridge summarizes the Biblical concept of the Fatherhood of God in the lines –

God's child is Christ adopted--Christ my all –
What that earth boasts were not lost, cheaply, rather,
Than forfeit that blest name, by which I call
The *Holy One*, the *Almighty God*, my Father?
Father! in Christ we live, and Christ is *Thee* –
Eternal *Thou*; and everlasting *We*!
The heir of Heaven, henceforth I fear not death;
In *Christ* I live! In *Christ* I draw the breath
Of that true life!

The foundation of all God's promises and works is His eternal Love. In a past eternity, it was that love which conceived salvation's plan, and determined all divine promises on our behalf.

"I am the Lord which exercise loving kindness." Jeremiah 9:24; 31:3 "Continue thy lovingkindness unto them that know thee." Psalms 36:10; 42:8 "He will rest in his love." Zephaniah 3:17 "With loving kindness have I drawn thee." Jeremiah 31:3 "I have loved you." John 15:9

"The love of Christ." Ephesians 3:19; Galatians 2:20

"God commendeth his love toward us." Romans 5:8

"He first loved us." I John 4:19

"God is love." I John 4:8, 9, 16; Deuteronomy 7:13; Isaiah 43:4; 9:25; Ephesians 2:4; II Thessalonians 2:16

In his prayer for inner fulness and knowledge, Paul makes it clear that to know the unknowable love of Christ one must be rooted and grounded in love. To be able to comprehend the breadth, length, depth and height of the love of Him whose love surpasses that of a woman's, one must have a heart saturated with such in divine love. To know the love of Christ, we must first know the Christ of love. Further, the knowledge the apostle refers to is not a mere mental understanding of the love in question, but an experimental knowledge—a knowledge born of faith. Such a love is both of the heart and of the head. The same principle is true of the love of the Spirit.

"The love of Christ which passeth knowledge." Ephesians 3:19

"I beseech you . . . for the love of the Spirit." Romans 15:30

The impelling motive in all effective service is the love *of* Christ and love *to* Christ. Paul never journeys far from such a double incentive (Galatians 2:20).

"The love of Christ constraineth me." II Corinthians 5:14

Constrained by love! How this destroys all ulterior motives in ministry. Love of self, love of crowds, love of applause, love of money—all lesser loves are consumed by the mastering love of, and for, Christ. Further on in the chapter Paul speaks of beseeching men to be reconciled to God. He could beseech men in Christ's stead, since he had a heart constantly warmed by the love of Him whom he dearly loved.

"O love the Lord, all ye his saints." Psalm 31:23

"They shall prosper that love thee." Psalm 122:6

"Thou shalt love the Lord thy God with all thy heart." Matthew 22:37

"There is no fear in love; but perfect love casteth out fear." I John 4:18

"He that dwelleth in love dwelleth in God." I John 4:16

For an inner understanding of the promised, divine love, we must live near the writings of John, the apostle of love. It is he who reminds us of God's initiative in love.

"Herein is love . . . he first loved us." I John 4:19

Here is the most fascinating form of love. We did not love God. Our natural mind was at enmity with God. Yet in our wicked and rebellious condition, He loved us and manifested His love in the sacrifice at the cross (Ephesians 2:4).

"In His love and in His pity, He redeemed us."

John further teaches that we must emulate the divine example and take the initiative in loving the unloving and unlovable. If we would be perfect in love, our hearts must go out to lost souls irrespective of their condition.

"Having loved his own, he loved them unto the end." John 13:1

A more effective translation would be, "He loved them to the uttermost." What a promise this is to cheer the heart! His love is not intermittent, spasmodic. We have an uttermost love as well as an uttermost salvation, the latter being the product of the former. It is not a mere coincidence that the conception of Judas' dark crime immediately follows. Christ loved the traitor to the end. Love must have striven to prevent Judas betraying the Master, but it failed. Is it not blessed to know that, even though we disappoint Jesus, He never casts us off? His is the love that will not let us go. It is not a love continuous upon human merit or response.

There is another aspect of the divine promise and doctrine of love that must be stressed, namely, its personal concentration. While it is blessedly true that God loves the world (John 3:16), it is likewise true that He loves each individual in the world.

"*One* . . . whom Jesus loved." John 11:15; 13:15

"The Son of God who loved *me*." Galatians 2:20

While I was sitting beneath a blazing sun in Florida, meditating on this amazing truth, the thought came to me—although this sun is for the world, and its beneficial rays for all mankind, yet here am I, allowing it to expend its fulness on me. The sun is for all, and yet for each. Thus is it with divine love. In that Bethany home Jesus was fond of visiting, there were three persons so distinct in personal traits, yet each was loved by Christ. Are you not overwhelmed that He loves *you*?

The Bible also makes it clear that divine love liberates. It is dynamic in its action.

"Conquerors through him that loved us." Romans 8:37

"Unto him that loved us and loosed us

from our sins." Revelation 1:5 R.V.
Paul links love on to deliverance from *injury*
–John, from *iniquity*. The promise is that
the love freeing us from sin will see to our
emancipation from all that would separate
us from the Saviour. Once we clasp the
hand of love divine, no one and nothing
can ever separate us from that love which
is in Christ Jesus our Lord.

Like John, Paul was ever practical in
the application of the truth he taught. Thus
he exhorted the Ephesians, "Walk in love,
as Christ also hath loved us" (5:2). How
incumbent upon us to live a life of love –
a love generated in the heart by the loving
Holy Spirit Himself.
"Through the Spirit, unto unfeigned love
of the brethren." I Peter 1:22.

Are we walking in love? We use two feet
in walking and take one step at a time.
Paul refers to the two feet of love – love in
church and love in the *home*. Saints are
to love one another as saints; and saintly
husbands are to love their wives (Ephesians
5:25). May grace be ours to walk so as
to leave behind the footprints of love!

Another Bible doctrine with which are
associated so many rich promises is that
of divine RIGHTEOUSNESS. To gather all that
is recorded of this divine attribute would
fill pages. Look at these pearls on such a
necklace of truth! Others were mentioned
in our meditation *Jehovah Tsidkenu*.

"Thy righteousness is an everlasting
righteousness." Psalm 119:42
"I will bring near my righteousness:
it shall not be far off." Isaiah 46:13
"My righteousness shall be for ever."
Isaiah 51:8
"I will betroth thee to me in righteous-
ness." Hosea 2:19
"In righteousness doth he judge and
make war." Revelation 19:11

The words "just" and "righteous," "justice" and "righteousness" are equivalent in
both the Hebrew and Greek, and the root
meaning of these terms is *straight, right*–
the quality of being just or righteous in
dealing with others. God's righteousness or
justice is His faithfulness in protecting His
government and laws and in rendering to each
person his dues. It is that attribute of God
which causes Him always to do right, whether
it be in inflicting punishment, in giving rewards, or in judging between right and wrong.

In dealing with any of the doctrines,
it will be found that the ever-blessed Godhead, as we have indicated, are one in the
gracious gifts enshrined in the promises, all
of which come to us from God the Father,
through the Son, by the Spirit. The Father
conceived the promises – the way to them was
opened up by the Son – the appropriation of
them is inspired by the Spirit. Thus –
God the Father is just, or righteous.
"Justice and judgment are the habitation of his throne; he shall judge the
world in righteousness."
Psalms 89:14; 96:13; 98:9, etc.
God the Son is just, or righteous.
"The just One." Acts 3:14; 7:52
"The righteous judge." II Timothy 4:8
"Jesus Christ, the righteous."
I John 2:2, 29; 3:7
God the Spirit is just, or righteous.
"He will reprove the world . . . of
righteousness." John 16:7-11
"Filled with the Holy Spirit . . . thou
enemy of all righteousness." Acts 13:9, 10

The gracious ministry of the Spirit is to
bring sinners face to face with the justice
and holiness of God, and to enable them
to realize the sufficiency of a divine righteousness, which is the only covering for the sinner. God has told us what He thinks of
the garment of self-righteousness we try to
weave in order to hide our nakedness in
His sight –
"All our righteousnesses are as filthy
rags." Isaiah 64:6
"Found in him, not having mine own
righteousness." Philippians 3:9
"Can the Ethiopian change his skin, or
the leopard his spots?"
Jeremiah 2:22; 13:23

Through the death of Christ, who came as
the personification of divine righteousness,
there was provided for a sinful and sinning
race a perfect covering. It is thus we sing –

When free grace awoke me, by light from on high
Then legal fears shook me, I trembled to die;
No refuge, no safety, in self could I see;
"Jehovah Tsidkenu" my Saviour must be.

Another divine attribute to which so many
blessed promises are related is that of God's
everlasting MERCY. How full the Bible is
of tributes to Him as the merciful God!
"The Lord thy God is a merciful God."
Deuteronomy 4:31
"I will shew mercy on whom I will
shew mercy." Exodus 33:19
"The mercy of the Lord is from everlasting to everlasting." Psalm 103:17
"Therefore will he be exalted, that he may
have mercy upon thee." Isaiah 30:18

"In my favour have I had mercy on thee." Isaiah 60:10; Jeremiah 31:20

"I will have mercy upon her that had not obtained mercy." Hosea 2:23

"God who is rich in mercy, for his great love wherewith he loved us."

Ephesians 2:4

"Great is his mercy toward them that fear him." Psalms 103:11-12; 130:7-8

"Let him return unto the Lord, and he will have mercy upon him."

Isaiah 55:7

"For thou, Lord, art . . . plenteous in mercy." Psalm 51:1

Mercy, or grace, spoken of as the unmerited favor of God, is the outcome of His love, and implies pity or compassion. It also includes forbearance, gentleness, and long-suffering. The word "lovingkindness" is often given for mercy in the R.V. (see Psalm 136).

Shakespeare, in reminding us that "the quality of mercy is not strained," writes of it as "an attribute of God Himself." It is, of course, an attribute of the Godhead. God has an inexhaustible depth of mercy (Psalm 111:4; Titus 3:5). Christ is the channel of such mercy (I Timothy 1:2; Mark 5:19; Jude 21). The Holy Spirit applies this mercy to the believing sinner (Galatians 5:22, 23). Apart from the divine, abundant mercy, there is no salvation for the sinner. The promise is that God is full of compassion and of great mercy (Psalm 145:8).

We all know how the tragic doctrine of SIN casts its dark shadow over the whole Bible. From Genesis to Revelation we can trace the trail of the serpent, the parent of all sin. Yet everywhere there is the bright promise that "where sin abounded, grace did much more abound." The Westminster Catechism states that, "*Sin* is any want of conformity unto, or transgression of, the law of God." the Bible uses four prominent words to describe such disobedience to the divine law –

"Transgression," which means *a passing over, violation, rebellion.*

"Sin," which is the more general term used, means *missing the mark,* wandering from a marked out path of uprightness and honor, doing or going wrong. "Iniquity" implies *crookedness* as opposed to straightness and uprightness, *that which is wrong* as opposed to that which is right.

"Evil" indicates *badness, wickedness, depravity.*

"Through one man sin entered into the world" (Romans 5:12).

Here is a striking illustration of Solomon's dictum about one sinner destroying much good (Ecclesiastes 9:18). All the tears, sorrows, losses, graves which sin has caused can be traced back to the one sin our first parents committed. Satan was not long marring the handiwork of God. But the promise for any sinner is that through the obedience and sacrifice of another Man, myriads have been delivered from the guilt and government of sin. And because influence is never neutral, each of us is helping others heavenward or hellward. Is *your* life a blessing or a blight?

"Fools make a mock of sin."

Proverbs 14:9

Only a *fool* could be guilty of such mockery. But belittle sin as he may, it ever rises to mock the fool who says, "There is no God! (Psalm 14:1). Mocking or minimizing sin does not do away with it. Satan has deluded some people into believing that he does not exist. If he is non-existent, then someone is carrying on his diabolical work. Further, if sin is only human frailty, or the just expressions of human nature, then it is a very destructive force. Sin is *sin,* and it must be hated and shunned, for its wages are death (Romans 6:23).

"Be sure your sin will find you out."

Numbers 32:23

Scripture, history, and experience testify to the fact that sin is a master detective. Moses knew what he was writing about, for the detection of his slaughter of the Egyptian meant forty years of solitude. Man may try to hide his sin and the effects of it, but at last it tracks him down. Sooner or later, "the chickens come home to roost." The sinner reaps what he sows. If exposure does not come in Time, there is always Eternity to reckon with.

"The soul that sinneth, it shall die."

Ezekiel 18:20

"Death through sin." Romans 5:12

Personal accountability is among the ethical instructions set forth by Ezekiel. Eternal death is for the sinner's own sin, and not another's (31:29, 30). Because all have sinned, all must suffer the second death, unless they rest in the death of the Saviour. "Death" does not mean cessation of being or annihilation, since the soul is indestructible. Death means separation. In physical death, there is the separation of the soul from the body.

In spiritual and eternal death, there is the separation of the soul from God. Surely such a terrible separation is a strong enough incentive for soul winning.

Paul makes it clear that every grave is the result of sin. Had there been no sin, there would have been no death. Doubtless we would have been translated like Enoch and Elijah. But through Adam, the federal head of the human race, sin came into the world, and death has come upon all men, for all have sinned.

"He that sinneth against me wrongeth his own soul." Proverbs 8:36

When fashioned by God, the soul possessed high and holy desires and also promises of heavenly bliss. Made for the heights, its nature has been sadly perverted by the corrupt influences of Satan and the world. Thus every time a person sins against God, he sins against that within his nature which, at one time, was God-like. Defiance of all God's loving desires for His creatures ever means the crucifixion of those appetites and aspirations calling out for the supreme and only source of entire satisfaction.

"Sin shall not have dominion over you." Romans 6:14

What a heartening promise this is! God has left no place in His program for sinning saints. Once delivered from the penalty of sin, there is no reason why we should continue sinning, for within us is the Holy Spirit so that we might not sin. If we do sin, Jesus pleads His efficacious blood on high (I John 2:1, 2). Are we dead to sin? Sin does not die, but by divine power we die *to* sin. The only way by which sin can be constantly dethroned is through the constant enthronement of Him who is stronger than Satan and sin.

"Christ died for our sins.". I Corinthians 15:3

"The blood of Jesus Christ, his Son, cleanseth us from all sins." I John 1:7

The mystery of the cross is that He who knew no sin was made sin – not a sinner! – for us. *Made sin!* Who can fathom the depth of this startling statement? The sinless One made sin. It pleased God to make His Son an offering for sin, and He died as the sinless Substitute for sinners.

What a Gospel to preach! How consoling was the promise of the cleansing blood to Martin Luther! When the devil came to the monk and reminded him of his sins,

Luther told the devil to make a list of them all and then write over the ugly catalog: "The blood cleanseth from *all* sins." That blood has perpetual efficacy because it was the blood of God's Son.

If troubled about your sin, which, if *you* try to cover, you will never prosper (Proverbs 28:13), run your eye over these promises regarding what God has done, and is willing to do, with sin—

He covers it (Romans 4:7)

He blots it out (Isaiah 43:25; 44:22; Colossians 2:14)

He removes it beyond recall (Psalm 103:12)

He hides it beyond discovery (Jeremiah 50:20)

He casts it into the depth of the sea (Micah 7:19)

He casts it behind His back (Isaiah 38:17)

He cleanses the sinner whiter than wool (Isaiah 1:18; Psalm 51:7)

He will not impute it once forgiven (Romans 4:8)

He will forgive it (Psalm 103:3; Colossians 1:14)

God is able to deal thus with sin because He laid it all on His sinless Son, and because He, by His death, bore it away (Isaiah 53:6; John 1:29).

All God's promises would be of no practical value if we did not have the revelation of His matchless GRACE. Because of His grace and His power, He can accomplish that which He pleases. "He will work, and who will let it?"

"I will pour upon the house of David . . . the spirit of grace." Zechariah 12:10

"Grace for grace . . . grace . . . came by Jesus Christ." John 1:16, 17

"By grace are ye saved." Ephesians 2:5

"According to the riches of his grace." Ephesians 1:3-7

Grace implies that we get from God just the oposite to what we deserve. Our sins deserve eternal death, but through grace we have eternal life. "Grace is a comprehensive word of boundless reach and infinite depth of significance," says Butler, "signifying unlimited favour to the undeserving, all who by reason of transgression have forfeited every claim to divine favour, and have lost all capacity for meritorious action."

"The God of all grace." I Peter 5:10

He is the Source and Giver of grace (Psalm 84:11; James 4:6), and such divine grace needs no supplement. How wonderful it is that the One sinned against was the One whose heart provided salvation from sin. The hands torn by man's sin offer free grace to all. Although God, because of His holiness, can never excuse iniquity, yet as the God of grace He deals kindly with the repenting sinner. He is not a tyrant or despot, but One whose grace is sufficient.

"Grace did much more abound."

Romans 5:20

Sin reigned! Grace reigns! What a contrast of sovereigns Paul presents in this chapter exalting the gift of grace! Abounding grace, however, making possible our liberty, does not mean license. We must shrink from the false doctrine that once saved we can do as we like. Divine grace demands that we must live as He likes. Grace must never be presumed upon. "Shall we sin that grace may abound? – God forbid." When grace reigns, all other claimants for the throne of the heart are deposed.

"Grow in grace." II Peter 3:18

It will be noticed that we do not grow *into* grace, but *in* it. We cannot grow unless we are rooted. Regeneration is a crisis. Once within the sphere of grace, we grow within it, just as the child begins to grow once it has life and is in the world. Are we growing? As in nature, so in grace, dwarfs are a monstrosity.

"Good stewards of the manifold grace of God." I Peter 4:10

Grace imputed and imparted must become grace communicated. Receiving the gift we must transmit it. Once Jesus saves us, we must tell others the story. With such good tidings, we dare not hold our peace.
The Bible makes it clear that salvation is all of grace, lest any man should boast. But what exactly is this promised SALVATION? Jesus, whose name means "salvation' (Matthew 1:21), came as the promised Saviour (Genesis 3:15).

"Christ our Saviour." Ephesians 5:23; Titus 3:6

"The appearing of our Saviour." II Timothy 1:10; Philippians 3:20
"The Father sent the Son to be the Saviour." I John 4:14; John 4:42
"Peace from the Lord Jesus Christ our Saviour." Titus 1:4
"Him hath God exalted to be Prince and Saviour." Acts 5:31; 13:23
"There is born this day . . . a Saviour." Luke 2:11
"Looking for . . . our Saviour Jesus Christ." Titus 2:13

As to the salvation so freely and fully provided by the Saviour, promises abound as to its fact and features.

"Our God is the God of salvation." Psalm 68:20; Isaiah 45:21; 49:26
"Saved is the Lord with an everlasting salvation." Isaiah 45:17
"Look unto me, and be ye saved, all the ends of the earth." Isaiah 45:22
"The world might through him be saved." John 3:17
"If any man enter in, he shall be saved." John 10:9
"Happy art thou . . . O people saved by the Lord." Deuteronomy 33:29

As to the extent and character of this salvation, it is –
"Great," "Eternal," "Uttermost," "Common" Hebrews 2:3; 5:9; 7:25; Jude 3; Isaiah 45:17

Such a salvation is likewise embracive, saving us –

From our sins (Matthew 1:21)

From coming wrath (Romans 5:9)

From our enemies, Satanic and human (Luke 1:69-71)

From all our trouble (Psalm 34:6)

From all uncleanness (Ezekiel 36:29)

From sinful dwelling-places (Ezekiel 37:23)

From our distresses (Psalm 107:13)

In studying the cardinal doctrine of salvation, we must bear in mind its three tenses or aspects which Paul so clearly defines, namely –

Its Past Tense – Salvation from the penalty of sin the moment we accept Jesus as personal Saviour. As soon as we receive Him, our past sin is for ever blotted out.

"The gospel of Christ . . . is the power of God unto salvation."

Romans 1:16; 10:9, 10

Its Present Tense – Salvation, day by day, from the power of sin. The first aspect represents a *crisis* – this second aspect is a process.

"For if, when we were enemies, we were reconciled to God (or, *saved*) by the death of his Son, much more, being reconciled, we shall be saved by his life." Romans 5:10

Here we have a double salvation – one by the death of Christ, the other by His life. In referring to Christ's life, Paul did not mean His earthly life. There is no salvation from sin by the life that He lived among men. He had to die to become a

Saviour. By "His life," Paul meant His present life in the glory – His exalted throne-life. Because of all He is up there, He is able to save us with an uttermost salvation (Hebrews 7:25).

Its Future Tense – Salvation from the entire presence of sin both within and around. When Jesus comes, the *saved* will be saved to sin no more. Salvation will be experienced from the old sinful, Adamic nature within, and from a sinning world. Then, and not till then, will "the Church be saved to sin no more." What a blessed promise and prospect this final installment of salvation holds for us!

Another great doctrine of our Christian faith related to further promises is that of REDEMPTION. The kindred terms "redeem," "redeemed," "redeemeth," and "redemption" appear over 150 times in the Bible. The New Testament word for "redeem" carries a three-fold significance –
1. Buying a captive in a market place.
2. To take away from the market place what was purchased.
3. To set free, or to let go.

Does it not take all these meanings to unfold the Gospel story of sin, bondage, and emancipation?
"Ye are bought with a price."
I Corinthians 6:20
The English word employed here implies the act of buying back from slavery or captivity or death by the payment of a price. It further carries the idea of substitution.
"Thou shalt redeem it with a lamb."
Exodus 13:13
"Ye were redeemed . . . with the precious blood of Christ." I Peter 1:18, 19
The price paid is called a "ransom," which brings us to the infinite cost of our redemption from satanic slavery.
"The price of his redemption."
Exodus 25:51, 52
"To give his life a ransom for many."
Matthew 20:28
"Who gave himself a ransom for all."
I Timothy 2:6
"The Lord that bought them."
II Peter 2:1
In one redemption there was a real transaction between God the Father and God the Son, the former sending the latter to redeem, and the latter willingly purchasing redemption with His own blood.
"Christ Jesus, who of God is made unto us . . . redemption." I Corinthians 1:30

"Who gave himself for us, that he might redeem us from all iniquity."
Titus 2:14
One of the marvelous aspects of the manifold provisions of God is the fact that they are all personified in Christ. Thus redemption is not *something* but SOMEONE. *He* was made *redemption*. Attention is focused, not so much on gifts but on the GIVER.
"The right of redemption is thine to buy it." Jeremiah 32:7, 8
The Old Testament supplies us with several illustrations of redemption by ransom, or price, the latter being gold or silver. There is the well-known incident of Boaz purchasing Ruth's inheritance and becoming her kinsman-redeemer. Jeremiah supplies us with another illustration of redemption in his purchase of Hanameel's field. The redeemer Moses wrote of and prefigured Jesus as the Redeemer.
"Their redeemer is strong."
Jeremiah 50:34
Both Solomon and Isaiah also join with Jeremiah in extolling the might of our Redeemer who, mighty as He is, can yet stoop to the sinner's weakness and empower him to live free from sin.
"Their redeemer is mighty; he shall plead their cause with thee."
Proverbs 23:11
"I the Lord am thy Saviour and thy redeemer." Isaiah 49:26
How mighty Christ must have been, when at Calvary He laid hold of the dark forces of hell and spoiled them of their power. Satan, the slave owner, was conquered, and the sin-bound were delivered from the curse and the grave. Then His resurrection added to His might. His became the strength of a glorious Conqueror. As another writer expresses it –
"The human race was wholly lost, sentenced to death, and excluded from the inheritance of spiritual and eternal life no mere created being could redeem. By the dominion of sin over them, they were captives of Satan and justly doomed to eternal woe. They had no kinsman to vindicate their cause, to interpose for them by power or force. The glory of the Gospel is that Christ came, and by giving Himself a ransom, provided a perfect redemption."
"With him is plenteous redemption."
Psalm 130:7
With His own blood Jesus obtained a

plenteous and an eternal redemption for all mankind. Millions in heaven and on earth have participated in His blood-bought salvation, and yet there is provision for millions more. How stupendous and far-reaching was the work of the cross! The tragedy is that although Christ died for all, only few, in comparison, have appropriated their redemption.

What were we redeemed from in the eternal redemption Christ obtained for us when He shed the blood of deity? (Acts 20:28). Go over those 150 references we have mentioned and see if you have claimed all your promised redemption rights—

From all iniquity (Titus 2:14; Psalm 130:8)

From the curse and bondage of the law (Galatians 3:13; 4:5)

From the power of sin (Romans 6:18, 22)

From a vain manner of life (I Peter 1:18)

From any kind of bondage (Exodus 6:6; Deuteronomy 15:15; Micah 6:4)

From all evil, trouble, distress, adversity (Genesis 48:16; II Samuel 4:9; I Kings 1:29; Psalm 25:22)

From deceit and violence (Psalm 72:14)

From destruction, death and Hell (Job 5:20; Psalms 49:15 R.V.; 103:4; Hosea 13:14)

From all our enemies (Psalm 136:24; Micah 4:10)

From the great enemy, the terrible one (Psalms 106:10; 107:2; Jeremiah 15:21; 31:11)

As one redeemed with a plenteous, precious, and eternal redemption, do you belong to the "Say-so Society"?—"Let the redeemed of the Lord say so" (Psalm 107:2). Paul reminds us that being redeemed we are not our own, but the property of Him who shed His blood for our redemption (I Corinthians 6:19, 20).

ATONEMENT is a further evangelical truth predicted and promised in Scripture. The provision and universality of Christ's atoning work is implied and illustrated in scores of passages. We confine ourselves to those references where the actual word "Atonement" is used in the Authorized Version. It is purely an Old Testament word, and is not properly found in the New Testament at all. The word Paul employs means "reconciliation," implying an exchange from enmity to friendship and is so translated in the Revised Version. As used in the Old Testament, "atonement" means *covering*. In Christian thought, however, Christ's full atonement represents His work of reconciling the world to God, and the satisfaction which He rendered His Father thereby.

"By whom we have now received the atonement." Romans 5:11

Paul's statement indicates the fact that Christ both *supplies* and *applies* atonement. God has nothing to offer apart from His Son. Our Lord's own word is emphatic on this point—

"No man cometh unto the Father, *but by me*." John 14:6

Christ, then, is the Mediator and the Medium. Through Him the sinner, estranged from God because of his sin, can be reconciled to God—not God to man. God has never had any need of being reconciled to man. Through the cross, fellowship is restored.

"When we were enemies, we were reconciled to God by the death of his Son." Romans 5:10

"Christ has for sin atonement made, What a wonderful Saviour."

"Make ye the atonement, that ye may bless the inheritance of the Lord."
II Samuel 21:3

What would you say is the greatest blessing flowing from Christ's atoning death? True, we are blessed with so many spiritual blessings in virtue of Calvary, the principal boon being deliverance from the penalty and guilt of sin. But the word "atone," when split up, reads "AT ONE," which gives us the heart of atonement, namely *made one with God*.

Jewels of gold... to make an atonement for our souls." Numbers 31:50

As we have indicated, the Old Testament word for "atonement" conveys the idea of something being covered, and the Israelite was allowed to appease God in various ways. In the narrative before us, the spoil of Midian was presented to the Lord to make an atonement for the soul. But the promise is that, under grace, acceptance with God cannot be bought. Some there are who try to buy their way into God's favor, but it cannot be done. All the jewels in the world could not purchase salvation for a conscience-stricken soul. A sinner must come as a beggar and, without money and without price, accept Calvary's gift of reconciliation. Once reconciled, then we can surrender all the jewels the Saviour's cause should have.

What the sinner must be reminded of is the fact that he can only be saved through *atonement*, and never through *attainment*. How many deluded souls there are who seem to think that they must do something in order to gain access to God! But by their religious activities and moral deeds they can never attain to salvation. Access to God, and acceptance by God, cannot be gained by human merit. Salvation can only be *obtained* by faith, never *attained* by works.

"Make an atonement; for there is wrath gone out from the Lord." Numbers 16:46

Sin occasioned the anger of God, but through the cross such righteous anger was appeased. This is why the believer is no longer under wrath, present or future. The unregenerated sinner, however, is still under condemnation. God is angry with him every day (Psalm 7:11). "The wrath of God abideth on him" (John 3:36). The promise offered the sinner is "Kiss the Son, lest he be angry" (Psalm 2:12).

"Do no work . . . it is a day of atonement." (Leviticus 23:28).

The application of this command is that God cannot save on a 50/50 basis, partly grace, partly works. When Jesus cried, "It is finished," he referred not to the cessation of His anguish, but to the consummation of man's complete deliverance from sin, and of a free access into the presence of God.

"An atonement for himself, and for his household." (Leviticus 16:17).

Under Jewish economy, household atonement played a prominent part in the ritual commanded by God. Before they left Egypt, the blood had to be sprinkled on the portal of the house, implying deliverance from death for *all* within the blood-marked home. Can we say that His blood is on us and on our children? Is our family circle complete in grace?

It is also evident that Christ's work of reconciliation was universal, although the realization of it is not.

"One died for all . . . He died for all."
II Corinthians 5:14, 15

"Ye will not come unto me, that ye might have life." John 5:40

If a sinner finally perishes, it will not be God's fault. Theologian Hodge says, "No man is lost for the want of atonement, or because there is any other barrier in the way of salvation than his own most free and wicked will." The atonement Christ provided is universal in that it covers the sinful nature inherited from Adam. This offers the promise of heaven for infants who die, and for those born idiots. When, however, a person reaches the years of accountability and refuses to accept a provided new

nature, allowing inherited sin to become practiced sin, then he becomes accountable to God. Yielding to the sinful nature, he must bear the fruit and punishment of it (Romans 5:12-14; 6:1-12; 8:2, 3).

"Atonement money for the service of the tabernacle." Exodus 30:16

What a practical lesson can be gleaned from the above requirement! God has ever been particular about the kind of money used in His service. The gold of the godless carries no value in the treasury of heaven. God's work, when done in God's way for God's glory, never lacks the divine supply. *Blood-money* – that is, the substance of blood-washed men and women – is what He uses for the spread of the Gospel. God has only one way of maintaining and extending His cause in the world, and that through the sacrificial giving of those who realize that Calvary has every claim upon all they *have* and *are*.

Among the manifold promises of God is the one proclaiming REGENERATION for the fallen sinner. This act of the Spirit is known as the "new birth" – a birth from above, the Divine work whereby the believing sinner is bought into a heavenly relationship. As the result of our physical birth we are initiated into a heavenly family with God becoming our Heavenly Father.

John's first Epistle is pre-eminently one of regeneration, the words "born" and "begotten" occurring 10 times. In his *gospel* John speaks of being "born again" and "born of the Spirit" (3:3-8). The Word of God is mentioned some 6 times as the instrument the Holy Spirit uses in the necessary work of regeneration (John 15:3; I Corinthians 4:15; Ephesians 5:26; James 1:18, 21; I Peter 1:23). Jesus emphasized the necessity of this work that Paul calls "a new creation" (Galatians 6:15). "Ye must be born again" (John 3:7). Apart from this spiritual birth, heaven cannot be entered.

"Except a man be born from above, he cannot see the kingdom of God."
John 3:3

While regeneration and CONVERSION are treated as identical acts, there is a difference between the two. *Conversion* is a human act, and one that can be repeated (Luke 22:32). *Regeneration* is a divine act, and once accomplished can never be repeated.

"What God doeth is for ever."
Ecclesiastes 3:14

Closely allied to regeneration is ADOPTION, which is, so to speak, the other side of the coin. *Regeneration* is "son-making" – *adoption* is "son-placing." The latter term is of Roman origin and represents the time when a senator's son became "of age" and heir to his father's possessions. At that time the father took his son into the Senate and publicly took off the toga of boyhood and put upon him the toga of manhood. We must not read into the word our modern thought of adoption in which a man takes a son not his own and gives him the place of a son in position and advantages. As God's children we cannot very well be born *and* adopted. If His, then we are His sons now, with all the spiritual rights and privileges of sonship.

"Now are we the sons of God."
                                    I John 3:1
The "adoption" of the Bible is not a present experience but a future promise. It is true that we are indwelt by the "Spirit of adoption," but as such He is the promise or pledge of a coming placement in God's House above (Romans 8:15).

"The holy Spirit of promise . . . of our inheritance." Ephesians 1:13, 14
We await our "adoption," which is a phase of and occurs when the body is redeemed at Christ's return.

"We ourselves groan within ourselves, waiting for the adoption, to wit, the redemption of the body." Romans 8:23
Redeemed by the blood and regenerated by the Spirit and therefore the sons of God (John 1:11, 12), we await our son-placing, or adoption as sons.

"That we might receive the adoption of sons." Galatians 4:5
"Having predestinated us unto the adoption of children by Jesus Christ to himself." Ephesians 1:5
A further promise connected with our divine relationship is that of SECURITY. In Christ we are not only saved but safe, or secure. The keeping power of God, which involves our preservation, permeates Scripture.

"Hold up my goings in thy paths, that my footsteps slip not." Psalm 17:5
"He is at my right hand, I shall not be moved." Psalm 16:8
"None of them that trust in him shall be desolate." Psalm 34:22
"He shall never suffer the righteous to be moved." Psalm 55:22
"The Lord is thy keeper." Psalm 121:5
"The Lord preserveth all them that love him." Psalm 145:20

"I know that I shall not be ashamed."
                                    Isaiah 50:7; 45:17
"He . . . preserved the way of his saints." Proverbs 2:8
"He will keep the feet of his saints."
                                    I Samuel 2:9
"No man is able to pluck them out of my Father's hand." John 10:28, 29
"There is therefore now no condemnation to them which are in Christ Jesus."
                                    Romans 8:1
"Nor any other creature, shall be able to separate us from the love of God which is in Christ Jesus our Lord." Romans 8:38, 39
"He is able to keep that which I have committed unto him against that day."
                                    II Timothy 1:12
"The Lord . . . will preserve me unto his heavenly kingdom." II Timothy 4:18
"Jesus the author and finisher of our faith." Hebrews 12:1, 2
"Kept by the power of God through faith." I Peter 1:15
"Now unto him that is able to keep you from falling." Jude 24
How sad it is that in spite of all these gracious promises relating to the eternal security of the believer, so many of God's dear children do not have the assurance their faith should beget. We recognize, of course, that faith is *not* assurance. Geike remarks that–

"It is often a great stumbling-block to humbler but faint-hearted Christians that they fancy they cannot be true believers if they have not full assurance that they are accepted by God. Many a worthy soul goes softly all his days, fearing to lay hold on the promises, from a sense of unworthiness and a dread of presumption. But it is very certain, whatever some may say, that assurance is not faith, but a result of it, attuned only gradually and sometimes not at all: the ripened fruit in the autumn of one's experience, for the most part, rather than a spring blossom."
For failing to lay hold of promised security, many are robbed of the peace and joy that come through believing. John reminds us that all who believe should *know* that they have eternal life (I John 5:13). Can it be, my reader, that you are among the number lacking this assurance of Christ's power, not only to save, but to keep? Well, ponder these further meditations on the divine ability to hold you fast–

"This is the Father's will . . . that . . . I should lose nothing." John 6:39
There are at least five things Jesus related to His Father in this wonderful verse. He was

sent by the Father. We were given to Christ by the Father. It is His will that, surrendered to His Son, we should never be lost. Being Christ's own, our security rests with Him. We are to be raised up at the last day.

Lose nothing! Yes, and Christ will see to it that not one of His given ones will perish. God wills our security, and His beloved Son provides it. Thus, when Satan casts doubt upon your eternal salvation, remind him that Christ has declared that He will lose nothing. All who are His will be raised up to meet Him at His appearing. The question of great importance is, Are you among the number given to Christ by the Father?

"They shall never perish . . . My hand . . . My Father's hand." John 10:28

With such a double grip we are doubly safe because the Father and the Son are one in their purpose to preserve their own. It must be further noticed that this is no condition attached to this promise and charter of security. Jesus did not say that we can only be eternally safe if we strive to keep ourselves in His hands. Once union with Him has been consummated, it can never be severed. *Communion* with Him can be ruptured, but *union* is eternal. If we can receive life from Christ today and lose it tomorrow, how can it be eternal in nature?

"He is able to keep." II Timothy 1:12

Paul, the apostle of assurance, never had any doubt regarding his *standing* in grace. Like the rest of us, his *state* concerned him. But he clearly taught that it is the work of the Holy Spirit to translate position into practice. Have you noticed the double committal and the double security in Paul's positive declaration? The Lord keeps what we commit to Him (1:12); and we keep what He commits to us (1:14). Paul's certainty as to his eternal security comes out again when he asserts that Christ would keep him from every evil work and preserve him unto the heavenly kingdom (4:18). Have you committed your soul to the Lord? Then believe, and be persuaded with Paul, that your heavenly Keeper will guard the deposit.

"The Lord is thy keeper." Psalm 121:5

For every sigh God has a psalm, and in this precious psalm the sigh of the heart for preservation has the psalm of divine security. Read this psalm through and underline the three-fold *keep* and the three-fold *preserve*. The emphasis of the psalm as a whole is upon the fact that our security is the Lord's responsibility. We do not have to struggle to keep ourselves saved. The sheep never trouble themselves about keeping the shepherd. That the Lord is well able to keep His own is evidenced by two of His characteristic features – He made heaven and earth; and He neither slumbers nor sleeps. Count up the realms in which you can expect His preserving power, and praise Him anew as the Keeper (Isaiah 27:3).

"Him that is able to keep you from falling." Jude 24

From falling and faultless! What a mighty Preserver we have! Daily He is able to keep us from stumbling, and then at His Advent presents us to Himself faultless . . . with exceeding joy. Falling has to do with our walk. But such falling does not affect our position in Christ. A closer walk with Him cannot make us more secure, but it will bring us greater peace and reward. What we must not lose sight of is the truth that, while we cannot help Christ to keep us eternally secure, we can yet assist Him to keep us from stumbling. As we keep ourselves in the love of God, keep ourselves from idols, keep ourselves unspotted from the world, we experience Christ's ability to keep us from sinning.

"If God . . . will keep me . . . then." Genesis 28:20, 21

Jacob's error was that of meeting God's "I will keep thee" with his "If God . . . will keep me." May we be delivered from the same folly of driving a bargain with God. "If" must not be in the vocabulary of the saint who takes God at His word.

Jacob was ever the man of sight, and taken up with material security. Preservation from danger, bread to eat, raiment to wear, was the patriarch's interpretation of the divine promise of blessing. Jacob's vow, however, must not be lost upon us. Eternal security carries with it the full sovereignty of our Keeper. "Then shall the Lord by my God." As our God, he has every right to all we are and have.

"Keep me as the apple of the eye." Psalm 17:8

Frequent references to "the apple of the eye" (Deuteronomy 32:10; Proverbs 7:2; Lamentations 2:18; Zechariah 2:8) are associated with the keen sensibility of the ball of the eye. It is a most expressive metaphor, denoting God's most careful protection and security. The eye is always preserved, no matter what may assail it from without. Such a delicate organ is continually protected by the lids and continually cleansed by its tear-ducts. God is willing to protect and purge His children, assymbolized by the apple of the eye. Because we have been redeemed by the blood of His Son, God will see to it that neither demons nor men rob Him of such a treasure.

How sweet and satisfying are the promises attached to the Bible Doctrine of JUSTIFICATION – a term implying the act of counting, declaring, or pronouncing one righteous, or free from guilt and exposure to punishment. As saved sinners, we are declared righteous before God because we are covered by the finished substitutionary work of His Son. The Westminister Catechism cites the doctrine thus –

"Justification is an act of God's free grace wherein He pardoneth all our sins, and accepteth us as righteous in His sight, only for the righteousness of Christ imputed to us and received by faith alone."

His justification, and the declaration of it in heaven, is made available the very moment Jesus is received as the Substitute.

"He hath not beheld iniquity in Jacob." Numbers 23:21

"In the Lord shall all . . . be justified." Isaiah 45:25

"My righteous servant shall justify many." Isaiah 53:11

"Being justified freely by his grace." Romans 3:24

"Therefore being justified by faith." Romans 5:1

"Being now justified by his blood." Romans 5:9

"The free gift . . . justification of life." Romans 5:18

"It is God that justifieth." Romans 8:33

"Ye could not be justified by the law of Moses." Acts 13:39

"Being justified by his grace." Titus 3:7

How stupendous is the amazing grace of God! It causes the justified one to stand perfect before the law, as if he had never broken it. Through Christ every demand of God upon the sinner as far as the law is concerned was met, and as soon as Christ is received as the Saviour and Substitute, the sinner is freely justified from all things.

"How then can man be justified with God?" Job 25:4

Job's question finds an answer in Paul's declaration that "God is just and the justifier of him which believeth in Jesus" (Romans 3:26). Just and yet justifier! How is God able to clear the guilty sinner upon whom He had pronounced death? Condemned yet pardoned! Jesus supplies the answer. He died in the sinner's room and stead. True to His justice, God punished sin, which He did in Christ. Appropriating the Sin-bearer, the believing sinner is forever cleared from the Law's just verdict.

"If I justify myself." Job 9:20

From Adam down, man has endeavored to justify himself. Plausible arguments excusing sin have been easy to find. But is a man full of talk justified? (Job 11:2). Elihu was angry with Job because he justified himself rather than God (32:2). Jesus condemned the Pharisees for justifying themselves (Luke 16:15). But in spite of all his self-justification, man stands condemned in the sight of a thrice-holy God. "In thy sight shall no man living be justified" (Psalm 143:2).

"Being justified freely by his grace." Romans 3:24

To be justified freely means not only that Christ's redemptive work provides a full, complete justification from the just claims of the Law, but also that the most unworthy can participate in such a provision. Paul speaks of the *free* gift. But are not all gifts free? Any article cannot be a gift if we have to pay for it. The value of a gift, however, is determined by the love borne to the one about to receive the gift. Merit, then, prompts and guides our giving. To give a precious gift to an enemy could be a "free gift" – given without cause or merit. Such is the giving of God. Although His enemies, and altogether without merit, He justified us.

"Justified by faith." Romans 5:1

In all of his writings, Paul emphasizes the truth that faith alone actualizes what Christ made possible by His death and resurrection. Light in the room where these lines are being written is possible because electricity is in the wires, and bulbs are waiting to give an unseen power, expression. But before the possible can become actual, I must put my finger on the switch at the door, producing thereby the contact between the possible and the actual. In effect, Paul says that faith is the *switch*.

"Justified by his blood." Romans 5:9

"Raised again for our justification." Romans 4:5

We link these two passages together for the simple reason that both Christ's death and resurrection form the basis of justification. When presenting the Gospel we must be careful never to disassociate His death from His resurrection. To say that we are justified by His blood is true, but only half true. Had Christ remained in the grave there would have been no salvation for a sinning race. But the promise was that He should rise again, which He did, and the sinner is saved as he believes in his heart that God raised His Son from the dead (Romans 10:9, 10).

"Whom he justified, them he also glorified." Romans 8:30

To be justified means to be brought up before God as if we had never sinned. What a miracle of grace! Yet such is the scope of redemption that our future is covered and assured. Love is to perfect what it begins. Having begun a good work of justification, the Lord will consummate it in our glorification. Positionally, we are with Him already in glory. The realization of our transformation into the likeness of the Justifier, however, will be ours when we see Him face to face.

"Justified by works." James 1:22, 25

There is no contradiction here of Paul's doctrine of justification by faith. James the Just was a very practical man who believed in the outward signs of inward grace. "As the body without the spirit is dead, so faith without works is dead also." Both Abraham and Rahab were justified by their works – that is, what they did was an evidence of what they believed. We cannot work for our justification, but by the life we live after we are justified we can demonstrate the reality of our heavenly calling. We labor for the Lord because we *are* His, not to *become* His.

Coming now to God's PARDONING, FORGIVING love, how rich are the promises assuring the sinner of his willingness to blot out his iniquity. Such gracious promises run through the Bible like a golden thread. Both *pardon* and *forgiveness* are constituent elements of *justification*. Although different phases of the same act and taking place at the same time, there may be a slight difference between pardon and forgiveness.

Pardon means the release from a penalty. The feelings of the pardoned one may or may not be changed.

"I tell you, this man went down to his house justified rather than the other."
Luke 18:9-14

Forgiveness implies the surrender of an inward feeling of injury or resentment, the removal of a feeling of anger and the restoration of a feeling of favor and affection –

"Through this man is preached unto you the forgiveness of sins: And by him all that believe are justified from all things, from which ye could not be justified by the Law of Moses." Acts 13:38, 39

N. M. Miller writes: "Humanly speaking, one may receive pardon without forgiveness. He may also receive pardon and forgiveness without remission. Remission, propitiation, and reconciliation, besides being definate acts of God based upon the finished work of Jesus, also represents phases of the work of Jesus which made these acts possible. As *Judge*, God pardons; as *Father*, He forgives."

"I will forgive their iniquity, and will remember their sin no more."
Jeremiah 31:34

"I will pardon all their iniquities, and I will pardon all." Jeremiah 33:8

"Who is a God like thee, that pardoneth iniquity." Micah 7:18-19

"Forgiving iniquity, transgression and sin." Exodus 34:6-7

"I, even I, am he that blotteth out thy transgressions." Isaiah 43:25

"Our God, for he will abundantly pardon." Isaiah 55:7

"There is forgiveness with thee, that thou mayest be feared." Psalm 130:4

"Thou art a God ready to pardon, gracious and merciful." Nehemiah 9:17

"Thou forgavest the iniquity of my sin."
Psalm 32:5

"For thou, Lord, art good, and ready to forgive." Psalms 86:5; 25:18

"To the Lord our God belong mercies and forgiveness." Daniel 9:9

"Forgiving iniquity and transgression and sin." Exodus 34:7; Numbers 14:18

"A Saviour, for to give . . . forgiveness of sins." Acts 5:31; 3:19

"Who forgiveth all thine iniquities."
Psalm 103:3, 12

"Through his blood, even the forgiveness of sins." Colossians 1:14; Ephesians 1:7

"Father, forgive them; for they know not what they do." Luke 23:34

"He is faithful and just to forgive us our sins." I John 1:9

What a beautiful glimpse of the divine character Nehemiah gives us! Not only have we a pardoning God, but One who stands with a pardon in His hand, so to speak, waiting for the sinner to accept it. "A God ready to pardon." This God of infinite kindness has not to be coaxed into pronouncing the criminal forever cleared from guilt. He is ready to pardon. If only sinners were as *ready* to receive this completed, offered pardon written out in the ruby blood of Him who died in the sinner's stead!

"The Lord God, merciful and gracious . . . forgiving." Exodus 34:6-7.

Nowhere in all the Bible is there a more satisfying revelation of God's character than here, where the Lord granted Moses the sublime revelation of His pardoning grace. No wonder Moses bowed his head toward the earth and worshiped! Mercy is "kept" for thousands, which implies that God has an inexhaustible store of it and can draw on it as sinners need it. As we read the entire verse, we find that forgiveness covers iniquity, the fruit of original corruption; transgression, the doing of what is prohibited; and sin, failure to do what is commanded.

"I, even I, am He that blotteth out thy transgressions." Isaiah 43:25

Is it not wonderful to realize that the God who freely offers to forgive is the One so constantly sinned against? Take the last phrase of the previous verse, which reads – "Thou hast wearied me with thine iniquities," and connect it with the above verse for a blessed glimpse of God. The One despised, outraged, scorned, and deserted for idols was the very One Israel was urged to return to. God further declares His willingness to forgive for His "own name's sake." Such a phrase implies that because of His loving, righteous character, expressed in many of His names, His actions must correspond to His attributes, which, praise Him, they do.

"But there is forgiveness with thee." Psalm 130:4

To rightly understand this aspect of promised forgiveness, we must look at the blessed "but" introducing it. Something opposite precedes it. We would have been of all men most miserable if we only had the third verse –

"If thou, Lord, shouldst mark iniquities, O Lord, who shall stand?"

How hopeless our case if we had an unforgiving God to deal with! All sinners, however, are encouraged to confess their sin because of the promise of God's unfailing and inexhaustible source of forgiveness. Further, forgiveness is manifested and freely bestowed that God may be feared, implying not a cringing fear, but reverential trust, obedience, confidence, and worship. Forgiving grace enables us to stand before the Lord.

"I have blotted out . . . thy transgressions . . . I have redeemed thee."
Isaiah 44:22

The basis of forgiveness is the redemptive work of the cross. Because "righteousness and truth kissed each other" at Calvary, a vindicated justice is now able to blot out our confessed sins. By His death, Christ purchased pardon for all. Few in comparison, however, have appropriated that pardon. Although redeemed, they are not "healed, restored, forgiven." Are you among the redeemed who know that God will remember sin against you no more for ever?

"Who is this that forgiveth sins also?"
Luke 7:49

In the parable of the creditor and the two debtors, Jesus has a good deal to say about forgiveness. There is evidently the degree of forgiveness. While one debtor owed ten times as much as the other, both were freely forgiven. But deeper love was expressed by the debtor to whom the creditor forgave most. It is thus that our Lord interprets the action of the woman whom others despised –

"Her sins, which are many, are forgiven, for she loveth much: but to whom little is forgiven, the same loveth little."
Luke 7:47

Another application is that Christ alone has the prerogative to forgive, since He is the *Creditor*. All souls are deep in debt to Him, and of themselves are utterly unable to discharge the debt. But as He paid it all, and all to Him we owe, He has every right to say, "Thy sins are forgiven." Forgiveness is also an evidence of His deity –

"Who can forgive sins, but *God* alone?"
Luke 5:21

A further promise begetting assurance of faith is that with God, to forgive is to forget –

"Their sins and iniquities will I remember no more" Hebrews 10:17

We may be sincere in our forgiveness of another, but yet find it difficult to forget. The nail is drawn from the wood, but the scar remains. God, however, removes both the nail and the scar. This tenth chapter of Hebrews provides us with a forceful illustration of heaven's forgiveness. In 11:29 we have the account of Israel's deliverance from Egypt, and then came the forty years of wandering. Sin, disobedience, and lust characterized the wilderness journey, but the next verse has no record of that dark period. What a jump! From the Red Sea to the walls of Jericho. We would have expected those forty years to have a line or two. But no! God remembered them no more. If He has forgiven your sinful past, then why should you continually rake it up?

"As we forgive." Matthew 6:12

The duty of mutual forgiveness is enjoined upon all who are the recipients of divine forgiveness. C. I. Scofield's comment is helpful at this point—

"This is legal' ground. Compare Ephesians 4:32 which is grace. Under law forgiveness is conditioned upon a like spirit in us, under grace we are forgiven for Christ's sake, and exhorted to forgive because we have been forgiven."

Christ not only taught forgiveness but exemplified it in His life and at His death. How full of rebuke, if we are guilty of maintaining an unforgiving spirit, is His prayer—

"Father, forgive them, for they know not what they do." Luke 23:34

Tennyson wrote of "The little hearts that know not how to forgive." The Lord grant us large hearts—Calvary hearts!

Among the manifold bestowals of God likewise included among the cardinal truths of the Gospel is that of PEACE, about which we had something to say when considering the divine title—"Jehovah Shalom." Such a possession, however, carrying with it so many promises, is worthy of fuller consideration. Wordsworth gave us the expression—

> *"Peace—*
> The central feeling of all happiness."

As the word "Peace" and its cognates appear some 400 times in the Bible, the problem of selection was not easy to settle. Among so many peace promises, the following glitter like the several facets of a diamond. Such a fundamental doctrine is approached from different angles.

1. There is peace *with* God, which is secured by Christ's finished work.

"We have peace with God through our Lord Jesus Christ" (Romans 5:1). This aspect of peace is not a mere feeling, but a permanent state or condition into which believers are brought, solely as the result of the cross, the value of which is placed to their account as the result of faith. No sinner can *make* his peace with God. Such peace was made when Christ died and rose again. God Himself was the One who

"Made peace through the blood of his cross." Colossians 1:20

"He is our peace . . . preaching peace." Ephesians 2:12-17; Acts 10:36

Peace, then, is not something but *Someone*. Peace is a Person, even Christ who removed the wall of partition between Jew and Gentile in order that both might be brought nigh to God. This state of peace we are introduced into by grace was established between God, who represented the divine government and Christ who represented the offending sinner. The sin-hating God met the sin-bearing Christ at Calvary and settled, once and for all, the sin question, providing a peace that knows no change.

2. There is the peace *of* God, which is imparted by the Holy Spirit.

"The peace *of* God, which passeth all understanding, shall keep (guard or garrison) your hearts and minds through Christ Jesus." Philippians 4:7

This particular promise of peace is communicated by the Holy Spirit upon the three conditions mentioned in the context, namely,

> Be careful for nothing—
> Be prayerful in everything—
> Be always thankful.

The first aspect of peace was the legacy of the Christ who died—this aspect is the gift of the living Christ by His Spirit. The first is the peace of conscience through the appropriation of the Saviour—the latter is the peace of heart found in full, unhindered fellowship with Him who bore "the chastisement of our peace" (Isaiah 53:5).

"Peace I leave with you . . . my peace" (John 14:27).

Materially, Christ had nothing to leave. He had no need to make a will. Yet the greatest bequest ever bequeathed is ours in *His peace*. Think of His calm, unruffled spirit amid turbulent forces surrounding Him! Why, He could sleep in a wave-tossed boat out in a raging storm! No wonder there is no peace comparable to His. Such a legacy is for every child of His—have you staked your claim?

3. There is the peace *from* God, which is a full expression of grace from the Godhead.

"Peace *from* God our Father, and the Lord Jesus Christ." Romans 1:7 (See also I Corinthians 1:3; II Corinthians 1:2; Galatians 1:3; Ephesians 1:2; Philippians 1:2; Colossians 1:2; I Thessalonians 1:1; II Thessalonians 1:2; I Peter 1:2; II Peter 1:2.)

When individuals instead of churches are

addressed, the form of the invocation or salutation is generally changed. Peace in this connection includes all the blessings we need for time and eternity. Grace is the unfailing fountain, and peace from the Godhead the everlasting stream – the outflowing of grace in practical benefits for those who are at peace with God, and who have peace through believing.

4. There is peace *on* earth, which will be fully realized when Christ returns.

"On earth, peace." Luke 2:14

"Neither shall they learn war any more."
Isaiah 2:4; Psalm 46:9

What heartening promises these, and similar ones are, for a blood-soaked, war-weary world! Amid threats of a universal, devastating nuclear war, the carol of the angels seems to be a contradiction. With Satan as god of this world, what else can we expect but strife and bloodshed? As a "murderer from the beginning," as Jesus called him, he is the instigator of international and communal feuds resulting in war. Almost two millenniums ago "the Prince of Peace" was crucified, and since then the world has been torn by a succession of wars. But world-peace is coming, and it will be experienced when Christ returns to earth as its rightful Lord and King.

The *Prayer Book Version* of Psalm 120:6 is most suggestive –

"I labour for peace; but when I speak unto them thereof, they make them ready for battle."

God always labors for peace, but the nations fail to recognize Him as the blessed Peace-Maker, and, piling up their destructive bombs, they make ready for another battle. But His day is coming when the nations will be forced to transform their spears into pruning hooks. Does not Paul declare the promise of ultimate peace in the words:

"The God of peace shall bruise Satan under your feet shortly." Romans 16:20

Six times over in the New Testament we have the designation – "The God of Peace," and its connections form a profitable Bible meditation. Peace is not only one of His attributes, but a part of His inherent nature (Philippians 4:7, 9; Colossians 3:15; II Corinthians 13:11; Hebrews 13:20). He *is* peace, and as such will destroy everything antagonistic to His peaceful nature. Is it not comforting to know that Satan, the origin of unrest and disorder, was dealt a death-blow at Calvary, and that before long

he will be finally vanquished. In this age of grace we need to heed the warning of Jesus that the message He would have us proclaim produces conflict rather than peace –

"Think not that I am to send peace on earth." Matthew 10:34

Universal peace on earth will only come when He ushers in His kingdom of peace, and He reigns supreme as King of kings.

There are a few further *peace-promises* which we can briefly consider before passing on to other divine attributes.

"He will speak peace unto his people." Psalm 85:8

"Great peace have they which love thy law: and nothing shall offend them."
Psalm 119:163

"Thou wilt keep him in perfect peace, whose mind is stayed on thee."
Isaiah 26:3-4

"Great shall be the peace of thy children." Isaiah 54:13

Promised and possessed peace can be fully enjoyed as we live in the will of God. As He speaks peace to His saints, He likewise warns them not to turn again to folly. If we are His children, then loving His Word and having the mind stayed on Him, we can experience peace, perfect peace – a peace passing all understanding, and misunderstanding as well.

"The meek . . . shall delight themselves in the abundance of peace."
Psalm 37:11

Have you heard the story of the old woman whose life had been a constant struggle against poverty, and who had never seen the sea? On being taken to the seaside for the first time, she exclaimed, "Thank God there's something there's enough of!" God has supplied countless millions with His peace, and yet there is more to follow. How exhaustless is His provision!

"Peace always by all means."
II Thessalonians 3:16

"All her paths are peace."
Proverbs 3:17

"The fruit of the Spirit . . . is peace."
Galatians 5:22

In Paul's beautiful benediction, he dwells upon four different aspects of peace. First of all, Christ is the Lord of peace. He is its Source and Substance. Secondly, He never delegates another to bring us His peace, but bestows it Himself. Thirdly, His peace is an abiding possession. Circumstances can never affect it. Whether sunshine or shadow, we have "peace always." Fourthly, this divine peace, Christ's own peace, comes to us "by *all* means." It is easy to be peaceful when all is well, but Paul implies that even adversities can contribute to our peace of heart. All roads can lead to this peace which, by the Spirit, we can possess.

"Follow peace with all men."
Hebrews 12:14

"The unity of the Spirit is the bond of peace." Ephesians 4:3

"Be at peace among yourselves."
I Thessalonians 5:13

"Follow peace with all men."
II Timothy 2:22

"See that ye fall not out by the way."
Genesis 45:24

The above *peace* verses bring us to the practical outward manifestation in our lives of the divine and inner peace we profess to have as the Lord's. There are some expositors who see in the exhortation of following peace with all men a reference to the hunter, "Follow peace, as the hound does the hare." It is to be feared that we have not the same enthusiasm for peace among ourselves as hounds have for hares. There were times when Paul found those fractious souls who loved trouble rather than peace, and so wrote—

"*If it be possible,* as much as lieth in you, live peaceably with all men."
Romans 12:15

Our responsibility is to seek peace and pursue it, even as the hound pursues the hare. If those with whom we seek to live in peace reject our overtures and retain their antagonistic attitude, we must yet maintain a peaceful frame of mind, as well as a peaceful attitude.

For Christian workers who seek to win those who are not at peace with God, here are one or two peace verses which are essential to keep in mind since they warn the sinner of the error of his ways—

"Peace, peace . . . no peace."
Isaiah 57:19-21

As the God of peace, He is consumed with a passion to make all men the recipients of His bounty. He has no pleasure in the death of the wicked. He is all for peace, and has peace for all. There is abundant peace for those "far off," not only geographically but spiritually. The least privileged and most sinful are called to appropriate God's offered peace. There is likewise peace for "him that is near." And who are

so near as the redeemed of the Lord?
"In the Person of His Son,
We are as near as He."

For the sinner it is "peace with God"; for the saint, "peace in God." But if the wicked are content to remain "afar off" from God, then in retaining their wickedness, they are like the troubled sea, ever restless, casting up mire and dirt.

"He shall make peace with me."
Isaiah 27:5

"The work of righteousness shall be peace." Isaiah 32:17

A writer of last century reminds us that peace is "that delightful sensation which arises from the assurance of safety, enjoyment, and security against want and misery." As by sin man is at enmity with God, or in a state of war with heaven, so to be delivered from such estrangement is called "peace with God." From this aspect of peace arises that of peace of conscience (Hebrews 10:22). Christ became the sinner's *Peace,* which was the effect or outcome of divine righteousness. Now the proffered promise to the sinner is that by faith he can accept a provided peace.

"There is no peace, saith the Lord, unto the wicked." Isaiah 48:20-22

What a graphic description the prophet gives us of the turmoil and conflict raging within the breast of the godless—

"The wicked are like the troubled sea, when it cannot rest, whose waters cast up mire and dirt." Isaiah 57:26

How fittingly this metaphor depicts the unsettled condition of the sinner! The craving for satisfaction which Christ alone can impart creates a ceaseless round of worldly pursuits and pleasures. He seeks peace, but it eludes him. Sometimes death is sought in order to end unsatisfied yearnings for peace. Suicide, however, only plunges the wicked into the fiercer restlessness of hell.

"Acquaint thyself with him, and be at peace." Job 22:21

What a gracious promise this is! Because peace was secured at Calvary, all that one with a troubled conscience can do is to acquaint himself with Him who is our Peace. When at peace with God, then, as Job promises, "good shall come unto thee." How can a person expect anything that is good, if a blood-purchased peace is not accepted? It is hoped that you are acquainted with God, and have a heart as tranquil as the lake Jesus calmed while here on earth.

Having considered some of the promises connected with many of the cardinal gospel doctrines, it must be emphasized that the realization of doctrinal promises is conditioned by REPENTANCE and FAITH on the part of the sinner.

"Repentance toward God, and faith toward our Lord Jesus Christ."

Acts 20:21

What is this *repentance* God commands? Is it not a change of heart and attitude Godward, resulting in a change of life? The two New Testament words translated "repent" mean *a sorrow of remorseful regret*, then *to change one's mind, or to have a better mind*. The latter meaning suggests a reversal of man's entire natural, intellectual, affectional, and moral outlook which is the miracle taking place at regeneration. Biblical repentance implies a complete right about face based upon deep sorrow and remorse for, and abhorrence of, sin – an abhorrence made possible by a sight of God's holiness and of the terribleness of sin. Repentance is illustrated in these three steps –

"I thought on my ways,
And turned my feet unto thy testimonies.
I made haste and delayed not . . . ."

Psalm 119:59, 60

Thomas Chalmers says of repentance that, "It describes that deep and radical change whereby a sinner turns from the idols of sin and self unto God, and devotes every movement of the inner and outer man to the captivity of His obedience."

"The Lord . . . saveth such as be of a contrite spirit." Psalm 34:18

"A broken and a contrite heart, O God, thou wilt not despise." Psalm 51:17

"He healeth the broken in heart."

Psalm 147:3

"Repent, for the kingdom of heaven is at hand." Matthew 3:2

"Except ye repent, ye shall all likewise perish." Luke 13:3

"God commandeth all men everywhere to repent." Acts 17:30

"That all should come to repentance."

II Peter 3:9

"Repent therefore, and turn again, that your sins may be blotted out."

Acts 3:19

"Repent: or else I will come unto thee quickly." Revelation 2:5, 16

"The goodness of God leadeth thee to repentance." Romans 2:4

"I acknowledge my faults." Psalm 51:3, 4

"Turn ye ever to me, saith the Lord, with all your heart and with fasting, and with weeping, and with mourning. And rend your heart and not your garments."

Joel 2:12, 13

"Godly sorrow worketh repentance . . . a repentance which bringeth no regrets."

II Corinthians 7:10 R.V.

Carlyle says of this necessary attitude – "Of all acts, is not for man repentance the most divine?" Jeremy Taylor expresses it in another way, "True repentance must reduce to act all its holy purpose . . . A holy life is the only perfection of repentance." Both saint and sinner have need to repent of sin.

Hand in hand with such repentance is faith, without which no sinner can be saved, and no saint can be fully blessed. There is a *saving* faith, and also a *sanctifying* faith. Faith and belief are more or less equivalent. *Faith* is *believing*. To have faith in God is to believe Him. Dr. R. Torrey says that –

"To believe God is to rely upon or have unhesitating assurance of the truth of God's testimony, even though it is unsupported by any other evidence, and to rely upon and have unfaltering assurance of the fulfilment of His promises, even though everything seems against fulfilment."

From the Gospel point of view, *believing* is *receiving* –

"As many as received him . . . to them that believe." John 1:12

"If thou believest with all thine heart . . . I believe." Acts 8:37

"If thou shalt . . . believe in thine heart." Romans 10:8-10

"That Christ may dwell in your hearts by faith." Ephesians 3:17

"Believe . . . that ye may know ye have eternal life." I John 5:13

"He that believeth on him shall not be confounded." I Peter 2:6

"Whoso believeth in him should have everlasting life." John 3:6

"He that believeth on the Son hath everlasting life." John 6:47

"Blessed are they that have not seen, but yet have believed." John 20:29

"By grace are ye saved through faith."

Ephesians 2:8

"Faith is an attitude," says Henry Drummond, "a mirror set at the right angle." Paul reminds us that faith is a divine product –

"The fruit of the Spirit . . . is faith."
Galatians 5:22
Whether faith is the opening of a beggar's hand to receive the gold of heaven, or active energy in devotion, or the bridge across the chasm between the soul and God, it is ever the gift and fruit of the Spirit. When Jesus said, "Have faith in God" (Mark 11:22), He meant, as the margin expresses it, *Have the faith of God*, that is, the faith which God gives (See Isaiah 28:16; 45:22; John 7:35,37; 12:46; Acts 10:43; I Timothy 4:10 etc.).

"There are diversities of gifts . . . faith by the same Spirit." I Corinthians 12:4, 9 "Saved through faith . . . it is the gift of God." Ephesians 2:8

We recognize the existence of a natural faith which we exercise apart altogether from grace. When we deposit letters in the mail box, we *believe* they will reach their destination. Boarding a train, we *believe* it will carry us to where we are going. Faith, however, to believe that we are lost sinners and need a Saviour, and that Christ alone by His finished work can save us, is a gift imparted by the Holy Spirit. Sometimes we hear it argued that it does not matter what a man believes, as long as he believes something. But what we believe in shapes our character and determines destiny. Our *belief* influences *behavior*.

"Whether ye be in faith."
II Corinthians 13:5

We must distinguish between *faith*, as *a principle of life*, and *faith*, as *a body of revealed truth*. When we speak of one "denying the faith," we mean that he rejects the revealed truth of God as found in the Bible. This is "The Faith" we are to "earnestly contend" for.

To be "in the faith," one must have the faith born of God. The modernist, attacking and rejecting the fundamental facts of The Faith, is not conspicuous for his personal faith and confidence in God. He is usually self-centered and self-satisfied.

"God hath dealt to every man the measure of faith." Romans 12:3

That faith is God's gift, and that to some is granted more faith than to others is evident from the Bible and experience. All believers have faith, otherwise they would not be believers, but some have a greater measure than others. And to whom much is given, much is expected. Four times over we have our Lord's rebuke of His disciples for their "little faith." Toplady said that

"Little faith goes to heaven no less than *great faith*, though not so comfortably." Jesus commended *"great faith."*

"According to your faith be it unto you." Matthew 9:29

Such a declaration suggests an expanding mercy. It implies the necessity of seeking an ever-enlarging measure of trust in the power of Him whose faithfulness is great. Promises of abundant blessing await those whose faith increases when tested.

"Strong in faith, giving glory to God."
Romans 4:20

Weymouth translates this phrase – "Under hopeless circumstances he hopefully believed." *He staggered not!* Abraham believed that God could cause the impossible to happen. Do we? "Act faith," our forefathers used to say. General William Booth's slogan for his Salvation Army soldiers was, "Keep up with your repeated acts of faith."

"Faith laughs at impossibilities,
And cries, 'It shall be done.'"

The old Methodist preacher gave us practical advice when he wrote: "If the devil puts up a stone wall in front of us, we are to believe right through it." Here, then, is the secret of strong faith – acting faith, repeated acts of faith.

"As ye have therefore received Christ Jesus the Lord (by faith), so walk ye in him . . . stablished in the faith." Colossians 2:6, 7

Says Lowell, "He who keeps his faith, he only cannot be discrowned."

"The trial of your faith, being much more precious than of gold that perisheth." I Peter 1:7

Such a trial is exemplified in the lives of Abraham, Joseph, the prophets, Paul, the apostles (see Genesis 22:1, 2; 40:14, 15; Psalm 105:17, 19; II Corinthians 11:24-28; Hebrews 11). Jesus sought to try the faith of the nobleman who was deeply concerned about his sick son. "Except ye see signs and wonders, ye will not believe" (John 4:48). But the nobleman's faith in Christ's ability to heal, even at a distance, won the day. When he reached home, he found faith translated in fact. Note in the narrative *personal* faith (4:50), *progressive* faith (4:51), and *prevailing* faith (4:52, 53). Is your faith being sorely tried? Keep believing! God is near, no matter how dark the night, and faith will triumph.

"Faith is the substance of things hoped for." Hebrews 11:1

This is more than a definition of faith –

it is a declaration of its action. Faith is certain the ship is coming home to port, although it cannot be seen. This remarkable eleventh chapter of Hebrews has been called "The Westminster Abbey of the Bible," because it contains the illustrious role of martyrs who were full of faith and faithful unto death. Look at this aspect—

The Path of Faith (11:1-7)
The Patience of Faith (11:8-22)
The Power of Faith (11:23-40)
The Pattern of Faith (12:1-12).

Here is the faith enabling the saints to realize all the promises of God. He has declared Himself in His Word and we believe Him.

As the story goes, Napoleon was once reviewing his troops near Paris, and the horse on which he sat was restive. The emperor thoughtlessly dropped the reins from his hand in the eagerness of giving a command, and the spirited animal bounded away. The rider was in danger of being hurled to the ground. A young private standing in the lines leaped forward and, seizing the birdle, saved his beloved commander from a fall. The emperor, glancing at him, said in his quick, abrupt way, "Thank you, Captain." The private, knowing the peculiarities of his chieftain, looked up with a smile, and asked, "Of what regiment, sire?" "Of my guards," answered Napoleon, and instantly galloped to another part of the field. The young soldier laid down his musket with the remark, "Whoever will may carry that gun; I am done with it," and proceeded at once to join a group of officers who stood conversing at a little distance. One of them, a general, observed his self-possessed approach and angrily said, "What is this insolent fellow doing here?" "This insolent fellow," answered the young soldier, looking the other steadily in the eye, "is a captain of the guards." "Why, man," responded the officer, "you are insane! Why do you speak thus?" "*He said it*," replied the soldier, pointing to the emperor, who was far down the lines. "I beg your pardon, Captain," politely returned the general, "I was not aware of your promotion."

In the application of the story, it is important to remember that there was nothing whatever to indicate the sudden passage of the young soldier from the ranks to a position of honor, except the word of the Emperor. Doubtless he felt glad as he laid down his musket, but he was not promoted because he felt glad; he felt glad because he was promoted. The truth is he was not thinking of his feelings, nor of his worthiness, nor of his unworthiness, but only of the promise of Napoleon, and trusting in that promise he was happy. To those looking on the outward appearance, as even the prophet Samuel was disposed to do when seeking a king (I Samuel 16:7), he was still a private, dressed in the coarse, rough garb of a common soldier. No epaulettes adorned his shoulders, no silken sash circled his waist, no sword dangled at his side, no badge of distinction glittered on his breast, no brilliant uniform decked his person. He seemed precisely like the thousands who were standing in the lines to be inspected as "food for powder," and after awhile to sleep in nameless graves; but in the bold assertion of his dignity, he could meet all the jeers of his comrades and all the scoffs of his superiors with the ready reply, *"He said it."*

Such is faith's triumphant answer to every accusation, every doubt, every fear. The troubled sinner, aroused to see that his body is but food for worms, and his soul fit fuel for the flames, has heard the precious word, "The Son of man is come to seek and to save that which was lost" (Luke 19:10); "Him that cometh to me I will in no wise cast out" (John 6:37); "He that believeth on me *hath* everlasting life" (John 6:47; "Beloved, *now* are we the sons of God; and it doth not yet appear what we shall be: but we know that, when he shall appear, we shall be like him; for we shall see him as he is" (I John 3:2). This is enough. He is led by the Holy Ghost to accept as true, and true for himself, the promises of the Gospel; and he knows by the testimony of the Saviour, who cannot lie, that he has passed out of death into life. His life for the present is hid with Christ in God, but he also knows that when Christ, who is his life, shall appear, he too shall appear with Him in the glory, exalted above the angels. Hence amid the temptations of the world, the humiliating displays of the flesh, and the wiles of the devil, he is ready always to give an answer to every man that asketh a reason of the hope that is in him by pointing upward and exclaiming, "HE SAID IT,"

(Genesis 32:12 – Thou saidst it.")

"Said I not unto thee, that, if thou wouldst believe, thou shouldest see the glory of God?" John 11:40

"Lord, I believe; help thou my unbelief." Mark 9:24

Once saved by grace through faith, and truly *in* the faith, the necessity of SANCTIFICATION, or *holiness*, must be faced. Safe in Christ, we must journey on to know Him in a richer and fuller measure. Too many tarry at the wicket gate of salvation. They are *saved*, but not *sanctified*. Their holiness is not perfected in the fear of the Lord. Great promises, however, are associated with a practiced sanctification of life. The Greek word *hagiasmos* occurs ten times in the New Testament. Five times it is given as "holiness" (see Romans 6:19,22; I Thessalonians 4:7; I Timothy 21:5; Hebrews 12:14), and five times as "sanctification" (see I Corinthians 1:30; I Thessalonians 4:3,4; II Thessalonians 2:13; I Peter 1:2). The Revised Version adopts "sanctification" throughout, which is better and less confusing. "Holiness" represents moral purity, freedom from all the defilement or uncleanness of sin. Inherent holiness is one of the attributes of the Trinity.

God the Father is absolutely holy (Psalm 99:3; Luke 1:49, etc.).

God the Son is absolutely holy (Hebrews 7:26; I John 3:3,5 etc.).

God the Spirit is absolutely holy (Psalm 51:11; Luke 11:13 etc.).

Each Person of the Godhead desires and demands our personal holiness. Promises of spiritual progress and power are attached to holiness of life. God promised to accomplish great and mighty things for His people once they were sanctified and ready for conquest – "Up, sanctify yourselves against the morrow" (Joshua 7:13; 8:1).

The primary root meaning of *"Sanctification"* is that of *separation*, a setting apart *from* and a setting apart *for*. We are separated *from* all that is alien to the holy mind and will of God and then separated *unto* Him for His service and glory. Let us consider a few of the passages dealing with the requirements and rewards of holiness.

"Be ye holy for I am holy."

I Peter 1:16

Peter's heart-moving appeal for personal holiness is based upon the holy character of God. "As he which hath called you is holy, so be ye holy." He desired His children to reflect His character. Further, "glorious in holiness, God is not only the foundation and pattern of holiness, but also

the source of our holiness. What He commands, He supplies. It is impossible for us to manufacture this required holiness. But the promise is that the very holiness He demands, He graciously bestows. Thus, as Augustine expressed it, "Give what Thou commandest, then command what Thou wilt" (I Thessalonians 5:23).

"Holiness becometh thine house, O Lord, for ever." Psalm 93:5

Here we encounter an aspect of holiness that we tend to forget in our congregational worship. While we may not have much sympathy for the rites, ceremonies, and liturgies in Romish and High Church circles, we have to confess that they seem to have an atmosphere conducive to worship which our Protestant Churches lack. While we may not countenance robes, vestments, incense, candles, and Latin prayers, we should yet seek to cultivate something of the reverence characteristic of ritualistic churches.

Roman Catholics have no need of notices at the entrance of their churches asking them to be silent. Are Protestants not guilty of laxity, thoughtlessness, and irreverence when it comes to church behavior? Too often the few minutes before a service begins suggest the rabble of a market rather than the sanctuary where a holy God waits to reveal Himself to those who are supposed to be His holy children. Paul has a pointed word about behaving ourselves in the church of God (I Timothy 3:15).

"The Spirit of holiness." Romans 1:4

As we have already indicated, each Person within the Trinity is described as being *holy*. Over 100 times in the Bible the Third Person is designated "the Holy Spirit." Why? Well, He came as the promise of a thrice-holy God (Isaiah 6:3), He represents the holy Son, He is inherently holy, He inspired holy men to write the Holy Scriptures, and His great task is to transform us into divine holiness. "Every thought of holiness is His alone."

As "the *Holy* Spirit," He is deeply grieved with anything we entertain that is antagonistic to His holy will. Paul sets forth some of the things that please or pain the Holy Spirit who seeks our sanctification (Ephesians 4:25-32).

"Upon every foot . . . holiness unto the Lord." Zechariah 14:20, 21

What can the insignia of holiness upon bills and pots mean but that the Lord expects our commercial and social life to bear the imprint of our allegiance to Him?

In these modern days when millions of cars have taken the place of horses, we can change the figure and say, "Upon every car, *Holiness* unto the Lord." Is yours a consecrated car? Do you use it in His service and for His glory?

Holiness on every pot implies that He is the Lord of the home, and "of all pots and pans." The next time you are tempted to grumble about so many dishes to wash, remember that even your kitchen can become a sanctuary if the glory of the Lord is brought into the most commonplace duties.

"A difference between holy and unholy."
Leviticus 10:10

The Mosaic enactments were necessary to prove that the Jews were a separated people. By their religious observances, camp life, food and raiment, they were conspicuously different from surrounding heathen nations. Promises of divine bounty were offered if such a distinction was maintained. Our tragedy is that of conformity to the world. As those who profess to be followers of a holy God, we are not as distinctive as we should be. Separation from the pleasures and pursuits of an unholy world is not as marked as the Bible demands. Is your life different from those around you who make no claim of being the Lord's? It was Mary Slessor, the renowned Calabar missionary, who said that "complete separation from the world spells power for God."

"What manner of persons ought ye to be in all holy conversation and godliness . . . blameless." II Peter 3:11-14

The apostle Peter presents the return of Christ as a powerful incentive to personal holiness. As we remember that He may be here at any moment, do we not find ourselves stirred to seek purity of life? We cannot live any kind of a life if we believe that Jesus is coming. John reminds us of the fact that this is a sanctifying hope—

"Every man that hath this hope in him purifieth himself, even as he is pure."
I John 3:3

Holy conversation! Does our language reveal the residence of the King within? Is our speech attractive because of its divine accent? "Conversation," as Peter uses the word, means our whole manner of life, including our lips.

"By our holiness we made this man to walk." Acts 3:12

In his first apostolic miracle, Peter desired it to be known that the lame man was directly healed by God, and not as the result of any commendable virtue Peter himself possessed. The bystanders were not to marvel at the miracle as if Peter's own character made it possible. Nevertheless, Peter's life contributed to the miracle. He was the channel of divine operation, and the channel must correspond to the source. God's holy work must be accomplished by holy workmen. All who bear the clean vessels of the Lord must be clean.

"The *life* was the *light* of men."
John 1:4

Life and light! What a vital combination they present! Our *life* is ever the *light* of men. What we *are* never fails to illumine the minds of others. It is not so much what we say, but the divine life pulsating through our whole life that counts for God.

"Go unto the people, and sanctify them."
Exodus 19:10

Scholars remind us that the kindred words, consecration, dedication, sanctification, and holiness, all spring from the same Hebrew root, and whether used of persons or possessions, they convey the one idea of separation unto God. When any of the terms is used of God, Christ, the Spirit, the angels, no separation from evil is involved, for they are sinless. C. I. Scofield remarks, "Doubtless a priest or other person set aside to the service of God, whose whole will and desire went with his setting apart, experienced progressively an inner detachment from evil; that aspect is distinctively of the New Testament, not of the Old Testament."

"Sanctified in Christ Jesus."
I Corinthians 1:2

Sanctification, as applied to ourselves, has a four-fold character—*positional, practical, progressive, prospective* and *perfect*. In the passage before us, Paul is dealing with our *positional sanctification*. By the cross, all believers were eternally set apart by, and for, God.

"By which will we are sanctified through the offering of the body of Jesus Christ once for all." Hebrews 10:10

"Ye are sanctified . . . in the name of the Lord Jesus." I Corinthians 6:11

From the moment of regeneration, the Christian is reckoned by God "holy," or "sanctified." Accepting Christ as Saviour, we become complete in Him (Colossians 2:10), and "saints" (I Corinthians 1:2). Peter seems to imply a *pre-conversion sanctification,* and so does Paul—

"Elect according to the foreknowledge of God the Father, through sanctification of the Spirit." I Peter 1:2

"God hath from the beginning chosen you for salvation through sanctification of the Spirit." II Thessalonians 2:13

The marvel and mystery is that God chose us in His sovereignty, and the Holy Spirit sanctified and separated us to believe the truth. "The sanctification of the Spirit is associated with the choice and election of God; it is a divine act preceding the acceptance of the Gospel by the individual." Our standing before God cannot be surrendered, nor in any way altered, by our state here below. Our positional sanctification is that relationship with God into which we enter by faith in Christ, and to which our sole title is the death of Christ (I Corinthians 6:11; Ephesians 5:25, 26; Colossians 1:22).

We now come to our *practical sanctification,* which involves a daily separation from evil things and ways. In Old Testament times, an Israelite might be *positionally* sanctified, yet be ceremonially unclean, and a believer under grace may be complete in Christ but most incomplete as far as holiness of life is concerned. This practical sanctification is the translation of our standing before God into a state here below. Our *practice* must correspond to our *position.*

"This is the will of God, even your sanctification . . . God calleth us not for uncleanness, but in sanctification."
I Thessalonians 4:3, 7 R.V.

This aspect of sanctification represents our separation from all sinful motives and acts, and also from false teachers (II Timothy 2:20). Complicity and conformity with the word and its ways must be shunned. Was this not the burden of our Lord's intercession for His own? –

"I pray not that thou shouldest take them out of the world, but that thou shouldest keep them from the evil."
John 17:15

Further, we must not strive after holiness of life simply because of promised blessings accruing from such, but because we belong to a holy God and are therefore under a solemn obligation to reflect His holiness.

Then there is a *progressive sanctification.*

"David waxed stronger and stronger."
II Samuel 3:1

"He that hath clean hands shall be stronger and stronger." Job 17:9

"The path of the just is as the shining light, that shineth more and more unto the perfect day." Proverbs 4:18

"By little and little I will drive them out." Exodus 23:30

The moment God graciously saved us we were instantaneously sanctified in His sight, but such a transaction did not make us perfectly holy. We were made partakers of a new nature, for in Christ we became a new creation. In regeneration, however, the old nature – the sinful, Adamic nature with which we were born – was not removed. This nature, the source and seat of sin, remains and will be with us until our death or translation at Christ's return. This was the dual nature Paul referred to when he said –

"I know that in me (that is, in my flesh) dwelleth no good thing . . . When I would do good, evil is present with me." Romans 7:15-25

The promise is that God can make us victorious over the old nature. The *crisis* – sanctification taking place at our regeneration – can become a *process* – sanctification, as day by day we claim all God provided for us. Here is the steady growth in grace as the result of our daily obedience to God's Word, a daily bringing of all our thoughts and ways into captivity to the obedience of Christ (II Corinthians 10:5).

The Holy Spirit does not reveal all our defects, failures, and unclaimed territory at once. As we continue looking into the mirror of the Word, and a clearer reflection of our sin becomes ours we claim the promise of cleansing and are thus progressively sanctified. When we obey the light we receive, further light is made possible. Thus we are transformed into the likeness of Jesus Christ day by day.

"We are changed into the same image from glory to glory." II Corinthians 3:18

When we have been brought to a more blessed understanding of the requirements and resources of God's holy will, there takes place a more complete dedication to that will. As the white light of divine holiness is focused upon our daily walk, unconscious impediments to fuller holiness become conscious and are immediately dealt with by the blood (I John 1:7).

"This is the will of God, even your sanctification." I Thessalonians 4:3

A progressive holiness, then is the *will* as well as the *work* of God. What He wills He is able to work, if only we will let Him. Our sanctification is a part of the divine will because God, being holy, desires His children to walk in a way pleasing to Him. By holiness of life, the saint recommends the Gospel of sanctification to those who find themselves miserably defeated by the forces of the old nature.

"The very God of peace sanctify you wholly." I Thessalonians 5:23

If our practical and progressive holiness is "the progressive conformity of heart and life to the will of God, and includes dying to sin and living in holiness," then every part of our being must bear the imprint of such a divine work. Moffat's translation of Paul's prayer is, "Consecrated through and through, spirit, soul and body, may you be kept without break of blame until the arrival of our Lord Jesus Christ."

There is the fourth aspect to distinguish, namely, our *prospective, perfect sanctification*, which will be consumated for all believers at the return of Christ. Holiness in its final and eternal form will mean that we shall be complete in every way, in spirit, soul, and body. When we see Him we shall be like Him – as perfectly holy as He is.

"I shall be satisfied when I awake with thy likeness." Psalm 17:15

"That he might present it to himself a glorious church, not having spot or wrinkle or any such thing, but that it should be holy and without blemish."
Ephesians 5:25-27

"When he shall appear, we shall be like him." I John 3:2

"The Lord Jesus Christ: who shall change our vile body, that it may be fashioned like unto his glorious body."
Philippians 3:20, 21

What glorious promises these are! To know that when our eyes behold Him we shall be forever delivered from the trammeling influence of the world, the flesh, and the devil. Then a perfect holiness will be ours.

In our quest for holiness we are encouraged by our Lord's own example, which He would have us emulate.

"Sanctify them . . . I sanctify myself."
John 17:17, 19

When He spoke of self-sanctification, the only aspect He had in mind was the setting of Himself apart for God's service. As the sinless One, He had nothing unclean to be separated from.

"Which of you convinceth me of sin."
John 8:46

"He hath made him to be sin for us, who knew no sin." II Corinthians 5:21

"Who is holy, harmless, undefiled, separate from sinners." Hebrews 7:26, 27

"The prince of this world cometh, and hath nothing in me." John 14:30

"Tempted . . . yet without sin."
Hebrews 4:5

Unflecked holiness was His. Spotless purity characterized His life and ways. God and man testified to His sinless character. Had He committed one small sin, He would have forfeited the right to die as the sinless Substitute for sinners. It is His sinlessness that gives His blood such abiding efficacy.

When Satan approaches us, he has a part of his territory he seeks to claim, namely, the old, sinful nature with which we were born. But Satan had nothing in Christ he could call his own, because He was holy in birth and in practice. This is the One who seeks to make us sharers of His holiness.

Among other Christian themes worthy of attention is RESTORATION to Divine favor is, in spite of our yearning for holiness, we yield to the lusts of the flesh and the lure of the world. So many promises of rectification are ours to claim if, and when, we confess our folly and failure.

"Return, thou backsliding Israel . . . for I am merciful . . . Return, . . . I will heal your backsliding."
Jeremiah 3:12, 22

"I will heal their backsliding, I will love them freely." Hosea 14:4

"A fountain opened . . . for sin and uncleanness." Zechariah 13:1

"If we confess our sins, he is faithful and just to forgive us our sins."
I John 1:9

"If any man sin, we have an advocate with the Father." I John 2:1

"Your sins are forgiven you for his name's sake." I John 2:12

"Then shall ye remember your own evil ways . . . and shall loathe yourselves." Ezekiel 20:43; 36:31

"Let him return unto the Lord, and he will have mercy upon him."
Isaiah 55:7

"If my people . . . turn from their wicked way . . . I will forgive their sin." II Chronicle 7:14

"The Lord your God is gracious and merciful, and will not turn away his face from you, if ye return to him."
II Chronicles 30:9

"I acknowledged my sin unto thee . . .

thou forgavest." Psalm 32:5

"Whosoever confesseth and forsaketh them shall have mercy." Proverbs 28:13

"I have sinned . . . Bring forth the best robe." Luke 14:21, 22

The above list comprises a few of the promises of forgiveness and restoration God offers His sinning saints. If we have yielded to temptation and grieved the Lord by our lapse into sin, let us not yield to any depressed feeling and say, "What's the use of trying to be a Christian? I have failed my Lord." He knows all about you, and while He can never condone your weakness, He has made ample provision for your recovery and victory. Sincerely confess your sin and rest in His promise of forgiveness (see Psalm 51:12; Luke 22:32; Isaiah 58:12; Mark 8:25; Psalm 23:3).

As we come to the doctrine of PRAYER, we find ourselves embarrassed by spiritual riches. What a marvelous array of prayer promises the Bible spreads before us! No matter where we look, God is presented as The One who hears and answers prayer. Without contact with heaven our spiritual life cannot be maintained.

"Prayer is the Christian's vital breath,
    The Christian's native air."

The Bible is the believer's prayer-guide. It unfolds the nature and necessity of prayer and is eloquent with promise as to its privilege and power. For a full treatment of this absorbing theme, the reader is directed to the author's volume on *All the Prayers of the Bible*. The following summary of prayer pointers, promises, precepts, provisions, poems and paragraphs might be found helpful, especially for the preacher on such a doctrine.

Here is a serviceable outline of our Lord's

Prayer Pointers:

We should pray in His name.

"Again I say unto you, that if two of you shall agree on earth as touching anything that they shall ask, it shall be done for them of my Father which is in heaven.

"For where two or three are gathered together in my name, there am I in the midst of them." Matthew 18:19, 20.

We should pray in a forgiving spirit.

"And when ye stand praying, forgive, if ye have ought against any; that your Father also which is in heaven may forgive you your trespasses." Mark 11:25

We should avoid vain repetitions.

"But when ye pray, use not vain repe-

titions, as the heathen do; for they think that they shall be heard for their much speaking." Matthew 6:7

We should pray with insistence.

"I say unto you, Though he will not rise and give him, because he is his friend, yet because of his importunity he will rise and give him as many as he needeth."
Luke 11:8

We should pray in sincerity.

"And when thou prayest, thou shalt not be as the hypocrites are: for they love to pray standing in the synagogues and in the corners of the streets, that they may be seen of men. Verily I say unto you, They have their reward." Matthew 6:5

We should pray from the heart.

"But thou, when thou prayest, enter into thy closet, and when thou hast shut thy door, pray to thy Father which is in secret; and thy Father which seeth in secret shall reward thee openly." Matthew 6:6

*We should pray with the
spirit and understanding.*

"Ye worship ye know not what: we know what we worship: for salvation is of the Jews. But the hour cometh, and now is, when the true worshippers shall worship the Father in spirit and in truth: for the Father seeketh such to worship him." John 4:22, 23

We should pray in truth.

"God is a Spirit: and they that worship him must worship him in spirit and in truth." John 4:24

We should pray with watchfulness.

"Watch ye therefore, and pray always, that ye may be accounted worthy to escape all these things that shall come to pass, and to stand before the Son of man." Luke 21:36

*We should pray according
to the will of God.*

"Saying, Father, if thou be willing, remove this cup from me; nevertheless, not my will, but thine be done." Luke 22:42

We should pray in faith believing.

"Jesus answered and said unto them, Verily I say unto you, If ye have faith, and doubt not, ye shall not only do this which is done to the fig tree, but also if ye shall say unto this mountain, Be thou removed, and be thou cast into the sea, it shall be done. And all things, whatsoever ye shall ask in prayer, believing, ye shall receive." Matthew 21:21, 22

"Whatsoever we ask, we receive of him, because we keep his commandments, and do those things that are pleasing in his sight."
I John 3:22

Prayer Promises

Space forbids collating all verses dealing with the many aspects of prayer. The Bible is predominantly a Book of prayer. It does not prove the reality of prayer. It is taken for granted that prayer does not need *proof*, but *practice*. Bible saints had no doubt about God hearing and answering prayer. Here are a few promises for us to appropriate –

"If my people, which are called by my name, shall humble thelselves and pray, and seek my face, and turn from their wicked ways: then will I hear from heaven, and will forgive their sin, and will heal their land." II Chronicles 7:14

"The. Lord is nigh unto all them that call upon him, to all that call upon him in truth." Psalm 145:18

"Seek ye the Lord while he may be found, call ye upon him while he is near." Isaiah 55:6

"Be careful for nothing; but in everything' by prayer and supplication with thanksgiving let your requests be made known unto God." Philippians 4:6

"Pray without ceasing. In everything give thanks, for this is the will of God in Christ Jesus concerning you."
I Thessalonians 5:17, 18

"Let us therefore come boldly unto the throne of grace, that we may obtain mercy, and find grace to help in time of need."
Hebrews 4:16

"The effectual, fervent prayer of a righteous man availeth much." James 5:16

"The eyes of the Lord are upon the righteous, and his ears are open unto their cry. The righteous cry, and the Lord heareth, and delivereth them out of all their troubles."
Psalm 34:15, 17

"Ask, and it shall be given you; seek, and ye shall find; knock, and it shall be opened unto you; For every one that asketh receiveth; and he that seeketh findeth; and to him that knocketh it shall be opened. Or what man is there of you, whom if his son ask bread, will he give him a stone? Or if he ask for a fish, will he give him a serpent? If ye then, being evil, know how to give good gifts unto your children, how much more shall your Father which is in heaven give good things to them that ask Him?" Matthew 7:7-11

"Again I say unto you, That if two of you shall agree on earth as touching anything that they shall ask, it shall be done for them of my Father which is in heaven. For where two or three are gathered together, in my name, there am I in the midst of them." Matthew 18:19

"Without faith it is impossible to please him; for he that cometh to God must believe that He is, and that He is a rewarder of them that diligently seek Him."
Hebrews 11:6

"If any of you lack wisdom, let him ask of God, that giveth to all men liberally, and upbraideth not; and it shall be given him. But let him ask in faith, nothing wavering. For he that wavereth is like a wave of the sea driven by the wind and tossed. For let not that man think that he shall receive anything of the Lord."
James 1:5-7

"Draw nigh to God and He will draw nigh to you." James 4:8

Prayer Precepts

The reader is encouraged to add to this list the gems of his own search, which, with eyes open, he will discover in the most unlikely places.

An old Jewish mystic says that "Prayer is the moment when heaven and earth kiss each other."

> They never sought in vain that sought
> the Lord aright.

> Prayer is a correspondence fixed with
> heaven.
> *– Robert Burns*

I would not exchange the prayer of your dead wife in my behalf for the united glory of Homer, Caesar, and Napoleon, could such be accumulated upon a living head.
– Byron to a Mr. Sheppard

> He prayeth well, who loveth well
> Both man and bird and beast;
> He prayeth best who loveth best
> All things both great and small;
> For the dear God, who loveth us,
> He made, and loveth all.
> *– Samuel Coleridge*

> Satan trembles when he sees
> The weakest saint upon his knees.
> *– William Cowper*

> Resort to sermons, but to prayers most;
> Praying's the end of preaching, O be
> drest!
> Stay not for th' other pin.
> *– George Herbert*

> And help us this, and every day
> To live more nearly as we pray.
> *– John Keble*

> Six hours in sleep, in law's grave study,
> six.
> Four spend in prayer, the rest on nature fix. *Sir E. Coke*

Begirt th'almighty throne
Beseeching or besieging.
                    – *John Milton*
Long tarries destiny,
But comes to those who pray.
                    – *Dean Plumptre*
Words without thoughts never to
heaven go.
                    – *William Shakespeare*
Battering the gates of heaven
with storms of prayer.
                    – *Alfred Tennyson*
Her eyes are homes of silent prayer.
                    – *Alfred Tennyson*
Making their lives a prayer . . . .
                    – *John Whittier*
The sure relief of prayer . . . .
                    – *William Wordsworth*
Prayer ardent opens heaven.
                    – *Edward Young*
In every storm that either frowns or falls,
What an asylum has the soul in prayer!
                    – *Edward Young*
The fewer the words, the better the prayer.
                    – *German Proverb*
   To the above we add: "For a pretense
make long prayers." Matthew 23:14
   Do you wish to find out the really
sublime?
   Repeat the Lord's Prayer.
                    –*Napoleon I*
A short prayer finds its way to heaven.
A short prayer enters heaven.
A long drink empties the cup.
                    – *Latin Proverbs*
Cease to hope that the gods' decrees
are to be changed by prayer.
                    – *Virgil*
Nor are any prayers, unless righteous,
heard by the gods.
                    – *Tacitus*
Prayer and work.
A sound mind in a sound body is a
thing to be prayed for.
                    – *Latin Proverbs*
He who labors, prays.
                    –*St. Augustine*
He who prays and labours lifts his heart
to God with his hands.
                    –*St. Bernard*
Prayer is a cry of hope.
                    – *A. de Musset*
Even silence itself has its prayers and
its longings.
                    – *Tasso*
Necessity teaches to pray.
                    – *German Proverb*
Forced prayers are no guide for

the soul.
                    – *Scotch Proverb*
Pray to God, but row to the shore.
Pray to God, but keep the hammer
going.
                    – *Russian Proverbs*
Fighting with their hands, and praying
unto God with their hearts.
                    – *II Maccabees 15:27*
He has mickle (much) prayer but little
devotion.
                    – *Scotch Proverb*
He who ceases to pray ceases to prosper.
He that would learn to pray, let him
go to sea.
Let him who knows not how to pray,
go to sea.
Labour as long-lived; pray as ever dying.
                    – *Unusual Proverbs*
Patience is the greatest prayer.
                    – *Buddha*
When the pirate prays, there is great
danger.
                    – *Fuller's Gnomologia*
Ye have little need o' the Campsie
wife's prayer
"That she might aye be able to think
enough o' hersel."
                    – *Scotch Proverb*
Work as though work alone thine end
could gain;
But pray to God as though all work
were vain.
                    – *D'arcy Thompson*
Prayer and practice is good rhyme.
Prayer knocks 'til the door open.
To join hands in prayer is well;
To open them in work is better.
Pray devoutly but hammer stoutly
Prayers and provender hinder no journey.
To pray well is to have well endeavoured.
Remote from man, with God he passed his
days,
Prayer all his business, all his pleasure praise.
                    – *Thomas Parnell in The Hermit*
Prayer is God's road which fetches forth
streams of blessing from the rock of
affliction.
                    – *C. H. Spurgeon*
Prayer is not to change God, but to
change us.
                    – *Charles Finney*
Trouble and perplexity drive me to prayer,
and prayer drives away perplexity and
trouble.
                    – *Melanchthon*
There is no enterprise which you cannot

submit to the test of prayer.

— *Hosea Ballow*

Between the humble and contrite heart and the majesty of heaven there are no barriers: the only password is prayer.

— *Matthew Henry*

Let prayers be the key of the morning, and the bolt of the evening.

— *Matthew Henry*

Prayer will make a man cease from sin, or sin will entice a man to cease from prayer.

— *John Bunyan*

The best and sweetest flowers of paradise God gives to His people when they are upon their knees. Prayer is the gate of heaven.

— *Thomas Brooks*

For spiritual blessings, let our prayers be importunate, perpetual, and persevering; For temporal blessings, let them be general, short, conditional, and modest.

— *Jeremy Taylor*

I have been driven many times to my knees by the overwhelming conviction that I had nowhere else to go. My own wisdom, and that of all about me, seemed insufficient for that day.

— *Abraham Lincoln*

Prayer is the soul drawing near to God . . . Whatever form it takes, it is that solemn moment when the soul in need turns to God.

— *Hugh McLellan*

Religion is no more possible without prayer than poetry without language, or music without atmosphere.

— *Martineau*

Prayer is the very sword of the saints.

— *Francis Thompson*

God answers sharp and sudden in some prayers,
And thrusts the thing we have prayed for in our face,
A gauntlet with a gift in 't.

Elisabeth Barrett Browning

Prayer and patience and faith are never disappointed.

— *Richard Newton*

I want a life of greater, deeper, truer prayer.

— *Archbishop Tait*

You know the value of prayer: it is precious beyong all price. Never, never neglect it.

— *Sir Thomas Buxton*

Prayer is not conquering God's reluctance, but taking hold upon God's willingness. — *Phillips Brooks*

Prayer is the first thing, the second thing, the third thing necessary to a minister. Pray, then, my dear brother; pray, pray, pray.

— *Edward Payson*

Who goes to bed, and doth not pray,
Maketh two nights to every day!

— *George Herbert*

Let never day nor night unhallow'd pass,
But still remember what the Lord hath done.

— *William Shakespeare*

Prayer is the voice of faith.

— *Horne*

Prayer is a virtue that prevaileth against all temptations.

— *St. Bernard*

A prayer, in its simplest definition, is merely a wish turned heavenward.

— *Phillips Brooks*

Prayer is a shield to the soul, a sacrifice to God, and a scourge for Satan.

— *John Bunyan*

Some Short Bible Prayers:

What outpouring of heart the saints of old were capable of! Their language, so expressive and intense, is a safe guide for us to follow as we approach "the mercy seat" where Jesus answers prayer. Many of these prayers should be memorized and made our own.

"Thou art my rock and my fortress; therefore for thy name's sake lead me and guide me." Psalm 31:3

"And now I am no more in the world, but these are in the world, and I come to thee. Holy Father, keep through thine own name those whom thou hast given me, that they may be one, as we are. Neither pray I for these alone, but for them also which shall believe on me through their word; that they all may be one; as thou, Father, art in me, and I in thee, that they also may be one in us; that the world may believe that thou has sent me. And the glory which thou gavest me have I given them; that they may be one, even as we are one; I in them, and thou in me, that they may be made perfect in one; and that the world may know that thou hast sent me, and has loved them, as thou hast loved me." John 17:11, 20-23

"Thy mercy, O Lord, is in the heavens; and thy faithfulness reacheth unto the clouds. Thy righteousness is like the great mountains; thy judgments are a great deep; O Lord, thou preservest man and beast. How excellent is thy loving-kindness, O God! therefore the children of men put their trust under the shadow of thy wings. They shall be abundantly satisfied with the fatness of thy house; and thou shalt make them drink of the river of thy pleasures. For with thee is the fountain of life; in thy light shall we see light. O continue thy loving-kindness unto them that know thee; and thy righteousness to the upright in heart. Let not the foot of pride come against me, and let not the hand of the wicked remove me." Psalm 36:5-11

"Have mercy upon me, O God, according to thy loving-kindness; according unto the multitude of thy tender mercies blot out my transgressions. Wash me thoroughly from my sin, and cleanse me from my iniquity. For I acknowledge my transgressions; and my sin is ever before me. Against thee, thee only, have I sinned, and done this evil in thy sight; that thou mightest be justified when thou speakest, and be clear when thou judgest. Behold, I was shapen in iniquity, and in sin did my mother conceive me. Behold, thou desirest truth in the inward part; and in the hidden part thou shalt make me to know wisdom. Purge me with hyssop and I shall be clean: wash me and I shall be whiter than snow. Make me to hear joy and gladness, that the bones which thou hast broken may rejoice. Hide thy face from my sins, and blot out all mine iniquities. Create in me a clean heart, O God, and renew a right spirit within me. Cast me not away from thy presence; and take not thy holy Spirit from me. Restore unto me the joy of thy salvation; and uphold me with thy free spirit. Then will I teach transgressors thy ways; and sinners shall be converted unto thee." Psalm 51:1-13

"Search me, O God, and know my heart; try me, and know my thoughts; and see if there be any wicked way in me, and lead me in the way everlasting." Psalm 139:23, 24

"For this cause I bow my knees unto the Father of our Lord Jesus Christ, of whom the whole family in heaven and earth is named, that he would grant you, according to the riches of his glory, to be strengthened with might by his Spirit in the inner man; that Christ may dwell in your hearts by faith; that ye, being rooted and grounded in love, may be able to comprehend with all saints what is the breadth, and length, and depth, and height;

and to know the love of Christ, which passeth knowledge, that ye might be filled with all the fulness of God. Now unto him that is able to do exceeding abundantly above all that we ask or think, according to the power that worketh in us, unto him be glory in the church by Christ Jesus, throughout all ages, world without end, Amen." Ephesians 3:14-21

"Let the words of my mouth, and the meditation of my heart, be acceptable in thy sight, O Lord, my strength and my redeemer." Psalm 19:14

Prayers for the Young:

While it is commendable to teach the young to express themselves in their own simple way when they say their prayers or grace, yet because they easily remember what is taught them, the following forms might prove helpful. How childlike prayers are remembered through the years!

MORNING PRAYERS

Jesus, gentle Shepherd,
Bless Thy lamb today;
Keep me in Thy footsteps,
Never let me stray.
Guard me through the daytime
Every hour, I pray,
Keep my feet from straying
From the narrow way. AMEN

Father, we thank Thee for the night,
And for the pleasant morning light;
For rest and food, and loving care,
And all that makes the day so fair.

Help us to do the things we should,
To be to others kind and good,
In all we do, in work or play,
To grow more loving every day.
                      — *Rebecca E. Weston*

Father, in the morning, unto Thee I pray;
Let Thy loving-kindness keep me through
  this day.
At the busy noontide, pressed with work
  and care,
Then I'll wait with Jesus till He hear my
  prayer.

When the evening shadows chase away the
  light,
Father, then I'll pray Thee, bless Thy child
  tonight,
Thus in life's glad morning, in its bright
  noonday,
In the shadowy evening, ever will I pray.
                      — *A. Cummings*

EVENING PRAYERS

Now I lay me down to sleep,
I pray Thee, Lord, my soul to keep,
If I should die before I wake,
I pray Thee, Lord, my soul to take,
And this I ask for Jesus' sake. AMEN

Father, unto Thee I pray,
Thou hast guarded me all day;
Safe I am while in Thy sight,
Safely let me sleep tonight.
Bless my friends, The whole world bless.
Keep me ever in Thy sight. AMEN

GRACE BEFORE MEAT

God is great and God is good,
And we thank Him for our food.
By His hand we all are fed.
Give us, Lord, our daily bread. AMEN

Come Lord Jesus, be Thou our guest,
And may this food to us be blessed. AMEN

Prayer and the Poets

Turning to the prayer section in almost all church hymnals, many choice and expressive poems can be found on all aspects of communion with God. Incomparable among hymn-writers on prayer is James Montgomery. One of the greatest of all prayer-hymns is his –

Prayer is the soul's sincere desire,
Uttered or unexpressed;
The motion of a hidden fire
That trembles in the breast.

Another of Montgomery's prayer-hymns begins:

Come to the morning prayer,
Come, let us kneel and pray;
Prayer is the Christian's pilgrim staff,
To walk with God all day.

Missionary zeal has been quickened by the oft-quoted poem in missionary talks and in periodicals –

THE POWER OF INTERCESSION

Away in foreign fields, they wondered how
    Their simple words had power;
At home some Christians, two or three,
    had not forgot
    To pray an hour.
We are always wondering – wondering how
    Because we do not see
Someone – perhaps unknown and far away
    On bended knee.

Other precious prayer poems follow:

Be not afraid to pray – to pray is right.
Pray, if thou canst, with hope; but ever pray,
Though hope be weak, or sick with long delay;
Pray in the darkness, if there be no light.
    – *Hartley Coleridge*

Then let us earnest be,
    And never faint in prayer;
He loves our importunity,
    And makes our cause His care.
    – *John Newton*

Prayer makes the darkened clouds withdraw;
Prayer climbs the ladder Jacob saw;
Gives exercise to faith and love;
Brings every blessing from above.

Restraining prayer, we cease to fight;
Prayer makes the Christian's armor bright;
And Satan trembles when he sees
The weakest saint upon his knees.
    – *William Cowper*

MAKE TIME TO PRAY

"No time to pray!" How sad the thought:
What gross dishonor here is brought
To Jesus Christ, who died to save,
And for us all His life He gave!

"No time to pray," we often hear.
Oh, stop this lie! and persevere;
Make time to pray, and you will know
His presence with you where you go.

"No time to pray; there's so much work."
So we communion this way shirk,
And opportunities go past
For which we must account at last.

O child of God, make time to pray!
And go apart with Him each day!
Thus only you can render Him
A joy which never will grow dim.

Watch and pray, watch and pray,
And cheer some weary heart each day.
This was the blessed Saviour's way.
He'll give you wisdom what to say.
Watch and pray, watch and pray,
Go, seek for some who've gone astray.
    – *Margaret Spencer Johnson*

BECAUSE YOU PRAYED

Because you prayed –
God touched our weary bodies with
    His power
And gave us strength for many a try-
    ing hour
In which we might have faltered,
    Had not you, our intercessors,
    Faithful been, and true.

Because you prayed –
God touched our lips with coals from
    altar fire,
Gave Spirit-fulness, and did so inspire
That when we spoke, sin-blinded souls
    did see;
Sin's chains were broken;
    Captives were made free.

Because you prayed –
The dwellers in the dark have found the
    Light;
The glad Good News has banished heathen
    night;
The message of the cross, so long delayed,
    Has brought them life at last,
    Because you prayed.
                        – *Charles B. Bowser*

DON'T FORGET TO PRAY

Ere you left your room this morning,
    Did you think to pray?
In the name of Christ our Saviour
Did you sue for loving favour
    As a shield today?
When you met with great temptation,
    Did you think to pray?
By His dying love and merit,
Did you claim the Holy Spirit
    As your guide and stay?
When your heart was filled with anger,
    Did you think to pray?
Did you plead for grace, my brother,
That you might forgive another
    Who had crossed your way?
When sore trials came upon you,
    Did you think to pray?
When your soul was bowed in sorrow,
Balm of Gilead did you borrow
    At the gates of day?
Oh, how praying rests the weary!
    Prayer will change the night to day;
So in sorrow and in gladness,
    Don't forget to pray!
                        – *Mrs. M. A. Kidder*

Because of the vastness and value of this
subject of prayer, we could devote more
space than the whole of this volume represents, to a consideration of every phase
of it. Let us confine ourselves, however,
to a few expositional

Paragraphs

"He that cometh to God . . . a rewarder of them that diligently seek him."
                        Hebrews 11:6

Here we have two general principles regarding prayer, namely, our *conception of*,
and then our *contact with*, God. Contact
depends upon conception. It is only as we
know Him that we can trust Him. Our
conception is of a two-fold nature – we must
believe that *He is* (meaning that He is
real) and also that He is the Rewarder
of those who accept His reality. Is God
real to you? Is yours the reward of seeking Him?

"Lord, teach us to pray." Luke 11:1

While it is true that men, even godless
men, cry to God in the deep crises of life,
the fact remains that prayer is not natural
to the unregenerated man. Once the Lord's,
he has to be instructed in such a holy art
by the very One he desires to approach.
And all effective prayer depends upon relationship. It was as *disciples* that one of
them voiced the request, "Teach *us* to pray."
To address a man as "father" implies the
relationship of sonship. Have you been
born into the divine family? If so, then
yours is the privilege and joy of addressing
God as your Father in heaven.

"Praying always with all prayer."
                        Ephesians 6:18

Outside an English church the sign was
found – "When your knees knock, kneel on
them." But why postpone prayer until an
emergency arises? Prayer is not a mere
fire escape from danger, but is our vital
breath. Paul urges us to pray *always*. The
qualifying phrase is at the end of the verse
– "in the Spirit." We are never in the spirit
of prayer unless the Spirit is in our prayer.
There is a vast difference between saying
prayers and praying in the Holy Ghost.

"We know not what we should pray
for." Romans 8:26

How helpless we are without the indwelling Intercessor, the Holy Spirit, our Instructor in prayer. At best we are only,

"Infants, crying in the night,
    With no language but a cry."

Knowing the mind of God, the Spirit can
enable us to present our petitions accordingly. He it is who takes our sighs, broken

and imperfect utterances, and recasts them until they rise as sweet incense to God. What we are prone to forget as we approach the mercy-seat where Jesus answers prayer is that God answers prayer not according to *our* intelligence but according to His own. Often we ask, but we receive not because we ask amiss (James 4:3).

"God forbid that I should sin against the Lord in ceasing to pray for you."
I Samuel 12:23

We seldom catalog *prayerlessness* as a sin, grievous in God's sight. Samuel, however, knew that if he failed to pray for the idolatrous multitude he would be guilty of sinning against the Lord, and against the people needing his prayers. Praying without ceasing for the lost is an arduous task.

"Whatsoever you shall ask in prayer, believing." Matthew 21:22

Here is Christ's blank check for all who pray – *whatsoever*. Surely this covers all our need. But how slow we are to cash our check. The truth likewise emphasized by Christ is that prayer must be accompanied by faith. Have you faith to praise God for the assurance of granted requests, even though the answers have not yet reached you?

The Bible offers abundant evidence that God not only hears but also promises to answer those prayers offered in accordance with His "sweet, beloved will." There are, as A. Proctor reminds us –

"Prayers, which God in pity
Refused to grant or hear!"

"The Lord is nigh unto all them that call upon him in truth." Psalm 145:18

Prayer is an acknowledgment of God's all-sufficiency and of our dependency upon Him for all things necessary for our life on earth. It is likewise an evidence of our helplessness and insufficiency to help ourselves. In the Psalm quoted above, David emphasizes two important factors in all true prayer. First, we have not to cry as if God were at a distance and deaf. The wondrous promise is that He is nigh unto all who call. Whenever we need Him, He is at hand. The second aspect is that He only responds to our approach if we call upon Him in truth, which means that our praying must be in accordance with His revealed will. It is only thus that He promises to hear and answer (I John 5:14, 15).

"He shall pray unto God, and He will be favourable unto him." Job 33:26

If we draw nigh unto God in all reverence, adoration, and faith, He then has delight in responding to our petitions. God never withholds any good thing from those who seek Him aright. There are times, however, when granted answers appear to be most unfavorable to our finite understanding. We pray to be kept in health, and sickness comes. We pray for relief from a burden, but it remains. Has God forgotten to be gracious? Of course not! Because of His infinite wisdom He knows what is best for His own. Therefore, if He permits sickness, He knows that this is the most favorable experience for us. Often a bed of pain makes a far more powerful pulpit than a healthy body.

"God gives the very best to those
Who leave the choice with Him."

"Lord, thou hast heard the desire of the humble; thou wilt prepare their heart, thou wilt cause thine ear to hear." Psalm 10:19

In this gracious promise, three divine actions are indicated. God hears the desire of the humble, even before it is expressed. He hears before we call. Then He prepares our heart, not only to pray aright, but to be in a fit condition to receive His answer. Further, He inclines His ear to hear. The necessary preparation of heart, in order to approach God in a way agreeable to Him, is the work of the Holy Spirit. Alas! too often we rush into God's holy presence and hurriedly express ourselves, as if the mercy seat were a quick-lunch counter. Effective praying must have earnest preparation of mind and of spirit.

"By a riverside, where prayer was wont to be made." Acts 16:13

Wherever we pray, God is present. He heard Jonah as he cried out of the belly of the whale. He answered the dying thief on the cross. If the spirit of prayer is sincere, the sphere makes little difference. Yet, if at all possible, it is so helpful to have a *sanctum*, a trysting place, where God and the soul can meet. Paul found his way to a sheltered spot by the riverside where a few devout hearts were in the habit of meeting for prayer and worship. Christ loved to pray on the mountainside or in a garden. Many of the saints in all ages have found themselves so near to God in the cathedral of nature. It would be interesting to learn where *you* pray best.

"Evening and morning, and at noon, will I pray." Psalm 55:17

Set times, as well as set places, contribute to the value of our prayer life. How *often* do you pray? David opened the door into heaven three times a day. As he commenced the day, he cried for strength and guidance. At noon, when both hands of the clock point upward, the psalmist stretched out both hands for further help. As the evening shadows fell, he again sought God for forgiveness and cleansing. Praise would be expressed for divine goodness through the day; and rest sought for the silent hours of the night. The ideal attitude is to live in the spirit of prayer. Is it as natural and easy for you, even in the busy mart, to turn aside and talk with God, as it is to converse with a friend at your side? Is prayer your native air?

"Make thy prayer . . . pray thy vows."
Job 22:27

To *pray*, then, means to *pay*. But how slow we are to learn that he who prays, pays. We get, but do not give. Our answered prayers do not lead us to fulfil our obligations, both Godward and manward. We keep the angels busy coming down from God with required provision, but we send them back empty-handed. How the angels love to carry home to a prayer-answering God the praises, gratitude, and fuller obedience of those He has so richly blessed! Have you forgotten the practical side of prayer? Then pay that thou owest.

"Whatsoever ye shall ask in prayer, believing, ye shall receive." Matthew 21:22

Faith in the willingness and ability of God to hear and answer prayer is essential to prevailing prayer. Jesus taught of God's power to respond to our faith-prayers:

Ask – Seek – Knock (Matthew 7:7, 8, 11)

The first three letters of these words spell A-S-K. God cannot be expected to respond to our asking if doubts lurk in the mind as to the possibility of an answer. When we come to Him, we must believe that He is ever the rewarder of those who believingly and diligently seek Him. George Mueller's orphans were daily fed and cared for, because his prayers were girded with faith and also with his holy life. Our prayers, when backed by faith, can only be effective as they ascend from a heart in tune with the infinite One above.

In conclusion, a word is necessary regarding the vital connection between *prayer* and the *promises* in general. The latter should always be the basis of all our prayers, for the promises as a whole are alike our warrant for asking and our security for receiving what we ask for. We must guard ourselves from asking anything that lies beyond the all-embracing scope of God's promises, for we have no authority to do so. But we may confidently ask for whatever is included in these promises, which God never fails to fulfil.

"Thou promisedst . . . and hast fulfilled . . . There hath not failed one word of all his good promise."
I Kings 8:24, 25, 56

Further, the great promises of God should be the material of our prayers. The saints of old knew how to turn promises into prayers. Does not God Himself command us to definitely plead for the performance of His promises?

"Put me in remembrance: let us plead together" Isaiah 43:26

When praying for deliverance from Esau, Jacob reminded God of His promises at Bethel and in Padanaram (Genesis 32:9-12). Twice over Moses pleaded God's promises in his intercessions for the people (Exodus 32:13; Numbers 14:17-19). David spread the promise before God and pleaded for its fulfilment – "Do as thou hast said" (II Samuel 7:28, 29; Psalm 119:49). Solomon began his intercessory prayer by asking that the promise made to David might be *verified* (I Kings 8:25, 26).

Then, it is essential to remember that the promises of God are given to stimulate our prayers, not to supercede them. While everything good for us is promised in anwer to believing prayer, *nothing is promised apart from it*. Once we are persuaded of the promises and embrace them, by believing prayer we claim their fulfilment. How our prayer life is enriched when we come before God with some gracious word of His own in our heart and on our lips! Let us plead the promises with greater fervor.

The motto of an old English family reads – *The promise made to the ashes of my forefathers has been kept*. The promises made by God to our fathers of old were kept, and those embracing us will likewise be kept. God will never fail in the performance of any promise made on our behalf. May we be as faithful in the fulfilment of the vows and prayers we present before His face!

Promises Relative to the Christian

The term "Christian," which came into vogue with the establishment of Christianity in the world, was originally coined as a nickname. The people of Antioch, watching Christ's followers and observing how like their Master they were, called them *Christians*, meaning, followers of Christ, just as *Wesleyans* were so named because they were followers of John Wesley.

Such an honored designation occurs thrice in the New Testament, in three different settings –

"The disciples were first called Christians at Antioch." Acts 11:26

"Almost thou persuadest me to be a Christian." Acts 26:28

"Yet if any man suffer as a Christian . . ." I Peter 4:16

When Jesus was on the earth, those who received Him and His teachings became known as "disciples," or "learners," and as such formed His Church *in representation*. Did not Christ have them in mind as part of the material of the Church He said He would build? Therefore all the promises He gave His disciples, many of which were fulfilled on their behalf after His ascension, are for the disciples of any age to claim. Think of the multitudes of saints who, individually, have rested and continue to rest in the promise He gave to His disciples in the upper chamber that He would come again! (John 14:1-3). Here are we, almost two millenniums after Jesus uttered so many wonderful promises when His followers were around Him, still feasting upon a daily realization of them on our pilgrimage to heaven.

What about the hundreds of Old Testament promises? Are they also for us in this Christian age? Can we, for instance, personally claim the numerous promises found in the ancient Psalms? Scofield's comment is apt at this point –

"The promises of the Psalms are primarily Jewish, and suited to a people under the law, but are spiritually true in Christian experience also, in the sense that they disclose the mind of God, and the exercises of His heart toward those who are perplexed, afflicted or cast down."

In this concluding section of our study of the promises, we shall endeavor to set forth their great scope, and classifying them, indicate their personal application. Written for *all* the saints, they were likewise written for *each* of the saints. Have we not personally proved what a pleasant and profitable exercise it is to take a specific promise

and plead it at the mercy seat? Often our prayers are *pointless* because we do not follow the example of David, the royal promise pleader, who delighted to direct his finger to some particular faithful promise and say to God, "Remember thy word unto thy servant, in which thou hast caused me to hope" (Psalm 119:49). We must cultivate the art of singling out promises suited to our present case and, pressing their heavenly ripeness into our own cup, praise the Most High who has given us such divine joy from a single cluster of the vintage of His Word.

How single texts shine out before the soul in its hours of darkness, like a light to each belated traveller! The lonely widow, the helpless sick, the pining exile, the friendless poor, the feeble old, the fainting and the dying, lift up their eyes and forget their misery when they think how their God has said,

"Fear not, for I have redeemed thee, I have called thee by thy name; thou art mine. When thou passest through the waters, I will be with thee; and through the rivers, they shall not overflow thee." Isaiah 43:2

How blessed the saint who thus, in whatever state he may be, has a divine secret that keeps him always heart-whole, and fills him with a joy that is unspeakable and a hope full of glory! Take the promises, O child of God, and plead them as *your* title to the inheritance, and they will be owned. They are *your* charter and covenant from God Himself. If we would personally enjoy the promises, we must see to it that they have a place in our hearts. We must take them as the sure words of One that cannot lie. We must make His words our living trust, as no less worthy of our reliance as if He had fulfilled them already.

The worth of any promise you may plead gathers an additional glory as you bear in mind that heaven and earth may pass away, but not one word of your Heavenly Father will fail till all be fulfilled. Further, you must remember that any promise, or all of them, are not *lent* to be recalled at any time, but *given*. They are not given of favor, nor for any merit, but are earnests of grace – words of love, not reward for service.

"He hath *given* us exceeding great and precious promises." II Peter 1:4

The milk and honey of all the promises are for you and me, without money and without price. *Given*, equally, with royal fulness, to all believers. Not to a happy, selected few among them, the elder sons, or favorites, of God's great family, but to all alike, with an impartial hand, as they have shown themselves fitted to receive. There is not a single promise in all the Bible that the poorest saint may not plead, if he or she only comes to God aright.

The promises of God are exceeding great and precious in their boundless diversity and scope. Human promises can meet but a few needs. Divine promises cover all our needs, as their abundance clearly proves. Let us now try to classify a quantity of those promises according to the manifold phases of life.

There are promises for the *temporal realm*, covering all of our material requirement here below.

There are promises for the *physical realm*, covering associations with the human body.

There are promises for the *marital realm*, covering the different aspects of our home life.

There are promises for the *spiritual realm*, covering the needs of the soul and of Christian experience.

There are promises for the *eternal realm*, covering all the future inheritance of the Christian.

PROMISES AND THE TEMPORAL REALM

As to all promised temporal blessings, there are one or two observations to bear in mind as to the right application of these varied promises. First of all, the majority of them are not to be applied universally, but with limitation, as far as may be for God's glory and our present good – which in effect are one. All outward things are of such a nature as to be capable of being either good or evil to us, as circumstances vary. Riches in some circumstances may be useful and valuable, in which case God will bestow them according to His promise. To others, wealth may prove to be pernicious and destructive, so it is withheld.

Certainly, God has promised us good things, but He knows that even temporal good may become spiritual evil; that health of body can result in debility of soul; the gain of earth result in the loss of heaven; the gratification of the present end in the jeopardy of eternity. Thus it is consistent with His promises to bless us with earthly blessings to have, as the spirit of any promise given, the aspiration in the promise to seek first His kingdom. If we indulge in the wish for temporal good at the hazard of coming short of His honor and glory, then we are not fit to plead any promise. Temporal mercies, if granted, would only end in our undoing. While there is a promise prepared for any need or emergency that may arise, we can only expect God to undertake for us as we claim a specific promise, as we acknowledge Him in *all* our ways (Proverbs 3:6). His good things are only added unto us as we seek and put Him first (Matthew 6:33).

While it is true that our daily course is, from first to last, "skirted with fair borders of promises that are green and blossoming when all around is bare," we must beware of a light and unwarranted estimate of the condition of receiving these promises. There is no room for presumption. Grace must be ours to pass the time of our sojourning here in fear – fear, not of any promise failing of performance, but of our sinful natures; fear lest a promise being left us of entering into His rest, any of us should seem to come short of it (Hebrews 4:1).

Then let it never be forgotten that we may, and can, enjoy the richness of the promises only when our hearts are quick with a healthy spiritual life of which God, by His Spirit, is the sole Source. To comprehend and appreciate the divine promises, there must be unbroken communion with Him who gave them.

Further, it must be noted that in this Christian era, the right to appropriate the promises is usually coupled with the Name of Jesus – "Whatsoever ye shall ask the Father in my name." Does this not imply that only believers in Him are recognized as having any interest in the promises which can only be inherited and obtained "through faith"? All these promises are "of God, in him," that is, the Saviour. The Father committed to the Son the bounties of His grace to give to men, and they can only receive them as they come to Him. All from God is in Christ Jesus. On God's part, they were all given in His Name, and it is only through faith in that Name that we can claim particular interest in the promises and in Christ as being the Pledge of their fulfilment.

Coming to Him, with any particular promise in mind, we' have no need to ask for any security of the verification of any word of His. Claiming the promise in the divinely appointed way, we have the sweet assurance that God will be as good as His word and undertake accordingly.

The multitudinous promises – "eighty-five for every day of the year," one writer computes – cover all our needs, whether for the body, home, mind and soul, and for the whole of life, both here and hereafter. These wonderful promises fit our varied needs as the key fits the lock, and we can never find ourselves in any situation without an appropriate promise. Our petitions for temporal, physical, and spiritual blessings should be as detailed and specific, as was the experiences of the saints of old. (See Genesis 24:12-14; 32:11; I Samuel 1:11; Matthew 21:12; Philippians 4:6.)

There are those general promises which blanket all that we may require. Daily God loads us with His benefits.

"What shall I render unto the Lord for *all* His benefits toward me?"
Psalms 103:2; 116:10

"Thou crownest the year with thy goodness." Psalm 65:8-13

As long as we have empty vessels to produce, the divine oil flows in to fill them. God never stops fulfilling His promises, as long as we keep pleading them by faith to cover our needs (II Kings 4:1-7). As Mrs. C. H. Morris wrote –

Like the cruse of oil unfailing is His grace
  forevermore,
And His love unchanging still;
And according to His promise with the Holy
  Ghost and power,
He will every vessel fill.

Centuries have elapsed since God gave Noah the promise that –

"While the earth remaineth, seedtime and harvest, and cold and heat, and summer and winter, and day and night, shall not cease." Genesis 8:22

He who created the universe guides and governs all things both according to His will and pleasure and for the benefit of His creatures. Here is a proof of His *faithfulness*. He remembers His promise and gives us *"all* things richly to enjoy." The unfailing fulfilment of His promise also offers a proof of His *infinite power*. Man may seek to alter many aspects of God's creation, but with all his genius and science he cannot clothe a field with golden corn. Then the promise to Noah is an evidence of His *goodness*. In spite of the accumulated sin of the human race, He continues to shower down His manifold blessings – giving man "rain from heaven, and fruitful seasons, filling their hearts with food and gladness." Man requires sustenance, and in the succession of seasons, human needs are met.

"The Lord is my shepherd, I shall not want." Psalm 23:1

This Shepherd Psalm as a whole reveals the Shepherd's ability to care for us in every way. If we are His sheep and His private mark is upon us, then we know that because of His kind, tender, and liberal heart all our fears of support are follies, our forebodings are sinful, and our anxieties groundless, for He is able to "supply all our needs, according to his glorious riches in Christ Jesus."

"They that seek the Lord shall not want any good thing." Psalm 34:10

This is another comfortable promise to cheer our hearts and to strengthen our assurance. In us, "there dwelleth no good thing," but how many "good things" God heaps upon us! We can rest assured that He will withhold nothing profitable from any of His children. "How much more shall your Father which is in heaven give good things to them that ask him?" (Matthew 7:11. See II Corinthian: 3:5).

"All things come of thee."
I Chronicles 29:14

"Shall he not with him also freely give us all things?" Romans 8:32

God is the Source of every good gift and every perfect gift. Temporal mercies and spiritual blessings are from Him. "All good things around us come from heaven above." Every crumb is from Him.

"Jehovah-Jireh – the Lord will provide."
Genesis 22:14

Under the titles of Jehovah we considered various aspects of God's bountiful provision. As we are dealing in this section with all our temporal necessities we can turn again to our *Jehovah-Jireh* and find in such a designation the guarantee of material supplies. He cares for all that concerns our life here below. Says Alexander Smellie, "If I trust Him, I shall get enough for comfort if not enough for luxury, enough to rid me from unworthy solicitude if not enough to free me from wholesome dependence and continuous faith. Every modest and present want He is sure to satisfy."

"The Lord hath blessed me hitherto."
Joshua 17:14

"Hitherto hath the Lord blessed us."
I Samuel 7:12

Each of us can raise our stone of *Eben-ezer*, and be confident that all the Lord has been, and is, He will be. Looking back over the past, we remember all the marvelous things He accomplished for us. How graciously he sustained in times of need and changed our burdens into wings! He promised to bless, and we found Him faithful. Not one promise of His failed—and never will (I Corinthians 10:13).

"God even our God shall bless us."
Psalm 67:6

"My God shall supply all your need."
Philippians 4:19

Our wants should remind us of God's promises; and the promises should be used to quell our fears and comfort our hearts. We may not know the needs of the future, *but He does*, so let us banish all care and rest and rejoice in Him who has promised to be our *Provider*.

"They who come to be supplied,
Will find Jehovah doth provide."

"Consider how great things the Lord hath done for you." I Samuel 12:24

Too often we dwell upon the miseries of the past and forget our mercies. But as He supplied us through all our yesterdays and satisfied us with His goodness. He will not withhold any good thing from us in the days to come. He gave us faith to trust Him, promises to plead with Him, and proofs of His care and provision without number. Should these not encourage us to face the days ahead with confidence?

"He will bless them that fear him,
both small and great." Psalm 115:13

How full of cheer is this promise for those of humble estate and whose fare is frugal! God cares for the small things in His creation, even for the sparrows. No one is too small for Him to bless. If poor, unnoticed, and unknown, you loom large in His eyes and have the promise of His best.

"No good thing will he withhold from
them that walk uprightly."
Psalm 84:11

"How shall he not with him also freely
give us all things?" Romans 8:32

What royal promises these are, if not in form, then in fact! These two verses suggest a conglomerate of promises. His

love, like a spring, rises of itself and over-flows for the supply of all our needs, all of which are so freely bestowed. Had there been any limit to His giving, He would have kept back His own Son.

"My God shall supply all your need."
Philippians 4:19

"Blessed of the Lord be his land, for the precious things of heaven, for the dew, and for the deep that coucheth beneath." Deuteronomy 33:13

While we delight in the spiritual significance of the above promises, we must not lose sight of their coverage of all that concerns our complex life. As the Creator of the heavens and the earth, God is able to meet all our needs, whether material or spiritual. How abundant and varied are His "precious things"!

Passing from the *general* promises of God's providential provision, we now come to a few of the *specific* promises related to material things. To live we must eat and drink, so we start with FOOD.

Are we not guilty of receiving the gifts and blessings of nature in the spirit of vanity and self-pride, as if by our own arm we had gotten this, that, and the other material benefit.

"What hast thou, that thou didst not
receive?" I Corinthians 4:7

"Every man also to whom God hath given riches and wealth and hath given him power to eat thereof . . . this is the gift of God." Ecclesiastes 5:19

With amazing regularity God showers His blessings upon the just and the unjust! Alas! these, however, become so common-place and we seldom pause to think of, and thank, the Giver of all.

A brief glance at the following passages should be sufficient to remind us of our dependence upon God for the temporal mercies of life, and should elicit our gratitude for them.

"Trust in the Lord . . . and verily
thou shalt be fed." Psalm 37:3

"Who satisfieth thy mouth with good
things." Psalm 103:5

"He satisfieth them with the bread of
heaven." Psalm 105:5, 40

"That thou givest them, they gather:
thou openest thine hand, they are filled
with good." Psalm 104:27, 28

"I will satisfy her poor with bread."
Psalm 132:15

"Thou openest thine hand, and satis-

fieth the desire of every living thing."
Psalm 145:16
"He giveth to the beast his food."
Psalm 147:9
"The righteous eateth to the satisfying of his soul." Proverbs 13:25
"Behold, my servants shall eat."
Isaiah 65:13
"Ye shall eat in plenty and be satisfied." Joel 2:26
"Behold the fowls of the air . . . your heavenly Father feedeth them."
Matthew 6:26, 30, 33
"If ye then . . . give good gifts unto your children . . . how much more shall your heavenly Father give."
Luke 11:11-13
"What ye shall eat . . . shall be added unto you." Luke 12:29-31
"Bread shall be given him; his water shall be sure." Isaiah 33:16
"Yet have I not seen . . . his seed begging bread." Psalm 37:15
"He fed them with bread." Genesis 47:7
"The God which fed me all my life long unto this day." Genesis 48:15
"The bread wherewith I fed you in the wilderness." Exodus 16:32
"These forty years . . . thou hast lacked nothing." Deuteronomy 2:7; II Samuel 3:29
"Who fed thee in the wilderness with manna." Deuteronomy 8:8, 16; Psalm 78:25
"Thou shalt feed my people Israel."
II Samuel 5:2; 7:7
"I have commanded the ravens to feed thee there." I Kings 17:4
"He fed them according to the integrity of his heart." Psalm 78:72
"The Lord will feed them as a lamb in a large place." Hosea 4:16
"Give us this day our daily bread."
Matthew 6:11
What a small petition this is – bread sufficient for a day. Why did Jesus not teach us to pray for bread enough to last a week – a month – a year? By this request, we are taught a twofold lesson. First of all, we must learn the lesson of continual dependence upon our Heavenly Father – coming to Him each new morning asking for the day's food, that we might never feel as if we can get along without Him. In the second place, our Lord teaches us that the true way to live is by the day. We are not to be anxious about tomorrow's needs. Did not the manna have to be gathered a day's portion at a time?

There are times when God permits FAMINE as a chastisement when He is disobeyed or forgotten. Is not famine mentioned as one of His four sore judgments? Yet even in days when food is scarce, God is able to preserve His own.
"Them that fear him . . . to keep them alive in famine." Psalm 33:19
"I have not seen . . . his seed begging bread." Psalm 37:25
"Ye shall eat the good of the land."
Isaiah 1:19. (See Genesis 45:18)
"In famine he shall redeem thee from death." Job 5:20, 21
"In the days of famine they shall be satisfied." Psalm 37:19
"He filleth the hungry soul with goodness." Psalm 107:9
"The Lord his God . . . which giveth food to the hungry." Psalm 146:7
"I will . . . lay no famine on you."
Ezekiel 36:29
"Although . . . the fields shall yield no meat . . . yet I will rejoice in the Lord." Habakkuk 3:16, 17
"Who separate us from the love of Christ, shall . . . famine?" Romans 8:35
"At . . . famine thou shalt laugh."
Job 5:20, 22
God's ability to care for His own in times of straightened circumstances is emphasized again and again in the Bible. Elimelech should have remained in Bethlehem (meaning *House of Bread*) in spite of the famine. As a Jew, he should not have gone down to Moab for bread (Ruth 1:1-3). Had not his covenant-keeping God promised to care for Him? No matter what scarcity may prevail, God can provide for His own.
Dr. George H. Morrison of Glasgow was wont to tell of a dear friend of his who used to collect for charities. The poor, as well as the rich, were visited. A dear old woman named Betty, who was poor, yet generous to a fault, was called upon. The collector found her sitting at "her tea." When she went to get her mite out of the chest, she threw her apron over the table to hide what was there. The girl peeped under the cloth and found the cup filled with water. "Why, Betty," the girl collector cried, "It isn't tea you've got there, it's water!" "Aye my dear," was the reply, "It's just water, but He makes it *taste like wine*." The old woman had found one of the secrets of life which Isaiah suggests in his chapter on liberality, in which he recommends that we "deal our bread to

the hungry" (58:7. See II Kings 4:1-7).

"Ye are of more value than many sparrows." Matthew 10:3

There are many lessons to be learned from "Doctor Sparrow," as Martin Luther called him. The lowly sparrow feeds at God's table and teaches us that a mighty Hand cares for our every need. The sparrow also reminds us that when its little span of life is ended, it dies under God's compassionate eye. All through, and at the end, His eye is on the sparrow.

Our pre-eminent need in the material realm is that of WATER, without which there could be no food to eat. Have you ever stopped to think how utterly dependent we are upon this further gift of God? While we may have to pay for the piping of the water to home and industry, the precious, indispensable commodity itself costs us nothing. God has given us the promise—

"His waters shall be sure." Isaiah 33:16
The Bible gives us abundant proof of the Divine ability to fulfil even this encouraging promise. Death from thirst faced Hagar's son, but God provided the well of water and Ishmael lived. In the wilderness, the Israelites thirsted for water, but God provided an unfailing supply which lasted for about forty years. "They drank of the Rock which followed them." Elijah knew what it was to languish by the side of a drying brook, and to live through a three and a half year drought. Jesus, in His humanity, knew how beneficial cool water was to a thirsty soul, and so begged for a drink from the woman at Sychar's well (see also Matthew 25:35-42). At the cross, Jesus thirsted and those around gave Him vinegar to drink, instead of the cooling water His parched lips needed.

"I will pour water upon him that is thirsty." Isaiah 44:3

"Neither shall they thirst any more." Revelation 7:15

The promise John has given us of eternal satisfaction holds more for those saints in the dry, uncivilized parts of the world than for those of us living in areas in which there is seldom any scarcity of life-giving water.

"Thou, O God, didst send a plentiful rain." Psalm 68:9

The Lord interposed and fulfilled this promise when three armies were perishing of thirst. Although there were neither cloud nor rain, yet He supplied an abundance of water which filled all the prepared ditches (II Kings 3:16,17). As the author pointed out in his volume on *All the Miracles of the Bible*, God is not dependent upon ordinary methods, but is able to surprise His people with novelties of wisdom and power.

"His heavens shall drop down dew." Deuteronomy 33:28

In the East, without dew everything is dry and withered. In the world of nature, things droop, fade, and die. But when the dew falls, nature becomes lively and vigorous. What a promise there is for our hearts in this natural occurrence! How we constantly need the gentle, silent, saturating dew of God's spirit to refresh and quicken us!

"The Lord shall open unto thee his good treasure, the heaven to give rain." Deuteronomy 28:12

Because God has promised that SEASONS will not cease, He sends in its season the copious showers that man and beast require. How unfailing is His bounty! As nature is the emblem of those celestial refreshings the Lord is ready to bestow upon His people, may we drink and live.

"Give me this water, that I thirst not." John 4:14, 15

"My soul thirsteth for God, the living God." Psalm 42:2

Did not our Lord remind us that while food is so necessary for our mortal life, we cannot live by bread alone? If God so willed it, we could live without bread, even as Moses and Jesus did for forty days; but we could not live without Him who is the Bread of Life. As Spurgeon puts it—

"Bread is a second cause; the Lord Himself is the first source of our sustenance. He can work without the second cause as well as with it; and we must not tie Him down to one mode of operation. Let us not be too eager after the visible but let us look to the invisible God."

It is consoling to know that God is faithful and will, according to His promises, provide for us in every strait. But to trust in these royal promises "does not abate our industry in all lawful and common means, or give us the right to expect to be fed like the ravens, or clothed like lilies, without working for feed and raiment. But it does check our trying doubtful courses even in our darkest hours." Although God sent the manna, the people had to gather it. It is not our sowing, or planting, but the bounty of God that gives us increase.

Further, we must guard ourselves against any view of the promises of temporal favors that would bind God down to grant them without conditions, or otherwise than His pleasure. All the blessings of life – food, riches, health, and prosperity – are dispensed with an eye to our higher good. The great end of Divine Providence towards us is to lead us nearer the provident One Himself.

Closely allied to the enjoyment of the food God provides is APPETITE, without which the best of food seems tasteless and wasteful. There are wealthy people who can afford the most costly foods, but who have little appetite to appreciate them. The Bible word for "appetite" covers *desire* and *lust,* good or bad. God is referred to as filling "the appetite of the young lions" (Job 38:39). Overeating is condemned by Solomon, who certainly knew what he wrote about –

"Put a knife to thy throat, if thou be a man given to appetite." Proverbs 23:2
"Yet the appetite is not filled."
Ecclesiastes 6:7
"Greedy dogs which can never have enough." Isaiah 56:11

A normal appetite supposes life and is regulated by nature, and a carnal appetite is satisfied with carnal things. In the spiritual realm, a Christian can only be satisfied with spiritual things. His appetite is fixed on its Object, and it is only as he feeds upon Him that he enjoys satisfaction (Psalm 107:9). Daniel and his three friends knew how to curb their appetites. They did not live to eat, but ate to live.

"Let them give us pulse to eat and water to drink." Daniel 1:2

They proved to those around them in the court that plain living was the ladder up which they mounted to high thinking. Those young men set themselves against undue indulgence of the body in eating and drinking, and so must we if we would be spared from indulgences unfitting the soul for the lofty and sublime delights of fellowship with heaven. A devout saint of a past century left on record his vow –

"I shall be spare of sleep, sparer of diet, and sparest of time that, when the days for eating, drinking, clothing and sleeping shall be no more, I may eat of my Saviour's hidden manna, drink of the new wine of my Father's kingdom, and inherit that rest which remaineth for the people of my God, for ever and ever."

How great is the goodness of Him who supplies us, not only with our necessary food, but also our equally necessary RAIMENT – more necessary in some climates than in others.

"Take no thought . . . for your body, what ye shall put on . . . Take no thought, saying . . . Wherefore shall we be clothed . . . Shall he not much more clothe you?" Matthew 6:30
"Whose adorning let it not be . . . the putting on of apparel." I Peter 3:3
"Their raiment waxed not old."
Deuteronomy 8:4; 29:5
"If God . . . will give me . . . raiment to put on." Genesis 28:20
"I will clothe thee with raiment."
Zechariah 3:4
"The body is more than raiment."
Luke 12:23, 28
"Having food and raiment."
I Timothy 6:8
"Buy of me white raiment that thou mayest be clothed." Revelation 3:18

Good clothes are expensive these days and those saints who are materially poor may have a little anxiety as to where new clothes are to come from. Well, theirs is the promise that as God clothes the fields with grass, He will surely care for the bodily covering of His children. "He who made man so that when he sinned he needed garments, also in mercy supplied him with them." Let us look at some of the above promises more closely.

"Take no thought for . . . what ye shall put on." Matthew 6:25

These are days when we spend a good deal of time and thought as to what we should put on. Christ did not teach negligence in respect to what we wear. Shabbiness, if avoidable, is no recommendation of saintliness. There can be a beauty of holiness in the tone and material of the very clothes we choose. Horace Bushnell once said that "it is possible to dress in the Spirit." Jesus Himself would be fittingly attired as He moved among men. We cannot conceive of His ministering in the Temple with unkept hair and careless attire.

If we interpret His mind aright, what Christ warned us against is the sinfulness of making idols of what we put on. Clothes can be worshiped. He further indicates that if we are His, and live as unto Him, there should be no concern about necessary raiment.

"The body is more than raiment."
                                    Matthew 6:25

The health and holiness of the body are of greater importance than its habiliments. As a child of God, your body has become a temple of the Holy Spirit, which means that you have to be more anxious over your body functioning as a medium of blessing than as a mere model, displaying the latest creations. The spiritual is more important than the material. To spend more money on clothes than we do for nutritious food, whereby the body can be kept healthy and thereby able to render the utmost service for God, is surely unworthy of one redeemed by the blood of Christ. The promise is that if God is able to feed the birds, and our bodies, He has also power to provide the raiment the bodies need. If He clothes the birds with such lovely plumage, He will not be indifferent regarding what His children should wear. He knows what things they have need of.

"Their clothes waxed not old."
                                    Nehemiah 9:21

One of the lesser miracles God performed for the Israelites was the preservation of their clothing during the forty years of wilderness journey (Deuteronomy 8:4; 29:5). With the best of care, the best of clothes wear out. If we could keep our raiment for forty years, it might look old and outmoded by the end of such a period, but what a tremendous saving would be ours! In spite of rigorous usage, the clothes with which the Israelites left Egypt served their purpose until the land of Canaan was reached. "They waxed not old" – language implying that they were as fresh-looking after such long wear and tear as when first made and put on. How encouraging to faith it is to remember that we serve a God who knows how to make things last!

"God . . . clothed them." Genesis 3:21

God, then, was man's first Tailor. Adam and Eve, conscious of their nakedness, sewed fig leaves together and made themselves aprons, or loin coverings. But such aprons afforded no efficient and permanent covering. Thus God made them "coats," coats of skin – longer than aprons and more durable than leaves. Man's first bodily covering was made of skins, and skins imply the death of animals. God condemned the leaves Adam provided by his own effort. Our self-righteousness is as a filthy rag in God's sight. Apart from the sacrificial covering of divine righteousness, we are naked

before God. "Naked, come to Thee for dress."

"They have no covering in the cold."
                                    Job 24:7

What a soft, sympathizing heart Job had! "For God maketh my heart soft" (23:16). This was why the heartlessness of those he condemns weighed upon his tender spirit.

"They caused the naked to lodge without clothing, that they have no covering in the cold." Job 24:7

When Old Man Winter comes around, are our hearts pained as we think of the very many who lack sufficient clothing to keep them warm? How grateful we should be if we have sufficient clothing to keep out the cold! Are there those living near you whose raiment is somewhat scanty, who are poor and unable to provide what they sorely need as the cold, wintry days approach? As you count your blessings, are you also sharing them with others?

"I was naked, and ye clothed me . . . When saw we we thee naked? . . . Inasmuch as ye did it unto the least of these, ye did it unto me." Matthew 24:35-40

"Buy of me . . . white raiment that thou mayest be clothed." Revelation 3:18

A study of raiment verses in the Bible reveals that God is in the clothing business in a large way. He Himself is described as being clothed with light, honor, and majesty, with garments of vengeance, in a vesture dipped in blood, in a cloak of zeal. As for ourselves, we are to be clad in garments of salvation, humility, and righteousness. Fine linen, clean and white – all promised and provided by God – should be our daily garb (see I Peter 3:3, 4). If it is true that clothes make the man, we have the right kind of clothes to make us the Christ-man. Solomon's practical advice is –

"Let your garments be always white."

"White" frequently denotes victory and the favor of God. If, however, we magnify ourselves against the Lord, He will clothe us with shame and dishonor. We are urged to *buy* of Christ the spiritual raiment we need; and such a purchase is made not with silver but surrender. Abandonment to His claims is the only currency He will receive for the performance of any of His promises.

Does it surprise you to learn that God's consideration for his own includes the SHOES they wear, as well as their clothes? There is that old time Negro spiritual about all God's children having shoes. Alas! many of His dear ones have shoes the soles of which are thin, and who wonder where the next pair will come from.

"Thy shoes shall be iron and brass."
Deuteronomy 33:25

"Thy shoe is not waxen old upon thy foot." Deuteronomy 29:5

"I sent you . . . without shoes."
Luke 22:35

"He will keep the feet of his saints."
I Samuel 2:9

"Their feet swelled not."
Nehemiah 9:21

"Feet shod with the preparation of the gospel of peace." Ephesians 6:15

God promised and provided shoes for His pilgrim people. Spurgeon's apt comment on stout shoes is –

"They are very needful for travelling along rough ways, and for trampling upon deadly foes. We shall not go barefoot – this would be unsuitable for princes of blood royal. Our shoes shall not be at all the common sort, for they shall have soles of durable metal, which will not wear out even if the journey be long and difficult. We shall have protection proportionate to the necessities of the road and the battle. Wherefore let us march boldly on, fearing no harm even though we tread on serpents, or set our foot upon the dragon himself."

Among our material requirements, MONEY occupies a most prominent place, and some of the divine promises are specifically related to what may become "filthy lucre" (I Peter 5:2).

"The silver is mine, and the gold is mine, saith the Lord of Hosts."
Haggai 2:8

"Thou shalt have plenty of silver."
Job 22:25

"For brass I will bring gold, and for iron I will bring silver." Isaiah 60:17, 18

"Wealth and riches shall be in his house." Psalm 112:3

"By humility and the fear of the Lord are riches." Proverbs 22:4

"Give me neither poverty nor riches."
Proverbs 30:8

Plantus, the Latin philosopher, is credited with having said, "By heaven, money is a beautiful gift." But it is a beautiful gift only when it is received as a trust from heaven and used in ways pleasing to Him to whom the silver and the gold belong.

It is most profitable to go over some of the Bible promises and references to money and to gather from them God's mind in the use of our material substance today.

"Thy silver and gold is mine."
I Kings 20:3; Haggai 2:8

Thy – MINE! What we call our own is not ours, but His. Money is hoarded, saved, or spent without any reference to God's will regarding its disposal. If the silver and the gold are His, and they are, because He created all metals, then He has the prior claim upon such. There would never be any lack of support for God's work at home or abroad if only all His children looked upon their substance as the Lord's money to which He has every right of access.

"Lay up gold as dust . . . thou shalt have plenty of silver." Job 22:24, 25

While Eliphaz was a religious dogmatist who said many true things, much of his philosophy was his own. In his third discourse, he propounded the old theory that Job must have sinned, therefore he was allowed to suffer. If only Job, poverty-stricken as he was, would return to God, material prosperity would come his way again. Plenty of silver would be his. Such advice, however, revealed the mercenary mind of Eliphaz.

But the Bible, history, and experience prove that some of the purest of men have been the poorest. The majority of God's children are not able to lay up gold as dust. What the Lord does promise is sufficient for our needs. When our money is used for God's glory it becomes treasure in Heaven. Eliphaz erred in urging Job to get right with God simply that he might have earthly riches. The spiritual riches gained through being right with God are of greater value.

"I have made gold my hope."
Job 31:24

The patriarch confessed that gold, and not God, had been his confidence. His hope had been in the gift and not the Giver. If it be true that money talks, then with a loud, commanding voice it demands worship, and gold-greedy hearts bow in allegiance to that which makes them as hard as the metal they worship. And worshiping the "golden calf," they too perish in the wilderness. The Laodicians are described as being "rich and increased with goods," but the Lord saw them as being "poor and miserable," and urged them to turn from gold to grace. The richest man is the poorest, if his heart is destitute of Him whose price is above rubies. Heaven's millionaires are those who revel in the riches of His grace.

"I will make a man more precious than fine gold." Isaiah 13:12

Because gold is the most valuable of all the metals, it is used to typify God's Word, tried saints, sound doctrine, and the New Jerusalem. In the promise before us, Isaiah reminds us that a man is worth more than money. But wherein is a man more precious than gold, even than a golden wedge of Ophir? Well, man has life; gold is inanimate. Man has personality, talents, feelings; whereas gold is merely metal and destitute of all the glorious powers of man. Man is eternal; but gold is only temporary. Man is indestructible (his body may perish but he, himself, can never be destroyed); but gold can be easily reduced to nothingness. Man has been redeemed by the precious blood of Christ; gold can never experience His love and grace. When war breaks loose, human life is of little value, yet the Word of the prophet stands that, "a man is more precious than gold," especially if he be a new man in Christ Jesus.

"Wherefore do ye spend money for that which is not bread?" Isaiah 55:1, 2

What the prophet is here condemning is the expenditure of money on useless things. As a nation we spend more money on cosmetics than Christian missions – more on crime than on education. A good many Church-going people spend more on amusements, sports, personal pleasure, and nonessentials than they do for the furtherance of the Gospel. Money prayerfully and wisely spent produces "bread" upon which God, ourselves, and others can feed. "Bread" represents that which is sustaining and satisfying and is therefore a fitting type of the good our gold can accomplish when it is used as a trust from God. Isaiah, likewise, has a paradox about buying without money. Faith and obedience form heaven's purchase price for all its spiritual commodities.

"Ye shall be redeemed without money." Isaiah 52:3

There are some valuable possessions money cannot buy. Money may "speak," but it cannot save. Gold can purchase a good deal, but when it comes to the redemption of the soul, which is most precious, all the money in the world would not be sufficient for such a transaction.

"Ye were not redeemed with corruptible things, as silver and gold . . . but with the precious blood of Christ."

I Peter 1:18, 19

Whether rich or poor, God's priceless salvation is offered to all in gift, "The rich shall not give more, and the poor shall not give less" (Exodus 30:15). As my Kinsman-Redeemer, Jesus paid the atonement money – paid it in the currency of heaven – "the silver and gold of His true body and reasonable soul." We do not have to bring even the temple half-shekel in our hands. Jesus paid the whole shekel.

While it is true, however, that money cannot buy us back from sin's bondage, once we become the Lord's, our substance must be dedicated to Him. Although saved from sin and hell without money and without price, we cannot serve our Saviour without money or without price. We dare not offer Him that which costs us nothing.

"He that loveth silver shall not be satisfied." Ecclesiastes 5:10

It would seem as if the more the natural man has, the more he wants. Thus, the *love* of money (and not the money itself) becomes the root of evil. It is always dissatisfying to love money for money's sake. Whether we have much or little, may the grace of satisfaction be ours. An ever deepening love for the Lord will deal most efficiently with any love in our hearts for the passing possessions of this world (II Timothy 4:8, 10).

"The prophets . . . divine for money." Micah 3:11

Paul speaks of those who, coveting money, "erred from the faith and pierced themselves through with many sorrows." There are times when the lure of money ruins the influence of God's servants. Micah asks, "How can the Lord work among us, if we judge for reward, teach for hire, preach for money?" Those who are called to minister the Word are under the solemn obligation of ministering to all without undue concern of the cash value of opportunities, knowing that since "the laborer is worthy of his hire," the Lord will provide all necessary remuneration. Has he not the promise that his every need will be supplied? A nationally-known preacher confessed to the writer that as he faced an audience he found himself weighing it, and saying to himself, "I wonder what I can get out of this crowd?" It should be the sincere desire of a prophet to give, not to get, all he can, and rest in the assurance that God is ever a good Paymaster.

"Does not your master pay tribute?"
Matthew 17:24

In these days of heavy taxation when various taxes claim a large part of our income, it is somewhat consoling to learn that the Master Himself willingly paid His annual tribute. He met every required demand. Rather than evade the tax-collector, He performed a miracle to provide sufficient tribute money for Himself and for Peter. The apostle found the silver piece in the fish's mouth. Money is found in other ways to meet church obligations. Schemes, many of which are unworthy of her high and holy calling, are undertaken to raise money. A strong, spiritual church where tithing is taught and practiced does not have financial problems.

"Put my money to the changers."
Matthew 25:27

"Gavest thou not my money into the bank?" Luke 19:23

We gather from these statements that there is a legitimate trading of money. A man is no less a saint because of a wise and safe investment of his money. As a Christian, he will be careful how and where he invests and how he uses accruing interest. He must not be fascinated by high and quick returns offered by unreliable companies, nor gamble with the markets and possibly lose precious money the Lord could have used in missionary causes. John Wesley laid down a safe policy for his followers to pursue –

"Get all you can:
Save all you can:
Give all you can."

"The thirty pieces of silver."
Matthew 27:3-10

Judas is a tragic illustration of the love of money being the root of evil. As the treasurer of the little band of disciples, Judas betrayed his trust, for he kept what was in the bag. Evidently he was chosen to handle the money matters of Jesus and His disciples because of his administrative ability. But his gift was his downfall. Disgusted over Mary's expensive expression of love, Judas only thought of her love-gift in terms of money. He expressed pity for the poor and said that the three hundred pence Mary spent on her alabaster box of ointment were wasted. Something like forty dollars seemed too much to waste in such a way. Yet how inconsistent Judas was!

He grumbled at Mary sacrificing forty dollars to anoint Christ for His burial, yet sold his Lord for some *nineteen dollars!* It is the abuse, not the right use of money which the Bible condemns.

"They brought the money, and laid it at the apostles' feet." Acts 4:37

Is there not something fascinating about the Pentecostal communism of the Early Church?

"Neither said any of them that ought of the things which he possessed was his own: but they had all things common."

Lands and houses were sold and the money put in a common purse for distribution as each person had need. Ananias and Sapphira were smitten with sudden death because of an acted lie on their partial surrender. Professing their all was on the altar, they kept back part of the price.

Dear old Matthew Henry, writing on earthly bubbles, has this to say:

"We must not covet an abundance of earthly things nor be still grasping at more and more of them, as never knowing when we have enough. We must not content ourselves with them, as all we need or desire: we must be content with a little for our passage, but not with all for our portion."

"Simon thought . . . that the gift of God may be purchased with money."
Acts 8:18, 20

The sorcerer, being accustomed to receiving payment for his sorceries and enchantments, evidently thought that Peter was a dealer in the peculiar power of the Holy Spirit, and that a gratuity was necessary for the transfer of such. But whatever faults Peter may have had, making a fast dollar in any way was not one of them. Neither Peter nor what he had could be bought. Judas was tempted to sell his Lord, but Peter had no temptation to dispose of spiritual power on a cash basis. The incident of the silver piece in the fish's mouth had taught him that his Master could supply all necessary money. The lesson of the narrative is evident. Spiritual treasures cannot be bought with material means. Nothing is sold over heaven's counter. A pauper can enjoy as much sunshine as a prince. God's provision is of grace, and can only be received by faith.

"The street of the city was of pure gold." Revelation 21:22

Some eighty per cent of the world's gold

is stored away at Fort Knox, in the United States, for safety and exchange. The precious ore is closely guarded because of its intrinsic value. Earth values, however, are not recognized in heaven, for over there gold is used as road metal. What men covet down here is used to pave streets up there. Here men worship gold; in heaven they walk on it! Do we realize that our personal attitude towards money is a true indication of character? What a person gathers money for, and uses it for, stamps the owner as miserly or liberal-hearted.

"He that hath pity upon the poor lendeth unto the Lord; and that which he hath given will he pay him again."

Proverbs 19:17

It is not Christian to give to the poor out of pity, nor to be seen and applauded, much less to get influence over them. Sympathy and compassion should prompt our giving. Neither must the poor be helped with expectation of return, whether in kind or gratitude. What we give is a loan to the Lord, and His promise to repay is better than gold or silver.

"But when thou doest alms, let not thy left hand know what thy right hand doeth." Matthew 6:3, 4

There are times when our right hand would be ashamed if it did know what the left hand gave to the needy. This is no promise for those who give to the poor in order to be seen of men. Those who desire recognition have their reward at once and cannot expect to be rewarded twice. Alms lose their influence when their giver whispers to himself, "How generous I am!" It is fatal to reward ourselves for giving. Both here, and hereafter, the Lord from whom nothing is hid will personally see to the rewarding of the secret giver of alms.

"Owe no man anything, but love."

Romans 13:8

Unnecessary debt is as much a breach of the divine precept as robbery or murder. All of us, especially if Christians, should live within our income and not disgrace the Lord's name by contracting debts we cannot pay. Rash speculations are inconsistent with our Christian testimony. We are exhorted to "adorn the doctrine of God our Saviour" in all things, but if in debt and not grieved by it, humbled under it, and striving to extricate ourselves from it, we blacken our profession. As Christians, payments should be prompt and punctual. Our promise should be as firm as a bond

—our word as sacred as an oath. *Love* for others is a debt we need never be ashamed of. In discharging this love debt we prove the Lord's blessing which maketh rich without any sorrow (Proverbs 10:22).

The Bible also has much to say about RICHES. As in human society, so in the Bible (which is a true mirror of society) the extremes of riches and poverty are met. Many children's hymns are weak and sentimental and also distort truth. For instance, there is one hymn, a verse of which reads—

The rich man in his castle,
The poor man at his gate,
God made them high and lowly,
And ordered their estate.

Such a sentiment is not true of the divine character. God cannot be blamed for the feudal system that produced such extremes. Some men become rich through their own industrious efforts, while other men become poor because of their indolence. The Bible certainly teaches that God does permit wealth for some and poverty for others.

"The Lord maketh poor, and maketh rich." I Samuel 2:7

"They that trust in their wealth, and boast themselves in the multitude of their riches . . . his glory shall not descend after him." Psalm 49:2, 6, 17

"They that will be rich fall into temptation and a snare." I Timothy 6:9, 10

"Let the rich rejoice in that he is made low." James 1:9, 10

"Let not the rich man glory in his riches." Jeremiah 4:23

"All the riches which God hath taken from our father." Genesis 31:16

"I have also given thee . . . both riches, and honour." I Kings 3:12, 13; 10:23

"The man that . . . trusteth in the abundance of his riches." Psalm 52:7

"If riches increase, set not your heart upon them." Psalm 62:10

"He that trusteth in his riches shall fall." Proverbs 11:28

"Riches certainly make themselves wings and fly away." Proverbs 23:5

"Every man also to whom God hath given riches and wealth."

Ecclesiastes 5:19

"The deceitfulness of riches choke the word." Matthew 13:22

"How hard it is for them that trust in riches to enter into the kingdom of God." Mark 16:24, 25; Luke 16:22, 23

"For in one hour so great riches is come to nought." Revelation 18:17

The above, and many other passages dealing with material wealth, surely prove two things—that God is the Source of it, and that few can endure the doubtful privilege of being rich. It is most difficult to have riches and not set the heart upon them. Affluence has the tendency to draw the soul away from God like a magnet draws iron. How grateful we should be that not a penny is necessary to buy anything the soul within requires!

"The poor of this world rich in faith."
James 2:5
"Poor . . . thou mayest be rich."
Revelation 3:17
"Poor . . . yet making many rich."
I Corinthians 6:10; 8:9
"I know thy poverty . . . but thou art rich." Revelation 2:9

Many of God's saints are poor in respect to this world's goods, yet rich in faith and heirs of the kingdom which God has promised to them that love him. Those saints in Smyrna were plundered and persecuted, tried and tortured, but Jesus said of them, "Thou art rich." So are all God's people *rich,* even if their pockets are empty. They are rich in the relation to the blessed Trinity, rich by donation because unsearchable riches have been bequeathed them, rich by faith, rich in expectation of a city whose Builder and Maker is God.

PROSPERITY and HONOR are among other promises associated with the material realm which the Bible takes cognizance of.

"The Lord shall make thee the head and not the tail."
Deuteronomy 28:2, 8, 13
"Every good thing which the Lord thy God hath given thee."
Deuteronomy 26:11
"Them that honour me, will I honour."
I Samuel 2:30
"Whatsoever he doeth shall prosper."
Psalm 1:3
"He shall give thee the desires of thy heart." Psalm 37:4
"I will set him on high . . . and honour him." Psalm 91:14, 15
"His horn shall be exalted with honour."
Psalm 112:6, 9
"In her left hand, riches and honour."
Proverbs 3:18; 4:8; 10:22
"By . . . the fear of the Lord are riches, honour and life." Proverbs 22:4
"God that performeth all things for me." Psalm 57:2
"They are the seed of the blessed of the Lord." Isaiah 65:23
"If any man serve me, him will my Father honour." John 12:26
"The Lord shall command the blessing upon thee." Deuteronomy 28:8

Israel was made "plenteous in goods" that, as a nation, she might be able to lend to all nations and borrow from none.

"The Lord shall open unto thee his good treasury." Deuteronomy 28:12

The work of Israel was blessed, not only because God delighted in her, but in order that she might become the medium of blessing to others. Prosperity was hers, not to retain, but to scatter. On January 21, 1835, George Mueller, the man of faith, entered in his *Journal* these words: "The Lord pours in, whilst we seek to pour out." Basil Miller, biographer of Mueller, remarks, "He had struck a partnership with God, and had promised to dispense whatever the Almighty provided." It was thus that Israel functioned. Have we learned the lesson of sharing what we receive?

"The prosperity of fools shall destroy them." Proverbs 1:32

Asaph was somewhat disturbed over the prosperity of the wicked. Profane, yet they were prosperous. Defiant, yet they were affluent. Godless, yet they escaped the trials and afflictions of life.

"I saw the prosperity of the wicked."
Psalms 73:3; 37:7

Asaph himself was pure in heart yet poor. Righteousness had failed to bring him any of the riches fools enjoyed. Consistent, he was yet chastened every morning. Such seemingly inequality "was too painful" for him. Then something happened. Asaph went into the sanctuary, and looking at the prosperity of the wicked from the Divine angle, he understood how transient their vaunted treasures were (73:17-19). Does not experience teach us that the gains of the godless often result in grief? Their wealth, which is often secured in dishonorable ways, produces misery. Opulence ends in a tragic overthrow.

"I spake unto thee in thy prosperity, but thou saidst, I will not hear."
Jeremiah 22:31

In so many ways, Israel had been honored of the Lord. As a nation, however, she committed the folly of glorying in her prosperity rather than in the God who sent it. Divine warnings passed unheeded. The goodness of God should have begotten humility and repentance, but the nation, puffed up with conceit over their divinely bestowed possessions, lived to see their treasures plundered by ruthless hands. Is not Israel's tragedy that of many a professed Christian? God was good in sending prosperity their way. But a more affluent position, instead of being used for God, gradually withered up their spirituality. Gains were not dedicated to the Lord who sent them, but used on the gratification of selfish desires. God lovingly warned them, but ears were deliberately closed to the divine appeal. Prosperity became their god, and the God of their prosperity was forgotten. Like Jeshurun, they waxed fat, and forsook the Rock of their salvation.

"The upright shall have good things in possession." Proverbs 28:10

The book of Proverbs, like the Psalms, are saturated with promises. Faith learns how to turn the promises into psalms of praise and proverbs of wisdom. If hidden in the hollow of the divine hand, all the malice and cunning of our foes cannot rob us of what God gives. "All are yours." Whether the possessions are material or spiritual, or both, we have them "in possession."

When God commanded His blessing upon the storehouses of His people, He made it clear that He always blesses what He bestows. Prosperity is no curse when blessed of the Lord. It is when men have more than they require for their immediate and future needs, and pull down their barns and build greater out of greediness, that the dry rot of covetousness or the blight of hard-heartedness follows accumulation, and God's blessing is lost. But when "Prudence arranges the saving, Liberality directs the spending, Gratitude maintains the consecration, and Praise sweetens the enjoyment," then His benediction rests upon our possessions.

As to POVERTY, the Bible holds out many sweet promises to those whose cup is not as full as others.

"He . . . loveth the stranger, in giving him food and raiment."
Deuteronomy 10:18

"He saveth the poor from the sword . . . the poor have hope." Job 5:15, 18

"He delivereth the poor in his affliction." Job 36:15

"The needy shall not be forgotten: the expectation of the poor shall not perish for ever." Psalm 9:18

"The poor committeth himself unto thee." Psalm 10:14

"For the oppression of the poor, for the sighing of the needy now will I arise, saith the Lord." Psalm 12:5

"Blessed is he that considereth the poor." Psalm 41:1, 2

"O God, hast thou prepared of thy goodness for the poor." Psalm 68:10

"The Lord heareth the poor."
Psalm 69:33

"But I am poor and needy; make haste unto me, O God." Psalm 70:5

"He shall judge . . . thy poor with judgment . . . He shall spare the poor."
Psalm 72:3, 13

"God . . . defend the poor and fatherless." Psalm 82:3

"He will regard the prayer of the destitute." Psalm 102:17

"He setteth the poor on high from affliction." Psalms 107:41; 113:7

"He shall stand at the right hand of the poor." Psalm 109:31

"I will satisfy the poor with bread."
Psalm 132:15

"He that hath pity upon the poor lendeth unto the Lord." Proverbs 19:17

"He hath delivered the poor from the hand of evil-doers." Jeremiah 20:13

"A certain beggar, named Lazarus . . . carried by the angels into Abraham's bosom." Luke 16:20, 22

"Let the brother of low degree rejoice in that he is exalted." James 1:9

"Hath not God chosen the poor of the world?" James 2:5

It would seem as if there are more gracious promises for the poor than for the rich. It appears that God has deep solicitation for the poor. His beloved Son, rich as He was for our sakes became poor – and how poor! He had to borrow a penny to enforce a lesson on allegiance both to God and to rulers. At the end, His friends had to bury him in another man's grave. In going over these promises related to the poor, there are one or two we can single out for particular notice.

"Blessed be ye poor: for yours is the kingdom of God." Luke 6:20

There is a sense in which all the Lord's people are poor; they see and feel that sin has stripped them of every excellence and has left them poor and naked. Yet He who giveth to all men liberally has endowed them with the riches of His grace and of glory. But as we are presently dealing with those who are poor, materially, how rich they are as they contemplate all the Lord has for them! Poor at present – fabulously rich by-and-by; for theirs is the kingdom of heaven if Jesus is their Saviour and Friend.

"The expectation of the poor shall not perish for ever." Psalm 9:18

What a heartening promise this is! All God's promises raise the expectation. What the promise has engaged to give, Providence seems loath to bestow. But no good word of His can possibly fail. If in straitened circumstances, my friend, God knows your need; therefore you can expect Him to support you under all your trials and supply you with all necessary good if you are striving to make Him your daily portion. Poverty is a hard heritage; but those who trust in God are never forgotten of Him, even though it looks as if they have been overlooked in His providential distribution of good things.

"The poor committeth himself to thee."
Psalm 10:14

Those who appear to be among the poorest are yet rich in faith and are blessedly content even though frugality is theirs. They may also appear to be the most friendless, yet theirs is the truest and best Friend, who has promised never to forsake them. They have committed themselves to Him, and have the assurance that He knows all about their struggles. As one expositor expresses it, "They have committed themselves –

To His grace – to be saved by it;
To His power – to be kept by it;
To His providence – to be fed by it;
To His word – to be ruled by it;
To His care – to be preserved by it;
To His arms – to be safely landed in glory.
"As having nothing, and yet possessing all things." II Corinthians 6:10

Paul knew what it was to suffer penury for Christ's sake. At times, he existed upon the gifts of fellow believers. If help was not forthcoming, he turned to his trade as a tentmaker to make ends meet. Because God was His inheritance, he was never downcast when he had nothing. His bare necessities were usually met, and having learned to rejoice in the Lord always, he was content. He lived not only *for* the Lord, but *upon* Him. No wonder Paul could say, although destitute of those material possessions calculated to make other people happy, that he possessed all things!

"Blessed is he that considereth the poor; the Lord will deliver him in time of trouble." Psalm 41:1

Our Lord affirmed, "The poor ye have always with you," and they are near us to *consider*. This precious promise is for those who think about the poor and let them lie on their hearts as a Christian duty. To throw a coin in a hurry as we pass a poor person is not to look into their case and devise plans for their relief, as this promise suggests we should. We receive singular personal providential help as the Lord sees how desirous we are of trying to bring the needy out of trouble. As we do unto others, so will the Lord do unto us.

"He shall deliver the needy when he crieth; the poor also, and him that hath no helper." Psalm 72:12

Spurgeon's comment on this verse is most helpful. "The needy cries; what else can he do? His cry is heard of God; what else need he do? Let the needy reader take to crying at once, for this will be his wisdom. Do not cry in the eyes of friends, for even if they can help you it is only because the Lord enables them. The nearest way is to go straight to God, and let your cry come up before Him. Straightforward makes the best runner: run to the Lord, and not to secondary causes."

No saint, no matter how poor, can say he has "no helper." If without material supplies and human friends, God can undertake in both capacities. He is the Help of the helpless and able to supply all temporal mercies. The advice of Solomon, who never knew what poverty was, is worthy of recognition –

"Better is a little with righteousness than great revenues without right."
Proverbs 16:8

"The liberal soul shall be made fat."
Proverbs 11:25

If we desire to flourish spiritually and materially, then we must not hoard up our possessions but share them with the more needy. Niggardliness may be the world's way to prosperity, but it is not God's way. Does not the Bible say, "There is that scattereth, and yet increaseth; and there is that withholdeth more than is meet; and it tendeth to poverty"? The more we give, the more we receive. If we hoard up what we receive, and do not have bowels of mercy, then, as Spurgeon puts it, "Too great riches might make me as unwieldy as corpulent persons usually are, and cause me the dyspepsia of worldliness, and perhaps bring on a fatty degeneration of the heart."

"Fret not thyself because of him who prospereth in his way."

Psalms 37:1,7; 73:3

The psalmist confesses that he fell into hidden envy when he saw the prosperity of the wicked. Nothing vexes a man so sorely as his bitter sense of unfairness in the ordering of things. But the wealth of heaven has no canker staining it and is far more precious than money. The prosperity of the wicked is of short duration, but the saint's pleasure is eternal.

"Yet a little while, and the wicked shall not be."

"He that doeth the will of God abideth for ever."

If our trust is in Him in whom alone is sweet contentment, then may He save us from all discontentment, envy, and fret. "The poorest of His saints is loftier in rank and riches and treasure than the world's millionaires and princes."

WORK of some sort or the other is essential for the majority of us if we are to eat, drink, and have sufficient necessary clothing and house accommodation. The good Book has it –

"If any man would not work, neither should he eat." II Thessalonians 3:10

Whether our labor is manual or mental, or both, we can find some practical advice in what the Bible has to say about the day's labor.

"Blessed shalt thou be in the field . . . Blessed shall be thy basket and thy store." Deuteronomy 28:3,5

The underlying principle in these promises is the same whether work is in a field or a factory. Obedience to God brings a blessing on our industry and also upon all the provisions our industry earns for us. If our work provides just enough for our needs, with very little to put by for a rainy day, we have the Lord's promise that His blessing will be ours, even if we do live from hand to mouth, getting each day's supply in the day. As long as it is from His hand to our mouth, what else matters?

"Be ye strong, therefore, and let not your hands be weak; for your work will be rewarded." II Chronicles 15:7

The God who accomplished great things for King Asa and Judah when they were feeble is able to strengthen us for life's responsibilities. Whether we think of our labor to live or service for God, the promised reward is the same. Our labor, as

His, is never in vain. Our present best reward is to go through our work with determined diligence.

"The Lord thy God shall bless thee in all that thou doest."

Deuteronomy 15:18

The spirit of the promise bound the Hebrew of old to treat work-people well. Bondslaves, in particular, had to be dealt with graciously, and when liberty was due, the masters had to start the freed slaves in a new life with a liberal portion. Employers have much to learn from these Mosaic exhortations. God cannot fulfil His promise of blessing on their behalf if they fail to treat their employees in a just and honorable way.

"He that gathered by labour shall increase." Proverbs 13:11

The lazy, idle rich, who never worked for their money, often see it diminish. Having never labored for it, they do not fully value it. Hard and honest work, whether related to the brain or the body, brings with it a right estimation of the money it secures. That which we inherit or receive as a gift does not seem as precious as that which mind or muscle produces. So, as Solomon puts it, "In all labour there is profit." The Lord places no premium upon indolence, whether it be in our work or His.

"Seest thou a man diligent in his business? he shall stand before kings."

Proverbs 22:29

Here is a declaration history confirms. As a lad, I can remember the excitement prevailing all over my home town of Woolwich, London, when the late William Crookes was elected to Parliament. Born in Poplar Workhouse, and having had a very hard life as a lad, he yet persevered until he achieved fame in national life. Thus though Bill Crookes, as he was affectionately called, came from obscurity by his unceasing diligence, he had royalty as his friends. We may never have the honor of standing in the presence of an earthly potentate, even though we labor hard and long at the work of our hands. But of this we are confident, that if we labor for the Master from the dawn to the setting sun, the blessed privilege will be ours of standing before the King of glory. Salvation will bring us into His royal presence, and service will determine our reward from His hand.

"Is not this the carpenter's son?"

Matthew 13:55

For something like fifteen years Jesus labored at the bench. He wrought at His trade, proving that an honest trade is no discredit to any man. One quaint writer has it, "He who spends his time in idleness is fit for any business in which Satan chooses to employ him." And of this we are confident, that nothing shoddy ever left that Nazareth carpenter's shop. The hands of Jesus could not make anything unless it was perfect. As He worked with wood and nails, others around witnessed the toil of divinity revealing the divinity of toil. And, as the majority of us have to labor hard and long, it is comforting to know that in Jesus we have one who understands. Yes, He knew what it was to earn His own bread by the sweat of His brow and the strength of His arm. This is just one respect in which He was made like unto His brethren.

" . . . His workmanship . . . good works . . ." Ephesians 2:10

We are not saved by any works of our own, but in being saved by grace we are created in Christ Jesus unto good works. These are all manner of duties, as well as thoughts, words, and actions, toward God or Man which are commanded in the law of God and proceed from a pure heart and faith unfeigned, and are referred unto God's glory. Further, these good works are not the cause of our entrance into the Kingdom, but the foundation of our reward within it. While we cannot work for our salvation, we can work like slaves for our position in coming glory. Faithfulness to the Lord, His truth, and His cause, form the basis of reward in Eternity. The word Paul uses here for workmanship suggests a unique creation, a masterpiece. "We are His poem" is given as one translation of the phrase, "we are His workmanship." Re-creation, then, nullifies fleshly works and produces good works.

"My father worketh . . . I work."
John 5:17

How untiringly the Father and the Son, and likewise the Holy Spirit, work for the spiritual and eternal welfare of souls! While it may appear as if truth is on the scaffold and wrong is on the throne, the Father and the Son are tireless in their united efforts to take the prey from the mighty foe. Divine forces are silently operating and will one day emerge victorious over all the dark, satanic powers arrayed against the Lord and His own. Often we hear the question, "Why does God not do something about war?" Beloved, let us never forget that God is not a detached spectator of world travail and anguish. While it is true that Satan is still the god of this world, God overrules even the machinations of our arch-enemy. God is not inactive, indifferent, or ignorant. As the omnipotent One, He reigns. Along with His dear Son, He is working out the best for His own.

" . . . a workman that needeth not to be ashamed." II Timothy 2:15

Study and *work* were favorite words in Paul's vocabulary. Here he is found using them to enforce our double relationship. Continuous study must be ours if we would have lives approved of God. Then, as diligent workmen, we must rightly divide His truth. All who handle the Word are spoken of as "workmen." The books of the Bible and reliable books about the Bible are our tools, and with them we have to work until we are able rightly to divide the Word of Truth. All preachers should be specialists in the Scriptures. Observation, however, compels us to admit that the Bible is the one Book a great many preachers know least about. One has only to listen to them to discover that they wrongly divide the Truth. They are peddlers in small wares, instead of skilful workmen, well able to handle the august themes of Holy Writ.

" . . . do your own business and work with your own hands."

I Thessalonians 4:11

Paul was spiritually practical. He knew how to combine and harmonize worship and work. Thus, sandwiched in between a solemn injunction regarding sanctity of life and the revelation of Christ's return, he has this matter-of-fact note about studying to be quiet, doing our own business, and working with our own hands. Evidently Paul had met those who made plenty of noise, and who knew a great deal about other people's business, but who did little with their own hands. They could talk a lot, but toil little. Paul was likewise a man who practiced what he preached. A prince of preachers, an astute theologian, and a gifted writer, he yet worked with his own hands at tent making in order to live. Declaring that they who preach the Gospel should live of the Gospel, Paul saw to it that he was not dependent upon others. There was a laborer who, worthy of his hire, yet made his trade support him.

Before leaving this section of our study devoted to the temporal realm, a brief consideration must be given to what the Bible has to say about the CARES of this life, the bulk of which are of a material nature.

"The cares of this world, and the deceitfulness of riches, choke the word."
Matthew 13:22

"Be not overcharged with . . . the cares of this life." Luke 8:34; 21:34
"Casting all your care upon him: for he careth for you." I Peter 5:7

A fixed and constant attention to the promises, a firm faith in them, and the audacious claiming of them delivers us from all fear, doubt, and anxiety associated with the cares of this world. The acceptance, and reality of the promises quiets the mind and fosters composure amid the crises and changes of life and prevents our spirits from sinking when faced with the severe and several troubles the flesh is heir to.

"In the multitude of my thoughts within me thy comforts delight my soul."
Psalm 94:19

When we fail to appropriate the promises, we deprive ourselves of their solid comfort and give way to unbelief or to forgetfulness of the Promiser Himself. We must never forget that there is no extremity, no matter how great, but that there is a promise suitable to it and, through it, sufficient relief.

"I would have you without carefulness."
I Corinthians 7:32

Certainly we are to be careful, but the *"carefulness"* here is *undue anxiety*, which can be very injurious. Such inordinate care divides the heart, distracts the mind, chokes the Word, leads to distrust, destroys our peace, and is inconsistent with our profession as Christians. Because we are His, the entire responsibility of our life is upon His shoulders. This means that we should consider our homes, our property, our business as being His, and trust Him to undertake and overrule in all things. Because of His veracity, fidelity, and immutability, no promise of His can be broken or forfeited. He has each one of us upon His heart. Therefore, to fret, worry, or yield to unbelieving anxiety injures our souls and is opposed to contentment and resignation; nourishes impatience and lack of faith; hinders our usefulness; hardens our hearts; cuts off supplies; and procures the divine rod and frown.

"I would seek unto God, and unto God would I commit my cause: Which doeth great things and unsearchable; marvel-lous things without number."
Job 5:8, 9

With such an all-powerful Creator, whose wonders are displayed in the universe and who is also our loving Heavenly Father, we should be content to leave our cares and cause to Him. The marvels in His created world will be matched by the gracious provision of His kindly providences for those who rest in His will. From an unknown source comes the following thought .

"Consider the little bee that organizes a city, that builds 10,000 cells for honey, 12,000 cells for larvae, and finally, a very special cell for the mother queen, a little bee that observes the increasing heat and, when the wax may melt and the honey be lost, organizes the swarm into squads, puts sentinels at the entrances, glues the feet down, and then, with flying wings, creates a system of ventilation to cool the honey that makes an electric fan seem tawdry – a little honey bee that will include 20 square miles in the field over whose flowers it has oversight. If a tiny brain in a bee performs such wonders, who are you that you should question the guidance of God? Lift up your eyes and behold the hand that supports the stars without pillars, the God who guides the planets without collision – *He it is who cares for you!"*

"The Lord hath been mindful of us: he will bless us." Psalm 115:12

All God has been, He is and will ever be. All the saints can set their seal to the first part of this sweet promise, for their part is strewn with numerous tokens of divine favor. Praise ascends as we meditate upon the way God has thought of us, provided, comforted, delivered, guided us. His mind has been full of us. Without a single break, He has cared for us, and the promise is that because He is unchangeable, He will continue to bless us.

"In nothing be anxious . . . let your requests be made known unto God."
Philippians 4:6 R.V.

In this blessed invitation to approach the mercy seat with all our requests, there is the latent promise of relief. Paul actually gives us a three-fold cord, a trinity of truth in unity.

We should be careful for nothing. While God expects us to use sanctified commonsense in the ordering of our lives, and to exercise our minds calmly and judiciously whether in our temporal or spiritual affairs, whatever goes beyond our careful planning and prudence in sin. It is a sign of distrust when we allow ourselves to be shaken with vague uncertainties and ceaseless alarms. For today and tomorrow we must trust God.

We should be prayerful for everything. Prayer safeguards us against and counteracts the manifold dangers surrounding us. "Prayer," Alexander Smellie reminds us, "corrects the feverish restlessness of my heart, brings me into God's atmosphere of calm. Prayer enables me to continue steadfastly in well-doing, giving me back old energy. Prayer endues me with marvellous influence over others, opening not only the door of the Celestial City but the door of human hearts, and my King comes in."

We should be thankful for anything. How lacking in gratitude we are! Note the scope of such thankfulness – *anything!* Not only thankful for the pleasant things of life, but the unpleasant experiences as well – for trials as well as triumphs, for losses as well as gains. The Master could take the bitter cup and give thanks. While it may be hard to thank God for sorrow, we can bless Him because He knows what is best for us, and for the fact that He cannot make any mistake in what He may permit a child of His to bear.

"Be not anxious for your life."
Matthew 6:25 R.V.

Some of the temporal needs our Lord refers to in the narrative we have already considered. We pause here to note His command regarding unnecessary, anxious thought. Does He not remind us that God spreads a table for the sparrows and clothes the wayside with lilies of exquisite beauty? And because we are dearer to Him than birds and flowers, because we have been redeemed by His blood, we must not distress ourselves over mundane things. Are we not children in the royal and wealthy family of the King of kings? Then, surely, there is no justification for us to be perplexed or to be burdened during the day and sleepless at night.

"Casting all your care upon him: for he careth for you." I Peter 5:7

The last part of this wonderful promise can be translated, "He has you upon His heart." If this is so, and it is, why are we so often fretted by the annoying cares of daily life? Why look forward to what may happen tomorrow? The same everlasting Father who cares for us today will take care of us every day. "When we cast all our sins upon Christ, there is no sin upon us, and so we enjoy pardon," says H. P. MacGregor. "When we cast all our care upon Christ, there is no care upon us, and so we enjoy peace. If we keep the cares, we cannot have the peace; if we cast the cares, we cannot help having the peace."

"One thing is needful . . . that good part." Luke 10:42

Martha was cumbered about many things. Jesus did not upbraid her for being solicitous about home responsibilities, but for their encroachment upon the more needful and good part, namely, meditation upon Himself. The many trifles of time must not affect, distract, and bewilder us, robbing us thereby of precious fellowship with the Master.

"As thy servant was busy here and there, he was gone." I Kings 20:40

If the heart is in a sanctified and healthy state, the home will not be neglected and neither will the deeper things of the soul.

"Seek ye first the kingdom of God."
Matthew 6:33

What a copious promise this is! "These things" – food, raiment, home – God undertakes to add unto us if we put Him first. If we give His business pre-eminence, He will give our business His primary concern. Spurgeon humorously remarks, "If you want paper and string, you get them given in when you buy more important goods; just so all that we need of earthly things we shall have thrown in with the Kingdom . . . Covetousness is poverty, and anxiety is mercy; trust in God is an estate, and likeness to God is a heavenly inheritance."

"Bring them hither to me."
Matthew 14:18

Does not this invitation cover the bringing of our trials, troubles and needs to Him? If we carry all things to Him, small things as well as great ones, then by doing so trials are surmounted, foes are conquered, tribulation is glorified in, and God becomes so real.

PROMISES AND THE PHYSICAL REALM

In the previous section we thought of many things connected with the body, such as food, water, and raiment, and of money, so necessary for the welfare of the body.

Now we come to examine another group of promises definitely connected with the body itself – aspects of our physical, natural life, the length of which is in the hands of God. It is somewhat surprising to find how wide is the coverage of these divine promises in respect to the stages, needs, and emotions of our life in the flesh.

One of Sir Winston Churchill's favorite admonitions to writers was –

"Clarity and cogency can be reconciled with a greater brevity . . . It is slothful not to compress your thoughts."

A characteristic feature of Bible promises, not only of the explicit ones we are now to consider, but *all* of them, is their "clarity and cogency." How they compress, in a most remarkable way, divine thoughts! Not a word is wasted. They are *multum in parvo* – much in little – and their designed brevity is impressive. Truth is stated in a clear, concise way as to be easily understood.

BIRTH

Our physical life on earth began with our natural birth. Such a birth gave us a human body, "fearfully and wonderfully made . . . in secret, and curiously wrought" (Psalm 139:14, 15).

"Better is the day of death than the day of one's birth." Ecclesiastes 7:1

At our birth we enter a world with all its sin, suffering, sorrow and separation; but at our death, if our hope is in Christ, we bid farewell to all the flesh is heir to. It is in this respect that death is gain, as Paul expresses it. We are born to live, but sooner or later we die. The proverb has it: "For life is nearer every day to death." If, however, we die in Christ, then death is the commencement of life for evermore.

"Many shall rejoice at his birth."
Luke 1:14

Zacharias and Elisabeth were assured that the birth of their divinely promised and provided son John would result in much joy. He came as the forerunner of Him whose birth was also to be accompanied with much joy. The birth of a child usually produces happy hearts. Unwanted children are not joyfully welcomed, much to the detriment of the babes themselves. Are you still a joy to those who gave you birth?

"Travailing in birth." Revelation 12:2

"I travail in birth." Galatians 4:14

We should never forget what our birth cost the mother who bore us. Many a mother forfeits her life in the birth of her child. She dies that it may live. But if spared, the agony and travail are soon forgotten in the joys of radiant motherhood, and as she faces the future with the promise of happy companionship:

"The children which God hath graciously given thy servant." Genesis 33:5

"He maketh the barren woman to keep house, and to be a joyful mother of children." Psalm 113:9

"Children are a heritage of the Lord, and the fruit of the womb is his reward." Psalm 127:3

"The promise is unto you, and to your children." Acts 2:39

Not many parents, we fear, realize that children come as gifts from God, who giveth to all life, and that as soon as they are born they have every right to the promises of God when able to understand and appropriate them.

"That which is born of the flesh is flesh: and that which is born of the Spirit is spirit." John 3:6

In this renowned chapter, so full of the promises of redemption and regeneration, our Lord emphasizes the necessity of a second birthday. If we are to carry with us the promises of eternal life, we must be born anew, or born from above. Our physical birth, by natural generation, introduces us into an earthly family. The second birth, by regeneration, brings us into the heavenly family and makes us children of God. Our natural birth is necessary to the spiritual birth. But it matters little where, or of whom, we were born naturally. The question of paramount importance is, Have we been born anew by the Spirit of God?

"The third day, which was Pharaoh's birthday." Genesis 40:20

"When Herod's birthday was kept."
Matthew 14:6

Birthdays, whether natural or spiritual ones, should always be associated with gratitude. As we reach each new milestone, we should be found reviewing the past with gratitude of heart for God's unfailing goodness, and stepping out into the future with renewed dedication to His service. Here are two Bible birthdays observed in different ways. Joseph interpreted to the butler and the baker what would happen to them as soon as Pharaoh's birthday came round. As prophecied, the butler was freed from prison but the baker died. It was a good day for the butler as, with wine, he added to Pharaoh's merriment on the anniversary of his birth. What a good opportunity it was to speak a kind word in Joseph's favor! But, the story reads, "Yet did not the chief butler remember Joseph, but forgot him." May no birthday of ours be marred by forgetfulness and ingratitude!

A terrible tragedy was enacted when Herod's birthday was kept. John the Baptist was beheaded. Yet for John himself, that orgy of a birthday was a happy occasion, since it witnessed his liberation from the toils, trials, and tears of earth. The moral, however, is this, that when birthdays are misspent they usually bring sorrow in their trail.

"The birth of Jesus Christ."

Matthew 1:18

This momentous birth changed the calendar of the world. This is why we have B. C. and A. D. and recognize this as the year 1964. In the fulness of time Jesus came as the promised Saviour. What a dark, sad world ours would have been if He had not been born of a virgin as prophesied and promised! The first birthday of His caused heaven to rejoice and hell to rage. The Christmas carol tells us that Jesus was "born to give us second birth." Do you celebrate two birthdays in a year? When you celebrate the day of your natural birth, are you happier over another day, which reminds you of all you are heir to because of Christ's incarnation and death?

Do you ever pause to wonder what thoughts Jesus had as His birthday came around? What emotions must have been His as He remembered that deity and humanity were combined in Mary's womb, and that He appeared as the God-Man in order to bring man to God. Countless millions in heaven and earth praise Him for His lowly birth, knowing that He came into the world to save sinners. Is the world better for your birth? Voltaire, the French sceptic, died groaning, "I wish I had never been born." What enrichment has your birth added to life? When you reach your next birthday, ask yourself the question, "As my years come and go, is my life telling for God upon others around me?"

"Joash was seven years old when he began to reign." II Chronicles 24:1

"From a child thou hast known the holy scriptures." II Timothy 3:15

How gratifying it is when children, like the child Samuel, grow up in the fear of the Lord! How preserved they are if their young minds are saturated with the truths of the Bible! Seven was a very early age for the son of Ahaziah to be crowned king. Joash had been but a year old when he was preserved from slaughter and kept hidden for six years. Now, on his seventh birthday, he is produced and acclaimed King of Judah. Is there a boy or girl in your home or Sunday school class celebrating a seventh birthday? Well, why not use the coronation of Joash as the basis of an appeal for decision? If he was not too young to be crowned king, surely the child at your side is not too young to learn about Jesus. He *began* to reign. That was the crisis. He began to *reign* – and reign he did, for he did that which was right in the sight of the Lord. The youngest can be taught how to reign in life by Christ Jesus.

YOUTH

The Bible holds attractive stories for young hearts. How gripping are its records of youthful exploits like those of David, for example! It has much to say about *youth*, and promises the favour of God to those who "in life's fair morning" are willing to "buy the pearl of truth."

Divine Blessing is promised if
the young honour the aged

"Thou shalt rise up before the hoary head, and honour the face of the old man, and fear thy God: I am the Lord."

Leviticus 19:32

Divine favour is promised if
a godly example is followed.

"My son, hear the instruction of thy father, and forsake not the law of thy mother." Proverbs 1:8; Jeremiah 3:4

Divine counsel is given youth to live aright.

"Rejoice O young man, in thy youth, and let thy heart cheer thee in the days of thy youth . . . but know"

Ecclesiastes 11:9

"Remember now thy Creator in the days of thy youth." Ecclesiastes 12:1

"Let no man despise thy youth . . . Take heed unto thyself and unto the doctrine."

I Timothy 4:11-16; Ezekiel 16:60

"The child grew, and waxed strong in spirit." Luke 1:80

"Jesus increased in wisdom and stature, and in favour with God and man."

Luke 2:52

It is to be regretted that in these days of increasing juvenile delinquency, "the shades of the prison-house" close upon many youths guilty of the most heinous crimes.

May God richly bless and prosper all those movements seeking to win the young for Christ! God uses the phrase, "The kindness of thy youth" (Jeremiah 2:2). Would that more young people could be found nourishing affection of truth and righteousness, and acting more kindly to those who gave them birth! Does not the poet remind us that an unkind, unthankful child is sharper than a serpent's tooth?

"I love them that love me; and those that seek me early shall find me."

Proverbs 8:17; see Hosea 11:1

What a blessed promise this is! While Solomon is personifying *Wisdom* in the verse before us and saying that Wisdom has her lovers and seek her seekers, Jesus Himself became the personification of the Wisdom of God. The promise is that if we love and seek Him, in return we shall enjoy His love, and find Himself. The appeal is to the young, those "early in life." How happy are the young whose morning of life is spent with Jesus! The younger we seek and find Him, the better. "Early seekers make certain finders."

"It is good for a man that he bear the yoke in his youth."

Lamentations 3:27

A good deal of rubbish is uttered about putting an old head on young shoulders, implying, of course, that youth should not be burdened with too much labor and responsibility. Bismark's advice was, "To youth I have but three words of counsel —Work, work, work." Jeremiah's word is as good as a promise. It was good, it is good, and it will be good to bear the yoke. Many a yoke prepares a young person for future honor. The yoke of affliction, of disappointment, of hard work make for character. Soft times in one's youth do not make for eminence. As a lad, Jesus toiled at the carpenter's bench and grew up with a love for those whose day's work was hard.

Some of the most conspicuous men in the ministry, in commerce, in politics, are those who as youths had to work hard in some realm or the other. Success has a sweeter taste if it has sprung from rough soil. Youthful burdens and responsibilities create sympathy, understanding, large-heartedness and contentment. Can it be that you, my reader, are young, with little time to spare? Other young folk are free and have plenty of time and money for sport and pleasure, but you have to keep your nose to the grindstone. Are there

times when your yoke is somewhat irksome? Well, remember that a yoke is made for two, and that Christ has promised to share your yoke. If your burden seems heavy, bear in mind that the Master offers to bear both the burden and its bearer.

"When the young man heard that saying, he went away sorrowful."

Matthew 19:22

The rich young ruler's tragic lack was the willingness to surrender the very thing that came between Christ and himself. He loved his money, and to be told to part with all that he had was a drastic condition of discipleship the wealthy youth was not willing to fulfil.

"He went away sorrowful, for he had great possessions." But the young Man pleading with the young ruler was not asking the impossible. He was only urging the youth to follow His step. Did He not surrender all when He left His Father's home above? Rich, for the ruler's sake—and ours, He became poor. Are you young, strong, and free, yet lacking in one thing? What hinders your abandonment to Jesus? With the young ruler it was his possession. What is it with you? As Jesus is the greatest Possession, let everything else go and secure Him.

"But a youth, and ruddy, and of a fair countenance." I Samuel 17:42

David's ruddy face indicated that his blood-stream was pure. This shepherd lad, a deep lover of nature, never wasted his substance in riotous living, and was, therefore, worth more to God than any dissolute shepherd of his day. It is not necessary for a young person to go the way of transgressors and sow wild oats. We are apt to glorify those who are saved out of a horrible pit. Certainly, great sinners, when fully emancipated, magnify the grace of God. But surely unspoiled lives are of greater value to the Lord! Damaged goods never yield the full price. This is one reason why we should labor for the salvation of girls and boys. To win them early, before they are partially destroyed by sin, means to capture their unimpaired physical and mental powers for Him who deserves the best.

"Let no man despise thy youth."

I Timothy 4:12

In his letter to Titus, Paul urged him to exhort young men to be sober-minded, exhibiting incorruptness, gravity, and sincerity. What an example for modern youth to emulate! Alas! the dissipation of so many young people today is a blot upon our national life. Timothy, in order to have a dynamic, influential youth, had to give attendance to reading, exhortation, and doctrine. The bulk of young folks today do not go in for much serious thinking and reading. Sport, pleasure, amusements dominate their spare time. If *you* are a God-fearing youth, diligent in your studies and work, a compelling witness will be yours. No man will despise your youth if the Master is the center and circumference of your life.

"Your sons and daughters shall prophesy, and your young men shall see visions."
Acts 2:17

While Joel's prophecy had a partial fulfilment at Pentecost, its absolute performance will be experienced during Christ's millennial reign. But we take the promise and apply it to youth of this or any age. Eyes anointed by the Spirit of wisdom and revelation are far-sighted. Youth, out of Christ, is near-sighted. They only see the present. They are of the earth, earthy. God grant us an ever-increasing number of sons and daughters able to prophesy or proclaim the undying story of Jesus and His love, and who are perpetually borne along by a vision of souls dying without Christ! What a mighty army of young people with a vision of myriads dying in heathen darkness has answered the call! Their vision resulted in a mission. Without a vision a young person is apt to become visionary. The thrilling stories of conquests in the regions beyond, however, prove that many a visionary became a missionary. Are you a mere dreamer, or by the Holy Spirit are you daily realizing your vision? John Drinkwater writes of–

"Age with all the best of all his seasons done
Youth with his face towards the upland hill."

"Thou hast the dew of thy youth."
Psalm 110:3

Without doubt this psalm sets forth the promise of the High Priestly and Kingly prerogatives of the Messiah. Christ recites this brief but blessed psalm as referring to Himself (see Matthew 22:44; Mark 12:36). The epistle to the Hebrews likewise quotes this psalm, interpreting it Messianically. By the dew, we are to understand freshness. In a very real sense Christ retains the dew of His youth. He did not come to the end of His earthly sojourn an old, decrepit man. Jesus had just turned thirty-three years of age when He entered the glory. *Thirty-three!* Because of the fact that the glory of a young man is his strength, our blessed Lord, as "the young Prince of Glory," retains the dew of His youth. The Ancient of Days, He yet has the perennial freshness of eternal youth. No wrinkles will ever gather on His brow. Time produces no change in His glorified body. His strength never wanes. And the promise is that when we see Him, we shall be like Him, youthful forevermore (see Isaiah 40:30-31).

MIDDLE LIFE

Middle age has other risks than that known as "middle age spread." A Christian reaching the half-way mark on life's pilgrimage should be aware of its perils. Often the middle years are the hardest and provide a severe test. What we must strive to do is to dispense with the lie that "we are too old at forty for the best things life holds." The child of God knows that the "forty-ish" years are fine training for the future. It was Lord Lytton who said that "There is a future left to men who have the virtue to repent and the energy to atone." Sir Winston Churchill was past middle life when he began to paint. To countless numbers of Christians, the joy in middle age is the unfailing friendship of God.

"I said, O my God, take me not away in the midst of my days: thy years are throughout all generations."
Psalm 102:24

"Forty years old was I when Moses the servant of the Lord sent me."
Joshua 14:7

"He that getteth riches . . . shall leave them in the midst of his days."
Jeremiah 17:11

"The Lord hath kept me alive . . . these forty and five years."
Joshua 14:10

"The man was above forty years old, on whom this miracle of healing was shewed." Acts 2:22

"When he was full forty years old, it came into his heart to visit his brethren the children of Israel." Acts 7:23

"The rest of his time . . . The time past of our life." I Peter 4:2, 3

Are not the above experiences and desires indicative of the promise of what God is able to do for those who want the rest of their years to tell for Him? They sug-

gest what Thomas Moore wrote about in 1780–
> "For hope shall brighten days to come,
> And memory gild the past."

A proverb has it that, "The vigor of our days passes like a flower of spring." But this is not so, spiritually, for the Christian.
> "O Lord, revive thy work in the midst of the years: in the midst of the years make known." Habakkuk 3:2

Have you come to the meridian years of life? Then if you are the Lord's, may He reawake your amazement at the marvels of His love, grant you the continuance of the child's unquestioning faith, enable you to retain your former modesty and meekness, and cause you to drink at the fountain of His undecaying strength. May He make Himself known to you in a new way in the midst of life's fatiguing years! With a growing radiance of character, the proverb of Horace the philosopher is true–"The autumn of the beautiful is beautiful." For such a trusting one "the glittering dreams of youth" are not past, and "the sun of life" is not overcast. A "rugged way may attend the noon of life," but He is near, the One of whom they said, "Thou art not yet fifty years old" (John 8:57).

Martin Luther was 41 when he married Katharine von Bora, an age and event which marked his complete surrender of monastic views and which was at once a scandal to the Roman Catholic Church and an example to the reformers.

It was also when he was 41 that Thomas Carlyle finished his work on *The French Revolution*, and giving it to his wife, he said that he could now tell the world, "You have not had for a hundred years any book that comes more direct and flamingly from the heart of a living man."

Harriet Martineaux wrote in 1844, as she approached her 41st milestone–
> "At past forty years of age, I begin to relish life and without drawback. I believe there never was before any time in my life when I should not have been rather glad to lay it down. During this last sunny period, I have not acquired any dread or dislike of death: but I have felt for the first time a keen and unvarying relish of life."

If "forty" is a critical period, and a crisis reveals character, then what Joshua accomplished on his fortieth birthday was commendable. Because of his implicit obedience he could say–
> "The Lord hath kept me alive as he

said, these forty and five years . . . Lo, I am this day four score and five years old. As yet I am as strong this day as I was in the day that Moses sent me; as my strength was, even so is my strength now, for was, both to go out, and to come in." Joshua 14:8-11

May you and I have the assurance that whether the future years bring health or sickness, loss or gain, that grace will be ours to have a bow abiding in strength!

OLD AGE

If we would experience what Wordsworth calls, "An old age serene and bright," then we must learn how to embrace the divine promises related to life's sunset years and thereby prove to be a lie the adage that "Youth is a blunder: manhood a struggle: old age a regret." Whittier, in *My Namesake*, has the prayer–
> "I pray the prayer of Plato old:
> God make thee beautiful within."

What a beautiful paragraph F. W. Boreham gives us in *The Home of the Echoes*–
> "Some day my life's little day will soften down to eventide. My sunset hours will come . . . And then, I know there will arise, out of the dusk, a dawning fairer than any dawn that has yet broken upon me. Out of the last tints of sunset there shall rise a day such as I shall never have known before; a day that shall restore to me all that the other days have taken from me, a day that shall never fade into twilight."

Is this not the glorious promise before any Christian, as he or she journeys on toward the end of the road? Let us collate some of the descriptions and promises the Bible gives us of old age.
> "Ye shall walk in all the ways which the Lord your God hath commanded you . . . that ye may prolong your days." Deuteronomy 5:33; 6:2
> "I am an hundred and twenty years old this day." Deuteronomy 31:2
> "I am this day fourscore and five years old." Joshua 13:1; 14:10, 11; 23:1
> "Thou art come to thy grave in a full age, like as a shock of corn cometh in his season." Job 5:26
> "Ye are very old: wherefore I was afraid . . . Multitude of years should teach wisdom." Job 32:6, 7
> "What man is he that desireth life, and loveth many days that he may see good?"
> Psalm 34:12, 14

"I am now old; yet have I not seen the righteous forsaken." Psalm 37:25

"Cast me not off in the time of old age." Psalm 71:9, 18

"The days of our years are threescore years and ten." Psalm 90:10, 12

"With long life will I satisfy him." Psalm 91:16

"For length of days, and long life, and peace, shalt they add to thee . . . Length of days is in his right hand." Proverbs 3:2, 16

"For by me thy days shall be multiplied, and the years of thy life shall be increased." Proverbs 9:11; 10:27

"Despise not thy mother when she is old." Proverbs 23:22

"Even to your old age I am he: and even to hoar hairs will I carry you." Isaiah 46:4; 40:29-31

The question of the philosopher is, "Who can deny that a long life may not be good enough – But a good life is long enough." The Bible promises that we can have a good life right up to the last mile. Perhaps these lines are being read by a dear old saint living on their savings, or on pension, or on Social Security. Yours has been a full life and you patiently await your happy release from the woes of this world. It may be that the passing years have brought you sickness, disease, loss of limb, death of dear ones. If so, make the old-time prayer yours –

> God grant me the serenity,
> To accept the things I cannot change,
> The courage to change the things I can;
> And the wisdom to know the difference.

When he was eight-four years of age, faithful Caleb could say, "I wholly followed the Lord." Life is not to be counted by the calendar, nor measured by the years. While we cannot prevent the years going by, we can retain enthusiasm and hope and the assurance that He who is the length of our days will sustain until traveling days are o'er.

"They shall still bring forth fruit in old age." Psalm 92:14

We read of Moses when he died at 120 that "his eye was not dim, nor his natural force abated." If winter has settled down upon your hair, accept the challenge of advancing years.

Samuel Johnson was 68 when he began to write his greatest work, *Lives of the Poets*, which he finished in his 72nd year.

John Wesley preached with power when he was 86 years of age.

Verdi at 74 produced his masterpiece, *Otello*; at 80, *Falstaff*; and at 85, the famous *Ave Maria*, *Stabat Mater*, and *Te Deum*.

Oliver Wendell Holmes at 79 wrote *Over the Teacup*.

Goethe completed *Faust* when he was 80.

Michaelangelo, greatest of artists, created works of genius when past 80.

Tennyson was 83 when he composed his famous poem, *Crossing the Bar*.

Titian at 98, painted his historic picture of *The Battle of Lepanto*.

Commodore Vanderbilt, between the years of 70 and 83, added one hundred million dollars to his fortune.

When he was 85, William E. Gladstone wrote to Lady Dorothy Neville – "The year hand on the clock of time is marked 85, and has nearly run its course; I have much cause to be thankful, and still more to be prospective." Prospective! That's the key word – undreamed horizons ahead!

Grandma Moses was an inspiration for all who feel life is over at any definite age. She was 76 before she owned her first paint brush. She lived to the 100 mark, her pictures are collectors' items, and her original scenes hang in major art exhibits.

Such an illustrious roll surely proves that life can begin well after 40, with courageous hearts determined to make every passing day count. "Youth is confident – manhood ware – old age confident again." If you are growing old in years, make the best possible use of whatever talent you possess, cultivating all the time an ever growing friendship with Him whose years have no end.

To the aged, many of the divine promises are so full of comfort and encouragement. Here are a few to muse over and store up in your heart.

"Cast me not off in the time of old age." Psalm 71:9

Because of the several references in this psalm to the aged, it has become known as, "The Old Man's Psalm." Old age is sometimes beset with fears of being unwanted. It is to be regretted that some old people are treated as if they are discarded. David had the promise that God would remember him in his declining years and enable him to become a kindly old man, sweet in mind and spirit.

"I am an hundred and twenty years old this day." Deuteronomy 31:2

How impressive is this testimony of the

veteran soldier and saint! In it, the aged servant of God testifies to God's enduring faithfulness. The promises made to Moses in his early years had been graciously fulfilled. God had disappointed all his fears, answered all his prayers, led him forth by the right way, and year after year had borne him up in His everlasting arms.

"Old men and children, let them praise the name of the Lord." Psalm 148:12

What a happy combination is here presented! Some of the aged are apt to be overcautious and unduly prudent. Youth, on the other hand, is apt to err by rashness and undue daring. He is "the best Christian who combines the thoughtfulness of the old with the boldness of the young; who has the skill to calculate and plan, and yet the decision and *abandon* to venture and achieve and win." How attractive it is when these diverse yet complementary qualities are combined! So, "let age approve of youth, and death complete the same."

"The years of thy life shall be many." Proverbs 4:10

Solomon's glowing promise is for those who find wisdom – the wisdom of heaven! But is this a promise literally fulfilled for all who are wise unto salvation? Many martyrs and saints are taken in their youth. John the Baptist was murdered just after his thirtieth birthday. Robert Murray M'Cheyne burned out for God before he was 30 years of age. But all the warriors who died young, and whose light was intense while it lasted, "fulfilled a long time in a short time," for one crowded hour of their glorious life is worth an age of ineffectual years. It is not the length of a life that counts, but the quality of it. Whether our years are few or many, may we learn to go softly through all of them (Isaiah 38:12). Life is a momentous trust, not to be trifled with but used for the glory of Him who gave it. "The righteous shall hold in his way." Job 17:9

"At evening-time it shall be light." Zechariah 14:7

How uplifting is this promise for all those who have reached life's evening-tide! In the natural world everything is dark, at evening time, but in the spiritual realm it is the opposite. Does not this promise feed Patience? The glorious morn is at hand, and it casts something of its light before. At times, it would seem as if when the aged die that their eyes are lighted with a holy lustre, and the harps of heaven are sounding for them. May such a triumphant sunset be yours and mine!

"Even to your old age I am he . . . . even I will carry you." Isaiah 46:4

This is another blessed promise for each of us as age creeps on. When we grow old our God will still be the great I AM who created us and bears us all through the years. Our hoar, or white hairs, speak of physical decay, but although aged, we enjoy this promise by the foresight of faith. The arms of Him who decayeth not are round about us to carry us when we can hardly carry ourselves. No Christian should dread old age, but grow old graciously by the grace of Him who carries us in the years of infirmity and physical decline.

"The fear of the Lord prolongeth days." Proverbs 10:27

This promise confirms the fact that the fear of the Lord leads to virtuous habits which, in turn, prevent that waste of life which sin and vice produce. The healthy fear of which Solomon writes kills worry – a sure life-shortener. Obedience to and confidence in God act like healing medicine. Here, then, is the secret of a long life if it is God's will that we should see a good old age and come to the grave as shocks of corn in their season. "The truest lengthening of life is to *live* while we live, wasting no time, but using every hour for the highest ends."

"The years draw nigh, when thou shalt say, I have no pleasure in them." Ecclesiastes 12:1-7

What a unique portrait Solomon here gives us of old age and the failure of the vital forces in the various organs of the physical frame! Old age with its attendant infirmities prompts many to say, "We have no pleasure in them." The body becomes too feeble for service, and sometimes the mind too clouded to appreciate the things of God as in earlier years. Thus, in a fascinating fashion, Solomon describes their infirmities.

The keepers of the house shall tremble.

The *house* is the body and the *keepers*, the hands – strong defenders and providers of the house. As protective members, the hands are constantly coming into use in a thousand ways. But usually in old age these "keepers of the house" tremble and shake from failure of nervous power or disease, and become as weak as the little hands of an infant.

The strong men shall bow themselves.

Commentators suppose that these "strong men" refer to our *legs*. Matthew Henry has it, "The legs and thighs which support the body, and bear its weight, bend." Adam Clarke has a similar comment, "The legs become feeble and unable to bear the weight of the body." It is rare, however, that legs and thighs bow themselves in old age. No curvature of the bones of the legs takes place. Therefore, as a Christian scientist explains it, "The strong men refer to the 24 vertebrae forming the spinal column or backbone. In old age a change takes place in the cartilages. They become shrivelled and lose their elasticity, causing the body to bend forward and a decrease in stature. The strong men "bow to the fiat of an august and almighty power."

The grinders cease because they are few.

"Grinders" is a very expressive term for our double teeth which grind or chew food in preparation for mastication. Teeth are called *molars,* from "mola," meaning, a mill, because their masticating surfaces are marked with ridges and corresponding depressions like the stones of a corn mill. In Coverdale's Bible, we have the translation, "The millers shall cease because they are few." Very few old people retain their natural teeth, and without them food is not properly masticated and indigestion ensues. Fortunately, modern dental science can provide efficient substitutes for our original teeth.

Those that look out of the windows be darkened.

The "windows" are the sockets in which the eyes are set, and those that look out of them are the eyes. It is not until these organs of vision are impaired that we realize their value and importance. Often in old age sight fails and blindness, partial or complete, overtakes the aged one.

The doors shall be shut in the street, when the sound of the grinding is low.

This further figure requires but little explanation. The lips, now called doors, have no longer the support of the teeth, and their sockets fall in. This shutting of the doors is a wise provision of nature to prevent the food falling out while being chewed. Often old people who have lost their teeth masticate with their lips closed, and the mastication being performed by the smooth surface of the gums produces less noise than when done by teeth." So "the sound of grinding is low."

He shall rise up at the noise of a bird.

This is a reference to the light sleep of old age. Usually those who are well advanced in years cannot enjoy the profound and continued sleep of youth. They are easily aroused even at "the voice of a bird."

The daughters of music shall be brought low.

What are these "daughters of music" but the ear and the voice-marvelous organs for producing and appreciating sounds. Old age often means that the voice loses its compass and melody, and the ear, its critical appreciation of musical sounds. The best of vocalists have to bow a painful farewell.

They shall be afraid of that which is high.

It is common knowledge that old folks are afraid to climb very high because of the difficulty in breathing and the feeling of giddiness that height causes.

Fear shall be in the way.

Watch an aged person walk. How cautiously they progress! Eyes bent downward, they are careful of the steps they take. They neither walk or ride with their former boldness.

The almond tree shall flourish.

It would seem as if this is a reference to the hair, the chemical constituents of which are naturally changed with age, leaving the hair of the head like an almond tree in full blossom. The grey or hoary head, a mark of age and wisdom in the East, is remembered by God and should have our respect.

The grasshopper shall be a burden.

The grasshopper, common in the East, makes momotonous, chirping sound, which active, busy persons scarcely notice. The mind of the aged, however, being less occupied, dwells on the increasing noise until it becomes a burden. Pleasures of sense become tasteless and sapless.

Desire shall fail.

Strong feelings succumb before the ravages of time and natural desires fail-even the desire to live.

The mourners go about the streets.

At last the promise is fulfilled for the aged Christian who, released from the trammelling influences of the flesh and the world, goes to his long home, and loved ones mourn his departure.

Solomon, knowing that the termination of life is not always as gradual and gentle as he depicted in the aspects of natural decay, goes on to describe those who die in a violent and sudden manner in the metaphors - "silver cord loosed" - "golden bowl broken" - "the pitcher broken at the fountain" - "the wheel broken at the cistern." In the face of the possibility of such a sudden, unexpected end, Solomon calls upon the youth to remember the Creator in the days of youth, so that when their dust returns to the God who gave it a blessed inheritance will be theirs.

While still dealing with the promises related to the physical realm, there are those experiences and necessities of the body to consider. Sleep, leisure, sickness, health, accidents, fear, tears, infirmities, afflictions, and death – these are physical emotions and requirements to which so many promises are associated.

SLEEP

Promises in respect to sleep - "soother of hearts" and "the friend of woe," form a most profitable meditation.

"The Lord God caused a deep sleep to fall upon Adam."
Genesis 2:21; 15:12; 28:16; Isaiah 29:10
"My sleep departed from my eyes."
Genesis 31:40; Esther 6:1
"A deep sleep from the Lord was fallen upon them." I Samuel 26:12
"When deep sleep falleth upon men."
Job 33:15; 4:13
"Lest I sleep the sleep of death."
Psalms 13:3; 76:5
"The Lord awaked as one out of sleep."
Psalm 78:65
"The children of men . . . they are as a sleep." Psalm 90:3, 5
"I will not give sleep to mine eyes . . . until I find out a place for the Lord." Psalm 132:4, 5
"Thou shalt lie down, and thy sleep shall be sweet." Proverbs 3:24
"They sleep not . . . their sleep is taken away." Proverbs 4:16; Daniel 2:1; 6:18
"Do this now . . . give not sleep to thine · eyes . . . How long wilt thou sleep, O sluggard?" Proverbs 6:4, 9, 10
"Love not sleep, lest thou come to poverty." Proverbs 26:13
"My sleep was sweet unto me."
Jeremiah 31:26; Daniel 8:18; 10:9
"Sleep is a perpetual sleep, and not wake." Jeremiah 51:39
"That I may awake him out of sleep."
John 11:11, 13; Daniel 12:2
"It is high time to awake out of sleep."
Romans 13:11; Acts 16:27
"I will both lay me down in peace,

and sleep." Psalm 4:8
"Behold he that keepeth Israel shall neither slumber nor sleep."
Psalm 121:4
"For this cause . . . many sleep."
I Corinthians 11:30; Mark 13:36
"We shall not all sleep."
I Corinthians 15:51; I Thessalonians 4:14
"Let us not sleep as do others." I Thessalonians 5:5, 7, 10; Jonah 1:6; Ephesians 5:14
"Awake, why sleepest thou, O Lord."
Psalm 44:23
"He that sleepeth in harvest is a son that causeth shame." Proverbs 10:5
"Peter was sleeping between two soldiers." Acts 12:6
"While men slept, his enemy came and sowed tares." Matthew 13:25

Because sleep is absolutely essential for our physical well-being, when God created our bodies He graciously provided such a boon. In these days of stress and strain, and also of excessive and exhausting night pleasures, multitudes find they cannot sleep naturally. Suffering from insomnia, they spend millions of dollars on sleeping pills and drugs and tranquillizers. A perusal of the above passages reveals that sleep is a divine gift and induced by honest labor. It is likewise used symbolically of natural and spiritual sluggishness and of death. A good, natural sleep is better than medicine. One-third of the human span of life is spent in sleep.

"The sleep of a labouring man is sweet"
Ecclesiastes 5:12

The poison destroying our energy is called fatigue, and the anti-dote is sleep. Sleep, not so much in quantity as in quality, increases our energy reserve. Sleep at its best is not a luxury but a necessity. Muscular and nerve relaxation is the role of sleep. This is why manual laborers enjoy their rest. Physical exertion induces sleep and proves to be most refreshing. Note Solomon's human touch in the narrative - "Whether he eat little or much." Those who labor with their minds may not have the same appetite as others who work with their hands. But both types of labor are exhausting and make sleep sweet. The idle rich are among the most restless. People who have to work hard are seldom dope fiends. They have little need of a sleeping draught. How many who have plenty of time on their hands and an abundance of this world's goods, long for the laborer's undisturbed, refreshing sleep!

Ezekiel gave a very rich promise indeed to Israel of old which, by faith, we can claim and use in a spiritual sense.

"They shall dwell safely in the wilderness, and sleep in the woods." 34:25

How gracious it was on God's part to enter into a covenant of peace with His sinful and rebellious people! As their Shepherd, He promised to rid them of all noxious influences and give them rest from their destroyers. Is not the good Lord able to make this promise good for His people today? What intrigues us about Ezekiel's promise is the ability of the Lord to grant His people security in places of greatest exposure, and to make the wilderness and woods, pasture fields for His flock. Spurgeon's brief, experimental comment is suggestive –

"If the Lord does not change the place for the better, He will make us the better in the place. The wilderness is not a place to dwell in, but the Lord can make it so; in the woods one feels bound to watch rather than sleep, and yet the Lord giveth His beloved sleep even there. Nothing within or without should cause any fear to the child of God. By faith the wilderness can become the suburb of Heaven, and the woods the vestibule of glory."

"When thou liest down, thou shalt not be afraid: yea, thou shalt lie down, and thy sleep shall be sweet."

Proverbs 3:24

"The Lord will strengthen him upon the bed of languishing." Psalm 41:3

There are times when the healthiest Christian is confined to bed by sickness. Yet even at such a time He who bore our sicknesses and infirmities is near. There is no physician like the Lord, no stimulant like His love, and no tonic like His promise. Let us therefore hug this assurance to our heart even if sickness or trouble is ours – "When thou liest down, thou shalt not be afraid." Peter could sleep soundly and sweetly although in a prison cell guarded by soldiers. But to have sweet sleep it is imperative to have "sweet lives, sweet tempers, sweet meditations, and sweet love."

"He giveth his beloved sleep."

Psalm 127:2

A seventeenth century philosopher wrote, "God's blessing be upon the man who first invented this, self-same thing called sleep; it covers a man all over like a cloak."

Further back, Ovid, the Latin philosopher gave us this description: "Sleep, rest of nature, O sleep, most gentle of the divinities, peace of the soul, thou at whose presence care disappears, who soothest hearts wearied with daily employments, and makest them strong again for labour."

But no man invented sleep, although by artificial means he can induce it. It was the Creator Himself who gave man the ability to draw a dark curtain over his eyes and conscious mind, and thus become oblivious to all around. The psalmists remind us in different ways that sleep is the gift of mercy to weariness. As a modern writer puts it, "It is for a night the end of sorrow, surcease from toil, a compassionate forgetfulness, the restorer of health and strength, a blessing for which we are not always grateful enough – until it begins to escape us. Whatever makes sleep natural, is the covert of God's kindness."

The qualifying clause in this promise, however, must be underlined – *His beloved!* This highest possible honor is ours through grace who have been accepted in God's Beloved, even Jesus Christ. Even although we may sometimes toss and turn at night, we have the assurance that on His bosom we can rest in perfect security.

Another delightful aspect of this comforting promise is that God is continually working on our behalf as we sleep. Actually, it reads, "He giveth His beloved *in* sleep," implying the rich blessings He imparts when we are in a state of mental repose. Moffat's translation reads – "God's gifts came to His loved ones as they sleep." Thus we have the double thought, the first being that sleep itself is God's gift. The other thought is that as we sleep God communicates to us gifts we must exercise and dreams we must realize in our working hours. What wonderful revelations came to many of the prophets of old, like Daniel, who as they slept they had visions and dreams of God's will and purpose which in working hours they remembered and rehearsed.

"Behold, he that keepeth Israel shall neither slumber nor sleep." Psalm 121:4

Is this not a remarkable promise? He who made man and provided for all his physical necessities, including sleep, is never in need of slumber Himself. It is said that Alexander the Great could sleep because his friend Parmenio watched. As those belonging to a greater King we too can sleep because He is our Guard. If, for some reason or another, we cannot sleep, is it not encouraging to know that our Keeper is ever awake and able to cheer our hearts with the reminder of His promises? As the omnipotent One, unconsciousness never steals over Him. He is ever alert and watches over the house and the heart of each of His own.

"Thou shalt lie down, and thy sleep shall be sweet." Proverbs 3:24

Once again, Solomon reminds us of the sweetness or refreshing benefits of sleep, the lack of which drives men mad and causes soldiers to lose decisive battles. If undisturbed sleep is ours, do we pray for those who, for various reasons, endure so many sleepless nights? If sleep is sweet to you, remember to pray for those whose watchfulness guards you as you sleep. Pray for the nurse in her night vigils, the policeman on his rounds, the physician on his urgent calls, the driver at the throttle, the pilot at his task. Let us also pray for the removal of those terrors which forbid sleep among the nations troubled by war. What must not be forgotten is that the truth that sleep is only sweet to those who walk in wisdom's ways and love her counsel.

"I laid me down and slept." Psalm 3:5
"I will make them to lie down safely."
Hosea 2:18

A recent advertisement boosting certain spring-air beds carried an impressive sales line—

"It is vital that you look to your sleep for the rejuvenating powers that will fit you for today's tremendous tasks.

Your capabilities can only be as great as your sleep permits them to be, for resistance to physical and mental letdowns is only in proportion to the quality of your sleep.

So give a thought to that bed of yours. Make it give you a sound, relaxing sleep—a *victory* sleep. Not by sleeping longer, but sleeping better."

But what is the use of a good bed if a person has a bad conscience? A true victory sleep can only be ours as we experience the life of victory which the God who never sleeps makes possible. Many a martyr has slept soundly on bare boards, the sustaining Lord making them as comfortable as feather-down.

The context of Hosea's promise of restful sleep speaks of *peace* even amid foes. It is blessed to know that the Lord is able to deal with those forces threatening the

peace of His people. "It is safer for a believer to lie down in peace than to sit up and worry. Fully supplied and divinely quieted, believers lie down in calm repose."

"On that night could not the king sleep."
Esther 6:1

On *that* night! What night? Why, the very night that cruel Haman had built the gallows to hang Mordecai and had commenced his proposed ruthless extermination of the Jews. It was on such a night of brutal preparation that the King could not sleep, or, as the original suggests, "The king's sleep fled away." Who caused it to flee? Who but the Creator of sleep Himself? Power is His to bestow or banish slumber. But why the king's sleepless night? As sleep fled from his eyes, the king commanded the book of records to be read to him. As a consequence, the unrewarded deed of Mordecai was brought to light, resulting in the unfolding drama of Esther and the preservation of the seed which was to produce Christ according to the flesh. What catastrophes would have happened if the king had slept that night! How do you react when you have a sleepless night? Do you toss and turn, moan and murmur? It is more restful, even if you cannot sleep, to pray, and remember those who deserve your gratitude.

"Love not sleep, lest thou come to poverty." Proverbs 20:13

Sleep, as we saw from the list of verses quoted, is used in many ways. While the farmer sleeps in his bed, the seed is growing in his field (Mark 4:27). While the sinner sleeps the sleep of sin, God is working for his good (Romans 13:11). While saints are sleeping, the Bridegroom will be coming to their door (Matthew 25:5). The injunction, "Love not sleep," is somewhat tantalizing, for who does not love a good sleep? What Solomon means is that we must love sleep only for its beneficial results, and not merely love to sleep our heads off. That some people are deeply in love with sleep is evidenced by the time they devote to it. Peter slept when he should have been praying. Drowsiness can clothe a man with rags. Some live to sleep—others sleep to live. Is it not a fact that all of us would be holier in life if we spent a little more time on our knees and less on our backs? If your daily work is of such a nature as to control so much of your time that you find it difficult to wait upon God, why not sacrifice an hour's sleep for prayer and Bible meditation and save yourself thereby from spiritual poverty?

"They that sleep, sleep in the night."
I Thessalonians 5:7

Man was meant to sleep at night, and he has the promise that God will protect him as he sleeps. Alas! the development of modern civilization, as well as the multiplication of worldly pleasures, have turned night into day for many who dissipate their energies to their own undoing. How these "night birds" add to the darkness of the night by their crimes, sin, and wickedness! But, as already hinted, are we grateful enough for those who rightfully labor as we sleep? The morning paper I read, the milk I drink, the early letters I expect, and many other necessary benefits are mine as each new day dawns because others served while I slept. Tonight in this land of liberty, I expect to have the usual quota of refreshing sleep. But as I rest, a great army of public servants will be alert that I may be safe and that my needs may be met. May God give them restful sleep when it comes their time to rest!

"He findeth them asleep."
Matthew 26:40

Solomon reminds us that to everything there is a season, even a time to sleep, but the disciples were guilty of sleeping at the wrong time, and every syllable of our Lord's rebuke "is as an arrow whose point has been dipped in wistful and wounded love." Had He not distinctly commanded them to tarry and watch with Him? He desired the fellowship of His own in that grim hour in Gethsemane, but they left Him to tread the winepress companionless. "The memory of the bloody sweat deterring them from sin, the recollection of the cup drained to its dregs teaching them to suffer and be strong; but what can scholars learn whose eyes are heavy and slumbrous?" How guilty and hazardous it is to sleep, when Christ bids us to be wide awake and pray! Sleep is inexcusable in the face of our Lord's demand, *"Could ye not watch?"* Many a night He spent pleading for me. Shall I grudge Him the loss of a few fast-fleeting hours?

"But some are fallen asleep."
I Corinthians 15:6

The Greeks used to speak of "the holy sleep" of death, and the simile was one our Lord used of the death of his friend Lazarus. When I snatch repose in slumber, I do not cease to be the man I was. My real self lives on, for sleep is only a parenthesis, an interlude, a temporary halt of physical and mental activities. Thus is it with death. When our existence in the present is over, we do not sink into nothingness and forgetfulness. We awake on the other side to an everlasting morning in the likeness of Him in whom we have an undecaying life. It is thus that a true Christian never says "Good-by." It is only "Good-night!"

ACCIDENTS

In his physical life, the child of God is subject to varied experiences and emotions, some of which we now consider. First of all, let us think of what we call "accidents." What do we mean by an "accident"? The dictionary describes it as "that which happens; an unforseen or unexpected event; a happening by chance; a mishap." In the Christian's vocabulary, however, the word "chance" is not to be found. He does not believe in "luck." Events he did not foresee were fully known to his All-Knowing Lord. But since the words "chance," "hap," "haply," and "happen" occur in the Bible, it may be profitable to examine their significance.

"That chanceth him by night."
Deuteronomy 23:10

"Her hap was to light on the portion of the field." Ruth 2:3

"Something hath befallen him."
I Samuel 20:26

"One event happeneth to them all."
Ecclesiastes 2:14, 15

"That which befalleth the sons of men," or "sons of men are chance."
Ecclesiastes 3:19

"If a bird's nest chance to be before thee in the way." Deuteronomy 22:6

"As I happened by chance upon Mount Gilboa." II Samuel 1:6

"There happened to be a base fellow."
II Samuel 20:1

"Time and chance happened to them all." Ecclesiastes 9:11

"Neither evil, nor evil concurrence."
I Kings 5:4

"By chance a certain priest was going down that way." Luke 10:31

"It may be . . . It may chance of wheat." I Corinthians 14:10; 15:37

"And Leah said, With fortune . . . That prepare a table for fortune, and that fill up wine mingled with fate." Genesis 30:11; Isaiah 65:11 R.V. also LXX

Hap is an old Saxon word for "luck," "chance," and is the translation of *mikreh*, meaning, "a fortuitous chance." G. H. Trevor in his article on "Chance" in *The International Standard Bible Encyclopaedia* informs us that the idea of chance in the sense of something wholly fortuitous was utterly foreign to the Hebrew creed. Throughout the whole course of Israel's history, to the Hebrew mind law, not chance, ruled the universe, and that law was not something blindly mechanical, but the expression of the personal Jehovah.

Israel's belief on this subject may be summed up in the couplet—
"The lot is cast into the lap:
But the whole disposing therefore is of Jehovah." Proverbs 16:33
A number of Hebrew and Greek expressions have been translated "chance," or something nearly equivalent, but it is noteworthy that of the classical words for chance, *suntuchia* and *tuche*, the former never occurs in the Bible and the latter only twice in the LXX.

The thought of God's overruling providence in the affairs of men is forcibly illustrated in Joseph's career. It was no accident or chance that the Ishmaelite merchants passed by as Joseph's brothers were planning his disposal. When Joseph revealed himself to his brothers after he came to eminence in Egypt, he looked back upon the event when he was sold as a slave and comforted them by saying—
"Be not grieved, nor angry with yourselves that ye sold me hither: for God did send me before to preserve your life." Genesis 45:4-15
The heathen believed that if their device for ascertaining the cause of their calamities turned out a certain way, they would call them a chance, or bad luck (I Samuel 6:9). It was Leah, not an Israelite, who spoke of "fortune" and "fate," "fortune" being used for *Gad*. Isaiah is here rebuking idolaters for apostasy to heathen deities, such as "the god of destiny." But the Christian does not believe in fortune or fate or chance. To the believing heart, there is nothing independent of the will of God, even although an event may be unexpected. Because of His omniscience, God knows the end from the beginning.

It was no mere chance that Saul lost his father's asses, or that David came into the camp as Goliath thundered forth his challenge, or that the Samaritan passed by as the traveller lay half dead, or that Paul was shipwrecked. "Chance" in the New Testament means a *meeting together with*, a coincidence of circumstances. "If haply" denotes *if therefore, if accordingly*, or *if in these circumstances*. When Paul spoke of "the things *which happened* unto me," he simply meant, "the things relating to me." No thought of chance as we used the term, or luck or fate, was meant.

It was no accident that wintry day when plans at the chapel went wrong and the regular preacher was snowed up. The plans of a boy under the gallery went wrong, for the snowstorm shut him off from the church of his choice. Those two seemingly wrong things together made one tremendous right, as F. W. Boreham points out in his chapter on Spurgeon's conversion in *A Bunch of Everlastings*. Out of those shattered plans and programs came an event that has incalculably enriched mankind, namely, the salvation of one of the princes among preachers, Charles Haddon. Do you recall the sonnet of Archbishop Trench?
"Thou cam'st not to thy place by accident;
It is the very place God meant for thee."
A young captain in the British Army found after a battle that his Bible had been struck by a bullet, which penetrated to the text, "Rejoice, O young man, in thy youth . . . but know for all these things God will bring thee into judgment." His Bible saved his life, and this somewhat accidental occurrence was the means of saving his soul.

Behind what we call accidents, whether of a physical or circumstantial nature, there is our ever-present God ruling and overruling. The promise the Christian rests upon is that "*all* things—even if they are untoward and unexpected—work together for good" (Romans 8:28).

Some time ago the papers carried a story of a lone survivor of a shipwreck marooned on an uninhabited island, who managed to build a hut in which he placed all he had saved from the wreck. He prayed to God for rescue and anxiously scanned the horizon every day to signal any passing ship. One day on returning from a hunt for food he was horror-stricken to find his hut in flames and all his possessions consumed. What a tragedy! Shortly after a ship arrived. "We saw your smoke signal and hastened here," the captain explained. The survivor thanked God for the accident.

We often say, "Accidents will happen." Apparent tragedies, broken bones, sickness, affliction, storms, missing a train or plane or ship, unexpected death, all these and other kinds of seemingly disasters have proved a blessing. When that French steamer sank in mid-ocean many years ago, a mother's four children were drowned but she was rescued. She wired her husband, a Chicago lawyer, "Saved . . . alone." He replied, "It is well . . . the will of God be done." Later he composed the beautiful hymn of trust – "It is well with my soul."

The death of Lazarus stunned his two dear sisters, but four days later they learned why Jesus allowed their deep sorrow. The terrible death of Jesus brought consternation to the disciples, but three days later their perplexity was dispelled. The death of Lazarus and the crucifixion of Christ were no accidents. They were God-planned events.

AFFLICTIONS

Saintly Samuel Rutherford used to say, "When I find myself in the cellars of affliction, I look about for the King's wine." What he implied was that he would look for the wine bottles of the promises and drink rich draughts of vitalizing grace. The Bible presents the record of many of the old-time saints who also knew what it was to languish in the cellars of affliction, and who experienced divine succor in all their afflictions, being made spiritually exhilarant so that they could rise above them on the wings of God's promises.

That the Bible is a Book about and for the afflicted can be gleaned from the fact that the word "afflict" and its cognates appear some 150 times. No fewer than eleven Hebrew words in the Old Testament and three Greek words in the New Testament are used to represent "affliction," both in an active and in a passive sense.

Actively, the term covers the various causes responsible for physical pain and mental distress. Many are depicted as eating this "bread of affliction" (Deuteronomy 16:3; Psalm 34:19).

Passively, the word describes those who are in a state of being in pain or trouble. "To visit the fatherless and widows in their affliction" (James 1:27). A perusal of the following pages reveals the chief form of affliction.

Individually, these are sickness, poverty, the oppression of the weak by the strong and rich, perverted justice. In this category we would place references to *adversity, perse-cution, suffering, trials, tribulation.*

Nationally, great place is given, especially in the Old Testament, to affliction as a national experience, due to calamities such as war, conquest by foreign powers, exile. In the New Testament the chief form of affliction was due to fierce antagonism manifested by the Jewish hierarchy and Rome to Christ and the Christian faith. Such affliction meant persecutions, imprisonment, and death.

"Thou in faithfulness hast afflicted me." Psalm 119:75

"My judgment is passed over from my God." Isaiah 40:27

"I create evil (that is, *calamity*). I the Lord do all these things." Isaiah 45:7

"The Lord hath forsaken the earth, and the Lord seeth not." Ezekiel 8:12; 9:9

"Shall there be evil in a city, and the Lord hath not done it?" Amos 3:6

These and other passages prove that the saints of old did not dwell on any secondary causes. They attributed everything, even affliction, directly to the First Cause and Author of all things. Although evil agents are also spoken of sending affliction (for example, the evil spirit responsible for Saul's mental disturbance, the lying spirit contributing to Ahab's fall, Satan's testing of Job, the woman Satan bound), yet all of these had no absolute sovereignty of their own. They acted by divine permission and in accordance with divine providence. They were "included in the divine will and in the circle of divine providence."

The problem perplexing God's people was the meaning and ministry of affliction. Why did God provide or permit their sore trials? Believing as they did in His love and justice, their afflictions seemed to be inconsistent with the divine character. Reasons given for the provision of afflictions are as follows:

They came as the result of the divine law of retribution. Job's friends tried to convince him that his great sufferings were due to his iniquity. The prophets regarded national calamities as the tokens of divine displeasure because of national sins. People reap what they sow (Galatians 6:7).

Further, afflictions were permitted in order to test the character or the faith of the afflicted. It was thus that God allowed Satan to test the reality of Job's trust in Himself by allowing him to suffer so much disease and misfortune (23:10-12). Shakespeare, in *Othello*, has the couplet, which

agrees with Scripture—
> "Had it pleased heaven
> To try me with affliction."

"He might prove thee, to do thee good at thy latter end." Deuteronomy 8:2, 16
"For thou, O God, hast proved us: thou hast tried us as silver is tried."
Psalm 66:10
"I have chosen thee in the furnace of affliction." Isaiah 48:10
"Behold, I will melt them, and try them." Jeremiah 9:7
"The Lord trieth the hearts."
Proverbs 17:3
If a light affliction was not freely accepted, a heavier one was laid upon those who failed to profit through God's more lenient chastisement.

> "Thou hast broken the yokes of wood; but thou shalt make for them yokes of iron." Jeremiah 28:13

When light affliction attained the end desired, Divine chastening was removed, for God's purpose is not to destroy, but to regenerate.

> Count each affliction, whether light or grave,
> God's messenger sent down to thee, do thou
> With courtesy receive him, rise and bow,
> And ere his shadow pass thy threshold, crave
> Permission first his heavenly feet to lave,
> Then lay before Him all thou hast, allow
> No cloud of passion to usurp thee
> Nor mar thy hospitality.

In addition to the *probational* character of affliction, the Bible takes cognizance of its disciplinary or purifying ministry. This is why the metaphor of refining metals in fire and smelting out the dross is used to describe the way affliction burns out pride and presumption (Exodus 15:25; Job 33:14-30; 36:8-15).

"Blessed is the man whom thou chastisest, O Lord." Psalm 94:12
"Before I was afflicted I went astray: but now have I kept thy word . . . it is good for me that I have been afflicted: that I might learn thy statutes." Psalm 119:67, 71
"I will . . . purely purge away thy dross, and take away all thy tin."
Isaiah 1:25
"I will bring the third part through the fire." Zechariah 13:8
"He is like a refiner's fire."
Malachi 3:2, 3
"The trying of your faith worketh patience." James 1:3
"When thou walkest through the fire, thou shalt not be burned." Isaiah 43:2

Gold, the symbol of worldly wealth, is only procured by means of water and fire. First, the precious ore is submitted to a process of water treatment. Then the gold passes through the fire, and in the furnace it is consolidated into the treasure we hold it to be. Without the fire and water we could never have the gold. Thus is it with the furnace of affliction. Often God casts us into the crucible to try our gold of faith and to separate it from dross and alloy (II Corinthians 12:7, 9; I Peter 1:7; 4:17).

The afflictions of Christ were of a vicarious and redemptive nature only. It is true that in His humanity He learned obedience by the things which He suffered. "Perfect through sufferings" (Hebrews 2:10). But Isaiah with profound spiritual insight reveals that Christ's pain and sorrow were on our behalf. "He was wounded for our transgressions" (Isaiah 52:13; 53). His terrible afflictions were not due to any sin of His own, because He was sinless. In all He endured, He bore the punishment our sin merited. Now, as His redeemed ones, we partake of His vicarious sufferings.

"Fill up . . . that which is lacking in the afflictions of Christ." Colossians 1:24
"The fellowship of his sufferings."
Philippians 3:10
"Ye are partakers of his sufferings."
I Peter 4:13
Abundant promises of purification, sustenance, and deliverance are offered those sorely afflicted. A brief exposition of some of these consoling promises may prove to be profitable. Taken as a whole, they indicate that, *affliction* can be of the greatest advantage to us, and the inflicting of it a token of favor. But the withholding of it may not be good for us. God is the best Judge of what we should experience and endure. Promises are ours that if we are fully yielded to God and submit entirely to His wisdom as to what is best for us, then we have every right to claim the fulfilment of His promises on our behalf.

"Seven days shalt thou eat . . . the bread of affliction." Deuteronomy 16:3
As already indicated, by "affliction" we are to understand calamity or distress of any kind. For the Jews, the Passover unleavened bread was to be looked upon as "the bread of affliction," because it was a reminder of the cruel physical bondage endured in Egypt where heartless taskmasters afflicted them. That such "bread" has a bitter taste, the saints of all ages can

testify. "Affliction Bread," while never palatable, is yet profitable for our spiritual health. It produces trust in God, strength of character, and sympathy of approach. Bread is our staple food. Possibly we have thought of our sorrows and trials as being wholly unnecessary – something we could have got on very well without. But sore afflictions make for spiritual advancement. We climb to God by the path of pain.

"The more they afflicted them, the more they multiplied and grew."

Exodus 1:12

"No man should be moved by these afflictions . . . we are appointed thereunto." I Thessalonians 3:3, 4

Abundant afflictions – as well as revelations – came the way of Paul, and grace was his to trace them to the divine source, and to look at them in the light of glory. Friendly hearts felt for him, but while Paul was grateful for their sympathy, he asked them not to be troubled over his sufferings. Because God had permitted them, all would be well. Over some old established British business houses, like Harrods of London, is the Royal Crest, bearing the sign, *By Royal Appointment*. It means that such a firm has been commanded to supply the Royal Household with particular goods. Do we look upon our afflictions, as Paul could, as coming "by Royal Appointment"? If our heavenly King appoints our adversities, then we too should glory in them. Sighs as well as smiles, are traced upon our dial by a God of love.

"When they persecute you . . . they will scourge you." Matthew 10:23

Jesus makes it clear in the narrative that tribulation is an indispensable mark of true discipleship. As with the Master, so with His servant, the way of the cross is the one the pilgrim must walk to the Celestial City. Full allegiance to Christ brings opposition, ridicule, and resentment. Perhaps affliction has changed its dress since apostolic times. Christians today are not torn limb from limb in the Roman Coliseum, burnt to ashes in the fires of Smithfield, beheaded as many of the Covenantors were; yet if we would live godly lives in Christ Jesus, we must suffer persecution (I Peter 4:12-16).

"I will bring the third part through the fire." Zechariah 13:9

In the days of the severest trial, God always has His chosen ones – *the third part* – whom He protects and preserves as a praise unto Himself. There are always the few in Sardis who, in spite of what they endure, walk with Christ in white. Although they form the little flock, so insignificant, yet to Him they are very precious. To Him, they are as white silver and yellow gold, and as the lapidary uses every method to beautify what he prizes most, so the heavenly Refiner chastens His own.

We are not promised immunity from affliction because we are His. Grace transmuted us into His silver and gold, and the fire follows as a necessary consequence. *Through the fire* He brings His own, with the fire refining but never destroying them. Then the promise is ours that although the sorrow may be severe, He never leaves us in the furnace. While in it, He is with us, as He was with the three Hebrew youths, and then in His own good time He brings us forth kindly with a new glow of life.

"It is good for me that I have been afflicted." Psalm 119:67

Looking back and speaking in the past tense, David could testify to the beneficial aspect of his affliction. "What is grievous to endure is sweet to remember." A saint, he became more saintly as the result of passing through the crucible of suffering. Before he was afflicted, he found himself straying. "Before I was afflicted I went astray" (Psalm 119:67). But his afflictions brought him near God. They weaned him from the world, resulted in submission, produced humility, excited diligence, stirred him up to prayer, conformed him to the divine image.

C. H. Spurgeon, who often suffered excruciating pain, confessed – "I owe more to the fire, hammer, chisel than to anything else in my Lord's workshop." J. R. Miller, in his heart-warming devotional volume, *Silent Times*, reminds us that many of the world's best things were born of affliction.

"The sweetest songs on earth have been called out by suffering. The richest blessings that we enjoy have come to us out of the fire. The good things we inherit from the past are the purchase of suffering and sacrifice. Our redemption comes from Gethsemane and Calvary. We get heaven through Christ's tears and blood. Whatever is richest and most valuable anywhere has been in the fire."

"Knowing that tribulation worketh patience." Romans 5:3

Here is a promise in essence, if not in form. We sorely need patience, and here is the way of securing it. As by swimming we learn to swim, so by enduring, we learn to endure. The beneficial ministry of tribulation is supernatural, for of itself tribulation worketh petulance, unbelief, and rebellion. If our burden is to become beneficial, then we must submit to the Lord's gracious operation. We must bear our trials and, understanding God's design in permitting them, remember the promise of support and thereby gather the fruits of affliction. Then, like Joseph, we too can become fruitful in the land of our affliction. From a pit, he went to a palace. Had it not been for his slavery, he would never have become the saviour of Egypt.

"Wherefore hast thou afflicted thy servant?" Numbers 11:11

While it may assuage the fury of the flame to know that God has chosen us in the furnace of affliction, there are times when, like Moses, we are disturbed over the tears we shed. Looking at the context, we see how God's treatment of Israel displeased their leader, who, somewhat burdened by the responsibility of so great a leadership, asked if he had to carry the multitudes in his bosom. Mystified over God's anger, Moses asked to be killed.

Are there not times when we cry, "Why?" or "Wherefore?" We can understand sinners suffering. Because of their flagrant sin, they deserve to suffer. In all they endure, nature is only extracting her dues for dissipation. But why are we sometimes robbed of health and vigor when we have such a desire to live and labor for God? For a full explanation of all God permits, we must wait until we reach heaven. Meantime, we can trust the infinite wisdom of our loving Heavenly Father and console ourselves with the remembrance that the Saviour's heart — *why* was wrung from the Saviour's heart —

"My God, My God, *why*" . . . ?

"He doth not afflict willingly."

Lamentations 3:33

Perplexed though we may be over the providential dealings of God, here is a promise to console our disturbed hearts. God never causes any child of His one unnecessary tear. Behind our afflictions, there is not only divine sovereignty but divine love, wisdom, and holiness. If God has to strike, it is always in love, and His arrow is aimed at our spiritual welfare. Further, when He afflicts it is only partially, occasionally, and sparingly, because He has no pleasure in our sighs and sorrows. His rod is never used hastily. He is slow to anger and of great kindness.

It is thus that we rest in the assurance that He never afflicts us without a necessary and sufficient cause — committed of sin, neglected duties, mercies slighted, lukewarmness, worldly-mindedness, abused privileges, warnings despised. At the back of all He permits, there is His good and gracious intention to make us fear our sin and flee from it; to beget deep contrition and godly sorrow; to produce in us His likeness — above all to prove that His authority is not surrendered because His love is great.

"Is any among you afflicted? Let him pray." James 5:13

An ancient proverb has it that, "Time cures affliction." But James reminds us that the only infallible cure is *prayer*. Plantus, the Latin philosopher, would have us know that "An undisturbed mind is the best sauce for affliction." But prayer alone can create this condition of mind.

"Man was born unto trouble . . . I would seek out God." Job 5:7, 8

James was no visionary. He always approached the problems of life in a practical way. Sanctified common-sense earned him the title of "James, the practical." To this austere apostle, faith without works was dead. Among his exhortations in view of Christ's return, he urged the saints to pray if in pain, to turn merriment into music, to supplicate God in sickness. And that prayer is a wonderful elixir when affliction is heavy upon us. It is the testimony of many a suffering saint. Too often, instead of praying about our pain, we are peevish. We complain, instead of communing with Him who knows what is best for every child of His. Prayer strengthens us to suffer, lightens our load, turns our pain into a pulpit, interprets all our baffling infirmities.

"Most gladly therefore will I glory in my infirmities." II Corinthians 12:9

"I also will leave in the midst of thee an afflicted and poor people, and they shall trust in the name of the Lord."

Zephaniah 3:12

Paul and the prophet Zephaniah agree that the Lord always has His faithful remnant — those who, although the poor of this world, are yet rich in faith and who, in spite of their afflictions, can trust in the Lord with all their heart. He has a trusting people today among the afflicted and poor — can we say that we are among them? Are we a part of that conserving salt checking the worldly corruption around us? Do we glory in our trials, knowing that the Lord carries both the burden and its bearer?

"The unpolished pearl can never shine –
'Tis sorrow makes the soul divine."

That the Bible abounds in promises of consolation and exhortation adapted to encourage the afflicted, is evident to its most casual reader. The Psalms particularly are rich in their precepts of endurance in any kind of affliction. There is the frequent reference to God's beneficent sovereignty behind all that He permits in the lives of His own.

"The Lord reigneth . . . clouds and darkness are round about them."
Psalm 97:1, 2

"All things work together for good to them that love God." Romans 8:28

"It is the Lord: let him do what seemeth him good." I Samuel 3:18

"The Lord do that which seemeth him good." II Samuel 10:12

"He made it again another vessel, as seemed good to the potter."
Jeremiah 18:49

God is love, and since He is on the throne of the universe, we have the promise and assurance that He orders everything after His perfect will.

"Behind a frowning providence,
He hides a smiling face."

A further unfolding is that whatever trials and afflictions may be ours, they are only of brief duration in comparison with the eternal joy to follow.

"Weeping may endure for a night, but joy cometh in the morning."
Psalm 30:5

"For a small moment have I forsaken thee, but with great mercies will I gather thee." Isaiah 54:7

"Ye now therefore have sorrow . . . your joy no man taketh from you."
John 16:22

"The sufferings of this present time are not worthy to be compared with the glory which shall be revealed in us."
Romans 8:18

"Our light affliction . . . far more exceeding and eternal weight of glory."
II Corinthians 4:17

These promises form the Christian's postulate of faith. A future blessedness will offer a solution to the problem of pain (Job 19:25-27); Psalm 37, etc). Embracing these promises, we fortify ourselves against the afflictions assailing us. The early saints derived comfort from the near approach of the Master.

"Be patient therefore, brethren, unto the coming of the Lord." James 5:7, 8 Amid our adversities and afflictions, we are exhorted to manifest the spirit of patience (Psalm 37:7; Luke 21:19; Romans 12:12; James 1:3, 4; 5:7-11; I Peter 2:20), the spirit of joy (Matthew 5:11; Romans 5:2; II Corinthians 12:10; James 1:2, 12; I Peter 4:13) – the spirit of the Master's patient endurance (John 16:33; James 5:7-11; I Peter 2:19 ; 3:17).

Then there are those promises, too numerous for us to fully enumerate, recommending the afflicted "to take refuge in the supreme blessedness of fellowship with God and of trust in His love, by which they may enter into a deep peace that is undisturbed by the trials and problems of life."

"Thou wilt keep him in perfect peace, whose mind is stayed on thee."
Isaiah 26:3, 4

"Let not your heart be troubled, ye believe in God." John 14:1-27

"The peace of God, which passeth all understanding, shall keep your hearts and minds through Christ Jesus."
Philippians 4:7

"The Lord upholdeth him with his hand." Psalm 37:24

"Many a time have they afflicted me . . . yet have they not prevailed against me." Psalm 129:1, 2

"The Lord raiseth them that are bowed down." Psalm 146:8

"In the time of trouble he shall hide me in his pavilion." Psalm 27:5

"Call upon me in the day of trouble: I will deliver thee." Psalm 50:15

"When thou passest through the waters, I will be with thee." Isaiah 43:2

"In all their affliction, he was afflicted."
Isaiah 63:8, 9

"Thou hast been . . . a strength to the needy in his distress." Isaiah 25:4

"He drew them out of many waters."
II Samuel 22:17

"He shall deliver thee in six troubles: yes, in seven there shall no evil touch thee." Job 5:19

"When I sit in darkness, the Lord shall be a light unto me." Micah 7:8

"The God of all comfort, who comforteth us in all our tribulation."
II Corinthians 1:3, 4

"He had compassion on her, and said unto her, Weep not." Luke 7:13

Bacon writing on adversity says, "Prosperity is the blessing of the Old Testament; adversity is the blessing of the New, which carrieth the greater benediction." But both sections of Scripture reveal a mixture of prosperity and adversity, with promises attached to each. "This is my comfort in my affliction" (Psalm 119:50).

Having had his share of adversity, David wrote out of his own experience when he said that—

"Many are the afflictions of the righteous, but the Lord delivereth him out of them all." Psalm 34:19

This was the psalmist's comfort then in all the crises he faced, that he had recourse to the Book of comfort. As he meditated upon God's statutes, they became his songs. But just how did the Word comfort and quicken David? Why, because amid all his cares and calamities, he knew from the sacred commandments that they could not last forever! The glorious hope of cessation from the tears and trials of life upheld him amid his woes.

It is likewise comforting to learn from the Word of God that the God of the Word Himself was with the psalmist, blessing him with peace and patience. David's greater Son has shown the saints of all ages how He also gathered comfort in His afflictions from the quickening Word. We also can know what it is to find "patience and comfort of the Scriptures" (Romans 15:4). Is it not blessed to realize that the Lord through His Word "comforts the afflicted, but afflicts the comfortable"?

"Fear thou not: for I am with thee . . . I will help thee." Isaiah 41:10

This promise guarantees us aid in those circumstances in which we cannot act alone. God says that He will supply strength within and help without. What else could we ask for from this Helper of the helpless? Whatever the cloud of affliction, the Christian can depend upon this bow of covenanting promise (Genesis 9:14).

"Though I walk in the midst of trouble . . . thy right hand shall save me." Psalm 138:7

"He hath smitten, and he will bind up." Hosea 6:1

He who bruises the heart is able to bind it up. As no surgeon would make an incision and then leave his patient to bleed to death, so the Lord heals every wound He permits. So we rest our case in the sure surgery of His hands, which are able to save us. Are *you* in the midst of trouble? Then talk these promises over to yourself, till the song of confidence and the solace of holiness are yours.

"The afflictions of the gospel according to the power of God." II Timothy 1:8

Partakers of a divine nature must be prepared to become partakers of the afflictions of the Gospel. When Paul wrote these words, he was languishing in a Roman dungeon, awaiting martyrdom. The apostle identifies his sufferings as filling up that which is behind of Christ's afflictions (1:24). For a catalog of these afflictions, we turn to the moving record Paul has left us (II Corinthians 11:16-33). Are we ashamed of the afflictions allegiance to Christ brings? There is no need to court hostility. Walking and witnessing in the Gospel demands that satanic and human antagonism will come our way. Grace to endure, however, will always be ours. The Holy Spirit indwelling us overcomes fear and causes us to triumph even in our adversity.

"Though I have afflicted thee, I will afflict thee no more." Nahum 1:12

"He will not always chide: neither will he keep his anger forever." Psalm 103:9

"He keepeth all his bones; not one of them is broken." Psalm 34:20

These promises have one thought in common, namely, the end of our afflictions and our emergence from them whole. How consoling it is to realize that when the billows roll over us that we shall emerge without real damage! Bruised we may be, but the bruises will be healed. Our sin deserves His rebuke, but once that sin is effectively dealt with, He smiles upon us once more. With Him is plenteous forgiveness. There are limits to His afflictions. When His chiding has served its purpose, the rod is removed. Once our testing has served its purpose, God will end it. After the storm comes a great calm.

INFIRMITIES

Infirmities, assuming many forms and allied more or less to afflictions previously considered, are likewise mentioned in the Bible. Promises are also related to these various infirmities of the flesh.

"This is my infirmity, but I will remember . . . the most High." Psalm 77:10

"A woman which had a spirit of infirmity eighteen years." Luke 13:11, 12

"A certain man . . . which had an infirmity thirty and eight years."

John 5:5

"Great multitudes came . . . to be healed by him of their infirmities."

Luke 5:15

"He cured many of their infirmities."

Luke 7:21

"Because of the infirmity of your flesh."

Romans 6:19

"How through infirmity I preached unto you." Galatians 4:13

"High priests which have infirmity."

Hebrews 7:28

"We then that are strong ought to bear the infirmities of the weak."

Romans 15:1

"Things concerning my infirmities."

II Corinthians 11:30

"I glory . . . in mine infirmities."

II Corinthians 12:5, 10

"Use wine for thine infirmities."

I Timothy 5:23

"Himself took our infirmities."

Matthew 8:17

"Touched with the feeling of our infirmities." Hebrews 4:15

"The spirit of a man will sustain his infirmity." Proverbs 18:14

"The Spirit who helpeth our infirmities." Romans 8:26

From this combination of passages we learn several truths. First of all, the infirmities mentioned are for the most part physical, whether natural or inflicted by others. In their infirmities, the saints turned to God for succor and relief, and if the infirmities were not removed, grace was given to use them as steppingstones to higher heights. Jesus is described as being "touched" by infirmities. In His humility, He experienced what some of these infirmities were. That is why He is able to comfort those who are being tested.

The Christian is indwelt by the gracious Holy Spirit, who knows all about the infirmities endured and so can sustain and relieve. He in the Spirit of man upholding him in his infirmity. If we ourselves are "strong," or free of any physical infirmity, then we should be considerate toward those who are infirm and help them as much as we can. Shakespeare, in *Julius Caesar*, says –

"A friend should bear his friend's infirmities

But Brutus makes mine greater than they are."

A Brutus is the wrong kind of a friend to have. But we have a Friend who sticketh closer than a brother, who bears our infirmities. We know so little about what is best for us, or what is coming upon us, or what Satan's designs are. Then we are so weak, as well as ignorant, weak to bear pain, weak to withstand evil, weak to obtain help. Most of our infirmities are constitutional, arising from our tempers, or dispositions, or bodily ailments, or the limits of our capacity. But although so infirm, One is near to teach us what we need, to lead us to the promises, to excite us to pray and assist us as we pray. He begets those unutterable groans for holiness to which God attends. What mighty power He gives to those who are faint! (Isaiah 40:29). May we be found daily seeking the Spirit's power to help!

TEARS

Still in the physical realm, we must consider the tears – so common to us all – and those sweet promises associated with the drying of all our tears.

"Art thou a child of tears

Cradled in care and woe?" – then look with me at what the Bible has to say about your tears.

"Thus saith the Lord . . . I have seen thy tears." II Kings 20:5; Isaiah 38:5

"Mine eye poureth out tears unto God."

Job 16:20

"I water my couch with my tears."

Psalm 6:6

"Hold not thy peace at my tears."

Psalm 39:12

"My tears have been my meat day and night." Psalm 42:3

"Put thou my tears into thy bottle."

Psalm 56:8

"Thou feedest them with the bread of tears." Psalm 80:5

"Thou hast delivered . . . mine eyes from tears." Psalm 116:8

"They that sow in tears shall reap in joy." Psalm 126:5

"There is a season . . . to weep."

Ecclesiastes 3:1, 4

"The tears of such as were oppressed, and they had no comforter."

Ecclesiastes 4:1

"I will water thee with my tears."

Isaiah 16:9

"The Lord God will wipe away tears from off all faces."

Isaiah 25:8; Revelation 7:17

"Oh that my head were waters, and mine eyes a fountain of tears."

Jeremiah 9:18; 13:17; 14:17

"Refrain . . . thine eyes from tears."
                                    Jeremiah 31:16
"Her tears are on her cheeks."
                          Lamentations 1:2; 2:11, 18
"Neither shall thy tears run down."
                                    Ezekiel 24:16
"Covering the altar with tears."
                                    Malachi 2:13
"She . . . began to wash his feet with tears." Luke 7:38, 44
"Serving the Lord with tears." Acts 20:19, 31; II Corinthians 2:4; II Timothy 1:4
"He offered up prayers and supplications with strong crying and tears."
                                    Hebrews 5:7
"No place of repentance, though he sought it carefully with tears."
                                    Hebrews 12:17
"Jesus wept." John 11:35; Luke 19:41

The above array of tear verses, to which we might have added all those taken up with "weeping," reveals the Bible to be a tear-drenched Book. Since sin entered the world, a torrent of tears have flowed – and they still flow! Says the ancient proverb, "We are born crying, live complaining, and die disappointed." If we entered the world with tears, it is truer to say that they are ours until we can cry no more. When we first see the light we weep; when we leave it we groan.

What are *tears* (which Keble describes as "The gift of tears, the best gift of God to suffering man")? They have been spoken of as liquid pain, or agony in solution. When our Creator fashioned our bodies, He equipped our eyes with tear ducts containing the salty water necessary for the cleansing of the eyes, and as the repositories of the expression of joy or grief. Tears, "the noble language of the eye," perform this dual ministry. We often cry when we laugh, as well as when our heart is broken. Ovid the philosopher says that "Sometimes tears have the weight of words."

What are the causes of the oceans of tears daily shed the world over? Wordsworth said that "Tears to human suffering are due." Had there been no transgression, there would have been no tears. Sin, suffering, and the separations of life – these are the main causes of our weeping. As the list of verses quoted shows, our tears are spoken of as our "bread" and "meat" – as much a part of our daily life as our necessary food.

Often it takes tear-washed eyes to discern the Bible's most precious treasures. Many a saint has a tear-stained Bible – one over which he or she has wept with joy because of the revelation of the glory and goodness of God, or over the insight gained into his own evil heart.

"When the Lord saw her, He . . . said unto her, Weep not." Luke 7:12

Jesus was no Stoic philosopher. He too knew what it was to weep. The saying that, "Only human eyes can weep" is only partially true. The God-Man shed His tears as well as those whose tears He dried. The shortest, sweetest, and most profound verse in the Bible is, "Jesus wept." But He alone had the right to speak the imperial word, "*Weep not,*" to the widow so grief-stricken over the death of her only child. The miracle He performed that day predicted the future, in which there will be no separation. At His coming, He will give us back our "unforgotten dearest dead," if they and we alike belong to Him who has the dominion over the king of terrors. At the sound of His majestic voice, the dead in Him shall rise first.

Because *death* is common to our race, more tears are shed over the passing of loved ones and friends than over any other experience we encounter. But the promise is that "God shall wipe away all tears from their eyes; and there shall be no more death" Revelation 21:4

Good Bishop Andrewes prayed for "the grace of tears" and because we are exhorted to "weep with those who weep," we have need to re-echo the same petition. We often sing about "weeping o'er the erring one," but are we moved by the compassion of His who beheld the city and wept? Says Alexander Smellie, "They caricature Christianity who would freeze the moisture of human eyes, and swathe the swellings of human hearts in the cerements of indifference." We have the adage that, "Men must work – women must weep." But strong men, as well as women, weep.

On Mirabeau's funeral day, a lady complained of the municipality for neglecting to water the boulevard. "Madame," a poor woman replied, "they reckoned on our tears." Does not Jesus reckon on our tears, our prayers, our service in the bringing of the lost around to a knowledge of His forgiving grace and mercy?

David could write about watering his couch with tears, and he knew how to weep over his sins. His penitential psalm (51) is stained with his tears of contrition.

If, as the poet has reminded us,
"A tear is an intellectual thing
   And a sigh is the sword of an angel
      king" –
then in the confession wrung from King
David's heart we have "a whole cruse of
tears and a whole armory of sighs." Yet,
as Archbishop Trench expresses it, "You
cannot cleanse your heart with tears," which
is the same truth enshrined in the gospel
hymn –
   "But drops of grief can ne'er repay
      The debt of love I owe."
Nothing can cleanse the soul of the sin we
weep over, but the precious efficacious blood
of Jesus Christ.

What a touching moment that must have
been when Mary washed the feet of Jesus
with her tears, and dried them with her
hair! Those warm tears were the expression of her love and gratitude to Him who
had forgiven her her sin. In *King Lear*,
Shakespeare pleads –
   "O, let not women's weapons, water-drop,
      Stain my man's cheeks."
But the tears of Mary stained her Lord's
feet, and if "a lady's tears are silent ora-
tors," then those tears of Mary were eloquent of her adoration of Him who had
forgiven much.

Are your tears flowing today? Are you
weeping over the effects of your own sin –
over the sins, ingratitude and forgetfulness
of others – over your adversities and problems – over the vacant place in your heart
and home through the death of a dear one?
Then here is the precious promise for your
grief-stricken heart –
   "The Lord God will wipe away tears
      from off all faces."

PHYSICAL FITNESS AND BEAUTY

A word or two in passing might be in
order as to Bible references to physical
fitness and beauty. Strength and beauty
are combined by Solomon in the proverb –
   "The glory of young men is their strength:
      And the beauty of old men is the grey
         head." Proverbs 20:29
While the whole trend of Scripture is that
of being physically fit to fulfil life's task
and to have a body God can use, it never
magnifies mere human strength. Often God
can do more through a weak and suffering body than He can through one at the
peak of physical perfection. Samson was
eminently endowed physically, but he utterly failed God. Paul had a very weak
body – one completely battered through ex-

posure to stoning, shipwreck, and prison
life. He also suffered from a serious eye
disease which made it difficult for him to
see. But the promise of a perfect body
at his Lord's return was his constant inspiration. It was this apostle who gave
this promise to young, stalwart Timothy –
   "Bodily exercise profiteth for a little:
      but godliness is profitable unto all things,
      having promise of the life that now is,
      and of that which is to come."
                                    I Timothy 4:8
It is more profitable to have a saved soul
in a weak body, than a strong body hous-
ing a miserable starved soul. If we cannot
be physically healthy, we can through grace
be strong in soul. "When I am weak, then
am I strong." If only more young men
were as zealous over the development of their
spiritual muscles as they are over their
physical ones, how mighty they would be
for God in a world of need!
   "Quit you like men, be strong."
                              I Corinthians 16:13
Passing from *brawn* to *beauty*, we look
at what the Bible has to say regarding physical attractiveness. Many women are praised
for beautiful countenances – Sarah, Rachel,
Abigail, Bathsheba, Esther. Some men also
were renowned for their beauty. David
had a ruddy and beautiful countenance, as
did his son Absalom. Our blessed Lord has
a beauty all His own. "How great is his
beauty" (Zechariah 9:17). And the promise is that we are to see Him in all His
beauty (Psalm 27:4; Isaiah 33:17).

What enormous sums are spent today on
the creation of facial beauty! The ever-
growing number of face creams, lotions, and
cosmetics of differing kinds testify to the
modern craze for glamor. Yet some of the
homeliest persons alive are the most beautiful within. It is said that Jesus had no
beauty that men should desire Him (Isaiah
53:2). God had some strong things to say
about those who painted their eyes (Ezekiel
23:40). The only woman in the Bible who
is named, and who was famed, for artificial
make-up was Jezebel. This most disreputable
woman "painted her face, and tired her head"
(II Kings 9:30).

If God has made us plain, we can yet
have "the beauty of holiness" and ever
desire to behold His beauty. "Let the beauty
of the Lord be on us" (Psalm 90:17). Has
He not promised to be not only "the *help*
of our countenance" but its health? "Who
is the health of my countenance, and my

God" (Psalms 42:5, 11; 43:5).

On the matter of preserving charm an elderly Quaker lady with a beautiful complexion was asked what kind of cosmetics she used. In reply she gave the following prescription –

For my LIPS   — TRUTH
For my VOICE   — PRAYER
For my EYES   — PITY
For my HANDS   — CHARITY
For my FIGURE — UPRIGHTNESS
For my HEART   — LOVE

"If your heart is honest, you would surely look bright."

Genesis 4:6,7 (Moffat). One of the marvelous by-products of a Christ-centered life is a radiant, cheerful expression. The late Bishop Warne of India was asked by a non-Christian what kind of oil the girls in his school used to make their faces shine. He replied that when the false and the ugly go out of life, the countenance shows a new radiance. The psalmist reminds us that the King's daughters should be all-glorious *within* (Psalm 45:13).

Drop Thy still dews of quietness,
Till all our strivings cease,
Take from our lives the strain and stress,
And let our ordered lives confess
The beauty of Thy peace.

FEAR

Fear is another physical emotion the Bible gives prominence to as having many eyes. Wordsworth says that –

"Fear hath a hundred eyes, that all agree
To plague her beating heart."

It may surprise you to learn that *fear* is used in various ways some 500 times in the Bible. To classify and briefly expound all of these references would require more space than we can allow in our study on the divine promises.

"Their houses are safe from fear."

Job 21:9

"There were they in fear, where no fear was." Psalm 53:5; Psalm 14:5
"Fear was on every side."

Psalm 31:11; 48:6

"I will mock when thy fear cometh."

Proverbs 1:26

"Be not afraid of sudden fear."

Proverbs 3:25

"The fear of man bringeth a snare."

Proverbs 29:25; Isaiah 8:12

"The Lord shall give you rest from fear." Isaiah 14:3
"Fear is on every side."

Jeremiah 6:25; 20:10; 49:29

"Who through the fear of death."

Hebrews 2:15

"There is no fear in love." I John 4:18
"The disciples cried out for fear."

Matthew 24:26; John 7:13; 19:38

"For fear of her torment."

Revelation 18:15

"Serve the Lord without fear."

Luke 1:71; I Corinthians 6:10

"He hath delivered me from all my fears." Psalm 34:4
"Therefore will not we fear."

Psalm 46:2

"Fightings without, fears within."

II Corinthians 7:5

"Fear none of those things."

Revelation 2:10

"Fear not, I am with thee."

Genesis 26:24; 46:3; 50:19

"Fear not, stand still and see the salvation of God." Exodus 14:13
"Fear not your enemies."

Deuteronomy 21:3; 31:8

"Fear not: for they that be with us are more than they that be with them."

II Kings 6:16; II Chronicles 20:17

"Say to them that are of a fearful heart, Fear not." Isaiah 35:4; 41:10, 13
"Fear not the reproach of men."

Isaiah 51:7; Daniel 10:12, 19

"Fear not, to take Mary."

Matthew 1:21; 28:5

"Fear not them which kill the body."

Matthew 10:28

"Fear not, believe only."

Luke 8:50; 12:32

"Fear not, I am the first and the last."

Revelation 1:17

"Though an host should encamp against me, my heart shall not fear."

Psalm 27:3

"I will not fear what flesh can do unto me." Psalm 56:4; 118:6; Hebrews 13:6
"They feared exceedingly."

Mark 4:41; Luke 9:34

"The thing which I greatly feared is come upon me." Job 3:25
"Why are ye fearful, O ye of little faith?"

Matthew 8:26

"Whoso hearkeneth unto me . . . shall be quiet from fear of evil." Proverbs 1:33
"Neither fear ye their fear, nor be afraid." Isaiah 8:12

Such an array of verses reveal the manifold causes of fears – true and false; the reasons why a Christian should not yield to unholy fear; and the blessed Promises of deliverance from all our fears. Virgil warns us against "Fearing even things which are safe." It makes a profitable meditation to gather together all the "Fear not's" of the Bible. One writer suggests that there are 365 of them – one for every day of the year.

What is fear? The dictionary explains it in a two-fold way. First of all, our human fear is a painful emotion marked by alarm, dread, or disquiet – anxious concern or solicitude. The tragedy is that the majority of our fears are imaginary. We are in fear where no cause of fear exists. "Why are ye fearful, O ye of little faith?"

In the second place, *fear* represents awe, profound reverence, especially toward God as the Supreme. This is not a "fear" like the former kind, resulting in physical and mental disorders, but a reverential trust and confidence. When we fear God, we do not cringe before Him, as those robbed of their liberty do before a cruel, heartless dictator. Love to God casts out the wrong kind of fear which ends in torment. Said Thomas a Kempis, "Fear God, and thou shalt not shrink from the terrors of men."

Many promises of blessedness are attached to such a holy fear of the Lord. Here are a few of them –

"In thy fear will I worship toward thy holy temple." Psalm 5:7
"The secret of the Lord is with them that fear him." Psalm 25:14
"Blessed is every one that feareth the Lord." Psalm 128:1
"Fear God, and keep his commandments." Ecclesiastes 12:14
"Sanctify the Lord . . . let him be your fear." Isaiah 8:13
"The fear of the Lord is his treasure." Isaiah 33:6
"Fear him which is able to destroy both soul and body in hell." Matthew 10:28
"Walking in the fear of the Lord." Acts 7:31
"Perfecting holiness in the fear of the Lord." II Corinthians 7:1
"Submitting yourselves one to another in the fear of God." Ephesians 5:26
"Love the brotherhood. Fear God." I Peter 2:17

We choose a few of the passages in which our own physical fears are mentioned to prove how senseless and baseless so many of them are, and to note the promised blessings of deliverance from them the Lord offers. Cowper asks the question –

"Who would lose, that had the power to improve,
The occasion of transmuting fear to love?"

Our brief meditation on each passage cited may enable us to transmute our fears to love.

"Fear not, little flock; for it is your Father's good pleasure to give you the kingdom." Luke 12:32

The context of this promise contains a rebuke of the disciples for the fear they entertained regarding sufficient food and clothing as they continued to follow Jesus. Was not God able to care for the birds and the fields? Then why should the disciples charge their souls with care about material things, when they had such a mighty God who was able not only to add unto them all they needed, but to give the Kingdom as well? "My God shall supply all your need." Philippians 4:19

The Christian is often referred to as a sheep which has no natural ability for fighting off its adversaries. Because it is helpless when attacked, fear is one of its chief characteristics. Our Good Shepherd knows that fear is our inherent weakness as we face our arch adversary the devil, and He so utters the assuring, "Fear not, little flock." He wants faith to supplant fear. "Fear is like sand in the machinery of life – faith is like oil."

"Be not afraid of sudden fear." Proverbs 3:25, 26

Although we are not listing the verses in which we are exhorted not to be *afraid*, the same are allied to all those dealing with *fear*, since they are alike.

Solomon is speaking of the occasions when God's righteous judgments are abroad, he urges his people not to yield to any fear because of God's promise to defend and preserve them. While the plagues afflicted the Egyptians, the Israelites were divinely covered. "Serenity under the rush and road of unexpected evils is a precious gift of divine love," says Spurgeon. No matter what desolation may overtake the wicked around us, as Christians, we are called upon to exhibit a quietness and confidence born of faith in the promise of divine protection.

"I will not fear what man shall do unto me." Hebrews 13:6

Here is a promise rich with the presence and power of the Lord. Because He will never leave us, we can be content with such things as we have, knowing that He always is at hand as a Helper. If we fear Him with all our heart, there will be nothing else to fear. The world around may seek to scorn and harm us, as many a Chinese saint is proving, but the animosity of the godless is calmly borne.

Vengeance is His, and He will repay.

"Who shall lay anything to the charge of God's elect? If God be for us, who can be against us?" Romans 8:31, 33 "Fear not; for thou shalt not be ashamed." Isaiah 54:4

In times of severe testing we must not be afraid lest, like Peter, we deny our Lord. We shall not be ashamed of Him whom angels praise. We shall not be ashamed of the truth of His infallible Word, nor of His love to us and our love and faith toward Him. When we choose the reproach of Christ rather than the treasures of Egypt, the Lord will be near to inspire us with holy boldness and courage.

"I the Lord do keep it: I will water it every moment: lest any hurt it, I will keep it night and day." Isaiah 27:3 "Fear not: I will help thee. Fear not, thou worm Jacob." Isaiah 41:13, 14

The reference of the *worm* to Jacob signified his utter weakness and nothingness. Apart from his divine Helper, Jacob had nothing and could no nothing. And what are we but mere worms of the dust; yet empowered by the Lord, worms can thresh mountains (41:15). How unworthy is unwholesome fear when we have the promise that His everlasting arms are underneath and around us! Is He not a very present help in trouble? He *can* help the weakest of His children for He is the omnipotent Lord. He *will* help because of His promise to undertake for His own in any state or place.

"He hath said, and shall He not do it? He hath spoken, and shall He not make it good?"

With such a declaration we should not be fearful or cast down no matter what circumstance may arise.

"Why are ye so fearful? how is it that ye have no faith?" Mark 4:40

The presence of fear was the evidence of the absence of faith. Fear and faith can never exist together. It is true that the disciples were in danger of being drowned and that the perilous storm encountered was enough to create fear. But what the disciples forgot was that the sleeping Christ in the boat was the one who said, "All power is given unto me." Had He not assured them that the very hairs of their heads were numbered? There are two impressive phrases in the miracle Jesus performed –

"There arose a great storm . . . He arose."

How suggestive is the combination. For the rising of any storm there is the rising of the Master. He is the Christ well able to meet any crisis or emergency.

Are you presently fearful? Is your frail bark being dashed about by the waves and billows of trial, sorrow, and loss? Keep looking up, friend, for He is near with His power to defend you, His wisdom to guide you, His fulness to meet your need.

"It is I: be not afraid." John 6:20

We read that it was dark, and that Jesus had not joined His disciples as He had promised and as they had anticipated. Thus in the darkness they mistook His walking figure for some kind of a ghost or apparition, with power to stride the wind-lashed water. They became alarmed. But how dishonoring were their fears. Had not their Lord just fed 5,000 hungry mouths? Their fears were also groundless because was He not the Master of ocean, earth, and sky? Such fear in a Christian is a flat denial of his faith, and likewise a fruitful source of soul-distress. No matter what losses or crosses may pain and perplex us, amid the darkness we should be assured by that loving voice of His, "It is I; be not afraid." As a devotional expositor expresses it –

"Should we hear the pillars of heaven crack, and feel the strong foundation of the earth give way; should the heavens be rolled up like a scroll, and the great white throne appear; still, amidst the wreck of matter and the crash of worlds, He cries, "Be not afraid; it is I."

"What time I am afraid, I will trust in thee." Psalm 56:3

Because of our human frailty we are prone to be cast down, and subject to tormenting fears. When David wrote this psalm, he had been taken by his foes, the Philistines, to Gath, and naturally he had every reason to be afraid; but his trust in God triumphed over his trials. David knew how to rely on God's promise, and he needed no comfortable feeling to underprop his confidence in God. If we have Him as the Object of our trust, then He should be trusted at *all* times (Psalm 62:8). If God be for us – and He is – who or what can be against us? Our frames of mind and feelings are unreliable and subject to change. A firm trust in God's covenant love, even when His providence appears to frown, is graciously rewarded. Our warrant is that He will never betray nor fail our trust in Him. "Though he slay me, yet will I trust Him."

"Thou shalt not be given into the hand of the men of whom thou art afraid."

Jeremiah 39:17

This promise seems to contradict the experience of many a Christian who experienced what it was to be delivered into the hands of cruel men of whom they had every reason to be afraid. We think of Christians in the fighting forces who were taken prisoners and whose sufferings were horrible in the extreme, and of faithful missionaries tortured and killed by man-eaters. Yet when the Lord's faithful ones are made to suffer, the heart receives sweet messages from Himself that He is near to deliver them, if not by liberating them, then by taking them to be with Himself.

Turning to the context from which this last verse is taken, we find that Ebed-melech was only a despised Ethiopian, a humble black man, yet he had been so kind to the prophet Jeremiah. For being mindful of God's persecuted servant, Ebed-melech received the special promise that God would be mindful of him and preserve him from those whose vengeance he feared. Such a promise was fulfilled, for although thousands were slain by the Chaldeans, the lowly Negro was not hurt. As for ourselves, we rest in the fact that men, even when in rage, can do nothing apart from divine permission.

"The Lord God of thy fathers hath said unto thee: fear not, neither be discouraged." Deuteronomy 1:21

What God has graciously given, we must possess. But is grace ours to possess our possessions? There may be many foes seeking to discourage our possession of all the Lord has treasured up for us. No one can deny our right to a freely bestowed inheritance. May we be strong in faith as we march to the conquest!

"Fear not: for they that be with us are more than they that be with him."

II Kings 6:16

The only big battalions God is in league with are those of heaven. This is why one with God is always in the majority for what is any great host of earth alongside the mighty, invincible hosts of heaven of which He is Lord. "Horses of fire are mightier than horses of flesh, and chariots of fire are far preferable to chariots of iron," says Spurgeon. Elisha's young servant was alarmed because he could not see how the lonely, unarmed prophet and himself could possibly escape the host of armed men. Then his eyes were opened to see a greater host with far superior weapons guarding the prophet shut up in Dothan.

As a "little flock" it may seem as if the Lord's people are weak and defenseless against the crafty adversaries of the truth, but greater is He that is in us than those arrayed against us. Blessed be God, we cannot lose as we fight the good fight of faith for we are on the winning side!

"Why art thou cast down, O my soul? and why art thou disquieted within me?"

Psalm 42:11; 43:5

A characteristic feature of the psalms which makes them so precious to every generation of sinful and sorrowing men is their deep, vivid, pervading sense of the relation between the soul and God. A direct, close, immediate, and holy intimacy was taken for granted. The psalmists were men who had found God for themselves and who possessed Him as their very own. "The Lord is *my* shepherd" (Psalm 23:1). In the two psalms before us, we listen to a colloquy between the singer and his own soul and God. In thrice-repeated refrain, the psalmist pathetically rebukes and chides his own soul for impatience, fearfulness, and despondency.

How often do we find ourselves taking the language of these psalms and making it our own? Why art thou cast down, O struggling, faltering, solitary, and yet loyal soul? Are we not personally dismayed at times by doubts and fears? Somehow the experiences of the psalmist are a mirror of our trials. There are the oppression of the enemy – the disappointment, desertion and betrayal – the labor unrewarded, the sacrifice unnoticed, the patience unpraised. May the same patience of hope be ours – "I shall yet praise him."

The principal figure in John Bunyan's *Pilgrim's Progress* is Mr. Fearing, who was "one of the most troublesome pilgrims that I ever met with in all my days." Multitudes of modern pilgrims seem to belong to the spiritual family of this Mr. Fearing. They are often cast down, dismayed, fearful. If only these timid souls could look up and realize what a great God they have, and continually encourage themselves in Him, how quickly the clouds would disappear!

Necessary and beneficial to the Christian's physical well-being are periods of *rest, leisure, holiday,* and *change,* of which our Lord Himself took cognizance. So active were the apostles in the work they were commissioned to do that they had scarcely time for regular meals, for there were "many coming and going." Thus the thoughtful Master constrained the laborers to take a season of leisure and of change from their daily activities.

"Come ye yourselves apart into a desert place, and rest a while." Mark 6:31

I was once associated with a most solemn-faced preacher who boasted that he had never taken a holiday. When asked why he never provided for the occasional rest and change which his mind and body required, he replied, "The devil never takes a holiday, so why should I?" What false reasoning! Who, in their right senses, wants to emulate the devil? It is more worthy – and healthier – to follow the example of Jesus, who often withdrew from His preaching and healing ministry to rest and meditate in a desert place.

The word our Lord uses for "rest" in the above passage means *intermission from labor, to refresh oneself, to take one's ease* (Luke 12:19). Vine tells us that in the papyri it is found as an agricultural term, for example, of giving land rest by sowing light crops upon it.

Ovid reminds us that, "Leisure nourishes the body, and the mind also is fed thereby; on the other hand, immoderate labor exhausts both." From another Latin philosopher we learn that, "He who does not know how to employ leisure, makes more of a business of it than there is business in business itself."

"Behold, I am with thee, and will keep thee in all places whither thou goest."
Genesis 28:15

What a promise this is to have before us when we set out on a vacation! Have you heard of the little boy who prayed, as the family were about to leave home for a holiday, "Well, good-bye, God! We're off for our holidays." Too often there are those who profess His Name but leave Him at home, and who, on vacation, engage in things and go to certain places they would not think of patronizing at home. As we prepare to leave, whether we journey far or near, we need journeying mercies and also God's presence and preservation, and we cannot have these unless there is the continual recognition of the fact that we are His. Whenever we go abroad from our accustomed abode, let us take with us our heavenly Escort, and the days of change and pleasure will be crowned with His favor.

If we live in the spirit of "The Traveler's Psalm" (Psalm 91), then our holidays will be *holy days*.

In his illuminating study, *Early Christianity*, Dean Farrar tells the story of a young man who traveled to see the apostle John. When at last he was ushered into the presence of the disciple Jesus loved, his face registered disappointment, for John, instead of being wrapped in meditation or engaged in prayer, was playing with a pet partridge. The old man was quick to discern the look on his young visitor's face, and he pointed to a bow standing in the corner of the room. "Notice, friend," he said, "that bowstring is released. It is needful to relax at times, otherwise the bow becomes useless through continual tension."

Is it not so with the human bow? Do not its strings need to be relaxed from tension at times in order to retain their powers? What is leisure, whether from our daily tasks, or for a longer period when we seek a change of sphere and scenery for a week or so? Is not true leisure "release from tension in order to renew resilience"? It is "the pause that refreshes." But if a *vacation* is to fulfil its function and renew us for our *vocation*, then one or two necessary principles must be observed before the promised renewal is to be ours.

It should be re-creative.

"Recreation" simply means to re-create, or restore the energy or nerve power drained by mental or physical labor. If our leisure or holidays do not renew our powers, then their wrong use will only enervate or weaken our nerve force and unfit us for life's responsibilities.

It should be restful.

If our vocation is heavy and taxing, then it is essential that our vacation be restful. Do not men, beasts, and machines work better after a rest? By rest we do not imply mere idleness or lounging around. Cowper wrote that "Absence of occupation is not rest." How true is the adage that "Satan finds mischief for idle hands to do." In order to lift our thoughts from the care and concern of our daily task, a change of interest is necessary. Swinging from the familiar to the unfamiliar, we must seek refreshing pastimes.

It should be educative.

Many use their vacation or leisure-time for participation in exhausting, worldly pleasures and pursuits, and are too dependent upon created, artificial amusements for a change. They forget that "a good man is satisfied in himself" and can find delight, inspiration, and invigoration in a more prolonged Bible meditation, in a good book, in innocent pastimes, in nature herself. If we would claim all the promises associated with rest, there must not be the wanton waste of the God-given commodity of time. *It should be all-inclusive.*

Paul reminds us that the glory of God must be the center and circumference of all we do.

"Whatsoever ye do, do all to the glory of God" (I Corinthians 10:31). *All* cuts out the wrong employment of our leisure. The sweeping universality of the apostolic rule implies that all life, and every act of life, must be consecrated by holy motives. The life of a Christian is not cut up into sections, with some parts we label "spiritual" and other parts, "secular." Everything a Christian does should be *Christian.* When we are able to "rest a while," our leisure is most beneficial as we follow the principle Paul lays down. To "do all to the glory of God" delivers the vacationist from all the miserable, self-seeking carnal and degrading pleasures, and lifts him out of the murky atmosphere of earthly things into a serene air of Heaven itself. How comforting is the prayer of Tobit, taken from the Apocrypha (Tobit 5:16) –

"God which dwelleth in heaven, prosper your journey.
And the Angel of God keep you company."

We now take up the consideration of those promises related to bodily sicknesses, healing and health, of which there are many scattered throughout the Word. Had sin not entered man's being to disrupt his physical powers, there would have been no sin, disease or death. With the development of sin, and sins, there came the multiplication of physical sicknesses and diseases. When God created Adam and Eve, they were holy and healthy, and He meant them to remain so, but Satan was not long in marring the divine masterpiece.

SICKNESS

As far back as Job, there were quack healers who tried to explain the cause of sickness and pain. "Ye are forgers of lies, ye are all physicians of no value" (13:4). There are those who deny sickness altogether: others affirm that all sickness is of Satan –

that we are sick because of sin in the life, that we suffer because it is the will of God for us. As nothing is more dangerous than half-truth, let us examine what the Bible has to say on the question of the Christian and his sickness, suffering, and pain.

"By man came death."
                              I Corinthians 15:21
"Ye shall not eat . . . lest ye die."
                              Genesis 3:3
As sickness, disease, and pain usually precede the accompanying death, we can safely assume that human sin was the original cause of sickness. Direct disobedience to divine laws result in suffering.

"Because of thy sins." Micah 6:13; see Exodus 15:26; Numbers 11:33
God is spoken of as being directly responsible for sending sickness and disease.

"The Lord will smite thee with the botch of Egypt and with the emerods, and with the scab, and with the itch, whereof thou canst not be healed." Deuteronomy 28:27, 28; II Samuel 12:15; II Chronicles 18:25, 26
Then the breaking of nature's laws and the strain of Christian service can result in sickness. Because of the vision Daniel received, we find him saying, "I Daniel fainted, and was sick certain days" (Daniel 8:26, 27). Because of his zeal and concern for the Philippian believers, Paul "was sick unto death" (Philippians 2:25-30).

Wrong thinking, which produces worry, hate, jealousy, criticism and murmuring, as well as a high pressure type of life, can produce ulcers and sickness.

"A merry heart doeth good like a medicine: but a broken spirit drieth up the bones." Proverbs 17:22
"Delivered him to his tormentors."
                              Matthew 18:34, 35
There are occasions when sickness or affliction is not the outcome of any individual sin (see II Kings 20:1; John 11:1; Acts 9:37; Matthew 8:14).

"Neither hath this man sinned, nor his parents." John 9:1-3
"This sickness is not unto death, but for the glory of God." John 11:4
In some mysterious way Satan and evil spirits are permitted to afflict the body with sickness and disease.

"All that he hath is in thy power; only upon himself put not forth thy hand. . . . Satan . . . smote Job with sore boils from the sole of his foot unto his crown." Job 1:6-21

"This woman . . . whom Satan hath bound."

Luke 13:10-16; 2:1-10; I Corinthians 5:5

Ignorance and carelessness as to food, rest, and mental habits can issue in physical disorders. "My people are destroyed for lack of knowledge" (Hosea 4:6).

The Bible answers the prophet's pertinent question, "Why is my pain perpetual, and my wound incurable, which refused to be healed?" (Jeremiah 15:18). The purpose and ministry of sickness and suffering can be classified thus –

To limit sin.

"If ye sin, ye shall surely die."

Genesis 2:17

Death with its attending pains and diseases is the consequence of sin.

To teach us God's laws.

"Before I was afflicted I went astray . . . It was good for me that I have been afflicted; that I might learn thy statutes." Psalm 119:67, 70

To perfect the person who sins.

"After ye have suffered a while, make you perfect, stablish, strengthen, settle you." I Peter 5:10

To reveal the Works of God.

"That the works of God should be manifest in him." John 9:2, 3

To prepare us for a coming glory.

"Think it not strange concerning the fiery trial which is to try you . . . When his glory shall be revealed, ye may be glad with exceeding joy." I Peter 4:12, 13; 1:7

"Our light affliction . . . worketh for us a far more exceeding, and eternal weight of glory." II Corinthians 4:17, 18

To equip us to comfort others.

"The comfort wherewith we ourselves are comforted of God."

II Corinthians 1:3-5

To chasten and discipline us.

"Whom the Lord loveth he chasteneth."

Hebrews 12:5-11

To complete the sufferings of Christ.

"Fill up that which is behind of the affliction of Christ." Colossians 1:24

To furnish us with opportunities of witness.

"It shall turn to you for a testimony."

Luke 21:12, 13

"Rejoicing that they were counted worthy to suffer." Acts 5:4

The Bible also leaves us in no doubt as to how we should act in seasons of sickness, pain, and suffering. If when the testing time comes we are embittered, peeved over what we are enduring, then our physical condition will swallow us up. We must trust God and await His divine unfolding.

"In all this Job sinned not, nor charged God foolishly." Job 1:22

"Though he slay me, yet will I trust in him." Job 13:15

"Rejoice, and be exceeding glad."

Matthew 5:11, 12

"My brethren, count it all joy."

James 1:2

"Think it not strange . . . Humble yourselves." I Peter 4:12, 13; 5:6, 7

Dr. A. T. Pierson classified sickness and suffering under the following groups, illustrations of which are to be found in the Bible.

1. *Organic and hereditary* – Timothy's frequent infirmities and his constitutional weakness illustrate this group (I Timothy 5:23).

2. *Retribution, penal, and judicial* – Paul refers to one who was visited with sickness for special sins (I Corinthians 11:30. See John 8:14; 11:25).

3. *Corrective, paternal, and disciplinary* – The case James contemplates can be placed in this category (James 5).

4. *Educative and preparatory* (See Psalm 35:13; Isaiah 38:12-16; Matthew 25:36; James 5:14).

5. *Voluntary and vicarious* – Epaphroditus and Trophimus were sick but their sickness was not of a disciplinary character calling for confession (Philippians 2:25-30; II Corinthians 12:7-10).

As the Lord is the Creator of the human body with all its organs, faculties and members, He is able to re-create it.

"The Lord God formed man of the dust of the ground." Genesis 1:26, 27; 2:7

"I am the Lord that healeth thee."

Exodus 15:26

"The Lord will take away from thee all sickness." Deuteronomy 7:15

"With thee is the fountain of life."

Psalm 36:9

"Is there no balm in Gilead? Is there no physician there?" Jeremiah 8:22

"I will take sickness away from the midst of thee." Exodus 23:25

"Neither shall any plague come nigh thy dwelling." Psalm 91:10

"There was not one feeble person among their tribes." Psalm 105:37

"Who healeth all thy diseases."

Psalm 103:3

"Himself . . . bare our sicknesses."

Matthew 8:17

As to Christ's healing power and His delegated healing power, see the author's volume *All the Miracles of the Bible.* Look up Matthew 9:29; 13:15; 17:20; 21:21, 22; Mark 9:23; 11:22-24; 16:15-20; Luke 4:18; John 10:10; 14:12; Acts 28:27; Romans 8:11; James 5:4-16; I Peter 2:34. Christ, as the living manifestation of the Old Testament *Jehovah*, the Healer who gave the laws of health to Israel, is the Great Physician of the New Testament with power to heal with, or without, means.

"He sent his word (instructions), and healed them, and delivered them from their destruction." Psalm 107:20

The laws of health whereby sickness could be prevented are explicit.

1. *Sanitation* - "Camp kept clean" (Deuteronomy 23:14). All filth had to be satisfactorily disposed of so that the camp would be fit at any time for Divine inspection and reception of the Divine presence.

2. *Sterilization of all Utensils* - "Be clean." . . . "Wash." . . . "Running water." . . . "Fire" (Leviticus 11; Numbers 31:23). Most modern antiseptic ideas were embodied in the instructions given to Israel.

3. *Diet and Hygiene* - Read Leviticus 11 and Deuteronomy 14, and note what Israel could eat and not eat. God eliminated the danger points from the diet of His chosen people. Eating with impunity as we do is responsible for many of our physical disorders.

4. *Quarantine* - "Outside the camp" (Numbers 5:4). Separation and isolation were enforced in order to check the spread of an infectious disease. The strictest quarantine was enforced (Numbers 5:4; Leviticus 13-14) - a safeguard we still observe.

5. *Necessary Physical Exercise* - "They set . . . the Levites in their courses" (Ezra 6:18); "A certain priest . . . of the course of Abia" (Luke 1:5). Physical exercise in some form or another is necessary for the maintenance of health. Sedentary workers, professional men, and even preachers break down through lack of exercise.

6. *Rest* - God ordained one day in seven for man and beast to rest so that energy must be conserved (Exodus 20:3, 10, 11; Mark 6:31).

As the natural means through which healing came, the Bible cites several -

The poisonous waters of Marah were healed by a tree (Exodus 15:25). Compare quinine, sulphanilamide, and modern medicines and drugs.

Figs as plasters for boils were used (II Kings 20:7); oil for wounds (Isaiah 1:6; Luke 10:34); salves for pain (Jeremiah 51:8); honey for osteomyelitis (Proverbs 24:13 ; unfermented wine (Psalm 104:15 ; I Timothy 5:23); spittal and clay (John 9:15, 16); leaves of a tree (Revelation 22:2). Luke is referred to as "the beloved physician" (Colossians 4:14), and as such he was the Lord's special provision for Paul, not only as a fellow traveler, but as a doctor ever near to care for the apostle's physical needs.

Christ's healing ministry was of a fourfold nature -

It was a miraculous intervention (Luke 4:39, 40; 5:17-22; etc.).

It was gradual - "He began to amend" (John 4:52).

It was instantaneous - "Immediately" (Luke 5:25).

It was permanent - "Enter no more" (Mark 9:25).

It was complete - "Made whole from that hour" (Matthew 15:22-28).

His purpose in healing was of a twofold character -

GODWARD, it proved His deity (Luke 5:24), fulfilled prophecy (Matthew 8:16, 17), satisfied His compassion (Matthew 14:14), obtained the glory of His Father (John 9:2, 3).

MANWARD, His miracles of healing were designed to save life, to set the infirm free, to empower and ennoble life, to add to life qualitatively, to reorganize life creatively, to reveal God's love in practical ways.

In the light of the divine promises of healing and of manifestations of divine power to heal all manner of diseases, how puerile is the claim of Rome!

"SAINTS" FOR SICKNESS

Are you worried over some "bodily ill"? Well, take a look at the following list of Roman Catholic "saints," the illnesses they "cure," and then test them out.

The list recently appeared in a Roman Catholic publication, *Our Sunday Visitor.* Here it is:

Epilepsy and nervousness - St. Vitus
Exposure to extreme cold - St. Genesius
Family troubles - St. Eustachius
Fever - St. George
Fire - St. Lawrence and St. Barbara
Floods - St. Columban
Foot diseases - St. Victor
Gall stones - St. Liberius
Glandular trouble - St. Cadoc

Gout – St. Andrew
Hazards of travel – St. Christopher
Headaches – St. Dennis
Insanity – St. Dympna
Insects – St. Tryphon
Intestinal disorders – St. Erasmus
Lightning and thunder storms – St. Barbara
Lumbago – St. Lawrence
Paralysis – St. Serverus
Pestilence – St. Hadrian
Skin diseases – St. Roch
Temptation at the hour of death – St. Cyriacus
Toothache – St. Apollonia
Tuberculosis – St. Pantaleon
Typhus and fevers – St. Adalard
(Naturally we do not guarantee a "cure" but think of all the money saved in doctors' bills! – Ed.)

– From *The Protestant Standard*

The question may be asked, "Does God heal today?" Certainly He can, and does, *but not always.* No gift of healing was used to restore Epaphroditus, Timothy, Trophimus and Gaius (Philippians 2:26, 27; I Timothy 5:23; II Timothy 4:20; III John 2). God is sovereign in His bestowal of physical healing. He can heal in response to prayer and faith, through skilful physicians and medicines, or independent of means. If, as a Christian, you are sick or diseased, realize that God is your Father and your Friend and that you can leave the matter of your healing entirely in His hands.

A closer examination of one or two of the promises connected with sickness and its banishment might prove to be profitable. First of all, the body, whether it is subject to ill health, sickness, or infirmity, or not, is not be be dishonored (Leviticus 19:28; 21:5; Deuteronomy 14:1). Because the body of a Christian is the temple of the Holy Spirit (I Corinthians 3:16; 6:19; II Corinthians 6:18) it must be kept pure for the Master's use (Romans 12:1; I Corinthians 6:13; I Thessalonians 4:4; 5:23).

"Thou wilt make all his bed in sickness." Psalm 41:3

What a sweet promise this is for all who are on beds of sickness! Nurses are specially trained in the art of bedmaking. Without undue discomfort or inconvenience to a sufferer unable to leave his bed, a careful nurse can change the bedclothes. To one forced to stay in bed, it means so much to have the sheets changed and the pillows turned and fluffed up. But can we conceive of God acting as tenderly as a nurse? He here promises to make our bed in sickness. Is this not a precious glimpse into the tender heart of God? When we are laid aside, He does not neglect us. The rustle of His seamless robe can be heard by the bed of pain. In every sick room He is present, seeking to ease the afflicted. He it is who imparts strength and courage to sufferers and who upholds and sustains the sufferer through long and difficult days. Are you on a bed of sickness? Then look up and trust your divine Nurse to do the very best for you.

"At even . . . He healed many that were sick." Mark 1:32, 34
"I will add unto thy days fifteen years." Isaiah 38:1-5; 15, 16

The entire world is like a vast hospital. Wherever we go there are multitudes of afflicted minds and bodies. Hospitals are enlarging all the time, and we never had as many physicians, surgeons, and agencies to alleviate a pain-stricken humanity as at this present time. Many are sick and beset by sicknesses that still baffle the medical fraternity. Why, even the common cold remains mysterious and without a definite cure!

God anointed Jesus of Nazareth to heal those who were oppressed of the devil. Is it not encouraging to remember that all sickness meets its Master in Him to whom the multitudes gathered in their need? And because His touch has still its ancient power, we, too can draw near to Him who is well able to dispel our suffering.

"Himself . . . bare our sicknesses." Matthew 8:17

Much misunderstanding has arisen over this identification of Christ with our human ills. Advocates of what is called "divine healing" (all healing, with or without medicine is divine) affirm that there is physical healing as well as a spiritual salvation in the atoning work of Christ. The argument is that at Calvary Christ bore our sicknesses as well as our sins; therefore we have no right to be ill. If sickness does beset us, then we can claim healing in virtue of the cross.

Such an interpretation, however, is not in keeping with Scripture as a whole. What Christ bore on the tree was our sins (I Peter 2:24). Interpreted in the light of the context, taking our infirmities and bearing our sicknesses simply means Christ's perfect sympathy with all who suffer. The sight of the fever-stricken mother and of demon-possessed souls drew forth the compassion of His sympathetic heart. Deeper still, in taking upon Himself the likeness of our flesh, He experienced something of its weariness and pain. As a true representative, He carried many of our sorrows. Tested and tried as we are, He is touched with the feeling of our infirmities.

"This sickness is not unto death, but for the glory of God." John 11:4

Because the sickness of Lazarus did result in actual, physical death, the answer of Jesus to Mary's and Martha's request for Him to hurry to Lazarus' side is apparently confusing. But what the declaration implies is that sickness in this case was not merely a natural occurrence that would produce death, but that it was being permitted for the glory of God. The man born blind was thus afflicted, not through any inherited or personal sin, but that the works of God might be manifest in him (John 9:3). The troubled sisters of Lazarus came to see God's glory in Christ's seeming denial and delay. Are these lines being read by one whose body is riddled by pain or disease? If so, do you realize that God is permitting your suffering in order that greater glory might be His? He is seeking to make your pain the platform upon which to display His grace. It is for this cause that your sickness is unrelieved.

"I was sick, and ye visited me."
Matthew 25:36

The gospels do not reveal whether Jesus was ever actually sick. Because of the limits of His humanity, He must have suffered some of its frailties. He did experience physical weariness and pain, hunger and thirst. He knew what it was to be a stranger, to go to prison, to be naked. In the narrative, Christ is identifying Himself with His needy brethren. "Inasmuch as ye have done it unto one of the least of these my brethren ye have done it unto me." What a Christ-like and Christ-pleasing ministry sick visitation is! To visit some shut-in, taking a few flowers or some fruit, leaves a ray of sunshine behind. Committing the sick to the Lord's tender mercy as we tarry at the bedside is a blessed task. Can you think of a lonely soul, confined to bed, whom a visit from you would cheer? Then know as you go administering consolation and hope that if you go in Christ's Name, you are actually ministering unto Him.

"The prayer of faith shall save the sick" James 5:16

In this promise James is found emphasizing the power of prayer rather than the healing of the body. Hence, his allusion to Elijah's effectual, fervent prayers. Then might it not be that the *saving* of the sick is a spiritual salvation James exhorts us to pray for? If sins are repented of and faults confessed, then in response to the prayers of believing saints, God may raise up the afflicted from the sickness their sins and faults caused.

Devotees of healing cults have been guilty of wresting the words of James out of their context. Let it not be forgotten that hundreds have been earnestly prayed over. Healing was claimed, yet those prayed for continued to suffer and ultimately died. At the same time, many do owe their restoration to health to the prayers of saints.

"Many are weak and sickly among you."
I Corinthians 11:30

Sickness is a fit simile for the soul's malady. Isaiah describes those who are away from God as having a whole head that is sick, with wounds, bruises and putrifying sores covering the body. Unbridled appetites resulting in carnality caused Paul to speak of those carnal Corinthians as "weak and sickly." Many today have life – they are born again, but they resemble those who have physical life but who are yet physically disabled. They lack robust spiritual health. They are spiritually impoverished, having just enough grace to keep them going. Just as the majority of sicknesses come through a germ finding its way into the blood stream, something foreign to life in Christ possesses the thought life and results in spiritual weakness. If sin-sick, we have the promise of the healing balm of Gilead.

As to promises relating to *Bodily Healing* and *Health*, the Christian can find encouragement in what the Bible says along this line. Here is a parade of the outstanding verses on promised healing –

"I am the Lord that healeth thee."
Exodus 15:26

"Thy servant our father is in good health." Genesis 45:28; III John 2

"His flesh shall be fresher than a child's."
Job 33:25

"The Lord will strengthen him upon the bed of languishing." Psalm 41:3

"Who healeth all thy diseases; who redeemeth thy life from destruction."
Psalm 103:3, 4

"I shall not die, but live, and declare the works of the Lord." Psalm 118:17
"It shall be health to thy navel, and marrow to thy bones." Proverbs 3:8; 4:22
"Thine health shall spring forth speedily." Isaiah 58:1-8
"I will bring it health and cure, and I will cure them." Jeremiah 33:6
"They that be whole need not a physician, but they that are sick."
Matthew 9:12
"The sick, and the Lord shall raise him up." James 5:15
"God . . . who is the health of my countenance." Psalms 42:11; 43:5
"I will restore health unto thee."
Jeremiah 30:17

The foregoing and other promises indicate that the Lord is a skilful Physician and well able to bring health both to the body and heart of any child of His. He is the perfect Master of all diseases, physical or spiritual. Is not His name *Jehovah Rophi* – the Lord my Healer? Then why not consult Him and lay our whole case before Him? His skill is unfailing and His power perfect; therefore we can take all that He prescribes.

"With long life will I satisfy him, and shew him my salvation." Psalm 91:16

In his discourse, Eliphaz speaks of some of the saints coming to the grave in a full age, like a shock of corn cometh in his season (Job 5:26). But it is not always so! God is good to many who journey beyond the allotted span and are blessed with long life, with few physical ailments. Reaching a ripe old age, they become ripe for glory. Comparatively free from sickness and disease throughout their long pilgrimage, they enter port with untattered sails. A long life, however, is something no believer can claim. The length of his sojourn on the earth depends upon the will of God. There are those, like saintly Robert Murray M'Cheyne, who was diseased from childhood and died at 28. It is not the length or health of life that counts, but the quality of it. From a long life God expects a greater harvest. Short lives, however, are often most effective for His kingdom.

"It shall be health to thy navel."
Proverbs 3:8

The margin gives us "medicine" for the word "health." By "navel" we are to understand the waist, that is, the part of the body in which are concentrated so many of our physical organs. Going back a few verses, we find Solomon stressing the necessity of obedience to God's Word, absolute confidence in His ability to undertake for His children, and their full acknowledgment of His wisdom as the true road, not only to holiness of heart, but health of body as well. Length of days and long life and peace are often promised possessions to those who abide in the will of God. There would be less need of physicians if only we had a greater number of Christians who were willing for the Lord to direct their paths and pursuits (Proverbs 4:22; 10:27).

"God . . . the health of my countenance." Psalm 42:11; 43:5

Already we have touched upon this promise. Paint and powder may be able to produce an artificial, healthy look, but the glow is only temporary. A shower of rain can work havoc with a cosmetic-produced complexion. Clear eyes, ruddy cheeks, and a well-nourished face depend upon pure blood for their healthiness. Millions spent on cosmetics would be unnecessary if only people learned how to tarry longer in God's beauty parlor. Good living, good food, good looks, and good company, all have their share in creating those blood streams responsible for a fresh-looking countenance. Depression registers upon the face. By our looks we reveal whether we are cast down or happy. Twice over the psalmist declares that God is the *health* of our countenance, which implies that as the Source of our health, He is able to maintain it.

"The tongue of the wise is health."
Proverbs 12:18

A good word is able to cheer the heavy heart (12:25). Godly merriment can produce a smiling countenance (15:13) and prove more effective than medicine (17:22). Is your talk a tonic? Are sufferers in mind and body somehow blessed, comforted, and heartened as you pass by with a smile of encouragement and a word of sympathy? If words are able to chase the shadows from a face, inspire sufferers to carry their cross courageously, and lift loads from heavy hearts, then God grant us an abundance of those comfortable, gracious, and acceptable words the Bible speaks about. If, somehow, your tongue has not functioned as a health-giving factor, why not ask God to take your lips, purge them of all that is cynical, critical, ironical, sharp, harsh and bitter, and make them the media of blessing to the sick and weary you meet on life's highway?

"Take some meat, for this is for your health." Acts 27:34

What a practical man Paul was! Eminently spiritual, he yet used sanctified common sense when it came to some of the crises of his life. He it was who urged Timothy to take wine for his stomach trouble. If we do not have Timothy's weak stomach, it is best to keep away from the wine. The context describes a terrible shipwreck when, for almost two weeks, sailors, soldiers, and prisoners had little to eat. Adrift and hungry, those 276 were downcast. They feared the worst. Then Paul got down to business. Starvation would not ease the situation. So taking what meat and bread there was, Paul gave thanks and persuaded the people to eat. And eat they did! "They were all of good cheer and took some meat." Have many of your hopes been shipwrecked? Is sorrow yours, and are you denying yourself food accordingly? Go and have a satisfying meal, and your cares will become lighter.

"The leaves of the tree were for the healing of the nations." Revelation 22:2

A good deal of our efficacious medicine comes from herbs and the leaves of trees. Certain herbs are most beneficial for bodily ailments. It is with this fact in mind that John describes the life in which there will be no sickness. Beneath the shade of the Tree of Life no disease shall ever afflict the glorified. Perpetual health is to be their portion. Back in the beginning, the leaves of a tree were despised by God as a sufficient covering for a discovered nakedness. How different are the leaves of the Tree of Paradise! With the curse gone, and a groaning creation gloriously transformed, the redeemed are to have unbroken health. Beloved, are you not thrilled at the prospect of becoming perfectly holy and perfectly healthy?

"I will bring it health and cure."
Jeremiah 33:6

While the prophet is taken up with Israel's restoration to divine favor, the principle enunciated is that all health is from God. Physicians may prescribe medicines and drugs, but they readily confess that although they are doctors, they cannot cure. Their diagnosis and treatments are essential, but in the end, the patient is dependent upon God for health and life. If it is His will to take the sick Christian to be with Himself, then all the physicians in the world would not be able to add a minute to life. God placed breath in our nostrils and at His pleasure it is retained or removed. Thus, if physicians and physics are needed, let their aid be mixed with faith in God's sovereign will and power.

The last experience we encounter in the body is that of *Death*, which is an appointment all must keep (Hebrews 9:27). "Our birth made us mortal – our death will make us immortal." A German proverb has it that "As soon as a man is born he begins to die." Dear old Bishop Hall expressed a similar thought when he wrote, "Death borders on our birth, and our cradle stands in our grave."

If the Lord should come in our lifetime, then we Christians shall not taste death. Like Enoch and Elijah, we too shall escape the grave. "O joy, O delight, should we go without dying." But otherwise, *death* is a physical certainty both saint and sinner must face. As W. M. Punshon vividly expressed it –

"No sex is spared, no age exempt. The majestic and courtly road which monarchs pass over, the way which men of letters have trod, the path the warrior traverses, the short and single annals of the poor – all lead to the same place: all terminate, however varied their routes, in the one enormous house which is appointed for all the living. One short sentence closes the biography of every man – 'And he died.' Such is the frailty of this boasted Man."

Before coming to a brief exposition of some of the numerous and precious promises connected with the death of a Christian, a collation of the most outstanding passages concerning the fact of, support in, and deliverance from Death may be found impressive:

"I kill, and I make alive."
Deuteronomy 32:39; I Samuel 2:6
"For we must needs die and are as water spilt on the ground."
II Samuel 14:14
"He will deliver his soul from going down into the pit." Job 33:28
"Mark the perfect man . . . the end of that man is peace." Psalm 37:37
"He will be our guide even unto death."
Psalm 48:14
"But God will redeem my soul from the power of the grave." Psalm 49:15
"Unto God belong the issues of death."
Psalm 68:20
"Thou carriest them away as a flood."
Psalm 90:4-7, 9

"They draw near unto the gates of death." Psalm 107:18

"To loose those that are appointed unto death." Psalm 102:20, 26

"The righteous hath hope in his death."
                                   Proverbs 14:32

"He will swallow up death in victory."
                    Isaiah 25:8; I Corinthians 15:54

"I will redeem them from death: O death, I will be thy plagues."
                                   Hosea 13:14

"Neither death . . . shall be able to separate us from the love of God."
                                   Romans 8:38, 39

"The sting of death is sin."
                    I Corinthians 15:56, 57

"Though our outward man perish."
          II Corinthians 4:16, 18; 5:1-4

"To die is gain . . . a desire to depart."
                    Philippians 1:21, 23

"Christ, who hath abolished death."
          II Timothy 1:10; Hebrews 2:14, 15

"I have the keys of hell and of death."
                    Revelation 1:18

That *death* is no respecter of age is proven by recorded deaths in the Bible. *Infants* and *children* die. Lord Byron says, "Heaven gives its favorites early death."

"David therefore besought God for the child . . . the child died."
                    II Samuel 12:16-23

"If I am bereaved of my children, I am bereaved." Genesis 43:14

"Rachel weeping for her children . . . they were not." Jeremiah 31:15-17

"I have lost my children and am desolate." Isaiah 49:21

"My beloved has gone down into his garden to gather lilies."
                    Song of Solomon 6:2

"He shall gather the lambs with his arm, and carry them in his bosom."
                    Isaiah 40:11

"A little child shall lead them."
                    Isaiah 11:6; Mark 10:15

The deaths of babies and young children make desolate our hearts and homes and disturb our future plans. Often, as in the case of Rachel, inconsolable grief over the death of children is ours. Yet heaven is nearer and dearer because of their presence there. Are they not in His garden as "lilies," unsullied by the sins of life? Did not God gather them early before their beauty started to fade? As lambs, they are in His bosom. David knew he could not bring his baby back, but that he would go to be with him. Therefore, David's grief was not ex-

cessive. He resigned himself to the will of God.

"Who plucked that flower?" asked the gardener, in anger, as he saw the broken stem of a rare and choice flower upon which he had bestowed great care. "It was I," said the Master, and the gardener held his peace.

Thomas Boston experienced that a little child's death is a bitter and poignant blessing. God's sword, like Cid's sword, wounds that it may heal. The crown of thorns can be transmuted into a crown of gold. "To bury his name was indeed harder than to bury his body," Boston murmured when he laid his infant Ebenezer to sleep. But there is no burying such a name, for Boston knew that his dear Ebenezer was in heaven, beckoning and alluring him to the heights above.

The Bible also reminds us that the scythe of death often cuts down our noble *youth*. That is why Solomon exhorts young people to remember their Creator (Ecclesiastes 12:1). The Shunamite lost her boy when he was "grown" (II Kings 4:18-26). Jairus had the anguish of knowing that his daughter had died (Mark 5:22, 23, 35-42). The widow's son, who was the bread-winner of the home, died, adding thereby to his mother's loneliness. Death in youth seems most unnatural. Nature has her seasons, such as seedtime and harvest, summer and winter, but Death has all seasons. No age is exempt. While youth is the time for joy, if the young are ready for death, then the true joy of life is increased. Although suddenly the thread is broken and the loom stops, the design is completed elsewhere for God's work is never half done.

Lazarus had likely reached *middle life* when death laid its cold fingers upon him. Our blessed Lord died just after His thirty-third year. Stephen was not much older when he died as the Church's first martyr.

"Every man at his best state is altogether vanity." Psalm 39:4, 5

"What is your life? It is even a vapour."
                    James 4:13-14

At the half-way stage of life, when it would seem that a man is at the zenith of his powers and accomplishments, he needs to be reminded about the brevity of life, and certainty of death.

"As for man his days are as grass; as a flower of the field, so he flourisheth . . . the place thereof shall know him no more." Psalm 103:15, 16

"Man that is born of a woman is of few days." Job 14:1

"Nevertheless man being in honour abideth not." Psalm 49:6-20

"There is but a step between me and death." I Samuel 20:3

Decay and death are written everywhere in nature, and the best of men must be reminded that they are only mortal men at the best, and that death is a step they must take at any given moment.

Prince Albert, who was stricken down upon his dying bed, as he approached the prime of life, said:

"I have had wealth, rank, and power. But if this were all I had, how wretched I should be now!

Rock of Ages cleft for me, Let me hide myself in Thee."

If one's trust is in the Saviour, then it does not matter when death knocks at the door. "To die is gain." As Christians, we have a glorious inheritance beyond the grave. We never say "Good-by!"

Back in the cradle of humanity, before sin issued in the numerous sicknesses and diseases affecting the span of human life, the *longevity* of people was amazing, as Genesis 5 clearly shows. The longest lived man of all time was Methuselah, who died at 969 years of age–31 years short of a millennium. Adam was 930 when he died. Moses reached 126 before God took him to heaven. The apostle John was in his 100th year when he entered glory. The normal span is given by the psalmist as 70 years–

"The days of our years are threescore years and ten; if by reason of strength they be fourscore years, yet is their strength labour and sorrow; for it is soon cut off." Psalm 90:10

Numerous precious promises are given to those whom the Lord satisfies with long life, and upon whom His beauty rests.

"We have a building of God, an house not made with hands, eternal in the heavens . . . Present with the Lord." II Corinthians 5:1-10

"I have fought a good fight . . . there is laid up for me a crown of righteousness." II Timothy 4:7-8

"Though after my skin worms destroy this body . . . shall I see God." Job 19:25-27

"Thou shalt come to thy grave in a full age, like as a shock of corn cometh in his season." Job 5:26

"Even to your old age I am he." Isaiah 46:4; Genesis 15:15; 25:8

"It shall come to pass, that at evening time it shall be light." Zechariah 14:7

"Lord, now lettest thou thy servant depart in peace." Luke 2:29, 30

While we are often mystified when death claims a baby, child, or young person, we somehow expect those who have reached the prescribed measure of their existence to die. "The young may die, but the old must." To them, death seems natural, and if they are the Lord's they are glad for release from many of the afflictions of old age. While the death of any saint is precious in His sight, the exodus of an aged saint is like an honorable discharge from a long warfare. At the end of a road, the weary traveler is welcomed home. Paul tells us how the aged should be found living as they await their decease–"sober, grave, temperate, sound in faith, in love, in patience" (Titus 2:2, 3).

We speak of being in "the land of the living," but actually we live in "the land of the dying." Because of this fact, it may enlighten and edify us to look more closely at some of the Biblical aspects of death.

"Mark the perfect man . . . the end of that man is peace." Psalm 37:37

If one has experienced the joy of sin forgiven, then death will not be a leap in the dark. Death to one saved by grace is a falling into the embrace of the Saviour. A peaceful end comes to those who were not idle in the market place. Every God-given opportunity was appropriated, and rest when it came was sweet. The end of the upright is always one of peace, because their future is bright with the promise of eternal bliss. What else can the Christian do but die happy and victorious, when he or she knows that heart and life are to be entirely emancipated from evil and that the sight of Christ's face, the society of the holy, and the full enjoyment of God for all eternity awaits them! But to have a peaceful end, it is necessary to have Christ as our Peace while we journey over the rough and rugged pathway of life. David makes it clear that it is only the perfect, or upright, whose end is peace. "Blessed are such dead who die in the Lord" (Revelation 14:13).

"The end of that man is peace." What a noble epitaph is this to have traced upon our tombstone! Will it be yours when your tired body and worn spirit come to the close of life's day?

"He will be our guide even unto death."
Psalm 48:14

We all need a guide, and what a privilege and joy it is to have God as our infallible Guide. Isaiah reminds us that God guides us continually (58:11), which means that every minute of every hour He is near to direct our steps. He never loses sight of the Lord, nor of ourselves as travelers. He never leaves nor forsakes us. As day follows day, and the years come and go, His watchful eye is upon us. We may not know the way, but we know the Guide, and so we trust Him where we cannot trace Him. But what happens when we reach the end of the road? Does our faithful Guide leave us? There He is with us as we journey through the valley (Psalm 23:4). There He is carrying us through the valley into the broad and beautiful country of heaven. The word "even" is given as "over," signifying that God is not only our Guide *even* unto death but *over* death into eternity.

"The power of death . . . the fear of death." Hebrews 2:14, 15

What great power Satan must have had before Calvary! He certainly possesses much power yet, but the cross was his "Waterloo." The keys of death and hell are his no longer. They dangle from Christ's girdle. The fact that the devil had the power of death may be one reason why he contended with Michael for the body of Moses (Jude 9).

The question is, If Christ destroyed the power of death, why do we not let Him deliver us from the fear of death? If its power has gone, then why dread it? Yet how many there are who, all their lifetime, are subject to its bondage. Are we not taught to sing to fear the grave as little as our bed? Have you a dread of death? If you are a Christian, such a fear is sinful, as well as without foundation. The Christless have every reason to fear death, for, to them it will be a brutal foe ushering them into a Christless eternity. But with you, as a child of God, it is different.

"Precious in the sight of the Lord is the death of his saints." Psalm 116:15

"Lord, now lettest thou thy servant depart in peace." Luke 2:39

War cheapens life and hardens the heart of man to the act of dying. Dictators and war lords think nothing of gambling with millions of lives. It means little to them that bloody battlefields are strewn with battered, lifeless bodies. But God is moved, even over the death of the wicked. With sadness He views the passing of the godless because He knows the terrible eternity awaiting those who die out of Christ.

The death of saints, however, is precious in His sight. Why does He count their death precious? Saints are those who have been redeemed by the blood of His precious Son, and who in virtue of the cross have heaven as their goal. For every saint, "the best is yet to be." Like Simeon of old, the saints can depart in peace, for their eyes have seen Christ, God's Salvation, and thus for them there is an eternity in fellowship with Him and with the glorious citizens of His court.

"O death, where is thy sting?"
I Corinthians 15:55

The sting (or *edge, anguish, virus*), of death is sin. But when sin is cancelled through Jesus' paying the debt, the sting is gone forever. We cannot deny that death has a certain sting. The final sting will only vanish when Christ returns. To watch a loved one die, and then to stand and witness the precious dust buried in God's green earth, produces a heart-sting. Death produces a temporary shudder because of the snapping of long and loving friendships. But the promise is that the dead in Christ are to rise first, and for them death will be swallowed up in victory. The Abolisher of death, the Christ who died and rose again and who is alive forevermore, will deal the death blow to man's last enemy. For the lost, in the blackness of darkness forever, the sting of death remains, because their eternal punishment is referred to as "the second death." May the Lord exercise us regarding the peril of the lost around us, and use us for their deliverance from death's eternal sting!

"Yea, though I walk through the valley of the shadow of death, I will fear no evil." Psalm 23:4

To the Christian, death is only a *shadow,* because Christ robbed it of its substance. Why be afraid of a shadow? What deathbed assurance this promise inspires! When Jesus came to pass through that dark valley of death, there was a moment when He felt forsaken of God. But for those redeemed by His blood, the promise is that "Thou art with me."

"There is but a step between me and death." I Samuel 20:3

For David there was the constant thought that death might be around the corner.

Saul's anger and jealousy made young David's a precarious existence. In the midst of life, he was in death. The spears of Saul almost got David, but every time they were aimed, God saw to it that they missed their mark. How true it is that we are nearer heaven than we realize! Healthy though we may be, with nothing organically wrong with our bodies, God may see fit to take the breath from our nostrils. We have no lease on life, therefore, because death is only a step away, we should be found sitting loose to things of earth. Our heart should be weaned from the world and its ways. We must live right with our Lord, and with those around, so that no regrets will be ours if we are brought abruptly to the end of our earthly career. May grace be ours so to live that, whenever the summons may reach us, we shall be ready to obey!

"Thou shalt rest, and stand in thy lot at the end of thy days." Daniel 12:13

For Daniel, this prophecy was also a promise. For us, the Lord is our Lot, and we shall be found in Him at the end of our days. We also have a *lot* in the heavenly Canaan, and come what may, we shall stand in it. Has the God of Daniel granted unto us a worthy portion no one and nothing can rob us of.

"I shall not die, but live, and declare the works of the Lord." Psalm 118:17

Many a Christian brought down to a sick bed has been inspired by this promise. Death seemed to be near, but the Spirit whispered the assurance that gripped the psalmist's heart, as by God's grace and power the afflicted one was spared and raised to render many years of service. Vigor returned to declare the works and words of Jehovah. While it may sound a paradox, yet it is true, although we may die, we shall not die, but live forever. The grave may claim my body, but not *me*.

"Because I live, ye shall live also." John 14:19

The prophets make it clear that personal accountability is an inescapable fact. Death, physical and eternal, is for the sinner's *own* sin, and not another's.

"Every one shall die for his own iniquity." Jeremiah 31:31

"The soul that sinneth, it shall die." Ezekiel 18:20

"Death through sin." Romans 5:12

While Adam, the federal head of the human race, brought sin into the world, and

death because of sin, Ezekiel and Paul declare that every grave is the result of personal sin. "Death has passed upon all men, for all have sinned." All the tears, separations, heartaches, and graves which death produces can be traced back to sin. Had there been no sin, there would have been no death. Like Enoch and Elijah, we would have been translated when wanted in heaven.

The death referred to does not mean cessation of being or annihilation, because the soul is indestructible. Death means separation. In physical death, there is the separation of the soul from the body; in spiritual and eternal death, the soul is separated from the presence of God throughout eternity. This is our strong incentive in service for the Master. "We . . . believe to the saving of the soul" (Hebrews 10:39).

Another evident fact the Bible observes is that no man can live beyond the period of divine permission. Science assures us that the span of life has been considerably lengthened. Life may be sweet to many of us and the desire to linger as long as possible, but the psalmist reminds us that—

"None can keep alive his own soul." Psalm 22:29

One interpretation of this declaration is that man must leave all and follow death when it beckons. Saint and sinner, prince and pauper alike, must obey the call. Another thought is that only the God who created the soul can supply the true life it must have if it is to function aright. Apart from Him who is "The Life," the soul is dead, spiritually dead–dead yet alive (I Timothy 5:6)–even as it struggles to live physically and socially.

If we do go home by the way of a grave, may our end be like the triumphant departure of those who have met death as a transition from earth to heaven.

"Let me die the death of the righteous." Numbers 23:10

John Wesley is reputed to have said that all his preachers died well. But to die well, we must live well. Job speaks of those who die in full strength being wholly at ease and quiet. Because the victorious death of a Christian is precious in God's sight, may ours be the glorious experience of D. L. Moody who, as he died, confessed, "This is glorious. Earth is receding, heaven is approaching. God is calling."

"There shall be no more death." Revelation 21:4

John found it difficult to describe heaven.

All he could do was to outline with a few negatives what will be missing in God's new order. Thus he gives us a series of "No mores," of which "no more death" is the second. What a blessed promise this is! Because death is to be finally banished, there will be no more sorrow, no more crying, no more pain, all of which are associated with man's last enemy. In Summer-land above, there are no funeral homes, no cemeteries, no more cruel separations. Now death is a grim reality. But with the dawning of God's new world, no eyes will ever be wet with tears. Now caskets, graves, and heartaches are ours. But when God makes all things new, sin and death will never again mar His creation.

PROMISES RELATIVE TO THE MARITAL REALM

No matter how one may look at the Bible, it is unique in every direction. "There is none like it," as David said of Goliath's sword. Its authorship is divine, its historicity unquestioned, its teachings eminently spiritual. Yet although its tone is so high and lofty, it is the most practical book in the world when it comes to dealing with the common and ordinary relationship of life. It is indispensable in that it touches life at every point. This is especially true when it deals with love and romance, courtship and marriage, home and parenthood. No phase of marital life is omitted.

In these modern days of disastrous sexual licence, pre-marital experiences, wide-spread divorces, and absence of real home life, how wholesome it is to turn to the Bible for guidance as to all that concerns love and home. Numerous promises are related to the right kind of love and marriage, to parents and children, and to homes that are fragrant with divine love and favor.

"The many make the household
But only *one* the home."

It is to be regretted that most books on *sex* and *marriage* written today stress the lower instincts rather than man's more noble and higher instincts. Many secular bookstores are saturated with literature pandering to evil lusts. Hollywood is not innocent when it comes to glamorizing adultery, divorce, and looseness of marriage vows. Materially, we never had it so good, but morally, the nation was never at a lower level than it is today. Hence the need of a study of God's Word on these vital matters, for the Bible gives dignity and rightness to the exquisite intimacies of love, marriage, and home. Today, it is difficult to separate sex from sin. Originally, sex was not connected with sin because mating and marriage were instituted by God before Adam and Eve had sinned against their Creator.

"God blessed them, and said unto them,

Be fruitful, and multiply, and replenish the earth." Genesis 1:28

To this first promise given to our first parents, many more promises throughout Scripture are directly, and indirectly, associated with love-union, marriage, wives and husbands, homes and children. Did not Paul worship the Father "of whom every family in heaven and earth is named?" (Ephesians 3:15). Because family life was divinely instituted, it is fitting that the Bible should contain clear and explicit precepts and promises regarding the exact nature and order of all that is connected with marital life.

In his sane, satisfying, and Scriptural volume on *Life and Love* – A Christian View of Sex, Dr. Clyde M. Narramore tells us that the God who inspired the Bible is the same God who made the marriage of man and woman a part of His creative plan. Because He wants His creatures to be well-adjusted in every area of life He desires that "courtship and marriage be the means of mutual contentment rather than frustration."

By ordaining marriage, God planned that men and women through physical union might share with Him a partnership in begetting new lives. God alone possesses the power to create, that is, to bring something out of nothing, but through marriage, mating, conception, and child-bearing, God permits a man and a woman to be His instruments in creating a new life – an immortal soul! What a wondrous thought! A partnership with God! Sex is a sacred and sobering area of life when seen in Scripture from the viewpoint of God's creative purposes. Dr. Narramore's factual and frank book should be read by all young people confused by sex relationship. It is packed with common sense and maintains a spiritual tone throughout its pages, and it is most valuable in that it proves that God in His great providence has given us all necessary instruction on such a vital subject.

As we seek to gather out the promises covering the manifold phases of marital life, we shall discover that the Bible is "a bold book," as Joseph Parker expressed it. "It hides nothing of sham: the Bible is not afraid of words which make the cheek burn; the Bible conceals nothing of moral cripplency, infirmity, or weakness or evil." An illustration of the absolute honesty of the Bible can be found in the chapter dealing with Jacob's progeny and policy (Genesis 30). There is no attempt to hush things up. No paint is used to obscure the pallor of the sickly face of that ancient family. Think of this ugly list –

1. Envy (30:1)
2. Anger (30:2)
3. Impatience (30:4)
4. Human devices for forestalling God's purpose (30:14-15)
5. Deceptive scheming (30-32)
6. The most absolute selfishness (30:41-45)

The same frankness in presenting an unvarnished record is found in Judah's sons, Er and Onan (Genesis 38). The wickedness of Er is declared but not described. Whatever it was, "it was wicked in the sight of the Lord" (38:7). Of the sin of Onan, which is described, we can only say that such a sin has slain its thousands and is one to be shunned as we would shun – if we could but see them – the flames and smoke of Gehenna. The evil of these two sons must have been great, for both of them were slain by God (38:7, 18). As to love and sex as a whole, the Bible takes cognizance of them and presents them in both the true and perverted light. Divine promises are given to the virtuous.

Although we have no way of knowing how Adam felt as he looked upon his God-given companion – the world's first woman, wife, and mother – he must have been enraptured as he gazed upon her undraped, perfectly formed figure and the beautiful countenance which Eve must have had as God's direct creation. For both Adam and Eve, it must have been love at first sight. For this first pair there was no courtship leading to conjugal love. As soon as Eve was formed out of Adam, each knew they were for each other and were divinely instructed as to all they were to do for, and to be to, each other. By intuition, Adam recognized the close relationship of Eve to himself; and that, as part of himself, she

would continue to be a part of himself. Is not this fact designed to show that any man and woman made one by marriage are to regard themselves as being of one flesh (Ephesians 5:31)? Those who are completely one in a spiritual sense are sure to be one in heart, in companionship, and in purpose, and can claim to all promises connected with such a union symbolizing the union between Christ and His Church. Promises were given to Adam and Eve as to their parenthood, power, and provision – which promises alas! were shadowed by their ensuing sin (Genesis 1:28-31; 3:14-19).

Love and marriage, then, received their sanction and their sacredness from the divine relation to them. God instituted marriage when He made the world, and Christ honored it when He attended the wedding at Cana (John 2). It was good for Adam intellectually, emotionally, socially, and spiritually not to be alone, and the provided love and companionship of a woman for Adam show how grievously they err who cast a reflection upon wedded bliss by "forbidding to marry" (I Timothy 4:3).

God placed honor upon womanhood, in that the first woman, like the first man, was a divine creation (Genesis 2:21-23). Adam was made of the common dust, but Eve was made of dust that had been "etherealized by passing through the hands of God" and was thus signally honored, as all should honor women (Ephesians 5:33). But women are not worthy of their origin when they degrade their dignity. A wife is not a real companion if she is "a field wife like Dinah; a street wife like Tamar: a window wife like Jezebel: a nagging wife like Job's wife: a worldly wife like Lot's wife: a cruel and vicious wife like Herodias."

Is it not sad to realize that Adam fell through the one he loved? Has not this story been repeated thousands of times in human history? Affection for earthly friends must always be subordinate to what God demands. If we do not love Him supremely, we cannot love Him at all. Giving Him the first place means the enrichment of our love to others.

"He that loveth father or mother . . . son or daughter more than me is not worthy of me." Matthew 10:37

As to romantic *courtship*, it is somewhat refreshing to read the Bible's unsullied, charming stories of the wooing for the affection of another with a view to a companionship for life. The Song of Solomon, a much misunderstood book, is devoted to the art of, and the right kind of heart, for the making of love. In C. I. Scofield's introduction to this ancient love-idyll, in his *Reference Bible*, we are told of the two-fold interpretation of Solomon's work. "Primarily, the book is an expression of pure marital love as ordained of God in creation, and the vindication of that love as against both asceticism and lust—the two profanations of the holiness of marriage. The secondary and larger interpretation is of Christ, the Son and His heavenly bride, the Church (II Corinthians 11:1-4)."

Answering the question as to how this book became a part of Holy Scripture, Dr. H. A. Ironside offers the solution that Jewish teachers thought of it as designed by God to give a right apprehension of conjugal love.

"They thought of it as the glorification of wedded life, and if we conceived of it from no higher standpoint than this, it would mean that it had a right place in the Canon. Wedded life in Israel represented the very highest and fullest and deepest affection at a time when, in the nations surrounding Israel, woman was looked upon as mere chattel, as a slave, or as the object of man's pleasure to be discarded when and as he pleased. But it was otherwise in Israel. The Jewish home was a place where love and tenderness reigned, and no doubt this little book had a great deal to do with lifting it to that glorious height."

But the spiritually-minded of all ages have seen in Solomon's Song, the deeper meaning of the mutual love existing between Jehovah and Israel, and of the union and communion between Christ and His Church. Samuel Rutherford's heart-stirring poem is based upon this glorification of wooing and wedded love.

"Oh, I am my Beloved's,
    And my Beloved's mine."

Another beautiful courtship, although somewhat brief, was that of Isaac and Rebekah. With these two like-minded hearts, it was another case of love at first sight. As soon as Isaac saw Rebekah, "he loved her" (Genesis 24:67). Guidance as to the right kind of a partner for Abraham's son had been promised. The servant of Abraham was entrusted with the mission to find a wife for Isaac (Genesis 24:7), and relying upon the divine promise of guidance,

he succeeded in his task. "He shall send his angel." The earthly messenger was guided by the heavenly messenger, and so the servant contacted Rebekah, which "thing proceeded from the Lord" (24:50). Says Henry Thorne, "Some matrimonial matches have been described as 'Lucifer matches,' but here, at all events was a marriage that was 'made in Heaven.' There would be more angels in our homes if young people looking for husbands and wives were more careful to seek the guidance of the Angel by whom the servant of Abraham was led."

The servant prayed for good speed, and he got it. God's promises had been fulfilled, and the relatives of Rebekah saw the leading of God in the mission of Abraham's servant, and they gave their consent to the proposed marriage. Says old Thomas Fuller of this sweet story, "Seeing heaven did ask the *banns*, why should earth forbid them?" How all young people attracted to each other should read and reread the story of a bride sought and won by a servant, and guided and protected by him across the desert until she met the one she was meant for!

It was soon after his mother's death, and Isaac found great consolation in Rebekah's companionship. Their united life, however, deserves close study by those who are wooed and won, It has been suggested that in searching for a wife for Isaac, Abraham was really looking for Jesus. Rebekah's marriage with Isaac was to be a link in the chain of events resulting in the fulfilment of the promise that secured blessing for all nations of the earth through the seed of Abraham. "Through the wedding day Abraham would see the day in which the Church should become the Bride of Christ." The meeting then, of Isaac and Rebekah was an integral part of—

"That far-off divine event
    To which the whole creation moves."

The union of Isaac and Rebekah was brought about by prayer. It was a divinely ordered alliance. What early shipwrecks in many marriages today would be prevented if only those drawn to each other had sought and obtained the guidance and benediction of heaven! After twenty years of marriage, Rebekah was still childless, which must have been a trial of faith for both hearts. So Isaac made this matter of care a matter of prayer, and as the prayer was in the line of God's purpose, it was sure of an answer.

"Isaac entreated the Lord for his wife,

because she was barren.''
Genesis 25:21, 22

"If we ask any thing according to his will, he heareth us." I John 5:14

Those long years of waiting prove that God is never before His time, nor after it. He knows just when to perform His promise.

The family life of Isaac and Rebekah and their twin sons, Jacob and Esau, sounds a warning about the folly and tragedy of favoritism in a family. Isaac's love for Esau was somewhat sensual. He loved Esau "because he did eat of his venison." Such an aspect of love was of a carnal nature. Highest love has regard not so much to what the one loved gives as to what he or she *is*. "Rebekah loved Jacob." That she had a good deal of influence over her son, but used it for a bad purpose, is seen in the command – "My son, obey my voice" (27:8; see II Chronicles 22:3). Evidently God had a preference for Jacob –

"Jacob have I loved, but Esau have I hated (loved less)." Romans 9:13

Samuel Morley is reported to have said, "I am much what my mother has made me." Therefore Rebekah cannot be blamed for her partiality, since Jacob was God's favorite. Still, on the human plane, when parents do not treat their children equally, but dote on one child to the indifference of another, homelife as God meant it is seriously impaired, as the later experiences in the home circle of Isaac and Rebekah prove. Was it out of spite that Esau grieved his parents by aligning himself in marriage with two ungodly Hittite women (26:26, 34)? Later on, he married his half-cousin, daughter of Ishmael (28:9). As Esau was around forty years of age, he knew his own mind, and he should have sought a companion in keeping with Hebrew requirements. "A sin," says Joseph Parker, "is sometimes aggravated by the age of the sinner."

Jacob and his beloved Rachel provide us with one of the sweetest stories of courtship in the Bible. Here is another illustration of a praying man being divinely led to a good woman who was to share his life. How incomparable in the realm of literature is the heart-gripping statement –

"Jacob served seven years for Rachel; and they seemed unto him but a few days, for the love he had to her."
Genesis 29:20

Having met God on the way, "Jacob lifted up his feet" (Genesis 29:1, margin),
which implies a light-hearted alacrity, and he continued the journey to the woman who was to capture his love. The promise of divine companionship and protection inspired him with great courage –

"I am with thee, and will keep thee in all places whither thou goest." 28:15

Jacob's first sight of Haran where he was to live for more than twenty years of his life – the same length of time his parents had to wait for his birth (27:23; 32:29) – must have cheered his heart. Incidents leading up to meeting the love of his life are dealt with in the narrative. There was the well, the gathered flocks, the shepherds Jacob called "brethren," and finally the apparent unpremeditated meeting of Jacob and Rachel. The moment he looked upon his cousin's beautiful face, he knew that this woman was to be his.

This union, like that of Isaac and Rebekah, was of God, whose providence ordered things so that they should meet at the well. Divinely directed lives are often shaped by circumstances, which human prescience could not have foreseen. What a fascinating record it would make if only we could have a group of stories of how men and women first met before entering into a matrimonial alliance!

Jacob's instant love for Rachel prompted him to come to her aid in the removal of the great stone at the well. Love nerved him into new energy (see II Corinthians 5:14). As her cousin, Jacob had the right to kiss Rachel, according to Eastern etiquette, but somehow we feel that when "Jacob kissed Rachel, and lifted up his voice and wept," that kiss remained an unforgotten one.

The unfolding story of Jacob's introduction to Rachel's family and of his covenant with Laban, her father, can be briefly told. Jacob manifested his love for Rachel by agreeing to serve seven years for her. He loved, not in word only, but in deed and in truth, and because love brightens labor, those seven years of service must have been bright for Jacob. Do we not have a parable and promise here of Christ's love for His Church?

"He loved the church, and gave himself for it."

Jacob was faithful to his promise, and at the end of the seven years, he went to Laban to claim his much-loved Rachel as his own. But what deception Laban practiced! After the wedding feast, in the light of the next morning, Jacob discovered that Leah, and not her sister Rachel, was his wife (29:21-30). Laban tried to condone his unrighteous, cruel act by pleading the custom that the younger could not be given in marriage before the first-born. He was a deceiver and should have thought of this custom seven years before when he made a covenant with Jacob.

True love, however, was not to be discouraged or daunted, so for another seven years Jacob toiled bravely on. Polygamy, in which Jacob became involved, was practiced by godly men before his time and after. But his experience with his two wives and their families reveals polygamy as a disgraceful crime against a serene home life. Rachel's envy over Leah's children was part of the evil fruitage of polygamy, which is a sin against divine arrangement. Her spirit of envy led to a wicked request – "Give me children!" Rachel made the common mistake of looking to man rather than to God, who alone can give life. Rachel's request aroused the anger of Jacob, but such anger over one he loved so truly and tenderly was a source of bitterness. Perhaps Jacob had not considered the bitterness of Rachel's disappointment over her barrenness as he might have done.

Rachel, however, was not forgotten of God. He "remembered her" (30:22, 23), and Joseph, who was to become the saviour of Egypt, was born. How full of God Rachel's life became! He heard her prayer and added unto her another son, Benjamin, whose birth cost Rachel her life. How often the brightest anticipations of life are clouded by the gloom of the grave! In the promise of Rachel's second son, however, there is the larger promise of "another Son," even Jesus. "The Son of Mary, like the son of Rachel, was both the son of sorrow (Ben-oni, Isaiah 53:3, 4), and the son of the right hand (Benjamin, Hebrews 1:2, 3)." Doubtless Rachel praised God for answered prayer in the birth of Benjamin, but such an answer was a crushing burden, and she sank beneath the weight of it. Yet to her there came the sweet promise, "Fear not."

It must have been a heavy hand that raised the pillar over the grave of the beloved Rachel. Earlier, he had dug another grave in which Jacob buried the images Rachel had brought from Haran. He had no regret at rearing a pillar over that grave. But this pillar at Bethel was a sad memento of a broken heart. What loneliness overtakes a true lover when half of his heart is taken to heaven!

Courtship of a sensual, debased sort was that of Amnon, when he fell madly in love with his half-sister, Tamar. After seducing the virgin girl, love turned to hate. And what hate!

"Amnon hated her exceedingly; so that the hatred wherewith he hated her was greater than the love wherewith he had loved her." II Samuel 13:16

What a tragic story is unfolded in this chapter! What solemn lessons it teaches! One evident lesson is that when sexual desires are stirred, they are only sinful when they result in a union outside the bond of marriage, and become fornication or adultery (Exodus 20:14, 17; I Corinthians 6:13-20). Promise of divine blessing is only for those who woo and marry in the Lord.

Absalom, Tamar's brother, was determined to have revenge on Amnon for the release of his ungoverned passion upon his sister, and he waited "two full years" (II Samuel 13:23) to punish Amnon. Sheepshearing was a time of feasting, and cunningly Absalom begged his father, King David, to allow all his sons to attend the feast. Amnon was David's eldest son and heir apparent, which, coupled with the memory of his own sin with Bathsheba, was the reason for David's guilty leniency towards Amnon's crime. David finally allowed Amnon to go to the feast as his representative, but it was to be a feast of death, for drunken Amnon was slain at Absalom's behest. What an evil brood one sin can beget!

The sin and shame of Judah offers another warning to those who contemplate a love-union (Genesis 38). He sinned against an explicit divine command when he consorted with Hirah, and then with Shuah. Hebrews were forbidden to marry heathen of surrounding countries. Does this not illustrate the New Testament command about being "unequally yoked together with unbelievers"? Judah's son of Shuah, Onan, was slain for his perversion of a sexual act, and Tamar his widow had vengeance upon her father-in-law for his breach of promise. She played the harlot and involved Judah, who became the father of her twin boys. The miracle of grace is that Judah, Tamar, and her sons, found a place in the greatest of all genealogies (Matthew 1:3). God's election is only by grace, for otherwise these stained characters would never have been chosen.

The foregoing preamble prepares us for a closer examination of those precepts and promises associated with *marriage, husbands and wives, fathers and mothers, home and children.*

MARRIAGE

In these days of extreme laxity in marriage ties, it is imperative to go back to the Bible in order to find out how God views such a solemn ordinance.

It was divinely instituted.

"They shall be one flesh . . . The man and his wife." Genesis 2:24, 25

It was designed for mutual happiness.

"It is not good that man should be alone." Genesis 2:18; Ecclesiastes 4:9, 10

It was meant to produce a godly seed.

"That he might have a godly seed." Malachi 2:15; Genesis 1:18; 3:15; 4:1

It is a lawful and honorable transaction.

"Let every man have his own wife." I Corinthians 7:2, 28

"Marriage is honourable in all." Hebrews 13:4; I Timothy 5:14

It should only be in the Lord who instituted it.

"She is at liberty to be married to whom she will: only in the Lord." I Corinthians 7:39

It is a partnership death alone can sever.

"An husband is bound by the law to her . . . so long as he liveth." Romans 7:2, 3; Matthew 19:6; I Corinthians 7:39

It should be with the willing consent of parents.

"Esau saw that the daughters of Canaan pleased not Isaac his father." Genesis 28:8; Judges 14:2, 3; Exodus 22:17; Deuteronomy 7:3

It carries a benediction of promise when rightly contracted.

"They blessed Rebekah and said . . . be thou the mother of thousands of millions." Genesis 24:60; Ruth 4:11, 12 (see Deuteronomy 7:3; Joshua 23:12; Ezra 9:2, 12; II Corinthians 6:14 for wrong transaction)

It should be the source of constant joy and satisfaction.

"Let thy fountain be blessed, and rejoice with the wife of thy youth." Proverbs 5:18

It is sacred because symbolic of the union between God and His own.

"Thy maker is thy husband." Isaiah 54:5; Jeremiah 3:14; Hosea 2:19, 20

"One flesh . . . even as the Lord and his church." Ephesians 5:23, 24, 32

There are one or two conclusions to draw from the consistent witness of Scripture as to the sacredness and blessedness of the marriage tie, of which Crashaw wrote—

"How sweet the mutual yoke of man and wife,
When holy fires maintain love's heavenly life!"

First of all, there must be the determination to avoid the folly of drifting aimlessly or carelessly into marriage. In dealing with Jacob's encounter with Rachel at the first well he came to, Dr. F. B. Meyer says, "There is nothing more important than the union of heart with heart, there is nothing into which people drift more heedlessly." How young people need to beware when they break away from safe moorings to launch out on the sea of matrimony! Too often a sudden attachment is made and then "a marriage is drifted into, or whirled into, as when a boat is swept down by the wild rapids."

There is no prolonged, serious thought about the significance of such a solemn step, no weighing of the arduous responsibilities to be assumed, no mutual observation as to whether the one is fitted for the other. Because in the purpose of God marriage is "for better or for worse," it dare not be entered unadvisedly or lightly. If sincere love dreams are to become true, marriage must be faced reverently, thoughtfully, and in the fear of God.

The sad and lamentable increase of *divorces* would be greatly curbed if only professed lovers would remember the old-time promise—

"In all thy ways acknowledge him, and he shall direct thy paths." Proverbs 6:3 *All* thy ways includes "the way of a man with a maid" (Proverbs 30:10), and *vice versa.* When two fall in love, they should seek divine wisdom enabling them to make sound judgments, and to discover whether they are truly mated. If they are not, then there will be disillusionment and disaster ahead. There is no disgrace nor dishonor if an engagement is broken, if a happy life together cannot be envisioned.

Because love is like a delicate blossom which can so easily be stifled, and marriage a bond of deep affection, a thorough knowledge beforehand of each other's different backgrounds, habits, ideas and ideals is imperative. But if there is no forethought or foresight, and marriage is drifted into, than a holy wedlock will become an unholy deadlock. It is far better to remain single and happy than to marry and be unhappy. Is it not preferable to be happily single than unhappily married? A striking illustration of thoughtlessness before marriage is that of Samson and Delilah. Ignorance of the Sorek woman's treacherous character cost Samson his sight, liberty, and life.

Another necessary consideration if marriage is not to become a lottery, a sort of game of chance, is that of previous instruction. For other responsibilities of life there are deliberation and instruction; why not training for marriage? Mothers should realize their sacred duty of talking thoughtfully to their daughters about the significance of marriage, on principles that should guide them, and of what will be expected of them when they become wives. Fathers should have quiet conversations with their sons on how they can make a satisfactory marriage. The Chief Medical Officer of The Ministry of Education in Britain in his recent yearly report described the shocking precocity and depravity of some 14- and 15-year-old girls and boys, and of the appalling promiscuous sexual activity, and he says that one root of such irresponsible behavior is *the lack of or inadequate parental guidance and example."*

"Thou shalt bring her home to thine house." Deuteronomy 21:12

"Happy shalt thou be, and it shall be well with thee." Psalm 128:2

"My beloved is mine, and I am his."
Song of Solomon 2:16

"Heirs together of the grace of life."
I Peter 3:7

"The thing proceedeth from the Lord."
Genesis 24:50

"I will give them one heart."
Jeremiah 32:39

"A man . . . and his wife . . . shall be one flesh." Genesis 1:27; 2:24

There are so many precious promises connected with true marriages, but they can only be fulfilled in behalf of those who decide to unite only after deliberately and prayerfully examining their love and all that a permanent lovebond involves.

Assuming that a couple, drawn to each, have calmly and prayerfully considered their growing love for each other, and ultimately marry in the Lord, has the Bible any advice and guidance to offer the *newlyweds?* Are there any promises for them to claim as they stand together at the portal of their united life? There are. Is it not a wonderful insight into the divine character that

those who have just plighted their troth are remembered by the Almighty One? Male Israelites were liable for military service from 20 years and upward (Numbers 1:3), but God made a merciful exemption in the case of those who were newlywed.

"What man is there that hath betrothed a wife, and hath not taken her? Let him go and return to his house, lest he die in the battle and another man take her." Deuteronomy 20:7

"When a man hath taken a new wife, he shall not go out to war, neither will he be charged with any business: but he shall be free at home for one year, and shall cheer up his wife which he hath taken." Deuteronomy 24:5

How considerate God is! The Mosaic laws and regulations were divine commands, and this one relative to a newly married man carried with it a promise of a year's uninterrupted bliss when both man and wife would have time to adjust themselves to their life together. What a thoughtful, practical God we have!

"With gladness and rejoicing shall they be brought." Psalm 45:15

"Behold the bridegroom and the bride cometh." Matthew 25:5 Syriac Version

"He that hath the bride is the bridegroom: but the friend of the bridegroom, which standeth by, rejoiceth greatly because of the bridegroom's voice: this my joy is therefore fulfilled."
John 3:29

"I will walk within my house with a perfect heart . . . he, that worketh deceit shall not dwell within my house."
Psalm 101:2, 7

What a blessed promise this is to make as home is commenced! To have a "perfect heart" means a heart without blemish or defect. As used by our Lord, "perfect" implies imitation of God in doing good to the unworthy (Matthew 5:48). David himself was "a man after God's own heart." Thus to have a perfect heart indicates godliness of character. Because the best home is the one with God as its center and circumference, it is profitable to fashion a home on spiritual principles. Setting out together to journey through life as companions, bride and bridegroom can mold a beautiful home as they endeavor to walk with God. It is He alone who can enable them to have an honor where His honor dwelleth. Trying to walk with God outside the house will avail little if it does not correspond to one's walk within the house. To be a saint away from home and a devil at home, is hypocrisy.

"As for me and my house, we will serve the Lord." Joshua 24:15

Are you thinking of setting up house, or, recently married, have you just entered one? Have foresight, wise expenditure, and gifts of friends provided you with all that is necessary in the way of utensils and furniture? But can it be that in all your preparation and provision you have omitted to establish a family altar? Have you not learned that home life can only become beautiful and preserved from disaster, as those who form it give God His due? What Joshua meant by his declaration was that idolatry would not be tolerated by any within his house. All within were bound together by a solemn vow to worship and serve God, and God only. Has this been your decision?

"Seek ye first the kingdom of God."
Matthew 6:33
"Seek those things which are above."
Colossians 3:1

What constitutes the kingdom of God and those things which are above? Are they not conformity to Christ, devoutness to His service, faith which trusts God's Word, love which has God for its Author, Christ for its principle Object, and spiritual things for its chosen subjects? These are among the things above which saints enjoy and rejoice in.

As life is faced together, there may be anxiety now and again as to food and clothing. There will be practical problems confronting you. But the cure for all anxiety is trust in God's knowledge and care. His promise is that all that is necessary will be "added," thrown into the bargain so to speak, if He is given the first place in heart and home. When Jesus tells you to take no thought for the morrow, He does not mean that you are to be careless or negligent regarding the future. Anyone failing to make all justifiable provision for his own is worse than an infidel, Paul declares. What Jesus warns against is unbelieving anxiety. Putting God first, seeking the things above, result in God taking over our present and future needs. If in your recently established home life God's interests are being placed first, then your interests will become His first concern.

"Be ye kind one to another, tenderhearted, forgiving one another." Ephesians 4:32

What precious advice this is to follow, whether newly married, or more firmly established in the ways of home. It is not long before desires and personalities have a tendency to clash. What sorrow ensues if one or the other insists on his will being done. With differing characteristics and inclinations, there can only be harmony as both husband and wife deal in the commodity of kindness. They must enter into a give-and-take bargain.

The two lovely "bears" – *bear* and *forbear* – must always be present when purposes cross and conflicts arise. God knows, far too many homes are wrecked simply because one insisted on his or her rights and wishes. When selfishness rides roughshod over what the other proposes, it ruins the peace of home. Mutual kindness, consideration, and forbearance keep my home intact. Grace is promised to make us gracious and kind, so why not appropriate what God offers?

"Heirs together of the grace of life."
I Peter 3:7

What a sweeter, purer home life the nation would have if only newly wed couples would make this appealing promise the motto of their united life! The young husband, for example, would learn that his partner is not to be his slave or drudge, but his equal and companion. He would also understand his wife's limitations as the weaker vessel and not overburden her accordingly. Surely Peter's phrase, "heirs together," is one of the most expressive terms of the union and communion existing between husband and wife. How precious a sight it must be for the eyes of God to gaze down upon! Two blissful hearts, united in grace as well as in marriage, bowing together at the family altar, committing all that concerns their life and home to His tender care. Being heirs together implies that there is mutual understanding in all things. God grant the country many more homes like the one Peter depicts!

"Two are better than one . . . the one will lift up his fellow."
Ecclesiastes 4:9, 12

Together, two trusting hearts can prevail against any intruder, especially when God is the third Party and forms the three-fold cord that cannot be broken. In any companionship formed, God must be the unseen Partner, Instead of a bi-unity, it must be a *trinity*. Each of you will require the other, and both of you will certainly need God before you travel far along the highway of your wedded life. As multitudinous cares, trials, and sorrows arise, may you remember that two with God is always a majority. Let prayer, faith, and holiness produce that dual companionship which is ever the bulwark of a good home.

"Wives . . . husbands, as it is fit in the Lord." Colossians 3:18

The fitness Paul writes about is not according to the accepted and accustomed standards of society, but according to divine standards—"as it is fit in the Lord." A thoroughly Christian home, will not be characterized by unwarranted demands. Forceful and unloving husbands, bitter and inconsiderate wives, who act against a God-enlightened conscience, are certainly not "in the Lord." How many loving couples started out with high and happy hopes, but who met with sad disappointment at the bend of the road where unreasonable demands were made? Are these lines being read by two young hearts who have recently promised to love and cherish each other until parted by death? Well, take Paul's words and have them ever before you—*As it is fit in the Lord.* Such an arrestive motto will safeguard as well as sweeten your whole marital relationship as you turn the motto into a motive for living.

J. R. Miller in his devotional volume, *Silent Times*, has a telling chapter on "The Home Conversation" which all newlyweds ought to read. In fact, all who form a home could profit from the practical advice Dr. Miller gives. We take great pains in seeing that our house is well furnished, but we are not as careful and deliberate about household speech as we are about the choice of carpets and furniture. Tongues are not loving, tender, and cheerful in their speech as they should be. There must be a strong endeavor to keep out all incessant petty strife, if the home is to become the brightest and sweetest spot on earth to those who dwell within its walls. Conversation should always be elevating, enlightening, and enjoyable and not as unprofitable as the talk Job referred to when he said—

"Make my speech nothing worth."
                                                        Job 24:25
"Excellent speech becometh not a fool."
                                                Proverbs 17:7
"Let your speech be alway with grace, seasoned with salt." Colossians 4:6
"Sound speech, that cannot be condemned." Titus 2:8

Dr. Miller says that, "Home should inspire every tongue to speak its most loving words, yet there is in many families a great dearth of kind, affectionate speech . . . A stranger might mistake the home for a deaf-and-dumb institution, or for a hotel where strangers were together only for a passing season." Home conversation should be devoid of all sharp, angry, or unloving words. Speech must be governed, as James reminds us when he speaks of having a bridle on our tongue, so that no one will fly into a temper and utter bitter words at the smallest irritation.

Another aspect of home life which two young people who have set up their new home must prepare against is that of sorrow, which sooner or later will cloud their happiness. At first, it seems as if nothing could ever enter the newly fashioned home to disturb its joy. Household life flows softly on, then the day comes when sorrow lays its heavy hand upon hitherto happy hearts. Such an hour of initial grief is always a crucial one. If there is no strong bulwark against sorrow's fierce sea, then the unaccustomed grief will not work out its beneficent purpose. We read of those who were so overwhelmed by the death of a friend revered and loved that—

"They took up the body and buried it, and went and told Jesus." Matthew 14:12

In a grave they buried John, and in the heart of Jesus they buried their sorrow. To have Jesus as our Confidant means that we have One well able to protect and console our hearts when the first shadow falls across the home. Having Him, we also have the promise of His succor and relief. A Christless home goes to pieces when sorrow strikes. With the door shut on Christ, all peace and blessedness are shut out. Thus, when the lamp of earthly joy goes out, utter darkness prevails. But if Christ has been installed as the "Head of the House," then when the dark days come, it eases the mind to go in hope to Jesus and tell Him all about our trials and sorrows. He has promised to hear and help us when we cry in our need, and He certainly will.

A motto chosen by two young people as they set up a humble Christian home reads—

HERE WILL I SIT BEST!

Here is the secret of a happy home life. Because each loved Christ, there was that mutual desire to be *Christian* in all their ways. The motto meant the cultivation of a gracious, sweet disposition, which is one of the elements of a beautiful life, and also the manifestation of considerateness, the one toward the other. Having–

"Christ as the Head of the house
The Unseen Guest at every meal,
The silent Listener to every
conversation,"

means that there will be the constant display of tenderness, thoughtfulness, self-denial, and love.

A home which puts Christ first and is bathed in prayer never breaks apart. When the first family was formed, family prayer began, with the head of the family as the priest.

"I know him, that he will command his children and his household after him, and they shall keep the way of the Lord." Genesis 18:19

"There can be no true family life without family religion, and family religion is best sustained by family worship," says W. C. Proctor. The proverb has it that, "A home without prayer is like a house without a roof." Manifold promises are for those whose home life is permeated with prayer. "A family that prays together, stays together." Family prayer is "the bond of family love, the cement of domestic amity, and the sweetener of home life."

HUSBANDS

We now come to examine the component parts of a good Christian home, and we begin with the husband, to whom many Promises are given. Scripture makes it clear that Husbands–

Should have but one wife.
"A man . . . shall cleave unto his wife, and they shall be one flesh."
Genesis 2:23-24; Mark 10:6-8;
I Corinthians 7:2-4
Should have authority over the wife.
"Thy husband . . . shall rule over thee."
Genesis 3:16; I Corinthians 11:3;
Ephesians 5:23
Should have deep respect for the wife.
"Likewise, ye husbands . . . give honour unto the wife." I Peter 3:7
Should always love the wife.
"Husbands, love your wives . . . so love his wife." Ephesians 5:25, 33
Should have constant delight in the wife.
"Rejoice with the wife of thy youth."
Proverbs 5:18; Malachi 2:14, 15
Should have a life-long companionship with the wife.
"What God hath joined together, let not man put asunder." Matthew 19:3-9

Should always comfort the wife.
"Elkanah her husband said unto her, Hannah, why weepest thou?"
I Samuel 1:8
Should not leave the unbelieving wife.
"How knowest thou, O man, whether thou shalt save thy wife?"
I Corinthians 7:11-16
Should place Christ before the wife.
"If any man come to me, and hate not his . . . wife." Luke 14:26; Matthew 19:29
Good husbands are exemplified in Isaac and Elkanah (Genesis 24:67; I Samuel 1:4, 5), while *bad* husbands are portrayed by Solomon and Ahasuerus (I Kings 11:1; Esther 1:10, 11).

In His marvelous condescension, God offers Himself as a *Husband* to His believing people–
"Thy Maker is thine Husband."
Isaiah 54:5
What a precious promise this is! He is our nearest and dearest One, who loves us more than any other. As a husband is united to his wife and they become one, so God is closely united to us, and more deeply interested in us than any earthly relative could be. He has espoused us to Himself, has made full provision for all our needs, and has prepared a home for us above. May we be found confiding in Him and ardently longing for our union with Him in heaven. As our divine Husband, having loved us, He will love us unto the end.

WIVES

Wives also receive much notice in the Bible, and have promises they can claim as the husband's helpmate. Precepts regarding Wives are clear and explicit.
They were not to be selected from among the ungodly.
"Thou shalt not take a wife . . . of the daughters of the Canaanites."
Genesis 24:3; 26:34, 35; 28:1
They are to love their husbands.
"Teach the young women . . . and love their husbands." Titus 2:4
They are to reverence their husbands.
"The wife see that she reverence her husband." Ephesians 5:33
They are to be faithful to their husbands.
"Benevolence . . . the wife unto the husband . . . Let not the wife depart from her husband."
I Corinthians 7:3-5, 10
They are to be subject to their husbands.
"Thy husband . . . . he shall rule over

thee." Genesis 3:16; Ephesians 5:22, 24;
I Peter 3:1
They are to obey their husbands.
"Obedient to their husbands."
Titus 2:5; I Corinthians 14:34
*They are to remain until death
with their husbands.*
"The woman . . . is bound . . . to
her husband as long as he liveth."
Romans 7:2, 3
As to the numerous duties, obligations,
and responsibilities of wives, there are many
Scriptures to guide them aright as they
seek to fulfil their function.
*They should be adorned with
modesty and sobriety.*
"Whose adorning let it be . . . the
ornament of a meek and quiet spirit."
I Peter 3:3; I Timothy 2:9
They should manifest good works.
"Well reported of for good works."
I Timothy 6:10; 2:10
They should be virtuous.
"A virtuous woman is a crown to her
husband." Proverbs 12:4; 31:10, 12;
I Timothy 3:11
*They should be a blessing
to their husbands.*
"Whoso findeth a wife findeth a good
thing." Proverbs 18:22; 31:23
*They should have the confidence
of their husbands.*
"The heart of her husband doth safely
trust in her." Proverbs 31:11; 31:28
*They should be diligent,
prudent, kind to the poor.*
"Let her own works praise her in the
gates." Proverbs 31:13-31
*They should try to win their
unbelieving husbands.*
"The woman that hath an husband
that believeth not . . . save thy husband."
I Corinthians 7:13-16; I Peter 3:1, 2
*They should seek religious
instruction from their husbands.*
"If they will learn anything, let them
ask their husbands at home."
I Corinthians 14:35
Rachel and Leah, the wives of Jacob,
were conscious that God must be obeyed
and said to Jacob, "Whatsoever God hath
said unto thee, do" (Genesis 31:16). What
can be more noble than that of a good wife
seeking to strengthen a purpose the Lord
hath kindled in her husband's heart! Would
that we had more of such a noble order.
Portraits of good wives are before us in
the wife of Manoah, Ruth, Abigail, Elisabeth,

Mary, Priscilla, and Sarah. Bad wives are
exemplified in Delilah, Michal, Jezebel,
Zeresh, Job's wife, Herodias, and Sapphira.

FATHERS

As time goes by, in the goodness of God
husbands become *fathers*, and wives,
mothers. Thus we approach further home
relationships and the promises related to
them. First of all, let us consider the
FATHERS, who occupy considerable space
in the Bible. All that we can do at this
point is to select a few Father verses to
emphasize required fatherly qualities and
the promises connected thereto.
"Honour thy father." Exodus 20:12;
Matthew 15:4; 19:19; Mark 7:10
Parental respect, sadly decadent in modern
life, is strictly enforced throughout the Bible.
Physical and material blessings are promised
those who duly respect their parents. Needless to say, some fathers are unworthy of
any honor. Because of their godlessness and
lack of any religious influence in the home,
they fail in the true function of fatherhood.
They are fathers in name only. Yet the
Mosaic command does not carry any condition. It does not say, "Honor thy father
if he be a good, moral man." Whether
good or bad, we are to be *Christian* in our
treatment of those who gave us birth.
Can it be that you have been a little
lax or thoughtless in your obligation towards
your parents? Is there a heart somewhere
starved for a word of appreciation? When
your father is dead and gone, it will be
too late then to say, "Thank you!" Say it
now, and send him a token of your gratitude. Let *today* be your FATHER'S DAY,
when you will let your Dad know how deeply
indebted you are to him for all he has
been to you.
"We had our fathers of our flesh which
corrected us." Hebrews 12:9
Nescessary correction is never brutal but
always beneficial. Sparing the rod does not
save the child. Faults unrebuked and un-
punished develop into gross sins. We have
far too many spoiled children in these days
of a false reasoning about repression of
the young, both in our homes and in our
schools.
The central point of the context dealing
with our Heavenly Father's chastening is
that such correction never reaches a Christian by chance. God's corrections always
have a special, beneficial objective, namely,
the perfecting of His children in holiness.
This is why we must not forget the

loving exhortation –

"My son, despise not thou the chastening of the Lord, nor faint when thou art rebuked of him."

As our children profit by discipline and come to reverence a loving father who has the highest welfare of his chastened child at heart, in like manner we are to act toward "the Father of spirits" and live. He would be unkind, if He did not correct us in measure. Is divine correction yours? Then let it yield the promised, peaceable fruit of righteousness.

"The fathers have eaten a sour grape, and the children's teeth are set on edge."

Jeremiah 31:29; Ezekiel 18:2

This repeated dictum emphasizes the importance of individuality. While a great deal of sinning can be laid at the door of heredity, the Bible reveals that individuality has its message not only of awful responsibility, but also of glorious promise and of undying blessedness. Everyone is free to break with a saddening and miserable past. Grace can overcome inherited tendencies. Judgment, however, will not be ours for what we were born with. "Everyone shall die for his *own* iniquity." Wrapped up in the mystery of natural generation is the communication to others of desires and appetites, good or bad.

At the back of the descriptive saying of both Jeremiah and Ezekiel is the idea, *Like father, like son!* This is one reason why young, unmarried men should be urged to keep their record clean. Unborn generations are to be influenced by their godliness and chastity. As they are today, so will their offspring be tomorrow. The stream will correspond to its source.

As a father, Lot miserably failed in the mission of shaping the character of his children after righteousness. He was a weak man, and he chose to dwell in Sodom only because it was a wealthy city. He aimed at prosperity and position and his children married into the world and were ruined. When Lot saw disaster ahead, he tried to act the father's part in warning his children, but it was too late–"He seemed as one that mocked unto his sons in law" (Genesis 19:14).

Nell Warren Outlaw tells the story of a noble father who merited the respect and devotion of his son. The grief-stricken parent was sitting beside his dying child when the boy looked up into his father's face and said, "Dad, am I going to die?" For a moment the father could not speak; then he haltingly answered by posing another question, "Are you afraid to die, son?" The boy looked confidently into the face and replied, "No, Dad, not if God is like you."

"I was a father to the poor." Job 29:16

Job, affected by the miseries of the poor and willing to provide for their wants, is here self-styled "a father of the poor." In church history the term "Father" is applied to Christian leaders of the first centuries. Roman Catholic priests are called "Holy father"–which is somewhat sacrilegious, since the designation occurs but once in the Bible and is then applied only to God (John 17:11).

There is a sense in which all of us can manifest the fatherly qualities of love and compassion. Do you know of a fatherless child near at hand? It may be one who has never experienced a father's caress and companionship. Well, if you have no child of your own, here is an opportunity of bringing sunshine into a lonely life, one looking with longing eye at other children who seem to be so happy as "Daddy" romps and plays with them. Look around for someone you can father!

"Ye are of your father the devil."

John 8:44

Our Lord had no hesitation in naming the devil as the parent of a numerous, evil brood. In His discourse after the feast, Jesus had some stern things to say to the Pharisees who wanted to know who His Father was (8:18, 19). They professed to have God as their Father (8:41), but while His Fatherhood is clearly taught both in this chapter and throughout John's gospel, Jesus also spoke of the fatherhood of the devil, naming him as the father of lust, murder, and lies. Without apology, He told the Pharisees that they were the offspring of such a hellish father. No wonder those enraged children of the devil took up stones to kill Him!

God the Father–Satan a father! But then, Satan has ever been an ape of God. The Father of light blesses, the father of darkness blasts. Our Father in heaven is merciful, the father of hell is murderous. When earthly fathers follow the hellish father, their own children are robbed of those holy influences leading to the loving Father of our Lord Jesus Christ.

"I will be a father unto you."

II Corinthians 6:18

Here we have one of those conditional promises common to Scripture. To lay claim to God's fatherly provision and protection we must be prepared to break off all carnal connections, for carnality and spirituality cannot be reconciled. If our separation from worldly persons and pursuits brings with it persecution and ostracism, God is as near as a Father to comfort and protect.

That God holds a sacred estimation of fatherhood is evidenced by the fact that He often uses such a relationship to illustrate His feelings towards His own.

"Abba, Father." Galatians 4:5-7

Our Lord was particularly fond of the term "Father" as He addressed God or spoke about Him. As His "only begotten Son," Jesus lived near to His Father's heart and always sought to do those things pleasing to His Father.

When an earthly father dies, God offers to take his place and care for those who are left behind, and thus He speaks of Himself as the Father of the fatherless (Psalm 68:5). The best of fathers in the world are those who are fully separated from the world, and who, endeavoring to be free from an unequal yoke with unbelievers, know what it is to have the Lord God Almighty as a Father.

Life is ever fragrant in a home when a father, loving his Heavenly Father and striving to please Him in all his ways, so orders his home life as to give his children a beautiful conception of the love, sympathy, and protection of the Father above. The greatest responsibility of any father is to reflect the character of God. As to children, they should remember that they can only expect the full promise of God as they heed the words of Solomon –

"Hear thou, my son, and be wise . . . Hearken unto thy father that begat thee."
Proverbs 23:19

"Like as a father pitieth his children."
Psalm 103:13

"Your heavenly Father knoweth that ye have need of all these things."
Matthew 6:32

A father, mirroring the Father-heart of God, is different from one with a heart of stone. He knows how to pity his children in their sins and sorrows. While never winking at their shortcomings and lapses, he upbraids with love. Remembering their frailty, a wise father never imposes too heavy a load on his children.

It is thus that God stoops to our weakness, mighty as He is. He never condones sin in any of His children. Transgression is ever more horrible and grievous in His own than in the godless.

"Father! – to God Himself we cannot give
A holier name."

But, knowing our frame and remembering that we are but dust, our Father above makes all necessary and just allowances, and He bestows His pity where it is deserved. To merit His pity, however, we must fear Him, which does not mean cringing before Him as a despotic Father, but the exhibition of reverential trust and holy confidence in Him.

Because He is our Father who loves us, and has promised to care for us, we should be found trusting and acknowledging Him. We should believe that there is nothing too hard for Him to effect, nothing too great for Him to produce, nothing too good for Him to bestow upon His children.

MOTHERS

When a wife has the added relationship of *Mother*, what added responsibilities and joys become hers! The Bible has much to say about MOTHERS, and it records promises of all the strength, grace, and wisdom necessary for the exercise of true motherhood.

"Honour . . . thy mother."
Deuteronomy 5:16

Some of the greatest characters of the Bible and of history have testified to what they owe to godly, praying mothers. Abraham Lincoln once said, "God bless my mother. All I am or hope to be I owe to her." What a different nation ours would be if only we had more Christian mothers! It is but fitting that one of the most celebrated national events is MOTHER'S DAY, inaugurated to recall with gratitude a mother's love, sacrifice, and influence, and to express our love and thankfulness to the one giving us birth and influencing our life. Ruskin says –

"Home is the place of peace . . . And wherever a true Mother comes, this home is always round her . . . Home is wherever she is."

It is to be hoped that you are not among those callous hearts who have a lonely, neglected, almost forgotten mother somewhere, whose heart is so hungry for a token of loving remembrance. Do not wait for the annual Mother's Day to come round to send her a bouquet of flowers with your love. Send one often with your expression of undying love and remembrance.

"A foolish man despiseth his mother."
Proverbs 15:20

"A child . . . bringeth his mother to shame." Proverbs 29:15

"There is a generation that . . . doth not bless their mother." Proverbs 30:11

"Her children arise up, and call her blessed." Proverbs 31:28

King Lemuel had a good mother, one he loved and revered. That is why he gives us the most appealing portrait of a perfect mother ever sketched. From her pure lips Lemuel learned that kings and queens must strive to maintain personal chastity. By her example, as well as by exhortation, she likewise urged her royal son to honor good women. Truly the price of such a wonderful mother *is* above rubies! All the works, children, and husband of such a God-fearing wife and mother praise her.

Godliness makes for the enrichment of home life. The finest mothers in the world are those who love the Lord and the Bible and who, amid all the cares, trials, and sorrows of the home, know how to steal away to Jesus and confide in Him (Genesis 25:22). As a mother, are you virtuous, and do you have a husband and children who can justly praise you for all you are and do? Then you must be thrice happy!

"I arose a mother in Israel." Judges 5:7

The distinguished wife of Lapidoth was endowed with a prophetic spirit and was therefore qualified to exercise all the functions of a chief judge in Israel (4:4). Dwelling between Ramah and Bethel under a palm tree, the Israelites came to her for judgment. It would appear as if she was the first female appointed by God to rule His people. How well she was equipped and how faithfully she discharged the duties of ruler! Her triumphant ode is one of the most sublime in literature.

As a war cry, it is most applicable in the dark days of any international conflict. Mothers are always heavy sufferers when war afflicts a nation. What sorrow over separations, suspense, vigils, grief and heartbreaks are theirs! In the hour of Israel's national need, God had His woman ready, and what a true mother she became to all in Israel. As our nation is beset by foes within and without, it will be its mothers who will suffer most if war-clouds break.

"Now there stood by the cross of Jesus his mother." John 19:25

Faithful mothers never forsake a cross.

Born to carry burdens, they shoulder them without complaint. Is there not something arresting about the attitude and position of Mary? The One dying on that cruel cross was her Son, the Child of her womb. Hers had been the privilege of bearing that illustrious Saviour. Now, in the moment of His intense agony, where is she? She *stood* by the cross. As the drooping eyes of Jesus lighted upon His mother standing by the cross His disciples had forsaken. He must have felt deeply for her. It was Mary's grim determination not to give way to her feelings until it was all over. For a moment the Father had deserted His Son, hence the poignant cry, "Why hast *thou* forsaken me?" But Mary maintained her sorrowful vigil and *stood* there. Do we not praise God for all the praying, heroic mothers Mary represents?

Are you among the number who can bless God for the piety and kindliness of a mother who not only stood by the cross, but never rested until you received the One who died upon that cross as your personal Saviour?

"Who is my mother . . . Behold my mother." Matthew 12:48, 49

Jesus was ever mindful of the mother who gave Him birth. As He died, His last consideration was that of the future welfare of Mary. This is why in commending her to John, He said, "Behold thy mother" (John 19:27). And from that moment John's home sheltered Mary. But in the context before us, our Lord reveals a new, privileged, and promised relationship. Jesus was notified that His mother desired to speak with Him, but He answered, "Who is my mother?" Then, stretching forth His hands towards His disciples, He said, "Behold my mother . . . whosoever shall do the will of my Father which is in heaven, the same is . . . my mother."

Have you, as a mother, entered this new and intimate relationship? Are you His disciple? Looking upon you, can Jesus say, "Behold my mother"? There is no relationship so dear and sacred as that of motherhood. To have those around who love and bless you for your motherliness must be a thrill. But such feelings are not comparable to those that pulsate in the heart of one joined unto the Lord. Are you in the family of faith, bound to Christ eternally? If so, then your sweet home will be as heaven's twin sister.

"The mother of harlots."
Revelation 17:5

The awful abominations of Romanism and of Babylon – the fountain head of all idolatry and corruption – have each been spoken of as "the whore, the harlot." Whoever or whatever this foul "mother" will be, there is evidence that she is to gather unto herself all forms of false religions. "Sitting upon many waters" implies that she is to acquire to herself a sphere of world influence, using them for unholy ends.

Here we have the degradation of a sacred term – *mother:* "the mother of harlots." Surely there is nothing so abhorrent as one who has prostituted her functions and privileges (Proverbs 23:27, 28; 30:20). No wonder John was smitten with wonder as he saw this woman drunk with the blood of saints and of martyrs. Do we pray and labor as we ought to for the salvation of those mothers, and potential mothers, who are lost in sin and shame? Never despair of the most abandoned, degraded woman, because Christ is able to raise her from the dunghill and place her among His princesses.

"The mother of us all." Galatians 4:26

As a figure of speech, "mother" is applied to a variety of objects, such as the earth, queens, cities, to the Antichrist, and to the Church of God. As used by Paul, the term speaks of the Church triumphant in heaven. The true Church is only "mother" to the "free." Unless delivered from sin and its curse, we are in bondage and not spiritually fit to receive and experience the mother care of Him who is the Head of the Church.

Eve, another type of the Church, is referred to as "the mother of all living," and the Church of the living God is only the mother of those who have been made alive in Christ. Such a spiritual mother has no dead children. If a mother according to the flesh, are you certain that you are a member of the Church which is His body? As you mother others, is yours the joy that comes through the mothering influence of the Jerusalem which is above? May each of us nestle near our heavenly Mother!

"As one whom his mother comforteth, so will I comfort you." Isaiah 66:13

What a precious promise this is for all our hearts! God, not only as our Father, but as our Mother also. A mother is the queen of comfort. As the personification of tenderness, she can enter into her child's grief. When her boy or girl is overwhelmed by little troubles and sorrows, it is mother, rather than to the father of the home, to whom the child turns for consolation. A kiss on the brow, a hug to the breast, and a gentle rocking in loving arms provide an infallible cure for distressed baby hearts. Of all comforters, the child loves best the mother.

Is it not condescending for God to promise to act the mother's part? Did He not remind Israel that He would dandle her on His knees and comfort her as one comforted by a mother? He it is who takes His handkerchief and dries our tear-stained eyes. Even though our sighs and sobs are our readiest utterances, He never wearies of our approach. Where is the true mother who is weary of the child's oft coming for consolation? The tragedy of life is that so many sorrow-laden hearts meet their trials without a knowledge of the One who offers Himself as Comforter, dearer than the best of mothers.

Manly virtues and womanly graces meet in Him. All that is best, holiest, sweetest, and most gracious in a noble man, and also in pure-hearted women, can be found in our Lord, who is the source of all. "Male and female created He them," and the characteristic feature of both are resident in His loving heart. He fuses together in His own adorable person the strong, tender, brooding, comforting, sacrificial love of the woman. This is why both man and woman turn to the same Lord for salvation and sanctification. Both are part of Him.

PARENTS

Jointly, fathers and mothers, are known as PARENTS, whose joint obligations also find mention in the Bible, and for whom there are explicit promises to be claimed and precepts to obey. If you are a parent, think of these most pertinent Scriptures. Parents are obligated –

To receive their children as from God.
"The children which God hath graciously given thy servant." Genesis 4:1; 33:5; I Samuel 1:27; Psalm 127:3; Ruth 4:13
To instruct them in
God's Word and judgments.
"Statutes . . . teach them thy sons."
Deuteronomy 4:9; 11:19;
Isaiah 38:19; Joel 1:3
To command them to obey God.
"Ye shall command your children to observe to do, all the words of this law." Deuteronomy 32:46; I Chronicles 28:9
To pray for their spiritual
and physical welfare.

"Give unto Solomon my son a perfect heart." I Chronicles 29:19; Job 1:5

"David therefore besought God for the child." II Samuel 12:16; John 4:46, 49

To bring them to Christ.

"Suffer little children, and forbid them not, to come unto me." Matthew 19:13-15

To train them to serve the Lord.

"Train up a child in the way he should go." Proverbs 22:6

Bring them up in the nurture and admonition of the Lord." Ephesians 6:4

To correct them when necessary.

"He that loveth his son chasteneth him betimes." Proverbs 13:24; 19:18; 23:13; 29:17; Hebrews 12:7

To provide for them.

"If any provide not for his own . . . he is worse than an infidel."

I Timothy 5:8; II Corinthians 12:14; Job 42:15; Luke 11:13

To love, bless, and pity them.

"To love their children." Titus 2:4

"Isaac blessed Jacob."

Hebrews 11:20; Genesis 48:15

"Like as a father pitieth his children."

Psalm 103:13

When parents love God and seek to bring their children up in His fear and are faithful in the discharge of their parenthood, then they are blessed by their children—

"Her children arise up, and call her blessed." Proverbs 31:28; Isaiah 65:23

CHILDREN

As to CHILDREN themselves, the promise of them and promises connected with them occupy a most prominent part in the Bible. Children, who are a heritage of the Lord, have claims and responsibilities all their own. Coleridge wrote of Children—

"God's own image fresh from Paradise,
Hallows the helpless form of infancy."

First of all, perhaps a classification of children passages might enable us to realize our attitude toward the young, and also something of their mission in the world. Under the previous section on parents, some of these passages were cited.

Children of believers have divine blessing.

"God said . . . I will establish my covenant with thy son for an everlasting covenant." Genesis 17:9, 19

"Thy seed, to love the Lord thy God."

Deuteronomy 30:6

"I will pour my spirit upon thy seed, and my blessing upon thine offspring."

Isaiah 44:4, 5

"For the promise is unto you, and to your children." Acts 2:38

"Thou shalt be saved, and thine house."

Acts 16:31

"Suffer the little children to come unto me." Mark 10:14

"All thy children shall be taught of the Lord." Isaiah 54:13

"Else were your children unclean; but now are they holy." I Corinthians 7:14

"They are the seed of the blessed of the Lord." Isaiah 65:23

"Blessed is the man that feareth the Lord . . . his seed shall be mighty upon earth." Psalm 112:1, 2

"His seed are blessed after him."

Proverbs 20:7

"Children . . . as arrows are in the hand of a mighty man." Psalm 127:3-5

Children should be a joy to their parents.

"A wise son maketh a glad father."

Proverbs 10:1

"My son, if thine heart be wise, my heart shall rejoice."

Proverbs 23:15, 16, 24, 25

"I rejoiced greatly that I found of thy children walking in truth." II John 4

Children are exhorted to be obedient to parents.

What is given to the Jew applies equally to the Christian. Promises of temporal blessing annexed to the fifth commandment (Exodus 20:12) are carried over into this Church Age.

"My son, keep thy father's commandments." Proverbs 6:20-22; 1:8, 9

"Because ye have obeyed the commandment of Jonadab your father."

Jeremiah 35:18, 19

"Children obey your parents . . . That it may be well with thee."

Ephesians 6:1-3; Colossians 3:20

As a Child, Christ was an Example for all children to follow

"He was subject unto them."

Luke 2:51, 52

"Woman, behold thy son."

John 19:26, 27

The proverb has it, "Happy is he that is happy in his children." How happy parents are when their children are loving, thoughtful, and obedient! How true it is that "there is beauty all around, when there's love at home"! How distressed and divided a home becomes when a child or children grow up selfish, unkind, and disobedient! Shakespeare in his *King Lear* describes these heartbreak children—

Ingratitude, thou marble-hearted fiend,
More hideous, when thou show'st thee in a child,
Than the sea-monster!

How sharper than a serpent's tooth it is
To have a thankless child!

Among numerous promises of children and promised blessings contacted with them, we indicate a few all parents should meditate upon—
"He will also bless the fruit of thy womb." Deuteronomy 7:13
"Thou shalt know also that thy seed shall be great." Job 5:25
"The children of thy servants shall continue." Psalm 102:28
"He maketh the barren woman . . . to be a joyful mother of children."
Psalm 113:9
"Thy children like olive plants round about thy table." Psalm 128:3
"His children are blessed after him."
Proverbs 20:7
"That it may go well with thee, and with thy children after thee."
Deuteronomy 4:40; 5:29
"The seed of the wicked shall be cut off." Psalm 37:28
"A good man leaveth an inheritance to his children." Proverbs 13:22; 11:21
"His children shall have a place of refuge." Proverbs 14:26
"He will command his children and his household after him." Genesis 18:19
Grace N. Crowell wrote this prayer for parents—
"I have a child to rear, Lord God, I ask
Thy help in doing my great, blessed task!

Let us look a little more closely at some of these promises, making for a more wholesome child-life.
"Children are an heritage of the Lord."
Psalm 127:3
In reply to Esau's question regarding the children accompanying Jacob, Jacob said, "These are the children which God hath graciously given thy servant." Christian parents agree with Jacob and Solomon that children come as heaven's gifts. But children are only as arrows in the hand of a mighty man and only bring happiness to the father whose quiver is full of them when they grow up for the Lord. John Evelyn of the sixteenth century, who lost his dear child, left this testimony—
"For such a child I bless God in whose

bosom he is!
May I and mine become as this little child!
While children come from God, since He is the Author of all life, the tragedy is that multitudes of them grow up utterly godless in life. Can your parents speak of you as an heritage of the Lord? Born of God-fearing parents, who prayed for you before you saw the light of day, are you living in such a way as to please God who gave you life, and to gladden the hearts of those who nurtured you through early years? Children from God should be godly.
"His children are blessed after him."
Proverbs 20:7
How many children there are who owe their material prosperity to a father who coupled integrity with industry! A stranger to anything dishonest, success came his way, enabling him to leave others provided for. Have you entered into a spiritual and material inheritance? Have you desires, a disposition, and possessions which a good father made possible? Well, it is your obligation so to use all you are and have for right ends so that others will be blessed after you. Unborn generations will be influenced by your present life. "No man liveth unto himself." Influence is never neutral. Each of us are presently sowing seeds that will bear a good or evil harvest in others who will follow us. If you are presently blessed because of godly parents, determine so to live that you will leave behind you footprints on the sands of time.
"I will pour my spirit upon thy seed, and my blessing upon thine offspring."
Isaiah 44:3
This is a promise every worthy parent seeks to claim. We are not long in discovering that our children do not have the Spirit of God by nature. Original or inbred sin is not long in appearing, but when it does, our fears for the salvation of our children are banished by the Word that came to the patriarch, "Fear not, O Jacob, my servant." Because our great Heavenly Father takes pleasure in the prayers of fathers and mothers, He will hear your request for the regeneration of your children.
"Children . . . live long on the earth."
Ephesians 6:1, 3
When it comes to honoring our parents, no condition is attached. Whether they are in the Lord or not, we have to honor them. Godless they may be, yet because they gave us birth, we must ever respect them. The

double promise of the commandment before us is full of import –

"That it may be well with thee,
And thou mayest live long on the earth."

Disobedient, unthankful children who constantly dishonor their parents often beggar themselves and shorten their own days. Are you enjoying the first commandment with promise? If these lines are being read by a young person who has the tendency to be too independent, and who feels that Father and Mother are behind the times – too old-fashioned and antiquated – then pause and ponder. "Obey and honor," mean happiness and life, and also pleasure for the Lord (Colossians 3:20).

"Fatherless children, I will preserve them alive." Jeremiah 49:11

Among the most interesting exhibits displayed in the Moody Museum, Chicago, is the old Bible of D. L. Moody's mother. Reposing in its glass case, it is open at this page, and alongside the verse before us is a cross. When Mrs. Moody lost her husband and was left with seven children to care for, she claimed this promise for the dark and difficult days ahead.

It may be that you are fatherless, and motherless, too. The comforts and delights of the old home have gone. Or can it be that this paragraph is being read by a widow who has the care of fatherless children? God's promise of preservation is for you to claim – that is, if you know Him as the Father of the fatherless and as the Saviour of sinners.

"A little child shall lead them."
Isaiah 11:6

When Christ returns to earth, the animal creation is to be so transformed that the young will have no fear of destruction. Then, a den of lions will be as safe as a playroom. Isaiah's much quoted phrase, however, can be used in various ways. Often children lead their elders in humility and innocence. With a little child on His knee, Jesus taught those around Him a much needed lesson on *humility*. It is not the first time that a parent has been led by the simple prayers and faith of a child to the feet of the crucified One. When brought up in good surroundings, children truly love the stories of Jesus, and as they turn to Him, they have an unaffected way of speaking about Him that causes older people to think. But returning to the interpretation of Isaiah's description of the Millennium, is it not blessed to know that the Lord is going to make the world a safe place for the dear children to live in?

"Behold I and the children which God hath given me." Hebrews 2:11

"The God of thy father . . . who shall bless thee . . . with blessing of the breasts and of the womb."
Genesis 49:25, Deuteronomy 7:13

"She shall be saved in childbearing."
I Timothy 2:15

What unbounded joy will be the portion of completed circles as they gather around the Lord in yonder glory! To know that not one is missing will be cause for eternal praise. How comforting it is to know that there are no children – who died before coming to the years of responsibility and accountability – in hell. Because their Adamic sin was covered by the blood of Jesus, He took their unstained hearts to be with Himself.

The tragedy is that so many family circles are presently broken. Parents are saved – children unsaved. The old-fashioned religion of godly parents is too strait-laced for children who feel they have outgrown the faith of mother and father. Are you heartbroken over the lack of spiritual desires on the part of your children? Then take heart from the fact that God hears and answers prayer. Plead on for that girl or boy still out of the fold, and sooner than you expect the God who hears and answers prayer will rejoice your heart and complete your circle in grace.

"Children . . . let them praise the name of the Lord." Psalm 148:12, 13

The psalmist in his "Hallelujah" psalm did not exclude the girls and boys. The paean of praise ascending from all God's work would not be perfect without children's voices. How happy is the home where the young love to sing God's praises! Enthusiasm for the things of God rejoices the hearts of parents.

"How blessed the man whose treasures rare,
Are 'living jewels' – children fair."

It may be that because of His desire to have infant praises in the chorus above, God takes some of the lambs to be with Himself. In these days when the TV, radio, and movies have such a strong fascination for the young and they quickly pick up trashy songs, it is to be hoped that you are keeping your children from worldly things. Hymns learned in childhood days have a way of sticking with one through life. Do not rob God of the praise of the young. Strive to teach infant voices to proclaim their early blessings on His name. Instruct them in all that pertains to godliness and you will have no regrets. Do you remember the lines of C. H. Spurgeon? –

> Ere a child has reached to seven
> Teach him all the way to heaven;
> Better still the work will thrive
> If he learns before he's five.

HOME

As to the HOME which parents and children fashion, the Bible holds out many Promises for the earthly nest. James Montgomery in his poem "Home" so beautifully described –

> "There is a spot of earth supremely blest,
> A dearer, sweeter spot than all the rest."

"Thou shalt know that thy tabernacle shall be a peace." John 5:24
"He blesseth the habitation of the just."
Proverbs 3:33
"The house of the righteous shall stand."
Proverbs 12:7; 14:11
"She that tarried at home divided the spoil." Psalm 68:12
Possibly David was drawing on his experience at Ziklag when he wrote the above line. Here is the full record –

> "As his part that goeth down to the battle is, so shall his part be that tarrieth by the stuff; they shall part alike."
> I Samuel 30:24

Is it your responsibility to stay at home caring for "the stuff"? Public life may have more change and glamor about it than the humdrum duties of home. Perhaps your husband is active in Christian work, whose service takes him from home a great deal, and you long for more of his company. It may be that you long to be more conspicuous in the Master's service, but there is little freedom from the care of children and home duties. Do not be discouraged. It is your devotion to home that helps to make the public work of your husband possible, and at the Judgment Seat when rewards are bestowed, the "spoil" will be divided.

> "He said to the ruler of this house, Bring these men home." Genesis 43:18

This is the first reference to "home" in the Bible. "House," meaning all Noah's loved ones and possessions, occurs for the first time in Genesis 7:1. Joseph would feel very much at home as all his brothers gathered around the table. Is it not the desire of our heavenly Joseph to bring us all to our "long home" (Ecclesiastes 12:5). And Christ's *At Home* day is not far away. Presently, we are "at home in the body." But before long, reunion will be ours, just as Joseph was happy to have his own around him in his Egyptian home. "Where I am, there ye may be also" (John 14:3).

> "Ye brought it home. I did blow upon it." Haggai 1:9

The Lord had some caustic things to say about people who could spend plenty on their lovely houses, but who were content with a shack of a place for the worship of His Name. Judgment, however, fell upon those who prided themselves upon their ceiled houses. The Lord blew upon their coveted possessions. What have you brought home? Are you proud of your costly furniture, rugs, pictures, antiques and rare editions? Have you spent more on these than on God? Beware lest He blow upon your home gods! Except the Lord builds – and controls – your home, you labor in vain in trying to build it (Psalm 127:1).

> "Keepers at home." "Shew pity at home." Titus 2:5; I Timothy 5:4; Habakkuk 2:5

Pious homes, made possible by those who love God and His Word, form the nation's greatest asset. When home life declines, so does the influence of the nation. Many a family has gone to pieces simply because parents have neglected their home and children. Parenthood involves sacrifices, and in order that young lives might be shaped and molded aright, a good deal of public life (even if one is fitted for it) must be lightly undertaken. Tragic results accrue from the keeping of other vineyards and neglecting our own. Keeping house and showing piety at home may not carry the glare and popularity of social or club work, but it does result in the production of young lives who are well guarded to face the temptations and trials of life as they reach them.

> "Come home with me, and refresh thyself." I Kings 13:7

Turning aside from the direct interpretation of this passage, we make the application that home is not merely a place to eat, drink, and sleep in. We are certainly grateful for comfortable homes and for all the temporal and material refreshment they provide, but a good home should offer mental and spiritual refreshment, as well as material benefits. Yours is a poor home if all you can offer those who enter it is a hearty meal. When you invite friends to visit your home, do they feel when they come to leave that you have given them something more satisfying than a good dinner? Do they leave knowing that they have received a spiritual stimulus? Has your home a spiritual atmosphere about it that charms those who sit at your table? Do friends who love to visit you, not merely for the fine table you spread but for the refreshment of mind, and spirit they exercise, bless God for such a home? To speak sweetly and naturally of the things of the Lord is more beneficial than serving cocktails.

"Go home . . . and tell." Mark 5:19

The maniac of Gadara, marvelously delivered of his unclean spirit and restored to normal manhood, besought Jesus, his Emancipator, that he might follow Him. The earnest request was refused, however, because Christ knew that this demon-possessed man could do more effective work among his own relatives and friends. The one-time maniac wanted to remain with Christ and preach, but he was told to go home and preach. Reversely, the man who was commissioned to preach asked to go home and bid farewell to his friends, but Christ forbade him (Luke 9:61, 62).

Home is often the most difficult place in which to witness for Christ. Somehow it is easier to speak to strangers about Him. Has your life been transformed? Have you been made the recipient of the Saviour's power? Then let the Holy Spirit make you a *home* missionary first. Try to win your own kith and kin for Christ. By lip and life recommend Him to those who are nearest and dearest to you. If God cannot use you in your home, there is little likelihood of Him using you outside it.

"At home there is as death."

Lamentations 1:20

In God's contest with Pharaoh, the last plague with its death of the first-born was a time of universal grief. Egypt became a nation with drawn blinds. "There was not a house where there was not one dead" (Exodus 12:30). Taking our world as a whole, we realize that death-plagued homes are on the increase. In times of wide-spread war, countless numbers of fathers and sons leave home, never to return. In peace time, cars, planes, trains, plagues, and diseases claim a colossal toll of life, leaving widows, fatherless children, and orphans to wage a battle against poverty. Has death shadowed your home? Has your heart been emptied of

a treasure? Well, you have the promise of divine comfort and provision, and the assurance that in your vacant heart is One whose presence is real. Jesus is the Friend death cannot rob you of. In the day of your adversity, consider Him (Ecclesiastes 7:14). As for your precious dead who died in Christ, they are with Him.

"If they will learn . . . ask . . . at home." I Corinthians 14:35

In public gatherings, the women were not allowed to seek interpretations of the tongues used, but were to ask their husbands when they got home the significance of what was said. The enjoined silence then was in no way connected with public witness by women, but was a matter of interrogation. Whatever they desired to know had to be learned at home, where, in privacy, the husband explained the message of the unknown tongue for the enlightenment and edification of his wife.

The broader application of this asking at home suggests its educative value. Learn at home! Many of us have profited by what we learn in "The College of the Home." Family life offers a liberal education. Through daily contact the lessons of patience, forbearance, unselfishness, and consideration are learned. As we learn by asking, there are questions we can ask our dear ones that we would hesitate to ask a school teacher. A godly mother, fully instructed in the Scriptures, adds considerably to her child's knowledge of life and things.

"From a child thou hast known the holy scriptures." II Timothy 3:15

"Man goeth to his long home."

Ecclesiastes 12:5

Jesus spoke of heaven as "the Father's home" and it becomes more of a home as our early homes are broken up and scattered to the four winds. Many of us have more ties binding us to the unseen home than to the seen and the temporal. Sin, sorrow, and death destroy our earthly home, but heaven can never be ravaged by such destructive influences.

What constitutes a home? Is it not love and harmony and godliness? Heaven is our "long home," and perfect harmony prevails therein for all are at one with each other and with the Lord. Hell spells eternal homelessness. It is to be hoped that all within your home are children of God carrying the assurance of the blissful home beyond the skies.

FATHERLESS

Still dealing with those promises related to the "marital realm," we come to those the fatherless can appropriate. It is somewhat surprising to find how much the Bible has to say about those who are orphaned. Both the character and companionship of children are seriously impaired when mother or father, or both, are removed by death. But God has many heartening promises for those thus bereft. The fatherless are—

The recipients of divine mercy.

"In thee the fatherless findeth mercy."
Hosea 14:3

The objects of divine care and protection.
"Jehovah . . . a father of the fatherless." Psalm 68:5

"Thou art a helper of the fatherless . . . To judge the fatherless."
Psalm 10:14, 18; Deuteronomy 10:18
"Defend the poor and the fatherless."
Psalm 82:3; Isaiah 1:17
"Ye shall not afflict any . . . fatherless child." Exodus 22:23; Isaiah 10:1-3
"I will be a swift witness against . . . those that oppress the fatherless."
Malachi 3:5
"Pure religion . . . to visit the fatherless." James 1:27; Jeremiah 5:28, 29
"The fatherless . . . shall eat and be satisfied." Deuteronomy 14:29
"I delivered the poor that cried, and the fatherless." Job 29:12; Jeremiah 7:6, 7
"Oppress not . . . the fatherless."
Zechariah 7:10; Exodus 22:22; Proverbs 23:10
"Thy fatherless children . . . I will preserve them." Jeremiah 49:11
"Cursed be he that perverteth the judgment . . . of the fatherless." Deuteronomy 27:19; 24:17; see Proverbs 23:10; Jeremiah 22:3; Ezekiel 22:7; Psalm 94:6

The *fatherless* is used typically of Zion in affliction—

"Remember, O Lord, what is come upon us . . . we are fatherless."
Lamentations 5:1, 3
"If I have lifted up my hand against the fatherless." Job 31:21

In his affluent days, Job's fatherly heart felt for those who had been orphaned. He speaks of those who overwhelm the fatherless, of the arms of the fatherless being broken, of the driving away of the ass of the fatherless (6:27; 22:9; 24:3, 9; 31:17). In his defence, Job protects his innocence in these respects. His morsel had not been eaten alone but shared with those who had

no father to provide for them. And in his sympathy Job stands out as a fitting type of our Heavenly Father, who is ever willing to share His bounty with the needy.

"Son, thou art ever with me, and all that I have is thine." Luke 15:31

When you meet a fatherless child whose life and home are somewhat empty, help all you can, and above all tell the sorrowful one of Him who is both able and willing to undertake.

"Thou art a helper of the fatherless."
Psalm 10:14

Has your earthly father been taken from you, and are you somewhat fearful as you face life without the care, protection, and fatherly counsel you came to depend upon? Be of good cheer! Here is One who has promised to help you, and to meet your every need. He is also your Judge, ready to defend the fatherless against those who would take a mean advantage of them. What must be made clear, however, is the fact that God can only be expected to function toward the fatherless as promised if they commit their ways to Him. Our Father in heaven must be loved and obeyed if those without earthly fathers desire to claim His promised provision and protection. His grace and guidance must be sought through His beloved Son. It is only thus that any of us, fatherless or otherwise, can appropriate the sympathy and sustenance of Him "who is the God and Father of our Lord Jesus Christ."

"A father of the fatherless."
Psalm 68:5

Has not Jesus reminded us in most exquisite language that the death of a lonely sparrow is noticed by our Heavenly Father? Responsible as He is for all life, surely He is able to care for those without parents! When death robs us of our loved ones, has He not promised to take us up?

What is the function of a true father? Do not his children rejoice in his companionship? What a refuge his friendship is! When others misunderstand, he understands. When others grieve us, he throws his strong arm around us and soothes our troubled heart. In our perplexities, father is at hand to guide us. How clever and ready he is to straighten out our problems! But when death removes him, somehow our light goes out. Yet there is Another ready to step into father's place and to be all, and more than all, than the one we have loved long since and lost awhile.

"In thee the fatherless findeth mercy."
Hosea 14:3

In this sweet promise there is an excellent reason for casting away all other confidences and relying upon God alone. When a child is left without a natural protector, He steps in and becomes the Guardian. Mercy is spoken of as the sympathizing, pitying goodness of God manifested to the lonely, wretched, and needy. It is seen specially in the gift of Christ, and in His great eternal salvation for the guilty. It is this mercy which all the fatherless, as all other sinners, stand in need of. Often the removal of an earthly father brings the children to a realization of their need of divine mercy. The writer recalls a Scottish family, the father of which was killed at work. When his body was brought home, four fatherless boys knelt around the casket and gave themselves to God. Sometimes the world has little sympathy for those who are left alone. There is the axiom—

"Laugh, and the world laughs with you,
Weep, and you weep alone."

All lonely, disconsolate hearts, however, can find in God one who truly cares. In all our affliction, He is afflicted.

"There is no place where earth's sorrows are more felt, Than up in heaven."
"Pure religion and undefiled . . . visit the fatherless." James 1:27

Keeping ourselves unspotted from the world, in respect to its tainted pleasures and pursuits, is only one aspect of pure religion. Another is that we are to go out into the world, visiting and relieving the fatherless and widows. How often do your feet carry you into a home or an institution where the fatherless are found? Are you a visitor of love, bearing in your hands a few necessities of life a fatherless child may need, and a message of cheer on your lips? Children bereaved of parents find it easier to believe in a Father above the bright, blue sky when someone with a kind, loving heart and face comes their way. God is not here in a human form to visit orphans and widows who need His succor. He counts on your hands and feet. Thus when you feel impelled to call on the needy to assist them spiritually and materially, you are visiting in His stead. You may never be able to preach an eloquent sermon, but grace can be yours to run errands of mercy for your Father above, who ever rewards those who offer the thirsty a cup of water in His Name.

It is not surprising to discover that our tender, compassionate God has included WIDOWS in His great promise box.

"Ye shall not afflict any widow . . . I will surely hear their cry."
Exodus 22:21, 22
"He doth execute judgment of . . . the widow." Deuteronomy 10:18; 14:29; 16:11; Psalm 68:5
"The Lord relieveth the widow."
Psalm 146:9
"He will establish the border of the widow." Proverbs 15:25
"Let their widows trust in me."
Jeremiah 49:11
"Plead for the widow." Isaiah 1:17
"I will be a swift witness . . . against those that oppress the widow."
Malachi 3:5
"I caused the widow's heart to sing."
Job 29:13
"If I have caused the eyes of the widow to fail." Job 31:16
"Their widows were neglected in the daily ministrations." Acts 6:1
"Honour widows that are widows indeed." I Timothy 5:3-5
"To visit the widows in their affliction." James 1:27

Commendable widows who were conspicuous for the devotion to God's service, are the widow of Zarephath who cared for Elijah (I Kings 17:8-24), Anna, who served God with fastings and prayers night and day (Luke 2:36-38), the poor widow who cast into the treasury all her living (Mark 12:41-44), and the old widows who diligently followed every good work (I Timothy 5:9-10). Typically, a *widow* is used of a desolate condition (Isaiah 47:8,9; Revelation 18:7; Luke 18:1-7), and of Zion in captivity (Lamentations 1:1).

Three classes of widows are to be distinguished.

1. Ordinary widows, referred to in the majority of the verses above.
2. Widows "indeed," that is, those who were destitute and in need of church relief.
3. Presbyteral widows, those over 60 years of age, who had had some form of Church service.

"Ye shall not afflict any widow."
Exodus 22:22

Widows received the utmost consideration and care under Mosaic Law. That is why the single brother of a husband dying without children was commanded to marry his widow. Two motives were behind this necessary enactment.

1. The continuation of estates in the same family.
2. The perpetuation of a man's name in Israel.

It was deemed a misfortune for a man to die without an heir and for his inheritance to pass into another family. That this law extended to more distant relations of the same line is proven by the example of Ruth, who married Boaz after she had been refused by a nearer kinsman. With this consideration for bereaved wives before us, surely we are right in affirming that any widow who is the Lord's can count upon His comfort in grief, His presence in loneliness, His defense in exposure, His provision in need.

"Elijah was sent . . . unto a woman that was a widow." Luke 4:36

"Behold I have commanded a widow woman to sustain thee." I Kings 17:8-24

Elijah's visit to this widow at Zarephath proves that God's ways are not our ways. We would have sent so conspicuous a prophet as Elijah to those who were affluent and able to care for a hungry man. But no, God sent His servant to a poor widow who had a struggle to make ends meet. God bless the widows who cheer many a preacher's heart! The writer remembers one who lived in almost semi-poverty. What a lonely life was hers! Yet she loved the ministry of the Word, and ever and anon out of her scant pension she would wrap a bill in a tract and slip it into my hand. That God has a way of multiplying what little godly widows have, especially when they are willing to share their meagre possessions with others, is evidenced by the miracle Elijah wrought when he saw to it that the widow's barrel of meal wasted not and her cruse of oil failed not. (See *All the Miracles of the Bible*.)

"When Jesus saw the widow, He had compassion on her, and said unto her, Weep not." Luke 7:13

With her son's death, the widow, who was apparently highly esteemed, probably lost her sole source of support. The young man, devoted to his mother, had kept the home together. This we know, Jesus was cognizant of all the circumstances, and thus His compassion was of a practical nature. Let it not be forgotten that experience taught Him to be kind to widows. At the cross He committed His own mother to John's care, which indicated she was a widow. If legend be true, Mary's husband, Joseph, died when Jesus was but a lad, and it fell to His lot as the eldest to assist His mother in providing for the family. Realizing that He was so kind, thoughtful, and true, we cannot imagine Him forgetting His mother while He tarried on the earth. Are you a widow and somewhat lonely and needy? Then look up to Him who will not forget you.

"Because this widow troubleth me, I will avenge her." Luke 18:5

Many a widow has been robbed of her possessions through the flattery and professed love of a religious humbug. The reason, however, that Jesus used this illustration of the widow was not merely to prove that He is the Protector of the defenseless, but to emphasize the necessity of importunity in prayer. Persistency on the part of the widow moved the unjust, reluctant judge to action. Her constant entreaty produced the deliverance from cruel adversaries that the widow so earnestly desired.

The question is, "Do we cry day and night unto God for the relief we need?" We have to confess that we are so half-hearted in our supplications. We do not have the tenacity of the widow who would not take *No* for an answer. God grant us more persistency in prayer!

"This poor widow hath cast in more than they all." Luke 21:3

The point we often miss in Jesus' estimate of giving is that when this widow gave her two mites, she gave her *all*. So when we talk about "the widow's mite," let us remember that it implies the surrender of all possessions. The righteous Pharisee prided himself on giving tithes of all he possessed. It is commendable to tithe, but the widow Jesus has immortalized was *no tither*. She cast in *all* the living she had, not merely a tenth of her penury.

Often a church is dazzled by gifts of the rich, but in proportion many a poor widow, obliged to work hard and long for a mere pittance, gives far more to the cause of Christ. Our Lord's commendation of our giving, then, is based upon what we have left after we have cast of our abundance into His treasury. The widow earned eternal remembrance because, after giving God what she felt He should have, had nothing over for herself. Today's widows do more for the church than we know about.

"A widow . . . who served God."
Luke 2:37

Would that all widows had the same record as this daughter of Phanuel! Alas, there are far too many merry widows who, free from home ties, are gay, worldly, and scornful of spiritual matters. We read of Anna that "she departed not from the temple, but served God with fastings and prayers day and night." In her adoration, she likewise gave thanks for the coming of Jesus and witnessed of Him "to all them that looked for redemption in Jerusalem."

May grace be ours to follow this godly widow in her devotion to the Lord and to His house! As she testified that Jesus was the One so many loyal souls eagerly anticipated, so let us speak of Him to all in need of His saving power. As we await His Second Coming, let us serve God day and night, and thus be ready to welcome Him when He returns.

"Honour widows that are widows indeed." I Timothy 5:3-6

Elderly widows who had fulfilled certain conditions were eligible for church relief and maintenance. Where relief could be ministered by those who had relatives, no support from the church was to be forthcoming. Perhaps Paul has an intimation of the tendency to shelve family responsibility at the expense of church funds! Thrice over we have the phrase, "widows indeed," meaning the godly who were in dire need. If they were worldly-minded, spiritually dead, then they had no claim upon Christian sympathy. Promised relief was not for them and only the widows who were desolate and who trusted in God could receive church aid.

Kindness to good widows is to be commended. Bereft of a protector and provider, life is hard and dangerous for many a widow. Defenceless, they are sometimes preyed upon by heartless men. God, however, has His eye upon godly widows in their affliction, and in His goodness He offers Himself as a Husband to the widow and as a Father to the fatherless. As the One who increased the widow's meager provision to feed the prophet, He never fails to supply the necessaries of life for those who trust and honor Him.

CHILDLESS

The last aspect of the "marital realm" to which promises are associated is that of the CHILDLESS. Swinburne's sentiment is only half a truth –

"Where children are not, heaven is not."

Many a childless home is fragrant with the presence of the holy Child Jesus. For a fuller treatment of what God accomplished for some Bible childless couples, the reader is referred to *All the Prayers of the Bible*, and *All the Miracles of the Bible*.

"He maketh the barren woman . . . to be the joyful mother of children."
Psalm 113:9

While children not only provided valuable help for an Israelite in his work and increased his prestige and his authority in the community, barrenness in a wife was deemed a great misfortune, which was sometimes partially remedied by giving her personal maid to her husband as a concubine – the latter's children being considered as the wife's children (Genesis 16:2; 30:3). "The highest sanctions of religion and patriotism blessed the fruitful woman because children were necessary for the perpetuation of the tribe and its religion. Every Hebrew wife aspired to become the mother of the promised Messiah. Hebrew women like Sarah, Rebekah, Rachel, Manoah's wife, Hannah, and Elisabeth were naturally sterile and God's special intervention shows not only His particular favour to Israel, but His purpose to fulfil His promise of the Messiah."

Occasionally we have met couples who longed and prayed for a child, but whose desires were not satisfied. No ray of sunshine entered their home. Baby smiles never brightened their lives. Then, one day, the miracle happened. Longing hearts were satisfied. God made them the joyful parents of a child. Others, alas! remain childless throughout life.

In these iniquitous days, it is tragic to realize that many whom God meant to be joyful mothers resort in various ways to pervert nature. Has God been good to you? After childless years, did He permit a young one to come your way? Proud and happy as you must be, are you full of praise to Him who alone has power to banish barrenness, and are you training your longed-for child in the ways of righteousness? Do you look upon your baby as a two-fold treasure, namely, as God's child – and yours?

"As the sword hath made women childless." I Samuel 15:33

"Blessed are the barren." Luke 23:29

These two passages have a somewhat loose connection. In the latter verse, there may be a reference to the terrible destruction of Jerusalem, when dead children were boiled and eaten. The beatitude of Jesus can also apply to the Great Tribulation era, when many a childless couple will thank God they have no children to experience the horrors of such a time.

When wars and revolutions overtake a nation or nations, many homes are ravaged and left bare. Then wombs that did not bear are saved a good deal of anguish and heartache. If the world should suffer another war–an atomic war–it will be a dark day for the sons and daughters of the human race. The ghastly horrors of war, which Samuel describes, leave thousands childless. During the last World War, the papers recorded the sad story of a widow who lost her three sons in one day. A true patriot, however, she declared that if she had other sons she would have gladly surrendered them for liberty's sake.

How all others will welcome the millennial reign of Christ, when swords will be beaten into ploughshares and a child will not die until it is an hundred years old!

> "The desolate hath many more children than she which hath an husband."
> Galatians 4:27

Paul, quoting from Isaiah, illustrates the difference between the children of the bond-woman and the children of the free (54:1). Commenting upon the Master's act of taking up the children in His arms and blessing them, Scofield remarks, "In Hebrew custom, a father's act" (Genesis 27:28). He then quotes Bengel as saying, "Jesus had no children that He might adopt all children." Often the desolate mother has more children than if she had a few of her own. Think of the thousands of children George Mueller and his wife cared for! If you have no child of your own on which to shower your love, the world is full of little lives who know nothing of affection and who could be warmed by your heart. Think of the orphans, hungry for kindness and sympathy, and determine to make some lonely child happy, by transforming their desolation into delight.

> "They had no child." Luke 1:7

Zacharias and Elisabeth were righteous before God, walking in all the commandments and ordinances of the Lord, blameless; yet they had no child. Holy as they were, God in His wisdom withheld children from them. Ultimately, however, God declared that nothing was impossible, and so Elisabeth had a son in her old age (1:36,37)–a miracle often repeated in the

Bible as we have already indicated.

Eternity alone will reveal why some holy hearts which crave for a child are never satisfied. It may be that when the mists have rolled away, such devoted lives will discover that if a child had been granted, he or she would have grown up to live a life of sin and shame. But God, knowing the end from the beginning, graciously denied the prayers and desires of the childless. It is not always easy to accept denials in this way. Why some perfectly natural longings are not gratified is a mystery beyond our human comprehension. "Now we see through a glass darkly." At "daybreak," however, we shall bless the hand that guided and the heart that planned.

> "Unto the eunuchs . . . will I give . . . a name better than that of sons and daughters." Isaiah 56:4, 5

The Greek word for *eunuch* means, "one who guards the bed, and indicates the task of those who, deprived of their virility by natural defect, or by manual operation, cared for the beds and apartments of royalty." God forbade the people to make eunuchs (Deuteronomy 23:1). When Jesus spoke of a eunuch, He must have had a different kind of person in mind.

> "There be eunuchs, which have made themselves eunuchs for the kingdom of heaven's sake." Matthew 19:12

These were not mere "eunuchs of men," but those who, impelled by higher motives, abstained from marriage and participation in all carnal pleasures, so that less encumbered with the cares of this world they could devote themselves more fully to God's service. How many there are who for Christ's sake have remained single in order to serve Him unencumbered by home ties! To such the promise is given of a better name than that of sons and daughters. Multitudes of spiritual children are theirs. Paul was wifeless and childless, but thinking of the host of his Thessalonian converts who would surround him at the Judgment Seat of Christ, he could say –

> "What is our hope, or joy, or crown of rejoicing. Are not even ye . . . Ye are our glory and joy."
> I Thessalonians 2:19, 20

> "He promised . . . when as yet he had no child." Acts 7:5

Abraham received the promise of an heir before he became a parent. He was appointed as the father of the faithful before he was a father. Without a son, Abraham yet believed that his seed would possess the land. Childless, he yet trusted God that both his natural and spiritual descendants would be as the stars in multitude.

It is encouraging to know that whether children are born to us or not, all of us can become spiritual parents. Paul spoke of young Timothy as his beloved son in the faith. Have you experienced the joy of bringing someone into the world of divine love and grace? If as yet you are spiritually childless, the promise is to you that with complete surrender to the Holy Spirit, you will never know what it is to be barren or unfruitful in the begetting of a spiritual family. The Lord enable each of us to travail in birth until Christ is formed in other lives (Galatians 4:19).

PROMISES RELATIVE TO THE SPIRITUAL REALM

The majority of the "better promises," (Hebrews 8:6) are those related to our life *in* Christ and *for* Christ. These manifold spiritual promises are bound up with the life that now is (I Timothy 4:8), and are ample and diversified and altogether beyond the utmost extent of possible need. No variety of condition, no peculiarity of character has been overlooked. God has thought of and provided for every phase of our spiritual life. As we are to see, we have an inexhaustible treasury of promises to draw from, and burdened as we are with varied needs, God will never turn us away empty. We have but to come for our supplies with simplicity of heart, and in the Name of Jesus, to prove that God will withhold no good thing from us.

There are many passages in Job and Proverbs expressing the earthly advantages attendant upon righteousness, and the dire consequences of sin, which also have spiritual application. These promises, observations and maxims are not confined to Old Testament saints, but are for all to follow. Even direct, temporal promises have an indirect spiritual end. As we have indicated in *All the Miracles of the Bible,* many of the miracles of Jesus were wrought not only for the sake of the temporal or physical benefits immediately conferred but for an ulterior and higher purpose, even for the confimation of truth in order to the spiritual deliverance of souls. See Matthew 6:31-38 where the promise of material things is only for those who seek first the Kingdom of God.

At the outset, it may be as well to remind ourselves of our "charter" as we come to classify our needs and the divine promises of relief.

"The children of the promise . . . the word of promise." Romans 9:8, 9

"We . . . are the children of promise." Galatians 4:28

"Fellow heirs . . . partakers of his promise in Christ." Ephesians 3:6

"This is the promise that he hath promised us." I John 2:25

As we proceed we shall discover that all the glorious promises gathering around our life here below have all the necessary requisites for the refinement and ennoblement of our nature, the enlightenment of our understanding, the regulation of our will, the purification of our affections. Glorious promises of pardon and mercy, of acceptance with God, of high honors, of the unceasing ministry of the Spirit and of angels, and of a more conscious fellowship with God and with His beloved Son are waiting to be claimed.

One of the most remarkable books on Bible study, recently published by the Zondervan Publishing House, is *Dake's Annotated Reference Bible,* a wonderful work the reader should immediately purchase. Dealing with Bible promises, Finis J. Dake says that all "the promises and blessings in Christ are still for believers today," and cites Ephesians 1:3; II Corinthians 1:20; Psalms 34:9, 10; 84:11; Matthew 21; 22; Mark 11:22-24; John 14:12-15; and 15:7, 16. As to conditions regulating spiritual promises, Dr. Dake enumerates those set down by Paul –

1. Be not unequally yoked with unbelievers (II Corinthians 6:14-16).
2. Come out from among them (6:17).
3. Be separate from them (6:17).
4. Touch not the unclean thing (6:17).
5. Cleanse self from all filthiness of flesh and spirit (7:1).
6. Perfect holiness in the fear of the Lord (7:1).

As to the number of new Testament promises, Dr. Dake says there are 750 of them in 250 classifications, and then enumerates these promises from Matthew to Revelation – lists, providing the Bible student and a preacher with abundant expositional material.

Seeking to link the promises on to the various phases of our spiritual life, we find the coverage to be very wide indeed. There is need for every promise, and a promise for every need. Examining the nature of these manifold promises, we shall discover that each great promise is, as Guy H. King puts it –

> A shaft to lighten the day's journey.
> A key to unlock the day's program,
> A moral to quicken the day's appetite,
> A tonic to energize the day's doing.

As we proceed with the large number of promises in this section of our study, it is essential to realize that every one of them is for the humblest Christian to appropriate. Each promise is for all to claim, and all the promises can be claimed by each believer.

THE SECRET OF ABIDING

The Bible has much to say regarding the promises connected with the abiding life. The word "abide" itself carries several meanings.

To *tarry* –
"We will abide in the street all night."
Genesis 19:2

To *dwell* –
"Laban said . . . abide with me."
Genesis 29:19

To *endure* –
"The nations shall not be able to abide his indignation." Jeremiah 10:10

To *be* –
"Let thy servant abide instead of the lad." Genesis 44:33

To *continue* –
"That shall abide with him of his labour." Ecclesiastes 8:15; John 14:16

To *stand firm* –
"Thou hast established the earth, and it abideth." Psalm 119:20

To *rule or govern* –
"He shall abide before God for ever."
Psalm 61:7

To *rest* –
"He that hath it shall abide satisfied."
Proverbs 19:23

To *wait for* –
"Bonds and afflictions abide me."
Acts 20:23

"Nevertheless to abide in the flesh is more needful for you." Philippians 1:24

As used to describe our life in the Lord, the term "abide" implies to *dwell in, to be at home with*.

"Abide in me, and I in you."
John 15:4, 5

"If ye abide in me, and my words abide in you." John 15:6, 7

"Abide in him . . . not ashamed before him at his coming." I John 2:28

"He abideth in him...abideth in the light...the word of God abideth in you ...he that doeth the will of God abideth for ever...abideth in you."
I John 2:6, 10, 14, 17, 27; 3:6

"No murderer hath eternal life abiding in him." I John 3:15

"He that is called therein abide with God." I Corinthians 7:24

We must abide in Christ, for apart from Him we are nothing, have nothing, and can do nothing. It is only through Him that we can do all things. Union with Christ saves us, and keeps us safe and serene. He bids us abide in Him, which we do by living in absolute dependence upon Him, and by openly confessing our attachment to Him, and walking in daily fellowship with Him. Promises of answered prayer, fruitfulness and eternal security are ours through this abiding life. Further, it is only as we abide in Him that sin is mortified, graces are nourished, lusts and Satan are subdued, and necessary supplies are granted. "Abiding in Jesus will give us a single eye; a burning zeal; holy discretion; and enable us to seize all opportunities to glorify His adorable Name."

Jesus made the word "abide" so rich in splendid possibilities that once we realize what it is to abide in Him, the word is never commonplace again. Jesus promises us that this abiding life will be a fruitful, God-glorifying life. His life flows into us as the sap flows into the vine.

THE PROMISE OF ABUNDANCE

What vast riches we have in Christ! He does not provide us with just enough to get along. He is not niggardly in supply. In Him, we have more than enough. Whatever our need, abundance is at our disposal.

"The abundance of all things."
Deuteronomy 28:47; 33:19

"The abundance of peace and truth."
Jeremiah 33:6; Psalm 37:11

"The abundance of the heart."
Matthew 12:34

"He shall have more abundance."
Matthew 13:12; 25:29; II Chronicles 25:9

"Abundance of grace and the gift of righteousness." Romans 5:17; I Timothy 1:14

"The abundance of their joy."
II Corinthians 8:2, 14; Philippians 1:26

"The abundance of the revelations."
II Corinthians 12:7

"Trusted in the abundance of his riches."
Psalm 52:7; Jeremiah 51:13

"A man's life consisteth not in the abundance of the things which he possesseth." Luke 12:15

"The Lord . . . abundant in goodness and truth." Exodus 34:6

"This service . . . is abundant also by many thanksgivings unto God."
II Corinthians 9:12; 11:13

"According to his abundant mercy."
I Peter 1:3

"They shall be abundantly satisfied,"
Psalm 36:8; Song of Solomon 5:1

"He will abundantly pardon."
Isaiah 55:6; Titus 3:6

"Life . . . more abundantly."
John 10:10; I Corinthians 15:10

"The more abundantly I love you."
II Corinthians 12:15

"He is able to do exceeding abundantly."
Ephesians 3:20

"An entrance shall be ministered unto you abundantly." II Peter 1:11

The above exceeding great and precious promises speak for themselves. To them, we can add all those passages taken up with the fulness of God and the fulness of His Spirit (see John 7:37-39; 14:12-18, 26; Acts 1:8; 5:32; Romans 8:14, 16; Ephesians 5:18 etc.). We are solemnly warned against trusting in the abundance of material things which can vanish with the wind.

THE LIBERTY OF ACCESS

"By whom also we have access by faith into this grace." Romans 5:2

"Through him we both have access by one Spirit unto the Father." Ephesians 2:18

"Access with confidence by the faith of him." Ephesians 3:12

"No man cometh unto the Father, but by me." John 14:6

Whether we think of salvation, worship, or ultimately heaven, the same truth applies – we have no access to God apart from the mediation of Jesus Christ. When Jesus explicitly declared that "no man" can approach God apart from Himself, He meant *no man*, no matter what religion or merit he has. Christ alone is "The Way" to the Father, as Hebrews declares –

"Boldness to enter the holiest by the blood of Jesus, by a new and living way."
Hebrews 10:19, 20

Closely allied to the promise, privilege and provision is the access of our acceptance before God through Christ. It is because we have been accepted through grace that we can venture nigh unto God.

"I will accept you with your sweet savour, when I bring you out from the people." Ezekiel 20:40, 41

"He hath made us accepted in the beloved." Ephesians 1:6

"God accepteth no man's person."
Galatians 2:6

THE TRIUMPH OVER ADVERSARIES

The foes arrayed against the Christians are strong, numerous, and varied. As a "soldier," the believer must expect to face enemies, but many promises are his that as he fights "the good fight," the divine Captain will make him more than a conqueror. Our chief adversary, accuser, enemy, is Satan –

"Your adversary the devil."
I Peter 5:8

"Avenge me of mine adversary."
Luke 18:3; Zechariah 3:1

"Who is mine adversary? Let him come near me." Isaiah 50:8

"The Lord stirred up an adversary."
I Kings 11:14

"He . . . will render vengeance to his adversaries." Deuteronomy 32:27, 43

"They also that render evil for good are mine adversaries." Psalms 38:26; 69:19

"Adversaries to my soul."
Psalms 71:13; 109:4, 20, 29

"There are many adversaries."
I Corinthians 16:9

"In nothing terrified by your adversaries." Philippians 1:28

"Mine enemies and my foes."
Psalms 27:2; 30:1; 89:23

"A man's foes shall be they of his own household." Matthew 10:36

"Until I make thy foes thy footstool."
Acts 2:39

The threefold source of all our foes is the world, the flesh, and the devil; while the threefold avenue of approach is the lust of the flesh – the desire to indulge; the lust of the eyes – the desire to possess; the pride of life – the desire to attract. But we have the promises of deliverance from all the contrivances and snares of Satan. Assistance and encouragement are ours in the spiritual warfare when we cash in on the many promises of grace and strength to mortify sin and to resist the devil: The highest perfection of holiness and happiness can be ours as we appropriate the victory over all satanic foes which Christ secured by His death and resurrection for us.

"Thanks be unto God who giveth us the victory." I Corinthians 15:57

"Thine, O Lord . . . is the victory."
I Chronicles 29:11

"Safety (victory) is of the Lord."
                                    Proverbs 21:31
"This is the victory that overcometh the world." I John 5:4, 18
"They overcame him by the blood of the Lamb." Revelation 12:11; 15:2
"We are more than conquerors through him that loved us." Romans 8:37
"Thanks be unto God, which always causeth us to triumph."
                                    II Corinthians 2:14
"I give unto you power . . . over all the power of the enemy."
                              Luke 10:19; Zephaniah 3:15
All the Christian's enemies are the evil brood of the one Christ named as "the enemy," as "the god of this world," as "the prince of darkness." Unceasingly, this subtle enemy strives to injure us, draw us away from God, destroy our peace. But as faith seizes the perfect work of Christ as its shield and the perfect Word of God as its sword, victory is secured over our infernal foe.

"The battle is the Lord's and he will give it into our hands." I Samuel 17:47
The question we must first settle is, Who is battling against our foes? Why, it is the Lord! We cannot be victorious over the enemy by our own will, wisdom, or might. If, like Israel, we look to the sword and spear defeat will be ours.

"The arm of flesh will fail us,
We dare not trust our own."
Witnessing for Him, we war in His strength, and with Him fighting through us, who can triumph over us?

"Be not afraid of their faces; for I am with thee to deliver thee."
                                    Jeremiah 1:8
If in the conflict against all the foes of righteousness we falter, or are afraid, then faith will weaken and defeat will ensue. Says Spurgeon, we should "fear to fear. Be afraid to be afraid. Your worst enemy is within your own bosom. Get to your knees and cry for help, then rise up saying, 'I will trust, and not be afraid.'"

"I am with thee, and no man shall set on thee to hurt thee." Acts 18:10
What assurance this divine promise begets! As long as Paul was accomplishing a God-given task in Corinth, he enjoyed a God-given protection from those who would have hurt him. If we know that we are in the will of God, living and laboring as He would have us, then no weapon formed against us can prosper (Isaiah 54:17). As

for those who oppose us –
"By the greatness of thine arm they shall be as still as a stone till thy people pass over, O Lord."
In the struggle, He is near to restrain, and our "dauntless faith in God brushes fear aside like the cobwebs in a giant's path."

"A troop shall overcome him: but he shall overcome at last." Genesis 49:19
"Thou shalt drive out the Canaanites, though they have iron chariots, and though they be strong." Joshua 17:18
"The weapons of our warfare . . . are mighty." II Corinthians 10:4
As we fight the Lord's battles, with the Lord's weapons, we experience the Lord's victory. Promises of such a victory permeate the Bible.

Here are a few thoughts on some of the *victory promises* –
"I have overcome the world."
                                    John 16:33
If we take the 'y' from 'victory,' we are left with *victor*, which the sin-bound soul becomes as soon as the blood-bought victory of the heavenly Victor is appropriated by faith. Anticipating the cross, Jesus used the past tense in His affirmation of conquest. But what did he mean by "the world"? Scofield comments that the word implies this "present world system." The ethically bad sense of the word refers to the "order," "arrangement" under which Satan has organized the world of unbelieving manking upon his cosmic principles of force, greed, selfishness, ambition, and pleasure. This world-system is often outwardly religious, scientific, and cultured, but seething with national and commercial rivalries and ambitions, and is upheld in any real crisis only by armed forces, and is dominated by Satanic principles. This, then, is *the world* Jesus overcame by His life, death, and resurrection.

"They are not . . . I am not . . ."
                                    John 17:16
Twice over in His high-priestly prayer, our Lord declares that His own are not of the world, even as He is not of the world. Unworldly, we are hated by the world, just as He was. But is this true to experience? Do we continually appropriate Christ's victory over Satan and over a system of principles and pleasures he inspires? Are we dead to the world, and is the world on a cross, insofar as we are concerned? We can be in the world and not of it, just as the diver is in the sea, but the sea

is not in the diver! The secret of our separation from all forms of worldliness is the keeping power of our heavenly Intercessor and Keeper. "I pray . . . that thou shouldest keep them from evil."

"This is the victory . . . our faith."
I John 5:4

During the last World War the "V for Victory" movement swept over conquered countries, bringing hope to multitudes who had been overcome by cruel aggression. They endured their terrible trials, believing that their day of emancipation was near at hand. And in the war that rages, faith is essential to victory. In the spiritual realm, victory is dependent upon faith. But John makes it very clear what particular aspect of faith assures victory. "Who is he that overcometh the world, but he that believeth that Jesus is the Son of God." If we reject the deity of Christ, we are not Christians (I John 5:1). But if we are truly born of God, and rest in the deity of His Son, then God will keep us from the satanic influences of the world that lieth in wickedness, and Satan himself will not be able to touch us (I John 5:18, 19).

"The word of God abideth in you, and ye have overcome the wicked one."
I John 2:14

Promised victory is likewise dependent upon the use of effective weapons. And, as the Word of God is the sword of the Spirit, we have in our hands the very weapon by which Jesus Himself triumphed over Satan in the wilderness. But we will never function as victorious Christians if the Word is merely in our hands. It must be in our hearts, for it is only as it abides within that we are able to overcome the enemy. Worldly-minded Christians are usually those who do not have a very close acquaintance with the Scriptures. Carnality, however, never thrives where there is a deep and daily mediation upon the soul satisfying truths of the Word of God. If you are not among the overcomers, revise your Bible habits, and mark the results.

"The God of peace shall bruise Satan under your feet shortly." Romans 16:20

Satan was defeated, prophetically, in Eden; actually, at Calvary; and is defeated practically in our lives as day by day we exercise faith in the overcoming principle. For the complete bruising of Satan we must wait until the Great White Throne of Revelation 20:10, when he is to be cast into the lake of fire forever and ever. Are you presently enduring a season of satanic antagonism? Is he working through those who cause divisions and offences contrary to the doctrines you have learned, and who serve not our Lord Jesus Christ, but their own belly? Well, in spite of their deceiving good words, and fair speeches (Romans 16:17, 18) take heart; your deliverance is at hand. Live near your mighty God, and a bruised Satan will be at your feet!

"More than conquerors." Romans 8:37

To be conqueror is surely something to be grateful for, but Paul is not satisfied with conquest. He declares that Christ is able to make us *more* than conquerors. Evidently, then, there is something more than a mere victory. For a time Germany was gaining victories in Russia. But the conquest appeared to be negative. What was Germany gaining? Nothing but scorched earth! She was a conqueror temporarily, but she would have been more than a conqueror if she could have taken the wheat fields, industries, dams, and resources, intact. The believer is more than a conqueror in that he carries the tremendous gains of conquest. Victors in Olympic games were entitled to communal and national privileges. In verses 35 and 36 we have the negative side, and in verses 38 and 39, the positive side of our victory in Christ.

"Thanks be to God which giveth us the victory." I Corinthians 15:57

In the last issue, victory, whether it is over the world, sin, Satan, or death, is not *acquired* but *appropriated*. It is given, not gained. Victory is ever of the Lord. We sing about "marching on to victory," but in reality we march *from* victory, not *to* it. By the redemptive work of Christ securing a complete victory, Calvary was Satan's Waterloo. As the result of his ignominious defeat there by Christ, he is fully aware that any saint can overcome his machinations by the blood of the Lamb. The question is, Are we daily accepting from the pierced hands which achieved this glorious victory, the prerogative of telling Satan to get behind us? What fools we are if we refuse such a gift!

Promises of past, present, and prospective *satanic defeat* are as exhilarating as they are explicit. Linger over these instances for your encouragement.

"The Lord . . . shall punish . . . the piercing serpent . . . that crooked serpent." Isaiah 27:1

Reading back into chapter 26, it would

seem that the prophet is predicting and proclaiming the destruction of all the Gentile world-power. And during such merited destruction the believing remnant on earth will have the privilege of hiding in divinely provided chambers (Isaiah 26:20). Behind all evil, scheming, and brutal nations there is Satan, the god of the world, who himself is spoken of as a serpent and a dragon. And the punishment to be experienced by the nations he has inspired is but a forerunner of his own doom. God will yet deal with Satan for all the sin and sorrow he has caused. He is a condemned being and he knows it. This may be one reason why Satan keeps Christians from the last book of the Bible. It records his certain doom.

"When the enemy shall come in like a flood, the Spirit of the Lord shall lift up a standard against him."

Isaiah 59:19

There are three aspects in this message: the enemy, the Spirit of the Lord, the standard. By the latter we are to understand a banner, flag, or colors, carried in time of war (Numbers 1:52). This can be looked upon as a type of the cross. Again and again, "the enemy" is identified as Satan. He is the arch-enemy of God and man. In virtue of Calvary, the Holy Spirit is able to meet and overcome the enemy in your life and mine. When his approaches are so tempestuous, almost overwhelming us as a flood, then the Spirit raises the cross, and the flood recedes. The cross, as wielded by the Spirit, is more than a match for the devil and his legions. When floods of temptation rush by, do we call upon the Holy Spirit to hold up the cross and thereby defeat the enemy? What a double safeguard is ours! The Spirit and the cross. And as the Spirit presents the cross, we become more than conquerors.

"Shall the prey be taken from the mighty." Isaiah 49:24

Let us never be guilty of underrating Satan's power. He is "the strong man." But while he is mighty, he is not almighty. He does not share God's attributes of omnipotence, omnipresence, and omniscience, and in this we rejoice. Men and women like ourselves form his prey and his captives. He it is who contends with us, but there is One greater than he. Isaiah describes Him as "thy saviour and thy redeemer, the mighty one of Jacob." "Greater is he that is in you than he that is in the world."

Alas, too often the believer becomes the prey of the mighty. With guile, Satan sets his snare, and the child of God is caught. But "the mighty One" is able to take the prey from the might. He can be plundered and robbed of his dupes and slaves. Christ stands ready to break all fetters and transform slaves into sons. Is He using you to take some of the prey from the mighty?

"That wicked one . . . whom the Lord shall consume." II Thessalonians 2:8

By this wicked or lawless one we are to understand Satan's masterpiece, the man of sin, who is to climax the sin of man. And "wicked" truly describes the Anti-christ, since he will personify all the iniquity and deception Satan is capable of producing and imparting. But the evil, cruel sway of this hell-inspired person is shortlived. In spite of his much-vaunted authority and satanic, miraculous power, one look of the returning Lord will be sufficient to wither this wicked genius. And when the hour of his destruction strikes, Satan will not be able to preserve his tool. "The beast was taken, and with him the false prophet that wrought miracles, before him . . . These both were cast alive into a lake of fire burning with brimstone" (Revelation 19:20). In the final depository of the wicked, the wicked one will endure forever the wrath his wickedness deserves.

"Thou shalt bruise his heel."

Genesis 3:15

Satan was permitted to bruise Christ, that is, persecute, vex, pain, trouble Him by all means. The physical sufferings of Christ are involved in the bruising of the heel. But, as the seed of the woman, Christ bruised the *head* of Satan. Christ was manifested that He might destroy the works of the Devil. All through His earthly life Christ had Satan at His heel, causing many a bruise, but at Calvary the Saviour came down upon the head of the serpent. By dying, death He slew. But one may argue: If he is a defeated foe, why is he permitted to flood the earth with tears, anguish, and blood? How is it that he is still able to plan and scheme the destruction of man? Well, his days are numbered, and Satan is well aware that his time is short. His ultimate subjugation is not far distant. "The God of peace shall bruise Satan under your feet shortly" (Romans 16:20).

"That He might destroy the works of the devil." I John 3:8

Satan is the original sinner. He is the first to sin, hence, the significance of John's phrase, "the devil sinneth from the beginning."

By his act of rebellion, the devil gave birth to sin, and all who have sinned are of this parent of sin. Because of his sin, Satan was cast out of the presence of God. Christ, by His sacrifice, brings the sinner into right relationship with God. The cross nullifies the doings of the devil. Every regenerated, transformed life is a fresh evidence of Christ's conquest of Satan. Of course, many satanic works are still evident. Thus Satan, although spoiled as he was at Calvary, is still abroad doing his dirty work. But by faith, all believers can appropriate Christ's destruction of the devil's works. He can be overcome by the blood of the Lamb. Jesus is stronger than Satan and sin, and, if we will it, Satan must bow to Jesus in your life and mine, just as he will in the universe as a whole before very long.

"The devil that deceived them was cast into the lake of fire and brimstone . . . and tormented day and night forever."
Revelation 20:10

Our last glimpse of Satan corresponds to the first. He deceived Eve (I Timothy 2:14). We all know the axiom of giving a dog a bad name. Well, the devil carries his name as a deceiver with him into the everlasting fire prepared for him and his angels. But what a deceiver he is! Did not our Lord declare that he is able to deceive the very elect? Eternal torment, however, is to be his for all his cruel deception. And, let us make no mistake about it, Satan knows that this description of his doom is in the Bible for all to read! And for the devil there is no pardon. A certain looking for of judgment is his. This is why he is working with feverish haste to hurry men and women off the face of the earth before they repent and turn to the Saviour. He is determined to have multitudes share his eternal torments. And our solemn obligation is to see to it that the lake of fire will have fewer occupants than Satan is eager to cast therein.

THE HEAVENLY ADVOCATE

The satanic foe we have just thought about is also described as our fierce *Accuser* –

"The accuser of our brethren is cast down." Revelation 12:10
"False accusers."
II Timothy 3:2; Titus 2:3

Whenever Satan endeavors to accuse a Christian before God, Christ is there as the Advocate to plead the inaccuracy of Satan's charge and to represent the Christian's innocence. If there is foundation for the charges, then the Advocate pleads His efficacious blood on behalf of the sinning one.

"We have an advocate with the Father."
I John 2:1
"He ever liveth to make intercession for us." Hebrews 7:25

This evidence of Christ's advocacy above does not excuse sin, "any more than because a building has a fire escape you should set the building on fire for the sake of using the escape! Or any more than the provision of lifeboats on a vessel allows you to sink the ship in order that you may find occasion of use for the lifeboats." But in case we do sin, we have an Advocate to see us through. It may be painful to be frank about our constant need of the Saviour's advocacy. The greatest saints did not hide their sin. But confessing it, they had the assurance of His advocacy on high, where He not only pleads for us against the accuser, answering all his accusations, but also presents His blood against our sin. As an Advocate, His arguments are powerful and His manner divine. All for whom He pleads are safe, for the Father heareth Him always.

But the Christian is doubly blessed and fortified in that he has another Advocate in his heart, as well as the One interceding on his behalf in heaven. The Holy Spirit is the One within who pleads our cause, exhorts, comforts, and prays. "Advocate" and "Comforter" are the same word – *parakletos*, meaning "one called alongside of to help." Thus Christ and the Holy Spirit are similar in their ministry for others.

"He shall give you another comforter."
John 14:16; 15:26; 16:17

As Christ intercedes with God *for* us above, so the Holy Spirit intercedes *in* us below (Romans 8:26, 34). Fausett comments –

"The Holy Spirit, testifying of Christ within us, answers, as our Advocate be-before our consciences, the law's demands; As the Spirit of prayer and adoption, He inspires in us prayers which words cannot fully utter."

The Holy Spirit is within to keep us from sinning. But if we do sin, the Lord Jesus pleads His cleansing blood for us.

THE FRIEND IN ADVERSITY

Being Christians does not guarantee immunity from the trials, sorrows, and afflictions of this life. Much rough polishing gives the diamond its luster.

"God, who himself saved you out of all your adversities." I Samuel 10:19
"The Lord . . . who hath redeemed thy

soul out of all adversity." II Samuel 4:9
"God did vex them with all adversity."
II Chronicles 15:6
"I shall never be in adversity."
Psalm 10:6
"Thou hast known my soul in adversities. Psalms 31:7; 35:15
"That thou mayest give him rest from the days of adversity." Psalm 94:13
"A brother is born for adversity."
Proverbs 17:17
"If thou faint in the day of adversity, thy strength is small." Proverbs 24:10
"In the day of adversity consider."
Ecclesiastes 7:14
"The Lord give you the bread of adveristy." Isaiah 30:20
"Remember them . . . which suffer adversity." Hebrews 13:3

The combination of the promises reminds us that it is folly to think that no adversity will come our way. When it does overtake us, we are to consider God, who is well able to uphold and sustain us amid all the testing He may permit. If He does not remove the cross, He will strengthen our shoulders to carry it.

"Have I no power to deliver?"
Isaiah 50:2
"O keep my soul, and deliver me."
Psalm 25:20
"Compass me about with songs of deliverance." Psalm 32:7

If *prosperity* calls for rejoicing, *adversity*, says Solomon, calls for reflection. Possibly there is a just cause for permitted adversity. Providence frowns because of sin indulged in, commands disobeyed, self exalted, and grace slighted. Thus adversity is sent to reprove, correct, and restore us. When we confess our shortcomings, God, who loves us freely, heals our backslidings. Divine promises assure us not only of deliverances from the trials of life but of the sanctifying purpose God has in permitting them. Further, as the Father of mercies, He always has in view the spiritual and eternal benefit of His children. Adversity is never allowed in caprice.

The Anchor of "Always"

Ever and anon, as we meditate upon God's precious Word, a key word seems to leap out of its sacred pages, and, laying hold on us, will not let us go until it blesses us. "Always" is one such word to which sweet promises are related. If you look at the context of the following promises and precepts, you will see that they speak for

themselves. May we hearken to their voice!
"Keep all my commandments always."
Deuteronomy 5:29; 11:1
"Fear the Lord thy God always."
Deuteronomy 14:23
"Shall eat bread always at my table."
II Samuel 9:10
"I would not live always." Job 8:16
"Will he always call upon God."
Job 27:10
"I have set the Lord always before me."
Psalm 16:8
"He will not always chide." Psalm 103:9
"I have inclined my heart to perform thy statutes always." Psalm 119:112
"I was daily his delight, rejoicing always before him." Proverbs 8:30
"Neither will I be always wroth."
Isaiah 57:16
"Lo, I am with you alway."
Matthew 28:20
"Me ye have not always." Mark 14:7
"I do always those things that please him." John 8:29
"I knew that thou hearest me always."
John 11:42; Acts 10:2; Philippians 1:4
"God, which always causeth us to triumph." II Corinthians 2:14
"Rejoice in the Lord always."
Philippians 4:4
"Have these things always in remembrance." II Peter 1:15

The Ministry of Angels

In a previous section we dealt with some of the promises angels were commissioned to proclaim to saints of old. We owe more to angelic ministry than we realize.
"The angel of the Lord encampeth round about them that fear him, and delivereth them." Psalm 34:7
"He shall give his angels charge over thee." Psalm 91:11
"In heaven their angels do always behold the face of my Father."
Matthew 18:10
"Angels . . . to minister for . . . heirs of salvation." Hebrews 1:14
"The angels of his presence saved them." Isaiah 63:9. See also Genesis 48:16; Acts 5:19; 12:11; Numbers 20:16; Daniel 3:26; 6:22, etc.

In our full treatment of the subject of angels in *The Mystery and Ministry of Angels*, we have shown the significance of *chariots* as applied to "angels" (II Kings 6:17; Psalms 68:17; 104:3; Isaiah 66:15).

"Angels descending, bring from above,
Echoes of mercy, whispers of love."

"Angels came and ministered unto him."
Matthew 4:11

Twice over, after grim contests, angels hastened to Christ with their ministry of consolation. The wilderness and Gethsemane encounters left Him physically exhausted. Yet a mystery of our faith is the fact that although Jesus was higher than angels, in His humanity He evidently needed their beneficent aid. Just what heavenly cordials they administered to the needy Christ we are not told. It is apparent, however, that soothed and strengthened by their attention, the Master faced further sorrows with a fresh determination.

"Equal unto the angels." Luke 20:36

Some of us can still remember how as children, we used to sing with great gusto, "I want to be an angel, and with the angels stand." Well, the fact remains that we shall never be angels nor have wings. Ours is to be a more exalted and privileged relationship. Why, we are to judge angels! When our Lord spoke of equality with angels He referred, of course, to their deathless and sexless nature. Angels adore the Lord – let us equal them here, nay, surpass their praises, because He shed His blood for us and not for angels.

"His angels he charged with folly."
Job 4:18

Angels can sin, Peter reminds us. And although they were angels, God did not spare them. Justly He charged them with their folly. If, then, angelic beings are capable of prostituting their lofty privileges and position, how great is our peril, since we have not the environment angels are used to. And yet we are encouraged even by the judgment of angels for such is an evidence of a divine holiness that must be recognized and exhibited.

"The angels of God met him."
Genesis 32:1

"God's host," Jacob called the angelic company which met him on his way to the old home. Fear of Esau was dispelled by the sight of the divine protectors and companions. If you are called upon to tread perilous roads, face arduous duties, endure grievous trials, go your way and the angels will meet you. There are those who believe that every Christian has a guardian angel. Glory may reveal how much we truly owe to the emissaries of heaven.

"Four angels standing on the four corners of the earth." Revelation 7:1

The varied ministry of these legions of God is one of the most fascinating themes of Scripture. Here they are found exercising relegated power over material forces. Holding in check mighty winds blowing from every quarter, the angels preserve the earth from disaster. The thought, however, we take for our hearts is this – It does not matter in what corner of the earth we may be or where our loved ones live, threatened dangers are ever under control of angelic protectors.

"Joy in the presence of the angels of God." Luke 15:10

Sinners repenting occasion the angels great rejoicing. They share the joy of the Shepherd Himself as lost sheep are found. Christ did not die for angels, yet nothing thrills them like the sight of sinners turning to the Saviour. Are we contributing to the joy of angels and to the satisfaction of Christ? We were wont to sing in Gospel meetings, "There are angels hovering round to carry the tidings home." Alas, the majority of churches, destitute of soul-saving activities, send the angels away with sad hearts.

"Nor angels . . . shall be able to separate us from the love of God."
Romans 8:38-39

That angels have enormous relegated power is seen in the work of the angel who smote 185,000 Assyrians. Peter speaks of angels as being "greater in might and power" than proud, evil men. Yet, so indissoluble is the bond between Christ and His own that no angel or archangel is able to break it. In Christ we are eternally secure. No force, heavenly, human, or hellish can divide the Saviour and the saved. Hallelujah!

THE ASPECTS OF ANGER

That there is a right kind of anger, wrath, or indignation, as well as a wrong kind, is apparent, even to the casual reader of the Bible. Man is capable of a righteous indignation, or of a false anger. When used of God, the above terms signify His just displeasure of sin, and provision of its deserved punishment. Herewith is a selection of verses presenting the right and wrong forms of anger.

"Anger resteth in the bosom of fools."
Ecclesiastes 7:9

"Wrath is cruel, anger is outrageous."
Proverbs 27:4

"Cease from anger, and forsake wrath."
Psalm 37:8

"Put off these: anger, wrath, malice."
Colossians 3:8; Galatians 5:19-21

"He that is soon angry dealeth foolishly."
Proverbs 14:17

"Be ye angry and sin not."
Ephesians 4:26, 31; James 1:19, 20
"Grievous words stir up anger."
Proverbs 15:1
"Whosoever is angry with his brother shall be in danger of the judgment."
Matthew 5:22
"He that is slow to anger is better than the mighty." Proverbs 16:32
"The anger of the Lord was kindled against Moses." Exodus 4:14, etc.
"The Lord is . . . slow to anger . . . will not keep his anger forever."
Psalm 103:8, 9
"They angered him at the waters of strife." Psalm 106:32
"The Lord was angry."
Deuteronomy 1:37; 4:21, etc., etc.
"A steward of God . . . not soon angry."
Titus 1:7

Marcus Aurelius wrote that, "Our anger and impatiences often prove much more mischievous than the things about which we are angry or impatient." How true! As Christians, we should beware of "flying off the handle" at the least irritation.

"Because of thine indignation and wrath." Psalm 102:17
"The staff in their hand is mine indignation." Isaiah 10:5, 25
"The indignation of his anger."
Isaiah 30:30, 34:2 etc.
"They were moved with indignation."
Matthew 20:24; 26:8 etc.
"The wrath of the Lamb . . . The great day of his wrath." Revelation 6:16, 17
"The wine of the wrath of God."
Revelation 16:10, 19; 16:1, 8
"Let every man be . . . slow to wrath."
James 1:19

The double wrath and indignation John depicts will be experienced by the godless hordes of earth during "The Great Tribulation" period, when the vials of divine, just anger will be emptied out upon a guilty world. Is it not blessed to know that because we are the Lord's we shall escape future wrath? It is only upon those who are not His that divine wrath abides.

"He that believeth not . . . the wrath of God abideth on him." John 3:36
The Christian, however, rests on the promise that through grace, he has been delivered from coming wrath (I Thessalonians 1:10).

"We shall be saved from wrath through him." Romans 5:9

Woe to the men on earth who dwell,
Nor dread their Maker's frown;
When God doth all His wrath reveal,
And shower His judgments down!

THE REASONS FOR NEVER BEING ASHAMED

There are many unworthy things a Christian should be ashamed of doing. But no one who follows Christ, however, should ever be ashamed of Him, or *a shame to* Him.

"They shall not be ashamed that wait for me." Isaiah 49:23
"I know that I shall not be ashamed."
Isaiah 50:7
"They looked unto him . . . their faces were not ashamed." Psalm 34:5
"Whosoever shall be ashamed of me . . . the Son of Man shall be ashamed."
Mark 8:38
"I am not ashamed of the gospel of Christ." Romans 1:16
"Hope maketh not ashamed."
Romans 5:5
"In nothing shall I be ashamed."
Philippians 1:20; II Timothy 1:12
"Be not ashamed of the testimony of our Lord." II Timothy 1:23
"God is not ashamed to be called their God." Hebrews 11:16
"As a Christian, let him not be ashamed."
I Peter 4:16

Do we not possess the Master's promise that if we fearlessly confess Him before men, He will proudly confess us before His Father?

For all our guilty past we have need to be thoroughly ashamed of our sin, which would have ended in death.

"Those things whereof ye are not ashamed." Romans 6:21
But all past sin is covered by the blood, and now our constant prayer should be for grace to witness a good confession for Him who was not ashamed to die as a criminal for our salvation. Can we truthfully sing –

I'm not ashamed to own my Lord,
Or defend His cause;
Maintain the honour of His Word,
The glory of His Cross.

THE BLESSING OF ASSURANCE

Biblical *assurance* implies an absolute certainty of the reality of an object –

"Whereof he hath given assurance unto all men, in that he hath raised him from the dead." Acts 17:32
The term also includes a firm persuasion in the soul of its interest in the person, blood, grace, righteousness, and intercession of Jesus Christ.

"The work of righteousness shall be peace; The effect of righteousness,

quietness and assurance forever."
Isaiah 32:17
"We know that if our earthly house were dissolved . . . we have a building of God." II Corinthians 5:1
"I know whom I have believed."
II Timothy 1:12
"A true heart in full assurance of faith."
Hebrews 10:22

Is ours that grace of assurance enabling us to be triumphant in the dark and difficult hours of life? Paul's spirit was calm and tranquil when he dictated those words, so full of promise, "I know whom (not *what*) I have believed."

William Nicolson, in his *Bible Student's Companion,* reminds us of a three-fold aspect of such blessed assurance –

1. Assurance of the *understanding* in a well-grounded knowledge of divine things founded on God's Word – "Unto all riches of the full assurance of understanding" (Colossians 2:2).
2. Assurance of *faith* does not relate to our personal interest in Christ, but consists in a firm belief of the revelation that God has given us of Christ in His Word, with an entire dependence upon Him – "In full assurance of faith" (Hebrews 10:22).
3. Assurance of *hope* in a firm expectation that God will grant us the complete enjoyment of what He has promised – "The full assurance of hope unto the end" (Hebrews 6:11).

In the light of apostolic assurance, how wrong it is for any Christian to affirm that it is nothing but assumption to say that they know they are saved, and that eternally. To doubt what God says is to make Him a liar. Jesus said that if we believe in Him, we *have* eternal life (John 3:36). How then can it be assumption to take Him at His word?

THE PROMISE IN BENEDICTIONS

The Bible possesses a few blessed *benedictions*, each of which is fragrant with some divine promise.

There is God's benediction for Israel, which we too can claim –

"The Lord bless thee, and keep thee.
"The Lord make his face shine upon thee, and be gracious unto thee;
"The Lord lift up his countenance upon thee, and give thee peace."
Numbers 6:24-26

There are the apostolic benedictions –

"Grace be with you all." Titus 3:15; Colossians 4:18; I Thessalonians 5:28; I Peter 5:14
"Grace be with all them that love our Lord Jesus Christ in sincerity."
Ephesians 6:24
"The grace of the Lord Jesus Christ, the love of God, and the communion of the Holy Spirit, be with you all."
II Corinthians 13:14
"The God of peace, who brought again from the dead our Lord Jesus Christ . . . make you perfect." Hebrews 13:20, 21
"Now unto him that is able to keep you from falling." Jude 24, 25

To such rich promises as these *benedictions* contain, we can add those suggested by the *salutations,* with which most of the epistles begin. These *salutations* were made up of the greeting and parting words used by early Christians, because they were so full of hope and promise.

THE CALL TO BLAMELESSNESS

Our Lord wore "the white flower of a blameless life," and as He is, so are we in this world. This is why the Bible insists on blamelessness on the part of a Christian.

"That ye be blameless in the day of our Lord Jesus." I Corinthians 1:8
"Be blameless and harmless."
Philippians 2:15
"Holy and unblameable and unreprovable." Colossians 1:22
"How holily, justly and unblameably we behaved." I Thessalonians 2:10
"Be found . . . without spot, and blameless." II Peter 3:14
"I pray God your whole spirit and soul and body be preserved blameless."
I Thessalonians 5:23

To be blameless means to be without open fault, or allowed guile (Luke 1:6). Is it not consoling to know that the call to such blamelessness carries with it the promise of performance? Paul prayed that the saints at Thessalonica might be preserved blameless unto Christ's coming. But he hurried on to say – "Faithful is he that calleth you, *who also will do it*" (I Thessalonians 5:23). God does not leave us to manufacture the blamelessness He calls us to. He graciously supplies it. Because He is faithful to His own promise, He will ultimately present us to Himself – faultless. He will perfect that which concerns us. The good work He commenced, He will consummate.

THE MUSIC OF THE "BLESSEDS"

Have you ever catalogued the blessed "Blesseds" of the Bible? What an imposing array they make, and how laden with heavenly promises they are! Take, for example, the "Blesseds" found in the Psalms, in the Beatitudes of our Lord, and in John's Apocalypse. Why, it would take a volume to expound them all! Here are some samples of these "blesseds" with promise—

"Blessed is every one that feareth the Lord." Psalms 128:1; 34:8

"Blessed is he whose transgression is forgiven." Psalm 32:1

"Blessed are they who have not seen, yet have believed." John 20:29

"Blessed are the meek for they shall inherit the earth." Matthew 5:3-11

"Blessed are they that hear the word of God, and keep it." Luke 11:28

"Blessed is he that readeth, and they that hear." Revelation 1:3

THE BEARER OF BURDENS

No Christian is exempt from burden-bearing—"Every man shall bear his own burden" (Galatians 6:5). The best of us have personal responsibilities we cannot transfer to another. Those we cast upon the Lord, we still carry, but with the assurance that He carries both ourselves and our load. At the outset of our Christian pilgrimage, we are apt to think of life as only pleasure. But as we journey along, we discover that there are burdens to shoulder, crosses to bear, trials to endure, losses to reclaim and that, as Christ's, we must not yield to despair.

"Mine iniquities . . . as an heavy burden they are too heavy for me." Psalm 38:4

"I removed his shoulder from the burden." Psalm 81:6

"My yoke is easy, and my burden is light." Matthew 11:30

"Bear ye one another's burdens." Galatians 6:2

"The strength of the bearers of burdens is decayed." Nehemiah 4:10

"Cast thy burden upon the Lord, and he shall sustain thee." Psalm 55:22

Is a heavy burden yours? Then roll it upon God's broad shoulders. When He takes it, then it is on Him, and not on you, and sustaining you He will make the burden a blessing. The margin has "gift" for *burden*, and often our burdens are gifts in disguise. If our poor shoulders are galled with some oppressive load. He is near as the great Burden-bearer to relieve the pressure. Having carried our sins, He now promises to take not only our burdens and cares, but ourselves.

I am the Burden-bearer; I
Will never pass the o'erladen by . . .
Wherever is a load to bear
My willing shoulder still is there.

THE CURE FOR CARE

"The very hairs of your head are all numbered." Matthew 10:30; Luke 21:18

"A bruised reed shall he not break." Isaiah 42:3

"He shall feed his flock like a shepherd." Isaiah 40:11

"Take no thought of tomorrow." Matthew 6:34

"I would have you without carefulness." I Corinthians 7:32

"No man cared for my soul." Psalm 142:1; Luke 10:40

"Cast all your care upon him, for he careth for you." I Peter 5:7

The last half of Peter's promise can be translated, "He has you upon his heart." If this is so—and it is—then He knows all His saints and all their personal needs, trials, and problems. Here we are enjoined to cast them all upon Him and to believe that He will care for them. As soon as cares appear we should cast them upon Omnipotence. Are you among the number who have learned to sing that uplifting song of trust and confidence?—

"I have no cares, O blessed will,
For all my cares are Thine."

THE BENEFIT OF CHANGES

Many of the changes in life are feared and unwanted, yet the Bible declares that these very changes can be spiritually beneficial.

"I wait, till my change come." Job 14:14; 17:12

"As a vesture shalt thou change them." Psalm 102:26

"Thinks to change times and laws." Daniel 7:25; 2:9

"Christ shall change our vile body." Philippians 3:21; I Corinthians 15:21

"Because they have no changes, they fear not God." Psalm 55:19

How it is that "change and decay" are around us! The changing seasons of nature symbolize the constant mutations of our mortal life "summer and winter." Human life has its changes. Human institutions and governments have their changes. Customs and fashions change. Such changes impress us with the constant activity of God and remind us that this is not our rest.

David's career was by no means a monotonous one. What vicissitudes were crowded into it! Constant changes were his, and when he wrote about those who have "no changes," he had in mind the changes that disturb, unhinge our plans and arrangements, and frustrate our hopes; changes which, like earthquakes, upheave our ordered life, comfort, and settled ease. Without such changes we are liable to drift into the perils of an undisturbed life; and pleasant monotony can breed ignorance of God. When a Christian's life is filled with blessings but never darkened by storms, there is the fear that the absence of change will rob him of deeper holiness of life, and of a fuller acquaintance of Him who is the changeless One. Life's changes always should, and constantly do, awaken trust and lead us nearer God.

Where do we stand in all this? Have we grasped the promise that no change can separate us from Him who is ever the same? Do we live merely for present enjoyments, scorning the disturbing and unwelcome changes of life? Are we blind to the fact that the upheavals we shrink from can make for ennoblement of character, that we can climb to God by the path of pain? If, on the other hand, we have learned how to make changes minister unto us – if loss has yielded gain – if material poverty has produced spiritual wealth, then ours is life indeed. We live on the victory side when we discover that all the changes unsettling and deranging our schemes and destroying our hopes but serve to remind us that we have no continuing city in this world of change. Do you know Moffat's translation of David's promise, "My expectation is from God"? (Psalm 62:5). It is, "Leave it all quietly to God." In His unchanging character, He is our Rock and Refuge amid the drastic changes overwhelming us.

THE CHILDREN OF COVENANT

A Christian, as a child of God, is the heir to several glorious promises. As children, believers hold a privileged relationship to the Father.

"They shall be called the children of God." Matthew 5:9
"We are the children of God."
Romans 8:16, 17, 21
"Ye are all the children of God by faith in Christ Jesus." Galatians 3:26
"In this the children of God are manifest." I John 3:10
"We know that we love the children of God." I John 5:2

Allied to the filial term "Children" is the kindred one, "Sons," and it is the most profitable to meditate upon our rights, privileges and promises as those belonging to our Heavenly Father. What impresses us most is the fact that we are named as children of the covenant who have every claim upon the "covenants of promise" (Ephesians 2:12).

"Ye are the children . . . of the covenant." Acts 3:25
"Redeemed his people . . . to remember his holy covenant." Luke 1:68, 72

One of the ruling ideas running through the whole of the Bible is that of a covenant between God and His redeemed children. The marrow of Puritan faith was all that the truth of a covenant expressed. So the Puritans made a solemn league and covenant with one another, because they knew that they had entered already into a solemn covenant with God which was more solemn still. In a past generation, the note of that word *covenant* sounded through the sermons and the hymns which they loved best. "Testament," as we know, is just another name for "covenant" – the title by which the apostles called the *gospels* and the *epistles,* since they constituted the very bonds and indentures of their fellowship in Christ Jesus.

When the Puritans spoke of a covenant-keeping God, they knew that His covenant implied fixity and security – a covenant ordered in all things and sure. They were persuaded that God had bound them to Himself by links which were settled and established beyond their altering. His covenant was deeper than their fluctuations of feeling and moods of emotion and was one that would endure through the chances and changes of outward affairs. Can we say that we share their estimation of the *covenant?*

"Behold my covenant is with thee . . . between me and thee." Genesis 18:4-7
"I said I will never break my covenant with you." Judges 2:1; Psalm 89:34
"Be ye mindful always of his covenant." I Chronicles 16:15-17
"I will make an everlasting covenant with you." Isaiah 55:3; II Samuel 23:5
"My covenant . . . day and night." Jeremiah 33:16, 25; 32:40-41
"Nevertheless I will remember my covenant with thee . . . an everlasting covenant." Ezekiel 16:60

Here is a promise that goes back and then forward. As with Israel, so with ourselves – God looks rather to *His* covenant with us than to *our* covenant with Him. Then he affirms that His covenant shall not fail. If *we* do not stand, *He* does. He cannot draw back upon His promises. His own dear Son ratified that covenant of grace with His precious blood, and He will therefore rest in His covenant engagements.

"He will ever be mindful of his covenant." Psalm 111:5

The context of this promise indicates that "those who fear God need not fear want." Through those long forty years in the wilderness the children of the covenant lacked nothing. God remembered His covenant to guard and provide for His people. It is so with the covenant of grace, of which Christ is the Surety and the Holy Spirit is the Administrator. God will not suffer one word of such a covenant to fall to the ground. He will ever be mindful of His covenant, He cannot forget it, neither can He act contrary to it. May *we* also be ever mindful of His covenant!

The Virtue of Courage

The saints in God's portrait gallery were meek but not weak. Facing tremendous odds, fierce antagonism, cruel ostracism, and brutal martyrdom they were wonderfully brave. Fearing God, they had no fear of man. They were willing to hazard their lives for the Lord they dearly loved. Think of the fearlessness of the Hebrew youths when thrown into the fiery furnace, of Daniel when cast into the den of lions, of John the Baptist as he awaited decapitation, of Stephen threatened with a terrible death by stoning, of Paul as he awaited the hangman's block on the Appian Way!

Where have you, in the annals of history, such an exhibition of courage as that to be found in the Bible? Read the illustrious role of dauntless warriors in the eleventh chapter of Hebrews. What courage was theirs as they were called upon to shed their ruby blood for the sake of truth and righteousness! In David's beautiful eulogy of Saul and Jonathan, he describes their daring, boldness, and strength as surpassing that of lions (II Samuel 1:23). Solomon says that "the righteous are bold as a lion" (Proverbs 28:1). Wherein were those Bible saints "stronger than lions"? The strength of a lion is natural, the strength of saints is supernatural. They were dauntless and lion-hearted because they were strengthened with all might from above. What an inspiration, then, is the divine record of the brave to our hesitant, fainting hearts! How we need to be baptized with the same courage they exhibited.

"I will trust, and not be afraid."
Isaiah 12:2
"I will strengthen them in the Lord, and they shall walk up and down in my name." Zechariah 10:12. See Daniel 3:19-25.
"God hath not given us the spirit of fear." II Timothy 1:7
"Be ye of good courage." Numbers 13:20; Deuteronomy 31:6; Joshua 1:6; etc.
"Everyone said to his brother, Be of good courage." Isaiah 41:6
"Be courageous, and be valiant."
II Samuel 13:28; II Chronicles 32:7; 19:11
"Only be thou strong and very courageous." Joshua 1:7, 9

The promise of continual prosperity is linked on to the courageous spirit required for absolute obedience to God's law. Certainly the mighty God will be with us in our holy war, but He demands of us strict adherence to His requirements. Unless we "observe to do," how can we expect Him to add strength and courage to our faith as we set out on a straightforward course, turning neither to the right nor to the left?

"He took courage and put away the abominable idols." II Chronicles 15:8

King Asa's reform, begotten as it was by the Spirit-inspired warning of the prophet Azariah, was as radical in its nature as it was wide in its range. "For a long season Israel had been without the true God, and without a teaching priest, and without law" (v. 3). Godless, religionless, and lawless; what a condition! And as even nature abhors a vacuum, the heart of the nation minus God, priest, and law, became the home of abominable idols. But a courageous king renewed the altar, revived the law, and recovered faith in God. And because moral courage is ever greater than mere physical courage, many a ruler finds it easier to lead his nation into war against invading foes than to cleanse his nation of immoral foes within. It likewise takes courage, does it not, to put away the idols out of our own hearts (II Chronicles 19:11)?

"Paul saw . . . and took courage."
Acts 28:15

The sight of a friend's face in a time of crisis puts fresh heart in us. Paul was ever so thankful when, on reaching the market of Appius, he met the brethren who had come from Rome to greet him. After such a perilous sea voyage, and knowing what imprisonment faced him, Paul's courage rose high the moment he met sympathizing friends. Adversely, bearers of evil tidings may wither up any courage we have (Joshua 2:11). Life at best is very brief; and the world is full of men and women who need encouragement. Do those who cross our pathway from day to day feel all the better for having met us? Is there something about our handshake, our contented look, our sympathetic words, that lead them to thank God and take courage (Isaiah 41:6)?

"Be strong and of good courage, and do it." I Chronicles 28:20

Denied the privilege of building the Temple, David handed over to Solomon his son the materials he had prepared in abundance for the house of the Lord God. In doing so, he urged Solomon to be strong and courageous in the accomplishment of the gigantic task. "Dread not nor be dismayed" (I Chronicles 22:13). And truly it required undaunted courage to continue through twenty years covered by the building of the Temple and Solomon's own house. Has God assigned you some hard, long task? And are you a little overwhelmed by what He has asked you to build out of materials He has, or will, supply? Well, David's promise to Solomon is good for you. And remember, "The Lord God will not fail thee or forsake thee, until thou hast finished all the work" (I Chronicles 28:20).

"When they saw the boldness of Peter . . . they marvelled." Acts 4:13

No wonder the members of the Sanhedrin were amazed over Peter's courageous defence of His Master. Why, was not this the same man who, a few weeks previous, had cowered before the taunt of a servant girl and stoutly denied the Lord he was now defending? Such a change from cowardice to courage filled the Jewish rulers with amazement. The secret of such a transformation is given in the words, "they had been with Jesus." The spirit of the Master had possessed the servants. Pentecost transferred the courage of Christ to His one-time faltering servant. And fearlessness in witness is not of the flesh. It is heaven-born (Ephesians 6:19, 20).

"David encouraged himself in the Lord his God." I Samuel 30:6

David was in a sorry plight. Ziklag had been burned with fire, and the best of the populace carried away captive. David wept until he had no more power to weep. And added to his sorrow was the determined effort of the people who had been robbed of their dear ones to stone him. Circumstances were against David, but he encouraged himself in the Lord his God. What does it mean to encourage ourselves in God? In David's case it meant inquiring of the Lord, or in other words, reminding his heart of all he had in God. He rested in the joy of who and what God was. In spite of his adversities, he believed God was able to undertake, so out he went and "recovered all."

"Wait on the Lord, be of good courage." Psalm 27:14

Courage and strength are sandwiched between a double "wait on the Lord," for David, ever a brave man, knew that there is a vital connection between communion and courage. All who would do exploits must live near to Him, whose power nerves us for any conflict. The heroes of Hebrews 11 "waxed valiant," but only "through faith." The heart of this promise is in the words, "He shall strengthen thine heart." If our heart is sound, the rest of our physical system works well. The spiritual heart empowered by God makes for calmness amid tempest. There is a mere animal, physical courage which is displayed amid the grim exigencies of war, and is all too evident in days like these when multitudes are willing to defend their liberty. Sometimes courage is actuated by wrong motives. When Absalom had the opportunity of smiting Amnon, for his seduction of Tamar, Absalom exhorted his servants to "be courageous and be valiant." Such a valor, however, was motivated by fleshly vengeance. But courage for God is courage from God. It is only as we wait, that we become brave (Psalm 31:24).

"He shall not be . . . discouraged." Isaiah 42:4

A characteristic feature of Christ's life among men was His courage. He was ever brave. The taunts of men could not frighten Him. As the Captain of our salvation, He remained valiant when assailed. Stedfastly He set His face toward Jerusalem, and never halted until at Calvary He laid hold of the forces of hell and robbed them of their terror. In spite of the intense opposition of Satan, demons and foes, the word "discouragement" was never found in His vocabulary. He was "brave, stedfast and true." Believing in His ultimate victory, He courageously endured the shame and ignominy of the cross.

Isaiah likewise reminds us that this same dauntless One will never yield to despair "til he hath set judgment on the earth." Is your soul discouraged because of the greatness of the way? Then ask the Lord for a baptism of His faith and fearlessness. Allied to the Master's courage was His compassion. He defied those who thirsted for His blood to do their worst. But as He died the death His enemies planned, grace was His to pray for the forgiveness of His murderers.

THE ROD OF CHASTENING

God's disciplinary methods with those whom He redeemed and loves occupies much space in His Word. We may shrink from such necessary chastisement, yet we are consoled by the fact that it is never vindictive and that the rod is in the hand of our loving Heavenly Father, whose one purpose in permitted chastening is our highest spiritual welfare. Deserved discipline results in conformity to His blessed mind and will. The sculptor knows that as the chips fly, the image grows. The proverb has it—"A gem is not polished without rubbing —nor a man perfected without trials."

We may not look upon "chastisement" itself as being much of a promise. Its ultimate purpose, however, is full of promised spiritual growth and fruitfulness.

"I will chasten him with the rod of men." I Samuel 7:14
"He is chastened also with pain upon his bed." Job 33:19
"I have been . . . chastened every morning." Psalm 73:14
"The Lord hath chastened me sore." Psalm 118:18
"Chasten thy son while there is hope." Proverbs 13:24; 19:18; Deuteronomy 8:5; 21:18
"As many as I love, I rebuke and chasten." Revelation 3:19; Proverbs 3:13; Hebrews 12:6
"We are chastened of the Lord." I Corinthians 11:32; II Corinthians 6:9
"No chastening for the present seemeth to be joyous." Hebrews 12:9-11
"Despise not thou the chastening of the Almighty." Job 5:17; Hebrews 12:5
"Blessed is the man whom thou chasteneth, O Lord." Psalm 94:12
"They poured out a prayer when thy chastening was upon them." Isaiah 26:16

"I, even I, will chastise you seven times for your sins." Leviticus 26:28
"I will chastise you with scorpions." I Kings 12:11; Hosea 7:12
"The chastisement of our peace was upon him." Isaiah 53:5

A consideration of the above passages convinces us that in loving-kindness God provides and permits chastisement, uses various methods of imposing it, and has a beneficial end in view in sending it. Because God is loving and faithful He will not suffer us to be tested beyond what we are able to endure (I Corinthians 10:13). Dr. F. B. Meyer has beautifully expressed divine tempering of the rod in these words—

"There is not a step He does not weigh; nor a path He does not winnow; nor a tear the shedding of which has not been to Him a subject of anxiety; not a stab of pain, the edge of which He has not felt before it touches us; not a sorrow the weight of which He has not felt before He allowed it to impinge."

"Whom the Lord loveth, he chasteneth." Hebrews 12:6

We dare not doubt His promise that He will perfect that which concerns us (Psalm 138:3). But sometimes the means He uses to accomplish His gracious design are not pleasant to the flesh. "I bear my willing witness that I owe more to the fire, and the hammer, and the file, than to anything else in my Lord's worship," says Spurgeon. "I sometimes question whether I have ever learned anything except through the rod. When my schoolroom is darkened, I see most." God's manifold temporal promises never justify our expecting to escape His discipline. As our Father, He keeps in His hands the right to chasten us for our good, that we may partake of His holiness. While He assures us that He will comfort us as a mother consoles her child, He also tells us that without chastisement, we are bastards—not sons.

"My son, despise thou not the chastening of the Lord." Hebrews 12:5

We must beware of despising divine chastisement, which we do when we think there is no occasion for it, or that we could do as well, if not better, without it. Neither must we be guilty of cultivating a carnal, flesh-pleasing desire to be delivered from necessary divine correction. When the rod falls we must ascertain the cause for its fall, and quickly learn the lessons the rod is intended to teach. If grace is ours to submit to God's disciplinary work, acknowledging His right to chasten and His love in doing it, then we can trust Him to end the duration of our trial when its mission has been accomplished.

"I will correct you in measure."
Jeremiah 30:11

Sin and disobedience necessitate this correction, and love sends it. His love is without measure, but His chastisement is measured. God, we are told, chastises every son He receives. Every son is chastised because every son sins. The assurance of this promise is that God does not reward us according to our sin. He chastens us in measure, not in wrath. He seeks, through the trials He permits to drive us to Himself, to humble us at His feet, to purify and cleanse our hearts. For the present, these chastenings are not joyous, but grievous. But *afterward* they yield the peaceable fruits of righteousness.

Saints of old because of personal shortcomings, or of national sins, felt "the need of chastising of themselves."

"When I wept, and chastened my soul with fasting." Psalm 69:10

"Chasten thyself before thy God."
Daniel 10:12

Summerizing the teaching of Psalm 38, Finis J. Dake, in his monumental *Annotated Reference Bible*, tells us that this great Psalm sets forth eight good results of "Chastening" –

1. It makes one pray (1, 16, 21, 22)
2. It awakens to the foolishness of sin (3, 5)
3. It makes one desire God (9)
4. It enables him to know his true friends (12-14)
5. It makes one compassionate and merciful to others (12-14)
6. It makes him penitent (6, 7, 17, 18)
7. It produces hope and faith (15)
8. It encourages a life of following that which is good (20).

THE MEDICINE OF CHEER

"Blessed" means *happy*, and because God is the blessed, or happy, One, He does not want His children to be gloomy, despondent, cheerless. Did not Solomon affirm that? –

"A merry heart doeth good like a medicine." Proverbs 17:22

"A merry heart maketh a cheerful countenance." Proverbs 15:13

"Let thy heart cheer thee in the days of thy youth." Ecclesiastes 11:9

"Be of good cheer; thy sins be forgiven thee." Matthew 9:2

"Be of good cheer, it is I, be not afraid." Matthew 14:27

"Be of good cheer; I have overcome the world." John 16:32

"Be of good cheer . . . thou must bear witness." Acts 23:11

"I exhort you be of good cheer."
Acts 27:22

"God loveth a cheerful giver."
II Corinthians 9:7

"He that sheweth mercy, with cheerfulness." Romans 12:8

Is not the design of the cheery promises we have cited above to beget in us a "cheerful godliness," and to make us "cheerful travelers" on the road of life? The world around will never be attracted to God by a cheerless godliness. How narrow, warped, and joyless the religion of some professed Christians seems to be! They appear to be destitute of the joy of the Lord. Often their very faces suggest that the Gospel is a funeral, rather than a feast.

"Happy art thou . . . O people saved by the Lord." Deuteronomy 33:29

When adversity comes our way, we are apt to be downcast. Our spirit sinks when we are sorely tried. But even in a shipwreck, with everything gone, Paul could urge both crew and passengers to cheer up. And such was no false encouragement. Paul believed God, hence his cheerful confidence that all would reach safety. We face a hostile world, but Jesus says, "Be of good cheer; I have overcome the world." What a promise this is to hide in our hearts, and when Christ bids us cheer up we dare not be cast down. To Him, the world is a beaten foe, and we can share His victory over it. Therefore, let us be of good cheer and sing heartily unto our conquering, soon-coming Lord.

THE PROMISE AND PROSPECT OF
CHRISTLIKENESS

The very name "Christian" implies that the one who bears it is like Christ. Because of their adherence to all Christ taught, and the exhibition of Christlike qualities, the disciples became known as "Christians." Our constant shame is that although we profess His Name, yet we are so unlike Him. Somehow life and likeness do not agree as they should.

Many of the promises associated with Christlikeness are prospective in character. They are taken up with our transformation into His image, when upon seeing Him, we shall resemble Him.

"As we have borne the image of the earthly, we shall also bear the image of the heavenly." I Corinthians 15:49
"I shall be satisfied when I awake in thy likeness." Psalm 17:15
"The Saviour . . . who shall change our vile body, that it may be fashioned like unto his glorious body."

Philippians 3:20, 21
"When he shall appear, we shall be like him." I John 3:2
"They shall see his face; and his name shall be in their foreheads."

Revelation 22:4

Our finite minds cannot fully comprehend all that is involved in this glorious change. This we do know, that we shall not only resemble Him in His glorious body, but also in love, adoration, and praise.

As we tarry in the flesh, our constant desire should be to have a growing likeness to Christ in life and character. Can we say that our lives reflect Him? Is it easy for those around us to believe in Him because of the ways in which we exhibit His character?

"Beholding, as in a mirror, the glory of the Lord, we are changed into the same image." II Corinthians 3:18
"In the image of God created he him."

Genesis 1:26, 27
"They are not of the world, even as I am not of this world." John 17:14, 16
"As he is, so are we in this world."

I John 4:17
"Be likeminded one toward another according to Christ Jesus."

Romans 15:5; Philippians 2:2, 20
"As thou art, so were they: each one resembled the children of a king."

Judges 8:18

Because Christ condescended to be made in "the likeness of men," He expects redeemed men to have His likeness (Philippians 2:7; Romans 8:3). This is not a matter of mere imitation. One of our hymns puts it—
"Be like Jesus, this my song."
But if we try to be like Him in the power of the flesh, we shall miserably fail. It is only as the Holy Spirit controls our heart, mind, and will that Christ becomes enthroned within the life. Then when He is Lord, our works, ways, and words are fragrant with the reality of His presence within the life. He lives out His life through our life. It was because Paul could say "Christ liveth in me," that the life he lived in the flesh suggested Christ. A good

deal of Christ-imitation is artificial – and artificial roses have no perfume!

THE BEST OF COMPANIONSHIPS

Some of the most precious promises in the Bible are those declaring God's willingness to dwell within His people and to be with them throughout life's pilgrimage. Surely this is a most privileged companionship. The loneliest saint is therefore not companionless. How abundant are these promises of divine presence! How they deepen within our hearts gratitude and love to Him who became *Immanuel,* meaning, "God with us!"

"As the mountains are round about Jerusalem, so the Lord is round about his people from henceforth even for ever." Psalm 125:2
"God is with thee whithersoever thou goest." Joshua 1:9
"Samuel grew, and the Lord was with him." I Samuel 3:19
"God himself is with us as our captain." II Chronicles 13:12
"As I was with Moses, I will be with thee."

Joshua 1:5; II Chronicles 1:1; 17:3
"With us is the Lord our God."

II Chronicles 32:8
"David waxed greater and greater; for the Lord was with him."

I Chronicles 11:9
"I am with thee . . . I will hold thy hand." Isaiah 41:10, 13
"He is at my right hand . . . at Thy right hand." Psalms 16:8, 11
"We will . . . make our abode with him." John 14:23
"Lo, I am with you alway."

Matthew 28:20
"The Lord stood with me and strengthened me." II Timothy 4:17
"I will never leave thee, nor forsake thee." Hebrews 13:5
"What nation is so great, who hath God so nigh unto them?"

Deuteronomy 4:7
"He be not very far from every one of us." Acts 17:27-28
"Certainly, I will be with thee."

Exodus 3:12
"Fear not, I am with thee."

Genesis 26:24
"My presence shall go with thee, and I will give thee rest." Exodus 33:14

These blessed promises of divine companionship are for each saint to appropriate. In all of our journeyings we are assured of the double favor of God's presence and rest. No matter how our journeys may separate us from home and loved ones, there is always One who accompanies us, making us the recipient of His fellowship, and also of His care, provision, and strength. While our travels may not provide us with much physical rest, the knowledge that the Lord of Hosts is with us (Psalm 46:7), lets us rest in the joy of all He is in Himself.

"Am I a God at hand, saith the Lord?" Jeremiah 23:23, 24

The truth Jeremiah is emphasizing in these verses is that of God's Omnipresence. There is no secret place where we can hide from Him. Ever at hand, He sees and knows all. When Paul said, "The Lord is at hand," he meant what the prophet did, namely, that the Lord is at hand, as close as that, and ready to undertake in all things.

"Be not far from me; for trouble is near." Psalm 22:11

"Though he be not far from every one of us." Acts 17:27; Psalm 139:7-10

"The Lord will be with you." II Chronicles 20:17

This short but sweet promise of the divine presence was the very one King Jehoshaphat needed at that time. A great multitude had come out against him, and he feared the outcome of the battle. But the king was assured that God was with him, and that all would be well. We, too, can lay hold of this promise because no matter where we may be, in conflict, in the house, in the office or factory, in company or alone, the Lord is with us.

"Lo, I am with you all the days." Matthew 28:26 RV margin

What a wonderful coverage this promise has! *All* the days—not some of them. The days ahead may be days of divine discipline, but with the Lord with us the discipline will be a blessing and not a bane. Affliction will only teach us to grasp His strong hand with a tighter hold and to pray more earnestly. F. W. Boreham, in *Mushrooms on the Moor,* says that "Anybody can grow fine flowers in the daytime. But what can you grow in the dark?" Well, even in "thick darkness," God is near and can enable us to produce the fruit of the Spirit. Perhaps the unseen days may prove to be days of temptation, of loneliness, of death. Yet whatever kind of days they may be, He will be with us to the end, and through the end, and beyond the end forever and ever.

"Christ liveth in me." Galatians 2:20

Since He lives within us, what else can He be but our dear and closest Companion? He is not only *outside* us as our Guide and Guard, but *within* us as the Guest who can never be evicted. Further, because of His presence within, He is the Source of that inner joy and peace the trials around cannot destroy. Indwelling us, the beams from His blessed life turn night into day. He is ever there to undertake at all times, and to make our life, as we journey with Him, the medium of blessing to others.

"Certainly I will be with thee." Exodus 3:12

How impressive is the "certainty" in this promise! Why, there is nothing more certain in a Christian's life than the promised presence of the Lord! Are we not honored to be favored with His august presence? Such a promise should arm against fear—nerve us against opposition—embolden us to witness for Him. Because His presence is sure, we should be found cultivating the realization of it.

"For God is with us." Isaiah 8:10

"The Lord of hosts is with us." Psalm 46:7

"Emmanuel . . . God with us." Matthew 1:23

Because a Christian is never alone, he should not feel lonely. Think of whom this constant Companion is—GOD! And He is with His own, not only as an observer, but as the Omnipotent One. He is with us as the *Lord of Hosts,* having all the forces of heaven and earth under His direction to befriend us. He is with us as the *Guide,* to direct our step; as the *Counsellor* to instruct us; as the *Friend* to supply our need and comfort our heart; as the *Saviour* to deliver us from sin.

The consciousness of such a divine presence checks levity, prevents impatience, encourages intercession, produces patience and diligence, and inspires fortitude.

"The Lord is nigh unto all them that call upon him." Psalm 145:18

We have not to ask Him to be near us and to go with us over life's highway. It is for us to believe His promise that He *is* ever nigh, whether we call on Him or not. Yet is it not comforting to know that whenever we have a sense of need, or a sense of guilt, He is near, lovingly to listen to our cry, and graciously willing to help in our difficulty, or distress?

"I am with thee, and no man shall

set on thee to hurt." Acts 18:10

God's presence was real to Paul. He lived as one who had the Almighty as his Companion and Protector. Knowing that God was with him, and for him, the apostle had no fear regarding those who were against him. He rested in the assurance that no harm could assail him unless the Lord permitted it. Paul believed, as we must do, that the One who is Master of Satan can certainly control Satan's agents and protect His own.

"I will be with thee: I will not fail thee, nor forsake thee." Joshua 1:5

"The Lord, he it is that doth go before thee; he will be with thee, he will not fail thee, nor forsake thee."
Deuteronomy 31:8

"I will never leave thee, nor forsake thee." Hebrews 13:5

As we can see from these kindred passages, the Old Testament promise became the basis of a New Testament one. Because He is the same yesterday, today, and forever, all that He was, He still is and will ever be. With Joshua we should never be dismayed, since the Lord is with us, in us, beneath and above us as the Omnipresent and Omnipotent One. It is because He cannot fail us, that He will not forsake us.

This promise is not only one of the most precious in the Bible, but also the most remarkable in that you can read it backwards and it means the same. Take it the wrong way round—

"Thee forsake, nor thee leave, never will I."

Now read it the Bible way—

"I will never leave thee, nor forsake thee."

So whether we read it the right or wrong way, the thought is the same, namely, that we have the promise of our Lord's abiding presence every day, and all the days.

"The angel of the Lord encampeth round about them that fear him, and delivereth them." Psalm 34:7

"Mine eyes shall be upon the faithful of the land, that they may dwell with me: he that walketh in a perfect way."
Psalm 101:6

Here we have two of these conditional promises common to Scripture. His promised presence and fellowship can only be realized as we "fear him" and walk before Him "in a perfect way." Seeking to live in unbroken fellowship with Him, we know that as the Angel of the covenant, His eye is ever upon us. Obeying and trusting God, we are sentinelled by such an invincible One. Dwelling with Him, walking before Him with a perfect heart, we are privileged to serve Him as His honored servants.

THE SPRING OF COMFORT

There is not another book of Comfort in the world comparable to the Bible. Because the God of the Christian is "the God of all comfort," we expect His Word to be laden with promises of consolation for sorrowing hearts in a world of tears. Disconsolate ones see these promises shine out in golden letters on its dark sky, and take heart to trust for their fulfilment. F. W. Boreham draws attention to the fact that "the Bible is packed from cover to cover with things that it never mentions. *Sympathy* is one of them. The *word* nowhere occurs; the *thing* is everywhere." This is evident, as we shall see, in what the Bible reveals of the Lord as the Sympathizing One.

"He hath sent comforters unto thee."
II Samuel 10:3. Contrast Job 16:2

"Lord, thou hast holpen me, and comforted me." Psalm 86:17

"Let, I pray thee, thy merciful kindness be for my comfort." Psalm 119:76

"Comfort ye, comfort ye my people . . . Speak ye comfortably." Isaiah 40:1

"The Lord hath comforted his people."
Isaiah 49:13-16; 52:9; 12:1

"Walking . . . in the comfort of the Holy Ghost." Acts 9:31; John 14:18

"The comfort of the Scriptures."
Romans 15:4

"Daughter, be of good comfort."
Matthew 9:22

"We ourselves are comforted of God."
II Corinthians 1:3-4

"Our Lord Jesus Christ . . . comfort your hearts." II Thessalonians 2:17

Promises of this nature are associated with our relief in seasons of stress and sorrow, and they reveal how deeply interested God is in all that concerns our earthly life.

"In all their afflictions he was afflicted." Isaiah 63:9

Says Thomas à Kempis, "When therefore spiritual comfort is given thee from God, receive it with thankfulness; but understand that it is the gift of God, not any dessert of thine." Coleridge has the couplet—

"Like dew upon a wither'd flower
Is comfort to the heart that's broken."

Such is the nature of the comfort of Him who came to comfort all who mourn, and to heal the broken-hearted.

"The God of all comfort."

II Corinthians 1:3

God is, indeed, the spring of all our comfort. All our springs are in Him. A writer for the heart has reminded us that, "Spiritual comfort is that refreshing pleasure of the soul which arises from the consideration of what God in Christ is to us, in respect of relation, of what He has done for us, and infallibly promised to do for us." The margin gives us the word "encouragement" for "comfort," the multitudes of harassed, downcast saints certainly need this aspect of divine ministry. How privileged we are to have God as the *Author* of Comfort – Christ as the *Personification* of it – the Holy Spirit, the *Medium* of it – the Scriptures, the established *Ground* of it – ourselves, as the *Recipients* of it!

"As one whom his mother comforteth, even so will I comfort you."

Isaiah 66:13

As a good and godly mother is "the holiest thing alive," we have here a precious insight into the heart of God. It is to mother that the child usually runs when there are tears to be kissed away. The father may fail to successfully calm a fretful child. It is soon asleep, however, on the pillow of mother's breast. Is it not blessed to know that in the trying, troubled hours of life, when as fretful children we need consolation and sympathy, we can come and lean on the bosom of Him who is our *El Shaddai* – "the Breasted One"? God is the perfect Comforter, because He combines all the qualities of noble-hearted fatherhood and gentle motherhood.

"Another comforter." John 14:16

In order fully to appreciate Christ's promised Gift, we have to get at the back of the simple word, "another," which in the original carries a twofold significance: first, something of the same kind; second, something of a different kind. Because Christ used the first word, the language has no meaning whatever if the Holy Spirit is not a personal Comforter. In effect, Jesus was saying, "My ministry has been one of consolation, for I came to comfort all who mourn. But I am going to leave you, and Another is coming to continue My ministry of comfort. Do not be disconsolate; I will send you Another like myself." And truly the Spirit is Jesus' other Self. How blessed we are to be indwelt by One like Jesus!

"Miserable comforters are ye all." "Thy comforts delight my soul." Job 16:2;

Psalm 94:19

What a difference there is between divine and human comfort! The one delights, the other depresses. Perhaps Job's friends meant well, but they went the wrong way about cheering Job in his time of need. Alas, clumsy hands only deepen a wound! When we meet those whose hearts are smitten with grief, what need there is of tact, lest, in spite of our good intentions, we speak and act in a way calculated to increase sorrow. A crushed spirit requires delicate handling. With God it is so different. He is so understanding, so kind, so tender. He not only means well, but doeth all things well. When our trials are at their worst, and human sympathy is unavailing, He knows how to clothe our heaviness with the garment of praise.

"God, that comforteth those that are cast down . . . comforteth in your comfort." II Corinthians 7:6, 13

There is a beautiful connection here, where Paul lays bare his heart in writing to the Corinthians. Trouble on every side, fightings without and fears within, were enough to cast any man down. But God knew about His persecuted, distressed, and troubled servant, and He hastened to his side, not in the form of an angel, but in a pair of human legs. The God of comfort comforted Paul by the coming of Titus. This messenger and his message caused a downcast apostle to take fresh courage. Are you so in tune with the Lord as to be the channel of His comfort? How many are there who praise Him for your coming? What a privilege it is to function as heaven's ambassador of comfort!

"The Lord answered the angel . . . with good words and comfortable words." Zechariah 1:13

But angels are not the only ones who need to hear comfortable words! God has a heart that feels for men, even though they have frustrated His hopes. Isaiah was bidden, "Speak comfortably to my people." Earth rejects Him, but He answers back with words, both good and comfortable, and comfortable because they are good words of pardon. And if God is careful about the way He answers angels, surely we ought to exercise the same care in answering those who, whether they deserve our pity or not, certainly need it. Even if they refuse to be comforted (Genesis 37:35; Psalm 77:2; Jeremiah 31:15), let us ever remain true sons of consolation.

"Comfort one another with these

words." I Thessalonians 4:18

What words? Well, we must read the narrative to find out the significance of this climactic exhortation. These articulate messengers of comfort were words of hope. Loved ones had died, and lonely hearts were anxious as to the whereabouts of, and union with, their dead. Would they rise again? Did the future offer any certainty of renewed fellowship? In answer to these questions, Paul unfolded the truth of Christ's return. Our holy dead are happy with Christ. At His coming, the bodies laid away are to rise again. Living saints are to be changed. The dead will be raised, the living changed, and both caught up together. Thus the Second Advent is a comforting hope. And in this vale of tears, there are multitudes of grief-stricken hearts who wait to be comforted with "these words." God pity the pulpit or Christian guilty of a sinful silence when it comes to the Lord's return! It is the message a weary world needs.

"I am he that comforteth you."

Isaiah 51:12, 13

The promise comprising these two verses does not need much comment. It speaks for itself. There is a promise to believe, feed on, and constantly plead before our Maker and the Creator of the ends of the earth, who promises to comfort our fearful hearts. Oppressors should not be feared, for their breath is in their nostrils and can be withdrawn at God's bidding.

How does God comfort those who are cast down? He comforts *in*, and *by* His Son; through His gracious Spirit, the inner Comforter; through His Word, so full of the promises of consolations; through His ordinances, in which He meets with us; through His providential dealings. We must guard ourselves against the comfort which does not come from Him, or lead to Him. As the Author of comfort, God must be the Center to which we always gravitate, and the Circumference within which we live, and move, and have our being. All our springs are in Him (Psalm 87:7).

"I will not leave you comfortless."

John 14:18

What our Lord said was that He would not leave His own as *orphans* in a world of hostility. Their hearts were troubled over the announcement of His coming departure. "Let not your heart be troubled" (John 14:1-3). But although He was to leave His disciples, they were not to feel forsaken or lonely. Another Comforter was coming to take His place. Amid the separations and trials of life it may be natural to feel that somehow the Lord has left it, but such a feeling is not Scriptural, because He has promised never to leave us.

How absolutely dependent we are upon the gift of His comforting presence! Yes, and His presence and His comforts go together. His promise is plain—"*I* will not leave you comfortless." Such a precious promise must be firmly trusted and pleaded. As "the everlasting Father," He cannot leave His redeemed ones as "orphans." His presence and comforts are sure.

"To comfort all that mourn."

Isaiah 61:2

Michael Drayton, of the sixteenth century, in his *Barrons Wars*, affirmed that:

"Ill news hath wings, and with the wind doth go;
Comfort's a cripple and comes ever slow."

Possibly human comfort is somewhat crippled and is slow in coming, but divine comfort, like the Comforter Himself, is immediately available as soon as need of it arises. Although happy are the people whose God is their Lord, yet in another sense they are all mourners. They mourn over committed sin, over inward depravity, or spiritual impoverishment, over unsaved relatives and friends, over the godless condition of the world, as well as over their trials and losses. A saying accredited to a divine of 1660 reads—

"I have only two comforts to live upon. The one is the perfections of Christ; the other the imperfections of all Christians."

But Jesus declared—

"Blessed are they that mourn, for they shall be comforted." The Man of Sorrow came as the anointed and apointed Comforter of His own and He ever lives to soothe and succor. He comforts us by pardoning our sins, by subduing our old nature, by using us in His service, by reminding us of His promises, by the ministry of His servants.

"My Saviour will my comfort be,
And set my soul from trouble free."

"The Lord hath comforted his people, and will have mercy upon his afflicted."

Isaiah 49:13

Spurgeon says that "this word of promise, that our God will have mercy upon His afflicted, has a whole peal of bells connected with it." Hear their music—

'Sing!' 'Be joyful!' 'Break forth into singing.'"

And as we think of all the comforts of God, we have something to sing about. Why should we sigh and sulk, as we sometimes do, when we have such a God of comfort, and all the comforts of God? As those redeemed by the blood of His Son, God means us to be singing people, happy because of His unfailing love and grace.

"Blessed are they that mourn, for they shall be comforted." Matthew 5:4

Already we have suggested that all the "Blesseds" of the Bible can be treated as promises, and here is one of them. Whatever future application this promise may have, the Christian can claim it *now*. Here our Lord unites mourning and comfort. It does not matter what the reason of your present mourning may be, whether it be over personal sins and sorrows, or the shortcomings of others, the Lord is at hand to ease the aching heart, to dry the tears, and to sanctify the grief. It is certainly true that we live in a world of sin, sighs, and sobs, but it is not altogether true to say that our comfort is in heaven. The Comforter is with us here on earth. Nay, He is within our hearts as the unfailing Source of comfort.

"I will allure her . . . and speak comfortably unto her." Hosea 2:14

Satan may desire to have us, but God's desire is ever toward us. How He strives to match subtle allurements of Satan with the powerful allurements of His grace and goodness! He here promises to draw us apart to some separated place where He can commune with us and assure us of all He is in Himself and of all He can be to us. This is likewise a promise which experience alone can explain. In the desert of affliction, He speaks "to our heart," which is the original of "speak comfortably." Comforted of God, it is our responsibility to emulate the divine mission and seek to comfort others. If His comforts delight our soul (Psalm 94:19), then may our ministry of comfort delight many a downcast heart.

"Who comforteth us . . . that we may be able to comfort them which are in trouble." II Corinthians 1:4

Is this not the reflection of the divine heart, Trench suggested in the lines? –

"Wouldst thou go forth to bless" – be sure of thine own ground!
Fix well thy center first, then draw thy circles round!

There can be added to the promises of comfort, those related to consolation, which implies the same virtue. Generally, this latter term signifies –

1. Spiritual joy

   "Be satisfied with the breasts of her consolation." Isaiah 66:11

2. Christ and all His benefits

   "Waiting for the consolation of Israel."
   Luke 2:25

   "Are the consolations of God small with thee?" Job 15:11; 21:2

   "The cup of consolation to drink."
   Jeremiah 16:7

   "Ye have received your consolation."
   Luke 6:24

   "Barnabas . . . the son of consolation."
   Acts 4:36

   "They rejoiced for the consolation."
   Acts 15:31

   "The God . . . of consolation."
   Romans 15:5

   "Our consolation aboundeth in Christ."
   II Corinthians 1:2, 6, 7

   "The consolation wherewith he has comforted you."
   II Corinthians 7:7; Philemon 7

   "If there be any consolations in Christ."
   Philippians 2:1

   "Everlasting consolation and good hope through grace." II Thessalonians 1:16

   "A strong consolation." Hebrews 6:18

How our sorrowful world needs a large army of Barnabases – sons and daughters of consolation – who, by their words and works help to relieve distress.

Plantus, the Latin philosopher, wrote –

"He does nothing who consoles a despairing man with his words; he is a friend who in difficulty helps by deeds, where there is need of deeds."

God is a perfect Consoler who consoles our despairing hearts, not only with promises of comfort, but with practical performance of same.

THE SECRET OF CONFIDENCE

The "confidence" whereof the Bible speaks, and to which several promises are attached, signifies, according to the Bible Concordance, different ideas.

1. It suggests assurance.

   "The great confidence which I have in you." II Corinthians 8:22

2. It speaks of boldness.

   "With all confidence, no man forbidding him." Acts 28:31

3. It implies trust.

   "Is not this . . . thy confidence?"
   Job 4:6

4. It represents an object trusted in.
"The house of Israel was ashamed of Bethel their confidence." Isaiah 48:13

5. It includes help.
"What confidence is this wherein thou trustest?" II Kings 18:19

6. It represents safety.
"They shall dwell with confidence." Ezekiel 28:26

7. It stands for a bold profession of Christ.
"Cast not away therefore your confidence." Hebrews 10:34, 35

8. It covers a persuasion of acceptance.
"In whom we have boldness and access with confidence by the faith of him." Ephesians 3:13

9. It carries the idea of a due resolution.
"That I may not be bold when I am present with that confidence, wherewith I think to be bold against some." II Corinthians 10:2

True and false objects of confidence are indicated, with judgment following the false objects and promised blessing related to true objects.

"The Lord hath rejected thy confidences, and thou shalt not prosper in them." Jeremiah 2:37

"Put ye not confidence in a guide or a friend." Micah 7:5

"It shall be no more the confidence of the house of Israel." Ezekiel 29:16

"No confidence in the flesh." Philippians 3:3

"Confidence in an unfaithful man." Proverbs 25:19

"Put not your confidence in man . . . in princes." Psalm 118:8

"I said to fine gold, Thou art my confidence." Job 31:24; 18:14

"What confidence is this wherein thou trustest?" II Kings 18:19

"Gaal . . . the men of Shechem put their confidence in him." Judges 9:26

There is no need to linger over these passages. They speak for themselves. Men and material things fail, and therefore we dare not rely wholly upon them. The promise of defeat and loss accompanies any false confidence (Proverbs 21:22). But for our encouragement, the basis of unshaken confidence is given.

"The Lord shall be thy confidence." Proverbs 3:26

"In the fear of the Lord is strong confidence." Proverbs 14:26

"They shall dwell with confidence." Ezekiel 28:26

"The day of the Lord Jesus, and in this confidence." II Corinthians 1:14-15; 8:22

"Access with confidence by the faith of him." Ephesians 3:12

"We hold fast the confidence . . . firm unto the end." Hebrews 3:6, 14

"Cast not away therefore your confidence." Hebrews 10:35; 11:1

"When he shall appear, we may have confidence." I John 2:28

"Then have we confidence toward God." I John 3:21

"This is the confidence that we have in him." I John 5:14

A proverb has it – "Confidence is never safe." It is safe, however, if God is its object. Another Latin proverb says, "Confidence placed in another often compels confidence in return." The Bible clearly teaches that full confidence in God never passes unrewarded. Isaiah would have us know that no matter what our lot may be –

"In quietness and in confidence shall be your strength." 30:15

THE GAIN OF CONTENTMENT

Shakespeare, in *Macbeth*, speaks of being –
"Shut up
In measureless content."

The Bible is indispensable in that it not only promises such "measureless content," but reveals the secret of it. Such contentment is beneficial spiritually, mentally, and physically. Many physical ailments, like ulcers, would disappear if only people were more content. Is not "worry" a form of discontent? Contentment also affects our mental outlook. It produces a peace, serenity, and satisfaction of mind so necessary to health. Spiritually, contentment enables a Christian to rest in the all-sufficiency of God, and is a virtue recommending the Gospel to those who are plagued with discontented hearts. Thomas à Kempis said, "Be thankful for the least gift, so shall thou be meet to receive greater." The contentment God imparts equips us to receive His ever-increasing bounty. We come to experience that, "Contentment is the true philosopher's stone."

"When Moses heard *that* (see v. 19) he was content." Leviticus 10:20

"Would to God we had been content." Joshua 7:7

"Be content, I pray thee." Judges 19:6; II Kings 5:23; 6:3

"Now therefore be content." Job 6:28

"Neither will he rest content, though thou givest many gifts." Proverbs 6:35
"Let not thine heart envy sinners."
Proverbs 23:17, 18
"Pilate, willing to content the people."
Mark 15:15
"Be content with your wages."
Luke 3:14
"I have learned, in whatsoever state I am, therewith to be content."
Philippians 4:11
"Having food and raiment let us be therewith content . . . Godliness with contentment is great gain."
I Timothy 6:6, 8
"Be content with such things as ye have." Hebrews 13:5
"Not content therewith." III John 10
How illuminating these passages on contentment are, especially when they are studied in the light of their context! A cultivated contentment is not sufficient. It must be allied, as Paul reminded Timothy, to "godliness." Such supreme contentment is born of faith in God's all-sufficiency to supply us with all He deems necessary for both our spiritual and material well-being. Too often discontent springs from the desire that things should come to us as we will, rather than as God wills best for us.

"I have learned, in whatsoever state I am, therewith to be content."

How far short the best of us are of this apostolic ideal! Materially, Paul's life was an impoverished one. Yet though poor, he made many rich. Psalm 111 should be read in connection with the lesson of contentment Paul learned. Evidently Paul was not always content. Before Christ met and saved him, his was the discontent of ambition. But as he came to know his all-sovereign Lord, everything was changed for him, for he gradually learned that He was able to do exceeding abundant above anything he could ask of Him.

The words to underline in Paul's assertion are – *in whatsoever state*. What is your present state or condition? Is it an unwelcome one, one which has the tendency to irritate you or cause you to complain and grumble? But is victory yours? Are you content *in* your state, knowing that as God's child your present sphere and position are of His ordering, so all must be well?

"Be content with such things as ye have." Hebrews 13:5

If one's life is laden with an abundance of good things, it is not difficult to be content. But if scarcity is ours, and we long for many necessary things others have and enjoy, do we meantime manifest the grace of "contentment," even although *things* are few and old? If you do not have what you wish, as a Christian, you certainly have what your Lord thinks best for you. He it is who chooses our inheritance for us. If content with present things, there is nothing wrong about hoping for better. In this promise we rest, that "no *good* thing will He withhold from them that walk uprightly." The promised companionship of Christ is the guarantee that all necessary things will be added unto us.

"Better is a little with the fear of the Lord, than great riches and trouble therewith." Proverbs 15:16
"Give me neither poverty nor riches; feed me with food convenient for me."
Proverbs 30:8
Do not these proverbs express the true spirit of contentment? The possession of riches arouses the envious, while pangs of poverty excite repining. Solomon indicates that if we would travel securely along the pathway of life, it is wise to choose the middle course. The qualifying clause is "the fear of the Lord." If He is our portion, then we shall be content. True contentment consists in a ready and cheerful compliance with the will of God – in a patient continuance in the calling God has ordained, in a grateful use of all that He has provided, in a constant endeavor not to covet what others have.

"His brethren were content."
Genesis 37:27
The contentment realized by the cruel brothers of Joseph meant that his precious young life was spared a horrible end. Judah's plea to sell Joseph rather than slay him satisfied a jealous feeling. But such a contentment as Joseph's brother experienced was false and fickle. The cries and moans of the lad, as in anguish of soul he pleaded for mercy, were ever in their ears and haunted them through the days. Jealousy, deceit, and cruelty can never produce true abiding contentment. When spite has been meted out upon someone we dislike, vengeance may seem to produce a feeling of satisfaction. "Revenge," we say, "is sweet." It is often likewise Satanic.

"Would to God we had been content."
Joshua 7:7
Constant discontent on the part of the

Israelites earned them the displeasure and judgment of God. How the people murmured during the wilderness journey! The journey over, Joshua at Ai suffered a humiliating defeat. But his wail of discontentment was unjustified. Israel had sinned, and they suffered. There is, of course, such a thing as a holy discontent which all of us must cultivate.

"Neither will he rest content."

Proverbs 6:35

The rage of a jealous-minded man can never be appeased. His vengeful spirit cannot be satisfied. Gifts expressing good will fail to pacify him. The passion for revenge can never be bought off. Have you ever noticed that there is nothing calm, serene, tranquil, about a jealous person? Since the contentment the Bible advocates is related to the mind, it is necessary to guard ourselves against disturbing elements. Wrong feelings toward another agitate our thought-life and breed discontent.

"Pilate, willing to content the people . . . delivered Jesus." Mark 15:15

Had Pilate acted the other way and released Jesus, he would have gone down in history as a courageous man. He was guilty, however, of placing position and prestige before conscience. His better nature, as well as his "better half," told him that Christ was innocent; but the crowd clamored for His death, so what could he do? Many a preacher has succumbed to Pilate's temptation. Willing to content the worldly-minded around them, they have soft-pedalled. Accommodating themselves to popular demand, because they are anxious to retain a good living, preachers have been guilty of silence in the sterner side of the Gospel. But one called of God, who is desirous of inheriting the promises, must be willing to content the heart of the One sending him, no matter what discontent or displeasure his faithful witness may produce.

"Godliness with contentment is great gain." I Timothy 6:6

The contentment God blesses is not a self-manufactured one. It springs from a right relationship with Him who is "the secret source of every precious thing." It is not a question of trying to be content under all circumstances, but the willingness to abide in the will of God that produces the coveted grace we are considering. Truly, this godly contentment is great gain! There is a personal gain. In a discontented world the power is ours to exhibit a poise, a confidence, a tranquility commendable to our Christian profession. Then there is the great gain in influence. Tempted to fuss, fume and worry, our God-given calm, even when we do suffer, brings those around whose minds are like a troubled sea, to a new understanding of the marvelous grace of our God – who also gains in honor and praise as the result of our contentment.

If discontent sits heavy on your heart, look up to God and seek the calm and confident trust He can instill. He is all-loving and all-wise, and because you are His, He knows all about your lot or state and is able to cause *all* things to work together for your good.

THE YEAR OF DAYS

In a year there are not only 365 days, but there are all kinds of days, and the promise is that no matter what kind of day follows day, "*as* our day, so shall our strength be."

"Dust shalt thou eat all the days of thy life." Genesis 3:14
"All the days of his separation."

Numbers 6:5
"Learn to fear me all the days."

Deuteronomy 4:10
"Observe to do . . . all the days that ye live."

Deuteronomy 12:1; Joshua 24:31; Judges 2:7, 18
"I will give him unto the Lord all the days of my life." I Samuel 1:11
"That they may fear thee all the days."

I Kings 8:40
"All the days of my appointed time will I wait." Job 14:14
"Goodness and mercy shall follow me all the days of my life." Psalm 23:6
"That I may dwell in the house of the Lord all the days of my life."

Psalm 27:4
"All the days of the evil are afflicted."

Proverbs 15:15
"She will do him good and not evil all the days of her life." Proverbs 31:12
"In holiness and righteousness before him, all the days of our life." Luke 1:75

To many of the promises related to the phrase "all the days," we could add the very many associated with "that day," "this day," "days to come," "in the days," "my days," etc. The reader will find it most profitable to look at the promises connected with these particular "days" as they are conveniently sectionalized in a Bible concordance. Whether our days are to be few or many, if we belong to Him who is the Ancient of Days we have the assurance that each day, and all the days, He will prove Himself to be our satisfying, daily portion.

"As thy days, so shall thy strength be."
Deuteronomy 33:25

We cannot possibly tell what is before us. It is so true that we do not know what a day may be bringing forth. We are not omniscient and therefore cannot read the future. But to God nothing is hid, and our tomorrows are known to Him, and His promise is that strength will be proportioned to the needs and trials each day may bring. "*As* thy days," implying that no matter what kind of days they may be, God will be at hand to give *when* we want, *as* we want, and *all* we want. The promise given to Moses was plain and positive, and God will not fail in its fulfilment on our behalf.

God does not give us a stock of grace, or grace in advance. When we face the need, the amount of grace and the nature of special grace required is vouchsafed. Therefore, how useless it is to dwell on possible painful apprehensions of the future, or to anticipate coming sorrows. Be of good cheer, promised strength will come with tomorrow's trials. When exigency arises, the everlasting arms will be around us to support us.

"Be not anxious for the morrow; for the morrow will be anxious for itself."
Matthew 6:34

Phillips' translation is somewhat straightforward –

"Don't worry at all then about tomorrow. Tomorrow can take care of itself! One day's troubles is enough for one day."

The method of living which our Lord is here emphasizing is that of facing each day as it comes. We are not to grieve over yesterday's failures, if forgiveness has been sought for them, or to be guilty of any anxiety or corroding care over tomorrow's responsibilities. Jesus is urging us to fence off each day by itself, with its own duties, needs, and trials, and live life to its full as each day comes round. "Live a day at a time," the proverb has it. Charles Kingsley says –

"Do today's duty, fight today's temptation, and do not weaken and distract yourself by looking forward to things which you cannot see, and could not understand if you saw them."

"Surely goodness and mercy shall follow me all the days of my life." Psalm 23:6

David, in this Shepherd Psalm of his, did not say that the goodness and mercy of the divine Shepherd would follow us *some* of the days of our life but through ALL of them, and all means ALL. These two guards, *Goodness – Mercy*, or as F. B. Meyer speaks of them, "the Shepherd's faithful sheepdogs," are our portion on dark and difficult days of life, as well as on those days when all goes well and our lives are serene and joyful. *Goodness* is ever-present to supply our every need, and *mercy* to forgive us if we sin against His goodness.

May grace be ours, then, to live each day appropriating the Shepherd's promised provision and protection, claiming daily strength for daily needs. "Give us this day our daily bread." But while we seek to live each day as it comes we must not forget that all our days are links in an endless chain. As J. R. Miller reminds us, "Each day receives an inheritance from yesterday, and at its close passes it down to the day which comes after . . . In countless ways yesterdays' life and today's are intertangled. Each day is but a little section of a great web, containing one figure of the pattern, the warp running through all the days and years. A life is a serial story, opening with infancy, closing with death, and each day is one little chapter in the story."

"The Lord shall cover him all the day long." Deuteronomy 33:12

What a precious promise this is to rest on each day, and all the days, of our life! Why should we charge our souls with daily worry when we have such a divine covering? The *shoulders* represent strength to bear or carry. To be borne, then, upon the shoulders of the Eternal means that He is our support and strength as day follows day. *All the day long*. It does not matter how long the day, or days, may be, we rejoice in the promise that we are beneath the canopy of divine love.

"Is it not good, if peace and truth be in my days?" II Kings 20:19

"My days are swifter than a weaver's shuttle." Job 7:6, 16; 9:25; 10:20; 17:1, 11

"Lord, make me to know . . . the measure of my days." Psalm 39:43

"My days are like a shadow that declineth." Psalm 102:3, 11, 23, 24

"Teach us to number our days."
Psalm 90:12, 14

A GARLAND OF DELIGHTS

Wordsworth speaks of one as being "a

phantom of delight," but the *delights* of which the Bible speaks, and which are so full of the promise of blessing and satisfaction, are no mere phantoms. They are all real, substantial, and satisfying, except those false objects of delight. Of these phantom-like delights, the Bible warns in no uncertain terms –

"They delight in lies." Psalm 62:4

"Scatter them that delight in war." Psalm 68:30

"He delighteth not in the strength of the horse." Psalm 147:10

"Thou delightest not in burnt-offering." Psalm 51:16

"The scorners delight in their scorning." Proverbs 1:22

"Who delight in the frowardness of the wicked." Proverbs 2:14

"As for gold, they shall not delight in it." Isaiah 13:17

"Did not choose that wherein I delighted not." Isaiah 65:12; 66:4

"Their soul delighteth in their abominations." Isaiah 66:3

"Every one that doeth evil . . . he delighteth in them." Malachi 2:17

Many of the above so-called "delights" are among what Shakespeare calls "violent delights" which have "violent ends." Have you ever thought of gathering together God's delights, that is, those objects that please and satisfy His heart? Cowper wrote of *Winter*, because of its "fireside enjoyment" and "homeborn happiness," as "king of intimate delights." Greater than *Winter* is the One who created it and He is the King of most intimate delights.

His delight is in His beloved Son

"As a father the son in whom he delighteth." Proverbs 3:12

"I was daily his delight." Proverbs 8:30

"Seeing he delighted in him." Psalm 22:8

"The messenger of the covenant, whom ye delight in." Malachi 3:1

"My beloved Son, in Whom I am well pleased." ("delighted," margin) II Peter 1:17

Between the Father and the Son there has ever existed that pure delight, possible only to Deity. The Father has always found delight in His Son, and the Son ever delights in the Father –

"I delight to do thy will, O God." Psalm 40:8; Hebrews 10:7

He delights in His people.

Can it be true that such poor, unworthy creatures as we are can be the objects of God's delight? Yes, the humblest believer can say, "Through grace, I am Jehovah's delight; the object of His highest love; the subject of His sweetest thoughts; and His portion forevermore." What a blessed promise and incomparable privilege is ours! The infinite God fixed upon us from eternity and then sent His Son, the supreme Object of His delight, to die for our sins. In a very real way God turned His Delight into a sacrifice on our behalf.

"If the Lord delight in us, then he will bring us into this land." Numbers 14:8

"The saints . . . in whom is all my delight." Psalm 16:3

"The Lord taketh delight in his people." Psalm 149:4 margin

"My delights are with the sons of men." Proverbs 8:31

"How fair and how pleasant art thou, O love, for delights!" Song of Solomon 7:6

"The Lord delighteth in thee." Isaiah 62:4

"Ye shall be a delightsome land." Malachi 3:12

He delights in the prayers of His people.

"The prayer of the upright is his delight." Proverbs 15:8

He delights in the way of His people.

"He delighteth in his way." Psalm 37:23

"He delivered me, because he delighted in me." Psalm 18:19; II Samuel 22:20

"Blessed be the Lord thy God, which delighted in thee." I Kings 10:9

He delights in His mercy towards us.

"Because he delighteth in mercy." Micah 7:18; Ephesians 2:4

"Lovingkindness, judgment, and righteousness . . . in these things I delight, saith the Lord." Jeremiah 9:24

He delights in honesty and integrity.

"A just weight is his delight." Proverbs 11:1

"Such as are upright in their way are his delight." Proverbs 11:20

"They that deal truly are His delight." Proverbs 12:22

"Righteous lips are the delight of kings." Proverbs 16:13

Pursuing this aspect of meditation further, we discover that we are commanded to delight ourselves in God. So we have a kind of "mutual-delight society." If we do delight ourselves in the Lord, we have the promise that He will give us the desires of our heart (Psalm 37:4). When Milton urged us, "To scorn delights and live laborious days," he was not referring to the divine delights which enable us to face laborious days.

"Then shalt thou have delight in the Almighty." Job 22:21, 26; Isaiah 58:14

We are to delight in His Word.

"His delight is in the law of the Lord."
Psalm 1:2

"Blessed is the man . . . that delighteth greatly in his commandments."
Psalm 112:1

"I will delight myself in thy statutes." Psalm 119:16 (see verses 22, 24, 35, 47, 70, 92, 143, 174)

"The word of the Lord . . . they have no delight in them." Jeremiah 6:10

"I delight in the law of God."
Romans 7:22

We are to delight in His Day.

"Call the Sabbath a delight."
Isaiah 58:13

We are to delight in His provisions.

"They take delight in approaching to God," Isaiah 58:2

"Thy comforts delight my soul."
Psalm 94:19

"Let your soul delight itself in fatness."
Isaiah 55:2

"They delighted themselves in thy great goodness." Nehemiah 9:25

"I delight to do thy will, O my God."
Psalm 40:8

"The meek . . . shall delight themselves in the abundance of peace."
Psalm 37:11

"I sat down under his shadow with great delight." Song of Solomon 2:3

"Will he delight himself in the Almighty?" Job 27:10

John Masefield speaks of one who "delighted all my undelighted hours." No one, and nothing, can delight all our undelighted hours like Him, Who is the blessed Object of our delight, and whose Promises and Provisions constantly delight our hearts.

THE REWARD OF DILIGENCE

Jesus will always remain as the most outstanding example of the quality of *diligence* in the Bible. When but twelve years of age He knew what He was in the world for.

"Wist ye not that I must be about my Father's business?" Luke 2:49

Unwearyingly He gave Himself to His God-given task, and setting His face stedfastly toward Jerusalem, He diligently pursued His purpose until on the cross He shouted in triumph: "It is finished!" Thomas a Kempis

says that, "A fervent and diligent man is prepared for all things." The Man Christ Jesus, most fervent and diligent, was certainly prepared to face satanic and human endeavors to thwart His divine mission.

That the Bible has a good deal to say about diligence, and of promised blessings associated with it, is evident from the following exhortations and examples –

"The hand of the diligent maketh rich."
Proverbs 10:4

"The hand of the diligent shall bear rule." Proverbs 12:24

"The substance of a diligent man is precious." Proverbs 12:27

"The soul of the diligent shall be made fat." Proverbs 13:4, 11; 14:23

"The thoughts of the diligent tend only to plenteousness." Proverbs 21:5

"Seest thou a man diligent in business? he shall stand before kings."
Proverbs 22:29

"He that tilleth his land shall have plenty of bread." Proverbs 28:19

"Whatsoever thy hand findeth to do, do it with thy might." Ecclesiastes 9:10

"In every work that he began in the service of the house of God . . . he prospered." II Chronicles 31:21

"Be strong and work: for I am with you, saith the Lord of hosts." Haggai 2:4

"I can do all things through Christ which strengtheneth me."
Philippians 4:13

"Therefore seeing we have this ministry, as we have received mercy, we faint not." II Corinthians 4:1

"Let us not be weary in well doing."
Galatians 6:9

"Thou hast been faithful over a few things." Matthew 25:23, 29

"Whosoever hath, to him shall be given."
Matthew 13:12

"Not slothful in business."
Romans 12:11; I Thessalonians 4:11

"Giving all diligence . . . give diligence."
II Peter 1:5, 10

"Be diligent that ye may be found of him in peace." II Peter 3:14

A study of the above passages shows that whether our business is spiritual or secular, or both, we should be found putting our very best into what our hands find to do. "God helps those who help themselves" is certainly true, for He places no premium upon indolence. Yet it is also true that God helps those who cannot help themselves. A Danish proverb has it, "Diligence makes an expert workman." A diligence inspired of God enables one to achieve the best. Their industry becomes "the parent of success." Shakespeare, in *King Lear*, says,

"That which ordinary men are fit for,
I am qualified in, and the best of me
is diligence."

The opposite to diligence is not forgotten by the Bible. *Indolence, laziness, slothfulness*, with their promises of impoverishment, and sorrow, are not forgotten.

"Drowsiness shall clothe a man with rags." Proverbs 22:21
"Be not slothful to go, and to enter to possess the land." Judges 18:9
"The slothful man shall be under tribute." Proverbs 12:24, 27
"The way of the slothful man is as an hedge of thorns." Proverbs 15:19; 18:9
"A slothful man hideth his hand in his bosom." Proverbs 19:24; 21:25; 22:13; 24:30
"Slothfulness casteth into a deep sleep."
Proverbs 19:15; Ecclesiastes 10:18
"Thou wicked and slothful servant."
Matthew 25:26; Romans 12:11;
Hebrews 6:12
"Go to the ant, thou sluggard."
Proverbs 6:6, 9; 13:4; 20:4
"If any man would not work, neither should he eat." II Thessalonians 3:10
Scripture also takes cognizance of the fact that ulterior motives can inspire *diligence*. Charles Kingsley said, "That there can be no true industry without the fear of God, and love to your fellow citizens." But Jesus described one who was most industrious, laboring most diligently at his task, but who yet was destitute of any fear of God and of love to his fellowmen. He thought only of amassing greater wealth. David Hume wrote that, "Avarice – the spur of industry." It was avarice that spurred on the farmer who said –

"I will pull down my barns, and build greater . . . I will say to my soul, Soul, thou hast much goods laid up for many years; take thine ease, eat, drink, and be merry." Luke 12:16-32

Because the rich farmer allowed himself to work so industriously merely to lay up more treasure for himself, and failed to be rich toward God, the very night of his boast was the night of his sudden death. If, through our diligence, we are blessed with an increase of goods, we must not forget the Blesser's share of glory and gain.

THE PROVISION OF DEFENCE

God's coverage and protection of His own is described in so many interesting ways. It would seem as if He ransacks the range of suitable metaphors to reveal His ability and willingness to shelter and preserve those who are covered with His wings. Scores of promises are connected with Him as our *Refuge, High Tower, Fortress, Hiding Place, Rock, Covert, Eagle Wings, etc*. It would take more space than this section allows to fully quote all the passages dealing with these most profitable metaphors. A few selected examples must suffice to convince us that we have in the Lord One whose omnipotence and omnipresence and omniscience make possible the most perfect protection for the weakest believer.

"The waters were a wall unto them."
Exodus 14:22; Numbers 22:24
"I, saith the Lord, will be unto her a wall of fire round about." Zechariah 2:5
"He only is a rock . . . my defence; I shall not be moved." Psalms 62:6; 89:18
"A tabernacle for a shadow . . . a refuge . . . a covert." Isaiah 4:6; 25:4; 32:2
"In the secret of his tabernacle shall he hide me." Psalms 27:5, 6; 61:4
"Abide under the shadow of the Almighty."
Psalms 91:1; 15:1; Deuteronomy 33:12
"He shall cover thee with his feathers . . . wings . . . shield."
Psalms 91:4; 17:8; 36:7
"In the shadow of thy wings will I make my refuge." Psalms 57:1-3; 46:1
"Thou hast covered my head in the day of battle." Psalms 140:7; 85:2
"He is the rock, his work is perfect."
Deuteronomy 32:3, 4; Psalm 62:5-7
"As birds flying, so will the Lord of hosts defend." Isaiah 31:5; Psalm 91:3-6
"They wait upon the Lord . . . shall mount up as eagles." Isaiah 40:31
"Thou art my hiding place."
Psalm 32:7; II Timothy 4:17, 18
"The Lord is my rock, and my fortress . . . my high tower." Psalm 18:2
"The Lord shall cover him all the day long." Deuteronomy 33:12; Proverbs 1:33
"The Lord is round about his people from henceforth and for ever."
Psalms 125:2; 32:10
"The Lord is a refuge for the oppressed, a refuge in times of trouble."
Psalm 9:9; Proverbs 14:26
"Fear not, I am thy shield." Genesis 15:1;
Psalm 3:3; Romans 8:31

With this array of wonderful promises before us, how can we possibly be afraid of what the present or future may hold for us? With God as our Canopy we are safe, and should be serene and satisfied. Because He is between us and all our foes and trials, we can rest in the assurance that not a shaft can hit till He sees fit (I Peter 3:13; Proverbs 3:24; Isaiah 43:2).

"He kept them as the apple of his eye."
Deuteronomy 32:10

Moses described, in a most accurate fashion, God's care of ancient Israel, when the people groaned under oppressive slavery and writhed under the last of heartless taskmasters.

"He *found* him in a desert land, in the waste howling wilderness;
He *led* him about,
He *instructed* him,
He *kept* him as the apple of his eye."

First God found the people. His eye of love was fixed upon them. Then He led them, sometimes along a straight, sometimes a circuitous path, from Egypt to the Promised Land. He instructed them by providential dealings, mercies, warnings, judgments, frequent interpositions of His power, by signal proof of His determination to bless them according to His promise. Yes, and He kept them as the apple of His eye, meaning, He shielded the people in the hour of peril, manifesting Himself strong on their behalf. Such privileged and promised watchful guardianship and unceasing vigilance are for the humblest believer.

Christian, have you been found of God? Is He leading you? Are you being instructed of Him? Then rest calmly and unhesitatingly upon the sure promise that you will be kept by His mighty power.

"As an eagle . . . so the Lord."
Deuteronomy 32:11, 12

Because the eagle has undisputed supremacy over the birds of the air, being known as the king of the skies, it is used in many interesting ways. For instance, its speed is remarkable.

"Swift as the eagle flieth."
Deuteromony 28:49; Job 9:26; Proverbs 30:19

None among the feathered creation can surpass the eagle in speed of flight. How swift God is in the deliverance of His own! Many bird nests are robbed simply because they are within easy reach. The eagle, however, endowed of God with wisdom, builds her nest on the highest crag of the rock where she knows her eggs and young will be safe.

"Make thy nest as high as the eagle's."
Jeremiah 49:14; Job 38:27

In this passage Jeremiah reminds Edom that her high and haughty spirit will be crushed. Who is higher than an eagle's nest, and who knows how to bring the mighty from their seat? As a symbol of divine activities, the ways of an eagle are very expressive (Exodus 19:4; Jeremiah 48:40). Moses used the eagle's tenderness and care of its young to describe God's kindness and provision. The stirring up of the nest, fluttering over the young, spreading abroad the wings, can all be applied to the promise of God's consideration of His own, as well as a manifestation of grace to the sinner.

"The name of the Lord is a strong tower: the righteous runneth into it and is safe."
Proverbs 18:10

"Thou hast made the Most High thy habitation." Psalm 91:9

How invincible and impregnable God is as our tower and habitation! Having the promise of such a sure defence we can sing, "A safe Stronghold our God is still." Sheltered in Him, and by Him, we can laugh to scorn all the embattled hosts of hell. The proud onslaught of the enemy is doomed to defeat. Who can harm us if we be followers of the Lord? Promises of His protection are stars of heaven kindled for our comfort in the darkest night.

"Lead me to the rock that is higher than I." Psalm 61:2

How great is our need of Someone who is above ourselves, our cares, our trials, and our needs! Provoking and perplexing troubles assail us, but this "mighty Rock in a weary land" is high above all the trouble and turmoil of earth. Look at Psalm 130 in this connection. How happy we are if we have found this lofty and peaceful retreat!

"Thou art in the clefts of the rock."
Song of Solomon 2:14

We are here promised, as the Bride of Christ, several privileges. To Him we are as a "dove" – blameless and harmless. As the Rock, He was cleft at Calvary, and we hide in Him. "The secret places of the stairs" speaks of our intimate, spiritual fellowship with Him, who causes His face to be seen and His voice to be heard in His precious Word. Because He waits to meet us in the secret places of the stairs, let us never disappoint our Beloved.

"In the shadow of thy wings will I make my refuge." Psalm 57:1

"As birds flying, so will the Lord of hosts defend Jerusalem." Isaiah 31:5

What a comforting promise this is! It is indeed heartening to know that as the birds flutter over their nests with quivering and palpitating wings, so the Lord protects us. No matter what perils may shadow us, even though it be the last shadow of death, all is well if we enjoy the shadow of God's guardian wings. He shelters, protects, and preserves His blood-washed ones. In the shadow of His wings, we have power and peace, and heaven itself.

"He shall cover thee with his feathers."
Psalm 91:4

We here have another aspect of the promised covering of the divine wings which we can accept without hesitation and find sure. Past centuries justify our reliance on such a promise. A great company no man can number have proved how faithful God has been to the promised covering of His soft feathers. Did our Lord have this precious verse in mind when He used the simile of the hen protecting her brood, allowing them to nestle under her wings? Because His promise must stand, let us shelter in Him and experience the overflowing peace that comes through the knowledge that He is guarding us.

"I am thy shield . . . The Lord God, is a sun and a shield."
Genesis 15:1; Psalm 84:11

Safety and protection are suggested by the simile of a shield, and God promises to be our impenetrable Shield. All who believe are blessed with believing Abraham, and so the promise God made to him, He will fulfil to us, and we certainly need Him as our Shield. Are we not surrounded by foes? Do not fiery darts fly in every direction? But God interposes Himself as our Shield – "so mighty a Defender." And because He is our defence, we must expect His protection. He Himself, and His salvation, and our faith, form the shield. So when foes alarm and dangers affright, let us look to Him as our protector.

"God is our refuge and strength."
Psalm 46:1

"I flee to thee to hide me."
Psalm 143:9

The provision of a refuge implies several things. First, there is the presence of *danger*, and a Christian is ever in danger from sin, self, and Satan. There is *fear*. Often one pursued is afraid, but for those who have God as a refuge, all fears are groundless. Then a refuge suggests *foresight;* God knew all about distant storms and provided Himself a covert accordingly. On our part, seeking the refuge speaks of *prudence*. We hid in Him before the storms break. From God's side, the provision of a refuge reveals His laudable concern for our safety and comfort. How privileged we are to have God as our eternal Refuge! When hounded by our sin, the world, or our problems, we can flee to Him, knowing that His ear is open to our cry, and His hand is ready to help and deliver us. "His throne is our asylum, His promise is our comfort, and His omnipotence is our guard."

THE TEST OF ENDURANCE

Too many of us are like the builder Jesus depicted, who began to build but was not able to finish. Paul wrote Galatians for those who lacked this grace of endurance. They began in the Spirit but drifted into the flesh. The Bible holds out many rich promises for those who persevere unto the end. That the perseverance of the saints finds place in Holy Writ is evident from these passages –

"When they persecute you in one city, flee to another." Matthew 10:23

"If ye continue in my words, then are ye my disciples indeed." John 8:31; 15:7

"Be ye stedfast, unmoveable."
I Corinthians 15:58

"Let us not be weary in well-doing . . . if we faint not." Galatians 6:9

"Hold the beginning of our confidence stedfast unto the end." Hebrews 3:14

"Let us hold fast the profession of our faith without wavering." Hebrews 10:23

"Cast not away therefore your confidence, which hath great recompence of reward." Hebrews 10:35

"Continue in the Son, and in the Father."
I John 2:24, 28

"Look to yourselves, that we lose not those things which we have wrought."
II John 8:9

"Be thou faithful unto death."
Revelation 2:10

An ancient proverb has it, "He that endures is not overcome." The above exhortations, coupled as they are to promised blessing and reward, reveal how Spirit-inspired perseverance can make us more than conquerors. Think of the further encouragement we have in the exercise of this grace of perseverance!

"They shall never perish . . . no man

is able to pluck them out of my Father's hand." John 10:28, 29

"Neither death, nor life . . . shall be able to separate us."

Romans 8:38, 39; 17:12

"Who shall also confirm you unto the end." I Corinthians 1:8

"Now he which stablished us . . . sealed us . . . is God." II Corinthians 1:21, 22

"He which hath begun a good work in you will perform it." Philippians 1:6

"Faithful is he that calleth you, who also will do it." I Thessalonians 5:23

"The Lord is faithful, who will stablish you, and keep you from evil."

II Thessalonians 3:3

"Who are kept by the power of God."

I Peter 1:5; II Peter 1:10

"Keep yourselves in the love of God."

Jude 21

"When I said, My foot slippeth: thy mercy, O Lord, help me up."

Psalm 94:18

"The Lord will perfect that which concerneth me." Psalm 138:8

"The righteous is an everlasting foundation." Proverbs 10:25

While these Scriptures, and others we could cite, set forth the Christian's eternal security in Christ, they do not provide him with any license to live carelessly, indolently, and despairingly. If the professing Christian is truly –

"A monument of grace
A sinner saved by blood" – then he is Christ's forever. But while he can never be lost, if saved by grace, lack of determination to be true to Christ in spite of adversity, can result in the loss of reward. This was what Paul meant when he voiced his fear about being a "castaway," or disapproved, not counted worthy of a prize from the Master's hand in the grand day of rewards. A Latin saying puts it, "Endure and persist; this pain will turn to your good by and by."

Longfellow reminds us that, "Patient endurance is godlike" – to which Scripture agrees. See Lamentations 3:25-27; Hebrews 10:36; James 5:8; I Peter 2:20; Proverbs 10:28. In a good many cases the word "endure" carries with it the idea of continuance, abiding –

"His anger endureth but a moment."

Psalm 30:5

"The goodness of God endureth for ever."

Psalms 52:1; 100:5

"Thou shalt endure." Psalm 102:26, 27

"Thy dominion endureth throughout all generations." Psalm 145:13

In other passages, however, to endure means to bear up courageously under trials and testings, to be stedfast, long-tempered, to bravely tolerate. For this kind of endurance, promises are offered.

"Then shalt thou be able to endure."

Exodus 18:23

"He that shall endure unto the end, the same shall be saved." Matthew 24:13

Since this statement of our Lord's has been misconstrued to teach what is called "the falling-away doctrine," it is necessary to examine it in the light of the context. Christ was *not* referring to a spiritual salvation when He spoke thus. As verse 22 makes clear, he had in mind a *physical* salvation –

"Except those days should be shortened, there should no *flesh* be saved."

The shortening of the Great Tribulation period will mean that many saints will be saved from suffering and martyrdom. Our spiritual salvation has nothing to do with endurance. We do not endure in order to be saved at some future date. We endure because be *are* saved.

"The enduring of the same sufferings which we also suffer." II Corinthians 1:6

"Your persecutions and tribulations which ye endure." II Thessalonians 1:4

"Endure hardness as a good soldier of Jesus Christ." II Timothy 2:3

"Therefore I endure all things for the elect's sake." II Timothy 2:10

"What persecutions I endured."

II Timothy 3:11

"Will not endure sound doctrine."

II Timothy 4:3

"Endure afflictions." II Timothy 4:5

"Blessed is the man that endureth temptation." James 1:12

"Behold we count them happy which endure." James 5:11

"If a man for conscience toward God endure grief." I Peter 2:19, 20

"Endured with much long-suffering."

Romans 9:22

"Patiently endured, he obtained the promise." Hebrews 6:15

"Ye endured a great fight of afflictions."

Hebrews 10:32

"For he endured, as seeing him who is invisible." Hebrews 11:27

"Jesus . . . endured the cross."

Hebrews 12:2

"Consider him that endured such con-

tradition of sinners against himself."
                                    Hebrews 12:3
"If ye endure chastening."
                                    Hebrews 12:7
The foregoing passages exhibiting both divine and human endurance, and the promised reward of them should serve to nerve us for the challenge of life. Says a philosopher of old, "Bear what is hurtful, that ye may preserve what is profitable." If we remain true and stedfast in the fight of faith, the dross vanishes and we retain the gold. Virgil had the proverb, "Endure and keep yourselves ready for prosperous fortune." As saints, we endure, not for any material gain, but that a full reward will be ours at Christ's Judgment Day.

A BUNCH OF EVERLASTINGS

How imperative it is to live with eternity's values in view! Alas, we are like Bunyan's man with the muckrake, seeing only what is at our feet, and not as conscious as we ought to be about the crown of gold above our head. They said of Corot, the renowned artist, that he always began the painting of his immortal landscapes with the skies. May it be with the skies and with God that we are careful to begin – not with the earth and with its tarnish and rust.

To gather under one heading all the promises of *eternal life, reward, and blessedness* is a profitable exercise for the reader to pursue. We deem "eternal" and "everlasting" to be equivalent terms. Think of this selection –

"The eternal God . . . the everlasting arms." Deuteronomy 33:27
"Eternal salvation . . . eternal redemption." Hebrews 5:9; 9:12
"Eternal Glory." II Corinthians 4:17; II Timothy 2:10
"A house . . . eternal in the heavens." II Corinthians 5:1; Luke 16:9
"Everlasting joy" – "Everlasting love." Isaiah 35:10; Jeremiah 31:3
"Everlasting kindness" – "Everlasting consolation." Isaiah 54:8; Jeremiah 10:10
"Everlasting kindness" – "Everlasting consolation." Isaiah 54:8; II Thessalonians 2:16
"The way everlasting" – "An everlasting King." Psalm 139:34; Jeremiah 10:10
"Eternal life" – "Power of an endless life." Titus 1:2; Hebrews 7:16

For a confirmation of your faith, go over all the passages related to eternal, or everlasting life. You will be surprised as you collate all promised future joys and blessings.

THE POWER OF FAITH

Since there are over 500 references to *faith*, and its kindred term, *believe*, in the Bible, it is realized how difficult it would be to list all of these verses and briefly expound the majority of them. In fact, exposition is not necessary, because all such passages speak for themselves. Each passage is a promise. Attached to them are numerous promises as to the power and reward of faith. D. L. Moody tells us how he prayed for faith, and "thought that some day faith would come down and strike me like lightning. But faith did not seem to come. One day I read in the tenth chapter of Romans, 'Now faith cometh by hearing, and hearing by the word of God.' I had closed my Bible, and prayed for faith. I now opened my Bible, and began to study, and faith has been growing ever since."

If we would be "strong in faith," one sure way of gaining "great faith" is to prayerfully study every passage where "faith," "believe," and "trust" are found in Scripture. Let us content ourselves with a few nuggets from such a heap of gold.

"Have faith in God." Mark 11:22
"According to your faith." Matthew 9:29
"Justified by faith." Romans 5:1
"The just shall live by faith."
                                    Romans 1:17
"I have prayed for thee that thy faith fail not." Luke 22:32
"Without faith it is impossible to please God." Hebrews 11:6
"The stedfastness of your faith in Christ." Colossians 2:5; Hebrews 10:23
"Ask in faith." James 1:6
"The joy of faith." Philippians 1:25
"Precious faith." II Peter 1:1
"Unfeigned faith." II Timothy 1:5
"Breastplate of faith." Ephesians 6:16; I Thessalonians 5:8
"Your faith groweth exceedingly." II Thessalonians 1:3
"This is the victory . . . even our faith." I John 5:4
"Full assurance of faith." Hebrews 10:22; 11:1
"Contend earnestly for the faith." Jude 3

Among the almost 300 references to "believe," "believers," "believed," we choose a few to encourage us to keep on believing –
"All that believe are justified." Acts 13:39
"I know whom I have believed." II Timothy 1:12

"I believe God." Acts 27:25

"Only believe." Mark 5:36

"Unto you that believe he is precious."
I Peter 2:7

"We believe that we shall live with him." Romans 6:8

"He that believeth shall never thirst."
John 6:35

"Whosoever . . . that believes on me shall never die." John 11:26

"Joy and peace in believing."
Romans 15:13

"If thou wouldest believe thou shouldest see the glory of God." John 11:40

"The exceeding greatness of his power towards us who believe." Ephesians 1:19

"No manner of hurt was found upon . . . Daniel . . . he believed in his God." Daniel 6:23

"Power . . . to them that believe on His name." John 1:12

"The Father himself loveth you . . . because ye have believed." John 16:27

The world says, "Seeing is believing," but the Christian's axiom is "Believing is seeing." Did not Jesus say, "Blessed are they who have not seen yet have believed"? Belief, or faith, means taking God at His word, even though we cannot fully understand with our feeble, finite minds much of that He says. "Faith . . . is the evidence of things not seen." Unbelief, about which the Bible has a great deal to say, is the root of all sin. It rejects the miraculous and stumbles over the clear, concise statements of God's Word.

THE CALL TO FAITHFULNESS

To be *faith-full* means more than being *full of faith*. The term implies being worthy of faith, fidelity, stability, stedfastness. When used of God, "faithfulness" expresses that attribute of deity by which He infallibly fulfils His purpose and the promises of His Word. It would seem as if all the writers of the Bible unite to magnify God for His unfailing fidelity which runs as a golden thread through Scripture.

"Thy faithfulness reached unto the clouds." Psalm 36:5; I Peter 4:19

"I have declared thy faithfulness."
Psalm 40:10

"Thy faithfulness is destruction."
Psalm 88:11

"Thy faithfulness to all generations." Psalms 89:1, 2, 5, 8, 24, 33; 119:5. We can name this great psalm, "The Psalm of Divine Faithfulness."

"To show forth . . . thy faithfulness every night." Psalm 92:3

"O Lord . . . thou in faithfulness hast afflicted me." Psalm 119:75

"In thy faithfulness answer me."
Psalm 143:1; Revelation 21:5; 22:6

"He is God, the faithful God."
Deuteronomy 7:9

"Faithfulness the girdle of his reins."
Isaiah 11:5

"Thy counsels of old are faithfulness and truth." Isaiah 25:1

"The Lord that is faithful."
Isaiah 49:7; Hebrews 10:23

"Great is thy faithfulness."
Lamentations 3:23; Hebrews 11:11

"I will even betroth thee unto me in faithfulness." Hosea 2:26

"He abideth faithful." II Timothy 2:23; I Corinthians 1:9; 10:13; I Thessalonians 5:24. (See also Psalm 119:86, 138.) All of these testimonies are heavy with the promise of God's unfailing care and provision of His own. There has never been the least flicker in the lamp of divine loyalty. "Thou are the same." As the faithful God, He must be true to His own nature (Isaiah 25:1; I John 1:9).

Then we have the exhibition of the same quality in the life and labors of Christ, who came revealing divine attributes.

"His seed . . . shall be established for ever." Psalm 89:36, 37

"The Lord is faithful, who shall stablish you." II Thessalonians 3:3; Hebrews 2:7

"The faithful and the true witness."
Revelation 1:5; 3:14; 19:11

Solomon asked the question, "But a faithful man who can find?" The Man Christ Jesus was faithful in all things. If ever One was faithful unto death, it was He. Then we have the example of those who believed in, and served, the faithful One.

"He was a faithful man, and feared God above many." Nehemiah 7:2

"Daniel . . . forasmuch as he was faithful." Daniel 6:4

"They which be of faith are blessed with faithful Abraham." Galatians 3:9

"Moses was faithful in all his house."
Hebrews 3:5

"He counted me (Paul) faithful."
I Timothy 1:12; Acts 16:15

"Silvanus, a faithful brother unto you."
I Peter 5:12

"Epaphras . . . a faithful minister of Christ." Colossians 1:7

"Tychicus . . . a faithful minister."
Colossians 4:7

"Timothy . . . my beloved son, faithful in the Lord." I Corinthians 4:17
"Onesimus, a faithful and beloved brother." Colossians 4:9
"Gaius . . . thou doest faithfully."
III John 5
"Antipas, my faithful martyr."
Revelation 2:13
"The church in Smyrna . . . faithful unto death." Revelation 2:14

Those saints at Smyrna sealed their faithful witness, like those described in the eleventh chapter of Hebrews, with their life's blood. May grace be ours to follow in their train!

Applied to ourselves, this virtue of faithfulness carries many promises of divine favor, preservation, and reward. Yet we are not to strive after fidelity because of its promised rewards. For us, faithfulness is obedience to a divine command – a binding as any of those of the Law – "Be thou faithful unto death." Revelation 2:10 Thus it is not something we can please ourselves about cultivating. There are many privileges we enjoy in Christian life, but faithfulness is not one of them. It is not our *privilege* to be faithful but our duty – and duty is debt, and debt is something we owe another. Faithfulness, then, is a debt that must be discharged in a three-fold direction, namely, Godward, among ourselves as Christians, and toward a lost world. Here are some of the aspects of faithfulness we must emulate –

"A faithful ambassador is health."
Proverbs 3:17; 25:13
"A faithful witness will not be."
Proverbs 15:4; 27:6
"The Lord preserved the faithful."
Psalm 31:23
"A faithful and wise servant."
Matthew 24:45; 25:21; Luke 16:10; 19:17
"Required . . . that a man be found faithful." I Corinthians 4:2
"The faithful in Christ Jesus."
Ephesians 1:1; Colossians 1:2
"Faithful in all things." I Timothy 3:11
"Be thou faithful . . . I will give thee a crown of life." Revelation 2:10
"They that are with him are . . . faithful." Revelation 17:14
"They were counted faithful."
I Samuel 22:14
"Mine eyes shall be upon the faithful."
Psalm 101:6
"A faithful man shall abound with blessings." Proverbs 28:20
"They dealt faithfully." II Kings 12:15; 22:7; II Chronicles 19:9; 31:12

"Let him speak my word faithfully."
Jeremiah 23:28
"Render to every man . . . his faithfulness." I Samuel 26:23
Oppositely, the promise of condemnation is attached to *faithfulness* –
"There is no faithfulness in their mouth."
Psalm 5:9
"O faithless generation." Matthew 17:17
"Be not faithless, but believing."
John 20:27
Happily, we are not left to ourselves to produce this faithfulness God commands and commends. What He commands, He supplies. "Faithful is he who called you, who also will *do* it." In describing the varied fruit of the Spirit, Paul says that, "The fruit of the Spirit . . . is faith" (Galatians 5:22). The Revised Version has it – "The fruit of the Spirit . . . is faithfulness." Thus, we do not, and cannot, produce it – we only *bear* it. As we constantly walk in the Spirit, He makes possible the loyalty and fidelity that is pleasing to the heart of our faithful God and that brings to us at the end of the day the promised reward, "Well done, good and faithful servant."

THE TYRANNY OF FEAR

In our section dealing with the physical realm, we drew attention to "fear" as a despot of the human emotions. Enumerating many passages related to fear, we pointed out that so many of our fears are groundless, and are a form of distrust in God's ability to undertake for us as He has promised. Often we are guilty of "fearing even things which are safe." Bishop Butler, in his *Sermons*, suggests that the foundation of all our hopes and fears is in a future life. But to a Christian, there should be no fear regarding either this present or the future, because God has promised to care for both. The many Scriptures dealing with fear prove Wordsworth's lines to be true –
"Fear hath a hundred eyes, that all agree
To plague her beating heart."
"There is no fear in love." I John 4:18
If our hearts have been warmed by that divine love, and our lives are absorbed by it, then all fear as to the future is cast out.
"Only fear Jehovah." I Samuel 12:24; Psalm 128:1; Proverbs 1:7
The basis of a godly fear – the only "fear" we should have – is all that God is in Himself, and all that He has accomplished on our behalf.
"My heart will not fear." Psalm 27:3

Robert Burns, the Scottish poet, is credited with having said –

"I backward cast my eye on prospects drear!
And forward, though I can see, I guess and fear!"

But guesses and fears should have no place in a Christian's thinking. Certainty is written all over the sure promises of God.

THE JOY OF FELLOWSHIP

"Fellowship," and all that it represents to a Christian, is a term confined to the New Testament. It occurs only twice in the Old Testament.

"Commit a trespass . . . in fellowship." Leviticus 6:2

"Shall the throne of iniquity have fellowship with thee?" Psalm 94:20

In both cases the fellowship is of the wrong kind, and is akin to the evil companionship referred to by Paul –

"That ye should have fellowship with devils." I Corinthians 10:20

"Have no fellowship with the unfruitful." Ephesians 5:11

Used in a right sense, the communion of the saints is a most privileged and precious experience – an intimate, filial fellowship. This is none of the "half-faced fellowship" Shakespeare wrote about. It is full communion here and now, with the promise of eternal communion. Breaking up the word "fellowship," we find it to mean exactly that – the other fellow in the ship.

"They continued stedfastly . . . in fellowship." Acts 2:42

"Ye were called into the fellowship."
I Corinthians 1:9

"The fellowship of the ministering."
II Corinthians 8:4

"The right hands of fellowship."
Galatians 2:9

"The fellowship of the mystery."
Ephesians 3:9

"Your fellowship in the gospel."
Philippians 1:5

"If any fellowship of the Spirit."
Philippians 2:1; II Corinthians 13:14

"The fellowship of his sufferings."
Philippians 3:10

"Ye also may have fellowship with us."
I John 1:3, 7

"Truly our fellowship is with the Father, and with his Son." I John 1:3

We sadly confess the lack of this many-sided fellowship among professing Christians today. Isolated in our own sphere of worship, we lustily sing –

"Blest be the tie that binds
Our hearts in Christian love."

But the fact remains that we appear to be hopelessly divided, with this Christian group refusing to have any fellowship with another group equally fundamental in doctrine. How far removed we are from the "fellowship one with another" which the apostle wrote about!

THE BEARING OF FRUIT

As branches of the Vine, it is our responsibility to bear fruit to God's praise and glory. If fruitless, then there must be obstruction in the life which prevents the sap in the Vine from reaching the branches. We have been promised a fruit-bearing life for which life provision has been made. Peter makes it clear that as the life – so the fruit –

"If these things (see list, v. 5 through 7) be in you, and abound, they make you that ye shall neither be barren nor unfruitful in the knowledge of our Lord Jesus Christ." II Peter 1:8

What a great promise for the Christian to claim! Peter enumerates the virtues forming the soil producing the fruit. Such fruit is the overflow of life, and we must be full before we can flow over. If we realize that we have been fruitless professors, let us closely observe the graces so essential to fruit bearing. There must be fruit within, if we are to bear fruit without. All the graces and the fruit are divinely provided. "From me is thy fruit" (Hosea 14:5).

The 200 or more passages taken up with fruit and fruitfulness cover natural fruit, moral, physical, and spiritual fruit, or blessings. Look at these passages carrying their own promise, encouragements, and warning.

"I create the fruit of the lips."
Isaiah 57:19; Proverbs 12:14;
18:20; Hebrews 13:15

Our speech and testimony are part of the fruit the Husbandman expects.

"Bless the fruit of thy womb."
Deuteronomy 7:13; Psalm 132:11;
Luke 1:42

"Blessed be the fruit of thy body."
Deuteronomy 28:4, 11

"Take root downward, and bear fruit upward." II Kings 19:20; Isaiah 37:31

Let us never be guilty of the folly of trying to have fruit without root.

"Bringeth forth his fruit in his season." Psalms 1:3; 104:13; Proverbs 10:3

"They shall eat the fruit of their own way." Proverbs 1:31; Isaiah 3:10

"My fruit is better than gold."
                                    Proverbs 8:19
"He bringeth forth fruit unto himself."
                                    Hosea 10:1
"Ye have eaten the fruit of lies."
                                    Hosea 16:13
"The fruit of righteousness." Amos 6:12
"The fruit of the wicked to sin."
                                    Proverbs 10:16
"Increase the fruits of your righteousness." II Corinthians 9:10; Hebrews 12:11; Philippians 1:10
"Ye shall know them by their fruits."
                    Matthew 7:16-20; 12:33; 13:8
"Fruit unto life eternal." John 4:36
"He bringeth forth much fruit."
                                    John 12:24; 15:5
"The branch cannot bear fruit of itself." John 15:2-16
"Ye have your fruit unto holiness."
                                    Romans 6:21, 22
"The fruit of the Spirit."
            Galatians 5:22; Ephesians 5:9
"They shall still bring forth fruit in old age." Psalm 92:13, 14
"Fruitful in every good work."
                                    Colossians 1:10
"God bless thee, and make thee fruitful." Genesis 28:3
"The fruits that thy soul lusted after."
                                    Revelation 18:14
How variegated is the fruit we are to bear! It represents every phase of life. May we be spared from functioning as empty vines!
"Every branch in me that beareth not fruit he taketh away." John 15:2
This is a statement that has caused some believers no little concern. Does it teach, as some affirm, that we can be saved today but lost tomorrow? Certainly not! First of all notice where the believer as a branch is—"*in Me.*" Once an integral part of Christ, such a union can never be dissolved. Communion may be severed but union—*never!* The words "taketh away" can be translated "lifted up." A gardener noticing a branch trailing in the dust, where it cannot enjoy the sun and the full benefit of nature's forces, lifts it up, gives it a higher position. Often fruit is not ours because we live too near the earth. Our affections are not set on high, so the divine Gardener comes along and separates us from worldly pursuits and raises us up from fleshly desires. Are you trailing along with the world?
"The branch cannot bear fruit of itself, except it abide in the vine." John 15:4

An aspect of the truth our Lord unfolds in this chapter is that He is not the root or the stem only; He is *the whole vine.* Thus what Christ covers is every branch, every leaf, and every tendril of the whole plant. The same idea is present where the name "Christ" is given to the whole body (I Corinthians 12:12). The Christian is to abide in Christ, as the branch abides in the vine. The function of the branch is to maintain connection with the stem, to receive the life-sap at one end, and to bear fruit at the other.
"We should bring forth fruit unto God."
                                    Romans 7:4
Our Father is glorified when we bear much fruit—fruit of holiness, fruit of devotion to Him, fruit of witness and soul-saving. But, *no union—no fruit.* In the narrative, Paul is writing about being married to Christ, which means we have renounced our own name and have taken His—that we live upon His fulness, walk by His Word, and seek to please Him in all things. Our good works represent the fruits of our oneness with Him.

THE BOND OF FRIENDSHIP

Because all of us are in need of human friends, it is most important to be wise and careful in the choice of friendship. Is this not one of the most serious responsibilities of life? It is essential to have those friends who will not fail us at any point, but who are at hand to sympathize and help in time of need, and also ready to share in our happiness. Such a tie of personal friendship is not a tie of duty merely, or of obligation, but a bond more close and intimate. The friends whose friendship we revere are those who act as an elixir of life. Says Bacon, "A true friend—redoubleth joys and cutteth grief in half." The Apocrypha has the line, "A faithful friend is the medicine of life." With this introductory preamble, we come to what the Bible has to say about the choice and function of friends, and of the promised friendship of Christ.

Scholars remind us that our English word "friend" suggests different meanings in the original. In some cases, it denotes "the idea of loving as well as being loved"—a term of endearment. Then there is the idea of comradeship or partnership, as when Jesus said to Judas, "Friend (companion), wherefore art thou come?" (Matthew 26:50). What a false partner Judas proved himself to be! He failed to realize that true friendship is "love without wings." Drop the

"R" from "friend," and you are left with FIEND – which Judas appeared to be.

We often think of Abraham as one of the most privileged men in the Bible because of his friendship with the Eternal.

"Abraham thy friend forever."
II Chronicles 20:7
"The seed of Abraham my friend."
Isaiah 41:1
"Abraham believed God . . . and he was called the friend of God."
James 2:23

Moses was another who experienced similar intimate friendship, for it is said of him that – "The Lord spake unto Moses face to face, as a man speaketh unto his friend" (Exodus 33:11). But the Patriarchs are not alone in such a blessed, heavenly friendship. Did not Jesus describe those who love and trust Him as His friends?

"Ye are my friends, if ye do whatsoever I command you." John 15:14
"I have called you friends."
John 15:15; Luke 12:4; John 11:11

But this promised, exalted friendship carries the condition of *Obedience* to our heavenly Friend's wishes and commands.

"The rich hath many friends."
Proverbs 14:20; 19:4

Alas, these so-called friends often vanish with the riches, as the Prodigal discovered when all was spent and not one companion in his riotous living days was at hand to give him a meal! An Italian proverb says, "Who finds himself without friends is like a body without soul."

"Faithful are the wounds of a friend."
Proverbs 27:6
"All my inward friends abhorred me."
Job 19:19, 21
"The Lord turned the captivity of Job, when he prayed for his friends."
Job 42:10
"A friend loveth at all times."
Proverbs 17:17. See 22:24
"A man that hath friends must show himself friendly." Proverbs 18:24
"Thine own friend, and thy father's friend, forsake not." Proverbs 27:10
"Iron sharpeneth iron; so a man sharpeneth the countenance of his friend."
Proverbs 27:17
"Friend, I did thee no wrong."
Matthew 20:13
"He may say unto you, Friend, go up higher." Luke 14:10
"A friend of the world is the enemy of God." James 4:4

What guidance the above cameos of friendship provide for those who seek companionship, or those friends Shakespeare describes in *Julius Caesar*, "He was my friend, faithful and just to me"! If we are blessed with loyal, true friends let us value them and follow the advice Samuel Johnson gave another, "A man, Sir, should keep his friendships in repair."

The fact remains, however, that no matter how dear and beneficial an earthly friend can be, the best cannot bring us as much as Christ, who wants to be a Friend and whose friendship is pure and heavenly (see II Timothy 4:10). "There's not a friend like the lowly Jesus." Human friendship cannot go all the way, but Christ's friendship is an eternal one. Says J. R. Miller –

"Whatever other friendships you may miss, miss not Christ's friendship; Whatever else you may leave out of your life, let no one leave Christ out of his life."

"This is my beloved, and this is my friend." Song of Solomon 5:16
"The Son of Man . . . friend of publicans and sinners." Matthew 11:19
"I say unto you my friends, Be not afraid." Luke 12:4
"Greater love hath no man than this, that a man lay down his life for his friends." John 15:13

It is quite understandable that a true friend should be ready to sacrifice his life for one he is bound to with the cords of deep affection. But the marvel of marvels is that our heavenly Friend, died on the Cross, not for the few, close friends He had around Him, but for His enemies –

"When we were enemies, we were reconciled to God by the death of his Son." Romans 5:10
"The enemies of the cross of Christ."
Philippians 3:18

Is it not somewhat striking that after Jesus had been delivered up to death, Pilate and Herod, hitherto at enmity, became friends (Luke 23:12)? What a reconciling factor the Cross is! But what a friendlessness was His at the end!

"My lovers and friends stood afar off."
Psalm 38:11
"Lover and friend hast thou put far from me." Psalm 88:18
"What are these wounds . . . Those with which I was wounded in the house of my friends." Zechariah 13:6, 7

Now He offers Himself, not only to sinners as a Saviour, but as a Friend to those saved by grace. He is the Friend who loves us at all times, and who sticks closer than a brother (Proverbs 17:17; 18:24). Is it not condescending of Him to allow us to call *Him* "Friend"? May we understand increasingly all that is implied in this covenant of eternal friendship with Him! Such a privileged friendship should purify life and nerve us to the best and noblest service.

One has read of a patient brought into a London hospital for a serious and dangerous operation. The surgeon asked her if she thought she was strong enough to endure it. She answered, after a moment's hesitation, "Yes, if Lady Augusta Stanley will come and sit beside me." In Christ, we have the Friend who never leaves our side. At all times, and under all circumstances, He is at hand to console, succor, and relieve.

Says Richard Baxter, "Oh, that we could always think of God as we do of a friend; as of one who unfeignedly loves us, even more than we do ourselves; whose very heart is set upon us to do us good."

THE ONE WHO NEVER FORSAKES

An aspect of divine companionship is that of the promise of the Companion Himself never to forsake us (Hebrews 13:5). Here, the word "forsake" means *to leave behind in any state or place.* He will never abandon us, no matter how we may be. Irrespective of our straits, He is there to undertake. Paul was heartbroken over the way his close friend had treated him—"Demas hath forsaken me" (II Timothy 4:10. See 4:16). In Christ, however, we have One who will never treat us thus. But this abiding One knows what it is, like Paul, to be forsaken not only by man, but by God.

"Thou hast forsaken me, saith the Lord."
Jeremiah 15:6

"They forsook the Lord God of their fathers." Judges 2:12, 13; 10:6, 10, 13, etc.

"Which have forsaken the right way."
II Peter 2:15

"Why is the house of God forsaken?"
Nehemiah 13:11

"My people . . . have forsaken me."
Jeremiah 2:13

"They forsook him, and fled."
Luke 14:50

It is interesting to compare this heartless desertion with the noble desertion of the disciples. When they first met Jesus and He called them to follow Him, we read, "They forsook all, and followed him" (Luke 5:11). But the thought of the peril associated with close discipleship frightened them and so we read, "When they saw the swords and staves, they forsook him" (Matthew 25:56).

The crown of the Saviour's anguish was the consciousness that as He bore the load of human sin, His own Father's face was turned from Him. So we have His piercing cry—"My God, My God, why hast thou forsaken me?" (Matthew 27:46). Martin Luther said of this cry, "That was God forsaken of God." It was because He was forsaken in that dark hour that He is able to say to every blood-washed child of His, "I will never forsake thee." And this bright promise runs through the Bible.

"The Lord will not forsake his people." I Samuel 12:22

"Yet our God hath not forsaken us."
Ezra 9:9

"The God of Israel will not forsake them." Isaiah 41:17

"Forsake not the works of thine hands."
Psalm 138:8

The Master has left us with the promise of reward if we are willing to forsake all for His dear sake. He plainly declares that unless we are prepared to forsake all, we cannot be His disciples (Luke 14:33). But if we forsake all, then we shall receive an "hundredfold, and shall inherit everlasting life" (Matthew 19:29). Moses forsook Egypt, as seeing Him who is invisible (Hebrews 11:27).

THE JOY OF FORGIVENESS

We would have been of all men most miserable had there been no divine forgiveness of sin. But how rich and full are the promises associated with such a blessed Gospel truth. What is forgiveness? One expositor says it means "The giving up of an inward feeling of injury or resentment, the removing of a feeling of anger and restoring a feeling of favour and affection." It would seem as if Paul had this significance in mind when in his synagogue sermon at Antioch he said,—"Through this man is preached unto you the forgiveness of sins: And by him all that believe are justified from all things" (Acts 13:38, 39).

Since the key passages on "forgiveness" are generally known, a brief classification of same will suffice.

God is the God of forgiveness.

"There is forgiveness with thee."
Psalm 130:4

"The Lord our God . . . forgiveness."
Daniel 9:9

"Thou, Lord, art . . . ready to forgive."
Psalm 86:5
"He . . . full of compassion, forgave."
Psalm 78:30
"Thou wast a God that forgavest them."
Psalm 99:8
"Who forgiveth all thine iniquities."
Psalm 103:3; Daniel 9:19; Amos 7:2, etc.
God alone is able to forgive sin.
"Who can forgive sins but God only?"
Mark 2:7; I John 1:9
"Father forgive them." Matthew 6:14;
Luke 23:24; Mark 11:25
"The Son of Man hath power . . .
to forgive sins."
Luke 5:24; Colossians 3:13
God forgives sins through the cross.
"God for Christ's sake hath forgiven
you." Ephesians 4:32
"A Saviour . . . to give . . . forgive-
ness of sins." Acts 5:31; 13:28
"In whom we have . . . the forgive-
ness of sins."
Ephesians 1:7; Colossians 1:14
God forgives sin on the basis of repentance.
"Repent ye." Matthew 3:2; 4:17; Acts
2:38; Luke 13:5
"Repent ye therefore . . . that your
sins may be blotted out." Acts 3:19
God says we are blessed if forgiven.
"Blessed is he whose transgression is
forgiven."
Psalms 32:1; 103:3; Romans 4:7
God commands the forgiven to forgive.
"Forgiving one another . . . as God
for Christ's sake hath forgiven you."
Ephesians 4:32; Colossians 3:13
"Lord, how oft shall . . . I forgive him?"
Matthew 18:21; Luke 11:4

THE OIL OF GLADNESS

Because the Bible has much to say about
"Gladness," and the Lord exhorts us
to be "exceeding glad," a summary of the
prominent passages with promises, specific
and borderline, might prove profitable. The
various Hebrew and Greek words used for
our English terms, "glad," "gladness," and
"gladly," mean *rejoicing, to be good* as
well as *glad, to leap, to make joyful, to
be of good cheer.* For a fuller treatment
of the classification of the different words,
the reader is referred to *Young's Analytical
Concordance.*

The constant exhortation to manifest a
joyful spirit, reflects the Divine character.
Christ was anointed with "The oil of gladness above his fellows" (Hebrews 1:9; Psalm
105:43). Such "gladness," as the Bible

describes, is not a mere fleshly emotion
– a worked-up excitement and so effervescent
that it quickly evaporates. It is a gladness
from, and *in,* the Lord.
"I will be glad and rejoice in thee."
Psalm 9:2
"Be glad in the Lord, and rejoice."
Psalms 32:11; 64:10; 104:34, etc.
It is also a "gladness" springing from the
provision and experience of God's saving
grace and mercy. Such rejoicing is one of
the evidences or Regeneration (Deuteron-
omy 28:47).
"He hath done great things for us . . .
we are glad." Psalm 126:3
"I will be glad and rejoice in thy
mercy." Psalm 31:7; Isaiah 25:9
"Seen the grace of God, was glad."
Acts 11:23
"For thou, Lord, hast made us glad
through thy work." Psalm 92:4
"We declare unto you glad tidings."
(to tell good news) Luke 1:19; Acts
13:32; Romans 10:15
The acme of gladness is the vision of the
Lord.
"Then were the disciples glad when
they saw the Lord." John 20:20
As those experiencing the gladness of grace,
we are repeatedly called upon to serve the
Lord, not grudgingly, but gladly.
"Love the Lord with gladness."
Psalm 100:2; II Chronicles 29:30, etc.
Strange though it may seem, we are urged
to be glad even in grief. Such victory over
adversity carries with it the promised re-
ward in heaven.
"Rejoice, and be exceeding glad, for
great shall be your reward."
Matthew 5:12
"Thou hast made us glad according to
the days wherein thou hast afflicted us."
Psalm 90:15
"Most gladly therefore will I rather
glory in my infirmities."
II Corinthians 12:9, 15

THE TREASURES OF GOODNESS

As there are almost one thousand passages in which "good," "goodness," and
their cognates are to be found, we cannot
do more under this section than indicate
some of the conspicuous features and promised blessings of God's goodness. Here again
the original of our English words is replete
with many interesting meanings. *Beautiful,
benefit, pleasing, life, kindness, strong* or
courageous, recompense, honor are among
the outstanding implications of "goodness."

God is good, as opposed to anything that is bad.

> "Thou art good, and doest good."
>
> Psalm 119:68

> "Praise the Lord, for the Lord is good."
>
> Psalm 135:2, etc.

As we have repeatedly indicated, God can never act contrary to His own character. All that He is *in* Himself, He is in all His association with man. Because of His kind, benevolent nature, He delights in promoting the happiness of His own by supplying their needs and relieving their distresses. His is a goodness in the absolute, highest, and most perfect sense.

God the Father is abundant in goodness.

> "The Lord . . . abundant in goodness."
>
> Exodus 34:6

> "The earth is full of His goodness."
>
> Psalm 33:5

> "How great is thy goodness." Psalm 31:19; Zechariah 9:17; Psalm 14:2

> "The goodness of God leadeth thee to repentance." Romans 2:4

> "Behold therefore the goodness and severity of God." Romans 11:22

> "His kindness (goodness) toward us in Christ Jesus." Ephesians 2:7

> "The good pleasure of his goodness."
>
> II Thessalonians 1:11

> "After the kindness (as above) and love of God toward man appeared."
>
> Titus 3:4

God's Word is like Himself.

> "Thy judgments are good." Psalm 119:39

> "Good is the word of the Lord."
>
> Isaiah 39:8

> "Stablish you in every good work."
>
> II Thessalonians 2:17

> "The words of faith and of good doctrine." I Timothy 4:6

> "Him that teacheth you in all good things." Galatians 6:6

God the Son is likewise good.

> "Who went about doing good."
>
> Acts 10:28

> "Good Master, . . . There is none good but one, that is, God." Mark 10:17, 18

> "Every good thing which is in you is Christ." Philemon 6, Ephesians 2:10

God the Spirit is also described as good.

> "Thou gavest also thy good Spirit."
>
> Nehemiah 9:20

> "The Spirit is good." Psalm 143:10

> "The fruit of the Spirit . . . is goodness." Galatians 5:22

How full of promise are all these manifestations of Deity! Further, we were created and redeemed that we might possess and exhibit such divine goodness. Run your eye over the hundreds of references where "goodness" is related to the Christian and you will be deeply impressed with your high and holy calling.

> "He that doeth good is of God."
>
> III John 11

> "Filleth the hungry soul with goodness."
>
> Psalm 107:9

> "With good will doing service."
>
> Ephesians 6:7; I Peter 2:12

> "Be ye followers of that which is good."
>
> I Peter 3:13; Romans 13:3

> "I will rejoice over them that do good."
>
> Jeremiah 32:41

> "Do good to them that hate you."
>
> Matthew 5:44

> "Good works" - "Good conversation."
>
> Hebrews 10:26; 13:18; James 3:13

> "Make you perfect in every good work."
>
> Hebrews 13:21

> "He which hath begun a good work in you." Philippians 1:6

> "I follow the thing that is good."
>
> Psalm 38:20; 37:3

Thomas Carlyle says, "How indestructibly the good grows and propagates itself even among the weedy entanglements of evil! . . . mysteriously does a Holy of Holies build itself into visibility in the mysterious deep!" Can we say that ours is the brand of imparted divine goodness propagating itself in a world of evil! MacDonald reminds us that—

> "To be good

Is more than holy words and definite acts." Tennyson had a similar saying—"'Tis only noble to be good." If the good Lord has the full control of your life and mine, then goodness becomes both a possession and an expression.

THE GRACE OF GRATITUDE

While the words "grateful," or "gratitude," are not to be found in the Bible, all they represent saturates its sacred pages. If you gather together the hundreds of references dealing with *thanks, thanksgiving,* and *praise,* all of which are related to "gratitude," you will have a formidable array of evidence that Christians should be a thankful people. As to the promises connected with praise to, and adoration of, God for all He is and does, the same are as varied as they are numerous.

The oldest idea in America is the national institution known as Thanksgiving Day, the origin of which goes back to the three-day festival held at the Plymouth settlement in October 1621. This occasion was so arranged that the people might "after a special manner rejoice together" when their harvesting was ended. Those *Mayflower* pilgrims, eager to leave England in quest of liberty to worship God as they pleased, expressed their gratitude to Him as soon as they reached Cape Cod. William Bradford, who became the first governor of the colony, left this unadorned yet eloquent record of their gratitude—

"Being thus arrived in a good harbour and brought safe to land, they fell upon their knees and blessed the God of Heaven, who had brought them over the vast and furious ocean, and delivered them from all the perils of miseries thereof, again to set their feet on the firm and stable earth, their proper element."

Another great Thanksgiving was observed in July 1630, when fourteen vessels arrived with 840 additional colonists. Other Thanksgivings followed, and by 1680 the custom became annual. In 1777, the Congress set apart December 18 as a day of solemn thanksgiving and praise. George Washington issued "Thanksgiving proclamations," but it was left for President Lincoln to establish the occasion as a national holiday. This he did, and in 1864, the last Thursday in November, the date still observed, was set when millions of Americans of all faiths pause to thank God for His bounty.

A study of all the Bible has to say about thanks and praise to God for all His goodness, however, shows that as Christians we should make every day, and not merely one day a year, our *thanksgiving day*. Nay, every moment of every day should be used to "praise God from whom all blessings flow." We honor Him more when we *live* on *Thanksgiving Street* all the time, than by visiting it once a year. First of all, we note that thanksgiving is commanded by God. But we bless Him twice over, when we do so on our own initiative out of hearts that are truly grateful.

"Offer unto God thanksgiving, and pay thy vows unto the most High."
Psalm 50:14
"What shall I render unto the Lord for all his benefits toward me?"
Psalm 116:12-14
"In every thing by prayer and supplication with thanksgiving, let your requests be made known unto God." Philippians 4:6

Dake, in his *Annotated Reference Bible*, cites at least 50 positive commands to praise and thank God for His manifold mercies.

In our thanksgiving we emulate the example of the angelic and heavenly host who praise God unceasingly for all His wondrous works—

"Those living creatures give glory and honour and thanks to him that sat on the throne." Revelation 4:9
"All the angels . . . saying, Amen: Blessing, and glory, and wisdom, and thanksgiving . . . be unto our God."
Revelation 7:11, 12; 11:15-17
"They sung a new song, saying, Thou art worthy." Revelation 5:9

We likewise follow the example of Jesus when we extol God for all the good gifts He bestows upon us.

"I thank thee, O Father, Lord of heaven and earth." Matthew 11:25
"He took the cup and gave thanks."
Matthew 26:27
"Jesus took the loaves; when he had given thanks." John 6:11
"Father, I thank thee that thou hast heard me." John 11:41

We should live in the spirit of praise because of its beneficial effect upon God, ourselves, and others.

"It is a good thing to give thanks unto God." Psalm 92:1-3
"I will praise the name of God . . . magnify him with thanksgiving."
Psalm 69:30
"Therefore will I give thanks unto thee, O Lord, among the nations."
Psalms 18:24; 30:12

Our praises should be associated with our prayers, for "Prayers and praises go together."

"Begin the thanksgiving in prayer."
Nehemiah 11:17
"Prayer and supplication with thanksgiving." Philippians 4:6
"Continue in prayer, and watch in the same with thanksgiving." Colossians 4:2
"Intercessions and giving of thanks."
I Timothy 2:1; II Timothy 1:3; Philemon 4
"Sacrifice of praise . . . giving thanks to his name." Hebrews 13:15; Psalm 92:1
"I will offer to thee the sacrifice of thanksgiving." Psalm 116:17

We are further exhorted to be thankful for all things, that is, for the unwelcome, as well as the welcome, experiences of life.

"In every thing . . . thanksgiving to God."
II Corinthians 9:11; I Thessalonians 5:18

"Giving thanks always for all things."
Ephesians 5:20; 1:16; I Thessalonians 1:2
"Gave thanks before God, as he did
aforetime." Daniel 6:10

Gratitude must be expressed for the *common* mercies of life, which are as numerous
as the stars of heaven – air to breathe, sun-
shine to enjoy, sleep at night, use of faculties,
comfort of home, gift of loved ones, food
and raiment, work and money to spend.
Too often these benefits are so lightly valued.
"Oh that men would praise the Lord for
his goodness!" Psalm 107:8
"He that eateth . . . giveth God thanks."
Romans 14:6, 7
"Meats . . . received with thanksgiving."
I Timothy 4:3, 4, 5; 6:17
"When thou hast eaten and art full,
then thou shalt bless the Lord thy God."
Deuteronomy 8:10, 11
"He took bread, and gave thanks to
God." Acts 27:35

Reflecting, however, upon the manifold
spiritual mercies of God what else can we do
but adore Him? Do not the innumerable blessings of grace inspire us to honor Him with our
hope and trust, make Him the object of
praise and adoration, quicken us to walk
worthily before Him in the land of the living, and increase our delight in His service?
"Bless the Lord, O my soul, and forget
not all his benefits." Psalm 103:1-5
Because of the explicit, spiritual nature of
these benefits, our thanks ascend to God
through Christ by the Holy Spirit.
"Offer unto God thanksgiving."
Psalm 50:14
"I thank Christ Jesus our Lord."
I Timothy 1:12
"I thank my God through Jesus Christ."
Romans 1:8; Colossians 3:17;
Hebrews 13:15
"Giving thanks unto God . . . in the
name of our Lord Jesus Christ."
Ephesians 5:20
Enumerating a few of the spiritual mercies
promised and provided and which merit con-
tinual praise, we have
The remembrance of divine holiness
"Give thanks at the remembrance of
his holiness." Psalms 30:4; 97:12
The goodness and mercy of God
"O give thanks unto the Lord . . . for
his mercy." Psalms 106:1; 107:1; 136:1-13
The effectual working of the Word of God
"Also thanks to God for . . . the word
of God, which effectually worketh."
I Thessalonians 2:13

The Gift of God's beloved Son
"Thanks be unto God for his unspeak-
able gift." II Corinthians 9:15
The provision of deliverance from sin
"Who shall deliver me . . . I thank
God through Jesus Christ."
Romans 7:23-25
"Now thanks be unto God, which always
causeth us to triumph in Christ."
I Corinthians 15:57
Among the plentiful supply of exhortations
on thanksgiving, let us pause a little over
a few of them that seem to have a pertinent
message for our hearts. If–
Faith makes all things possible;
Hope makes all things bright;
Love makes all things easy –
Gratitude makes all things doubly
beneficial.
"Every creature of God is good . . . if
it be received with thanksgiving."
I Timothy 4:4

Gratitude produces contentment in all
conditions and places a bridle on one's
desires. It checks gloom, destroys envy,
and returns with blessings on the head of
the thankful one. We taste the sweetness
of any divine mercy twice over when we
are sincerely grateful for it.
"Oh that men would praise the Lord
for His goodness." Psalm 107:31
With amazing regularity God meets the
need of all. Provisions are poured down,
but praises seldom rise. Men fail to think
of what they owe, and therefore forget to
thank. The common ordinary blessings of
life are received as a matter of course.
Mercies, spiritual and material, come our
way, but the Hand providing them is forgotten. The poet speaks about the winter
wind as being kinder than man's ingratitude. But if man's inhumanity to man makes
countless thousands mourn, what must God's
feelings be like when He blesses so much
and is blessed so little? His compassions,
which fail not and are new every morning,
are of greater worth when, in receiving them,
we instinctively and immediately say,
"Thank you, Father!" Like an earthly parent,
God too loves grateful children.
"I will declare what He hath done for
my soul." Psalm 66:16
Thank of what He has done for your
soul! He it was who saw you lost and
helpless, and in His love and mercy provided a way of deliverance. It was your
sinful condition that brought the Saviour
from above to die on Calvary. By His "blood,

sweat, and tears" He secured a priceless redemption for your soul. But He has not only saved your soul. He has made it safe forever. And day by day, as you realize that the responsibility of your saved life is upon His shoulder, He meets your every need. To adapt what a gifted writer has said of Philip, one of the less brilliant of the disciples, "I may not be able to reason and debate. I may have little skill in logic and apologetic. My words may be destitute of the orator's passion and poetry and color. But at least I can say, 'Come, and you shall see; come, and you shall find for yourself how good He is.'"

"With thanksgiving let your requests be made known unto God."

Philippians 4:6

Paul is found presenting an interesting combination as he outlines the secret of the peace of God. As we pray, we must praise. Asking, we must adore. Requesting further favors, we must remember past provision. Our supplications must be accompanied with song. Too often we approach the throne of grace as beggars. Ours is the spirit of the Prodigal, "Give me, give me." We are so taken up with immediate cares, needs, and problems that we do nothing but request. Eager to take from God, we forget what He expects from us. Greedy, we take all we can, but fail to satisfy God's bountiful heart as it yearns for the gratitude of those He blesses. Well, the next time we pray, let us remember to mix praises with our prayers.

"Giving of thanks, be made for all men."

I Timothy 2:1; 4:4

Certainly, we have a lot to be thankful for in a democracy like our own, in which rulers are intent upon men leading "a quiet and peaceable life in all godliness and honesty." The statement "giving of thanks, be made for all men" is qualified, we think, by the next verse. When we pray for those who rule us, God moves their hearts and brings them to sympathize with the way of life which is good and acceptable in the sight of God our Saviour. While we could pray for those cruel dictators and war lords who, as Christless as cruel, are bent on the destruction of peace, freedom, and godliness, we could not very well give thanks for them. We can intercede for their salvation, for God is able to save the most inhuman among these brutal rulers, but surely we cannot thank God for them as we can for the kings and authoritative leaders of many

of the nations which were engaged in the overthrow of hellish aggression.

"Neither were thankful." Romans 1:21

Heathenism, with its absence of the clear knowledge of God, is destitute of thankfulness. The heathen have no songs of praise. We have multitudes around us who know not God, or if they do profess a knowledge of Him, glorify Him not as God and who, consequently, seldom pause to praise the Giver of all. Such gratitude arises from the Spirit-filled life and expresses itself in "psalms, and hymns, and spiritual songs, singing and making melody" in the heart to the Lord. Alas, however, the vast majority of church-going people know little of this outburst of praise. Thanks are seldom expressed for food, raiment, health, and other common mercies without which they could not live. There is not that thanksgiving leading to thanksliving. The heart is empty of that gratitude for spiritual and secular blessings, which ever results in a life of complete surrender to the Lord. Let us shun the company of the thankless!

"Thanks be unto God for His unspeakable gift." II Corinthians 9:11-15

God's bounty in giving produces thanksgiving. Paul was a grateful soul, and he was therefore quick to appreciate the kindness bestowed upon him. To his beloved converts at Thessalonica he wrote, "What thanks can we render to God again for you?" Paul never sent belated thanks. Gifts and favors were immediately recognized as, of course, they should be by us all. Because there is no darker sin than ingratitude, may we always be found basking in God's promised favor because of our constant praise that ever glorifies Him.

"He that eateth . . . giveth God thanks."

Romans 14:6

In the chapter dealing as it does with the law of doubtful things, Paul has some pointed things to say about eating and drinking. As we eat, we are to eat unto the Lord. If gluttonous and over-indulgent at the table, we do not eat for the glory of God. Too many dig their graves with their teeth. They live to eat. As Christians we should eat to live. Grace before meals, however, appears to be the significance of Paul's injunction. We fear that too many who profess to be the Lord's are negligent about giving thanks for temporal mercies set before them. Food is consumed with never a thought for the Giver of all good things. In some Christian homes there is the custom of reading the Word of God at the table before its provisions are taken advantage of. Surely the Lord loves to be the unseen Guest at such tables!

"He that was healed . . . giving him thanks." Luke 17:12-19

That one leper, having been instantly cured, turned right back to Jesus and immediately expressed his sincere thanks. The other nine took the gift of healing but forgot the Healer. They pushed on their unmindful, unthinking way, feeling perhaps that they had only gotten what was their due. Possibly the thankless nine felt the Healer was no longer necessary to them. The pressure of urgent want was past. If it is true that—

"Man's ingratitude to man
Make countless thousands mourn"—
the grateful heart of Jesus was stabbed by the ingratitude of those nine lepers He had healed; hence, His question of heart-feelings – "Were there not ten cleansed? Where are the nine?"

"Lacked ye anything?" Luke 22:35

If there is constant praise and thanksgiving for what He daily bestows, doubt never lurks in the mind regarding God's ability to undertake for us. Praise has a way of feeding faith. The promise is that they who seek Him and bless Him shall not want any good thing. He knows all about our needs, remembers His promises, and is always at hand to undertake.

THE LAW OF GROWTH

The most consecrated Christian cannot reach maturity in this life. He stretches forth for such a prize, which will be his when he awakes in his Lord's likeness. Constant, unretarded spiritual growth should characterize those saved by grace. They are never static. If not following on to know the Lord in a richer measure, then are they falling back into the beggarly elements of this world. Blessed be God, we have not only promised grace, but promised growth in grace!

"Thou shalt see greater things than these." John 1:50

Here we have the promise of an ever expanding experience of God's power. No matter how great the things we have seen, greater manifestation of divine provision are ahead. Greater heights of fellowship and deeper depths of experience await us. "The best is yet to be." The promises related to spiritual growth reveal both its necessity and nature. How blessed we are if, ...

through the Spirit, we are growing up into the full stature of Christ!

"Bless the lads . . . let them grow into a multitude in the midst of the earth."
Genesis 48:16

The promise given by Jacob to Joseph concerning the progenity of his two sons can be used spiritually. Are there, as a part of our growth, others who through us came to know the Saviour?

"Thou hast planted them . . . they grow (or *go on*)." Jeremiah 12:2

"He shall grow up before him as a tender plant."
Isaiah 53:2; Zechariah 6:12

"Jesse, and a branch shall grow out of his roots." Isaiah 11:1

"He shall grow as the lily . . . grow as the vine." Hosea 14:5, 7

"Consider the lilies of the field how they grow." Matthew 6:28-34

"Growth unto an holy temple in the Lord." Ephesians 2:21

"Desire the sincere milk of the word, that ye may grow thereby." I Peter 2:2

"Grow in grace, and in the knowledge of our Lord." II Peter 3:18

"Your faith groweth exceedingly."
II Thessalonians 1:3

"Grow up into him in all things."
Ephesians 4:15

Are you a growing Christian? As the days and years go by, do you find yourself with a deeper love for Christ, an ever-increasing desire for holiness of life, a greater passion for the souls of others, a cleaner separation from the entanglements of the world? All promised grace and power are at your disposal for that increase of spirituality, ever pleasing to the Lord.

THE OFFER OF GUIDANCE

Are we not privileged to have God not only as our Guard, but as our Guide? He offers us not only defense, but direction. The Bible presents us with a few gracious promises of guidance which, if we appropriate, will result in a life lived in the will and way of God. He promises us paternal instruction, correction, counsel, and guidance. The whole trend of Scripture is that God is beforehand with every need of man, and that He is with him to lead him to the place and provision of His own appointing. Allied to the promises concerning our heavenly Guides, and the aspects of their guidance, are similar ones connecting with divine leading and direction. Taken together, all of these promises present indisputable evidence of the infallibility of the Guide, and of His unerring escort. With the Bible as our guidebook, then, let us seek to understand the information it presents to travelers from *The City of Destruction* to *The Celestial City.*

"In all thy ways acknowledge him, and he shall direct thy paths." Proverbs 3:6

The fulfillment of our promised direction is dependent upon our acknowledgment of God in every phase of life. First of all, there must be the frank confession that we are utterly unable to guide and direct our steps. Left to ourselves we swerve from the King's highway and go astray.

"It is not in man that walketh to direct his steps." Jeremiah 10:23

"A man's heart deviseth his way: but the Lord directeth his steps."
Proverbs 16:9

"I will direct his ways." Isaiah 45:13

How necessary it is to trust the Guide with the greatest simplicity, speaking to Him frankly about present matters, and future decisions, and then joyfully following Him wherever He may lead. If this is our unvarying attitude then we shall prove that "The path of the just is as a shining light" (Proverbs 4:18). See Psalm 5:3; I Thessalonians 3:11; II Thessalonians 3:5.

There may be occasions when, because of our finite understanding, divine leading seems so contrary to reason. The Israelites thought it strange that the roundabout route was the quickest way to reach the Promised Land.

"God led them not through the land of the Philistines, *although that was near* . . . But God led the people about, through the wilderness of the Red Sea."
Exodus 13:17, 18; Deuteronomy 32:10

Had Israel tried to go through the land of the Philistines as an unarmed people, they would have been completely discouraged, so it was quicker to skip the short cut and take the long way round. The heavenly Guide knew best – He always does.

Divinely chosen journeys are not always straight ones. Israel had to learn that the longest way around was the quickest and surest way there. God is never very partial to short cuts. As our Guide, He refuses to be hurried. It may be that you have prayed for guidance in a certain matter, and although you are confident that God is guiding and governing, somehow you feel that with such a Guide you should have been at your destination before this. Alas, we are

so blind! We cannot see the danger spots on the road which are making God's detours necessary. We do not know the way, but if we know and trust the Guide, He will see to the fulfilment of His plans for our life (Psalm 78:52, 72).

"The Lord alone did lead him."
Deuteronomy 32:12; Nehemiah 9:19

"He it is that doth go before thee."
Deuteronomy 31:1-8

Here we have clear expression of the idea of divine *leadership.* But *rest* and *guidance* are also involved in such a gracious promise. In the cloud for a covering and a fire to give light at night we have the further provision of *shelter* and *illumination.* "Light in the night" is something from, yet in addition to, the light of guidance. The Lord does not leave His people in gloom and distress; He is a Light to them amid darkness.

"Lead me, O Lord, in thy righteousness, because of mine enemies." Psalms 5:8; 23:2; 25:5. See also Psalms 70:20; 80:1; 106:9; 139:24.

"He shall gently lead those that are with you." Isaiah 40:11

"The Lord thy God . . . which leadeth thee in the way that thou shouldest go." Isaiah 48:17; John 10:3

Amid all the wonders and glories of heaven, our heavenly Guide will still have the full control of us, for the blessed promise is that He will not only protect and provide but –

"He shall lead them unto living fountains of waters." Revelation 7:17

What a contrast He is to those whom He described as "Blind leaders of the blind" (Matthew 15:14; Acts 1:16; Romans 2:19).

That all three Persons of the Trinity are united in the guidance of the Christian is evidenced by the fact that the Holy Spirit, as well as the Father and the Son, is promised as a guide.

"The Spirit of truth . . . he will guide you unto all truth." John 16:13

"Then was Jesus led up of the Spirit."
Matthew 4:1

"Led by the Spirit of God."
Romans 8:14; Galatians 5:18

The Bible as a torch, or light, guides the footsteps of the believer through the dark, and the guiding Spirit leads him into a clear understanding of many dark and hidden things, so that what cannot be comprehended by the intellect is apprehended by the heart. Can we say that whether it be truth or life, that we are Spirit-led? Jesus promised the Spirit as another infallible Guide (Acts 8:31).

"The Lord shall guide thee continually."
Isaiah 58:11

"The meek will he guide in judgment."
Psalm 25:9

"I will guide thee with mine eye."
Psalm 32:8

"The Lord guided them on every side."
II Chronicles 32:22; Exodus 15:13

"To guide our feet into the way of peace." Luke 1:77

The Bible contains certain definite principles which are invariable and unchanging. One of these principles is that when divine guidance is in harmony with the trend of our circumstances, and the revealed truth of God, we may step out boldly and be confident that we are walking in the way of His will. If, somehow or the other, you have lost your way, and find yourself entangled in the dark wood of doubt, stand still and await God's salvation. Do not seek your own way, or consult only with flesh and blood. Abstaining from self-will and self-direction, await the guidance of Him who is the continual Guide.

As correct guidance depends upon the ability and knowledge of the guide, let the above promises assure you of the Lord's ability to lead you aright. The One who promises to direct your step continually is *perfect*. With such a Guide, how can you err, and why should you be afraid of what is ahead? Then He is *patient*. He knows how timid you are to step out after Him on some unknown road. He is also *powerful*, which means that He is well able to deal with all hellish and human forces endeavoring to impede your progress. He guards as He guides. Is He not also *perceptive?* All needs of the journey have been anticipated and bountifully provided for. Because He knows the end from the beginning, nothing can take Him by surprise. There are no crises with Christ.

"By springs of water shall he guide them." Isaiah 49:10

While the promise of the text is related to a preserved and restored Israel, John borrows some of its phraseology to describe the bliss of the redeemed once the swelling tide of death has been crossed. Guidance is to be ours until we see the Guide Himself face to face. Over the present perilous and thorny path of life we have the unfailing direction and companionship of our unerring Leader. When we reach the end of the way, the same mighty Hand will still be upon us, translating us from the dusty lanes of earth to the golden streets above. But surely we are warranted in giving this promise a present application. Our precious Guide knows where all the sources of refreshment are and can lead us to them for the banishment of our thirst.

"I will guide thee with mine eye."
Psalm 32:8

As it is common in the East to direct servants by signs, either by hands or eyes (Psalm 123:2), we have here a symbol of the pilgrim's alertness for the Guide's next move. Slaves would watch with great attention the will of their masters; the least wink or movement of the eye or motion of the fingers, though imperceptible to strangers would be sufficient to command service. Are we so watchful as to know our Lord's slightest wish? Can it be that we fail to recognize His desires? May grace be ours to be alive and quick to hear each whisper of His voice! As glad vassals of a Saviour's throne, may our eyes be ever open to discern His will as He bids us follow His steps.

"Thou art the guide of my youth."
Jeremiah 3:4

Looking back over past years, many of us can see how the Lord ruled and overruled in our lives, even though we had no thought of Him. With the perfect perception we would expect such an infallible Guide to have, He looked away down the corridor of time and graciously prepared us for His service. Thinking of all we have experienced, we find ourselves blessing the heart that planned. Wayward and godless though we were, unseen eyes were watching and unseen hands directing our steps. And if these lines are being read by one who is young, strong, and free, may his be the sweet consciousness that our Heavenly Father offers to be his Guide.

"The Lord saved . . . and guided them on every side." II Chronicles 32:22

Grace and guidance are related. To be saved means to be safe. Sinners, who deliberately reject the salvation of God have no right to expect His guidance. Sitting with a notebook and pencil and recording what may come into the mind, as a certain cult urges its followers to do, is no safe method of guidance. Tragedies have followed this unbiblical way of getting to know what to do. First of all, there must be the basis of salvation before guidance can be asked and given. God must get rid of our guilt before He can grant us any guidance we crave. Then, once delivered, we are ready to be directed.

"He . . . guided them by the skilfulness of his hands." Psalm 78:12

Wisdom and skill are both His. His hand cannot possibly lead astray or lose a traveler. If we seek His guidance we shall receive it; but He will not comfort our distrust or half-trust of Him by showing us the chart of all His purposes concerning us. He will show us only into a way where, if we carefully and trustfully go forward, He will show us a still further way. Because of His skill as a Guide, it is safe to trust Him.

"Commit thy way unto the Lord; trust also in him; and he shall bring it to pass." Psalm 37:5

"Him shall he teach in the way that He shall choose." Psalms 25:12; 107:7

If we are bent on going His way, and not our own, life becomes delightfully relaxed and peaceful. If, on the journey, we encounter any experiences which appear as accidents impeding our progress, we rest in the fact that there are no unfortunate occurrences in the divine purpose.

"He chose our inheritance for us."
Psalm 47:4; Isaiah 42:5

"I will bring the blind by a way that they know not of." Isaiah 42:16

Are you not amazed by the boundless condescension of God? Blind men cannot find a way which they do not know. Even when they have found a way after traversing it many times, they still pick their step carefully with the aid of their white stick or "seeing" dog. By nature we are blind to God's ways, but He promises Himself as a Guide of the blind. Our eyes are veiled to the future, but nothing is hid from Him in whom we trust. The unknown is known to Him.

"For the Lord your God is he that goeth with you." Deuteronomy 20:4; Mark 16:7

God is not only on before, but with us –our Companion as well as our Guide. If we are oppressed by fearful apprehensions of an uncertain future, then we can bid our fears depart, for He goes *before* us (Deuteronomy 31:8). Then as we go, He is *with* us as our august Ally to strengthen us for the warfare of faith.

"Thou shalt guide me with thy counsel, and afterward receive me to glory." Psalm 73:24

"He will be our guide even unto death."
Psalm 48:14

When we seek the counsel of the infallible God in preference to our own judgment or the advice of friends, we have the assurance that as the great Jehovah He will direct our steps each day, and all the days, until we reach the end of our days. We have His promise that He will lead us, and never leave us, right up to the time when we meet Him at heaven's gate. The margin suggests a sweet thought when it says that "even unto death" can mean "even *over* death," that is, over death into resurrection. He will never let go our hand even when we reach heaven, because even there we shall have Him as our blessed Guide forever. His guidance then means not only life security, but eternal security. When ultimately at home with the Lord, memory purified and perfected will intensify eternal gratitude as we "Remember all the way which the Lord our God led us" (Deuteronomy 8:2).

The Shadow of the Hand

Among the almost 1,500 Bible references to hands, there are a few relating to God which carry with them promises of provision and protection. Throughout Scripture hands are represented in very many expressive actions and customs.

The right hand was the place of honor and power.

"Upon thy right hand did sit the queen."
Psalm 45:9; I Kings 2:19

"The Lord said unto my Lord, Sit thou at my right hand." Psalm 110:1

"The right hand of power."
Mark 14:62

"Thou that saveth by thy right hand."
Psalm 17:1; Exodus 15:6

The right hand was illustrative of protection and support.

"Thou hast holden me by thy right hand." Psalm 73:23; Isaiah 41:13

"He is at my right hand, I shall not be moved." Psalms 16:8; 109:31; 110:5

Men smote the Lord with the palms of their hands, but He in love and mercy assures us that He has graven our names upon the palms of *His* hands (Isaiah 49:16; Matthew 26:67). If we want to remember something, we tie a piece of string round a finger. Our names *graven* – never to be effaced–on His hands carries the promise of His everlasting remembrance of us.

Because in creation and redemption we

are "The work of thy hand" (Isaiah 64:8), we are privileged to have the hiding shadow of that hand (Isaiah 49:2).

"My times are in thy hand." Psalm 31:15

What a rich promise this is the psalmist gives us! How blessed we are when we can sing –

> All my times are in His hand:
> I'll therefore trust, nor yield to fear,
> But cast on Jesus all my care.

All events are under divine control. Nothing is left to chance. As Christians, we do not shape our lives by any star, as astrologists would have us do. The One who made the stars rules and overrules in the affairs of your life and mine. In infinite wisdom and love, He appoints all that should come our way. By His power, He causes all things to work together for our good – whether the "times" be good or bad.

"My purpose shall stand, and I will do all my pleasure."

His purposes cannot be frustrated and His promises and purposes cannot fail.

"All his saints are in his hand."

> Deuteronomy 33:3

This further promise does not say that *some* of his saints – the most obedient and holiest – are in His hand, but *all* His saints. There is a sense, of course, in which every Christian is a saint – that is, separated and set apart by God for His service and sanctified by the operations of the Spirit. All believers, then, are saints, although some are more saintly than others. But all are in His hand of mercy, of power, and of providence. All in His hand are His property, to be protected and provided for by Him: and because His hand is large enough to hold all, it is strong enough to preserve all. His is the hand of a "living God" (Hebrews 10:31).

"Neither shall any man pluck them out of my hand . . . No man is able to pluck them out of my Father's hand."

> John 10:28, 29

Do we not have here the promise of a double security? Truly, the Christian is safe because of the double grip Jesus spoke about. His statement is explicit – "no man" – and this is a generic term implying that even the believer himself cannot wriggle out of the mighty hands of the Father and the Son. With our hands in these wonderful hands of deity, we are forever safe and secure.

The Pursuit of Happiness

Although "happy," "joy," and "rejoice" are distinctive terms each carrying different original meanings, yet they are used to express the God-created emotion of pleasure, felicity, and bliss. "Happy" is a word equivalent to *blessed*. Says Carlyle, "There is in man a higher than love of happiness: he can do without happiness, and instead thereof find blessedness." But when Jesus said, "Blessed" (Matthew 5:3-11), He used the same word given as "happy" (John 13:17). Therefore, in this classification of promises we are bunching together several passages where happiness, joy, and rejoicing are used, leaving the blissful verses to tell out their own message.

"Happy art thou . . . who is like unto thee, O people saved by the Lord." Deuteronomy 33:29; Psalm 144:15

"Happy is the man whom God correcteth." Job 5:17

"Whoso trusteth in the Lord, happy is he." Proverbs 16:20; 28:14

"These things, happy are ye if ye do them." John 15:17

"Happy is he that condemneth not himself." Romans 14:22

"If ye suffer for righteousness sake . . . If ye be reproached . . . happy are you." I Peter 3:14; 4:14

"Behold, we count them happy which endure." James 5:11

Such an emotion is not temperamental or intermittent, but deep and constant. The happiness which the Bible enjoins is begotten of faith and obedience and is therefore not a mere effervescent feeling but part of the fruit of the Spirit. In contrast, the so-called happiness of the unsaved is short, vain, and uncertain (see Job 20:5; Luke 12:20; Ecclesiastes 2:1; 7:6). As all the Beatitudes of Christ are promises, read "happy" for "blessed," and note some of the promised results of this heaven-born bliss.

Among the 500 or so passages dealing with joy and rejoice, there are several precious promises for the Christian to observe and obtain. We cannot muse upon all of these joy-verses without realizing that God expects His people to be a contented, satisfied, and happy company.

"God given to a man . . . joy." Ecclesiastes 2:26; Psalm 4:7

"The joy of the Lord is your strength." Nehemiah 8:10

"My mouth shall praise thee with joyful lips." Psalm 63:5

"Sing unto God . . . rejoice with

him." Psalm 68:4
"Blessed is the people that know the joyful sound." Psalm 89:15, 16
"The voice of rejoicing and salvation is in the tabernacles of the righteous."
Psalm 118:15
"They that sow in tears shall reap in joy." Psalm 126:5
"They joy before thee . . . as men rejoice." Isaiah 9:3; 41:15
"Ye shall go out with joy."
Isaiah 55:12; 61:7, 10, 11
"Although the fig tree shall not blossom . . . Yet I will rejoice in the Lord."
Habakkuk 3:17, 18
"My joy . . . your joy might be full."
John 15:11
"Rejoice in the hope of the glory of God." Romans 5:2; Isaiah 61:10; Psalm 97:12
"Ye rejoice with joy unspeakable and full of glory." I Peter 1:8
"All patience and longsuffering with joy." Colossians 1:11
"Thou servedst not the Lord thy God with joy."
Deuteronomy 28:47; Philippians 3:3
"I am exceeding joyful in . . . our tribulation." II Corinthians 7:4; Romans 12:12
"My spirit hath rejoiced in God my Saviour." Luke 1:47; 10:21
"When men revile you . . . Rejoice, and be exceeding glad." Matthew 5:11, 12
"As sorrowful yet always rejoicing."
II Corinthians 6:10; I Thessalonians 5:16
God expects His children to be joyful, because He Himself is described as the One capable of happiness – "He will rejoice over thee with joy" (Zephaniah 3:17), etc. Fullest gladness springs from grace and is an evidence to the world of that triumph over trial and adversity which the Lord makes possible. All the resources of God are unreservedly poured out upon us, so what else can we do but "Rejoice in the Lord *alway*" (Philippians 4:4). Such heavenly elation enables us to live our common life in an uncommon way.

"Rejoice in the Lord alway! and again I say, Rejoice." Philippians 4:4
Often we find this a very difficult precept to keep, especially when we are sometimes bewildered through the experiences God permits. The dispensations of Providence are somewhat perplexing, so much so that we are ready to cry out, "All these things are against us!" But God does not call upon me to rejoice in frames or feelings, but in *Himself*. In weakness, we can rejoice in His almightiness. Omnipotence is always on our side. In darkness, we can rejoice in His wisdom. He knows the path we take, and His methods of purifying and instructing us are always well ordered and sure. Never once is He betrayed into a false step. In the trials of life we can rejoice in His love for us. He cares for us, and therefore we can rest on His faithful promises.

The Beauty of Holiness

Here, again, we have several different Biblical words which all imply, more or less, the same truth – namely, our conformity to the divine image. "Holiness," "cleanliness," "godliness," "sanctification," and "separation" are terms which, although they may imply various shades of meaning, can yet be grouped together. The over-all truth is that God has not only promised us holiness of life, but has made every provision for it.

Dealing as we are in this volume with the promises of God, we must always bear in mind that the ultimate purpose of these promises is the separation of our lives from everything unworthy of our profession.

"Having these promises . . . let us cleanse ourselves." II Corinthians 7:1
Further, because of His holiness, God pledges the fulfilment of His promises.

"Once have I sworn by my holiness that I will not lie unto David."
Psalm 89:35; Amos 4:2
As there are some 1500 verses taken up with separation, godliness, cleanliness, holiness, and sanctification, they would take up a volume in themselves. All that we can attempt in our general coverage is to indicate some of the key passages the Bible uses in connection with the Christian's sanctity of life.

The basis of the pronouncements and promises of "holiness" is the holiness of God Himself – what He is, He desires His people to be.

"Ye shall be holy: for I the Lord your God am holy."
Leviticus 19:2; I Peter 1:15, 16
"Who is like unto thee, O Lord . . . glorious in holiness."
Exodus 15:11; Psalm 22:3
"God hath spoken in his holiness."
Psalms 60:6; 145:17; Isaiah 57:15
"Be ye followers of God, as dear children." Ephesians 5:1
That such likeness to the divine character is absolutely essential can be gathered from solemn warnings like these –

"No . . . unclean person . . . hath any inheritance." Ephesians 5:5

"Holiness, without which no man shall see the Lord." Hebrews 12:14

What holiness is this without which we cannot see the Lord? Christ was made of God unto us not only righteousness, but sanctification, and without this provision no man shall see the Lord. Righteousness is that which meets a just claim and Jesus satisfied every righteous claim that the Law had upon us. But God is a gracious and loving Father, as well as a righteous Judge, and had a heart needing to be satisfied. Nothing but a perfect response to the claims of His infinitely pure and holy nature could satisfy His heart. Christ, as the perfect Man – God's Ideal – actually accomplished and was so made unto us, became on our behalf – *holiness*. We cannot provide what God commands. By faith we accept the promised and provided holiness in Christ.

"Put on thy beautiful holiness."
                                    Isaiah 52:1

Included in the Christian's wardrobe are the garments which he must wear during his earthly pilgrimage and in which he must appear before the Holy One – the vestures of his eternity. Among Bible saints adorned in such garments was Barnabas, of whom it is said that "He was a good man, and full of the Holy Ghost and of faith" (Acts 11:24). Being filled with the Spirit was the secret of his Christlike character. The nine-fold fruit of the Spirit (Galatians 5:22) was reproduced in the one known as "the son of consolation." Is the same Holy Spirit bearing His fruit in us?

"Worship the Lord in the beauty of holiness." Psalm 29:2

"Partakers of his holiness."
                          I Corinthians 9:10

"We should be holy and without blame."
              Ephesians 1:4; Isaiah 35:8

"God hath . . . called us with a holy calling." II Timothy 1:8-9

"Unblameable is holiness." I Thessalonians 3:13; II Peter 3:11; Colossians 1:22

"Ye have your fruit unto holiness."
              Romans 6:22; Luke 1:74, 75

Sanctification, as we previously indicated, has a two-fold implication when used of the Christian. It involves a separation *from* all known sin, and a separation *unto* God for service. Christ sanctified Himself but only in the sense of setting Himself apart for God's purpose. As the One, "holy, harmless, separate from sinners," He had no sin from which to be separated.

"This is the will of God, even your sanctification." I Thessalonians 1:3, 4

"Chosen you to salvation through sanctification." II Thessalonians 2:13

"Sanctification through the Spirit."
              I Peter 1:2; Romans 15:16

"Sanctified through the truth."
                          John 17:19; Jude 1

"The very God of peace sanctify you wholly."
      I Thessalonians 5:23; Hebrews 2:11

Are we separated from all that is of flesh as we ought to be? One of the beautiful tiles adorning the "Dome of the Rock" in Jerusalem, bears the motto –

"He who clings to this world will lose the other."

If worldly-minded and unseparated, we shall certainly lose our promised reward.

"Separate yourselves . . . Touch nothing of theirs." Numbers 16:21, 26

"Wherefore come out from among them, and be ye separate, saith the Lord, and touch not the unclean thing: and I will receive you." II Corinthians 6:17, 18

David's host wanted to mingle with the Philistine's army, which was decidedly wrong, hence the question, "What do these Hebrews here?" (I Samuel 29:3). Delivered from sin and the world at their conversion, it is wrong for any of God's people to return to the beggarly elements of the world. "Arise ye, and depart, this is not your rest." It is dangerous to stray onto Satan's ground and to be found in the enemy's ranks. What do they here? The presence of a Christian in the world is unnatural and traitorous. He should be found in full fellowship with the spiritually-minded, and unspotted from the world.

It is incumbent upon all followers of God to bear His likeness and to be godly in all their ways. The psalmist reminds us that they who make gods are like unto them. How true this should be of a Christian who has the thrice holy God as his Father!

"All that will live godly in Christ Jesus."
              II Timothy 3:12; Psalm 12:1

"Exercise thyself rather unto godliness."
                          I Timothy 4:7, 8

"Godliness with contentment is great gain." I Timothy 6:6

"Things that pertain unto life and godliness." II Peter 1:3, 6, 7; 2:9

"He hath set apart him that is godly for himself." Psalm 4:3

We can suitably add to all verses related to the ideal and quest of holiness, those that are taken up with *purity* of life.

"He that hath clean hands, and a pure heart." Psalm 24:4

Keep thyself pure."

I Timothy 5:22; Hebrews 9:13

"He shall sit as a refiner and purifier of silver." Malachi 3:3

"He that hath this hope in him purifieth himself." I John 3:3

"Blessed are the pure in heart: for they shall see God." Matthew 5:8

"What manner of persons ought ye to be in all holy conversation and godliness." II Peter 3:11

As Christians, we are expected to be different from the ungodly. But are we? As the redeemed we have the promise and prospect of a new heaven and a new earth, wherein dwelleth righteousness, but are we rejoicing in our destination? Is the coming of Jesus the object of our desire and hope? Are we laying up treasures in heaven? Are we to be found of Him?

"We should walk in the newness of life."

Romans 6:4

As a new creation in Christ Jesus, we possess a new nature, are brought under new obligations, are expected to keep new objects in view and be influenced by new principles. No longer do we imitate the world or follow custom. We walk by new rules and follow the Saviour's bright example. Daily we should prove the power and purity of our new life and daily pray—

"Create in me a clean heart, O God."

Psalm 51:10

The best of us have to cry, "O God, remove guilt and pollution, produce purity and peace in my heart. Cleanse me by the precious Blood of Jesus, by Thy Word, and by the influence of the Holy Spirit." The world's greatest saints have been frank in their confession of personal sin. Martin Luther said, "When a man like me comes to know the plague of his own heart, he is not miserable only, he is absolute misery itself."

Jacob Behmen, the father of German philosophy, confessed, "Do not mistake me, for my heart is sometimes as full of malice as it can hold."

Philip Neri shouted to those who lauded him, "Begone! for I am good for nothing but to think and do evil."

Bishop Andrews, of saintly character, sobbed, "I am made of sin." His literary executors said that they could hardly decipher his private prayer book because it was stained with its author's tears of contrition.

Saint Teresa, one of the most cheerful women of her age, used to say, "I am the wickedest woman in the world."

Paul at the end of an unexampled life of service and suffering said, "I am the chief of sinners."

"Go unto the people, and sanctify them."

Exodus 19:10

"This is the will of God, even your sanctification." I Thessalonians 4:3

"Consecration," "dedication," "holiness," and "sanctification" spring from one Hebrew root. When used of man, they imply a progressive, inner detachment from evil. Such an experience is not only God's *will* for us but His *work* in and through us. Our daily life must not be alien to His will. Because of His own inherent holiness, He wills our personal holiness. Are we becoming more Godlike in this respect? By our separation from all uncleanness, we recommend the Gospel of sanctification to those around who find themselves miserably defeated by the forces of the old nature.

The Apron of Humility

Commenting on Peter's exhortation, "Be clothed with humility . . . Humble yourselves" (I Peter 5:5, 6), Ellicott gives us these most interesting sidelights on the verses:

> The Greek verb is a rare and curious one. It means properly "tie yourselves up in humility." Humility is to be gathered round about us like a cloak and *tied up* so that the wind may not blow it back, nor the rain beat inside it. But there is a still further and more delicate shade of meaning in the word. There was a peculiar kind of cape, well-known by a name taken from this verb (we might call it a "tie up"), and this kind of cape was worn by slaves, and no others. It was a badge of servitude. Thus Peter bids them all gird themselves for one another in a slave's "tie-up" of humility. None are to be master in the Church of Christ. And the humility is to be the very first thing noticed about them, their outward mark and sign.

Philipps translates the phrase, "Wear the 'overall' of humility in serving one another." Then when Peter urges us to "humble ourselves," it is "not merely as submissive bearing of the strokes which it pleased God to let fall upon them, but it was to be shown in the bearing toward one another." And "the mighty hand of God" is not to be regarded as that which is chastising them, but as the protecting shelter which they are humbly to seek.

The most outstanding personification of Humility the world has ever seen is that of the Lord Jesus Christ, who without any assumption whatever could say of Himself, "I am meek and lowly in heart" (Matthew 11:29). Christ lived what He preached and commanded of others. His was a "stainless peace of humility," and He urged His own to accept this virtue from Him. In all His ways, He rebuked "the pride of life," because *pride* is a sin God abominates. Before He was born, God promised Him exaltation for the lowliness He was to experience – a promise Paul records:

"Thou hast made him a little lower than the angels, and hast crowned him with glory and honor."

Psalm 8:5, 6; Hebrews 2:6

"He humbled himself . . . Wherefore God hath highly exalted him."

Philippians 2:7-11

The reader who desires to make a study of Christ's humility can elaborate on the following aspects set forth with clarity in the Bible.

- In taking upon Himself our nature (Philippians 2:7; Hebrews 1:16)
- In His birth and obedience to parents (Luke 2:4-7, 51)
- In His station in life (Matthew 13:15; John 9:29; 13:14, 15)
- In His voluntary poverty (Luke 9:58; II Corinthians 8:9; Mark 6:3; John 9:29)
- In His submission to ordinances (Matthew 3:13-15)
- In His willing servitude (Matthew 20:28; Luke 22:27; Philippians 2:7; John 13:5)
- In His identification with our infirmities (Hebrews 4:15; 5:7)
- In His association with the despised (Matthew 9:10, 11; Luke 15:112)
- In His refusal of worldly honors (John 5:41; 6:15; Zechariah 9:9)
- In His obedience to His Father (John 6:38; Hebrews 10:9)
- In His exposure to suffering, reproach, and death (Isaiah 56:6; 57:7; Matthew 26:37-39; Psalms 22:6; 69:9; John 10:15, 17, 18; Philippians 2:8; Hebrews 12:2)

Paul, who lived near to the heart of this humble One, came to reflect his Master's humility. Like Him, Paul "lay in the dust life's glory dead."

"Serving the Lord with all humility of mine." Acts 20:19

"I am the least of the apostles."

I Corinthians 15:9

"Less than the least of all saints."

Ephesians 3:8

"Not to think of himself more highly than he ought to think." Romans 12:3

"Though I be nothing."

II Corinthians 12:11

Do not the above confessions give us Paul's estimation of himself? The more he knew of himself and of his Lord, the more Paul humbled himself. Out of a lowly heart he could sing –

"I loathe myself when God I see
Content if Christ exalted be."

This is the apostle who counsels to imitate the Master's example, and his own – "Let this mind be in you, which was also in Christ Jesus" (Philippians 2:5). And the promise is ours, that the lower we lie before God, the happier and holier we shall be. Man's pride and misery is that he *must* be something. But the Christian is willing to become nothing that Christ may be all in all. Apart from Christ, we are less than nothing. If we continue empty, He will fill us. Let us beware of thinking too highly of ourselves or fancying that we deserve more than we receive, either from God or men. Humble, we are satisfied – helpless, we are strong.

Coming to ourselves, there are numerous precepts and promises connected with humility to be observed. Tennyson speaks of "True humility, the highest virtue, mother of them all." Confucius says, "Humility is the foundation of all virtues." Trench expresses a similar exaltation of humility in the lines –

"God many a spiritual house has reared,
but never one
Where lowliness was not laid first, the
cornerstone."

The experiences of Bible and church saints prove the dictum of Sir James Barrie in *The Little Minister* that, "Life is a long lesson in humility." We can briefly summarize the teaching of the Bible regarding this necessary quality in the following ways –

It is necessary to the service of God.

"What doth the Lord require of thee . . . to walk humbly with thy God."

Micah 6:8

God has no respect toward them who are proud, but condescends to walk with the humble. His grace humbles us – and it is only as we have true humbleness of mind that we can be happy and content. Of ourselves, we have nothing to be proud about or to boast of. The more we discover of the workings of our evil natures, the more our self-abasement. All that we can admire and boast of is the loving mercy and infinite compassion of God in saving such vile, unworthy sinners. As to the many promises connected with humility, let the mind dwell on these aspects –

It leads to riches, honor, and life.
"By humility . . . are riches, and honor, and life." Proverbs 22:4
"Before honor is humility."

Proverbs 18:12

"Honor shall uphold the humble in spirit." Proverbs 29:23

It brings the favor of God.
"Yet hath he respect unto the lowly."
Psalms 138:6; 147:6
"He forgetteth not the cry of the humble."
Psalms 9:12; 22:26; 25:9
"To revive the spirit of the humble."
Isaiah 57:15; 66:2; 29:19
"He shall save the humble person."
Job 22:29; Isaiah 61:1
"He that humbleth himself shall be exalted." Luke 14:11; 18:14; James 4:10
"The humble shall hear thereof, and be glad." Psalms 34:2; 37:11
"Lord, thou hast heard the desire of the humble," Psalm 10:17
"He forgetteth not the cry of the humble."
Psalm 9:12, 18
Do not these gracious promises remind us that humble, grateful hearts may have anything from the Lord? Because of His great love for us and delight in us, He will never despise nor condemn our petitions if lowliness of mind is ours.

It leads to increasing grace and blessedness.
"Blessed are the poor in spirit; for theirs is the kingdom of heaven."

Matthew 5:3

"Better is it to be of an humble spirit with the lowly." Proverbs 16:19
"He will beautify the meek with salvation." Psalm 149:4
"He giveth grace unto the lowly."
Proverbs 3:34; James 4:6
Humble hearts seek grace and secure it. When we humble ourselves because of our sins against humility, the Lord enriches us with His promised grace. Says Spurgeon –
"Humble hearts lie in the valleys where streams of grace are flowing and hence drink of them. Humble hearts are grateful for grace and give the Lord the glory of it, and hence it is consistent with His honour to give it them."
A French proverb has it, "Humility is the altar on which God wishes us to offer Him

sacrifice." It is upon this altar of Humility that we offer the sacrifice of praise continually.
It is the garment saints should wear.
"Put on therefore, as the elect of God . . . humbleness of mind." Colossians 3:12
"Walk . . . with all lowliness and meekness." Ephesians 4:1, 2; Luke 14:10
"Be clothed with humility."

I Peter 5:5, 6; John 13:14

Here are verses tantamount to a promise. We stoop to conquer. Humility leads to honor. Meekness means spiritual might. The lowly are lifted up. Once we cherish right views of our own littleness, unworthiness, insignificance, and vileness apart from grace, and then go on to possess the meek and quiet spirit of great price in God's sight, then we are in the position for Him to bless us. Humility is the most beautiful garment for a justified sinner to wear, for God has promised to dwell with the humble.

What we guard ourselves against is the false humility Paul speaks of – "Let no man beguile you of your reward in a voluntary humility . . . which things have a shew . . . of humility" (Colossians 2:18, 23). The proverb expresses it, "Pride, perceiving humility honorable, often borroweth her cloak." Let us beware of spurious humility. Proud of being humble is surely the worst form of pride. This is what Charles Dickens satirized in his character, Uriah Heep, who proudly confessed, "We are so very 'umble." In one of his devotional books, Dr. DeHaan has the thought – "Humility is that strange possession which you lose the moment you find out you've got it."

Associated with "humble" and "humility," words meaning *to make low, poor* and *afflicted; to trample upon; bruise,* we have the kindred term of "gentleness," which is derived from the same root as humility.
"Thy gentleness hath made me great."

Psalm 18:35

In these days of military might, men think it strange that greatness should spring from gentleness. But such meekness is not weakness. The most gentle are the truly great.
"The fruit of the Spirit is . . . gentleness." Galatians 5:22
"Put on therefore . . . meekness."

Colossians 2:12, 13

"The good and gentle." I Peter 2:18; James 3:17; II Timothy 2:24; I Thessalonians 2:7
"I beseech you by the . . . gentleness of Christ." II Corinthians 10:1

In our Sunday school days we learned to sing of the Master, "Gentle Jesus, meek and mild" – and He assuredly was the personification of gentleness and meekness. Yet what strength of character was His; what righteous indignation He manifested against satanic and hostile religious forces; what defiance of man to do His worst; what magnificent heroism in the face of a most brutal death! References to Christ's kindness can be linked on to His gentleness.

The continuing influence of the gentle Christ puzzled proud Napoleon in the loneliness of his exile. "Tell me, Bertrand, how it is that while I dwell alone and friendless on this barren rock, the dead hand of the Nazarene Carpenter can reach down the centuries and draw millions to follow Him?" Napoleon's friend replied, "The Nazarene Carpenter lived for others – Napoleon lived for himself." One of the most popular of modern historians in his judgment of Napoleon said of him, "Success intoxicated him and made him mad." The greatness of the Master's gentleness had been missed. Someone protested to General William Booth that self-preservation was the first law of nature. "Yes," was the old General's retort, "but the first law of grace is self-sacrifice." It was because of His gentle heart that Jesus could not save Himself.

"Be not high-minded, but fear."
Romans 11:20

This heart-appeal of Paul, who had sacrificed all for "His dear sake," forms a fitting conclusion to this section covering the promises related to humility and lowliness. The more we realize what deep debtors we are to the free, sovereign, and distinguished grace of God, the less tendency we shall have of thinking more highly of ourselves than we ought to. Remembering that in ourselves we are still weak, prone to wander, open to the subtle and designing attacks of Satan, serves to keep us humble and habitually dependent upon God. May grace be ours to cultivate humility of mind, and gentleness of spirit!

The Key of Knowledge

While it may have been advantageous to deal with terms like "knowledge," "wisdom," "understanding," and all verses taken up with "tuition" (or tutoring), noting numerous promises given with each, we feel that the following amalgamation will prove to be sufficient. Several hundred references cover the above aspects of one general theme. In the main, the scores of promises linked on to knowledge and wisdom are to be found in the Psalms and Proverbs. A diligent search of these with the aid of Young's Concordance will amply repay the student.

Another reason why we group the indicated terms together is because in many cases they spring from the same original root, and Scripture places these possessions in pairs –

"Incline thine ear unto widsom . . . thine heart to understanding."
Proverbs 2:2, 5
"The wisdom and knowledge of God."
Romans 11:33, 34

While knowledge and wisdom may be akin, we can yet differentiate between the two. A person may have an abundance of acquired knowledge covering many fields, yet lack sufficient wisdom in the full use of his wide knowledge, or in the ordering of his life and in personal decisions. On the other hand, a man may have had very limited educational advantages. Learning of schools was not his, yet his wisdom in many matters may be unique. Such a man was D. L. Moody, who, being forced to leave school when he was but a boy, lacked the secular knowledge which, through the schools he founded, he ultimately gave to thousands. But although uneducated, what remarkable insight, wisdom, and sagacity were his! Says Solomon, "Wisdom is the principal thing."

Let us look in the first place at what the Bible promises in connection with *knowledge*, which, in some cases, means "understanding."

"The Lord is a God of knowledge."
I Samuel 2:3
"Shall any teach God knowledge?"
Job 21:22
"He that is perfect in knowledge . . . mighty . . . in wisdom." Job 36:4, 5
"Knowledge . . . wisdom and instruction." Proverbs 1:7
"The lips of knowledge are a precious jewel." Proverbs 20:15
"My people are gone into captivity . . . they have no knowledge."
Isaiah 5:13; Hosea 4:6
"Whom shall he teach knowledge . . . make understand doctrine?" Isaiah 28:9
"The Lord God hath given me knowledge of it." Jeremiah 11:18
"Such knowledge is too wonderful for me." Psalm 139:6; Romans 11:33
"To know the love of Christ which passeth knowledge." Ephesians 3:19

"Then shall we know, if we follow on to know the Lord." Hosea 6:3

Paul presents us with one of the paradoxes of our faith, namely, knowing the unknowable. Along with the above passages, the reader can add the promises that can be found under the word "know." How rich and satisfying these are!

"Revealed . . . unto babes."

Matthew 11:25

The wise and prudent do not know everything. Mental and cultural equipment are not necessary for an appreciation of God and His ways. Babes are not characterized by a deep understanding, but they do have the ability to believe what is told them. In the confidence they repose in their elders, whose ways are beyond their little minds to fathom, we have the lesson our Lord emphasizes in the passage before us. Are we simple enough to receive a divine revelation? Have we reached the point where we can tell the Lord that, left to ourselves, we have and know nothing? Do we believe that mere worldly wisdom is foolishness to God? Is ours the attitude of a babe, believing all that our Father has declared? The difficulty God confronts is that of pride in human attainments. Many people know too much. From such the deeper things are hid.

"The natural man . . . cannot know them." I Corinthians 2:14

What is the exact nature of this spiritual knowledge we are presently considering? Paul makes it clear that it is a right understanding and notion of spiritual things, a daily progress in the appreciation of God's will and of His saving and sanctifying grace. Further, this spiritual knowledge reaches its perfection in Christ, is revealed unto us by the Holy Spirit, and produces faith, love, and obedience. The natural man is a person, a sinner by birth and then by practice, and one destitute of the regeneration the Holy Spirit makes possible. This "natural man may be learned, gentle, fascinating, but the spiritual content of Scripture is absolutely hidden from him." The spiritual man is the renewed man, Spirit-filled and walking in the Spirit in full communion with God. In which class are you?"

"God giveth to a man . . . knowledge."

Ecclesiastes 2:26

Secular knowledge comes by acquirement, spiritual knowledge by asking. The first is ours by research, the second by reception. And are we not guilty of folly when we refuse to take God at His Word and receive from His bountiful hand a knowledge of His love and will which passeth knowledge? Here is one of the mysteries of faith – we can know the unknowable! Further, this divinely imparted knowledge may be considered as experimental (II Timothy 1:12); affectionate (I John 3:19); influential (Psalm 9:10; Matthew 5:16); humiliating (Job 42:5, 6); satisfying (Psalm 36:7; Proverbs 3:17); superior (Philippians 3:6). Truly, such knowledge is too wonderful for me! One may be unlettered and ignorant, judged by the world's standards of knowledge, and yet have that Christian prudence and holy experience in the ways of God (see II Corinthians 8:7; II Peter 1:5, 6).

"If any man will do His will, he shall know." John 7:17

Our Lord affirmed that the truth He taught was not conceived in His own mind, but received from God. "My doctrine is not mine, but his that sent me." Which takes us back to a previous thought that divine knowledge is given, not gained. How can we become recipients of divine truth? Whether we have letters after our name suggesting learning or not, how can we arrive at an understanding of the doctrine Jesus received and repeated? Well, there must take place the harmony of two wills – namely, the human will and the will of God. Any conflict between these wills blocks the communication of knowledge. Not until there is perfect agreement between God's will and our own are we in a fit condition to receive the mind of God. Knowledge, therefore, is based upon obedience. Do, and thou shalt know. Disobedience closes the door of revelation. May grace be ours to will God's will.

"Knowledge . . . in the face of Jesus Christ." II Corinthians 4:6

Divine light, knowledge, glory, all reflected in a face! Doubtless the actual countenance of Christ suggested the illuminating, glorious knowledge of His Father. The apostle, however, is using face as a figure, Christ in His entirety was the personification of divine wisdom. By His works, ways, and words, He manifested the mind of God. Thus, with Christ, knowledge was not an attribute merely, it was Himself. Therefore, the more His people know Him, not know certain truths about Him, but know what it is to have a personal relationship whereby He and we are one, then with such a tie, we are ready for the impartation of all He knows. Perhaps we can be permitted to make an application. Knowledge in a face! Is this true of your face and mine? In a more limited measure, is the light of the knowledge of the glory of God seen in our faces? Let us never forget that the face can be the mirror of heaven!

"The earth shall be full of the knowledge of the Lord." Isaiah 11:9

Holy men of God, in describing millennial blessings, envisaged the time when men everywhere will understand divine things from the divine standpoint. Now there is widespread ignorance of God and His Word, but when Christ is here in person, the knowledge of the Lord will cover the earth, even as the waters cover the sea. They that erred in spirit shall come to understanding, and they that murmured will learn doctrine. "They shall teach no more any man his neighbor, and every man his own brother, saying, Know the Lord: for they shall all know me, from the least of them unto the greatest" (Jeremiah 31:34). This is a world in which the Lord is presently despised and rejected. The earth, having had as it has such a terrible blood-bath, is surely not an earth full of the knowledge of the Lord. Earth's travail is hers because of her ignorance of the Lord.

"Instruction," a kindred term sometimes meaning *to discern, to understand, to teach, to become known,* and *to chasten,* carries with it specific promises for the Christian who, as a disciple, is a *learner.*

"He instructed him." Deuteronomy 32:10; 4:36; Isaiah 28:26
"Thou gavest . . . thy good Spirit to instruct him." Nehemiah 9:20; Psalm 32:8
"Who hath known the mind of the Lord, that he may instruct him." I Corinthians 2:16; Isaiah 40:14

Here where Paul speaks of having "the mind of Christ," he uses a word suggesting the "thinking faculty" of Jesus. What a possession for the Christian to receive!

"Whoso loveth instruction loveth knowledge." Proverbs 12:1; 19:20; 23:23
"Profitable . . . for instruction in righteousness." II Timothy 3:16

How privileged we are to have the all-wise God as our Instructor—"His God doth instruct him to discretion" (Deuteronomy 4:36).

Coming to "wisdom," with meanings of *understanding, intelligence, knowledge,* it would take more time than we can allot to plough through the 500 or more passages where "wise," "wisely" and "wisdom" are found. Proverbs particularly extols Wisdom and offers appealing promises to those who seek her.

"Wisdom is the principal thing; therefore get wisdom." Proverbs 4:7
"The Lord give thee wisdom and understanding." I Chronicles 22:12; Daniel 2:20
"If any of you lack wisdom, let him ask of God." James 1:5
"The wisdom that is from above is first pure." James 3:17
"Christ Jesus, who of God is made unto us wisdom." I Corinthians 1:24, 30
"The wisdom of this world is foolishness with God."
                I Corinthians 3:19; Proverbs 23:4
"Give me now wisdom and knowledge."
                II Chronicles 1:10; Exodus 28:3, etc.
"Joshua . . . was full of the spirit of wisdom." Deuteronomy 34:9
"I wisdom." Proverbs 8:12

The Scofield *Reference Bible,* one of the most helpful aids to Bible study we know of, gives us this enlightening comment on Solomon's eulogy of wisdom in the chapter before us. "That wisdom is more than the personification of an attribute of God, or of the will of God as best for man, but is a distinct adumbration of Christ, is sure to the devout mind. Proverbs 8:22-36 with John 1:1-3; Colossians 1:17 can refer to nothing less than the eternal Son of God." And to this agrees the declaration of Paul that God has Christ to be unto us WISDOM as well as righteousness, sanctification, and redemption. Christ, too, is the hidden wisdom discernible only by faith (I Corinthians 1:30; 2:7).

"Wisdom is better than strength."
                                        Ecclesiastes 9:16

Tucked away in this chapter is a story of a little city besieged by a powerful king, and yet delivered by the wisdom of a poor man (9:14-18). And the way this forgotten, poor, wise man saved his small city led Solomon to confess, "Wisdom is better than strength . . . Wisdom is better than weapons of war." We are slow to learn, however, that the arm of flesh will fail us. By the mere strength of the flesh we can never prevail over superior forces arrayed against us. And carnal weapons offer the Christian no spiritual defense whatever. Our only hope of victory is in trusting in the wisdom coming to us from above the sun.

"Wisdom . . . shall be the stability

of thy times." Isaiah 33:6

Is it not somewhat of a mockery to speak of stability in a time like this? Chaos and despair afflict the earth. The bottom is falling out of things. Civilization is at the crossroads. Even our own personal life suffers the disruptive influences of war. And yet the prophet tells us that stability can be ours in an unstable age. With panic around, we can be at peace. Tranquility can be ours as we endure tribulation. And the secret of such stability is the wisdom of God. We may not be able to read the meaning of our tears, nor understand the anguish of earth. Faith, however, rests in the only wise God who never errs.

"Wisdom . . . God giveth liberally."
James 1:5

Wisdom is not achieved by research but accepted by faith. Knowledge is attainable by the effort of man. There are those who know a great deal. They have attained high eminence in literature, science, or theology. Much study has brought valuable knowledge. Wisdom, however, is not gained, but given. "God gave Solomon wisdom" (I Kings 4:29). And here in James we are reminded that the most illiterate saint, in so far as earthly knowledge is concerned, can yet become the possessor of profound wisdom. And if true that divine wisdom can be ours for the asking, are we not fools to remain unwise?

"Fools despise wisdom." Proverbs 1:7

Solomon's unique collection of proverbs appears to revolve around two sets of individuals – namely, the wise and the fools. And the Book as a whole is an exposition of the worth of the wise and the futility of the foolish. The wise delight in wisdom from above, while fools despise such wisdom schools can never impart. Solomon links true wisdom on to the emulation of parental piety. "My son, hear the instruction of thy father, and forsake not the law of thy mother" (1:8). But how many godless children there are who have outgrown the religion of their parents! Like fools, they despise the very source of power that gave them the noblest parents a child could have.

"Say unto wisdom, thou art my sister." Proverbs 7:4

Some people are very proud of their relatives, especially if they are famous. On the other hand, some relations are heartlessly forgotten. Well, in the wisdom from above which is first pure, then peaceable, gentle, easy to be intreated, full of mercy and good fruits, without partiality, and without hypocrisy (James 3:17), we all have a relative we should never be ashamed to own. Many of our connections are too poor to help us in a time of need. It is a struggle for them to make their own ends meet. But in the wisdom of God we have a sister who is endowed with priceless riches, and who is able to bless us with untold mental and spiritual wealth.

"This is your wisdom."
Deuteronomy 4:6

In teaching a new generation the lessons of Sinai, Moses made it clear that true wisdom consisted in obedience to the revealed Word of God.

"Keep therefore, and do the statutes; for this is your wisdom and your understanding in the sight of the nations." While wisdom "dwells with prudence," often a man acquires fame for his prudence and sagacity but reveals at the same time a conspicuous lack of wisdom. True wisdom springs from the fear of God, the love of God, and the right condition of heart before God. Prudent, are you wise? Wisdom, the Word of God begets is better than rubies.

Here again are promises for each of us to believe and claim.

"The Lord give thee understanding in all things." II Timothy 2:7

"God gave Solomon wisdom and understanding, exceeding much."
I Kings 4:29

"Through thy precepts I get understanding." Psalm 119:104

"Lean not unto thine own understanding." Proverbs 5:5-7

"In all wisdom and spiritual understanding." Colossians 1:9

"The full assurance of understanding."
Colossians 2:2

"The eyes of your understanding being enlightened." Ephesians 1:18; 4:18

"Great is our Lord . . . his understanding is infinite." Psalm 147:5; Isaiah 11:2

"Buy wisdom, and instruction, and understanding." Proverbs 23:23

As wisdom, knowledge, and instruction are associated with *tuition*, we briefly examine what the Bible says about the divine Tutors and their teaching. In the Persons of the Trinity, we have the three greatest Teachers it is possible to have.

"That which I see not teach thou me." Job 34:32; Psalms 27:11; 32:8; 86:11; 143:10

"Behold, God . . . who teacheth like him." Job 36:22; Psalm 25:4

"We know that thou art a teacher come from God." John 3:2

"They shall be all taught of God." John 6:45

"The Holy Spirit . . . shall teach you all things." John 14:26; 16:13; I Corinthians 2:14

"A teacher of the Gentiles in faith and verity." I Timothy 2:7

"Ye ought to be teachers . . . ye have need that one teach you." Hebrews 5:12

"Ye know all things . . . ye need not that any man teacheth you."
I John 2:20, 27

"Lead me in thy truth, and teach me." Psalm 25:2

God has only one way by which He can teach us His will–namely, by His Spirit through His Word. The Bible is the Christian pilgrim's lesson book and guidebook, and what perfect knowledge and tuition it promises. The path he is to follow is clearly indicated; the mountains of difficulty are revealed, along with the valleys of doubt and fear along the road he is to travel. Dangers to be encountered, and enemies in ambush are also made known. But without divine teaching, the Book is sealed –dark and unmeaning. When our eyes are opened by the heavenly Tutor, then its truths become our guide and stay, amid the wilderness of this world, and our hope and expectation of a blessed life in the great beyond. God teaches us that all His promises, precepts, and preservatives are ours.

"May God teach thee, my beloved!– may God teach thee."

Dr. G. Campbell Morgan wrote–

"With matchless patience, and pity, and tender love, this Teacher waits, stoops, and woos us, and ever for our highest good and deepest peace. Let us then by *consecrated watching*, maintain the attitude of advancement; and so, as we are able to bear, He will lead us on until we come to the perfect light, and life, and love of God."

"I will destroy the wisdom of the wise, and will bring to nothing the understanding of the prudent."
I Corinthians 1:19

This promise for the believer is likewise a warning to the worldly-wise unbeliever. Sometimes those who are professedly learned try to belittle the faith of the Christian, but God knows how to bring to naught the fleshy wisdom of the wise. He is well able to make clean work of much of our modern philosophy and prove how He is able to take the things which are not, to destroy the things which are.

"Then shall we know, if we follow on to know the Lord." Hosea 6:3

An efficient secular education means years of schooling and hard study. It is thus with heavenly knowledge which comes to us by degrees. At times, our progress may seem to be slow and our understanding somewhat dull, but the heavenly Instructor is so patient and has a unique way of making wise the simple. Our obligation is to keep close to Him and follow the trackway of Him who always teaches us to profit.

"The Spirit of truth . . . he will guide you into all truth." John 16:13

What an infallible Teacher and Guide the Holy Spirit is! He has a perfect knowledge of the Word and will of God, and can instruct us aright. *All truth* is an arrestive phrase. There is nothing one-sided or out of balance in the Spirit's revelation.

"I will instruct thee." Psalm 32:8

We know so little, and are so slow to learn, but the Lord promises to instruct and make us wise unto salvation. Under such divine instruction we learn so many necessary things–the true nature of sin, the vanity of the world, the fulness and preciousness of Christ, the glories of His grace. If we are honest with the light we receive, then humility, self-loathing, confidence in God, zeal for His glory and devotion to His service become ours, as well as all the promised blessings of obedience.

"That which I see not teach thou me." Job 34:32

Because as our Counsellor, God cannot perish (Micah 4:9), He ever lives to counsel us freely, fully, and cheerfully. Truths within His Word and many of His dealings may perplex the mind, but He is near to lead us into a clearer understanding of all things. "I will counsel thee, mine eyes shall be upon thee." "Teach Thou me" should be our daily prayer, and if it is, self will become vile–the world, vanity–sin, bitter–Christ's blood, most precious–divine righteousness, glorious–God's love, our joy–the Spirit, our strength–the promises, our constant stay.

The Rainbow of Love

We use the simile of the rainbow because "Love," as displayed in Scripture, is presented in many beautiful colors. We have the love of the Father, the Son, and the Holy Spirit for us as believers, and also divine love for a world of sinners lost and ruined by the Fall; our love to the Persons of the blessed Trinity and for all they love; our love for each other in the household of faith; our love for sinners; our love for the Word, and also for the appearing of Christ.

As there are, roughly, some 600 passages devoted to love, and its associate terms, the task of dealing fully with the salient features of such a divine and human emotion is beyond the purpose of this volume. All we can do is to indicate some of the promises connected with divine love, and with our love for those things God deems precious. Love saturates the Bible, and it is somewhat significant that the first reference to love is to be found in Genesis 22:2 – "Take now thy son, thine only son Isaac, whom thou lovest." The pattern of love is here set forth for us – it must reveal itself in sacrifice. The command to Abraham to surrender the son he loved affords a glimpse of the Father-heart of God, whose love was to be manifested in the sacrifice of His only begotten Son.

"O love, all love excelling."

First of all, let us take a few references reminding us of the love of the *Trinity* toward us, for we are loved by the Father, by the Son, and by the Holy Spirit. And truly in the spiritual realm there is no truth so uplifting to the Christian as that of being the object and recipient of this promised three-fold love.

"Yea, he loved the people . . . all his saints." Deuteronomy 33:3; 77:8; Isaiah 48:14

"God so loved the world."
John 3:16; I John 4:11

"Because he hath set his love upon me."
Psalm 91:14

"I have loved you . . . I will love him." John 13:34; 14:21; 21:20

"The Son of God who loved me."
Galatians 2:20

"The love of the Spirit." Romans 15:30; II Corinthians 6:8; Ephesians 4:30

"Yea, he loveth his people."
Deuteronomy 33:3; Psalm 91:14

Are you not cheered by the blessed present tense, "loveth," suggesting that all that God was, He still is. How privileged we are to be loved of the Lord! Those He declared He loved were oppressed, rebellious, stiff-necked, hard-hearted, and unworthy creatures – and we are no better! Yet He loves us, pities us, separates us from others around and promises to bless us. What a glorious mystery God's infinite and eternal love is! It is a love of unexampled kind – a love that promises never to forget us.

"O Israel, thou shalt not be forgotten of me." Isaiah 44:21

The only thing our loving God says He will forget is our sins.

"I will love them freely." Hosea 14:4

Here is another aspect of God's promised love we often lose sight of. He loves us *freely,* because of His free grace. There is no reason for His love, save His love itself (Deuteronomy 7:7). God loves His own as naturally as parents love their children – freely, without any cause whatever in them. Although we deserved His hatred and wrath, He loved – and loves – us. He saw nothing in us to move Him to love us; and now we are His, nothing can separate us from that love (Romans 8:38). Hug this truth to your heart – "The Father Himself loveth *you*" even you!

"The love that God hath to us."
I John 4:16

The emphasis here is on the article *the.* What is the nature of His love, and who can describe it? Twice over John tells us that "God *is* love" (I John 4:8, 16). Love is not only one of His glorious attributes, but His own inherent being. He *is* love – the Source and Supply of it. Finite mortals cannot fully comprehend His infinite love. Yet while we cannot understand it, we can bask in it for divine love is our present heaven. Our friends, feelings, and frames may change, but His love is like Himself, unchangeable. Such marvelous love "that wilt not let us go." is the spring of our happiness, and the cause of our safety.

"Beloved of God." Romans 1:7

Paul, who reveled in the revelation and the experience of divine love, here calls his Roman friends by a most endearing term, "Beloved of God" – "there is music in the very fall and cadence of the words, like the bells of the Angelus ringing through an evening sky." God is not the God of the dead but of the living. He loves *me.* He is mine and I am His, now and forever.

"The very thinking of the thought, without praise or prayer,

Gives light to know, and life to do, and marvelous strength to bear."

"Having loved his own . . . he loved

them unto the end."

John 13:1; Revelation 1:5

While these precious words are used of the love Christ manifested for His disciples, they are true of the love of each Person of the Trinity. Divine love is unchangeable and eternal. The R.V. margin expresses, "He loved them to the uttermost," and, as Alexander Smellie puts it, "This is love in its essence, love in its consummate blossom and fruit, love in its ultimate and final perfection." Because such love is from everlasting to everlasting, nobody and nothing can sever us from it.

Having loved us *from* eternity, God will love us *through* eternity. He will never cast away His people which He foreknew (Lamentations 3:31; Romans 11:2). "Having loved . . . he loved." It was love that made us "His own," and it is the same love that keeps us "His own." Is this not one of the secrets of divine love? His is the only heart that knows no variableness nor the shadow of turning. May we constantly take refuge in the constancy of God's love.

Aflame as it is with God's eternal, sacrificial, beneficial love, the Bible has also a great deal to say about our love to Him, and to His Word and work.

"We love him, because he first loved us." I John 4:19

"Love him and keep his commands." Deuteronomy 7:9; I John 5:2; John 14:15; Psalm 119:97, etc.

"Let them that love him be as the sun when he goeth forth in his might." Judges 5:31

"I love the Lord." Psalms 116:1; 145:20

"The things which God hath prepared for them that love him."

I Corinthians 2:9; 8:3

"Grace be with them that love our Lord Jesus Christ in sincerity." Ephesians 6:24

"Unto all them that love his appearing." II Timothy 4:8; James 1:12; 2:5

"Oh, love the Lord, all ye his saints." Psalm 31:23

Is not the Lord worthy of our highest love? Is He not the Center and Circumference of everything lovely? We think of Himself, of His Word, of Calvary, of His goodness, and we ask, What else can we do but love Him? He it is who gave us life, who provided us with newness of life, who bought us, who has promised us eternal bliss. To love Him is happiness, holiness, and heaven.

"Walk in love." Ephesians 5:2; I John.

4:21; 5:1, 2; II John 5, etc.

Christianity is love – the love of God shed abroad in the heart of the Christian, transforming his nature into love. What is received is reflected. Being loved of God, and loving Him in return, we walk by the rule of love toward others. Love becomes the ruling motive in the life, eliminating jealousy, ill-will, malice, selfishness, and bitterness. The Holy Spirit is the Spirit of love, and because He was the One responsible for our regeneration, love is the brightest and surest evidence of His work within the heart.

"The Lord preserveth all them that love him." Psalm 145:20

If we truly love Him then we can claim His promise to preserve us from sin, the flesh and the devil. Through His free and sovereign grace, He offers to preserve us from all our foes, and preserve us in troubles from its natural effects. But as He preserves us by use of means, let us walk before Him in love, wait upon Him, love His Word.

"Whom having not seen ye love."

I Peter 1:8

Our eyes have never seen His glorious form as those who were privileged to see Him, in the days of His flesh. Nevertheless, He is real, although unseen (John 20:29). His Word reveals His glory and grace, and the Holy Spirit enables us to visualize all that He is in Himself, because He delights in taking of the things of Christ and shew them unto us. To love Him with all our heart, mind, and soul means to manifest our love to Him by holy actions and a fruitful life. James Smith says –

"We love His adorable person; His countenance is majesty; His heart is love; His hand is omnipotence; His eye is bountifulness; His bowels are compassion; and His presence and smile are heaven.

"We love His precious salvation, its freeness, completeness, and glory.

"We love His delightful promises, which anticipate our wants, meet our wishes, and fill our souls with peace.

"We love His throne, where He meets us, attends to our requests, and blesses us indeed.

"We love His holy precepts, which exhibit His authority, display His love, and call us to holiness.

"We love His heaven-born family, who wear His likeness, are the excellent of the earth, and resemble the children of a King."

THE FACT OF MYSTERY

Because of our finite minds we cannot fully understand all God permits. In the process of time, many of His providential dealings become clear, but there are others heaven alone will explain. "Afterward" and "hereafter," as we shall see, are the key words the Bible gives us as the solution of the strange mystery of many divine providences.

Another reason why we cannot fathom many of God's seemingly mysterious ways is because we cannot see them in their completeness. Before the sculptor is a block of marble, and as he takes his mallet and chisel and works on it, the chips fly, but we still see nothing but marble. But the sculptor can see the angel in the marble and when ultimately the statue is finished, we are amazed.

"I have yet many things to say unto you, but ye cannot bear them now."
John 16:12

Lack of spiritual apprehension prevented the disciples receiving fuller truth. He had to leave a good deal unuttered, unrevealed because the soil was not yet ready to receive the seed. It is thus with ourselves as we come to certain aspects of Scripture which we find hard to understand.

"Shall I hide from Abraham that thing which I do?" Genesis 18:17
"The secret of the Lord is with them that fear him." Psalm 25:14; Amos 3:7
"The darkness and the light are both alike to thee." Psalm 139:12; I John 1:5
"I will bring the blind by a way that they knew not of." Isaiah 42:16; 50:10
"Why hast thou forsaken me?"
Matthew 27:46
"What I do thou knowest not now, but thou shalt know hereafter."
John 13:7

As those who are the Lord's, and who believe in His love and perfect wisdom, we must acknowledge His right to conceal His working until He fully accomplishes His designs. Presently, we must take comfort from the Master's promise that sooner or later we'll read the meaning of our tears. He will account for all the trying dispensations of His providence. Silently, we must submit to what He allows for He knows what is best, and is never guilty of taking a wrong turning. "Thou shalt know hereafter." Before long, perplexity will be resolved into the clearness of noonday. May grace be ours to trust Him where we cannot

trace Him!

"Thou art my lamp, O Lord . . . lighten my darkness." II Samuel 22:29

When darkness seems to veil His lovely face, we must trust Him as our Lamp. Sometimes darkness is ours because of the anguish and desolation of an unexpected bereavement. Why are our tears so salt? Why such a bitter parting? Why such a cruel loss? To some of the most sorrowful enigmas of experience God seems to give no explicit answer. He who partook of human sorrow cried, "My God, My God, *why* hast thou forsaken me?"

As the natural sun sometimes sinks in clouds, so occasionally the Christian who has a bright rising encounters the cloud. At such an evening time it is not always light. But the promise is that in God's light, he shall see light. The *why* and the *wherefore* of the dark cloud may be kept from him to test faith, discipline the tried one in trustful submission, and to acquiesce in the prayer, "Thy will be done."

"Now we see through a glass darkly; then face to face." I Corinthians 13:9-13

Over against a world of mystery Paul places the paradise of revelation. We must guard ourselves against being taken up exclusively with the gloomy "now." In the great mirror of eternity all events and experiences of our checkered life will be reflected, and we shall discover that—

"Behind a frowning providence
He hid a smiling face."

As we await the dawn we must not pry too curiously into His severe dispensations which will appear as "only the severer aspects of His love." Patiently, we must await the grand day of revelation.

"Now no chastening for the present, seemeth to be joyous, but grievous; nevertheless afterward."
Hebrews 10:5-15

This great passage assures us that the rod of chastening we cannot understand is in the hand of our Heavenly Father who loves us. J. R. Miller has the beautiful thought in one of his chapters on *Afterward*.

"Today's tears tomorrow are turned to lenses through which eyes, dim no longer, see far into the clear heavens, and behold the kindliness and radiance of God's face."

Presently so many things are dark and obscure, but the morning shall surely come and with its light all we suffered will be seen in true perspective.

"All things work together for good."
                                    Romans 8:28

As, in the presence of mystery, we cling to this comforting promise, we must not forget its conditions. We can only know that *all* things, even the most untoward experiences of life, are working together for our good, if we "love God" and are "called according to his purpose." When mistrust says, "All these things are against me," let faith rebuke the hasty conclusion, and say, "Shall not the judge of all the earth do right?" While we cannot *see* all things working together for our good, we can *believe* that they are. Amid life's manifold interpositions and perplexities may we be found passive in the hands of God, praying, "Undertake Thou for me." Grief-gripped in Gethsemane, Jesus could pray, "Nevertheless not my will, but thine, be done" (Luke 22:42).

THE JOY OF OBEDIENCE

A young Christian with a desire for aids to Bible study approached Dr. Theodore Monod, the renowned French saint and theologian, and sought his advice as to the best commentary. Replied the gifted scholar, "The best commentary on the Bible is *obedience. Do* and thou shalt *know.*" What a wise answer! Did not our Lord Himself say, "Happy are ye if ye *know* these things and *do* them"? If we obey the light we receive from the Word today, God will grant us further light tomorrow. If, however, we disobey today's light, then disobedience will close the door of revelation.

Further, the Bible makes it clear that the believer walks, spiritually, on two legs –*trust* and *obedience*–the one leg being essential to the other. It is thus we sing–

Trust and obey, For there's no other way,
To be happy in Jesus, But to trust and obey.

Summarizing what the Bible has to say on this all-important theme, the following aspects are inescapable–

1. *Exhortations to Obedience*

The obedience God demands is not only a virtue, it is a necessity–a possession of the highest importance if a Christian desires God's best. Generally, the term means "to hearken," or "to hearken submissively." As we hear God's voice through His Word, we submit ourselves unreservedly to His revealed will. The one thing above everything else God asks for is obedience.

"Hath the Lord as great delight in burnt offerings and sacrifices as in obeying the voice of the Lord? Behold to obey is better than sacrifice, and to hearken than the fat of rams." I Samuel 15:22

"Ye shall walk after the Lord your God . . . and obey his voice."
                            Deuteronomy 13:4

"Obey the voice of the Lord your God."
                    Jeremiah 26:13; 38:20, etc.

As Christians we were elected according to divine foreknowledge to obedience.

"Elect . . . unto obedience . . . As obedient children." I Peter 1:2, 14

We are also under the obligation of hearkening unto and obeying God's voice–"We ought to obey God rather than men" (Acts 4:19, 20; 5:29). Such commanded obedience must be sincere and from the heart–"Ye have obeyed from the heart" (Romans 6:17; Deuteronomy 11:13). Disobedience is a characteristic of those out of Christ, all of whom must obey the truth or perish in their sin.

"The children of disobedience." Ephesians 2:2; Titus 1:16; 3:3; Isaiah 42:24, 25, etc.

"What shall the end be of them that obey not the gospel of God?" I Peter 4:17; II Thessalonians 1:7-9, etc.

2. *Examples of Obedience*

Scripture abounds with examples of the obedience of the saints of Rome which had been shown "abroad unto all men" (Romans 16:19). The vast, angelic host above obey every divine behest. "Ye his angels . . . that do his commandments" (Psalm 103:20, 21). Perhaps the most conspicuous example of obedience in the Old Testament is Abraham, whose strong faith resulted in obedience to God's Word regarding the unknown future.

"By faith Abraham . . . obeyed: and he went out, not knowing whither he went."
                Hebrews 11:8; Genesis 12:4

Through obedience, Abraham believed God's promise and was made a blessing to the world because of his obedience to God's voice.

"Thy seed shall . . . be blessed; because thou hast obeyed my voice."
                    Genesis 22:18; 26:3-5

Then Israel was deemed to be God's peculiar people because of obedience–which, alas, was spasmodic in their history.

"Now therefore, if ye will obey my voice indeed . . . Ye shall be unto me a kingdom of priests, and an holy nation."
                            Exodus 19:5-6

Israel likewise received a promise of blessing pronounced upon obedience, and a promise of curse upon disobedience (see Deuteronomy

11:26-28; 27:10; 28:62; 30:2-9, 20). How tragic it is that the wilderness life of Israel was a judgment for disobedience, rebellion, and unbelief! Her long series of judgments which ended in the captivities were the dire and direct outcome of disobedience to God's revealed will (see Joshua 5:6; Judges 2:2; 6:10, etc.).

While in Old Testament times obedience was vital and formed a relationship not to be broken, the New Testament is just as insistent upon obedience. Here the Lord Jesus is the great Example of the Christian's obedience. He not only lived a life of perfect obedience to His Father, He was obedience *personified*.

"Suffer it to be so now: for thus it becometh me to fulfil all righteousness."
Matthew 3:15
"I have kept my Father's commandments." John 15:10
"Lo, I come to do thy will, O God."
Hebrews 10:9
"Though he were a Son, yet learned he obedience." Hebrews 5:8, 9

What must not be forgotten is the fact that perfect as Christ's obedience to the Father was, it is in no way a substitute for our personal obedience. It was His obedience that made ours possible (Romans 8:3, 4). Because He raised the Word of God to the highest moral and spiritual importance, He made our obedience to it a test of love and a condition for answered prayer, abiding, and fellowship (John 14:21-24; 15:7, 10). Thus, with Christ's example of obedience before us, we seek to make John Milton's decision our own.

3. Essentials of Obedience

For the guidance of the Christian, the objects demanding obedience are clearly defined, and all of them are involved in loving God Himself.

We must obey God's voice.

"Obey my voice." Exodus 19:5; Deuteronomy 13:4; 27:10; Jeremiah 7:23; Acts 5:29, 32

We must obey God's Word.

"Obey the commandments of the Lord your God." Deuteronomy 11:27, 28; Ecclesiastes 12:15
"The keeping of the commandments of God." I Corinthians 7:19; I John 5:3

There are two facts to observe in connection with this phase of our obedience. The first is that the commandments demanding obedience are not grievous – "His commandments are not grievous" (I John 5:3; Matthew 11:30). The second fact is that our position in our Lord's coming kingdom depends upon our obedience, even to the least of His commandments.

"Whosoever shall *do* and *teach* them, the same shall be called great in the kingdom of heaven."
Matthew 11:19; 7:24-27

We must obey God's obedient Son.

"Bringing into captivity every thought to the obedience of Christ."
II Corinthians 10:5
"The church is subject to Christ."
Ephesians 5:24; John 14:15, 21

We must obey God's Gospel.

"Obedience to the faith . . . Obeyed from the heart that form of doctrine."
Romans 1:5; 6:17
"They have not all obeyed the gospel."
Romans 10:16, 17

We must obey God's ordained rulers.

"Let every soul be subject unto the higher powers."
Romans 13:1; I Peter 2:13

Tennyson has reminded us that "Obedience is the courtesy due to kings." The promise is that the day is coming when obedience to the King of Kings will be universal in character.

"All dominions shall serve and obey him." Daniel 7:27

4. Expressions of Obedience

The Christian's willing, joyful, and unquestioning obedience to God's will and Word expresses itself in various directions.

It is expressive of sonship and of the possession of eternal life.

"Hereby we do know that we know him, if we keep his commandments."
I John 2:2-5; John 17:3
"By the obedience of one shall many be made righteous." Romans 5:19

It is expressive of our love for, and friendship with, Christ

"He that hath my commandments and keepeth them, he it is that loved me."
John 14:21
"Ye are my friends if ye do whatsoever I command you." John 15:14

It is expressive of our knowledge of God, and of answered prayer.

"Hereby we do know that we know him, if we keep his commandments."
I John 2:3
"Whatsoever we ask, we receive of him because we keep his commandments."
I John 3:22

*It is expressive of a peace
nothing can destroy.*

"O that thou hast hearkened to my commandments; then had thy peace been as a river." Isaiah 48:17, 18

It is expressive of a mutual indwelling.

"He that keepeth his commandments dwelleth in him, and he in him."

I John 3:24

*It is expressive of our love to God,
and to one another.*

"We love the children of God, when we love God, and keep his commandments." I John 5:2, 3

*It is expressive of Lordship.
Christ is the Lord we obey.*

"To whom ye yield yourselves servants to obey." Romans 6:16

It is expressive of a saving and sanctifying faith (Romans 1:5; 16:26). The faith indicated by Paul possesses a strong element of submission. Obedience and disobedience is a point of contrast from the saved and the unsaved as the comparison between I Peter 1:14 RV and Ephesians 2:2 show. Disobedience whether in the Christian or in the unbeliever is *sin,* and one God must punish (Jeremiah 3:25; 40:3; 44:23; I Samuel 15:23).

5. Encouragements to Obedience

Much promised blessing is ours if our obedience is from the heart (Deuteronomy 11:13; Romans 6:7); accompanied with willingness (Psalm 18:44; Isaiah 1:19); unreserved (Joshua 22:2, 3); constant and undeviating (Philippians 2:12; Deuteronomy 28:14); resolved upon and prepared for (Exodus 24:7; Joshua 24:24; I Samuel 7:3; Ezra 7:10); prayed for (Psalms 119:35; 143:10). Of course, we do not seek to obey simply to gain the promised rewards of obedience. We obey because we are commanded to, and because we delight in obedience. Here are some of the promises linked on to obedience.

"If thou shalt indeed obey his voice . . . I will be an enemy unto thy enemies." Exodus 23:22

"If ye will obey his voice . . . then shall both ye and also your king that reigneth over you continue following the Lord your God." I Samuel 12:14

"If ye be willing and obedient, ye shall eat the good of the land." Isaiah 1:19, 20

"Obey my voice, and I will be your God." Jeremiah 7:23

"A blessing if ye obey the commandments." Deuteronomy 11:27; 28:1-13

"Blessed are they that hear the word of God, and keep it." Luke 11:28.

His children, guilty of disobedience, miss promised joy (Psalm 112:1; 119:24, etc.). "He that endeavoreth to withdraw himself from obedience, withdraweth himself from grace."

The following inscription to be found in Lubeck Cathedral, contains an appeal demanding a right response.

WHY CALL YE ME LORD?

(Luke 6:46)

Ye call me MASTER . . . . and OBEY me not.
Ye call me LIGHT . . . . . . and SEE me not.
Ye call me WAY . . . . . . and WALK me not.
Ye call me LIFE . . . . . . and DESIRE me not.
Ye call me WISE . . . . . . and FOLLOW me not.
Ye call me RICH . . . . . . and ASK me not.
Ye call me FAIR . . . . . and LOVE me not.
Ye call me ETERNAL . . . and SEEK me not.
Ye call me GRACIOUS . . and TRUST me not.
Ye call me NOBLE . . . . . and SERVE me not.
Ye call me MIGHTY . . . and HONOR me not.
Ye call me JUST . . . . . . and FEAR me not.
If I CONDEMN you . . BLAME me not.

THE NEED OF PATIENCE

How necessary it is for each of us to pray the prayer set for the fifth Sunday after Epiphany in the Church of England Prayer Book –

"O Lord my God, patience is very necessary for me, for I perceive that many things in this life do not fall out as we would. Give me strength to resist, patience to endure, and constancy to persevere."

Out of the 40 odd passages where the word "patience" is to be found, only two references belong to the Old Testament –

"I waited patiently for the Lord."

Psalm 40:1

"The patient in spirit is better than the proud in spirit." Ecclesiastes 7:8 Akin to "patience" is "longsuffering," which are the same words in some of the references in the original, for example, Matthew 18:26, 29, where patience means to forbear, or to bear or suffer long, which is the equivalent of longsuffering in, say, Romans 2:4. We have to confess that we are not *long* on the suffering aspect of life. We become so impatient, irritated with so many of the small matters of every day life. The promises and precepts related to patience can be summarized thus –

1. Patience is necessary to the inheritance of the promises of God.

"Be . . . followers of them who through faith and patience inherit the promises." Hebrews 6:12

"Ye have need of patience . . . ye might receive the promise."

Hebrews 10:36

Abraham had to wait a long time before God's promise to him was fulfilled, But this great saint was not short on patience.

"After he had patiently endured, he obtained the promise." Hebrews 6:15

Says Thomas a Kempis, "Do not repine, neither do thou lessen thy crown by impatience." Abraham never lessened his promised crown by an impatient spirit. Although long tried, he was richly rewarded. God tried His servant by delaying the performance of His promise, and he was likewise tried in many ways by those around him – men tried him by jealousy, distrust and opposition; Hagar tried him by contemning Sarah; Sarah tried him by her peevishness; but Abraham patiently endured.

This great heart, and man of great faith did not question God's veracity, nor limit His power, nor doubt His faithfulness, nor grieve His love. Ultimately, Abraham received the promise because he bowed to divine sovereignty, submitted to infinite wisdom, was silent under delays, waiting God's time to fulfill His promise.

2. Patience is represented by many in Scripture.

There is the patience of God.

"The God of patience." Romans 15:5

"Longsuffering to usward."

II Peter 3:9

"The Lord is longsuffering."

Numbers 14:18; Exodus 34:6

Is it not a marvel that man's persistent sin and rejection does not exhaust His patience? Then we think of His multitudinous promises on man's behalf, and also for a better world, that seem to be so long in materializing.

There is the patience of Christ.

"He was oppressed, and he was afflicted, yet he opened not his mouth."

Isaiah 53:7

"He answered him never a word."

Matthew 27:13, 14

The fruit of the Spirit – longsuffering (Galatians 5:22) – was prominent in our Lord's earthly life. How patient He was with friends and foes alike! For a dramatic and appealing presentation of patience, there is nothing to compare with the silent majesty of Jesus amid all the scorn, spitting, shame, and suffering of His final hours and death. Patience was not only one of His conspicuous virtues – He *was patience.*

"For the joy that was set before him, endured the cross . . . Endured such contradiction of sinners against himself, lest ye be wearied and faint in your minds."

Hebrews 12:1-3

Mention has been made of *Abraham* as a conspicuous example of patience. As a patient waiter he was not disappointed. His believing expectation was realized. Does not his sweet content condemn a hasty spirit, reprove all murmuring, commend endurance, and encourage quiet submission to God's will and way? As we have already indicated, Abraham was tried, but strong in faith he waited, and receiving the promise, was satisfied. May grace be ours to imitate his example and share the joy of promised blessing!

Job is another distinguished as a man of patience. "Ye have heard of the patience of Job" (James 5:11; Job 1:21). George Herbert says that "God takes a text, and preaches patience." How true this is as we think of the text James gives us. An old German proverb has it, "Job was not so miserable in his sufferings as happy in his patience." How beautifully God rewarded his patience and trust!

Others who exemplified this estimable quality are the prophets (James 5:10), Simeon (Luke 2:25), Paul (II Timothy 3:10), and John (Revelation 1:9). These and multitudes more which time fails us to tell of, matched their patience against apparent divine delay, and also against surrounding trials and adversities.

3. Patience is related, with promises, to every phase of Christian life and experience. Here are some of its associations –

Its relation to spiritual maturity

"Let patience have her perfect work, that ye may be perfect and entire, wanting nothing." James 1:4

Impatience retards the spiritual growth of the Christian, dishonors his profession, grieves the Holy Spirit whose fruit is patience. Do we not have to guard ourselves continually against the impatient spirit? Every Christian is supposed to possess patience, to exercise it, and develop thereby growth in grace. Patience is not only of great benefit to ourselves; it proves to others the reality of the grace we profess to have.

Patience supposes the trials and tribulations Jesus warned us of, all of which "worketh patience." If the word "patience" signifies to remain stedfast under a burden, then such a virtue is opposed to all fretfulness, murmuring, despondency, and haste. Godly patience produces willing submission, silence before God, a serene satisfaction with all His dealings, trust in His love, and the appropriation of His promises of sustenance and strength.

Its relation to experience

"Tribulation worketh patience; and patience, experience." Romans 5:4

"Buffeted for your faults . . . take it patiently." I Peter 2:18-23

It is not so easy to endure grief and suffer wrongfully, yet if patient in such adversity, divine vindication will be ours.

Its relation to promised rewards

"Bring forth fruit with patience."

Luke 8:15

"Patient continuance in well doing seeks for glory and honor and immortality and life." Romans 2:10

"Let us not be weary in well doing; for in due season we shall reap, if we faint not." Galatians 6:9

Frank W. Boreham, urging us to possess our soul in patience, tells us to –

Give God Time – and even when the knife flashes in the air, the ram will be seen caught in the thicket.

Give God Time – and even when Pharoah's host is on Israel's heels, a path through the water will be suddenly opened.

Give God Time – and when the bed or the brook is dry, Elijah shall hear the guiding voice.

Its relation to the fruit of the Spirit

To Godliness – "To patience godliness."

II Peter 1:6; I Timothy 6:11

To self-control – "To temperance (self-control) patience." II Peter 1:6

To faith – "your patience and faith." II Thessalonians 1:4; Hebrews 6:12; Revelation 13:10

To longsuffering – "All patience and longsuffering." Colossians 1:11

To compassion – "Patience toward all men." I Thessalonians 5:14

To joy – "Patience . . . with joyfulness." Colossians 1:11

To service – "Let us not be weary in well-doing." Galatians 6:9

It is not enough to be active – we should be *doing* good. Too much of our *doing* misses the mark. What is done well is done in a Christ-like spirit, the spirit of love,

humility, and prayer. If we would act for the good of others, communicating encouragement, comfort, and relief, we must act in the fear of God and for His glory. If we are prone to be weary and discouraged as we go about doing good, it may be, because of disappointments and lack of appreciation, we must cling to the promise that in *due season* we shall reap if we faint not. God will not forget our labor of love.

Its relation to promised future rewards

"Let us run with patience the race that is set before us." Hebrews 12:1

At the end of the race, there is the reward for the runner who has run well. When He comes, the Lord will crown the hopeful, brave, stedfast, militant grace of patience with His benediction. Does not patience assure us that we shall carry home our harvest sheaves?

"Wait patiently for him."

Psalms 37:7; 40:1

"Quietly wait for the salvation of the Lord." Lamentations 3:26

"With patience we wait for it." Romans 8:23-25; 15:4; Galatians 5:5

"Waiting for the coming of the Lord Jesus." I Corinthians 1:7, 8; II Thessalonians 3:5

"Be ye also patient . . . the coming of the Lord draweth nigh." James 5:8

In our patient meditation, we have seen that God is a God of patience, Christ the great Example of patience, the Holy Spirit the Agent producing patience, the Christian the witness manifesting patience, and faith the parent of patience. Now James reminds us that the Second Advent will be the consummation of our patience, and with such a blessed hope in view we can in patience possess our souls. Knowing that as we await the blissful future, God is overruling in all things for our good and His glory; that as we await Christ's return with resignation and hope, His grace will sustain us to bear, without complaining, all He may appoint for us. As we linger amid the shadows, we experience what it is to have patience as a principal motive-force in self-government, and to keep "the word of His patience" (Revelation 3:10).

THE BLESSING OF PERSECUTION

We are apt to think of persecution for Christ's sake as a *bane* rather than a *blessing.* The Bible has much to say about the persecution coming from the ungodly, and under which Christ was so patient (Isaiah 50:6; 53:7). For the sake of God and godliness, the Christian must expect to suffer (Jeremiah 15:15; II Timothy 3:12). Facing the hostility of those who will not have Christ to reign over them we must not despair but "rejoice" (Matthew 5:12; I Peter 4:13). Glorifying God in the fires, we have the assurance that even persecution cannot separate us from Him (I Peter 4:16; Romans 8:35). That He can overrule and make even the wrath of man to praise Him is evident from the fact that persecution often makes for the furtherance of the Gospel (Acts 11:19). The blood of martyrs becomes the seed of the Church.

All we are doing in this brief meditation is to look at some of the promises which God has attached to persecution—

"I will be an enemy unto thine enemies." Exodus 23:22; Jeremiah 1:8

This is one of those conditional promises of Scripture. God promises to be a Foe to our foes *if* we obey His voice and witness fearlessly for Him. If we are living in full harmony with the will of our divine Protector, then we need have no fear about our persecutors, for our protection is His care.

"No weapon formed against thee shall prosper." Isaiah 54:17

What a blessed promise this is to cling to when the sharp weapons of slander, falsehood, insinuation, ridicule, and hatred are formed against us! God knows how to blunt the instruments of the wicked, and stop the mouth of liars. Our heavenly Defense is ever near to deliver. Think of these promises—

He never forsakes His saints when persecuted—"Persecuted but not forsaken" (II Corinthians 4:9).

He is able to deliver out of persecution (Daniel 3:25, 28; I Corinthians 1:10; II Timothy 3:11).

He assures us of the reward of blessedness if persecuted (Matthew 5:10; Luke 6:22). "Reproaches and afflictions . . . In heaven a better and an enduring substance" (Hebrews 13:33, 34).

If, as Nathanael Howe put it, "The way of the world is to praise dead saints and persecute living ones," we have the consolation of knowing that as living saints we are not alone. In the furnace of affliction is Another whose grace alone can make saints fearless, and His form is "like the Son of God" (Daniel 3:25).

THE NATIVE AIR OF PRAYER

Having previously considered the doctrinal side of "the Christian's vital breath," all that remains for us to look at are some of the promises connected with the holy exercise of prayer. We lose so much for want of prayer, for lack of faith in prayer and a firm persuasion of the ability and willingness of God to grant our requests for the sake of Him in whose Name they are presented. It is of no use coming to God with great words and little confidence.

All of God's promises should be turned into prayer, and we should always pray up to the amount of any promise to be claimed. We must also pray up to the influence of Him in whose Name we plead, believing that He is able to do far more than we ask of Him.

"The prayer of the upright is his delight." Proverbs 15:8

The terms of this promise, declaring a present fact, must not be lost sight of. It is the prayer of the *upright* God has delight in. Our first concern then is to be upright, having that integrity and righteousness which grace makes possible. If crooked ways are ours, then we shall find heaven deaf to our prayers. Errands to His throne are always beneficial when the messengers are pure in heart.

"Call upon me and I will answer thee." Jeremiah 33:3

Here is a great promise that encourages us to pray. Prayer is not a mere pious exercise. It moves the Hand that created and controls the world. How gracious of God it is to distinctly promise to answer prayer, and to answer it so magnificently! Our petitions can never be too large for Him to perform.

"If ye shall ask anything in my name, I will do it." John 14:14

This is another promise, the fulfilment of which is dependent upon the observance of a condition. Christ will answer prayer if presented in His *Name*—which means on the basis of His merit. If presented thus, then our prayer will be in accordance with His will and purpose. Remembrance of this wide, wise promise causes us to examine the nature of our prayers. Do we ask for that which Christ approves? Dare we put His seal to our prayers?

"The effectual fervent prayer of a righteous man availeth much." James 5:16

It is impossible to over-estimate the effect of prayer when it is *effectual, fervent,* and presented by a *righteous* petitioner. The legacy of such a prayer is of priceless worth, influencing the present and a future generation. Centuries after his ascension, Elijah is still remembered for his dynamic prayers. Although a man of like passions as ourselves, his supplications availed much. Elijah was definite in his prayers. He likewise prayed for others rather than for himself. If only we can practice his secret, then we too shall conquer heaven.

"Prayer and supplications, with fastings." Daniel 9:1

Fasting does not mean merely abstaining from food – it represents "an attitude of *detachment* from the things of time and sense, whether it be food or pleasure or lawful ambition. Prayer represents the complimentary attitude of *attachment* to the things of God." Then Dr. Griffith Thomas goes on to say, "We shall readily determine under the guidance of the Holy Spirit what particular forms our fasting shall take, thus helping our spiritual development."

"Praying in the Holy Ghost." Jude 20

The reader will find a full treatment of this aspect of prayer in the writer's volume *All the Prayers of the Bible*. It is certain that we cannot pray in the Spirit unless He is in us. There may be times when physical weakness makes it hard to think correctly or to frame prayer in suitable language. In such a time we can fall back on Another who is at hand to help in our infirmity and to pray in us and through us.

"She went to inquire of the Lord." Genesis 25:22

What a delightful aspect of prayer this is! Rebekah sought the mind of the Lord regarding her condition, and her excellent example is worthy of imitation. If we are in trouble, we can like Job pray, "Show me wherefore thou contendest with me," and the reason will be revealed. If we seek the Lord with an inquiring spirit, we shall be assured that what He allows is a proof of His love. "I will be inquired of."

"Pray without ceasing." I Thessalonians 5:17

Because the ear of God is always open, we can come to Him at any time. Our needs are so constant; therefore our prayers should constantly ascend to God, who is ever ready to listen to us. What Paul actually implies in his exhortation is an effort on the part of the Christian to acquire the *habit* of prayer – which should be as natural and constant as breathing. Occasional, spasmodic praying indicates a spiritually unhealthy state.

"All earthly things with earth shall fade away;
Prayer grasps eternity; pray, always pray."

"I will call upon thee, for thou wilt answer me." Psalm 86:7

Do we not have the same warrant David had? If his purpose and assurance are ours, God will answer prayer. We must, of course, be definite in our petitions and pray in accordance with the divine will as revealed in the divine promises and precepts. Prayer too must be in submission to God's will, and offered with importunity and perseverance. If there is anything alien to His will in the life, then God cannot answer prayer. Life and motives must be pure if God is to respond to our cry.

"Ask what I shall give thee."
I Kings 3:5; Luke 11:9-13

Asking is one of the chief elements of prayer. Jesus told the woman at the well that had she known of the divine Gift she would "have asked." The problem is not with our Heavenly Father's unwillingness to give but with our unreadiness to ask. How condescending He is in beseeching us to ask for what we need. "Ask of Me comfort and strength, faith and courage, purity and power." Asking thus, we receive, even as a child receives good things from the earthly parent.

Waiting is another phase of prayer.

"On thee do I wait all the day."
Psalms 25:5, 21; 52:9

"It is good . . . to quietly wait."
Lamentations 3:26; Proverbs 27:18

"They that wait upon the Lord."
Isaiah 40:31; Proverbs 20:22

We not only wait *upon* Him in worship and praise, we also wait *for* Him to act on our behalf, and ultimately appear for our deliverance from this world. There is, of course, a distinction between waiting *on* the Lord and waiting *for* Him. Promises are attached to both attitudes.

"Let us come boldly to the throne of grace." Hebrews 4:26

Because of the privilege of prayer we come to God in all humility, yet with all boldness. It is to a *throne* we come which speaks of divine sovereignty. But it is a throne of *grace* which is the very kind we need as poor, unworthy, needy supplicants. How deep in debt we are to God's unmerited grace! Let us be careful to remember that no long and painful journey is necessary to reach the throne and the God of grace who sits upon it – it is ever nigh at hand.

THE PARADISE OF REMEMBRANCE

The late Gypsy Smith, the famous evangelist, once wrote in my autograph album, "Remembrance is a paradise from which we need not be driven." Does not the Bible show us how to live continually in such a paradise? You may wonder why we are finding a place in our study on *promises* for *remembrances*. If the context of the majority of references to "remember" or "remembrance" are studied, it will be found that they are bound up with promised blessings. All divine remembrances are promises. The word that is usually employed for "remember" means *imprint*, and implies facts, experiences, and truths deeply inscribed upon the mind. Verses fall into two general categories, namely, God's remembrance of us – Our remembrance of God's goodness and grace.

1. Divine Remembrances

When "remember" is used by God, it is only in a metaphorical sense, because God never forgets. He condescendingly uses language to assure our finite minds that He ever has His own before Him. Without comment, we group divine remembrances together, allowing them to speak for themselves.

"I will remember my covenant which is between me and you." Genesis 9:15, 16; Psalm 105:8; Luke 1:72

"God remembered Abraham." Genesis 19:29; Exodus 32:15; Psalm 105:42

"God remembered Rachel."
Genesis 30:22; I Samuel 1:19

"He forgetteth not the cry of the humble."
Psalms 9:12; 112:6

"He remembereth that we are dust."
Psalm 103:14

"Put me in remembrance: let us plead together." Isaiah 43:26

"Then saith the Lord, I will remember thee."
Jeremiah 2:2; 44:21; Psalm 137:6

"He will remember their iniquity."
Hosea 9:9

"Remember how he spake unto you."
Luke 24:6

Most graciously the Lord provided us with One whose function it is to aid our faulty memories and keep alive in them His own precious truths –

"The Holy Spirit . . . shall bring all things to your remembrance, whatsoever I have said unto you."
John 14:26; John 2:22

The most solemn and moving request for remembrance was made by Jesus, when instituting the Supper commemorating His death. He asked, "This do in remembrance of me" (Luke 22:19; I Corinthians 11:24, 25).

2. Human Remembrances

Many are the Biblical exhortations urging us to remember all that God has accomplished for us and of the promised blessing of such remembrance. A French proverb has it, "Who loves well is slow to forget." The deeper and more intense our love for the Lord, the more we are conscious of all mercies. Memory is kept alert by the Holy Spirit, who never fails to stir up remembrance of divine promises and requests. It is interesting to note that two Psalms (38 and 70) bear the title, "A Psalm of David, to bring to remembrance." The Psalms themselves reveal the import of such a unique "dedication." Night and day there were those aspects of divine goodness which David did not want to forget.

"Remember this day, in which ye came out of Egypt." Exodus 13:3; Numbers 11:5; Deuteronomy 5:13

"Remember all the commandments of the Lord." Numbers 15:39

"O Lord God, remember me, I pray thee." Judges 16:28

"Remember his marvelous works that he hath done." I Chronicles 16:12; Job 36:24

"Remember the Lord, which is great and terrible." Nehemiah 4:14; 13:14, 29, 31

"Give thanks at the remembrance of his holiness." Psalms 30:4; 97:12

"I remember thee upon my bed."
Psalms 63:6; 77:3, 6

"Lord . . . remember how short my time is." Psalm 89:46, 47; Job 7:7

"Lord, remember David, all his afflictions." Psalm 132:1

"When my soul fainted within me I remembered the Lord." Jonah 2:7

"His disciples remembered."
John 2:17; Malachi 3:15

"Remember thy Creator in the days of thy youth." Ecclesiastes 12:1

As our Beloved comes into His garden to eat of His pleasant fruits, may we be ready to offer Him our garland of praise, not only for His remembrance of us, but also for those things about us, He will not remember.

"Remember, O Lord, thy tender mercies and lovingkindness . . . Remember not the sins of my youth, nor my transgressions." Psalm 25:6, 7

"O remember not against us former iniquities." Psalm 79:8; Jeremiah 31:34

The lamentable, heartless lack of remembrance is described as being grievous both to God and man.

"Yet did not the chief butler remember Joseph, but forgot him." Genesis 40:23

"The children of Israel remembered not the Lord their God." Judges 8:34

"The king remembered not the kindness . . . done to him." II Chronicles 24:22

"They remembered not his hand."

Psalm 78:42. See verse 35.

It was lack of remembrance that made hell more terrible for the rich man—"Son, remember" (Luke 16:25).

"His remembrance shall perish from the earth." Job 18:17

Tennyson reminds us "that a sorrow's crown of sorrow is remembering happier things." The rich man's crown of anguish was the remembrance of the rejection of those divine pleasures Lazarus chose.

Happily the Bible provides us with instances of sweet human remembrances, found principally in Paul's writings. What a grateful heart the apostle had! He never seemed to forget his friends.

"I thank my God upon every remembrance of you." Philippians 1:3

"Ye have good remembrance of us always." I Thessalonians 3:6; I Corinthians 4:17

"Without ceasing I (have remembrance) of thee in my prayers."

II Timothy 1:3, 5, 6

"Stir up your pure minds by way of remembrance." II Peter 3:1; 1:13

Concluding this particular aspect of our meditation on promises, let us return to the loving exhortations of Nehemiah—

"Remember the Lord" (4:14).

Whatever, or whoever, we forget, may we be found always remembering Him who never forgets us. We must have Him in mind at all times, because He is the Source of our supply and the only proper Object of faith and worship. James Smith, in his "Daily Remembrancer," sets out the ways by which we can *remember the Lord*—

Remember the promises He has made, the deliverances He has wrought, the blessings He has conferred, the invitation He has given, and the relations He now fills.

Remember Him in calamity, to trust Him: in prosperity, to praise Him; in danger to call upon Him; in difficulty, to expect his interference.

Remember to obey His commands, to attend to His exhortations; to keep His company; to seek His blessing; and to aim at His glory in all

you do.

Remember Him, for it is your duty: it is your privilege.

Remember Him, in order to strengthen your faith; as an antidote to your fears; as a source of encouragement to your souls; and as a preventative to sin.

Remember that He is holy, just and good: and He will be glorified in all them that draw nigh unto Him.

THE BEARING OF REPROACH

Is it not comforting to know that God's promises cover the bad treatment we receive, as well as the good? As used in Scripture, "Reproach" means *shame, contempt, being reviled.* Jesus leads the way when it comes to being rejected by men. What contempt was heaped upon Him!

"He shall send from heaven, and save me from the reproach of him that would swallow me up. Selah." Psalm 57:3

The title of this psalm informs us that when David wrote it he was fleeing from Saul and was obliged to hide in a cave. It must have been humiliating for such a noble soul as David to be hunted as a fugitive. But his faith in God's protection was strong. If necessary, He would send from heaven and deliver His servant. No wonder David shouted "Selah," a word meaning "Think of that!" Usually occuring either before or after some glorious truth the writer has uttered, this exclamatory term draws attention to the utterance in question. And to the mind of David, whom Saul derided, it was something to think about that the Lord would deliver him out of the jaws of those who waited to swallow him up. Is your soul among lions? Because of your allegiance to Christ, are you the object of scorn? Well, leave God to deal with those who reproach you (Psalm 144:5, 7).

"Reproach hath broken my heart."

Psalm 69:20

The way in which this psalm is used in the New Testament proves it to be prophetic of Christ's humiliation and rejection. And that His sensitive spirit was ultimately crushed by the shame He endured is evident in His cry of desolation. Full of heaviness, Christ looked for some to take pity, but there was none. Calling upon God to draw nigh and deliver Him from the reproach and dishonor of His adversaries, He yet knew that the waterflood would overflow Him. Thus, at Calvary, the loving, holy, and kind heart of Jesus broke. He was saved *in* His reproach, but not *from* it. Willingly He bore the terrible load of scorn and shame that His very despisers might have a way to heaven. Diligently Christ had kept the divine testimonies, yet reproach and contempt were not removed from Him (Psalm 119:22). He died, even as He had lived, the object of derision.

"The reproaches of them that reproached thee fell on me." Romans 15:3

In quoting "the reproach psalm," Paul links the believer to the self-abnegation Jesus practiced. Had He wished, Christ could have saved Himself a good deal of the derision that came His way; but silently He bore it all. Reviled, He reviled not again. Suffering, He threatened not, but committed Himself to Him that judgeth righteously (I Peter 2:19-25). And as He is, so are we in this world. We cannot have His redemption without His reproach. The offense of His cross has not ceased. True discipleship involves going to Him without the camp, bearing His reproach (Hebrews 13:13). Do you know what it is to endure shame for the Saviour's sake? Because of your allegiance to Him, are you being ostracized by your religious, yet carnal, friends? Well, count it a privilege to be identified with your Lord in His rejection!

"Fear ye not the reproach of men." Isaiah 51:7

By the mouth of the prophet, God promises Israel that all her oppressors will be righteously punished. As a people in whose heart was His law, they are bidden to treat their revilers with contempt. Two striking metaphors are used to describe the slow yet certain destruction awaiting Israel's foes. "The moth shall eat them up, like a garment, and the worm shall eat them like wool." Moths and worms are very destructive to clothes and books in hot countries. Even in our own land we take every precaution to protect our garments against moths. And the Lord knows how to set in motion those hidden forces which silently consume the animosity of those who despise us for Christ's sake. Our difficulty is that of leaving vengeance in God's hands.

"Esteeming the reproach of Christ greater riches than the treasures in Egypt." Hebrews 11:26

In some unrevealed way, Moses, like Abraham, must have rejoiced to see Christ's day. Looking down the vista of the ages, the deliverer of Israel endured reproach, as he saw Him who is invisible. And what a choice Moses made! Refusing all the pomp and privileges of the palace, he surrendered his claim as the adopted son of Pharaoh's daughter and identified himself with the afflicted people of God. Had he maintained his royal estate, the treasures of Egypt would have come his way, but rich in prospect, Moses felt that the reproach of the Lord's people outweighed any riches he might possess. Alas, in modern times, too many professing Christians esteem the treasures of Egypt greater riches than the reproach of Christ. With their eyes on the muckrake, they fail to see the crown of God above their heads.

"If ye be reproached for the name of Christ, happy are ye." I Peter 4:14

As partakers of Christ's sufferings, believers must not think it strange when the fiery trial appears to try them. They must guard themselves against suffering wrongfully. No Christian would have the least desire to suffer as a murderer or as a thief or as an evildoer. Unfortunately, few of us escape the last classification as a "busybody in other men's matters" (I Peter 4:15). If we suffer, it must be because we are *Christians* who are like Christ and for Him. And when reproach comes, we are not to be glum, but glad. We are not to bemoan our cruel treatment at the hands of others, and parade ourselves as martyrs, but count ourselves happy warriors. And Christ Himself makes it clear that the secret of our song in suffering is our future reward for any reproach we bear for His dear sake (Matthew 5:11; see II Corinthians 12:10).

"My heart shall not reproach me so long as I live." Job 27:6

Because sin is a reproach to any people, especially the Lord's people (Proverbs 14:31), every Christian should strive to emulate the vow of Job. Condemnation in abundance will come to us from a world that is blind to spiritual values. What we must guard against is that of having a heart within censuring us for our worldly ways. If our heart condemn us not, then we can look a hostile world in the face and bear its reproach courageously. As long as we live as unto the Lord, we have nothing to fear.

THE SOURCE OF CALM REPOSE

The Bible offers us an imposing number of precious promises linked to "rest," "quietness," "stillness," "peace," "repose," "serenity," and the supernatural virtue indicated by such is the only perfect antidote to all our anxiety, despondency, and dismay. Shakespeare would have us know that, "Our foster-nurse of nature is repose." But God Himself is presented as the Fount of spiritual serenity.

Run your eye over the following verses dealing with *quietness*, and see if you agree with the sentiment, "What is virtue but repose of mind." In the main, to "quiet" means to pacify.

"When he giveth quietness, who then can make trouble?" Job 34:29

"Then are they glad because they be quiet." Psalm 107:30

"I have behaved and quieted myself."
                                        Psalm 131:2

"Whoso hearkeneth unto me . . . shall be quiet." Proverbs 1:33

"Better is a dry morsel, and quietness therewith." Proverbs 17:1; Ecclesiastes 4:6

"Take heed, and be quiet." Isaiah 7:4; Zechariah 6:8; I Peter 3:4

"In quietness and confidence shall be your strength." Isaiah 30:14; 32:17

"That we may lead a quiet and peaceable life." I Timothy 2:2

"That with quietness they work and eat their own bread." II Thessalonians 3:12

How practical the Bible is! It tells me that if a man shuns work, he shall not eat. Then although my sphere may be humble and conspicuous, it can yet be hallowed and sacred. The most homely toils and labors can teach us lessons of trust and quietness. Even the kitchen can become the audience-chamber of the King.

"There is sorrow on the sea; it cannot be quiet." Jeremiah 49:23

But there is One who can quiet the angriest sea, because He made it and it obeys its Creator.

"He maketh the storm a calm."
                                        Psalm 107:29

"The wind ceased, and there was a great calm." Mark 4:31

Christ's miraculous power to calm troubled waters extends to the spiritual realm. Amid all that tends to disturb, agitate, and upset the mind of the Christian, Christ is near to command all that would annoy His peace to be still. As Tennyson plucked a daisy from the lawn, he said, "All that the sun is to that flower, giving it life and strength and beauty and fragrance, the Lord Jesus is to me." Along with promises of *quietness* and *calmness*, we have the kindred ones of *rest* and *peace*, the latter being already considered.

"Return unto thy rest, O my soul."
                                Psalm 116:7; Hebrews 4:9-11

"This is my rest: here will I dwell."
                                        Psalm 132:14

"The Lord shall give thee rest."
                                        Isaiah 14:3

"Come unto me, and I will give you rest." Matthew 11:28, 29

"I will give thee rest." Exodus 33:14

True rest of heart is only found in the presence, favor, and love of God. Apart from Him, our inner life is like a troubled sea – driven to and fro with perplexing doubts and fears. Along with the promise of His "presence," God also vouchsafed to Moses the promise of "rest," and the one springs from the other. Thus Moses went forward with quiet, unshaken confidence in God. Amid all *outward* trials, he had an *inward* quiet – the quiet of a loved, confiding child. True, Moses had to face long and arduous years of leadership, but with the *quiet* of a soul reposing on its God, Moses delighted in His service. Labor is rest to the loving spirit – congenial work is not toil. T. H. Darlow reminds us that the inner peace the Lord supplies "does not mean stoical passivity or sentimental self-absorption."

"He will rest in His love."
                                        Zephaniah 3:17

If God rests in His own perfect, unchangeable love, we should also learn how to rest in the same invariable love.

"God from his purpose shall never remove,
    But love thee, and bless thee, and rest in His love."

Are we able to confess with John, the apostle of love, "We have known and believed the love that God hath to us! God is love"? Here is the rock where we may rest with confidence – a pillow we can repose on in peace (Psalm 29:11).

"Be still, and know that I am God."
                        Psalms 46:10; 4:4; 23:2; Ruth 3:18

We have a feeling that plenty of activity is a sign of strength, but the Bible reminds us that our strength is to sit still. This stillness, however, is not a dreamy laziness, but a tranquility of soul that springs from faith in God's sovereignty. *I am God.* At times, reason may be confounded, and faith staggered, but a glimpse of Him whose path is in the deep waters hushes our fears and silences our despair. None can stay His hand. "Relax – I am the mighty One," is a suggestive translation given to the divine call.

"In quietness and confidence shall be your strength." Isaiah 30:15

Does not this wonderful assertion of Isaiah appear as one of the most brilliant of God's promises? Quietness, confidence – *strength*! What is the nature of this quietness helping to beget strength? Is it not expressive of our submission to God's holy will, and of a prayerful waiting upon Him as directed by His Word? Are we not enjoined to be silent before Him, assured that our best interests are secured by His promises? It is good to quietly wait for His salvation. Allied to quietness is confidence – a confidence reposing in God's unalterable Word, and in the confirmation of His promises in every generation. As we quietly confide, strength becomes ours to witness for Him; and as we honor Him by our confidence, He honors us by working in and through us.

"The Lord shall be thy confidence."
Proverbs 3:26

Our quiet confidence, then, is not *something* but Someone. As the *Lord,* He is our confidence. A calm, serene, and confident faith comes from knowing and believing His Lordship. As He presents Himself, His power and love and faithfulness, a blessed peace and sacred satisfaction becomes ours, and we make Him our confidence by believing His promises, frequenting His throne, and seeking His glory in all things. All who trust in Him as the *Lord* come to experience the inner calm of which David wrote so expressively –

His soul shall dwell at ease."
Psalm 25:13

Here is another aspect of the repose all the regenerated should realize. Shelley has told us that "Kings are like stars — they rise, they set, they have the worship of the world, but no repose." How different it is with ourselves as "kings and priests unto God"! We do not covet the worship of the world, yet amid all the trials and tribulations of the world we have a spiritual repose nothing can destroy. We *dwell at ease,* meaning that we are free from slavish fears, from corroding cares, from all fret and worry. Ours is a state of blissful contentment and solid peace. With God as our portion, His eternal covenant as our stay, His precious promises as our security, His glorious atonement as our plea, His complete salvation as our shield, His unceasing advocacy as our guarantee, His home as our final abode, what else can we do but dwell at ease! Because He is the Storehouse of every blessing, all fears are silenced, unbelieving doubts are contradicted, and God is exalted in our lives.

"Return unto thy rest, O my soul."
Psalm 116:7

"My peace I give unto you."
John 14:27

He who is our Peace makes possible every blessing of peace for those who are *at* peace with God. The sweetness of this peace was made possible by the shedding of the Saviour's blood, which is "the way of peace" (Romans 3:17). Such peace is not only reconciliation to God, but tranquillity and comfort of mind. As we confide in His promises and walk in His precepts, undisturbed peace is maintained. "From this day will I bless thee" (Haggai 2:19). What day is this? The day we completely identify ourselves with God's will and determine to abide in Him, will be the day His peace will begin to flow as a river (Proverbs 16:7). Is this not a promise to plead as each day begins? As we begin and continue the day with Him, He will bless us with peace, contentment, and prosperity. As we seek to live each day in unbroken fellowship with the Lord, we come to experience with Jeremy Taylor that "prayer is the peace of our spirits, the stillness of our thoughts, the evenness of recollection, the seat of meditation, the rest of our cares, and the calm of our tempest; prayer is the issue of a quick mind, of untroubled thoughts; it is the daughter of charity, and the sister of meekness." Such a constant attitude of heart leads us to say with Shakespeare –

I feel within me
A peace above all earthly dignities
A still and quiet conscience.

THE FOUNTAIN OF SATISFACTION

"He is well paid that is well satisfied," the great English bard reminds us in his *Merchant of Venice.* The Bible promises the Christian complete satisfaction – a satisfaction without alloy. To *satiate* means to be fully satisfied.

"I will satiate the soul of the priests."
Jeremiah 31:14, 25

"They shall be abundantly satisfied."
Psalms 36:8; 22:26; Deuteronomy 14:29

"My soul shall be satisfied as with marrow." Psalms 63:5, 4; 104:13

"The people shall be satisfied with my goodness." Jeremiah 31:14; Deuteronomy 33:23; Psalm 103:5

"O satisfy me early with thy mercy."
Psalms 90:14; 107:9

"The Lord shall satisfy thy soul in drought." Isaiah 58:10-11; Psalm 37:19

"Who satisfieth thy mouth with good

things." Psalm 103:3

In the Lord we have an unfailing source of satisfaction. All our springs are in Him. In the pleasures and pursuits of the world there may be temporary satisfaction for the godless, but no lasting life and joy.

"They shall not satisfy their soul."
                         Ezekiel 7:17; Micah 6:14

The Christian's pure and abiding satisfaction springs from his salvation, and the consummation of his enjoyment will come when, at his resurrection, he wakes in his Lord's likeness (Psalm 17:15). How true it is that "None but Christ can satisfy."

THE HONOR OF SERVICE

How privileged we are to serve the Lord! Service was one reason why He saved us, for we were saved to serve. Some there are who try to serve Him without being saved. Others, alas, although professedly saved, never seem to do much for the One who emancipated them from the guilt and government of their sin. How resplendent the Bible is with promises of strength and rewards for service!

"I know thy works, and thy labor."
                                    Revelation 2:2
"Faith worketh by love."
                    Galatians 5:6, 9; James 2:20, 26
"It is God which worketh in you."
                                 Philippians 2:13
"One soweth, and another reapeth."
John 4:35-38; Ruth 2:7, 15, 16; Psalm 126:5, 6
"I will make you fishers of men."
                                   Matthew 4:19
"Ye shall bear much fruit." John 15:1, 2, 8
"He that winneth souls is wise." Proverbs 11:30; Daniel 12:3; Psalm 51:12, 13
"Let thy work appear unto thy servants."
                                    Psalm 90:16
"Serve the Lord with fear . . . Serve the Lord with gladness."
                             Psalms 2:11; 100:2
"No man can serve two masters."
              Matthew 6:24; I Thessalonians 1:9
"For the service of God." Ezra 6:18; 7:19

We could fill pages with references taken up with God's servants and the service they can render Him. The question is, Are we serving Him in a way that pleases Him, and serving to the limit of our capacity? Though serving Him faithfully, we may not see immediate results of our labors, but we have His promise that "after many days" our scattered bread will be found (Ecclesiastes 11:1). As the Husbandman, God has planted us in His vineyards and expects

us to be fruitful. But His lament was – and is – "Many pastors have destroyed my vineyard" (Jeremiah 12:10). Are we among the number cultivating "the vineyard of the Lord of hosts" (Isaiah 5:7)?

"Son, go work today in my vineyard."
                              Matthew 21:28-41

When the Lord of the vineyard returns, will He receive of the fruit of His vineyard? What each of us must realize is that when God graciously saved us and made us His own that He endowed us with gifts or talents to be used in His service, and likewise promised rewards if these gifts were fully and rightly employed (see Romans 12:6-8; Ephesians 4:7-13). The quantity of talents may vary (Matthew 25:15-28; Luke 19:12-19), but whether we have a single talent or many, what we have must be on the altar for God and used to the limit for His glory. The boy had little to give Jesus – only five small loaves and two fishes. But all he had was fully surrendered and the Lord multiplied and used the gift.

Many of the Lord's servants have a larger part of the vineyard to care for than others, and theirs is a greater responsibility. To whom much is given, much is expected. But whether our sphere of service is conspicuous, or obscure, makes little difference. What the Lord of the harvest expects is the very best from us wherever, in His providence, we have been placed. At the Judgment Seat it will be the quality of service, not its quantity, that will bring the promised reward (Revelation 2:10).

The primary object in all service for the Master is the winning of others who know Him not. The salvation of lost souls is the fruit He expects, and has promised us all necessary wisdom and patience for. There is, of course, fruit unto holiness without which we cannot win the lost. Let us look at one or two phases of this soul-winning in which every Christian ought to be active.

"They that watch for souls."
                                   Hebrews 13:17

Among the admonitions of this chapter, none are so forcible as the one to be found in the above verse, which is one all of us, and particularly pastors and evangelists, should ponder. Can we say that we are watching for the souls of others, striving to bring others into the fold? Do we, after they are in, watch over them tenderly until they are established in the faith?

"His blood will I require at thine hand."
                                    Ezekiel 3:18

No Christian can read the solemn commission of Ezekiel and remain indifferent to the eternal destiny of souls. Jeremiah likewise urges us not to have the blood of others upon our skirts (2:34). Is it not a sobering thought that there might have been fewer souls in hell if only we had been more faithful in our witness? May grace be ours ever to warn the lost of the terrible eternity awaiting them if they die out of Christ!

"If your soul were in my soul's stead."
Job 16:4

Obadiah counseled Edom to remember the days when she stood on the other side. Once a captive and a foreigner, Edom was bidden to have sympathy for those whose distress was similar to what she herself had experienced. As a saved soul, do you remember the day when you stood on the other side? Never forget the pit from which you have been digged. Think of your sin and misery before Christ met you and transformed your life, and then never rest until you have the joy of bringing others a similar joy of sins forgiven.

"The redemption of their soul is precious, and it ceaseth for ever."
Psalm 49:8

To redeem the souls of men, God emptied heaven of the best He could find. In the sacrifice of His Son, the Father went to the limit for a prodigal race. Calvary likewise represents the value God places upon the soul of man. The gain of the whole world is reckoned poor exchange for the soul. But what is it that gives the soul its preciousness? Is it not the fact that it is of divine creation and is destined to exist forever? And, further, such was the stupendous sacrifice of Christ that the redemption of souls has ceased forever. Once for all, and for all, Christ died for sin. And now, all that a sinner can do is to accept by faith a completed redemption on his behalf.

"The soul that sinneth, it shall die."
Ezekiel 18:20

Personal accountability is among the ethical instructions set forth by Ezekiel. Eternal death is for the sinner's own sin, and not another's (Jeremiah 31:29, 30). And because all have sinned, all must suffer the second death, unless they rest in the death the Saviour died for sinners. The soul that sinneth - *it shall die!* This, of course, does not mean cessation of being or annihilation, because the soul is indestructible. Death

means separation. In physical death, it is the separation of the soul from the body. In spiritual and eternal death, it is the separation of the soul from God, now and throughout eternity. And surely the rescue of souls from such a death is a strong enough incentive in service!

"We . . . believe to the saving of the soul." Hebrews 10:39

Are we among the number who believe that souls can be saved? At times, we hear some degenerates referred to as being beyond redemption. But surely this is not true! No matter how hard and godless a man may be, while there is life there is hope. To claim that a gospel-hardened soul is hopeless to win is to limit the power of God. We are encouraged, then, to labor on, even for the very worst, because all the time that the door of mercy stands ajar, the vilest sinner may return.

"Save a soul . . . and hide a multitude of sins." James 5:20

A strong motive in evangelism is the fact stressed by James, namely, the rescue of a soul from spiritual and eternal death, and the blotting out of the past sins of such an one converted to God. And what an incentive this is! When we think of those conspicuously evil, and who, because of the multitude of their sins have a terrible eternity awaiting them, do we not find ourselves laboring unceasingly to bring these sinners to the covering blood? Solomon reminds us that "love covereth all sin." May greater grace be ours to love the lost out of their sins, and to lead them to cast a guilty past forever in the crimson stream!

The Shadow of Sin

It will have been observed that under the section, "Promises Related to Christian Doctrines," *sin* was dealt with from the doctrinal viewpoint. As we are presently dealing with promises for the Christian in the spiritual realm, we pause to consider some of these promises connected with deliverance from one's own sin. If one says he has no sin, he deceives himself - but nobody else (I John 1:8).

"Let a man examine himself."
I Corinthians 11:28

Paul addressed himself to the Christians at Corinth when he wrote thus. It was Plato who said that "the unexamined life was not worth having." The self-examination the Bible enjoins is no morbid introspection. Such an action is necessary to discover whether we are growing or declining, whether we have harbored sin to confess and abandon, and whether we are being enlightened as to sin's nature and subtle workings. While we are to examine ourselves carefully, deliberately and prayerfully, we must realize that God Himself is the Searcher of hearts (Psalm 139:1, 23, 24). And there is no need to be afraid of the revelation for "What the light reveals, the blood can cleanse."

"He shall save his people from their sins." Matthew 1:21

Note the phrase, *His people*. True, He came to save the lost (I Timothy 1:15), but Paul also tells us that Christ is the Saviour, "specially of those that believe" (I Timothy 4:10). So He is a Saviour of saints as well as sinners – and saints have many sins to be saved from. And we are encouraged by the promise that, having delivered us from the *guilt* of our sins when we first believed, He is able to deliver us from government of sin, as we keep on believing.

Our great comfort is that the Lord has made full provisions for sins of commission and omission, for unknown as well as known sins. That there are sins of ignorance, and the promise of forgiveness for such is clearly stated, "It shall be forgiven them; for it is ignorance" (Numbers 15:25). Spurgeon says that, "Because of our ignorance we are not fully aware of our sins of ignorance." Yet each of us have many such sins. What we may not deem as sin today will, with fuller light tomorrow, be seen as alien to God's holy will. But Christ's glorious atonement provided pardon for *all* sin, and in this fact we rejoice.

"If any man sin." I John 2:1

A. Lindsay Glegg, speaking to young people, counseled them to remember three things about sin.

1. *Never expect to sin.* Why should you desire to sin with such a Saviour?
2. *Never excuse sin.* Sin is still *sin*, whether we speak of it as a failure, weakness, or shortcoming.
3. *Never excite sin.* There is no half-and-half affair about it. Sin must not be parleyed with.

If we sin, John's *if* is of rich encouragement and good cheer. "We have an Advocate." How sadly disappointing the best of us are to God. Sin is forever casting its shadow over our pathway, but the promise is that day by day our Intercessor makes no pause. Pleading the merits of His own righteousness

and efficacious blood, our desperate case is relieved and all our necessity met. How blessed we are to have such a Paraclete in Heaven! He is our *Mediator* (Galatians 3:20; John 14:6; Ephesians 2:18).

Because of His holiness, God is, and must ever be, the eternal enemy of sin. He cannot be reconciled to it. He looks upon it with abhorrence. Therefore, the only way He can receive and bless us is through a Mediator, which Jesus is. He stands between God and us. He, it is who represents us to God, and we are accepted in Him. He is the Daysman between, presenting our persons, petitions, and praises to God in His own merit. It is because He lives for us up there, that grace can be ours to live victorious lives for Him down here.

"The lord is faithful . . . keep you from evil." II Thessalonians 3:3

The Lord is able to establish us, and faithful to His promise He will keep us from known evil if ours is the thirst for holiness. Often He is not able to keep us from some phase of evil simply because we desire it. If we hate what He hates, then He will keep us from it.

"Sin shall not have dominion over you."

Romans 6:14

Paul describes sin as a sovereign and it will reign over us if we give it any sympathy. How comforting is the promise and provision Paul speaks of! As a Christian, sin may wound you, but cannot establish sovereignty over you as you obey Him who is able to make you more than a conqueror. One of the greatest scholars of John Wesley's day, and one of the most influential figures in the Church of England, was Bishop Butler. His *Analogy of Religion* is still read. But when he came to die, all his learning and influence and dignities were of no worth to him. He could only remember his sinfulness. The proud waters were pouring over his soul. "My Lord," said his Chaplain in an endeavor to comfort him, "you forget that Jesus Christ is a Saviour." "True," the dying man replied, "but how shall I know that He is a Saviour for *me*?" "My Lord, it is written, 'him that cometh to me I will in no wise cast out.'" "True," said the Bishop, "I have read that word a thousand times, but I have never known its value till now. Stop there, for now I die happy." There is everyone's question answered: How shall I know that He is a Saviour for *me*?

"Ye shall loathe yourselves."

Ezekiel 20:43

"Ye shall not do this thing."

II Kings 17:12

Ours must be the effort to share God's hatred for sin. Wretched self and sin must be loathed and, truly repentant for defilement, we must cast ourselves upon His grace. He who accepts repentance is the One who gives it, and becomes in a repentant believer one of the most sanctifying results of salvation. The Lord warned His people against idolatry when He said, "Ye shall not do this thing!" Is there not a danger of us falling in the same sin of idolatry? We may not bow to idols of wood and stone, but there are the idols of wealth, fashion, art, and friends seeking my allegiance. But if He is to be Lord of all, then our dearest idol must be cast from its throne (Ezekiel 36:25).

"Thou, Lord, art good and ready to forgive." Psalm 86:5

If we have sinned, what a gracious promise this is to claim. Although a saint, the psalmist cried unto the Lord and was heard. Because of his repentant heart, he experienced the grace and liberality of God. How we should strive to have short accounts to settle. Says dear old Matthew Henry - "Repentance is a daily duty: He that repents every day for the sins of every day, when he comes to die will have the sins of only one day to repent of. Short reckonings make long friends."

THE VALLEY OF SORROW

The Bible is a Book, heavy with sorrow. A river of tears, divine and human, runs through its sacred pages. It begins with God's great sorrow of heart over the intrusion of sin into His newly created universe, and His pronouncement of sorrow for the human race because of sin. *"In sorrow* shalt thou eat of it all the days of thy life" (Genesis 3:17). From then on, the river of sorrow deepens and widens, and ends with the sorrows of hell for the finally condemned. All one has to do is to glance over the selected passages and discover the various reasons for man's sorrow of heart. The regions of sorrow are manifold, and because there is not a person in the world without a sorrow of some sort, we turn to the comfort of the Scriptures.

"I know their sorrows." Exodus 3:7

"I am a woman of a sorrowful spirit."

I Samuel 1:15

"I would harden myself in sorrow." Job 6:10

"I am afraid of all my sorrows."

Job 9:28; 17:17

"God distributeth sorrows in his anger."

Job 21:17

"I was dumb with silence . . . my sorrow was stirred." Psalm 39:2

"I am poor and sorrowful."

Psalm 69:29; Ecclesiastes 7:3

"By sorrow of heart the spirit is broken."

Proverbs 15:13

"The Lord shall give thee rest from thy sorrow." Isaiah 14:3; 5:30

"The day of grief and desperate sorrow."

Isaiah 17:11; 65:14

"The Lord hath added grief to my sorrow." Jeremiah 45:3

"These are the beginning of sorrows."

Matthew 24:8

"They were exceeding sorrowful."

Matthew 26:22

"I should have sorrow from them of whom I ought to rejoice."

II Corinthians 2:2, 5

"Godly sorrow worketh repentance."

II Corinthians 7:10

"Lest I should have sorrow upon sorrow." Philippians 2:27

"Because I have said these things unto you, sorrow hath filled thine heart."

John 16:6; Acts 20:38

While the original words used for "sorrow" include grief, pain, affliction, sadness, and evil, it is a word linked to love, for where there is no heart, there can be no sorrow. Further, while there may be what the poet calls "silent sorrow," sorrow usually produces tears. *Tears!* What a meditation! This we do know that when we give tears to our sorrow, the heart is relieved of its ache.

"Hold not thy peace at my tears."

Psalm 39:12

"My tears have been my meat day and night." Psalm 42:3; 38:6

"Put thou my tears in thy bottle."

Psalm 56:8

"She hath washed my feet with tears."

Luke 7:44

"Serving the Lord . . . with many tears." Acts 19:30, 31

"He had offered up prayers and supplications with strong crying and tears."

Hebrews 5:7

As Christians, what we should never cease to praise God for is the fact that ours are not the sorrows and tears of those without hope. While not immune from sorrow, we do not sorrow as those without hope (I Thessalonians 4:13).

"The sorrows of hell compassed me about." II Samuel 22:6; Psalm 18:5

"Many sorrows shall be to the wicked."

Psalm 32:10

There are three thoughts that seem to emerge from what the Bible has to say about sorrow. The first encouraging truth is that *because we belong to God, His loving heart is touched with our grief.* He is ever near to console and relieve. "In sorrow, He's our comfort." When the tempest of sorrow seems to sweep everything before it, we have a safe hiding place in Him Who offers Himself as a Covert (Isaiah 32:2).

Another comforting thought is that *in all our sorrows we have a Friend who experienced sorrows no others ever have.* Jesus became "A Man of Sorrows" and "carried our sorrows" (Isaiah 53:3, 4; Lamentations 1:12). He wept (John 11:35; Luke 19:41; Hebrews 5:7). Do not His sorrows and tears make Him of great value as a Sympathizer for our sorrow-stricken hearts?

Then there is the glorious promise that *all our sorrow is to be turned to joy,* if not here, then hereafter. "Earth has no sorrow heaven cannot heal."

Here are some consoling promises to hide within our hearts –

"Sorrow is turned into joy before him." Job 41:22; 42:12

"The mouth which was turned unto them from sorrow to joy." Esther 9:22

"Neither be ye sorry; for the joy of the Lord is your strength." Nehemiah 8:10

"Refrain . . . thine eyes from tears." Jeremiah 31:16

"Your sorrow shall be turned to joy . . . No more anguish." John 16:20, 21

"I will gather them that are sorrowful." Zephaniah 3:18; Proverbs 10:22

"They that sow in tears shall reap in joy." Psalm 126:5; Job 35:10; Psalms 35:5; 42:7, 8

For tears – triumph: for grief – gladness: for sorrows – songs. Such is the promise for those whose eyes are wet with silver tears. If our sorrow becomes a window bringing to us a clearer vision of our glorious Lord, and He, by His Spirit sanctifies our grief, then all we endure will bring us a harvest of joy.

"The days of thy mourning shall be ended." Isaiah 9:20

"The Lord God will wipe away tears from off all faces." Isaiah 25:8; Revelation 7:7; 21:4

How precious have these promises proved to pilgrims in this valley of tears! Sin, sickness, separation have added their quota to our mournful experience. One tear is scarce dried when another is ready to flow. But the future is bright with the promise and prospect of dry tears forever, for "no eyes are wet with tears in Summerland." Sinning, sighing and sorrow are to cease – Hallelujah! Our weeping may endure for a night, but joy will come on that glorious morn. God shall wipe away all tears! None else but our God of love can bid our sorrow and weeping cease. Tears are only for earth. There are no tears in heaven! As we await the loving ministry of the divine handkerchief, may the apostolic ministry be ours – "As sorrowful, yet alway rejoicing" (II Corinthians 6:10).

THE SECRET OF STRENGTH

When we come to many of the promises of God we find ourselves embarrassed with spiritual riches. There seems to be so much land to possess. This is particularly true when dealing with promises related to *strength* and *power,* which we group together because of their similarity in nature. There are over 700 references to this possession. In fact, in many cases the same original term is used of both words. *Power,* for example, in Romans 1:16 is the same word given as *strength* in II Corinthians 12:9. It would take a very large volume to elucidate and expound all references dealing with the power of God, of Christ, of the Holy Spirit, of angels, of saints under God, and of satanic forces. Because of the greatness of this aspect of our study, we must make a few selected passages suffice.

"The Lord is my strength and song." Exodus 15:2; Psalm 28:7

"Thou art the God of my strength." Psalm 43:2; 31:24

"Because of his strength will I wait upon thee." Psalm 59:4

"Power belongeth unto God."

Psalm 62:11

"Let him take hold of my strength." Isaiah 27:5

"The Lord will come with a strong hand." Isaiah 40:10, 26

"They that wait upon the Lord shall renew their strength." Isaiah 40:31

"The Redeemer is strong." Jeremiah 50:34; Habakkuk 3:19

"All power is given unto me, Go

ye." Matthew 28:18, 19; Ephesians 6:10 "The weakness of God is stronger than men." I Corinthians 1:25; Philippians 4:13

"Strengthened with all might, according to his glorious power." Colossians 1:11 "The Lord will give strength unto his people." Psalm 29:11

All God has promised, He will perform. But the promises that become a reality to the Christian are those that are believed and received *personally*. Have you experienced how strong God is to support you in every trial? His strength is ever sufficient – enough, but perhaps none to spare —suitable to your circumstances and needs. The saints in every age have found God to be a truth-telling and promise-performing God; and in this age, He pledges Himself to be your strength. As His strength is appropriated, grace is given to fight courageously, pray fervently, praise daily, and believe confidently. "Give *me* Thy strength, O God of power."

"I will go in the strength of the Lord God." Psalm 71:16; II Chronicles 20:20

We can go anywhere when girded with divine strength. Of ourselves we are weak, and the more conscious we are of our utter weakness the better, for then God is able to display His power. Apart from Him, we have no strength against our foes, no wisdom, no might to encounter difficulties. But in Him our strength is as the strength of ten if our hearts are pure. All necessary power has been promised us, and as we appropriate it by faith, we go forth to prove that He is faithful who hath promised. Relying upon His veracity, we are sure of succor and victory. To those who have no might He increaseth strength. Let us never be guilty of limiting Him (Psalm 78:41).

"As thy days, so shall thy strength be."

Deuteronomy 33:25

Like those whom Moses led, we too, are pilgrims traveling through a dreary wilderness to our Promised Land, and the promise given to the Israelites is good for our hearts. Our days may require patience, guidance, great strength, but the Lord offers Himself as our Sufficiency. As we think of present trials, and anticipate the future, sometimes we are apt to give way to despondency and doubt, but God is near who has promised us inward satisfaction and outward preservation. Therefore, let us be "strong in the Lord and in the power of His might." My Christian friend, He has promised strength no matter what kind of day you face, strength to encounter the tempest when it rages, strength to breast the foaming surges, strength to grapple when the last enemy meets us. Strength will not be given *before* we need it, but imparted just when we need it.

"No power: help us, O Lord our God: for we rest on thee." II Chronicles 14:11

What a plea and promise for us to make our own! "Lord, it is nothing with thee to help." Simple faith becomes fearless as it sees the invisible God at hand to succor. How helpless big battalions are when He manifests His strength! Our victory rests not in the arm of flesh or the resources of man, but in God's readiness to interpose for our deliverance. His arm is never shortened that it cannot save.

"The people that do know their God shall be strong and do exploits."

Daniel 11:32

How lacking we are in the valor and vigor of the saints of old! As a Christian I need more iron in my blood, more courage in my piety, more of the bracing worth of my godliness, more purpose in prayer and service. An old song of the Ashanti warriors as they rushed into battle was, "If I go forward, I die; if I go backward, I die. Better go forward and die." Daniel and his friends were valiant for God. Their adversaries were powerful, but God enabled His servants to be strong and defiant. If only we could catch something of their heroic spirit and think of a world of enemies as only a drop in the bucket of Him who nerves us for the conflict. "He who comes forth fresh from beholding the face of God will never fear the face of man."

"My strength is made perfect in weakness . . . when I am weak then am I strong . . . Mighty deeds."

II Corinthians 12:9-12

As Paul provided the weakness, God manifested the strength. Perhaps you are not weak enough for God to use as a platform upon which to display His power? What a paradox of Christian experience the Apostle gives us! To him, it was an antidote against spiritual pride – a counterpoise to the dazzling weight of glory he had had. Shipwrecked helplessly upon divine resources, Paul obtained divine relief. His extremity became God's precise opportunity of displaying His power.

"Let the weak say, I am strong."

Joel 3:10

The strength the Christian receives is not self-begotten but divinely imparted to be displayed in the sorest trials. Abraham was never so weak, yet so strong as when offering up his beloved Isaac on the mount. Martyrs as they face terrible deaths felt their entire weakness, yet prayed for and received strength to die victoriously. How the Lord magnifies His mercy in giving power to the faint, and increasing the strength of the weak! Milton asks, "Shall I abuse this consecrated gift of strength?" Samson was guilty of such abuse, and abusing his consecrated gift of unusual strength, he lost it.

"The Lord Jehovah is my strength."
Isaiah 12:2

As we pray for strength, what really happens is the fuller possesion of our impotent life by the God whose very name means "The Strong One." Mighty as He is, He yet stoops to our weakness and clothes us with His omnipotent Self. Further, it is blessed to realize that all He is, in Himself, is at the disposal of the humblest believer! The Gospel of the personal pronoun is a sadly neglected Gospel. "The Lord Jehovah is *my* Strength." Is He *your* strength? Simple, weak, unnoticed though you may be, do you constantly appropriate all you have in Christ for your very own needs? If the grace of appropriation is yours and daily you lay hold on Him who is the unfailing reservoir of strength, then you likewise know what it is to have Him as your Song, and likewise your Salvation. Why, the Lord is a trinity in Himself: Strength, Song, and Salvation!

"He increaseth strength." Isaiah 40:29

Youths become faint and weary, and utterly fall, but waiting upon the unwearied Lord, strength is renewed or exchanged, until the strengthened ones have power to mount up with wings as eagles, to run and not be weary, to walk and not faint. There is a thought here, however, we must not lose sight of. It is "to them that have no might" He increaseth strength. If mighty in our own estimation, then God has no strength for us. Can it be that we are too big for God to help? Puffed up with pride over our personal talents and capabilities, there is not that feeling of helplessness driving us to our knees for heavenly strength and grace. Paul could confess, "When I am weak, then am I strong." What a paradox! Weak yet strong. And yet, is it not true that if we provide the weakness, the Lord will provide the strength, and strength ever increasing, as further needs arise? When there is need of much strength, the Strong One is near.

"They go from strength to strength."
Psalm 84:7

One translation has it "from troop to troop," alluding to the journey to the temple thrice a year. When travelers had overtaken one troop, they ambitiously strove to overtake another troop. Amid all difficulties or opposition, we must persevere. The valley of tears must be fashioned into a wall of blessing. Adversities must be made as stepping stones to higher heights. The motto of the Royal Air Force of England is "Through Difficulties to the Stars" It may not be easy to climb to God by the path of pain, yet such a heavenly ascent can be ours. Are you going from the strength of yesterday to the greater strength of today? Has the grace you experienced in past trials girded you with the grim determination to endure the fiercer test just around the corner? As soldiers, the Lord's people are called upon to endure hardness. If our trials are met halfway, or in the spirit of complaint, we shall murmur more tomorrow. But rejoicing in tribulation, we make it a servant to minister unto us.

"I will strengthen them in the Lord."
Zechariah 10:12

God is revealed as the unfailing Source of strength. Apart from Him, Paul tells us that we are "without strength" (Romans 5:6). Through Christ, however, we are mantled with strength and can do all things, because He is within to strengthen us. Are we strong in the Lord and in the power of His might? As it takes a living fish to go against the stream, do we resist the strong currents of the world? Others around, because they are dead in sin, have no power of resistance. They easily drift with the stream of worldiness. But if Christ's, then we dare not be weak and impotent when sin's seductive charms are presented. Strengthened in, and by, the Lord, we meet the tempter and triumph gloriously over him. Zechariah goes on to say that when this divine strength is continuously appropriated, grace is ours to "walk up and down in His Name." Strength means liberty. We can walk up and down the lanes of earth, going and doing, not where and what we like, for such liberty would become license, but our liberty is in His Name, which means it bears the fragrance of His character.

"Strengthened . . . in the inner man."
Ephesians 3:16

In his Colossian letter, Paul asked that the saints might be "strengthened with all might, according to His glorious power." Sufficiency of strength can be expected from One who has unlimited power, both in the heavens and on the earth. But what do we know about this inner, hidden reservoir of strength? It is affirmed that deep below the angry, troubled surface of the sea there is a peace pocket. Above there may be raging storms, tempest-driven waves, cross currents of every kind, but below is an undisturbed calm which nothing above can affect. Is this true of ourselves? Have we the consciousness that the strong Son of God is within, empowering us to stand firm against the turbulent forces of sin and hell? What we are able to do depends upon what we have within. If the outer man is to be brave, courageous, victorious, then the inner man must be dominated by the Man Christ Jesus.

"Say to them that are of a fearful heart, Be strong, fear not." Isaiah 35:4

Ministers of the Gospel are here directed to strengthen and comfort the saints. And what a Godlike occupation this is! We dare not lift the veil upon the anguish and horror of war in many of the conquered countries. Think of the disturbed feelings we would have if we knew that our town was about to be overrun with brutal hordes of soliders who have no regard for the sanctities and decencies of life! To know that loved ones are about to be slain, our women raped, our homes destroyed, would produce terrible fear. And yet, what a baptism of misery multitudes have had. Look at the fear-stricken countenances of all the European peoples! It is encouraging to have the antidote to fear. What is it? Why, the judgment of God upon all the awful, inhuman crimes of rulers who are determined to transform the world into a camp of slaves. "Vengeance will come, the retribution of God: He will come, and will deliver you."

"The Lord will strengthen him upon the bed of languishing." Psalm 41:3

The open battle may have more notice and glory about it than a hidden bed of sickness. But surely it is harder to fight the good fight of faith on our back than on a battlefield. Courage for Christ is commendable as with a healthy body we serve the Lord out in the street, factory, or office.

But to be bright, hopeful, blissfully submissive to the Lord when the body is riddled with pain or disease is not so easy. There may not be much glamor about a sick bed, yet so often the Lord enables His suffering saints so to triumph over physical ailments as to fashion their bed into a pulpit from which His grace is magnified. Can it be that you are upon a bed of languishing? How active for Christ you used to be! What strength He vouchsafed toward you as you witnessed for Him! Well, your ministry has not ended. Its aspect has changed. Now you must make your suffering serve Him and for this altered ministry He waits to strengthen you.

THE BALM FOR TROUBLE

Troubles and trials are as old as the human race. "Man is born to trouble, as the sparks fly upward" (Job 5:7; Genesis 3:17-19). Whether our troubles are self-caused, produced by others, or permitted by God, the Bible is full of grand promises regarding God's ability to preserve *from* and *in* trouble.

"He shall deliver thee in six troubles . . . in seven."
Job 5:19; Psalms 31:23; 32:6

"Thou shalt preserve me from trouble."
Psalm 32:7; Proverbs 12:21

"A refuge in times of trouble."
Psalms 9:9; 46:1; 37:39; 41:1; Nahum 1:7

"Thou hast considered my trouble."
Psalm 31:7; Lamentations 3:22-33

"Though I walk in the midst of troubles, thou wilt revive me." Psalm 138:7

"He stayeth his rough wind in the day of the east wind." Isaiah 27:8; Job 34:23

"We are troubled on every side."
II Corinthians 4:8

"I will be with him in trouble."
Psalm 91:15

Rejoicing as we do in God's promise to guard us in trouble, we must not lose sight of its errand. Sin is the parent of trouble, which came into the world when man departed from God's command. Trouble is often occasioned by transgression. Sometimes it is permitted as a preventative to a greater evil. Through trouble, God corrects, improves, and brings us nearer Himself. If trouble is presently ours, let us rest in the promise that God is with us, and that He regulates the heat of the furnace. He will not suffer us to be tried more than we are able to bear. He is with us to increase our strength, and will deliver us in His own time and way. The old war-time song to which soldiers marched during World War I contained some sound advice. It goes—

"Pack up your troubles in your old kit bag,
And smile, smile, smile."

The Christian can afford to smile, not a mere artificial smile, but one born of deep joy, because all his troubles are packed up in the bag of resignation to the sweet and perfect will of God.

"Why are ye troubled?" Luke 24:38

A good deal of our trouble is unnecessary. Often we are troubled without cause. "Let not your heart be troubled," was Christ's message to His own. What troubles us? Is it sin? Well, He will pardon, subdue, and deliver. Is it the world? He has overcome it, and waits to make us sharers of His victory. Is it the devil? Christ conquered him, and the promise is that He is able to deliver us out of the snare of the fowler. Is it the cares and troubles of life? Then He offers Himself as the Source of all supply. So why be troubled? Is it not better to trust?

"The just shall come out of trouble."
Proverbs 12:13; 11:8

If all our days are troubled ones, the promise is that all present troubles will end in everlasting peace. We are to look beyond our troubles and this troubled world, to the world above where the wicked cannot trouble us. As we wait our release, God forbids our fear and commands our faith, since our life is hid with Christ in Him.

"Call upon me in the day of trouble: I will deliver thee." Psalm 50:15

Multitudes of troubled hearts have found consolation in this most blessed promise. How illuminating is C. H. Spurgeon's exposition of the psalmist's word—

1. *An urgent occasion*—"The day of trouble."

It is dark at noon on such a day, and every hour seems blacker than the one which came before it. Then is this promise in season: it is written for the cloudy day.

2. *Condescending advice*—"Call upon me."

What a mercy to have liberty to call upon God! What wisdom to make good use of it! The Lord invites us to lay our case before Him, and surely we will not hesitate to do so.

3. *Reassuring encouragement*—"I will deliver thee."

Whatever the trouble may be, the Lord makes no exceptions, but promises full, sure, happy deliverance. He will work out our deliverance by His own hand. We believe it and the Lord honors faith.

4. *An ultimate result*—"Thou shalt glorify me."

Ah! that we will do so most abundantly. When He has delivered us we will loudly praise Him; and as He is sure to do it, let us begin to glorify Him at once.

"He knoweth the way that I take."
Job 23:10; Psalms 17:3; 66:10

"The trial of your faith." I Peter 1:7; Habakkuk 3:17-18; Isaiah 42:3

"A great trial of affliction."
II Corinthians 8:2

"Trial of . . . mockings and scourgings."
Hebrews 11:36

"The fiery trial which is to try you."
I Peter 4:12

THE BLESSEDNESS OF TRUST

As "trust" occurs around 200 times in the Bible, it is easy to see its importance and the value God places upon it. Blessed promises, shining like a galaxy of stars, are also offered to those who trust in the Lord with all their heart. While there is a similarity between *faith* and *trust*, several interesting meanings are attached to the latter.

1. *To lean on, trust, be confident.*
"He trusted in the Lord God of Israel." II Kings 18:5

2. *To cause to trust.*
"Thou makest these people to trust in a lie." Jeremiah 28:15

3. *To roll upon.*
"He trusted on the Lord that he would deliver him." Psalm 22:8

4. *To stay self upon.*
"Judgment is before him: therefore trust." John 33:14

5. *To take refuge.*
"Under whose wings thou art come to trust." Ruth 2:12

6. *To wait with hope.*
"Though he slay me, yet will I trust him." Job 13:5

7. *To trust one's self upon.*
"Delivered his servants that trusted in him." Daniel 3:28

8. *To hope.*
"In his name shall the Gentiles trust."
Matthew 12:21

9. *To persuade.*
"He trusted in God: let him deliver him." Matthew 27:43

10. *To have confidence, believe.*
"Who will commit to your trust."

Luke 16:11

11. *To hope first or before others.*

"The praise of his glory, who first trusted in Christ." Ephesians 1:12

If the initial *T* is taken from TRUST, we are left with RUST. When we fail to *trust*, we quickly *rust*, spiritually. The promises and precepts regarding trust are summarized for us by David in the six words—

"Trust in him at all times." Psalm 62:8 Here we are given the true Object of our trust—*Him;* and also when trust in Him proves to be sufficient and satisfying—*at all times.* Not sometimes, when the sun is shining, and all is well, and our lives so radiant with the favor of heaven; but *all* times—even those times when trial, disappointment, and adversity fill the life.

> Simply trusting every day,
> Trusting through a stormy way;
> Even when my faith is small,
> Trusting Jesus, that is all.

Let us look at some of the encouragements offered to those who "Trust in the Lord with *all* (their) heart" (Proverbs 3:4).

God's everlasting strength

"Trust ye in the Lord . . . the Lord Jehovah is everlasting strength."
Isaiah 26:4

God's bountiful goodness

"The Lord is good . . . he knoweth them that trust him." Nahum 1:7

God's excellent lovingkindness

"How excellent is thy lovingkindness . . . therefore the children of men put their trust under the shadow of thy wings." Psalm 36:7; I Peter 5:7

God's gracious liberality

"Trust . . . in the living God, who giveth us richly all things to enjoy."
I Timothy 6:17

God's former deliverances

"Who delivered us . . . we trust that he will yet deliver us."
II Corinthians 1:10

"They that know thy name put their trust in thee." Psalm 9:10

"Thou art my trust from my youth."
Psalm 71:5

God never fails to honor the trust and confidence of those who believe and appropriate His promises. No matter how turbulent the waters, He is with us as our Confidence and Deliverer (Isaiah 43:2; Psalm 65:5).

Certain strong, unmistakable characteristics of trust appear as we compare Scripture with Scripture, enabling us to test the reality and quality of our personal reliance upon God.

It is not of the flesh.

"Have no confidence in the flesh . . . trust in the flesh." Philippians 3:3, 4; II Corinthians 1:9

It is not in carnal weapons.

"I will not trust in my bow, neither shall my sword save me." Psalm 44:6 "The weapons of our warfare are not carnal" II Corinthians 10:4; I Samuel 17:38, 39, 45

It is only in divine resources.

"In the Lord put I my trust." Psalms 11:1; 31:14; II Corinthians 1:9

"For I trust in thy word." Psalm 119:42

"I have trusted in thy mercy."
Psalms 13:5; 52:8; 62:8

"The God of my rock; in him will I trust." II Samuel 22:3

"His heart is fixed, trusting in the Lord." Psalm 112:7

"Though he slay me, yet will I trust him." Job 13:15

"Such trust have we through Christ to God-ward." II Corinthians 3:4

"Deliver me . . . for I put my trust in thee." Psalms 25:20; 31:1; 4:5

"In thee is my trust; leave not my soul destitute." Psalm 141:8

"Trust thou in the Lord: he is their help and shield." Psalm 114:9-11

"Under his wings shalt thou trust."
Psalm 91:4, 9

Such a wonderful array of promises and prayers assure us that we shall never be confounded nor disappointed if we are found hiding under those great wings of God. As chicks trust the mother bird as they nestle under her soft feathers, so as we rest in the divine promises, we are secure. While the Lord covers and protects us, we trust and are safe.

Not only is it necessary for us to trust in the Lord at all times, the witness of Scripture is that He graciously responds to, and rewards our reliance upon Him. He is the Rewarder of all those whose confidence reposes in Him. Think of these promises of blessing accruing from a personal trust—

"He that trusteth in the Lord, mercy shall compass him about." Psalm 32:10

"Thou wilt keep him in perfect peace . . . because he trusteth in thee."
Isaiah 26:3

"He that putteth his trust in me shall possess the land." Isaiah 57:13

"Whoso trusteth in the Lord, happy is

he." Proverbs 16:20; Psalms 5:11; 33:22
"Trust also in him; and he shall bring
it to pass." Psalm 37:5
"Save them, because they trust in him."
Psalm 37:46; Proverbs 29:25
"They that trust in the Lord shall be
as mount Zion." Psalm 125:1
"He that putteth his trust in the Lord
shall be made fat."
Proverbs 28:25; Psalm 44:4

The *fat* to which Solomon refers as one
result of trust represents prosperity – spiritual or material. But as we are thus blessed
we must guard ourselves against trusting in
our increase (Psalm 62:10). Our trust must
ever be in God, and not in any uncertain
riches He may permit us to have. Gifts
must never take the place of the Giver.
In this connection, it is necessary to follow what *trust* can keep us from –

"In God have I put my trust: I will
not be afraid." Psalm 56:11; Isaiah 12:2
"I have trusted in the Lord, therefore
I shall not slide." Psalm 26:1
"None of them that trust in him shall
be desolate." Psalm 34:22
"Trust in the Lord, and do good."
Psalms 37:3; 2:12; 34:8
"Blessed is the man that trusteth in
the Lord, and whose hope the Lord
is." Jeremiah 17:7

The psalmist's exhortation to *trust* and *do*
–which is the divine order–is worthy of
emulation. Faith, then works; salvation, then
service. "We trust God for good," says
Spurgeon, "and then we do good. We do
not sit still because we trust, but arouse
ourselves, and expect the Lord to work
through us and by us. We neither trust
without doing, nor do without trusting."
The "verily" in the promise is the assurance
that God will supply our every need as
we *trust* and *do*.

That the Bible is not silent regarding the
false objects in which the wicked trust is
evident from many Scriptures (Psalms 78:22;
118:8, 9; Isaiah 28:15; 59:4; Jeremiah 2:37;
17:5; Job 18:14, etc.). My soul come not
nigh their dwelling!

THE PATHWAY TO VICTORY

God expects His people not only to live,
but to live victoriously. Has He not made
full provision for *conquest*, as well as *conversion?* A defeated Christian gives the lie
to the divine promise of becoming more
than a conqueror.

"Through God we shall do valiantly:
For he it is that shall tread down our

enemies." Psalm 60:12

Promised dominion over sin and Satan can
be found not only in specific promises themselves, but also in all that the Lord is in
Himself. All-victorious, He waits to make us
sharers of His victory. Almighty, He seeks
to clothe us with His invincible might.
With such an omnipotent One to gird us,
there is no reason for weakness, defeat, and
spiritual impoverishment. As He *is*, so should
we *be*.

Promises concerning the overcoming life
were previously considered (Revelation 2:5,
11, 12, 21; 12:11; 21:7, etc.). Here are further
encouragements for the Christian to live
triumphantly –

"The Lord wrought a great victory that
day." II Samuel 23:10, 12
"Thine, O Lord, is . . . the victory."
1 Chronicles 29:11
"O sing unto the Lord a new song:
for he hath done marvelous things . . .
the victory." Psalm 98:1
"We are more than conquerors through
him." Romans 8:37
"The God of peace shall bruise Satan
under your feet shortly." Revelation 16:19
"Wherefore let him that thinketh he
standeth take heed lest he fall."
I Corinthians 10:12, 13
"But thanks be to God, which giveth
us the victory." I Corinthians 15:57
"Them that had gotten the victory over
the beast." Revelation 15:12
"Shout unto God with the voice of
triumph." Psalm 47:1 (see Job 20:5;
Psalm 94:3).
"He hath triumphed gloriously."
Exodus 15:1
"I will triumph in the work of thy
hands." Psalms 92:4; 106:47
"Which always causeth us to triumph."
II Corinthians 2:14; Colossians 2:15

With all these glorious promises before
us, what else can we do but apply the words
of Cowper to our timorous hearts –

Up! God has formed thee with a wiser view,
Not to be led in chains, but to subdue!
Calls thee to cope with enemies, and first
Points out a conflict with thyself — the worst.

An impressive fact that looms largely in
all that the Bible has to say about our personal dominion is that it is all of Him who
went forth "conquering, and to conquer."
Apart from Christ we are nothing, have
nothing, and can do nothing. Of old, the
people were reminded that victory of their
enemies came not by sword, by battle, by

bow, by horsemen (Hosea 1:7). God delivered His people, and that not by ordinary means. Thus all the honor was His, for He was able to give victory without battle. It is for this reason that God often determines to deliver us without second means, that the glory of conquest might be His alone.

"Sin shall not have dominion over you."
Romans 6:14

There is no reason why a Christian should not be constantly victorious over sin. God had made infinite provision for him. Has He not promised that sin shall not reign in the mortal body? Is not the Holy Spirit within us to keep us from sin? If the Lord who is stronger than Satan and sin is enthroned within the life, then all our foes feel the power of His mastery. No one and nothing can triumph over Him.

"The Lord knoweth how to deliver the godly." II Peter 2:9; Jeremiah 39:18

If only we could experience more fully the Lord's promised deliverance in the hour of conflict, how magnificently would our lives glorify Him. We may not know how to overcome our enemies, but He does. True faith is bound to be tested, but in the trial the Lord is present, personally undertaking the victory of the tried one. Have we learned to leave the *how* with Him? With no desire to pry the Lord's secrets, we leave the crushing of the tempter to Him (James 1:12).

"Resist the devil, and he will flee from you." James 4:7

The secret of successful resistance is clearly defined by James. As the text as a whole implies, it is by submission to God. Thus yielded to Him, we have Him to deal with our antagonist, who has no fear of us but who greatly fears the victorious Lord. Divinely-inspired resistance spells the retreat of the devil. Defeated, he returns with greater fury to overcome us, but clad in the whole armor of God, we are able to withstand all satanic assaults.

"The victory that overcometh the world . . . even our faith." I John 5:4, 5

John informs us that there are three pronounced characteristics of the victors in the battle against all the principalities and powers arrayed against the Christian – born of God, personal faith, belief in Christ's deity. Truly such a three-fold cord makes us invincible. The three-fold repetition of "overcoming the world" indicates certainty of promised victory. If we would be found

among the valiant overcomers, we must be assured of our regeneration; we must be strong in faith; and we must have a firm grasp of all the Lord is in Himself.

"The Son of God was manifested, that he might destroy the works of the devil."
I John 3:8

"Principalities and powers . . . he triumphed over them." Colossians 2:15

"Thanks be unto God, which always causeth us to triumph in Christ."
II Corinthians 2:14

"He led captivity captive."
Ephesians 4:8

This combination of passages proves that Christ's victory by His death and resurrection was secured for us. So a perfect deliverance can be ours through Him who laid hold of the cruel forces of darkness and stripped them of their vaunted authority. And His victory was not a bare one. He triumphed *gloriously*. He was more than a conqueror. Is it not comforting to know that His triumph can be ours? The question is, Have we the appropriating faith which makes actual in our lives all that our glorious Victor, Prince Divine, made possible by His death?

Too many of us are frustrated and defeated. We seem to have no might against the enemy. At times we try to struggle against those things alien to God's holy will, but all too easily we yield. If only grace would be ours to possess our possessions!

THE WAY TO WALK

The "walk" of the Christian means his whole manner of life, both before God and men. The Bible also stresses the importance of *talk* as well as *walk*. Several promises are related to our *lips*, as well as our *life*, and the reader will find it profitable to go over the verses in his Bible Concordance dealing with speech. But let us confine ourselves to the promises attached to the Christian's walk with God and his walk before men.

The first reference among the almost 400 verses dealing with "walk," or "walking," as related to man, is found in Genesis, where twice we are told that "Enoch walked with God" (5:22, 24). This beautiful cameo sets the pattern for the further revelation of the believer's privilege of having God as his walking Companion. In spite of his family responsibilities and the degenerate age in which he lived, Enoch maintained unbroken fellowship with his heavenly Companion. The second occurrence of the phrase,

"Enoch walked with God . . . God took him," led Andrew Bonar to suggest that God and Enoch were in the habit of having a daily walk together, and that at the end of one day God said, "Enoch, why should we part? Come home with Me," and so he walked all the way home to heaven with his Friend.

Various aspects of our walk should be closely studied by the reader. All we can do at this point is to indicate *how* we are to walk.

"Noah was a just man and walked with God." Genesis 6:9; Micah 6:8
"The Lord before whom I walk."
                    Genesis 24:40; 17:1; Psalm 116:9
"I will walk among you, and will be your God." Leviticus 26:12
"Ye shall walk in all the ways which the Lord your God hath commanded you." Deuteronomy 5:33
"The good say wherein they should walk." I Kings 8:36; Isaiah 2:3
"As for me I will walk in mine integrity." Psalms 26:11; 101:6; 15:2; Isaiah 33:15
"I will walk before God in the light of the living." Psalm 56:13
"Teach me thy way, O Lord, I will walk in thy truth." Psalm 86:11. (See also Ezekiel 18:9; 37:24; I John 4:6; Leviticus 18:4; II Chronicles 6:16; Isaiah 38:3; Luke 1:6.)
"We will walk in his paths." Isaiah 2:3; Deuteronomy 8:6; Judges 8:22, etc.
"We should walk in newness of life."
                    Romans 6:4
"We walk by faith." II Corinthians 5:7
"Walk worthy of the vocation." Ephesians 4:1; Psalm 101:6; Isaiah 57:2
"Walk worthy of the Lord." Colossians 1:10; 2:6; I Thessalonians 2:12
"This is the way, walk ye in it."
                    Isaiah 30:21
"Walk in love . . . walk as children of light." Ephesians 5:2, 8
"Ought ye not to walk in the fear of God?" Nehemiah 5:9; Acts 9:31
"Blessed is the man that walketh not in the counsel of the ungodly."
                    Psalm 1:1
"They shall walk with me in white, for they are worthy." Revelation 3:4

An examination of the setting of the above exhortations will reveal a variety of promises for the Christian whose walk is well pleasing to the Lord. There are a few particular aspects we can pause over. For example –

"They walked contrary unto me."
                    Leviticus 26:40
"Can two walk together, except they be agreed? Amos 3:3

Full fellowship with God is impossible if there are those things in our life contrary to His will. We cannot walk in step with Him unless there is perfect agreement between us. Harmony of thought, desire, and action make for a most pleasant walk together. It must have been so between God and Enoch.

"As ye have therefore received Christ Jesus, the Lord, so walk ye in Him."
                    Colossians 2:6

How did we receive Him as Saviour? Was it not by *faith?* We must, therefore, continue as we commenced, namely in faith. Having believed, we keep on believing. Fellowship with the Lord is precious and vital when we have full confidence in Him and our faith centers round all that He has promised.

"They shall walk up and down in his name, saith the Lord." Zechariah 10:12

The prophet here gives not only a promise as a solace for saints who are physically sick, but one for those whose spiritual walk has been hindered because of frustration. Are there not those who have become faint and fearful that they will never rise from their bed of doubt? The Lord, as the Great Physician, can banish the disease of fear, and taking the weak one by the hand say, "Arise, and walk." He can give His people liberty to walk with Him in holy contemplation, and inward leisure to exercise such liberty.

"He that walketh uprightly walketh surely." Proverbs 10:9

In the above citation of passages there are those suggesting the true walking posture. We are to walk with God – uprightness. The One we walk with was upright in all His ways. No guile was found in His mouth. None could convince Him of sin. We too must be firm in our integrity if our walk with our righteous Lord is to be amiable and profitable. We must walk in the light as He is in the light – and is *The Light*.

"If we live in the Spirit, let us also walk in the Spirit." Galatians 5:25

Is not the thought of the Holy Spirit always at hand as a personal Companion a cure for all loneliness? Lonely moments will never be ours if we continually think of Him as an ever present Friend with whom we can walk and talk. It is the Holy Spirit, and He alone, who enables us to persevere to the end. In Him, and with Him, we walk and are not faint. He enables us never to turn our back but to march forward. "It is a grander thing to walk resolutely and untiringly on than to mount up with the wings of an eagle."

If we endeavor to experience such a privileged walk in the Spirit, then we shall strive to entertain nothing in the life that would grieve Him (Ephesians 4:30). If grieved, then the walk is halted and His influence suspended. But if we sow to the Spirit, the promise is that we shall reap life everlasting. Walking with Him and in Him, there must be perfect agreement between us. As the *Holy* One, He must have likeness to Himself in those who seek to walk in Him.

"Walk circumspectly." Ephesians 5:15

The Christian must be careful where he treads. His own heart is deceitful and desperately wicked. He lives in an enemy's land, surrounded by temptations which the god of this world seeks to use in the diversion of the saint into *By-Pass Meadow*. Thus as a loving child, he must keep near to his Father's side, walking in the midst of unsuspected snares, watchfully, prayerfully cultivating a more precious fellowship with his Guide and Companion. His constant aim should be to honor the Lord in all things. There must be the avoidance of the very appearance of evil.

"Walk humbly with thy God."

Micah 6:8

Because God hates *pride*, how can He walk with one who emulates what He abhors? A vision of His august holiness produces self-abasement. "Mine eyes have seen the King–I am a man of unclean lips" (Isaiah 6:5). If we would walk as Jesus walked, it must be in all humility of mind. It is only thus that we can possess the utmost God has promised.

"We walk by faith." II Corinthians 5:7

Abraham's walk was certainly one of faith, for he went out not knowing whither he went. As we walk through the wilderness of this world amid all its clouds and crises, trials and tribulations, we must rest on God's sure promises, believe that He is ever near, and trust His immutability. We may not know the road ahead, but He does, and if He leads, all will be well.

No matter how long a walk we may take, we take it step by step. Some of the orig-

inal words used of "walk" in the Bible imply *to step rightly* (Galatians 2:14), *to walk or step in order* (Philippians 3:16), *to go on habitually* (Genesis 5:22, 24, etc.). So we have promises and instructions connected with the steps we take as we seek to walk with God. Both our *steps* – and *stops* – are ordered of the Lord.

"There is a step between me and death." I Samuel 20:3

"Thou numberest my steps." Job 14:16; 18:7; 31:37

"My foot hath held his step, his way I have kept." Job 23:11; 31:7

"Thou hast enlarged my steps under me." Psalm 18:36

"None of his steps shall slide." Psalms 37:31; 73:2; Proverbs 4:12

"Order my steps in thy word." Psalm 119:133; Proverbs 16:9

"It is not in man that walketh to direct his step." Jeremiah 10:23

"The step of a good man. . . . Though he fall, he shall not be utterly cast down." Psalm 37:23, 29

We have to confess, and that with shame, that although we are the Lord's we yet falter and fall. David says that the wicked fall and are not able to rise (Psalm 36:12). A Christian, however, is upheld by the Lord's hand, and so if he falls, he is not utterly cast down. "The law of his God is in his heart; none of his steps shall slide" (Psalm 37:31). "He walks surely who walks righteously," says Spurgeon. "We are moving along the great highroad of God's providence and grace when we keep to the way of His law."

"The steps of a good man." Psalm 37:23

We are here given a qualified promise. We cannot expect our goings to be established of the Lord if our ways are not fully committed to the Lord's keeping. Alexander Smellie asks,

"Suppose I had to travel for one single hour through a region to which the government of my Father did not extend. I could never emerge from that wilderness; I must die in its desolation. But it is a baseless fear."

"Who walk in the steps of that faith . . . of Abraham." Romans 4:14

"Ye should follow his steps." I Peter 2:21

"He will not suffer thy foot to be moved." Psalm 121:3

"Thou shalt walk in thy safety, and thy foot shall not stumble." Proverbs 3:23

If we follow the steps of Abraham and in the steps of Jesus, whose day Abraham saw, then our walk will be a safe one. Our feeble foot is apt to stumble, but divine grace is able to keep us from stumbling. "What with pitfalls and snares, weak knees, weary feet, and subtle enemies, no child of God would stand fast for an hour were it not for the faithful love which will not suffer our foot to be moved."

"I will save her that halteth."

Zephaniah 3:19

What a sweet promise this is! On the King's highway there are many cripples. The best of us halt in faith, in prayer, in patience, and service. What lame ones we are. But the promise is that God saves His ready-to-halt ones, so that they can run their race with diligence. Waiting upon Him for renewal of strength, we come to know what it is to walk and not be faint. When God becomes our all, our walk with and before Him is uninterrupted, and promised fellowship is realized. It is said that St. Patrick had this prayer inscribed on his breastplate—

> God be in my head,
> And in my understanding;
> God be in my eyes,
> And in my looking;
> God be in my mouth,
> And in my speaking;
> God be in my heart,
> And in my thinking;
> God be at mine end,
> And at my departing.

THE FOLLY OF WORRY

Although the word "worry" is not in the Bible, all it represents occupies a large place in Biblical precepts and warnings. As Christians, we should shun worry, because it is unbelief parading in disguise. When God urges us not to "fret" ourselves (Psalm 37:1, 7), He is actually telling us not to worry. Worry is not a virtue, a grace, or a duty but a sin against God and ourselves. There are some folks who would not be content if they were not worrying. Why, they sometimes *worry over their worrying.* The suggestion that they should be anxious about nothing is resented, yet Paul's promise is a radical cure for corroding care.

"Be not anxious . . . Be careful for nothing." Philippians 4:6

Tranquility of soul is the only proper antidote for worry. Even though you are a Christian, cares will come your way; but when they do you must cast them upon the Lord. I can hear someone saying, "Yes, that's all very well, but my case is exceptional. You have no conception of what I am facing." Still the quiet answer is, "In nothing be anxious." There are no exceptions to this rule. The secret of not worrying is in the promise of Jesus that all the things we worry about will be taken care of if we only put Him first.

When Jesus said to His disciples, "Take therefore no thought for the morrow" (Matthew 6:34), He knew that worry was not only a sin against God, but detrimental to one's spiritual and physical life. "Take no thought" literally means, *Do not worry.* Jesus did not mean that we are to completely disregard what may lie ahead. He would have us know that it is useless being over-anxious about tomorrow because all our "tomorrows" are in the hand of God.

But these troublesome guests – *Worry* and *Fret* – can be expelled if only the promise is believed that "all things work together for good" to those who are the Lord's. Does He not superintend every movement of every one of His own, and have their best and highest interests at heart? If we therefore worry, we are not trusting His love and wisdom and providence. When we worry we sin against Him and His promises.

Our health authorities are definitely *worried* over the disastrous effects of "worry" in the lives of an ever-growing number of people. The strain of modern living has become so intense that men and women, in order to forget the troubles they worry over so much, are developing at a fast pace the tranquillizer habit. A British report says that the doctor's biggest worry is – *worry!* One in five patients visited are mentally and emotionally disturbed. And this worry costs Britain some five million pounds in money a year in *mind pills.* Aspirin-type drugs bring almost the same amount. Around four billion aspirin-like tablets are swallowed yearly. Some 1,500,000 pounds, or well over four million dollars, goes to drug firms for a whole alphabet of vitamin pills. In America, the figures are even more colossal. In the U.S.A., Americans average one tranquillizer a day. In Britain, one in three use some sort of sedative daily. In Russia the people take enough pills to cause *their* doctors concern. It is claimed for this fast growing number of tranquillizers that they relieve anxiety and reduce tension without clouding our thought or making us feel lazy and sleepy. These pills slow down the agitation of the mind and reduce worry. But the effect is only temporary and so more and more pills have to be taken. Thus the detrimental habit is formed.

If faced with sleeplessness because of a temporary period of difficulty and trial, a drug under doctor's orders may be perfectly in order. The thing that must be guarded against is allowing drugs or pills to become habit-forming, and allowing oneself to become dependent on them.

For a Christian, any tranquillizer is a poor and dangerous substitute for the sane, simple, and sure remedy the Bible offers for worry and tension of any sort. Trust in God is far more effective than the most potent tranquillizer. Prayer can work greater miracles than pills. Spiritual victories are better than vitamins. A recipe that cannot fail can be simply put –

"To keep all worry and tension away, Take one of God's promises every day."

Paul's medication is the very best for all kinds of mental agitation. No care, but all prayer.

"Careful for nothing . . . everything by prayer." Philippians 4:6

Joyful communion with God produces a heavenly peace which garrisons the *mind*, preventing the intrusion of foes like *worry* and *fear*. He who directs angels, feeds sparrows, and calms storms is our Father well able to keep us in perfect peace. To think on all the noble virtues also makes for an untroubled mind (4:8, 9), as does the blessed contentment Paul practiced (4:1, 11). Why should I worry when God has promised to supply my every need according to His riches in glory? (4:19)

Are you a worrier, and does your worry result in physical troubles for which medicine is needed? Why not pack and move from the gloomy quarter on *Worry Street* to *Thanksgiving Avenue*, where folks live who do not need tranquillizers, pills, drugs, and tablets, for theirs is an inner peace which nothing can distrub.

"Stayed upon Jehovah, hearts are fully blest,

Finding, as He promised, perfect peace and rest."

PROMISES RELATIVE TO THE ETERNAL REALM

Now that we have come to the last phase of the scope of God's promises, we turn our eyes to the glorious future. Hitherto, we have thought of the hundreds of promises connected with our life in Christ here on earth. But Paul reminds us that godliness not only carries the "promise of the life that now is," but also "of that which is to come" (I Timothy 4:8). Having already dealt with death, the natural end of an earthly pilgrimage, we come to those inspiring promises so bright with future bliss. The good hope in death is that when we quit the body we have the promised prospect of resurrection, reunion, perfection of personal and social happiness in the full enjoyment of the Saviour's presence to all eternity.

THE PROMISE OF HEAVEN

One hardly knows where to begin when it comes to a brief classification of all that awaits the Christian when he or she comes to prove that to "die is gain" – and what a gain heaven is! No wonder Paul said that to depart and be with Christ was far better than anything earth could offer. What a wonderful promise to sustain us as we continue battling against the forces which are hostile to our faith here below! Under its

inspiration we press toward the glorious goal. In heaven our unfinished service, incomplete consecration, partially appreciated divine gifts, undeveloped capacities will all reach perfection.

So far in our study we have seen that our daily course, from first to last, is "skirted with fair borders of promises that are green and blossoming when all around is bare." But as we are to see, our life to come is also rich with promises of an exceeding and eternal weight of glory. We know that heaven is a definite *place*, as well as a state, because Jesus, who is *The Truth*, said so – "I go to prepare a *place* for you: that where I am there ye may be also" (John 14:3).

The kind of place He is preparing for His own in the Father's home will be worthy of Himself, and will suit us admirably. Our present abode may be incommodious and uncomfortable, but heaven will be spacious, magnificent, and worthy of our great Architect and Builder. This was the promise Abraham received – "He looked for a city which hath foundations, whose builder and maker is God" (Hebrews 11:10).

"The Lord will give grace and glory." Psalms 84:11; 73:24

Grace is our present possession, *glory* our future gift. It is *grace* that prepares us for *glory*. God's saving, sustaining, sanctifying, and satisfying grace carries with it the promise of glory, in which God will perfect that which concerns us. "After we have eaten the bread of grace, we shall drink the wine of glory." Bernard of Cluny exclaimed –

"I know not! Oh, I know not! what joys await us there!
What radiancy of glory! What bliss beyond compare!"

As your eye runs over the following list of promises, remember to look up the context in each case for a full understanding of each promise.

"An inheritance incorruptible . . . reserved in heaven for you."
I Peter 1:3, 4; Ephesians 1:18
"It is your Father's good pleasure to give you the kingdom."
Luke 12:22; Matthew 13:43
"We have a building for God . . . eternal in the heavens."
II Corinthians 5:1, 8
"Today shalt thou be with me in paradise." Luke 23:43; 16:22
"An entrance . . . into the everlasting kingdom." II Peter 1:10, 11
"Blessed are they that do . . . enter in through the gates of the city."
Revelation 22:14; 21:27
"Seek those things which are above."
Colossians 3:1
"Father, I will that they also, whom thou hast given me, be with me where I am." John 17:24
"At thy right hand are pleasures for evermore."
Psalm 16:11; I Corinthians 2:9
"Joint heirs with Christ . . . that we may be also glorified together."
Romans 8:2, 17, 18, 30
"Absent from the body . . . present with the Lord." II Corinthians 5:6-8

The revealing truth, however, is that the Bible when describing the glories of heaven deals in negatives rather than in positives. In the majority of passages we are told what is *not* in heaven, instead of what *is* in the heavenly realm. Job, with his dim revelation of the hereafter, thought of heaven as the place where "The wicked cease from troubling: and the weary be at rest" (7:17; Revelation 14:13).

There are three ways of describing to others scenes with which they have had no previous acquaintance.

1. A statement of those things which are not there, but which are found elsewhere within their sphere of observation.
2. A statement of those things which are found in them in common with those scenes with which they are familiar.
3. A statement of those things which are peculiar to them, and which are found in no other scene within their knowledge.

All three methods are employed by the sacred writers in their presentation of heaven. John gives us a specimen of the first method in his comforting portrayal of heaven. Think of his array of negatives – his "no mores."

"No night – no candle – no sun or moon – no defilement – no tears – no death – no sorrow – no pain." Revelation 21:4, 22, 27; 22:5-7

The certain things here mentioned as belonging to our earthly sphere have no existence in heaven. Yet this very *negative* description has a power to make on us a deep impression that heaven is a scene of transcendent blessedness.

1. *In heaven there is no specialty in forms of worship* – "no temple."

This promise would give the orthodox Jew the idea of a city to be avoided, for of old the temple was his glory. But through the ages, temples and their methods of worship have helped to nourish superstition and sectarianism. The absence of a temple in heaven, however, does not mean the cessation of worship. "No temple" really means "all temple" – united worship everywhere. "The Lord God Almighty and the Lamb are the temple of it." God and His Son are to be not only the objects of heavenly worship, but the very temple of perpetual devotion. Worship is not only to be rendered – the saints are *in* the Father and the Son in their worship.

2. *In heaven there is no necessity for second-hand knowledge.*

The sun and the moon are but secondary organs of light, for God is the Fountain of all light. He is the Father of lights. The sun catches His radiance and spreads it abroad. Here and now, second-hand knowledge is indispensable. We learn from the Bible which came to us from holy men of God – we learn from ministers, authors, parents, and teachers. But in heaven, our spiritual intelligence will be perfected by direct contact with the Source of all true knowledge.

3. *In heaven there will be no apprehen-*

sion of danger – "the gates of it shall not be shut." All that causes fear, affliction, death, will never mar the peace of the celestial host.

4. *In heaven there will be none of the inconvenience of darkness* – "no night there." Presently, night is the symbol of ignorance and interrupts labor. Night hides the beauty of the world and provides a cover for thieves. No twilight, no darkness will shorten the eternal day. The promise is that "the sun shall no more go down . . . the Lord shall be thine everlasting light." Wondrous secret of a nightless world, in which the everlasting light of Three in One will supersede all material luminaries.

5. *In heaven there will be no admission of sin* – "there shall in no wise enter into it any thing that defileth." Included are all those who are registered on the grand roll of redemption – the saints of all ages. *Excluded* are impurities of all kinds and degrees, and all sinners. What a blessed promise the nightless, sorrowless, tearless, sinless heaven is! Do you not long for the glorified state in which there is no exhaustion? *They rest not.*

"The glory of God did lighten the city."
Revelation 21:23

That the saints of God thought of heaven as a city is evident from Hebrews 11:10, 16. And this eternal city will be the temple of His divine majesty, in which His excellent glory will be revealed in the most conspicuous manner. It will be the sacred center of light, joy, and glory. How we long for the descent of this glorious city of God in which the Light will be the Shekinah glory of God and the Lamb! No sun by day, nor moon by night, and likewise no more artificial illumination. Darkness will be forever gone. When sunlight floods the heavens, glaring neon signs are scarcely noticed and are certainly not wanted. Thus will it be when the glory of God and of the Lamb illumine the heavenly city. God is Light, and Christ is the Light of the world, and together they will afford ample illumination for the glorified to walk and serve by. Beloved, are you not lost in wonderment as you think of a city without darkness?

"Absent from the body . . . present with the Lord." II Corinthians 5:8

The Lord is ever up-to-date! He is always "at home" as believers arrive from the dusty lanes of earth. And not only so, but there is no transition, no purgatory, no awaiting outside in some ante chamber until we are ready to enter the Father's home on high. As soon as the soul of the saint leaves his body, he enters immediately into the presence of the Saviour. It was this certainty Christ gave the dying thief, "Today shalt thou be with Me in Paradise!" Thus, there is no Biblical warrant for the cruel invention of Rome's purgatorical fires, which provides her corrupted form of Christianity with huge financial resources. Neither is there any warrant for the soul-sleep theory. The moment we take our last breath on earth, we take our first breath in heaven. As soon as farewells are said on earth, we experience reunion in heaven. One moment we are absent from earth, the next moment we arrive above.

"To die is gain." Philippians 1:21

If we have endeavored to follow Christ, then death will be gain indeed, and when He calls us, we shall go to Him with the gladness of a boy bounding home from school. Paul affirms that heaven to him was the presence of Christ. Often we are asked the question, "Where is heaven?" The answer is, "Thou shalt be *with Me* in Paradise." And surely this will be the greatest gain of death. Our eyes have never seen that radiant form of His. The veil of flesh hangs dark between His blessed face and mine. Now I walk by faith, but before long I am to see Him face to face. Would that I could live continually anticipating the thrill of seeing Jesus for the first time! What joy will fill my glorified heart! No wonder Paul says that to depart and be with Christ is far, far better.

"There remaineth therefore a rest to the people of God." Hebrews 4:9

While this rest may be the rest of faith, hence our labor to enter into it, yet we can give the verse a larger application. Heaven is the home of eternal rest for the people of God. After the cares and burdens and perplexities of life, we have the unruffled calm of the Lord's immediate presence. But such an eagerly anticipated rest will not mean eternal inactivity, for John tells us that in the New Paradise the servants of God and of the Lamb are to serve Them. And what restful service that will be! Service without complaint, weariness, cessation, and thought of self-glory. Resting from our earthly labors, we will enter upon labors more glorious, magnificent, and glorifying to God, for serving Him we are constantly to see Him and bear His Name in our foreheads. Presently our best work for the Master is marred by ulterior motives, but upon seeing Him we shall offer perfect service. What a day!

"Blessed are the dead which die in the Lord." Revelation 14:13

The word "blessed" as we know means *happy*. Happy, so says the Spirit, because they rest from their labors, from the toils of earth, and have works that follow them into heaven. Dr. Leon Tucker, commenting on this verse, speaks of it as a beatitude for tribulation days. "From henceforth" means *from that time*. If any desire to use this Scripture as an application in the present time, they may, but the *interpretation* has to do with *that time*. It is held out as a special source of strength to those who hold against the Beast and who would rather die than receive his mark, or his name, on their forehead. Who can imagine what this will mean to the suffering ones in the dreadful days of the Tribulation? There is a special beatitude of benediction pronounced upon them to steady, stay, and secure them in that day. Oh, blessed beatitude, blessed benediction!

"We have a building of God . . . eternal in the heavens."

II Corinthians 5:1

It would seem as if Paul teaches that once we leave this earth, our spirits are to have a temporary covering, or tent-house, until the reception of a glorified body at the coming of Christ, when the body of our humiliation is to be changed into a body like unto His own glorious body. God has a tent for each of us until we receive "a building of God, an house not made with hands, eternal in the heavens." In our present tabernacle we groan, being burdened. And what groans the old body gives us! The ills to which our flesh is heir give us weary days and long nights. Truly the whole creation groaneth and travaileth together in pain! But a glorious emancipation is at hand. At times we get a little impatient. Our bodily ailments get us down. Health is denied us, and we long for our exit from a body of sickness and of sin. And how we bless God, because we know that the redemption of the body is not far distant!

"Behold, the half was not told me."

I Kings 10:7

King Solomon typifies the Lord Jesus Christ in many ways. In the narrative before us the Queen of Sheba is pictured as being amazed at the magnificence of Solomon's wealth and wisdom. She had heard of his fame and she came to witness his greatness and prove his wisdom. And once she saw and heard everything, we read that "there was no more spirit in her." The queen did not believe what she had heard in her own land of Solomon's might and majesty, but once her eyes had feasted upon Solomon's glorious kingdom she confessed that Solomon's wisdom and prosperity exceeded the fame she had heard. Thus will it be with us. Here on earth we read and hear a great deal about the Lord Jesus Christ, and of the marvelous provision of heaven, but when we ultimately reach the palace of the King and gaze upon His glory and discover how He is adored by the vast hosts above, we will be found confessing, "the half was not told me."

THE PROMISE OF THE SECOND ADVENT

As we come to think of those promises related to the Second Advent of our Lord, a word is necessary regarding the true significance of such an Advent. It must be made clear that it does not represent a single event, but a series of events. Just as the First Advent of Christ covered over 33 years and included several events and crises, so His Second Advent takes in His return to the air for His Church, the Great Tribulation era, His appearance on the earth as its rightful Lord and King, His millennial reign, and His role as Judge.

Generally speaking, Christ's glorious Advent is in two stages. When the day comes on God's calendar for His Son to return, He is not coming all the way to earth at once, without a break. First of all, He is to tarry somewhere between heaven and earth and the saints are to be caught up to meet Him in the air (I Thessalonians 4:17). This will be His private manifestation, when He will return as the Bridegroom for His Bride – the true Church. Then after a period of some seven years, the period symbolized by Daniel's seventieth week, or the period known as the Great Tribulation, Christ will journey from the air to the earth, as Zechariah declares in his prophecy – "His feet shall stand in that day upon the Mount of Olives" (14:2, 4).

This *day*, as we shall later see, will inaugurate our Lord's millennial reign as the Prince of the kings of earth (Revelation 1:5).

First of all, He comes *for* His saints, then He comes *with* them, for when He sets up His kingdom, ours is the promise that we are to assist Him in the governmental control of all things.

"They lived and reigned with Christ a thousand years." Revelation 20:4, 6

The aspect presently concerning us is that of the *Rapture,* or "His appearing," as Paul loved to express it. I need hardly say that I heartily accept the pre-millennial teaching of the New Testament. Before Christ comes to establish His Kingdom, He must receive His Church unto Himself as He promised. "I will come again, and receive you unto myself" (John 14:3). This reception will take place when the Church is caught up to meet her Lord in the air (I Thessalonians 4:16, 17). This is the blessed consummation she patiently awaits.

Cunningham Geike, in his volume on *The Precious Promises,* remarks that "roses are sweet on the stalk, but it is only when you distil them that you get their full strength. A jewel may be bright in the casket, but it must be held up in varying lights to see it in its full glory. It is with the wide heaven of any of the promises as with the evening skies, at first we see only a single star, but as we look again and again, clusters and galaxies shine out as the darkness deepens, till the whole night is radiant." How true is this sentiment as we consider the glorious promises of our Lord's return. In the world's gathering darkness, these advent promises seem to shine with a greater brilliance.

If we had no other promise of Christ's coming, the one He left His own would be sufficient. Because He is faithful who promised, we know that He will not go back upon His Word. Then, was it not His dying wish that His Church should be with Him (John 14:3; 17:24)? In a sinless heaven the whole of the ransomed family – the Head, with all its members; the Vine, with all its branches; the Shepherd, with all His flock – will be together forever. Hence the necessity of the fulfilment of His own precious promise.

"I will see you again." John 14:22

Are we found pleading this promise? Here and now, we dimly see Him through the lattice of Scripture, but before long He will return to take us to His abode for the vision of His glory that will never fade.

"I will come again." John 14:3

As the character of a person has a good deal to do with the fulfilment of any promises he may make, so we can reckon on the realization of Christ's promise to return. Note the certainty of His return, "I *will* come again." And we are among the number who believe that when Christ said, "I," He meant Himself. Had He had in mind the gift of Pentecost, or the destruction of Jerusalem, or the spiritual experiences of the believer, or death, as some expositors affirm, Christ would have been explicit and would have said so. But we are simple-hearted enough to believe that He is coming again according to His Word, and that when He appears, He is to receive us unto Himself. It is esteemed a signal honor, indeed, if one is received by an earthly potentate or ruler. But an audience with a king or president is insignificant beside the honor which the humblest believer will have of being received by the King of kings and Lord of lords.

"This same Jesus . . . shall so come in like manner as ye have seen him go into heaven." Acts 1:11

Why did the two men from heaven put in that word "same"? It can be omitted without altering the sense of the passage. Evidently they knew that doubters of His personal return would arise, and so to make their message more emphatic, the two men from heaven declared that the Christ who had just left the men of Galilee would be the Christ to return. And it is He for whom we look, and none other. What comfort it must have brought to those amazed disciples to learn that the Master was coming back! It was this hope that inspired some of those disciples to write as they did of the Blessed Hope. Peter, for example, lived the rest of his life under the impact of the truth of Christ's personal return. Those disciples of old witnessed His ascent, but He went up and left them behind. His descent will be more blessed, for when He comes, He will draw His own up to Him in the air!

"For the Lord Himself shall descend from heaven . . . comfort one another with these words."

I Thessalonians 4:16, 18

It is interesting to notice that the New Testament writers approach the truth of the Second Advent from their own angle. For example, when Peter writes of it he stresses the aspect of *endurance.* James has the application of *patience.* John connects *purity* with the hope of Christ's coming. And Paul in his Thessalonian letter emphasizes *comfort*. Truly, there is no theme calculated to console our hearts like that of Christ's return! And is it not comforting to know that all earth's sorrows are to vanish when Jesus comes? Yet is it not sad to think that multitudes of people in so many of our churches are denied the heart-warming influence of the truth of the Blessed Hope? The pulpit does not accept such a message of consolation. Hazy ideas about a "kingdom" or a "golden age" are sometimes preached to people with aching hearts. Are you exercising the ministry of comfort by telling the sorrow-laden that the King is coming?

"The glorious appearing of . . . our Saviour." Titus 2:13

Paul makes it clear that every relationship of life profits when Christ's return is believed and lived. Could anything be more practical than the denial of ungodliness and worldly lusts, and a life characterized by sobriety, righteousness, and godliness in a corrupt world like our own? Surely a truth that lifts us above sordid passions and makes us better persons and more profitable to God and man cannot be deemed impractical. Jesus Himself was ever careful to give His Second Advent a practical turn. "Do business," He once said, "till I come." Foes there are of Christ's return, but our responsibility is to preach and teach such a vital aspect of Biblical truth. Any man who withholds the Advent message from his people is guilty of a grievous robbery. To keep souls in ignorance of the most glorious advent awaiting believers is to rob them of one of the greatest incentives to sanctity, service, and sacrifice which the New Testament offers.

"Changed . . . in the twinkling of an eye." I Corinthians 15:51, 52

One of the mysteries unfolded by the apostle Paul is the truth that not all believers will die. Not all are to sleep, but all are to be changed. And, what a sudden transformation it will be! Quicker than the unexpected flash of lightning will our change into Christ's likeness take place. We are told by men of science that the winking of an eye is the quickest movement of the human body. Greek scholars affirm that the original implies *"half"* a wink. If this be so, then God help us to live as those who are ready to leave the earth at any moment. Christ went away suddenly, and because He is coming in like manner as

He went into heaven, we must remain loose to things of earth. Since "the dawn is purpling in the East," we must stand as men that wait. Our complete change may be nearer than we realize. God forbid that the sudden appearance of our Lord should overtake us unawares!

"Unto them that look for him shall he appear the second time." Hebrews 9:28

On Christmas Day it is but fitting to bring the two Advents together. At His First Advent, Christ came as a Babe; at His Second Advent He will come as a Bridegroom. The first time He came it was as a Saviour from sin. At His second appearing He will come to take all saved sinners to be with Himself. At His birth, Christ took upon Himself a body in order to redeem the lost. When He returns, it will be to gather the redeemed, which are His spiritual Body, unto Himself. In the manger we have His condescension. Returning to the air, He will have His coronation. At His Second Advent, He will reap the reward of all the anguish, sorrow, disappointment, and sacrifice related to His First Advent. As myriads of the saved gather to meet Him in the skies, He will see of the travail of His soul and be satisfied. Thus when we celebrate Christ's birthday and think of all He accomplished as He lived among men, let ours be the forward look.

"Surely, I come quickly."

Revelation 22:20

As it is well-nigh two thousand years since the Lord left us with this promise of a speedy return, do we not feel like asking, "Why tarry the wheels of Thy chariot, O Lord?" But *who* is proposing and promising to come quickly? Is it a foe threatening us? No, it is Jesus, the Lover of our souls. He is coming for the completion of our salvation, and to claim us as His Bride. John, elated by the Lord's promise, echoed the desire of the true Church all down the ages— "Even so, come, Lord Jesus." With such a certain promise before us, may we be found living as children of the dawn, with our faces toward the sunrise. Soon, very soon, it would seem as if His blood-bought ones will hear His musical voice saying, "Rise up, my love, my fair one, and come away."

"They shall be mine, saith the Lord of Hosts." Malachi 3:17

When Christ comes for those redeemed by His blood, jealous of His honor and concerned for His glory, He is to treat them as His *jewels*, prized and acknowledged before the vast angelic host as His own precious possession. If we are His, then we can claim His promise to receive us, preserve us, and place us among His jewels forever.

"The blessed hope . . . This hope . . . Rejoicing in hope." Titus 2:13; I John 3:1-3; Romans 12:12; Joel 3:16

Such a glorious hope will be realized to the full some golden daybreak. As we linger amid the shadows, the trials encountered may tend to rob us of joy, yet we always rejoice in hope. We know that an eternal inheritance is reserved for us, and this excites desire, produces patience, prevents despondency and fills us with peace. The blessed hope was freely given, plainly promised, and is carefully preserved, and thus we are not ashamed of such a hope. Let us lift up our heads, for sooner than we think ours may be the joy of partaking of this hope, which is the anchor of our souls, sure and stedfast.

"We look for the Saviour."

Philippians 3:20

Who are those who eagerly expect the Lord from heaven? Paul tells us in the narrative where this promise is found – all who are "found in Him." The One we look for is the Promiser Himself. Presently He is at the right hand of God where He waits, expecting to make a footstool of His enemies. But before He comes to earth to punish His foes, and silence the groans of creation, He is to appear for His people to deliver them altogether from the bondage of corruption, and to crown them with glorious liberty. Coming as the *Saviour*, He will save us from sin within and around. Then, and not till then, will "the Church be saved to sin no more." The foundation of such a hope is a sure one – His oath, His promises, His covenant character, His finished work assure us of its fulfilment.

While the fact of Christ's coming is certain, the time of His appearing is uncertain. Thus to predict dates is contrary to our Lord's explicit teaching. Our obligation is so to live that if He should appear in the next hour we should not be ashamed before Him at His coming.

"Ye know not on what day your Lord cometh." Matthew 24:42 R.V.

What day! Life is made up of all kinds of days, and our Lord may come on any one of them. Surely this thought should hallow all our days. He may come on the day when we are immersed in our legitimate ordinary business and toil. If we seek to glorify Him in our daily work then if He should appear while at our usual tasks, His smile of approval will be ours. If He should come on a day of weakness and suffering, when because of pain the day seems long, then what relief will be ours from the burden! If He comes on the day when joy and success are ours, and we find ourselves basking in His favor, we shall not be sorry to leave earth's blessings for greater ones above. *This day*, let us live as though our Lord were to show Himself to us ere it closes.

"Of that day and that hour knoweth no man." Mark 13:32

How wise it is of the Lord to keep us in ignorance regarding the exact day and hour of His appearing! If we knew for certain that it was far away, we might be tempted to put off our preparation for such a day. Negligent and unwatchful, we should not be found living "with belted sword and spur on heel." If, on the other hand, we knew the day was very near, there might be the tendency to overlook and neglect all things else. We might become too heavenly-minded to be of any earthly use. The angels had to reprove the disciples for gazing up into heaven (Acts 1:11). Because we do not know when Christ is to return for us, such "ignorance is bliss." Faith is tested and developed; love for His appearing is intensified; vigilance is maintained. Daily we live as those who may hear the heavenly Voice at any moment saying, "Come up higher – inherit the kingdom prepared for you from the foundation of the World."

"At even, or at midnight, or at the cock-crowing, or in the morning."

Mark 13:35

Because we cannot tell when He will manifest Himself, we must be always wakeful, spiritually. Whether He comes at evening when the work of the day is done, or at midnight when the world slumbers, or at the cock-crow, when dawn appears, in the morning when the day is bright and strong, may the King finds us ready when He summons us home. Meantime, as we rest in our invisible Lord, let us likewise rest in the hope that we shall see Him whom our souls love.

"They all slumbered and slept." Matthew 25:5, 13; Psalm 130:6

"I say unto all, Watch." Mark 13:34-37; Luke 12:36; Isaiah 21:8-12; I Thessalonians 5:6

Because of the Promises Jesus made, the Precepts He left us, and the Warnings He uttered, we must always be watchful and active. But can we say that we are awake to our responsibilities, our privileges, our expectations? Are we looking, longing, and praying for Christ's coming? Do we love the thought of His appearing? It is high time to awake out of sleep. Both death and the return of Christ are uncertain, so we must *watch*. He has purposely concealed the time of His coming, in wisdom, in mercy, and for our good. He commands us to *awake*, and keep awake. We are to watch the events of the times, and sensing His nearness, be ready to hail His appearing.

"The end of all things is at hand . . .
What manner of persons ought ye to be
in all holy conversation and godliness."
I Peter 4:7; II Peter 3:11, 12

We cannot live just any kind of life if we believe that Jesus is coming again. Such a hope is a sanctifying one (I John 3:1-3). The end is at hand when labors must cease, commerce terminate, earthly relationships dissolve, pleasures and sorrows end, and the last church service be held. Therefore let us be temperate in all things, watch unto prayer, and serve God to the limit of our ability and capacity.

In connection with our Lord's promised return there are several features it is necessary to distinguish as He descends "from heaven with a shout, with the voice of the archangel, and with the trump of God." The first wonderful event is —

Resurrection — "The dead in Christ shall rise first" (I Thessalonians 4:16).

This phase of resurrection must not be confused with the resurrection of martyred saints as the Millennium is inaugurated (Revelation 20:4), nor with the "resurrection unto damnation" (John 5:29; Revelation 20:11-15). The Bible nowhere teaches a general resurrection when saints and sinners alike are raised and parted "right and left," as the hymn puts it. What is promised at Christ's Coming to the air is a particular resurrection — a resurrection out from among the dead — *only* the dead in Christ. The wicked dead are left in their graves until later when they will be raised to hear their final doom.

When Paul refers to "the *dead* in Christ," he was, of course, describing the bodies of believers who had died. Believers themselves *never* die. The moment they leave the body they are present with the Lord. This is why they return *with* Him (I Thessalonians 4:14). At present, all the saints in heaven, whose bodies rest in graves, do not have their eternal, glorified body. God is spoken of as having a covering of light, and it would seem as if Paul teaches that the saints in glory awaiting the redemption of the body have a temporary covering (II Corinthians 5:1-4).

Thus the promise is that when Jesus comes, all believers in His presence will descend with Him, and that at that moment, their dust or ashes, no matter where buried or scattered, will be wrought upon by the power of God, and body will meet spirit on that wonderful resurrection morn. The further promise is that it will be a body "like unto his glorious body" (Philippians 3:21).

"In Christ" is a characteristic phrase of Paul's, and it represents all those who are saved by grace and regenerated by the Spirit. These are they who "died in the Lord" (Revelation 14:15).

"This corruptible must put on immortality." I Corinthians 15:52, 53

In this great resurrection chapter, called the *Magna Charta of Resurrection*, Paul deals with the marvel of marvels, namely, that the sleeping ashes of the sepulcher will stir at the tines of the archangel's trumpet. Dishonored dust will rise with a glorified body like its risen Lord's. Ransomed dust will awake and Christ's "dead men shall arise." Writing to the Thessalonians of their blessed dead, Paul said, "Them also which sleep in Jesus will God bring with — or through — Jesus," who is "the Resurrection and the Life."

"I will ransom them from the power of the grave." Hosea 13:14
"He will swallow up death in victory." Isaiah 25:8; I Corinthians 15:54
"O, my people, I will open your graves." Ezekiel 37:12, 13
"Our Saviour, Jesus Christ, who hath abolished death." II Timothy 1:10
"God hath both raised up the Lord, and will also raise up us by his own power." I Corinthians 6:14
"My flesh shall also rest in hope." Psalm 16:9; Job 19:26
"I shall be satisfied, when I awake, with thy likeness." Psalm 17:
"All that are in the graves shall hear his voice." John 5:28

Here we have a confirmation and elaboration of Daniel's contribution to the doctrine of resurrection. All are to leave the graves either for a resurrection of life or a resurrection of damnation. What is striking in our Lord's declaration is the fact that resurrection will be at the command of Christ and accomplished by His power. Having vanquished death and all its powers, He now carries the keys of death and hades at His girdle. For an illustration of His commanding voice resounding through the grave, compelling death to obey, we have only to turn to the record of Lazarus at Bethany. That majestic voice of Christ will have a two-fold effect. To those who are His, that voice will have the sweetest tones ever heard. But to those who died rejecting His grace, the sound of that voice will call them to their ultimate doom. The important thing before the grave is to hear the voice of Jesus saying, "Come unto Me, and rest."

"Neither can they die any more."

Luke 20:36

The Sadducees differed from the Pharisees in that they rejected the resurrection. In reply to their catchy question about the woman with seven husbands, Christ had some important things to say. First of all, He declared that the relationships of earth are not continued in heaven, that His own are to die no more, that they are equal with angels, that they are known as the children of God. Then, going back to Moses, Christ clinches His answer by reminding the Sadducees that Moses called God, "the God of Abraham, of Isaac, and of Jacob." And because He is the God of the living, and not of the dead, the implication was that Abraham, Isaac, and Jacob were still alive and somewhere when Moses declared they had his God as their God. All who die in their sins have another death. Their eternal separation from God is called "the second death." But having died once, the believer dies no more. He ever lives unto Christ.

"He which raised up the Lord Jesus shall raise up us also by Jesus."

II Corinthians 4:14

Turning back to John 11:25, we find Jesus saying, "I am the resurrection and the life: he that believeth in me, though he were dead, yet shall he live." And here is Paul confirming the resurrection of Christ and declaring that all believers are to share in it. "Whosoever liveth and believeth in me

shall never die." Paul likewise makes it clear that the Holy Spirit was identified with Christ's resurrection. "The Spirit of Him that raised up Jesus from the dead" (Romans 8:11). And the selfsame Spirit will have something to do with our resurrection. In fact, His indwelling is a proof and pledge of our triumph over death. As the Lord and Life-Giver, the Spirit will operate upon our dust and produce the glorified body. There is, of course, a spiritual union with Christ in death and resurrection to be realized here and now. "As Christ was raised up from the dead by the glory of the Father, even so we also should walk in newness of life." Is this risen life yours?

"Our Saviour, Jesus Christ, who hath abolished death." II Timothy 1:10

The resurrection of Christ is one of the most important facts recorded in the New Testament. The truth indeed is that the whole system of Christianity stands or falls by it (I Corinthians 15:14, 15). As one of the old divines expressed it, "The Resurrection was God's receipt for Calvary." And that no one is truly saved if the resurrection is discredited is clear from Paul's teaching in Romans 10:9 – "If thou . . . shalt believe in thine heart that God hath raised him from the dead, thou shalt be saved." Never tell a sinner that all he needs to do in order to be saved is to believe that Jesus died for him. This, of course, is true, but it is only half the truth. The apostles preached Jesus *and the resurrection*. We need more than a dead Christ. If Christ be not raised, we are yet in our sins, and faith is vain (I Corinthians 15:17). Christ is alive forevermore, and as the risen, glorified, reigning one is well able to resurrect those who are dead in trespasses and sins.

Transformation

Next in order of events is the instant transformation of all living saints when Jesus appears –

"We which are alive and remain shall be caught up." I Thessalonians 4:15, 17

"Who shall change our body of humiliation." Philippians 3:20, 21

"We shall not all sleep, but we shall all be changed." I Corinthians 15:51, 52

These precious promises prove that all the saints of God living on the earth at the time of Christ's return to the air will be transformed immediately, "in a moment, in the twinkling of an eye," into His likeness. When we see Him, we shall be like Him (I John 3:2). Does such a promise not thrill your soul? Think of it! One day as you are busy here and there living and laboring as unto the Lord, He will suddenly appear and just as suddenly your body will be glorified and you will meet Him in the air.

Reunion

"Caught up together . . . We which are alive and remain shall not prevent (*precede,* or *go before*) them which are asleep." I Thessalonians 4:15, 18

Together! Now we are not together, for death results in painful and sorrowful separations. Life for you may be lonely because half of your heart is in heaven. The dear dust of your loved one reposes in God's green acre. But here is the comforting promise that when Jesus appears the dead raised and the living changed are to meet and rise together as a complete Church to greet the Saviour.

"The glory which shall be revealed in us." Romans 8:18

How Paul loved the truth of the Lord's appearing! It is from his *letters* that we have the fuller revelation of "the blessed hope" – which truth came to him as "the word of the Lord" (I Timothy 4:15). The apostle lived with eternity's values and realities in view. He hoped for that he was not privileged to see (8:25). What amazed Paul was not so much the fact that he was bound for heaven, as the thought that all God's children, once together, would function as reflectors of heaven's glory. Presently, we reflect the sorrows and trials of earth. Our bodies are mirrors, reflecting pain, anguish, and sin. But when the redemption of the body is experienced, then our glorified bodies will become glory-reflectors. At the glorious meeting in the air there will be realized "the general assembly and church of the firstborn, which are written in heaven" (Hebrews 12:23).

What a marvelous event and experience this will prove to be! No wonder it is referred to as "the Rapture," which, although it is not a Biblical term, yet expresses a definite Biblical truth, for "rapture" is from the Latin *rapio,* meaning *to snatch or remove away suddenly.* As used of the union and removal of the Church of the living God, "rapture" implies *to carry away to sublime happiness,* and was what Paul doubtless had in mind when he wrote of it as "that blessed hope" – "blessed" here meaning *happy* or blissful.

Further, when Paul said, "We – together,"

he referred to all Christians who had died and all Christians alive at Christ's return. The Lord will not leave behind one hoof in the Egypt of this world. "*All* who are Christ's at his coming" (I Corinthians 15:23). Such is the blessed promise!

Another aspect of Christ's promised Return is the thought of all God's children being brought together as one family. "The whole family in heaven and earth" (Ephesians 3:15). Positionally, we are now one family, but when Jesus comes to take us home, then all Christians will be *together* as a family forever. We could not be members of the same glorified family around His royal table and yet not recognize each other. The question is sometimes asked, "Shall we know one another in heaven?" Well, if heaven represents perfect bliss, how could we be happy in such a place if everyone and everything were strange to us?

Even now we are not happy if we are out of tune and sympathy with those among whom our lot is cast. Introductions are necessary when we meet persons hitherto unknown to us. It is deemed a breach of etiquette to speak to those to whom we have not been introduced. But in heaven there are no social distinctions and no restraints. All is love. Thus when we see Moses, we shall be able to speak to him, as well as to all the other Bible and Church saints. And the promise is that as we shall know Jesus by "the print of nails in His hand." Yes, "we shall know each other better when the mists have rolled away."

When Abraham died, we read that he was "gathered to his people" (Genesis 25:8), meaning godly souls like himself in the other world (Genesis 25:29; 37:25; 49:33; II Samuel 12:23).

"Then shall I know even as also I am known." I Corinthians 13:9-13

As memory is immortal (Luke 16:25), and identity is never destroyed, in our glorified bodies recognition will be intensified. Moses, raised from the dead on the Mount of Transfiguration, was still recognizable as *Moses.* When Jesus came forth with His resurrection body, identity was not destroyed by death. "It is the Lord" (John 21:7).

THE PROMISE OF REWARDS

What holy ecstacy will be ours when we see Him whom we love and serve! This will be "our gathering together unto Him." One reason for all the Church being caught up is –

"To meet the Lord in the air: so shall

we ever be with the Lord."

I Thessalonians 4:17

"Where I am, there ye may be also." John 14:3

"I will see you again, and your heart will rejoice." John 16:22

How elated we shall be when this promise of our future meeting with Christ is realized! What a joyous return His will prove to be! We know that in grace and goodness He comes to us again and again. But these spiritual comings of His will be eclipsed by His personal return when He comes the second time to claim His own. Once He and we meet, what can we expect to take place? It would seem that first of all there will be the Bema, or Christ's Judgment Seat, with its promised rewards, as predicted by Paul –

"We shall all stand before the judgment seat of Christ." Romans 14:10

"The day shall declare it, because it shall be revealed by fire."

I Corinthians 3:11-14

"Judge nothing before the time, until the Lord come." I Corinthians 4:5; 5:5

"We must all appear before the judgment seat of Christ." II Corinthians 5:10

When Paul used the pronoun *we,* he was referring to those who are "the Lord's" (Romans 14:8), that is, to all those saved by grace. This particular judgment must not be confused with that of the *Great White Throne* (Revelation 20:11-15), which is for the wicked dead. The Bible does not teach a general judgment when saints and sinners will be arraigned before the august Judge and then parted "right and left." No bornagain believer will be found at the Great White Throne, just as no unregenerated sinner will be found at the Judgment Seat of Christ.

The latter judgment is spoken of as the Bema, which was the raised place where the judge sat as he witnessed the Grecian games and then distributed the prizes won. It is in this capacity Christ will act after the Church meets Him. Why is such a judgment necessary, and what is to be judged? It is necessary to determine our place and position in our Lord's coming Kingdom, since the saints are to assist Him in the governmental control of all things. What will *not* be judged is our past sin, which God has promised to "remember no more" (Hebrews 10:17). What, then, will be manifested at that day?

1. Our present life as known by the Lord. (I Corinthians 4:3-5)

2. Our present conduct towards fellow believers. (Romans 14:10)

3. Our present service for rewards. (I Corinthians 3:11-15)

There are rewards for us in this present life. Obedience to God's Word brings us "great reward" (Psalm 19:11). For separating ourselves from the world, God becomes our "exceeding great reward" (Genesis 15:1). Then service brings us "a good reward" and "a sure reward" (Proverbs 11:18; Ecclesiastes 4:9). Our Lord tells us that even "a cup of water" given in His Name earns a reward (Matthew 10:42). But the rewards obtained at the Judgment Seat are those we earn here on earth for faithfulness. We dare not do anything merely for the sake of a reward. Such an attitude earns the rebuke of our Lord's displeasure (Micah 3:11; Isaiah 45:13). It is because He has redeemed us and made us His own that we serve Him. The rewards promised us are spoken of as crowns.

"My reward is with me, to give to every man according as his work shall be." Revelation 22:12

"Whatsoever is right, that shall ye receive." Matthew 20:7

"Verily there is a reward for the righteous." Psalm 58:11

Are we striving for masteries, in view of the coming day of awards? Do we always bear in mind that each soul's biography is being written in heaven, and will be revealed at "that day"? Will ours be a "full reward" then, or are we to stand before the Judge with a saved soul but a lost life – nothing to our credit; no stars in our crown because there is no crown for us? Saved, yes, but only as by fire. What are some of these rewards to be earned?

"The crown of glory." I Peter 5:3, 4

Glory is the portion of all believers in Christ, but "the crown of glory" is for those who "lay down their lives for the brethren," or who are "ensamples to the flock," who "feed the flock," and share the Chief Shepherd's loving interest in each and all who compose "the little flock" (see Hebrews 6:10; Mark 9:41; Jeremiah 31:16).

"An incorruptible crown."

I Corinthians 9:25

The crown presented to a successful runner was a garland of palm leaves, which after a few days would change color and become dry. For such a valueless and temporary reward, an athlete was willing to endure weeks of self-denial and arduous training. The apostle looks upon himself as a runner in a more glorious race. In order to win, not a few leaves, but a reward eternal in value and nature, he was willing to "buffet (his) body and lead it captive." With his service in mind, Paul expressed the fear that unless he observed all the rules of the race he would be ultimately disapproved, lose his reward, which is the meaning of "become a castaway." A teacher asked the boys in her Sunday School class how one could keep the body under. A bright-eyed fellow immediately replied, "Please, teacher, by keeping the soul on top." It was thus that Paul fought, not as one beating the air, but as one who was victorious over all the passions and lusts of the flesh.

"A crown of righteousness."

II Timothy 4:8

This particular crown Paul expected for loving Christ's appearing is so named because it is based upon the merit of Christ, the righteous One, and is only given to those whom He makes righteous, and who consequently long and live for His return. All the judgments of the Bema will bear the character of the Judge. No saint need stand in fear of favor or partiality. As the righteous Judge, He will do and bestow what is right. It is interesting to observe that the word "love" occurs in verses 8 and 10 in different connections. We have a study in contrasts: love His appearing – loved this present world. And the one love blasts the other. If we truly love Christ's appearing, the love of the world is not in us. But if, like Demas, we allow the world to capture our affections, then we have little desire for the coming of the Master. Are you determined to earn the reward the Lord has for those who long for His appearing?

"Our crown of rejoicing."

I Thessalonians 2:19

Here is the soul-winner's crown. Those won for the Lord are said to be a crown to those who win them for the Saviour. By calling his converts his *crown*, Paul implies that their salvation, stability, usefulness, and final triumph are to be desired with more avidity than a monarch's crown, and will confer ten thousand times more honor and real joy. Do you covet this particular crown? Are you winning the lost for the Saviour? Will souls be at the Judgment Seat because of the earnestness and consistency of your witness? What a tragedy

it will be to stand before Him with a saved soul but a lost life, no souls to one's credit, no stars in one's crown, empty-handed and rewardless. Preachers and parents alike can go in for this crown of rejoicing. Have you experienced the thrill of leading a soul to the Saviour? If not, begin right away to work for this conspicuous reward.

"A crown of life."

Revelation 2:10; James 1:12

This specific crown is strikingly expressive of the glory, felicity, and immortality of heaven. It suggests life in its fulness, completeness, "unendingness." This crown can also be used over against the "second death" which John mentions in the next verse. Faithfulness, it would seem, is to be the basis of reward in eternity. While we cannot work for heaven, we can labor as slaves for our position in coming glory. Therefore, it is not our fame but our fidelity that will bring the Master's "Well done." Further, we can look upon "the crown of life" as the martyr's crown. The Lord has a special reward for those who come to Him through dangerous fire and flood. Martyred Himself, Jesus has a peculiar interest in, and welcome for, all those who seal their testimony with their blood. It is thus that He is pictured as standing, waiting to lead the ovation of heaven as Stephen, the Church's first martyr, was about to leave his battered body.

"That no man take thy crown."

Revelation 3:11

The loss of a crown denotes the forfeiture of honor, splendor, and dignity. . While a saint cannot lose his soul, he can lose his reward. The crown that should have been his can remain without a wearer throughout eternity. What is it that robs a Christian of his crown? Well, John tells you! It is the lack of loyalty and steadfastness. "Hold fast that which thou hast." What have we to hold? Surely we must never part with the virgin birth, deity, efficacious death, physical resurrection, and Second Advent of our Lord. Other treasures we must guard are the spirituality of the Church, the infallibility of the Scriptures, the separation of the believer, and the necessity of a positive witness in a world of need. Alas, so many have lost their crown! Truth and conscience have been surrendered. Adrift upon the sea of doubt, they have no chart or compass, and no certain port to make for. Beloved, let us determine that no ruthless hand will take our crown!

"They cast their crowns before the throne." Revelation 4:10

What are we to do with the crowns we earn? We love to say, "I shall wear a golden crown, when I get home." But are we going to strut around with our diadems, as if to suggest, "See what I have won"? No! All honor will be surrendered to Him who alone will be worthy to "receive glory and honour and praise." Rewards become gifts to the King. From then on, we shall serve Him day and night forever without reward, save that of the unending joy of His presence.

The Promise of the Lamb's Marriage

The blissful, eternal union existing between Christ and His Church is indicated by the figures of the Bridegroom and the Bride (John 3:29; Romans 7:4; II Corinthians 11:2; Ephesians 5:25-33). At the Rapture, Christ appears as the Bridegroom to take His Bride, the Church, unto Himself. But such a pledged relationship must be consummated and Christ and His Church forever united as one. Hence, the Marriage of the Lamb.

"Let us be glad and rejoice, and give honour to him: for the marriage of the Lamb is come, and his wife hath made herself ready." Revelation 19:7, 8

The tense used, "*is* come," signifies a completed act, proving that the union has been consummated, following the events of the Judgment Seat of Christ. All is well between believers, and between believers and the Lord, so the "wife" appears in "the righteousness of the saints." While the Judgment Seat takes place in the heavenlies, the marriage of the Lord takes place in heaven, as no other location would fit a heavenly people (Philippians 3:20). "That Christ is spoken of as the *Lamb* points to His atoning sacrifice as the ground upon which the spiritual union takes place."

The marriage feast or supper (Revelation 19:9) is to take place on earth after Christ's return to it. This occasion involves Israel (Matthew 22:1-14; 25:1-13; Luke 14:16-24). Thus, "the wedding supper" becomes the parabolic picture of the entire millennial age during which the Bridegroom will display His Bride to all.

"Glorified in his saints, and to be admired in all them that believe."

II Thessalonians 1:9, 10

The Promise of the Millennium

Proclamations of and promises relative to the Millennial Reign of Christ are abundant in both Old and New Testaments. In fact, the only aspect of the Second Advent which Old Testament saints understood was that of Christ's glorious reign on earth. They saw the Cross and the Millennium, but not the valley of the Church in between the two mountain peaks.

"The sufferings of Christ, and the glory that should follow." I Peter 1:11

As the mystery of the Church (Ephesians 3:3-7) was not revealed in Old Testament days, the saints then knew nothing of the Church's consummation at the Rapture. They went from the Ascension right over to the Day of the Lord, the Great Tribulation era, and the Millennium, about which much of our Lord's teaching on the Kingdom is taken up.

"I appoint unto you a kingdom . . . my kingdom." Luke 22:28-30; 12:32

"Receiving a kingdom which cannot be moved." Hebrews 12:28

"The everlasting kingdom of our Lord and Saviour Jesus Christ." II Peter 1:11

"I have set my King upon my holy hill of Zion." Psalms 2:6; 10:16; 149:2

As the subject of the Millennium is too vast for our present study, all that we can do is to indicate some of the promised blessings of our Lord's reign. William Newell summarizes this period of the thousand years' reign as being "the direct administration of Divine Sacrament on earth by our Lord and His saints. Its earthly center will be Jerusalem and the nation Israel, though Christ and His saints will rule in heavenly resurrection bodies in the New Jerusalem and will take the place now occupied by the angels (Hebrews 2:5-8). Satan will be in the abyss during the thousand years, and his 'host of the high ones on high' will be 'prisoners gathered in the pit and shut up in the prison' during that time"(Isaiah 24:21-23).

"Millennium," a term made up of the Latin *mille,* meaning a *thousand,* and *annus,* a *year,* is used as "a thousand years" six times by John (Revelation 20:1-7), and represents the last dispensation for man before the final removal of the curse (Revelation 22:3). Among other definitions of this glorious period the Bible mentions are–

1. The dispensation of the fulness of times. (Ephesians 1:10)
2. The world (or age) to come. (Matthew 12:32; Ephesians 1:21, etc.)
3. The kingdom of Christ and of God. (Ephesians 5:5; II Timothy 4:1; Revelation 11:15)
4. The kingdom of heaven. (Matthew

3:2; 4:7; 7:21 etc.)

5. The times of the restitution of all things. (Matthew 19:28; Acts 3:20-21)
6. The consolation of Israel. (Luke 2:25)
7. The redemption of Jerusalem. (Luke 2:38)
8. The kingdom of His dear Son. (Colossians 1:13; II Peter 1:11)

Prophecies and promises connected with Christ's millennial reign are prominent in different parts of Scripture, particularly in the Psalms (see Psalms 72, 85, 89, 110 etc.). Among the millennial promises we have–

The promised glory of the Lord
"The glory of the Lord shall be revealed, and all flesh shall see it together." Isaiah 40:5; 4:5

The promised exaltation of Christ
"At the name of Jesus every knee should bow." Philippians 2:6-11

The promised throne for Christ
"To give unto him the throne of his father David." Luke 1:32; Psalms 2 and 110

The promised perfect government
"Thy kingdom come, thy will be done on earth as it is in heaven." Matthew 6:10; Hebrews 10:12, 13; Psalm 45:6, 7

The promised abundance of peace
"The meek shall inherit the earth, and shall delight themselves in the abundance of peace." Psalm 37:11
"Blessed are the meek, for they shall inherit the earth." Matthew 5:5

The promised physical changes on earth
"The desert shall rejoice, and blossom as the rose." Isaiah 35:1-7; 65:20-25
"All the land shall be turned as a plain." Zechariah 14:4-15

The promised holiness highway for earth's redeemed
"An highway shall be there . . . The way of holiness." Isaiah 35:8-10

The promised universal reign of Christ
"His dominion shall be from sea to sea, and from the river to the ends of the earth." Zechariah 9:9-11; Micah 5:2-5; Isaiah 9:6, 7

The promised abolition of war
"He maketh wars to cease unto the ends of the earth." Psalm 46:8-11
"They shall beat their swords into ploughshares." Isaiah 2:4-5

The promised deliverance from corruption
"The creation itself also shall be delivered from the bondage of corruption into the liberty of the glory of the children of God." Romans 8:20-22; I Co-

rinthians 15:24-28; Ephesians 1:10

The promised transformation of the animal creation
"The wolf and the lamb shall feed together." Isaiah 65:25

The promised general recognition of God
"The earth shall be full of the knowledge of Jehovah as the waters cover the sea." Isaiah 11:9; Habakkuk 2:14
"Jehovah alone will be exalted in that day." Isaiah 2:12-22; Psalm 46:9

The promised righteousness of Israel as a nation
"Thy people also shall be all righteous." Isaiah 60:21

The promised reign of the Church with Christ
"Do you not know that the saints shall judge the world?" I Corinthians 6:2, 3
"I saw thrones, and they sat upon them." Revelation 20:4; Luke 22:28, 29

The promised bondage of the devil
"Satan . . . bound for a thousand years, and cast into the abyss." Revelation 20:1-3

The promised longevity of man
"The child shall die an hundred years old." Isaiah 65:20-25; Revelation 21:3-7

The promised period of righteousness, truth, and peace
"Righteousness and peace will kiss each other." Psalm 85:10, 11, 13; Isaiah 2:3; 11:4-9; Micah 4

The passages cited indicate that the Millennium will be an age of wide-spread blessedness. With sin and rebellion under cover, because the devil is imprisoned and not able to continue his control of evil forces, and Christ reigning with an iron rule, the earth will breathe a purer air. The kingdom He will establish and reign over for a thousand years will continue into the new earth, and will therefore be eternal in nature.

THE PROMISE OF ETERNAL BLISS

Our finite minds cannot grasp the measureless eternity before us. Presently, we measure our time by days, weeks, months, and years. But with the commencement of eternity–the ages of ages–time will cease to be. This we do know, that through divine grace we are "portions of eternity," destined to spend this eternity with the Eternal One Himself. The depth of such a blest eternity has not been fully revealed, but we do rejoice in the knowledge that, as the children of God, we are part of that flowing river which will ultimately join–
"The hidden, the boundless sea,
Rolling through depths of eternity."

"He hath set eternity in their heart."
Ecclesiastes 2:11 RV

Within the breast 'of both saint and savage can be found the hope of immortality. Man may try to believe in oblivion at death, but ever an anon, the God-implanted desire for continuance beyond the grave expresses itself. Revelation and intuition confirm that death is not the end of all, but simply an episode on the way to the great beyond. Whether eternity is to be blessed or tragic depends upon our relationship to Jesus Christ before we die.

"From everlasting to everlasting thou art God." Psalm 90:2; Hebrews 13:8

This great promise implies that all God has been and is, He will be forever and ever. He is the Changeless One. Throughout eternity, ours will be the joy and privilege of basking in His eternal love and grace and glory (I Peter 5:10; II Corinthians 4:17; II Timothy 2:10). Not until our eternity with the Lord begins can we know that it is to appropriate the promises of eternal *joy* (Isaiah 35:10), eternal *love* (Jeremiah 31:3), eternal *Fatherhood* (Isaiah 9:6), eternal *kindness* (Isaiah 54:8), eternal *consolation* (II Thessalonians 2:16), eternal *arms* (Deuteronomy 33:27), eternal *life* (John 6:47; 10:28; I John 5:11), eternal *salvation* (Isaiah 45:17).

"Behold, I make all things new."
Revelation 21:5

All things will need to be made new, for they are sadly battered and worn by sin. Through grace we are new creatures in Christ Jesus, and when He comes our bodies will be new – like unto His glorious body. Transformed into His likeness we shall be altogether new and holy. Then there will come from His hand the new heaven and a new earth, as full of beauty, if not more glorious, than His first creation (Isaiah 65:17; II Peter 3:13).

"His servants shall serve him: and they shall see his face: and his name shall be in their forehead." Revelation 22:3, 4

Eternal blessings are ours in part now. We serve Him, but not as devotedly as we should. We see His face, but only as reflected in His Word. His Name is on our forehead, although we are not branded as His as we should be. But in eternity, these beginnings will be perfected. Then we shall serve Him without weariness or mistake. Then we shall see His face, and what joy this will be to see our blessed Saviour as He is. Then His Name will be photographed

upon our brow. As Spurgeon puts it, "The secret mark of inward grace develops into the public sign-manual of confessed relationship." The vast angelic host will know us as being Christ's.

What is the practical outcome of our contemplation of all the Lord has for us when "time shall be no more"? Does not Peter sum up our present obligation for us in his exhortation – "Wherefore, beloved, seeing you look for such things, be diligent that you may be found of him in peace" (II Peter 3:14)?

Heirs of a new world, we should be found living unworldly lives. Soon to see His face, we should seek to live as always in His presence. If we think seldom and superficially of His return, millennial reign, and eternal dominion, our spiritual life will be immeasurably weakened. Sailors on the Southern Ocean sing –

"Midnight is past, midnight is past,
The Cross begins to bend."

It is high time for us to awake out of sleep, for midnight will soon be past. And when the eternal sun arises, may we be found ready to enter our everlasting inheritance. In such a glorious future, the promises will still be our perpetual delight, even though they will be fulfilled.

"For ever, O Lord, they word is settled in heaven." Psalm 119:89, 90

Does this not mean that the original of the Bible, as given to holy men of old, is in heaven? In eternity we shall have the Promiser Himself, and then His promises will shine with a fresh and eternal beauty. Then we shall discover truths hid from us while we were in the flesh. "Then shall we know."

Now that we have reached the end of our study of the divine promises, the writer hopes that the reader has felt something of the thrill he experienced while preparing these gleanings from the promise treasury. David, the sweet psalmist of Israel, the royal promise pleads, delighted in placing his finger upon a particular promise and prayer – "Remember thy word unto thy servant, in which thou hast caused me to hope." Often our prayers are *pointless* because we do not take an individual promise and plead it at the mercy seat. Perhaps this book in your hands will help you to turn promises into prayers. The promises provide the most powerful incentives to service – they are the necessary spiritual food of the Christian – the highest cordials in the hour of need.

May we be found treasuring them up in our hearts! "Here are laid up the true riches of a Christian, and his highest hopes on this side of heaven." Perhaps one can be permitted to take the desire Dr. Isaac Watts expressed in his *Preface* to Dr. Samuel Clarke's book of *Precious Bible Promises,* originally published in 1750, and make it his wish for the reader–

"Those who have little leisure for reading may find their account in keeping this book always near them; and with the glance of an eye they may take in the riches of grace and glory, and derive many a sweet refreshment from hence, amidst their labours and travels through this wilderness. It is of excellent use to lie on the table in a chamber of sickness, and now and then to take a sip of the river of life, which runs through it in a thousand little rills of peace and joy.

"May the Holy Spirit of God, who indited all these promises, and our blessed Mediator, who, by His ministry and by His blood, has sealed and confirmed them all, render them every day more and more powerful and prevalent to draw the hearts of men towards God, and to fit them for the enjoyment of these words of grace in their complete accomplishment in glory. Amen."

PROMISES RELATIVE TO CHRISTIAN LITERATURE

It would be a colossal task to try and estimate how the promises of God have inspired and enriched Christian devotional literature down the ages. Countless thousands of sermons have been preached on the promises, and a multitude no man can number have been blessed accordingly. Through God's gracious promise of forgiveness and salvation, sinners have been delivered, backsliders restored, saints built up in their most holy faith. When the roll is called up yonder, it will be found that among the ransomed, myriads were made the Lord's through one promise or another. It is to be hoped that this volume will help to provide many a preacher with material for a series of messages on *The Promises of God.*

Then think of the perpetual use of the promises in various kinds of promise boxes, one of which my wife and I used for years. Yearly calendars for the home, each day bearing a text and brief exposition also continue the encouraging and sanctifying mission of the promises. Almost every Christian home uses these promise calendars– and what a blessing they prove to be!

In the development of this study, I had to search many hymn books and books of poems for suitable verses to attach to respective promises, and I was amazed to discover how these have permeated hymnology and poetry. I leave it to others to develop this feature. In quoting the following samples, I want to express my sincere gratitude to hymnists and poets, ancient and modern, for their gems I have extracted and used throughout this work. From Charles Wesley's enormous quantity of hymns, we

have these two promise-exalting verses–

> I rest upon Thy Word;
> Thy promise is for me;
> My succour and salvation, Lord,
> Shall surely come from Thee.

> *   *   *   *   *

> Jesus, we Thy promise claim,
> We are gathered in Thy name:
> In the midst do Thou appear,
> Manifest Thy presence here.

From S. M. Taylor we have the verse–

> Seek this first. His promise trying,
> It is sure — all need supplying —
> Heavenly things, on Him relying,
> Seek ye first.

F. R. Havergal, the saintly blind poetess, often extols the divine promises in her heart-moving poems. Here is a verse from one of these–

> Promise and command combining
> Doubt to chase and faith to lift, —
> Self-renouncing, all resigning,
> We would claim this mighty gift.

Isaac Watts, the Church's renowned evangelical poet, loved the promises and summarized his faith in same in these lines–

> Firm as His throne His promise stands,
> And He can well secure
> What I've committed to His hands,
> Till the decisive hour.

From G. M. J., the initials following one or two hymns in the old *Alexander Hymn Book,* we have this example–

> Confide in His Word, His promises so sure;
> In Christ they are Yea and Amen;
> Though earth pass away, they ever shall endure,
> 'Tis written o'er and o'er again.

From Sankey's *Sacred Songs and Solos,*

we take this stanza —

> Faithful is Thy promise,
> Precious is Thy Blood —
> These my soul's salvation,
> Thou my Saviour's God!

Redemption Songs, with its 1000 hymns and choruses, contains several verses in which the promises are praised —

> Hear the promise of the Lord,
> As recorded in His Word.
>
> •   •   •   •   •
>
> Still, still rest on the promise;
> Cling, cling fast to His Word;
> Wait, wait — if He should tarry,
> We'll patiently wait for the Lord.

The only hymn we can think of given over entirely to the exultation of the promises of God is No. 13 in *Redemption Songs*. Each verse commences with "Standing on the Promises," and the chorus goes —

> Standing, standing,
> Standing on the promises of God my Saviour
> Standing, standing,
> I'm standing on the promises of God.

Another aspect revealing the perpetual influence of the promises is the daily devotional section in many Christian periodicals, like *The Christian*, and *The Life of Faith*, published in London. For several years running it was my privilege to write the daily portions for *Revelation*, of which the late Dr. Donald G. Barnhouse was editor, and who continued this feature himself for many years in a most profitable way. Other monthly and weekly magazines, like the now defunct *Our Hope*, use the same popular feature, so helpful for devotions and family worship.

Then several Christian organizations like *The Back-to-God Hour*, Chicago, issue a monthly series of daily promises, readings, and prayers for home use. *The Radio Bible Class*, Grand Rapids, puts out a similar monthly brochure called *Our Daily Bread*, which is excellent for devotional purposes.

In the realm of daily readings for a year, in which the emphasis is more or less on the promises, we have a vast library to choose from. How these attractively produced volumes enrich our spiritual life! At the outset of our study we drew attention to some of these particular daily reading books. Others we have consulted and which have been a help are *The Daily Remembrance*, by James Smith; *The Pathway of Promise*, by I. A. M.; *The Christian's Daily Companion*, by M. A. Wykes; *Broken Bread*, by Evan H. Hopkins; *Come Ye Apart, Silent Times, Secret of a Helpful Life*, by J. R.

Miller; *A Daily Sequence*, which follows the Christian seasons, by Mr. Lyttelton Gell; *The Promises of Jesus*, by William J. May; *The Precious Promises*, by Cunningham Geikie; *Rainbow in the Cloud*, by Lolo E. Kilfit; *Daily Meditations*, found in the excellent McCall Barbour booklets; *Daily Light on the Daily Road*, by Harper and Brothers; Pocket Book of *Promises of Scripture*, by Dan Smith; *Help for Today*, by Finis J. Dake; *At Home in the Bible*, by T. H. Darlow; *At the Gates of Dawn*, by F. B. Meyer; and Scripture Union readings. There are scores of others one could list, but which were not consulted.

Finally, it would be interesting to discover how the promises have found their way into sermonic literature. Personally, I have always had a flair for books made up of sermons preached by renowned preachers. For over half a century I have made a study of the style and presentation of the sacred Word by others, in order to enrich my own ministry of the Word. Like many another preacher I am deeply in debt to C. H. Spurgeon. Go over his thousands of *sermons*, which can now be had in a convenient set, and you will be amazed to find how many of them are based on divine promises, which the renowned preacher had a peculiar love for as he confesses in his *Faith's Checkbook*, now issued by Moody Press. Another famed preacher of a past generation who loved to preach on the promises, and whose sermonic literature every preacher ought to possess, was Dr. Dinsdale Young. What a master he was at the art and craft of preaching! Then there was G. H. Morrison, of Glasgow, whom I heard with great profit when a student in the city. His many volumes of sermons, preached in his much-loved Wellington Church, afford a striking illustration of taking not only the promises, but some of the most out-of-the-way Bible phrases to proclaim the message of God. Time and space fail us to recite the illustrious roll of multitudes of others, like John Bunyan and William Gurnall, who could allegorize the promises in such dramatic ways. If we have any opportunity of proclaiming the Word, it is our privileged task, not only to *preach* the promises, but *practice* them and prove their worth thereby.

Well, the author's hard, yet happy, task is at an end, and he prays that many who read his book will be inspired to inherit the promises. Keep this volume on hand for devotional and study purposes. Send a copy to a shut-in friend, that it may lie on a table in the chamber of sickness so

,that now and again your needy friend may read with profit promises suited to their very trials. Birds that fly high never concern themselves about crossing streams. Your gift of a copy of *this* book, in your hands, may enable some distressed Christian to mount up with wings as an eagle, and flying high, look at their trials from heaven's angle. May grace be yours to love and live the Promises of God!

> The field of promise, how it flings abroad
> Its perfume o'er the Christian's thorny road!
> The soul, reposing on assured relief,
> Feels herself happy amidst all her grief:
> Forgets her labors, as she toils along,
> Weep tears of joy, and burst into a song!